Introduction to Clinical Psychology
Scientific Foundations to Clinical Practice

Michael Wierzbicki

Marquette University

Allyn and Bacon

Boston   London   Toronto   Sydney   Tokyo   Singapore

Series editorial assistant: Susan Hutchinson
Manufacturing buyer: Suzanne Lareau

Library of Congress Cataloging-in-Publication Data

Wierzbicki, Michael.
    Introduction to clinical psychology : scientific foundations to
clinical practice / Michael Wierzbicki.
        p.   cm.
    Includes bibliographical references and index.
    ISBN 0-205-15517-0
    1. Clinical psychology.   2. Psychotherapy.   I. Title.
    [DNLM: 1. Psychology, Clinical.   WM 105 W648ia 1999]
RC467.W539   1999
616.89--dc21
DNLM/DLC
for Library of Congress   98-15832
                                                 CIP

Printed in the United States of America
10 9 8 7 6 5 4 3 2 1   02 01 00 99 98

Introduction to Clinical Psychology

Contents

Preface   xiii

C H A P T E R   1

Clinical Psychology: A Historical Introduction   1

HISTORY OF CLINICAL PSYCHOLOGY   2
  Ancient Views of Abnormal Behavior   3
  Rise of Modern Views of Abnormal Behavior   4
  Modern Developments in Clinical Psychology   7
SUMMARY   12
STUDY QUESTIONS   13

C H A P T E R   2

Scientific Foundations of Clinical Psychology   15

PHILOSOPHY OF SCIENCE   15
  Assumptions of Science   16
  Stages of Science   17
  Scientific Theories   20
  Scientific Progress   21
RESEARCH METHODS IN CLINICAL PSYCHOLOGY   25
  Single-Subject Designs   26
  Correlational versus Experimental Research   27
  Other Important Designs in Clinical Psychology   31
THE SCIENTIST–PRACTITIONER MODEL OF CLINICAL PSYCHOLOGY   36
SUMMARY   39
STUDY QUESTIONS   41

C H A P T E R   3

Theories of Personality and Psychopathology   43

PSYCHOANALYSIS   45
   Structure of Personality   45
   Development of Personality   46
   Dynamics of Personality   48
   Psychopathology   50
   Treatment   51
   Evaluation   52

BEHAVIORISM   54
   Structure of Personality   55
   Development of Personality   56
   Dynamics of Personality   58
   Psychopathology   58
   Treatment   60
   Evaluation   60

HUMANISM   61
   Structure of Personality   62
   Development of Personality   62
   Dynamics of Personality   62
   Psychopathology   63
   Treatment   63
   Evaluation   64

COGNITIVE THEORIES   65
   Structure of Personality   67
   Development of Personality   68
   Dynamics of Personality   68
   Psychopathology   69
   Treatment   69
   Evaluation   69

BIOLOGICAL THEORIES   70
   Structure of Personality   72
   Development of Personality   74
   Dynamics of Personality   75
   Psychopathology   75
   Treatment   76
   Evaluation   76

SUMMARY   77

STUDY QUESTIONS   79

C H A P T E R   4   **Clinical Assessment: An Introduction   81**

BRIEF HISTORY   81

ROLE AND TYPES OF ASSESSMENT IN
CLINICAL PSYCHOLOGY   82

SCIENTIFIC ISSUES   84
Criteria for Evaluating Tests   84
Test Theory   88

APPLIED ISSUES   89
Standardized Test Administration and Interpretation   89
Test Construction   91
Ethical Issues   93

SUMMARY   95

STUDY QUESTIONS   96

C H A P T E R   5   **Assessment of Psychological Ability   97**

HISTORY OF ABILITY TESTING   98

INTELLECTUAL ASSESSMENT   99
Intelligence Tests   101

ACADEMIC ASSESSMENT   106
Achievement Tests   108
Aptitude Tests   110

NEUROPSYCHOLOGICAL ASSESSMENT   110
Neuropsychological Tests   114

SCIENTIFIC ISSUES   117
Reliability of Intelligence Tests   117
Validity of Intelligence Tests   118

APPLIED ISSUES   120
Ability Testing in Diagnosis and Treatment Planning   120
Labeling   122
Test Bias   122

SUMMARY   129

STUDY QUESTIONS   129

C H A P T E R   6   **Behavioral Assessment   131**

HISTORY   131

THEORY   132

THE INTERVIEW   133
  The Clinical Interview   134
  The Structured Interview   139
BEHAVIORAL OBSERVATION   141
  Naturalistic Observation   143
  Standardized Behavioral Assessment   143
  Behavior Checklists   144
  Self-Monitoring   146
COGNITIVE ASSESSMENT   149
  Think Aloud   149
  Cognitive Skills Assessment   149
  Cognitive Self-Assessment   150
APPLIED ISSUES   152
  Reactivity to Measurement   152
  Selection and Training of Observers   153
SCIENTIFIC ISSUES   155
  Assumptions of Behavioral Assessment   155
  Reliability and Validity of
    Behavioral Assessment   155
SUMMARY   157
STUDY QUESTIONS   159

CHAPTER 7   **Personality Assessment   161**
MEANING OF PERSONALITY   161
USES OF PERSONALITY TESTING   162
HISTORY OF PERSONALITY ASSESSMENT   163
  Classical Approaches   163
  Pre-Modern Approaches   165
PROJECTIVE PERSONALITY ASSESSMENT   165
  Projective Tests   166
STRUCTURED PERSONALITY ASSESSMENT   172
  Structured Personality Inventories   173
SCIENTIFIC ISSUES   178
  Evaluation of Projective Tests   178
  Evaluation of Structured Tests   182
APPLIED ISSUES   184
  Detection of Faking   184
  Response Sets   186

Use of Computerized Interpretations   188
SUMMARY   191
STUDY QUESTIONS   192

C H A P T E R   8

**Psychological Treatment:
An Introduction   193**
BRIEF HISTORY   193
SCIENTIFIC ISSUES   195
Psychotherapy Process   195
Psychotherapy Outcome   197
APPLIED ISSUES   204
Ethical Issues   204
Case Management   210
SUMMARY   212
STUDY QUESTIONS   214

C H A P T E R   9

Psychoanalytic Therapy   215
FREUDIAN APPROACHES TO PSYCHOTHERAPY   216
Psychoanalysis   216
Freudian Contemporaries   220
Neo-Freudian Therapies   223
Contemporary Variants   225
APPLIED ISSUES   226
How Long/Expensive Is Psychoanalysis?   226
Who Benefits from Psychoanalysis?   227
Who Should Provide Psychoanalysis?   228
SCIENTIFIC ISSUES   229
Difficulty Evaluating Psychoanalytic Treatment   229
Empirical Evaluation of Psychoanalysis   231
SUMMARY   233
STUDY QUESTIONS   234

C H A P T E R   1 0

Humanistic Therapy   235
HUMANISTIC APPROACHES TO PSYCHOTHERAPY   236
Theory of Psychopathology   236
Goal of Psychotherapy   236

Techniques of Psychotherapy   237
Variants of Humanistic Therapy   240

APPLIED ISSUES   248
Selection and Training of Psychotherapists   248
Providing Psychotherapy to the Healthy   250

SCIENTIFIC ISSUES   251
Effectiveness of Humanistic Psychotherapy   252
Influence of Rogerian Therapeutic Qualities   252

SUMMARY   254
STUDY QUESTIONS   255

CHAPTER 11   **Cognitive and Behavioral Therapies   257**

BEHAVIOR THERAPY   257
Theory of Pathology and Nature of Behavior Therapy   258
Techniques of Behavior Therapy   259

COGNITIVE THERAPY   266
Nature of Psychopathology   267
Techniques of Cognitive Therapy   268

APPLIED ISSUES   274
Symptom Substitution   274
Problem Relapse   276
Use of Analogue Subjects   277
Ethical Problems   278

SCIENTIFIC ISSUES   280
Early Reviews of the Effectiveness of Behavior Therapy   281
Meta-Analytic Reviews   281

SUMMARY   282
STUDY QUESTIONS   284

CHAPTER 12   **Biological Treatment   285**

MEDICAL TREATMENTS   286
Psychiatric Medication   286
Electroconvulsive Therapy   294
Psychosurgery   295

PHYSIOLOGICALLY ORIENTED TREATMENTS   295
Introduction to Stress-Related Disorders   296
Treatment of Stress-Related Disorders   298

BEHAVIORAL MEDICINE   302
  Behavioral Medicine Programs   303
APPLIED ISSUES   304
  Psychologists and Prescription Privileges   304
  Social Consequences of the Rise of Psychiatric Drugs   305
SCIENTIFIC ISSUES   306
SUMMARY   307
STUDY QUESTIONS   309

CHAPTER 1 3   **Child, Family, and Group Therapy   311**

CHILD THERAPY   312
  Historical Introduction   312
  Theoretical Approaches   312
  Applied Issues   316
  Scientific Issues   319
FAMILY THERAPY   319
  Historical Introduction   319
  Theoretical Approaches   320
  Applied Issues   323
  Scientific Issues   325
GROUP THERAPY   326
  Historical Introduction   326
  Theoretical Approaches   327
  Applied Issues   332
  Scientific Issues   333
SUMMARY   336
STUDY QUESTIONS   338

CHAPTER 1 4   **Training and Professional Roles of Clinical Psychologists   341**

GRADUATE SCHOOL TRAINING   342
  History   342
  Current Programs   344
PROFESSIONAL ROLES   346
  History   346
  Work Settings and Activities   347
  Recent Trends   348

APPLIED ISSUES   349
    Selecting Clinical Psychology versus Other Mental
        Health Fields   349
    Applying to Graduate School in Clinical Psychology   351
SCIENTIFIC ISSUES   353
    Evaluation of Graduate Training and Career Choice   353
    Evaluation of the Boulder and Vail Models of Training   354
SUMMARY   357
STUDY QUESTIONS   359

Glossary   361

References   377

Name Index   409

Subject Index   418

Preface

This book is intended to be the primary text in introductory courses in clinical psychology, presented either at the advanced undergraduate level or at the beginning graduate level.

I had two primary objectives in writing this book. First, I intended to write a textbook in this area that is more accessible to advanced undergraduate students than the other works currently on the market. To this end, this book is somewhat shorter and more readable than the other textbooks that introduce students to clinical psychology. To enhance the didactic value of the book, I have also provided summaries and study questions at the end of every chapter, and a glossary at the end of the book.

Second, I intended to write a textbook that integrates the material around a central theme. Many existing texts simply enumerate the many roles of the clinical psychologist, such as the most commonly used approaches to assessment and treatment. However, these texts fail to provide a coherent theme—historical or theoretical—that can be used by the student to help organize and master the material. I have presented the material in this book around the major theme of the *philosophy of science.* The philosophy of science addresses fundamental scientific issues, such as the assumptions of science, the characteristics of scientific theories, and the nature of scientific progress.

This theme has several advantages. First, it provides a way to *integrate theoretical and applied material.* For example, this textbook examines the major roles of the clinical psychologist (to explain, assess, and treat abnormality). There are chapters that examine the scientific issues related to each role, followed by chapters that describe the various approaches that clinical psychologists have adopted to perform this role.

Chapter 1 presents a brief overview of the history of clinical psychology. In Chapter 2, the fundamentals of scientific theories, the criteria used to evaluate theories, and the nature of scientific progress through the replacement of one theory with a superior theory are presented. Chapter 3 summarizes the major theories of personality and psychopathology, including the psychoanalytic, humanistic, behavioral, cognitive, and biological viewpoints.

In Chapter 4, the scientific issues related to psychological assessment are examined. Chapters 5 through 7 discuss the major types of clinical assessment, including intellectual, psychodiagnostic, and cognitive–behavioral. Chapter 8 focuses on the scientific and practical issues underlying psychological treatment. Chapters 9 through 13 examine psychoanalytic, humanistic, cognitive–behavioral, biological, family, group, and child therapy. When specific therapy and assessment techniques are presented in later chapters, their theoretical foundations and the scientific criteria used to evaluate them will have been well established. Chapter 14 discusses the training and professional roles of clinical psychologists. This chapter brings the text full circle, in that it addresses the changing professional roles of clinical psychologists and illustrates how the scientific foundations of clinical psychology are applied in practice.

The theme of philosophy of science also permits a presentation of the historical development of clinical psychology. A brief history of clinical psychology appears in the introductory chapter. In addition, throughout the book, the historical development of specific types of assessment and treatment are presented, along with discussions of how theoretical and empirical developments influenced such changes.

Finally, the theme of philosophy of science also supports an empirical emphasis. This book has an empirical orientation. It emphasizes that clinical applications should be founded on scientific fact. In this way, the book supports the scientist–practitioner model. This is the traditional model of training, which holds that clinical psychologists (1) are psychologists first and foremost, (2) should be trained in scientific research methods and the breadth of psychology, and (3) should use clinical methods that have a scientific foundation. Chapter 2 describes research methods used by clinical psychologists.

Throughout the text, empirical evidence is presented concerning theories of psychopathology, assessment instruments, and psychotherapies.

I would like to thank several individuals whose help made this book possible. First, thanks to Robert Lueger, Stephen Saunders, John Grych, Anthony Kuchan, Mary Anne Siderits, Anees Sheikh, along with all my other colleagues and students, for their encouragement and stimulation. Thanks also to my research assistants, Robert Nohr and Ann Rolling, for their help in locating the material cited in the text. I also appreciate the many helpful comments and suggestions from the psychologists who reviewed early drafts of this book: Stephen T. Black, Millsaps College; Clint A. Bowers, University of Central Florida; Bernard S. Gorman, Nassau Community College; Robert G. Meyer, University of Louisville; and Eric A. Zillmer, Drexel University. Finally, I want to acknowledge Alexis, Jane, and Kaye, without whose patience and support this book would not have been completed.

Introduction to
Clinical Psychology

1

Clinical Psychology
A Historical Introduction

I. History of Clinical Psychology
  A. Ancient Views of Abnormal Behavior
  B. Rise of Modern Views of Abnormal
    Behavior

C. Modern Developments in Clinical
  Psychology
II. Summary

Johny was a 10-year-old boy with a history of seizure disorders since infancy. When he started school, he was found to have learning problems in reading and spelling. At age 10, he was a socially isolated child with few friends. His interactions with others were odd; talking with Johny often left one with the unsettling feeling that one could not "connect" with him. In one therapy session, Johny revealed that he had found a dead cat that he frequently played with and now regarded as his pet.

Mr. G. was a 57-year-old inpatient in a mental hospital. Since his 20s, Mr. G. had been hospitalized numerous times, receiving many different diagnoses, ranging from mental retardation to schizophrenia. Mr. G. was no longer verbal or able to follow directions. His level of adaptive functioning was childlike; for example, he was unable to tie his shoes or feed himself. He also exhibited odd motor behavior—stiffness, jerki-

ness. During his hospitalization, he was diagnosed, for the first time, as having Huntington's chorea, a progressive neurological disorder that would ultimately be fatal. Mr. G. had seven children, from 18 to 35 years of age, all of whom now had to face a fifty-fifty chance that they had inherited this condition.

These two cases illustrate unusual and extreme forms of abnormal behavior. I worked with these individuals in my role as a clinical psychologist, the specialty within psychology that addresses abnormal behavior.

This book introduces students to the field of clinical psychology. This chapter defines and then provides a historical overview of clinical psychology. Later chapters will discuss the methods that clinical psychologists use to explain, assess, and treat disorders, such as those exhibited by Johny and Mr. G.

Psychology is commonly defined in introductory textbooks as the scientific study of behavior and mental processes (e.g., Wortman & Loftus, 1992). Many specialty areas of psychology focus exclusively on one type of behavior or mental process. For example, social psychologists are interested in group behavior; cognitive psychologists are concerned with cognitions or thought processes; developmental psychologists study how behaviors and mental processes develop as a function of age. *Clinical psychology* is the specialty area of psychology that is concerned with abnormal behavior and mental processes.

Clinical psychology is a popular field. Approximately ten percent of the doctoral degrees awarded annually in the United States in science and engineering are in psychology (Strickland, 1987). Of recent doctoral degrees in psychology, about 37 percent were in clinical psychology (Rosenzweig, 1991).

Clinical psychologists perform three major functions with regard to the study of abnormality. The first function is to explain abnormality. Theorists of psychopathology must define abnormality, distinguish abnormality from normality, and then attempt to explain its development.

The scientific issues that underlie the theoretical study of psychopathology are discussed in Chapter 2. These issues include the nature of theories and the nature of scientific progress. Chapter 3 summarizes the major theories in clinical psychology of both psychopathology and personality, including psychoanalytic, behavioral, humanistic, cognitive, and biological approaches.

The second function of clinical psychologists is assessment. After defining abnormality and explaining its development, clinical psychologists must then develop methods to recognize and measure abnormality. Chapter 4 discusses the scientific and theoretical issues underlying clinical assessment. Chapters 5 through 7 describe the major types of assessments conducted by clinical psychologists, including intellectual, personality, behavioral, cognitive, and neuropsychological.

The third major function of clinical psychologists is treatment. Clinical psychologists are not concerned, of course, simply with assessing and explaining abnormality. They are also concerned with providing effective interventions to remediate abnormality. Chapter 8 discusses the scientific and theoretical issues that underlie psychological treatment. Chapters 9 through 13 then discuss specific forms of treatment that stem from the major theoretical schools. In addition, these chapters present material on the historical development, practical applications, and research evaluations of these treatments.

Chapter 14 describes the training and professional activities of clinical psychologists. This will illustrate how clinical psychologists engage in the basic functions of explanation, assessment, and treatment of abnormality. Finally, Chapter 14 discusses future directions of clinical psychology. In this way, the textbook will go full circle, from an examination of the history of clinical psychology in Chapter 1 to the future of clinical psychology in Chapter 14.

It should be stressed that, although the roles of psychopathologist, assessor, and therapist are presented separately in this text, clinical psychologists engage in all three activities simultaneously. For example, when working with a client, the clinical psychologist conducts a diagnostic assessment, develops theoretical explanations of the cause of the disorder, and suggests appropriate treatments. Readers should remember that clinical psychologists engage in these activities simultaneously and so attempt to integrate the material.

It should also be emphasized that, as a specialty area of psychology, clinical psychology is a science. As such, clinical psychologists contribute to the scientific development as well as the applied aspects of the field. For this reason, readers should also remember that clinical research and practice go hand in hand.

HISTORY OF CLINICAL PSYCHOLOGY

Psychology is a young field. The origin of psychology as an independent discipline is often listed as 1879, when Wilhelm Wundt established the first laboratory devoted exclusively to psychological research (Boring, 1929).

Clinical psychology is younger still. The term *clinical psychology* was introduced by Lightner Witmer when he founded the first psychological clinic at the University of Pennsylvania in 1896 (Achenbach, 1982).

The nature of clinical psychology was the subject of much debate within the psychological community. For much of the first half of the 1900s, experimental and clinical psychology enjoyed an uneasy relationship. On two occasions, clinical psychologists left the American Psychological Association (APA) to form their own professional organization, only to return later to the APA (McNamara, Jones, & Barclay, 1982; Strickland, 1988).

Even clinical psychologists did not always agree on their proper role. For example, whereas the major role of clinical psychologists in the 1920s was assessment, by the 1940s the need for increased numbers of providers of treatment services in World Wars I and II led many clinical psychologists to adopt the role of psychotherapist (Strickland, 1988). However, many clinical psychologists resisted this increased focus on therapy over assessment.

This section of the chapter discusses the history of clinical psychology. It starts with a brief presentation on ancient views of abnormal behavior, addresses influences from the 1700s and 1800s that led to a greater interest in psychological explanations of abnormal behavior, and then summarizes major events in the 1900s. Because this historical overview is necessarily brief, interested readers are referred to other works that describe at more length the history of abnormal psychology (e.g., Bromberg, 1975), clinical psychology (e.g., McNamara & Barlow, 1982), and psychiatry (e.g., Kraepelin, 1917/1962).

Ancient Views of Abnormal Behavior

Abnormal behavior has always received attention from physicians, philosophers, and theologians. Records show that ancient civilizations (including Chinese, Greek, Roman, Egyptian, and others) recognized abnormal behavior as such and attempted to isolate the afflicted individual (Davison & Neale, 1994). Ancient civilizations typically adopted either a religious or a physiological approach to explain and treat abnormality.

Religious Model The religious approach holds that deviant behavior results from some form of spiritual possession or curse. The book of Deuteronomy in the Old Testament contains the statement, "The Lord will smite thee with madness." Suinn (1988) described the case of a daughter of an Egyptian pharaoh, whose illness and recovery were attributed to evil and benign spirits. Even the Greek philosopher Plato thought that "mental disorder was . . . partly divine in origin" (Bromberg, 1975, p. 13). In all of these cases, abnormal behavior was attributed to supernatural influences beyond the scope of natural laws.

This religious view of deviant behavior is thought to date to prehistoric times. Anthropologists have located skulls from a prehistoric time that have had sections surgically removed (a procedure called *trephining*). The regularity of the wounds and the fact that there is evidence of healing followed by repeated incisions, suggest that the skull sections had been removed deliberately and did not occur from accidental injury. Although anthropologists cannot be certain of the purpose of the procedure, many believe that trephining was intended to permit the release of "evil spirits" that inhabited the individual (Suinn, 1988).

The religious explanation of abnormal behavior persisted for thousands of years. For example, *Malleus Malleficarum (The Witches' Hammer)* was written in 1486 to guide the clergy in identifying individuals who consorted with witches. This book, which initiated the Spanish Inquisition and the witch hunts of the 1500s and 1600s, included the statement that "sudden loss of reason was a symptom of demonic possession" (Davison & Neale, 1990, p. 10). *The Witches' Hammer* specified appropriate interventions for a person possessed against his or her will, including severe measures such as torture and burning at the stake, and less extreme alternatives such as exorcism.

Witches were hunted and "treated" in this way for the next two centuries. Perhaps the most well-known example of witch hunts is the case of the Salem witch trials where, in 1692, several persons, who may have been suffering from a variety of mental disorders (Spanos & Gottlieb, 1976), were executed.

It is easy to dismiss such historical examples as the result of inadequate knowledge of the psychological and physiological causes of mental illness. However, it is important to recognize that the religious model of illness remains influential today. An example of this is saying "God bless you" following a sneeze, which dates back to a time when it was thought that a person was especially vulnerable to demonic possession when sneezing.

Religions such as Santeria believe in the reality of curses that may produce illness. Certain New Age religions suggest that channeling, which leads individuals to speak as though they were another person, is a form of spiritual possession. Even mainstream religions hold that spiritual influences may produce or treat mental and physical disorders. For example, Roman Catholic priests occasionally perform the exorcism rite to counter demonic possession. Fundamentalist Christians often use prayer and faith healing to treat illness.

Physiological Model   Some ancient civilizations also invoked a physiological model to explain and treat abnormal behavior. Hippocrates (460–377 B.C.) may be the most well-known ancient physician who adopted this approach. Hippocrates introduced an early method of classifying mental disorders and suggested that they had physical rather than supernatural causes. He recognized the effects of stress on both physical and mental disorders and advocated a variety of naturalistic treatments, including stress reduction, diet, and primitive medications.

Hippocrates introduced a physiological theory of illness that he extended to psychological disorders and even to normal psychological characteristics. He observed that there are four basic bodily fluids (blood, phlegm, black bile, and yellow bile) and proposed that psychological characteristics and illness are associated with imbalances in these fluids. Hippocrates proposed that an excess of black bile is associated with depression and that an excess of phlegm is associated with a sluggish character.

Of course, we recognize today that Hippocrates's theory is "all wet." Still, it is noteworthy that we continue to use words based on each of these four fluids to describe psychological traits (melancholic = depressed; sanguine = happy, optimistic; phlegmatic = sluggish; choleric = irritable, angry).

Other ancient physicians also recognized the importance of physiological influences on both behavioral and medical disorders. For example, Asclepiades (124 B.C.) introduced a form of physical therapy to treat illness. Celsus (25 B.C.–A.D. 50) recommended various herbs for the treatment of depression and delusions (Bromberg, 1975). Galen (A.D. 130–200) contended that the brain is the basis of human functioning. He also suggested that illness often results from brain disease and he proposed a variety of naturalistic treatments for depression and anxiety, such as exercise, massage, and bathing (Bromberg, 1975).

Rise of Modern Views of Abnormal Behavior

Although both the religious and physiological models of abnormal behavior were present during ancient times, the religious view may well have been the more predominant view from ancient times through the Middle Ages and into the Renaissance. However, the rise of modern science in the 1600s and 1700s and the Enlightenment of the 1700s set the stage for a revival of the physiological view and the development of new approaches to explaining and treating abnormal behavior. The social and psychological views, along with the revived physiological model, contributed to the development of contemporary psychological theories of abnormal behavior.

Social Model   Historians have labeled the eighteenth century as the Enlightenment. This period was characterized by an increased awareness of human rights and individual freedom, social values and responsibilities, and the view that the human condition can be improved through education and improved environmental circumstances.

These attitudes helped set the stage for the social reforms that followed the American and French Revolutions. They also set the stage for the development of the view that abnormal behavior may result from social ills and treated through environmental interventions.

Philipe Pinel (1745–1826) was a French physician who was appointed head of La Bicetre lunatic asylum in 1793 (Bromberg, 1975). Pinel attempted to apply to the treatment of the mentally ill the same principles of liberty and equality that played such an important role in the French Revolution. Pinel disagreed with the prison-like atmosphere of the hospital. Patients were confined to dark, small quarters; they were often restricted or even chained; and they were frequently beaten. Pinel treated mental patients more humanely; releasing their chains, providing better food, permitting greater freedom of movement, and forbidding beatings. Pinel reported that this more humane approach to the treatment of the mentally ill, which he called *moral treatment,* produced remarkable successes, even with patients who had been treated for decades previously without success.

Following Pinel, other physicians introduced similar changes in their institutions. In 1796, William Tuke established the York Retreat, a rural, resort-like hospital for the mentally ill in England. In 1820, Eli Todd established the Hartford Retreat in Hartford, Connecticut, based on moral treatment.

The social approach to explaining and treating abnormal behavior continued through the 1800s and into the 1900s. For example, Dorothea Dix campaigned from 1841 to 1881 for improved treatment conditions for mental patients. In 1908, Clifford Beers wrote *A Mind That Found Itself: An Autobiography,* a firsthand account of the dismal conditions in mental hospitals in the early 1900s, which led to an increase in the public's awareness of the need for improved treatment of the mentally ill.

Another example of the development of the social approach to explaining and treating abnormal behavior is the work of Jean Itard in treating the "Wild Boy of Aveyron." In 1799, a boy was captured by hunters in a forest outside Aveyron, France. The boy was about 11 or 12 years old and had apparently been living on his own for a long time. His behavior was quite wild. For example, he did not speak, he avoided people, and he resisted wearing clothing. The boy was brought to Itard, a French physician, who named him Victor. Itard believed that he could educate Victor through patience and caring. Although Itard eventually taught Victor to wear clothing, to eat with utensils, and to keep himself clean, Victor never learned to speak in complete sentences. Despite Itard's marginal success in training Victor, his treatment led to an increase in and attention to the special education of the mentally retarded.

The social approach to explaining and treating abnormal behavior remains influential today. For example, research on demographic correlates of psychopathology often finds that lower socioeconomic status is related to higher rates of mental health problems. Psychologists and other social scientists have provided services to this group in order to prevent such problems.

Similarly, many mental hospitals continue the tradition begun by Pinel. *Milieu therapy* is the current term for the treatment approach that attempts to provide an environment that is as humane and therapeutic as possible. According to milieu therapy, everything in the patient's environment—including the meals, the attractiveness of the physical grounds, the recreational activities available, and the formal therapy provided—should be aimed at fostering the patient's recovery.

Physiological Model   Although the physiological approach to explaining and treating abnormal behavior was present even in ancient times, it has enjoyed a tremendous increase in influence in the last several centuries. This change is due to the increased influence of science in this period and to its success in explaining and treating physical and mental disorders.

The classic example of the success of the physiological model is the condition *general paresis.* This disorder is characterized by progressive loss of motor and psychological functioning and is ultimately

EXHIBIT 1.1   Steps in Discovering the Physiological Cause of General Paresis

Year	Discovery	Year	Discovery
1798	Haslam described the symptoms of general paresis, including delusions of grandeur and dementia	1897	Krafft-Ebing reported that all paretic patients previously had syphilis
1860	Microscopic analysis revealed widespread destruction of nervous system tissue in paretic patients	1913	Naguchi and Moore found that the spirochete, the infectious agent in syphilis, was present in the brains of paretic patients
1884	Fournier reported that significantly more paretic patients (64%) previously had syphilis than other mental patients (10%)		

fatal. It is caused by deterioration of the central nervous system due to action of spirochetes, the infectious agent in syphilis.

In the 1700s, patients in the final stages of general paresis were institutionalized, often in mental hospitals, because they were psychotic (out of touch with reality) or demented (unable to control basic psychological functions). Over about a 100-year period, scientists learned that general paresis has a specific physiological cause. Exhibit 1.1 summarizes the steps in the discovery of the physiological cause of general paresis.

Herman von Helmholtz (1821–1894) also contributed to the revival of the physiological view to explaining behavior. Helmholtz, a physicist and a physiologist, attempted to apply Newton's laws of mechanics to biological and even to psychological systems. Newton's first law of thermodynamics states the principle of the conservation of energy—energy is not lost but is converted to other forms of energy. Helmholtz suggested that this law holds even for human nervous system functioning. Helmholtz is known for measuring the speed of the conduction of nerve impulses and for establishing a German school of thought that became known for its physiological reductionism.

This German school of physiological reductionism was influential among physicians, psychiatrists, and psychologists in the mid- to late-1800s. For example, nineteenth-century psychiatrists, such as Henry Maudsley and Emil Kraepelin, adopted a clear physiological approach to explaining and treating mental disorders. Even Sigmund Freud, who later focused his attention on psychological processes, initially adopted a physiological reductionistic position. In the 1890s, Freud began a project (which, however, he never completed satisfactorily) in which he attempted to reduce psychological processes to underlying physiological processes. Early in his career, Freud was comfortable with the claim that psychiatry (and psychology) could ultimately be reduced to neurology.

The physiological approach to explaining and treating abnormal behavior remains influential today. Although this view experienced a somewhat lessened influence in the first half of the 1900s (largely due to the increased influence of the psychological theories of psychoanalysis, behaviorism, and humanism), the physiological approach experienced a significant increase in emphasis in the latter half of the twentieth century. As will be discussed in Chapter 3, the physiological theory of personality and psychopathology is an active and influential viewpoint in contemporary clinical psychology.

Psychological Model   A third contemporary approach to explaining and treating abnormal behavior is the psychological model. There are, of course, numerous historical influences on and antecedents of this position. For example, Hippocrates recognized the effects of emotional stress on physiological disorders. Galen also recognized this, suggesting that perhaps 60 percent of his medical patients have emotional problems. However, although the psychological viewpoint had been hinted at in ancient times, it wasn't until the late 1700s that it received extensive attention.

One of the early figures who focused attention on the psychological model of illness was Franz Anton Mesmer (1734–1815). Influenced by contemporary scientific research on magnetism, Mesmer believed that there is a form of animal magnetism that affects living organisms and can be harnessed and directed into people. Mesmer treated patients in a mysterious, near-religious ceremony. He wore long robes and carried a scepter that he claimed had been imbued with animal magnetism. He walked behind his patients, who were seated around a table called a *banquet* that also had allegedly been magnetized. Mesmer then tapped their head or shoulders with the scepter. Patients convulsed, and after regaining consciousness, often reported that their physical symptoms had been alleviated.

Of course, Mesmer's construct of animal magnetism was invalid. A scientific commission (chaired by Benjamin Franklin) investigated mesmerism. After a series of controlled experiments (including the placebo design—see Chapter 2), the commission concluded that there is no physical action underlying mesmerism: the action is psychological rather than physical.

Although this research led most scientists to dismiss Mesmer as a crank, some physicians in the 1800s became interested in the psychological principles underlying and the applications of mesmerism. For example, in the mid-1800s, James Osteal employed mesmerism to induce anesthesia so that he could perform surgery. James Braid reinterpreted mesmerism as a neurological state, akin to sleep. He introduced the term *neuro-hypnotism* to describe the practice, which was later shortened to *hypnotism*.

By the end of the 1800s, the technique of hypnosis had become well established. Even though it was recognized as having a psychological and not a phys-

iological basis, sufficient evidence had been presented to demonstrate that hypnotism is a valid phenomenon with significant effects on psychological and even physiological processes.

Wundt established the first psychological laboratory in 1879, a date often marked as the origin of psychology as an independent discipline. Wundt founded a school of psychology called *structuralism*. Structuralism attempted to break down mental processes into their basic elements—a practice sometimes called *mental chemistry*. Wundt and his students helped to establish psychology as an independent science.

So, by the late 1800s, psychology had been established as an independent discipline. Structuralism and other approaches to psychology were well established. It was natural that, at this time, psychiatrists began to develop psychological models to explain mental illness.

By 1889, Janet had introduced a psychological explanation of *dissociation,* in which troubling ideas were split off from the rest of consciousness, resulting in a variety of symptoms (Bromberg, 1975). Sigmund Freud (whose ideas will be presented in detail in Chapter 3) began to develop psychoanalytic theory at this time. From 1893 to 1895, Freud published with Josef Breuer a series of papers that developed a psychological theory to explain *hysterical conversion disorder* (physical symptoms for which there is no physical cause but which instead are produced by psychological factors). In 1907, Carl Gustav Jung published *The Psychology of Dementia Praecox,* a psychoanalytic theory of schizophrenia.

From these examples, it is clear that, by the late 1800s to the early 1900s, the psychological view of the causes and treatments of abnormal behavior had become widespread.

Modern Developments in Clinical Psychology

Lightner Witmer introduced the term *clinical psychology* when he established the first psychological clinic at the University of Pennsylvania in 1896. Here, children who had school problems received treatment based on the educational principles of Wundt and Kraepelin (Shakow, 1968). Interestingly,

EXHIBIT 1.2   Important Events in the Development of the Field of Clinical Psychology

Year	Event	Year	Event
1892	Founding of the American Psychological Association	1952	*Diagnostic and Statistical Manual of Mental Disorders (DSM)* published by American Psychiatric Association
1896	First psychological clinic established by Witmer at the University of Pennsylvania	1953	*Ethical Standards for Psychologists* published by APA
1907	First clinical journal, *Psychological Clinic*, founded by Witmer	1956	Conference on training standards held in Stanford
1908	First clinical internship established at the Vineland Training School	1958	Conference on training standards held in Miami
1909	First child guidance clinic established by Healy in Chicago; section on clinical psychology established within APA	1963	Community Mental Health Centers Act passed by U.S. Congress
1917	Clinicians broke away from the APA to form the American Association of Clinical Psychology (AACP)	1965	Conference on training standards held in Chicago
1919	AACP rejoined APA as its section on clinical psychology	1968	*DSM-II* published by American Psychiatric Association; first Psy.D. program introduced at University of Illinois
1931	Committee on training standards appointed by clinical section of the APA	1973	Psy.D. model endorsed as an alternative training model at the Vail conference on training standards
1936	First text in clinical psychology published by Louttit	1977	Standards for Providers of Psychological Services published by APA
1937	Clinical section broke away from APA to form American Association for Applied Psychology (AAAP)	1980	*DSM-III* published by American Psychiatric Association
1945	AAAP rejoined APA; Connecticut passed the first law for the certification of psychologists	1987	*DSM-III-R* published by American Psychiatric Association; conference on graduate training in psychology held in Salt Lake City
1949	Conference in Boulder held on training standards in clinical psychology; scientist–practitioner model of training unanimously supported	1988	American Psychological Society founded

although he introduced the term clinical psychology, Witmer was an academic psychologist who did not work as a full-time clinician at any time during his career (Brems, Thevenin, & Routh, 1991).

Following the origin of clinical psychology as a distinct specialty, many advances followed rapidly. This section of the chapter briefly summarizes the development of the field as a profession, the important steps of which are listed in Exhibit 1.2. In addition, Exhibits 1.3 through 1.5 list, respectively, some of the important theoretical, assessment, and treat-

ment developments in clinical psychology from the end of the nineteenth century through the twentieth century. Most of these developments will be discussed later in the book, in those chapters that address clinical theories, assessment techniques, and therapies.

After Witmer introduced the specialty of clinical psychology, the role of the clinical psychologist remained uncertain. The different interests and needs of academic experimental psychologists and applied clinical psychologists led to a series of separations

EXHIBIT 1.3 Important Theoretical Advances in Clinical Psychology

Year	Theoretical Advance	Year	Theoretical Advance
1893–1895	*Studies on Hysteria,* published by Freud and Breuer	1948	*The Behavior of Organisms,* detailing the principles and applications of operant conditioning, published by Skinner
1911	Individual psychology movement founded by Adler following his split with Freud	1955	*The Psychology of Personal Constructs,* detailing a cognitive theory of personality, published by Kelly
1913	Behaviorism introduced by Watson	1958	*Ego Psychology and the Problem of Adaptation,* introducing ego psychology, published by Hartmann
1914	Analytic psychology movement founded by Jung following his split with Freud		
1920	Fear classically conditioned by Watson and Rayner	1968	*Personality and Assessment,* questioning the stability of personality traits, published by Mischel
1923	Structural model of personality articulated by Freud	1972	Cognitive social learning model of psychology presented by Mischel
1942	*Counseling and Psychotherapy,* introducing a humanistic theory of therapy, published by Rogers	1977	*Social Learning Theory,* published by Bandura

EXHIBIT 1.4 Important Advances in Clinical Assessment

Year	Advance	Year	Advance
1905	First modern intelligence test published by Simon and Binet	1949	Draw-A-Person Test used as a projective test by Machover; neuropsychological test battery developed by Halstead; Wechsler Intelligence Scale for Children (WISC) published
1916	Stanford-Binet published by Terman, introducing the intelligence quotient (IQ) as an index of intelligence		
1917	Army Alpha and Beta Tests developed to screen large numbers of persons for intelligence	1954	*Clinical Versus Statistical Prediction* published by Meehl, finding that statistical prediction always equalled or surpassed clinical prediction
1921	Rorschach Inkblot Test published	1955	Wechsler Adult Intelligence Scale (WAIS) published
1935	Thematic Apperception Test published by Morgan and Murray	1966	Standards for psychological tests published by APA
1937	Term *projective test* used by Frank	1967	Wechsler Primary and Preschool Scale of Intelligence (WPPSI) published
1938	Bender-Gestalt Test published	1974	Exner system for scoring the Rorschach published; WISC-R published
1939	Wechsler-Bellevue Test published by Wechsler, introducing the deviation IQ measure of intelligence	1981	WAIS-R published
		1989	MMPI-2 published
1943	Minnesota Multiphasic Personality Inventory (MMPI) published by Hathaway and McKinley	1992	WISC-III published

EXHIBIT 1.5   Important Advances in Treatment During the 1900s

Year	Advance	Year	Advance
1893–1939	Psychoanalysis developed and refined by Freud	1958	Systematic desensitization described by Wolpe
1924	Fear treated by Jones using behavioral techniques	1962	*Rational-Emotive Therapy,* a cognitive model of therapy, published by Ellis
1932	Psychoanalytic therapy applied to children in the form of play therapy by Klein	1966	Behavioral treatment of psychotic children described by Lovaas; Attention placebo introduced by Paul
1940	Aversive conditioning used to treat alcoholism by Voegtlin	1968	Token economy described by Ayllon and Azrin
1942	*Counseling and Psychotherapy,* describing a humanistic model of therapy, published by Rogers	1969	*Principles of Behavior Modification* published by Bandura
1946	Psychoanalytically oriented psychotherapy, a briefer form of psychoanalysis, described by Alexander and French	1976	Problem-solving therapy described by Spivack, Platt, and Shure
1947	Rogerian therapy applied to children in the form of play therapy by Axline	1977	*Cognitive Behavior Modification,* published by Meichenbaum; meta-analysis used by Smith and Glass to review studies of psychotherapy outcome; the average client who receives therapy found to have a better outcome than the average client who receives no therapy
1951	*Client-Centered Therapy* published by Rogers		
1952	Research on the effectiveness of psychotherapy reviewed by Eysenck; no evidence found that therapy is superior to no therapy	1979	Cognitive approach to treating depression detailed by Beck
		1995	A list of empirically validated psychotherapies published by the APA

and reconciliations between them (McNamara et al., 1982; Strickland, 1988). For example, clinical psychologists broke away from the APA in 1917 to form the American Association of Clinical Psychology (AACP), only to return in 1919 to the APA, as its section on clinical psychology. Clinical psychologists left the APA once again in 1937 to form the American Association for Applied Psychology (AAAP); the AAAP rejoined the APA in 1945.

The dividing issue was whether clinical psychology is an art or a science. Psychology had traditionally been regarded as a science, with psychologists trained to conduct scientific research in the laboratory. Clinical psychologists were now applying psychological principles in clinical settings. Although clinicians claimed that their techniques were applications of psychological principles, other psychologists argued that clinical techniques were not based on scientifically validated principles.

Even among practitioners, the proper role of the clinical psychologist was debated. For example, the major role of clinical psychologists in the 1920s was psychological testing (Strickland, 1988). Alfred Binet developed the first modern intelligence test in 1905. In 1916, Lewis Terman translated this test into English and published norms for its use in the United States. During World War I, Robert Yerkes chaired a committee that developed the Army Alpha and Beta tests, which could be used to screen large numbers of military recruits for intellectual deficits. These intelligence tests were extremely useful for identifying children and adults who were mentally deficient and who were in need of special educational services.

In the 1920s and 1930s, projective personality tests became popular. Based on Freudian personality theory, *projective personality tests* were designed to understand a person's underlying psychological processes, based on responses to ambiguous test items. Herman Rorschach published his Inkblot Test in 1921; Henry Murray published the Thematic Apperception Test in 1937; Lauretta Bender published the Bender–Gestalt Test in 1938.

Thus, by the 1930s, clinical psychologists had a wide range of tests available for both intellectual and psychodiagnostic assessment, and psychological assessment continued to be the major function of clinical psychologists. However, the need for increased numbers of providers of treatment services in World War II led many clinical psychologists by the 1940s to adopt the role of therapist (Strickland, 1988). The increased demand for clinical services and the increasing numbers of psychologists seeking to provide clinical services led the APA to formally address the educational and training requirements of clinical psychologists.

In 1944, the APA decided to train clinical psychologists in existing doctoral training programs in psychology (Reisman, 1981). The APA established a committee to make recommendations concerning the educational requirements of clinical psychology training programs. The committee report (Shakow, Hilgard, Kelly, Luckey, Sanford, & Shaffer, 1947) established the foundations for what has become known as the *scientist–practitioner model* of training in clinical psychology.

This model (which will be examined in more detail in Chapter 2), suggested that the clinical psychologist is a psychologist first and foremost. As a psychologist, the clinical psychologist must be trained in both scientific methods and general psychological principles, then in applied clinical techniques.

A two-week conference was held in 1949 in Boulder, Colorado to discuss this and other possible models of clinical training. The participants unani-

mously endorsed the scientist–practitioner model (Barlow, Hayes, & Nelson, 1984), henceforth also referred to as the *Boulder Model*.

From the 1940s through the present, there has been an increased demand for clinical services (Reisman, 1981) and a shift among psychologists toward applied rather than academic careers (Canter & Canter, 1982; Pryzwansky & Wendt, 1987; Reisman, 1981). With the increased demand for and interest in applied clinical positions, there has been an increased demand for programs that emphasize the practitioner over the scientific component of clinical training.

For these reasons, subsequent conferences on clinical training at Vail in 1973 (Korman, 1974) and Salt Lake City in 1987 (Bickman, 1987) endorsed a practitioner model of training as an alternative to the Boulder Model. The *Vail Model* emphasizes professional training over scientific training. However, this model continues to recognize that clinical practice should be founded on scientifically demonstrated principles and techniques, and so has been referred to occasionally as the *practitioner–scientist model*.

The Vail Model forms the basis of Psy.D. programs, which were introduced in 1968 at the University of Illinois (Peterson, 1968). By the 1980s, this model of clinical training had become well established (Peterson, 1985). By 1993, there were 50 Psy.D. programs in the United States, of which 22 were APA accredited (Norcross, Hanych, & Terranova, 1996).

Following the APA's endorsement of the scientist–practitioner model, many of the traditional assumptions and practices of clinical psychologists were subjected to empirical testing. Wierzbicki (1993a) discussed the empirical evaluation of six major issues that were examined at this time: the effectiveness of psychotherapy; the stability of personality; the reliability of diagnosis; the reliability and validity of projective tests; the relative accuracies of clinical and statistical predication; and the validity of clinical judgment. In every case, research in the 1950s and 1960s led clinical psychologists to question the validity of traditional assumptions and practices and stimulated the development of alternative approaches.

Thus, alternatives to Freudian psychoanalytic theory (including behavioral, cognitive, humanistic, and biological viewpoints) became popular in the 1950s and 1960s. Treatments that were based on these theories and that were more readily tested than psychoanalysis became popular at this time. Alternatives to projective personality testing (including structured personality inventories, and behavioral, cognitive, and neuropsychological assessment) became widespread from the 1950s to the present. In every respect, endorsement of the scientist–practitioner model had a significant impact on the roles of the clinical psychologist. The specifics of these innovations in theory, assessment, and treatment will be discussed later in the book.

SUMMARY

Clinical psychology is that branch of psychology that studies abnormal behavior and mental processes. It addresses the cause, assessment, and treatment of abnormality. Like other areas of psychology, it adopts a scientific approach.

Although clinical psychology is only about 100 years old, its historical roots extend back to ancient times. Three historical approaches to explaining abnormality are the religious, physiological, and psychological models.

Prehistoric man probably used a religious approach to explain and treat abnormality. Ancient civilizations (including Greek and Roman) recognized religious, biological, and psychological influences on abnormality. However, the religious viewpoint was probably the most influential view held until the rise of modern science in recent centuries.

Biological explanations of mental illness became popular in the 1800s, bolstered by successes in explaining disorders such as general paresis. Psychiatrists in the 1800s, including Freud early in his career, adopted a biological reductionistic approach to explaining and treating mental illness.

The social model of abnormality became influential following the Enlightenment of the 1700s. Pinel demonstrated that improved environmental conditions (moral treatment) had dramatic effects on mental patients. Other physicians and social leaders followed Pinel's lead, advocating more humane treatments of mental patients. Itard's treatment of Victor, the Wild Boy of Aveyron, also helped to increase the public's awareness of the need for improved education and care for the mentally retarded.

The psychological model also became influential following the Enlightenment. Wundt established the first laboratory devoted to psychological research, and helped to establish psychology as an independent science. One of the first to apply psychological techniques in efforts to treat disorders was Mesmer. He showed that mesmerism (later called hypnotism) could have dramatic effects on apparently physical symptoms. By the end of the 1800s, hypnotism was recognized as a powerful psychological technique. By this time, Freud and his contemporaries had developed a variety of psychological theories to explain disorders.

In the first half of the twentieth century, clinical psychologists employed theories that emphasized environmental influences. However, current thinking recognizes that both biological and psychological factors have a significant influence on abnormal behavior.

Witmer introduced the term *clinical psychology* in the 1890s and established the first psychological clinic in 1896.

Clinical psychologists had a somewhat uncertain role in the first half of the 1900s. Clinical psychologists were criticized by experimental psychologists for not basing clinical applications on established scientific principles. Clinical psychologists themselves debated whether their field was an art or a science, and whether their proper role was assessment or treatment. These disagreements led clinical psychologists to separate from and then rejoin the APA on two occasions.

Following World War II, the APA recommended that clinical psychologists be trained within existing doctoral programs. A conference on the training of clinical psychologists was held in Boulder, Colorado. This conference endorsed the scientist–practitioner (Boulder) model of clinical training, in which the clinical psychologist is trained as a scientifically-oriented psychologist and as a clinician.

Adoption of the scientist–practitioner model of training led clinical psychologists to examine their field scientifically. This led to a series of debates in the 1950s and 1960s, over the empirical support for many traditionally held assumptions and practices. As a consequence, clinical psychologists introduced new theories, assessment techniques, and treatments that were more readily testable and that received more empirical support than previous approaches.

In recent decades, there has been an increase in the demand for clinical services and in the number of clinical psychologists who seek applied rather than research or teaching positions. This has led to the development of Psy.D. training programs, also called the practitioner–scientist model of training. In this model, students are trained as clinicians first. Rather than conduct scientific research themselves, practitioner–scientists provide services that have a scientific foundation. This model of training has been endorsed by the APA as an alternative to the traditional scientist–practitioner model.

S T U D Y   Q U E S T I O N S

1. What are the major functions of the clinical psychologist?
2. What is the relationship between clinical psychology and psychology in general?
3. What are the major perspectives historically used to explain and treat abnormal behavior?
4. Describe the influences on the rise of the physiological approach to explaining abnormal behavior.
5. Discuss contemporary examples of the religious approach to explaining abnormal behavior.
6. Describe the major influences on the rise of the psychological approach to explaining abnormal behavior.

7. What conflicts arose in the first half of the 1900s concerning the role of the clinical psychologist?
8. What is the scientist–practitioner model?
9. What effect did adoption of the scientist–practitioner model have on the traditional assumptions and practices of clinical psychology?
10. What is the practitioner–scientist model? Discuss the similarities and dissimilarities between the Boulder and Vail Models of training.

2

Scientific Foundations of Clinical Psychology

I. Philosophy of Science
  A. Assumptions of Science
  B. Stages of Science
  C. Scientific Theories
  D. Scientific Progress
II. Research Methods in Clinical Psychology
  A. Single-Subject Designs
  B. Correlational versus Experimental Research
  C. Other Important Designs in Clinical Psychology
III. The Scientist–Practitioner Model of Clinical Psychology
IV. Summary

This text is based on the central theme of the philosophy of science. The purpose of this chapter is to introduce students to the scientific foundations of clinical psychology. In doing so, this chapter will discuss the philosophy of science, present the research methods used in clinical psychology, and describe the scientist–practitioner model of clinical psychology. This material will set the stage for examination, in later chapters, of the scientific bases of the clinical psychologist's roles as assessor, therapist, and psychopathologist.

PHILOSOPHY OF SCIENCE

Philosophy of science is a branch of the area of philosophy called *epistemology*. Epistemology is the philosophy of knowledge and deals with such eso-teric questions as: What do we know? How do we learn what we know? How certain is our knowledge?

Philosophy of science emerged as a distinct discipline in the first half of the twentieth century, influenced by the increasing importance of science to modern society and by the rise in *analytic, positivistic,* and other relatively *scientific* approaches to philosophy. Individuals important in the development of the philosophy of science include Karl Popper, Herbert Feigl, Rudolf Carnap, Ernest Nagel, and Carl Hempel.

Philosophy of science examines the assumptions and methods of science. What is understood implicitly by scientists is articulated and stated explicitly by philosophers of science. Thus, the goals of philosophy of science are (1) to identify and examine the assumptions of science; (2) to clarify the nature of scientific progress; and (3) to articulate these ideas for scientists and others.

Many students are not familiar with the basic assumptions and methods of science. However, the full appreciation of a science such as psychology demands such a background. What follows is an introduction to the philosophy of science. Interested readers should pursue further reading on this subject (c.f., Feigl & Brodbeck, 1953; Hempel, 1965; Nagel, 1961).

Assumptions of Science
Science is basically a method of attempting to learn about the world. However, it is only one of many approaches that people use. For example, popular alternatives to science include mysticism, revelation, rationalism, and intuition.

What distinguishes science from other enterprises are its assumptions. Science has been compared to a game (Agnew & Pyke, 1969). Like a game, science is played by a set of rules. If one is to "play" the game of science, then one must play by its rules: (1) determinism, (2) empiricism, and (3) order.

Determinism   *Determinism* is the assumption that all events have causes. When a phenomenon occurs, science assumes that it was caused. For example, if an individual begins to hear voices from beings in another dimension, emanating from the electrical outlets in the room, a clinical psychologist assumes that these hallucinations have a cause.

Furthermore, science assumes that a cause is related to its effect in several ways—temporally, spatially, and theoretically. Science assumes that causes occur before, have some physical connection to, and are lawfully or meaningfully associated with their consequences.

Although the principle of determinism sounds simple and common-sensical, it should be recognized that the basic principle can be debated at length. For example, quantum physicists have introduced the concept of the *positron* or *anti-electron*, which, according to their mathematical equations, can theoretically move backward in time. If so, then the temporal relationship between cause and effect may be questioned at the quantum level. Similarly, as physicists have identified various forces that act over distance, the spatial relationship between cause and effect has been extended. Also, as scientists have introduced novel principles, the notion of a lawful or theoretical relationship between cause and effect has been broadened.

Particularly troublesome to the scientific assumption of determinism is its applicability to human behavior. Philosophers and theologians have wrestled with determinism for thousands of years (e.g., Hook, 1958; Russell, 1945). A definitive solution to the issue of the determinism of human behavior is beyond the scope of this book (and probably the entirety of mankind's written record). For this reason, the principle of determinism will be left in its basic form articulated above and will be regarded as a working assumption of science, rather than as a metaphysical statement about human nature.

Empiricism   Science also operates under the assumption of *empiricism*. This is the assumption that science restricts its attention to observables or measurables. Like determinism, the principle of empiricism is one that is common-sensical and readily understood by nonscientists.

This is the assumption of science that led early behaviorists, such as John Watson and B. F. Skinner, to omit mental processes from psychology. They insisted that a scientific psychology restrict its attention to observables—behaviors. If a client complains of a lack of meaning in life, the assumption of empiricism leads the psychologist to consider not simply the client's description of this dilemma, but also the observable changes that have occurred in the client's behavior (social, occupational, self-care).

However, as was the case with determinism, the assumption of empiricism can be questioned. For example, astronomers have introduced the concept of a *black hole*—a phenomenon that, by definition, *cannot* be directly observed.

For several decades, philosophers of science and scientists have recognized that science can and does include nonobservables. However, the inclusion of nonobservables must be done cautiously and only after meeting rigorous restrictions.

Science includes nonobservables called *hypothetical constructs*. Hypothetical constructs are nonobservable constructs that are presumed to exist and are theoretically related to observable constructs (MacCorquodale & Meehl, 1948). Thus, one can conduct tests concerning the nature of a hypothetical construct by examining the state of the observable constructs to which the hypothetical construct is presumably related. In this way, hypothetical constructs, although not directly observable, become indirectly observable.

The black hole can be regarded as a hypothetical construct. Although it cannot be observed directly, statements about black holes can be tested through observations of concepts that are theoretically related to black holes. In the same way, psychologists regard mental processes and other internal psychological characteristics as hypothetical constructs. For example, self esteem cannot be viewed by others; still, self-esteem can be assessed through its relationship to observables, such as expressed confidence. Although mental constructs are not directly observable, they can be assessed at least indirectly through their theoretical relationships to observable constructs, such as overt behaviors or physiological states.

Order   A third assumption of science is *order*. This is the assumption that the universe is lawful—that nature is orderly. Science assumes that there are laws that govern the operation of its subject matter. The causes, presumed to exist by the assumption of determinism, are thought to act in a consistent and stable fashion.

The goal of a science, then, is to discover those laws governing its domain. In the science of psychology, the goal is to discover those laws that govern behavior and mental processes.

These three assumptions, of course, operate simultaneously. Any event has a cause that is detectable and that operates lawfully so that observations of similar cases can lead to the discovery of the cause. In this way, science is an optimistic enterprise. It is based on the premise that the scientist can and will ultimately understand universal laws.

As an example of this, suppose a psychologist observes that depression runs through a client's family, with relatives of the depressed patient having a higher risk for depression than the general population. The scientific clinical psychologist assumes that there is a cause for this phenomenon and that this cause is detectable. Moreover, the psychologist assumes that this cause is lawful and therefore leads depression to run through other families as well. The psychologist can then observe many families and ultimately discover why depression runs in families. Eventually, the clinical psychologist can use this information in efforts to prevent or treat depression.

Stages of Science

Science discovers these fundamental laws through a four-stage process. The four stages of science are to (1) describe, (2) explain, (3) make predictions about, and (4) control its subject matter.

Describe   The first stage of any science is to observe and describe its subject matter. It is a truism that science begins with observations. These observations should be both complete and accurate.

A basic part of scientific training is to learn how to use those measuring instruments that are appropriate to the field. As scientists, clinical psychologists learn to use methods for observing and measuring abnormal behavior: clinical interviews; tests of personality, intelligence, and cognitive processes; behavioral observations, and so on. These assessment techniques will be discussed at length in Chapters 4 through 7.

One of the important tools in this initial stage of science is the operational definition. An *operational definition* is a specification of a concept in terms of the operations or procedures used to measure the concept. The key idea here is measurement. For example, anxiety can be operationally defined in any of several measurable ways: physiological measures (such as elevated pulse or blood pressure); behavioral measures (such as fidgeting or avoidance of certain objects or situations); and self-descriptions of anxiety level.

Operational definitions are important for several reasons. By defining concepts in measurable terms, operational definitions lead scientists to think clearly and precisely about their concepts. Secondly, by defining concepts in measurable terms, operational definitions ensure that scientists meet the assumption of empiricism. Finally, operational definitions clarify communication within the field, because they specify exactly how a concept is measured. For example, clinical psychologists are interested in many constructs that, by their very nature, are difficult to pin down (e.g., personality, intelligence, and abnormality). Everyone knows what they mean by these terms, yet there are many different approaches to understanding them. One clinical psychologist may define anxiety in terms of a physiological measurement whereas another may define it in terms of self-rated anxiety. Although these psychologists may disagree as to which definition is more useful, they know exactly how the other conceptualizes the construct.

Explain   After having made extensive observations, the scientist ultimately begins to suspect that there are patterns underlying these observations— that variables seem to be related to one another in regular and lawful ways. These suspected relationships are *hypotheses,* or statements of the potential empirical relationship between variables. Hypotheses are potential in that they cannot be presented with certitude; they reflect one's best guess concerning the observations made to date.

After generating a number of hypotheses, the scientist begins to suspect that there are patterns underlying the various hypotheses—the hypotheses themselves seem to have an underlying order. At this point, the scientist develops a theory to try to explain the hypotheses. A *theory* is a set of general principles and concepts that are used to explain a set of observations.

For example, suppose a clinical psychologist observes the behavior of children and their parents. She will find that parents who smoke cigarettes tend to have children who, more than average, smoke cigarettes; parents who drink alcohol excessively tend to have children who, more than average, grow up to drink alcohol excessively; parents who physically abuse their children tend to have children who, more than average, grow up to become abusive parents. The psychologist will eventually observe many ways in which the behavior of children resembles that of their parents. Each of these observed similarities in the behavior of children and their parents can be stated as a hypothesis.

Now, the clinical psychologist will eventually attempt to explain the numerous observed similarities between children and their parents. For example, she may suggest that children observe such behaviors in their parents and learn them through observation. She may further elaborate this model by addressing issues such as why children model their parents' behaviors more than the behavior of other people. The clinical psychologist has proposed a theory or set of laws that explain why the behavior of children resembles that of their parents.

Scientific theories serve two major functions. As already noted, they provide possible explanations of observations. A second major function of theories, as elaborated below in the discussion of the third stage of science, is that they guide research by generating predictions that lead to new observations.

Predict   The business of science is not completed in Stage 2 with the development of theories to explain observations. Simply proposing a theory is not sufficient. No matter how plausible a theory sounds, it is possible that the explanation is incomplete or inaccurate. Other scientists may propose alternative explanations for the observations.

In the example of the similarity between the behavior of children and parents, a second psychologist might suggest an alternative to a modeling theory. Perhaps children and their parents express similar behaviors because of their shared genes. If the observed behaviors have genetic influences, then the behavior of children resembles that of their parents—not because they learned these behaviors from their parents, but because they inherited their parents' genes. Similarly, other psychologists may agree with the initial theory that children learn these behaviors from their parents; however, they may suggest that learning principles other than modeling are important. For example, perhaps it is direct instruction by parents or the parents' use of punishment and reinforcement that trains the behavior in their children. Psychologists may also suggest that children model their parents' behavior but use different principles to explain why imitation occurs (e.g., Freud's explanation of why children identify with the same-sex parent is based on sexual motivation).

Because simply proposing an explanation for observations does not ensure that the explanation is correct, science moves on to Stage 3, the stage of prediction and experimentation. In this stage, scientists pit competing theories against one another in order to determine which is the most accurate. If two theories explain equally well all of the observations made to date, then the scientist must imagine circumstances under which the theories will predict different outcomes. Such predictions represent new hypotheses. These circumstances are established and an experiment is conducted. The results may determine which of the competing theories is more accurate (or that neither theory is accurate and so some third theory must be considered).

Thus, the third stage of science requires that proposed theories generate predictions about new possible observations. It is through the investigation of such predictions that the accuracy of theories is evaluated.

Thus, science is a cyclical process involving both empirical observation and abstract conceptualization. Empirical observations are made, from which general principles are induced. These principles are then used to deduce predictions concerning new possible observations; empirical investigation then determines the accuracy of the predictions. In this way, science relies on both induction and deduction and on both empirical and abstract processes.

Control   After having determined which of several proposed theories seems to be the most accurate, science proceeds to its fourth stage. Here scientists apply their understanding of the theoretical laws in order to control their subject matter.

Many people object to the word *control* when discussing psychology. Clearly, it is not the goal of psychologists to establish themselves in positions of authority where they control the behavior of people in general.

The term *control* can easily be replaced with the term *application*. Psychologists apply their understanding of the laws of behavior and mental processes to achieve desired results in specific cases. For example, clinical psychologists use their understanding of the laws of learning, motivation, development, and other areas of psychology to help clients modify their deviant behavior or experience relief from distressing emotions.

The fourth stage of science therefore, can be thought of as the application stage. Scientists who understand the theoretical principles, developed and established in previous stages, apply them in specific circumstances in order to achieve specific goals. Exhibit 2.1 summarizes the four stages of science.

EXHIBIT 2.1   The Four Stages of Science

Stage	Tasks
Describe	Make careful, accurate observations.
	Introduce operational definitions for constructs.
Explain	Observe relationships between variables that can be stated as hypotheses.
	Develop multiple theories, or sets of laws, to explain the hypotheses.
Predict	Generate predictions from each theory.
	Test the predictions by conducting experiments.
	Select only those theories that withstand these tests for further consideration.
Control	Apply principles from the most well-validated theories to obtain desired results in specific cases.

Scientific Theories

The next two sections of the chapter present in more detail the second and third stages of science. This section of the chapter addresses the nature of scientific theories—the characteristics and criteria used to evaluate theories. The following section discusses the nature of scientific progress—what occurs when scientists test competing theories and find that one is superior to another.

Remember that theories are proposed in Stage 2 to explain events observed in Stage 1. However, just because a scientist has proposed an explanation for the observations does not mean that the explanation is correct. Two or more competing theories can be generated to explain the observations. The theories will be tested in Stage 3. However, even before theories are tested empirically, there are several characteristics that can be used to evaluate them: comprehensiveness, parsimony, applied value, internal consistency, and falsifiability.

The criterion of *comprehensiveness* is straightforward and readily understood. All else being equal, scientists prefer a more comprehensive theory over a less comprehensive one. A theory that explains many phenomena is preferred to one that explains fewer phenomena.

The second criterion for evaluating theories is *parsimony*. This is a nonparsimonious term that means simplicity. All else being equal, scientists prefer simple over more complex theories. This preference is so basic to science that it has been termed the *law of parsimony*. (See Exhibit 2.2 for historical presentations of this law.) Scientific theories are simple if they utilize few concepts and laws and if they introduce fewer new concepts and principles than competing theories. Such simple theories are considered elegant.

Two additional points about parsimony should be made. First, just because one theory is simpler than another does not mean that the simpler theory is correct. Empirical testing may later show that the complex theory is more accurate than the simple one.

Scientists prefer the most parsimonious theory when all else is equal. The simplest theory is the one that is most easily understood, most easily used to generate predictions, and most easily tested. Thus, by beginning with the most parsimonious theory, scientists will make the most rapid progress.

Second, it should be noted that the criteria of parsimony and comprehensiveness run counter to one another. As a theory becomes more comprehensive, it becomes less parsimonious; as a theory becomes more parsimonious, it explains fewer phenomena. Scientists strive for a balance between parsimony and comprehensiveness. They seek theories that are simple enough to be readily understood, tested, and applied, yet are comprehensive enough to be interesting and important.

The third criterion used to evaluate theories is applied value. Scientists prefer theories that, even though they may have been developed to account for observations in one arena, may be applied to new and

---

EXHIBIT 2.2   The Law of Parsimony

The law of parsimony states that, all else being equal, scientists prefer a more parsimonious theory over less parsimonious theories. Parsimony has been regarded as an important feature of scientific theories for centuries. An early statement of the law of parsimony is attributed to William of Occam (1300?–1350?). He wrote of science that "it is vain to do with more what can be done with fewer" (Russell, 1945, p. 472). That is, if science can possibly explain a phenomenon without presuming the existence of some hypothetical construct, then it should do so. Thus, the law of parsimony is often called *Occam's Razor*.

C. Lloyd Morgan (1852–1936), influenced by Darwin's theory of evolution, also stressed this principle. Morgan argued that, when explaining animal behavior, scientists should use the simplest explanation possible, without attributing to animals higher processes such as mind or will. Morgan (1894) wrote: "In no case may we interpret an [animal] action as the outcome of the exercise of a higher psychical faculty, if it can be interpreted as the outcome of the exercise of one which stands lower in the psychological scale" (cited in Herrnstein & Boring, 1966, p. 468). Thus, the law of parsimony is also called *Morgan's Canon*.

different arenas. The ability to be applied to multiple problem areas or contexts is called *heuristic value.*

The three criteria presented so far address practical considerations. It is readily apparent that comprehensiveness, simplicity, and applied value are desirable features of a scientific theory. The remaining two criteria, however, may be less readily apparent. These criteria address the degree to which a theory can be tested and so they both become important as science moves from Stage 2 (explanation) to Stage 3 (prediction).

The fourth criterion used to evaluate scientific theories is *internal consistency.* This means that, when the laws of a theory are applied to a set of circumstances, the theory cannot predict contradictory outcomes. Systems that predict contradictory outcomes will always be supported; they will be correct regardless of which outcome occurs. Thus, it is not possible to find flaw in the system and so it is not possible to replace the system with a more accurate one. Progress grinds to a halt.

The fifth and final criterion used to evaluate theories is *falsifiability.* This means that scientific theories must, in principle, be able to be falsified. That is, the theory must be able to generate predictions that need not be true. Scientists use the theory to generate predictions, carry out studies to check the accuracy of the predictions, and then revise or replace the theory as needed.

Falsifiability is also known as refutability or testability. Scientists must be able to test a theory's predictions. If a system cannot be used to generate predictions or if it can predict contradictory outcomes, then it is not falsifiable.

Karl Popper (1959, 1963) regarded falsifiability as the defining characteristic of a scientific theory. That is, scientific systems must, according to Popper, be able to generate predictions that need not be true. If a system cannot generate such testable predictions, then it is not science.

There are many examples of irrefutable systems. For example, consider the familiar childhood bet: "Heads I win, tails you lose." No matter what the outcome of a trial, the system wins. More complex examples of systems that cannot be refuted are certain philosophical and theological systems. For ex-

ample, consider a philosophical system that holds that all experience is illusory. This system cannot be refuted, because any evidence presented to counter the claim is explained away as part of the illusion. Similarly, the religious belief that the universe was created at 9:00 this morning cannot be refuted, since all of the evidence (historical, geological, astronomical) raised to counter the claim can be explained away as having been created intact this morning.

Of course, these examples do not pose difficulties for scientists. Philosophers and theologians do not claim to be scientists and so their systems do not have to meet scientific criteria. Philosophical and theological criteria are used to evaluate systems in these domains.

However, systems are occasionally presented as scientific but fail to meet the scientific requirement of falsifiability. Popper called such systems *pseudosciences* (or false sciences). Parapsychology is perhaps the most familiar example of a pseudoscience. Three of the most widely held beliefs about parapsychological phenomena are that they do not occur in the presence of skeptics, that they do not occur in a formal atmosphere (such as a scientific laboratory), and that psychics lose their powers over time. This set of beliefs is irrefutable! Suppose one conducts a card-guessing experiment. Every possible result is consistent with the system. If subjects exceed chance results, then this supports the claim that parapsychological phenomena occur. If subjects guess fewer cards correctly than expected by chance, then this supports the claim that skepticism and formal atmospheres inhibit such phenomena (parapsychologists refer to below-chance results as *psi-missing,* a type of negative ESP). Even chance results can be used to support the system, since analyses of individual subjects will show that some exceed chance at the start of the study but level off (i.e., lose their powers) by the end of the study.

Scientific Progress

This section of the chapter discusses the nature of scientific progress—how scientists operate when testing competing theories. The views of both Karl Popper and Thomas Kuhn will be presented on this issue. Their views represent contrasting models of the way in which scientists behave and science progresses.

Karl Popper   Karl Popper is an eminent philosopher of science who introduced the concept of falsifiability as the defining characteristic of science (Popper, 1959, 1963). According to Popper, falsifiability is the *line of demarcation* that distinguishes science from nonscience.

Popper viewed science as a series of *conjectures and refutations* (the title of one of his major books). According to Popper, scientists operate in Stages 2 and 3 as described above. That is, scientists generate theories that are conjectures or best guesses as to the nature of reality. They then proceed to test the theory. Scientists do not merely attempt to confirm the accuracy of the theory. Rather, they try to disconfirm or refute it. By demonstrating that a theory is inaccurate, scientists can discard the theory and adopt a superior one. Thus, science, according to Popper, is a series of conjectures (proposals of theories) and refutations (disconfirmations of theories followed by their replacement with better theories).

According to Popper, science advances more by refuting a theory and replacing it with a better theory than it does by simply obtaining confirmations of the theory. Contrary to what many nonscientists think, science attempts not merely to obtain evidence that supports an idea but rather to seek evidence that disconfirms an idea.

There is a clear asymmetry between proof and disproof of a theory. It is easier to refute a theory than to prove it. For example, consider the statement: "All crows are black." Logicians often use this example to demonstrate the asymmetry between proof and disproof. In order to prove with absolute certainty that this statement is true, it is necessary to observe all crows and to find that in fact *all* crows are black. Because there is only a finite number of crows, it is conceivable that this statement could be proved true. However, because the number of observations required to prove this statement is so large, and because there may be uncertainty as to whether all crows have in fact been found, it is not possible in practice to prove that the statement is true. Even after observing one million black crows, one still has not proved the statement with utter certainty.

On the other hand, it is simpler to prove with absolute certainty that the statement is false. The refutation requires the observation of only a single non-black crow. If one wants to evaluate the truth of such logical statements, it is more rational and economical to search for disconfirmations than confirmations.

The asymmetry between proof and disproof is also found in statistical hypothesis testing. When conducting statistical tests, the investigator establishes a null hypothesis (H_0) and an alternative hypothesis (H_1). The investigator then gathers data and determines the probability that these observations would occur, assuming that H_0 is true. If the result is improbable (likely to occur less than five percent of the time when H_0 is true), then the investigator rejects H_0 and accepts H_1. However, if the observations are not unlikely, then the investigator does not reject H_0. This does not mean that H_0 is true, but simply that it has not been rejected. Statistical hypothesis testing, then, exhibits a similar asymmetry between the proof and disproof of statistical hypotheses.

Suppose a researcher wanted to conduct a statistical test of the statement: "All crows are black." Now, statistical tests of such extreme statements are rarely conducted, so let us modify it slightly: "Virtually all crows (or at least 999,999 out of a million) are black." The null and alternative hypotheses are:

H_0: The percentage of black crows is at least 99.9999.

H_1: The percentage of black crows is less than 99.9999.

Suppose further that the researcher observes 100 crows and finds that 1 is white. The formula used to test whether an observed proportion is equal to a theoretical proportion is:

$$z = ((y/n) - p_0) / \text{SQRT}((p_0 \cdot (1 - p_0) / n),$$

where y is the number of observed "hits," n is the number of observations, and p_0 is the theoretical proportion. Substituting the number of observed black crows (99), the number of observations (100), and the theoretical proportion (.999999) yields a z statistic of approximately -100, which is highly unlikely to occur by chance alone. This makes sense. If only one crow in a million is white, then the probability of seeing that white crow in a set of 100 crows is low.

Now suppose that the researcher makes 100 observations and finds that all 100 crows are black. This study yields a z statistic of approximately 0.01. This is a likely result if H_0 is true, and so the researcher does not reject H_0. However, this does not mean that H_0 is true. After all, the actual proportion of black crows may be one in a half-million rather than one in a million. The result of the study is consistent with this hypothesis (and with countless other hypotheses) as well.

Popper suggested that the same asymmetry between proof and disproof that exists for simple logical statements and for statistical hypothesis testing also holds for entire scientific theories. Suppose a theory consists of a set of laws. To prove that this set of laws is true with utter certainty requires a set of observations comparable to that required to prove the truth of the statement "All crows are black." That is, to prove absolutely that a theory is true requires the observation *of all possible applications* of the theory: all conceivable predictions from the theory must be tested and found to hold true. Even if this is a finite number of observations (and it may not be finite but infinite), the number of possible predictions generated by a theory is likely to be so large that it can never be proved true in practice.

On the other hand, the refutation of a theory requires simply the observation of a single white crow. That is, if the theory generates a single prediction that is incorrect, then the theory must be replaced.

Thus, according to Popper, scientists should seek disconfirmations of theories in order to evaluate them most effectively. Science advances most rapidly when old ideas are proved incorrect, because they can then be replaced by superior ideas.

This mode of thinking is counterintuitive. However, it is easy to show that it is the most efficient way of evaluating hypotheses. See the example in Exhibit 2.3.

According to Popper, scientists should be paragons of rationality. They should be objective, impartial, open minded, and self-critical. When they develop ideas, they should be the first to examine them for flaws. When flaws are discovered in their systems, they should welcome such discoveries and be flexible enough to embrace new and alternative ideas.

Thomas Kuhn A very different view of scientists and the nature of scientific progress was presented by Thomas Kuhn. Kuhn is a historian of science who is best known for his 1962 book, *The Structure of Scientific Revolutions*.

According to Kuhn, scientists are much less rational than Popper suggested. Kuhn described science as operating within the context of a scientific paradigm. A *paradigm* is the dominant theory within a science. However, the paradigm includes more than the general principles of a theory; it also includes the research questions and methods that are considered appropriate.

Most of science, according to Kuhn, operates within the paradigm without attempting to refute it. Kuhn refers to this stage of science as *normal science*. In normal science, scientists apply the existing paradigm to problems that the paradigm suggests can be solved. They are engaged in mundane puzzle solving that simply extends the boundaries of the paradigm.

After a period of normal science in which scientists solve one minor puzzle after another, an anomaly may be discovered that resists solution within the paradigm. This anomaly may not stimulate much of a response because the paradigm may regard it as unimportant and unworthy of attention. However, if the anomaly cannot be ignored, then a scientific crisis occurs.

Scientific crises are characterized by the development and evaluation of numerous alternatives to the existing paradigm. There is a flurry of creative theorizing and critical examination. At this point, Kuhn's description of science resembles Popper's.

Ultimately, one of the alternatives to the existing paradigm becomes recognized as the most satisfactory. This new model can explain all the phenomena of interest to the old paradigm as well as the anomaly that resisted solution within the old paradigm. At this point, the new model becomes the new paradigm and

EXHIBIT 2.3   The Efficiency of Disconfirmation in Testing Hypotheses

Wason and Johnson-Laird (1972) described a classic study that demonstrated that the most effective way to evaluate hypotheses is to try to refute them.

Subjects were given a group of numbers (2, 4, 6) and told that these numbers met a simple mathematical rule. Their task was to discover the rule through experimentation; an experiment consisted of suggesting a new group of three numbers and learning whether this group met the rule. Subjects could then announce the rule when they were confident that they had deduced it.

Subjects who did not receive further instructions tended to use a confirmatory strategy. That is, they thought of a rule (e.g., "even numbers increasing by two") and generated experiments consistent with the rule (e.g., "4, 6, 8"; "10, 12, 14"). After learning that these groups met the rule, subjects quickly announced that they had discovered the rule. Upon being informed they were wrong, subjects formed other hypotheses (e.g., "even or odd numbers increasing by two") and conducted confirmatory experiments (e.g., "1, 3, 5"; "3, 5, 7"). After performing several experiments that confirmed the rule, subjects again announced they had identified the rule, only to learn they were incorrect. Subjects typically followed this confirmatory strategy throughout the experimental period, often failing to identify the correct rule ("any three numbers where $x < y < z$").

Wason and Johnson-Laird gave this same problem to other subjects, but instructed them that the most efficient manner of testing a hypothesis is to suggest a number sequence that is incompatible with it. Now, to test the rule, "even numbers increasing by two," subjects would try a sequence such as "1, 3, 6"). In this case, if one learns that the sequence is consistent with the rule, then, in a single trial, one has disproved the hypothesis. In this condition, subjects rapidly identified the rule, using relatively few experiments to reach the correct conclusion.

This study is a classic demonstration of the efficiency of a disconfirmatory strategy—the scientific method—in evaluating hypotheses. It should be noted, however, that this is a counter-intuitive manner of thinking. It is a process that must be developed through training and practice.

However, even scientists have difficulty remembering to use this strategy when they are not in their laboratory. Mahoney (1976) replicated the Wason and Johnson-Laird (1972) study, using both scientists and ministers as subjects, and found that scientists actually performed more poorly than ministers! According to Mahoney (p. 156), scientists tended to "be more speculative than non-scientists—generating more hypotheses, more quickly, and with fewer experiments per hypothesis!"

normal science resumes, with scientists devoting their efforts to puzzle solving within the paradigm.

Despite the scientific revolution, some scientists do not accept the new paradigm. Their devotion to the old paradigm leads them to reject the evidence for the new paradigm. Kuhn compares their devotion to the old paradigm to religious faith. They retain their old belief regardless of the evidence.

Younger scientists tend to adopt the new paradigm more readily than older scientists. They do not have the same emotional attachment to the traditional paradigm as older scientists. They train and conduct their initial research at the time when the old paradigm is being questioned. Because they have less commitment than more experienced scientists to the old paradigm, they adopt the new paradigm rather easily.

Interestingly, because older scientists are more established within the field than younger scientists (e.g., occupy more senior faculty positions, hold more positions as directors of research or of graduate training), it may take some time for the new paradigm to become firmly entrenched. Max Planck (1949) acknowledged this process in physics: "A new scientific truth does not triumph by convincing its opponents and making them see the light, but rather because its opponents eventually die, and a new generation grows up that is familiar with it" (pp. 33–34).

Comparison of Popper and Kuhn   Popper and Kuhn have both provided influential descriptions of science. Even though their views are quite different, they are both accurate to some extent. Popper and

Kuhn had different purposes in developing their models. Popper, the philosopher of science, provided a prescription for how scientists should behave in the ideal. Kuhn, the historian of science, described how scientists have behaved in reality.

Their views of science agree most clearly in how science progresses. Popper argued that all of science is a process of conjectures and refutations. He described scientific progress as occurring through the refutation of old ideas and their replacement with superior ones. Kuhn agreed that this type of process occurred; however, he believed that this occurred only during periods of scientific crisis. During normal science, Kuhn thought that scientists behaved rather mundanely only to confirm or to extend the existing paradigm.

It is important for students to be aware of both views of science. As future scientists (or at least consumers of scientific claims), it is important to recognize the nonrational influences on science that limit the accuracy of scientific claims. As potential clinical psychologists, it is also important to be aware of how different theoretical movements developed and supplanted previous approaches. Chapter 3 will present the major theories of personality and psychopathology in clinical psychology. Students should attend to the historical ebb and flow of these views and consider how both Popper's and Kuhn's models of science can be applied to them.

RESEARCH METHODS IN CLINICAL PSYCHOLOGY

The previous section of the chapter discussed the philosophy of science and the nature of scientific progress. As presented above, empirical observation and testing of theoretical predictions are essential to science. Throughout this textbook, research results that illustrate findings in assessment, psychotherapy, and psychopathology will be presented. Before reading the results of specific studies, it is important that students be familiar with the research designs that generated these results, and of the relative strengths and weaknesses of these designs. This section of the chapter examines the various research methods that are appropriate in a scientific study of clinical psychology.

Before discussing specific research methodologies, it is important to know two criteria that are used to evaluate research designs. The first of these is external validity. *External validity* is the extent to which the results of a study generalize to other subjects and situations. External validity is a function of the degree to which the subjects and situations in the study are representative of the subjects and situations to which the investigator wishes to generalize the results.

Researchers have often been criticized on the grounds that their investigations have limited external validity. For example, B. F. Skinner, the noted behaviorist, conducted much of his research on rats and pigeons. When he generalized his results to humans, he was criticized on the grounds that the findings need not generalize across species. Similarly, Sigmund Freud, the founder of psychoanalysis, has been criticized on the basis of low external validity. Freud's observations were conducted primarily on middle-aged, neurotic, upper-middle-class women. Although his ideas may apply to that population, they need not generalize to the rest of us.

The second criterion used to evaluate research designs is *internal validity*. Internal validity is the extent to which the results were caused by the experimental treatment. That is, did the variable in question actually produce the observed results?

For example, a psychologist may be interested in examining the effectiveness of a new treatment for a particular disorder. If the psychologist observes that 20 of 20 clients improve after receiving treatment, the psychologist may be tempted to conclude that the therapy caused the improvement. However, if the condition is time limited (e.g., the common cold, an adjustment disorder), then the improvement would have occurred with or without treatment. In this case, the improvement may have been caused by time alone (and the organism's natural healing processes) rather than by the therapy.

Internal validity is a function of the degree to which the investigator has controlled for and thereby ruled out alternative possible explanations for the observed results. In the example above, the investigator could add a no treatment (or delayed treatment) *control group* to the study, to rule out the possibility that the improvement was caused by the passage of time alone.

Single-Subject Designs

The first important research method in clinical psychology to be discussed is the *case study*. Incidentally, this is the research method used most extensively by early clinical psychologists. For example, the work of Freud and other early theorists was based primarily on case study research. In fact, the case study method may well have been the most commonly employed research method by clinical psychologists prior to 1960.

The case study is an intensive investigation of an individual subject (where "subject" in this context need not be a single individual but may be a couple, family, or other narrowly defined group). Case studies involve the detailed description of the subject, often over an extended period of time.

In clinical case studies, the subject presents with some form of pathology and receives therapy. Much information is gathered concerning the subject's history, symptomatology, and response to treatment.

Case studies are rich sources of information, and so they are useful in the first stage of science. Because so much information is obtained, case studies are also rich sources of hypotheses concerning the possible causes of the client's disorder and the effects of treatment. Thus, case studies are also useful in the second stage of science, when hypotheses are generated and theories are proposed.

However, case studies are relatively weak in the third stage of science, when testing the validity of explanations proposed in the second stage. Even experienced, diligent, well-trained, and motivated researchers may overlook some crucial evidence that would refute their theories. Also, observations may be biased to support the researchers' beliefs. Because case studies do not permit researchers to control for and rule out such alternative interpretations, they have relatively poor internal validity.

Case studies also have questionable external validity. Some argue that every individual is unique and so the results of a case study cannot generalize to others. Others argue that the representativeness of a case study must be judged for each and every case: some cases are representative of the group to which the results are being generalized whereas other cases are not. Thus, the external validity of a case study depends, as with other studies, on the extent to which the subject is representative of the population to which the results will be generalized.

Even though the internal validity of case studies is weak, case studies remain useful for several practical reasons. They are less expensive and less time consuming than large group studies. Therefore, investigators may use case studies in pilot research to determine whether their ideas have potential. Before committing themselves to expensive, time-consuming, large-scale studies, researchers may begin with case studies to determine whether their ideas warrant further study.

A second practical reason for case studies is the study of rare or unusual cases. If one is interested in a rare condition (e.g., multiple personality disorder) or the response to unusual environmental conditions (e.g., natural disaster, assault by a serial killer), then one must rely on case study research. There may simply be too few cases to support a larger group study.

Because the traditional case study has limited internal and external validity, psychologists have developed several superior single-subject designs. Traditional case studies can be described as having a simple AB design (where A represents the state prior to the intervention and B represents the state following the intervention). As noted above, this design does not provide much support for the claim that the treatment in state B actually caused the observed changes.

One improvement over the case study method is the *ABAB reversal design*. This method, introduced by behavior therapists, simply repeats the two elements of the traditional case study method. That is, there is a baseline period prior to treatment (A), the implementation of the treatment (B), removal of the treatment and return to a baseline condition (A), and finally a reimplementation of the treatment (B). If the client's condition improves during the first treatment period, worsens when treatment is removed, and improves once again when treatment is restored, then the researcher has more confidence than in the traditional case study that the treatment may be causing the improvement. However, because there is still the possibility that an unknown variable has varied along with the treatment and may be causing the improvement, the ABAB design does not prove that the treatment is the cause of the observed improvement.

Another improvement over the original case study that was pioneered by behavior therapists is the *multiple baseline design*. This research design can be used when the investigator has targeted several distinct symptoms for treatment. The investigator first assesses the level of each symptom during a baseline period. Treatment is then introduced for one symptom. If this symptom improves while other symptoms fail to improve (or improve to a lesser degree), then the investigator introduces a treatment for the second target symptom. This pattern is repeated until each symptom has been targeted for treatment. If each symptom improved most when it was the target of therapy, then the investigator has more confidence than in the traditional case study that the treatment caused the improvement.

Correlational versus Experimental Research

A basic distinction in research designs is that between correlational and experimental research. Correlational and experimental studies are distinguished by both the methods used and the conclusions drawn by the investigator. In a *correlational study,* the investigator observes and measures two or more naturally occurring variables, the levels of which are not set or determined by the investigator. For example, clinical psychologists often examine how socioeconomic status, environmental stress, and parental psychopathology are related to psychological problems. Because psychologists cannot determine the levels of these factors, but must instead assess them as they occur naturally, this type of research is correlational.

Correlational studies measure the strength of the relationship between variables, quantifying the relation in the form of a *correlation coefficient*. By convention, the symbol r is used to represent a correlation coefficient. Because correlation coefficients will be cited throughout the book to illustrate the results of specific studies, it is important to understand three basic characteristics of correlation coefficients.

1. Correlation coefficients range from -1 to $+1$.

2. A correlation coefficient of 0 means that there is no relationship between two variables—the variables are independent of one another. That is, knowledge of one variable conveys no information about the other. For example, social security numbers are independent of depression level: it is not possible to predict one from the other. On the other hand, a correlation coefficient of ± 1 means that there is a perfect correlation between the two variables: knowledge of one variable permits an exact prediction of the other variable. For example, a measurement of room temperature in degrees Fahrenheit permits us to predict with complete accuracy the room temperature in degrees Celsius. Correlation coefficients between 0 and ± 1 have intermediate strengths, with the association becoming weaker as r approaches 0.

3. A positive correlation is one where, as one variable increases, the other variable also increases. For example, as stress level increases, psychopathology also increases. If the data yielding a positive correlation coefficient are plotted on a graph, the points fall around a line with an upward slope. Conversely, a negative correlation means that, as one variable increases, the other variable decreases. For example, as depression increases, problem-solving ability decreases. If the data yielding a negative correlation are plotted, the data points fall roughly around a line that has a downward slope. Exhibit 2.4 presents examples of both a positive and a negative correlation.

Although correlational studies measure the strength of an association between variables, *they do not permit the investigator to draw causal conclusions.* This is the major limitation of correlation studies. It may be tempting to conclude from a correlational study that one variable causes the other. For example, because stress level is positively correlated

EXHIBIT 2.4   Examples of a Positive and a Negative Correlation

In a study of individuals who sought treatment for mild to moderate depression, Wierzbicki (1995b) examined the relation between level of depression and engagement in pleasant and unpleasant activities. Clients rated their level of depression using the Beck Depression Inventory (BDI; Beck, Ward, Mendelson, Mock, & Erbaugh, 1961); they reported their engagement in pleasant and unpleasant activities using the mood-related items of the Pleasant Events Schedule and Unpleasant Events Schedule (PES, UES; Lewinsohn & Amenson, 1978).

Depression was found to be significantly correlated with engagement in both pleasant and unpleasant activities. As depression increased, clients reported

engaging in more unpleasant activities ($r = .37$) and fewer pleasant activities ($r = -.37$). Thus, depression was about as strongly associated with pleasant and unpleasant activities, but the relationships were in opposite directions.

The data points from 65 subjects are plotted on the graphs below. As you can see, lines drawn on the graphs to best summarize or represent the data have upward and downward slopes. Also, note that the data points do not cluster very tightly around these lines. As correlation coefficients become larger, the data points cluster more tightly around these lines until, at $r = \pm 1$, the points all fall on the line.

A Negative Correlation between Depression and Engagement in Pleasant Activities

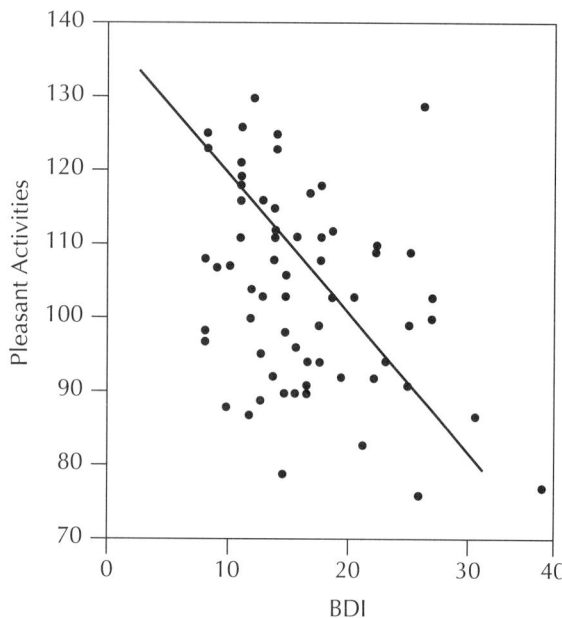

A Positive Correlation between Depression and Engagement in Unpleasant Activities

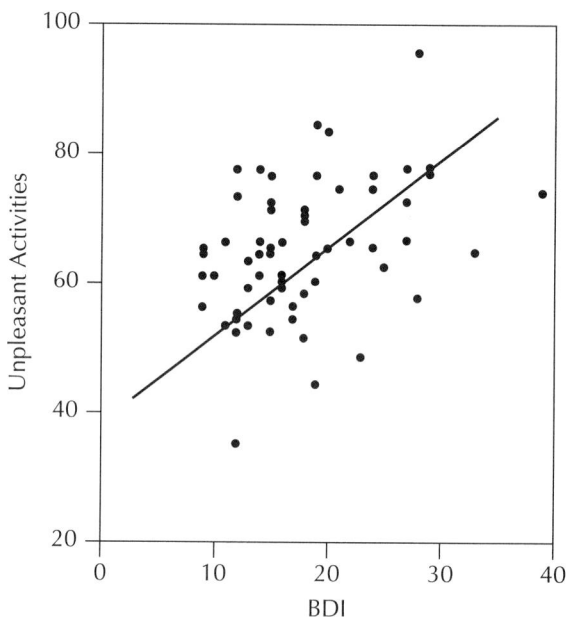

with level of psychopathology, one may be tempted to conclude that stress causes psychopathology. This is certainly consistent with much of what is thought about the causes of psychological disorders. However, despite the intuitive appeal of this interpretation, it is not permitted from the research design. After all, the correlational study has not controlled for,

and thereby ruled out, alternative explanations for the relationship.

Perhaps the causal arrow goes in the direction opposite to that which was initially suspected. That is, perhaps people with high levels of psychopathology experience more stress in their lives; it may be the psychological problems that cause their life

---

EXHIBIT 2.5   Possible Relationships between Stress and Psychopathology That May Account for the Correlation Between Them

a.   Unidirectional Causality:

Stress ⟶ Psychopathology

or   Stress ⟵ Psychopathology

b.   Reciprocal (Bidirectional) Causality:

Stress ⟷ Psychopathology

c.   Indirect Relationship through the Causal Effect of an Unknown Third Variable:

Z (e.g., genetics)

Stress ⟶ Psychopathology

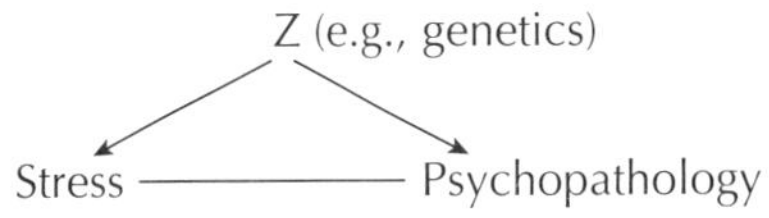

d.   Indirect Relationship through the Causal Effects of a Set of Unknown Third Variables:

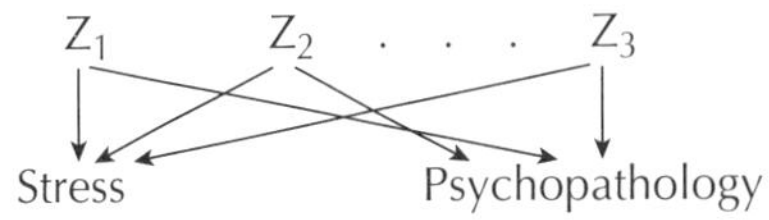

Z_1 Z_2 . . . Z_3

Stress   Psychopathology

---

stress. Perhaps the causal arrow goes in both directions; there may be a reciprocal relationship between the variables.

Another possibility is that some third variable (or set of variables), as yet unidentified, determines the levels of both stress and psychopathology and is the cause of the association between them. Biological (e.g., genetic), psychological (e.g., defensive functioning), or environmental (e.g., dietary, familial) factors may all influence both stress and psychopathology. Exhibit 2.5 illustrates some of the circumstances that may lead to an observed correlation between two variables. Because correlational research does not eliminate such alternative interpretations, the internal validity of correlational designs is limited.

There are many elaborations of the basic correlational study that enable researchers to examine more complex relationships among variables. These include the multiple correlational study, the cross-lag correlational study, and factor analysis.

Multiple correlation measures the association between a criterion variable and a set of predictor variables. For example, if a psychologist wishes to study college performance, she might consider numerous variables that may be correlated with academic performance. A multiple correlation coefficient can be calculated between a student's college grade point average (GPA) and a set of predictors including high school GPA, score on a test of college aptitude, household income, and parent's education level.

Cross-lag correlational studies examine the association between variables at two (or more) points in time. Comparison of the correlations between variables assessed simultaneously and subsequently may suggest the direction of the causal relationship between them. For example, psychologists have long recognized that depression is correlated with social skills: people with high levels of depression tend to exhibit poor social skills (i.e., speak in a monotone, avoid eye contact). But what is the causal

EXHIBIT 2.6   Factor Analysis: Its Rationale and Methodology

Although factor analysis is an advanced statistical technique, it has a simple and intuitive rationale. Factor analysis examines the interrelationships among responses to a large set of items. The technique identifies subsets of items that are answered in related ways. By examining these sets of items, researchers can try to identify the basic dimensions or factors that underlie all of the items.

For example, suppose the instructor in this course administers a cumulative final exam, consisting of 200 multiple-choice items. The instructor could factor analyze the final exam, trying to identify the test's basic dimensions. If a student has a special interest or advanced knowledge in one section of the course material (e.g., psychotherapy), then the student is likely to do well on many of the questions in that area. Conversely, if a student dislikes some portion of the class material or fails to prepare sufficiently during one quarter, the student will not do very well on questions over that material. Thus, a factor analysis of all items on a cumulative test in this course should identify factors that correspond to the major topics in the course (e.g., assessment, psychotherapy, theories of psychopathology, psychoanalytic theory, etc.).

---

direction? Does depression lower social skills or do poor social skills lead to social failure and so induce depression? A researcher can measure level of depression and social skills at two different times and then compare the cross-lag correlations. If the depression (time 1)–social skills (time 2) correlation is greater than the social skills (time 1)–depression (time 2) correlation, then this shows that depression precedes (and so may have a causal influence on) social skills.

Factor analysis is a multivariate technique that examines the interrelationships among a large number of variables in an attempt to identify the basic dimensions that contribute to scores on the variables. Because factor analysis is an important tool in theory development and test construction, it will be discussed in more detail in Exhibit 2.6.

Even though these advanced correlational techniques permit the examination of complex relationships among variables, they still do not permit researchers to draw causal conclusions. Demonstration of causality is restricted to experimental research.

In an *experiment*, the investigator manipulates or determines the level of variables. This manipulation is the feature that distinguishes experiments from correlational studies.

In an experiment, the researcher samples from a population and randomly assigns subjects to two or more groups. (If random assignment is not employed and groups are established by some other means, such as by using previously existing groups, then the research is not a true experiment but is instead what has been called a *quasi-experiment* [Campbell & Stanley, 1966]. Quasi-experimental research, like correlational research, does not permit the investigator to draw causal conclusions.) When random assignment is used to form groups, the laws of probability and statistics ensure that the groups are equivalent at the start of the experiment (as long as the groups are sufficiently large).

Groups are then exposed to identical conditions; any factor that may influence the variables of interest in the study are controlled or kept constant across groups. Thus, because groups were initially equivalent and have been exposed to constant conditions, they remain equivalent throughout the study.

At this point, the researcher introduces the experimental manipulation. Groups are exposed to different levels of the *independent variable (IV)*. At the end of the study, groups are compared with respect to the *dependent variable (DV)*. If the groups differ on the DV, then the investigator can conclude that the difference was caused by the IV.

To illustrate this, suppose a clinical psychologist is interested in testing a new psychotherapy for clients who suffer from frequent panic attacks. A large number of clients with this problem is recruited and randomly assigned to two groups: one receives the new treatment while the other receives no treatment (or is assigned to a waiting list to receive later treatment). Other factors that may be associated with panic are kept constant (such as use of medication, engaging in vigorous exercise, and so on). Following treatment, the psychologist assesses the frequency and severity of panic symptoms in both groups. If the treatment group is found to have fewer symptoms than the control group, then the psychologist can conclude that psychotherapy caused more improvement than no treatment. In this example, the IV (the variable manipulated by the researcher) is treatment and the DV (the variable assessed to determine whether the IV has an effect) is panic disorder symptoms.

Experiments enable us to draw causal, and so more powerful, conclusions than correlational research. This does not mean, however, that experiments are necessarily superior to correlational research. The internal and external validity of individual experiments must be evaluated. If subjects or situations in the experiment are nonrepresentative of the subjects and situations to which one wishes to generalize the results, then the experiment has low external validity. This criticism has occasionally been directed against laboratory experiments that establish artificial settings that differ from the "real world." Similarly, laboratory research with highly selected subjects, such as college freshmen, may not generalize to the general population.

The internal validity of experiments must also be examined on a case-by-case basis. For example, experiments that have not succeeded in maintaining conditions constant across experimental groups have low internal validity.

Other Important Designs in Clinical Psychology

In addition to the research designs presented above, there are several other methodologies that are useful in the study of clinical psychology.

Placebo Study   The first of these is the placebo study. A *placebo* is an inert or an inactive treatment that should not have any therapeutic effect. In medical research, a placebo might be a sugar pill or an in-

jection of a saline solution. The *placebo study* is an experiment that determines whether a treatment causes more improvement than a placebo. The placebo study is essential in determining the effectiveness of new forms of treatment.

Recall the example described in the last section in which a psychologist found that panic disorder patients who received treatment had a superior outcome to untreated patients. This result supports the conclusion that treatment causes a superior outcome to no treatment. However, this result does not explain *why* the treated clients experience greater improvement. It is possible that treated clients improve, not because of the effectiveness of the new treatment, but because of the very act of receiving an alleged treatment. After all, a substantial number of patients respond favorably to placebos. (See Exhibit 2.7 for an overview of the effectiveness of placebos.)

To determine whether a new treatment is in fact an effective treatment, it is essential to conduct a placebo study. In a placebo study, clients are randomly assigned to groups that receive the treatment or a placebo (additional groups may be added, for example, that receive no treatment or an alternative form of treatment). Clients are blind with respect to whether they are receiving a placebo or the new treatment. If the individual who administers the placebo or treatment is also blind with respect to the type of treatment being administered, then the design is referred to as a *double-blind study*. Following this experimental manipulation, outcomes are compared across groups. By comparing the new treatment to a no treatment control group, the psychologist determines whether the treatment is more effective than the passage of time alone. By comparing the new treatment to the placebo, the researcher determines whether the treatment is more effective than a placebo or whether it is, in fact, nothing more than a placebo itself.

The use of placebos has been commonplace in medical research since early in the twentieth century. In psychotherapy research, however, the use of placebos is a rather new development. Gordon Paul (1966) pioneered the use of placebos in psychotherapy research when he introduced the attention pla-

EXHIBIT 2.7   The Effectiveness of Placebos

The placebo effect has long been recognized by physicians. Even the ancient physicians, Galen and Hippocrates, suggested that emotional and other psychological factors are important influences on medical disorders.

Beecher (1955) reviewed 15 studies of the placebo effect and found that, on average, about 35 percent of medical patients respond to placebos. Shapiro and Morris (1978) reviewed the placebo effect in both medical and psychological research and reported that from 0 to 100 percent of patients respond to placebos, varying across populations, disorders, and treatments. A brief overview of the popular media shows that many essentially inactive treatments enjoy wide popularity (e.g., crystals, acupuncture to stop cigarette smoking, starch-blockers to "melt" off fat).

Placebos have not been used as widely in psychotherapy research as in medical research. However, following Paul's (1966) introduction of the attention placebo to psychotherapy research, many clinical psychologists have compared the efficacy of psychotherapy to a placebo.

Prioleau, Murdock, and Brody (1983) reviewed 32 studies that compared psychotherapy to a placebo and found only a modest superiority of psychotherapy. Bowers and Clum (1988) reviewed 69 studies that compared behavior therapy to no treatment, a placebo, or some

other therapy, and concluded that behavior therapy is more than twice as powerful as placebo treatments.

Even though placebos are known to produce significant effects on both medical and psychological conditions, the reason why they work is not known. Shapiro and Morris (1978) cited numerous possible explanations for their effectiveness.

For example, clients who receive a placebo may, because they expect to recover, relabel their symptoms so that they no longer judge them to be as severe as before. This leads to a reported decrease in severity of symptoms, although no real improvement occurs.

Similarly, clients who receive a placebo may become optimistic about their prospects for recovery and so be motivated to behave in healthier ways (e.g., eat a better diet, decrease their alcohol intake, avoid stress). It may be these healthier behaviors and not the placebo that cause the improvement.

Another possibility is that placebos work through classical conditioning. In the client's past, the act of being treated has repeatedly been associated with medical treatments that influence physiological recovery processes (e.g., release of endorphins to alleviate pain, activation of the immune system). In this way, "being treated" may be classically conditioned to elicit similar physiological processes.

---

cebo. When clients receive an attention placebo, they receive attention from a professional; however, there is no interaction that can be regarded as therapeutic.

Analogue Study   Another type of study often used in clinical research is the analogue study. An *analogue study* uses subjects who only resemble in some way the population to which one wishes to generalize the results. The research subjects are analogous to the actual population of interest in some way.

For example, early research on the behavioral treatment of phobias was conducted, not with actual clients seeking treatment for debilitating phobias, but with college students with high scores on measures of common fears (e.g., snakes, public speak-

ing). Similarly, much of the early work on cognitive theories of depression was conducted with college students rather than depressed clients.

Clinical psychologists have used analogue studies in several contexts. They have used analogue studies in treatment research. For example, prior to using new treatments with clinical subjects, analogue studies can be conducted within *subclinical populations* (that is, subjects with mildly elevated levels of certain symptoms, but whose symptoms are not severe enough to warrant a clinical diagnosis) to conduct the initial evaluations of and to refine the treatment. Clinical psychologists have also used analogue studies in research on causal models of psychopathology. For example, prior to research within clinical populations, research can be conducted within subclinical populations to examine the correlates, antecedents, and even the causal influences of mild levels of particular symptoms.

Analogues are used for ethical reasons as well. There may be ethical concerns about exposing patients to new and untested treatments. For this reason, laboratory animals may be used in the initial trials of new medications. Only later will human subjects be involved in the research. Similarly, subclinical analogues may be employed in the initial phases of the development of a new treatment. If the treatment proves to be ineffective, then the analogue subjects would not have suffered from the failure to be provided with an effective treatment to the degree that clinical patients would have.

Another ethical concern arises when investigators are testing causal models of psychopathology. It is clearly unethical to expose subjects to conditions that may produce severe psychological disorders. However, if the conditions are expected to produce mild and transitory elevations of a symptom, then the information to be gained from testing a causal model of subclinical pathology may outweigh the risk of producing such mild problems. Exhibit 2.8 describes the Velten (1968) procedure, which induces mild levels of elation or sadness and which has commonly been used in analogue studies of depression.

In addition to ethical concerns, there are also practical reasons for conducting analogue research. The availability of subjects and the cost of research with clinical subjects may lead psychologists to conduct initial studies in analogue populations.

The major limitation to analogue studies is clearly their external validity. By definition, analogue studies examine subjects from one population and generalize their results to another. The external validity of analogue studies can obviously be questioned. However, given the ethical and practical concerns raised above, analogue studies remain an important method of initial inquiry. Despite their

---

EXHIBIT 2.8   The Velten Mood Induction Procedure

Clinical psychologists have conducted many analogue studies of mood disorders. For such research, it is useful to have procedures that systematically induce positive or negative mood. One commonly used mood induction technique is the Velten mood induction procedure (VMIP; Velten, 1968). This is a cognitive technique in which subjects read and imagine a set of statements applying to themselves.

Velten developed sets of statements with different affective tones. Some were negative (e.g., "People annoy me; I wish I could be by myself," "Just a little bit of effort tires me out," "I just can't make up my mind; it's so hard to make simple decisions"). Some were positive (e.g., "Life is firmly in my control," "I'm really feeling sharp now," "Things will be better and better today"). Some were neutral (e.g., "The Orient Express travels between Paris and Istanbul," "Slang is a constantly changing part of the language"). Velten showed that subjects who read these different sets of statements experienced significant differences in mood, as assessed by self-report, reaction time, motor speed, and spontaneous verbalizations.

Others have also shown that reading Velten's negative statements induces depressed affect. Clark (1983) reviewed the research literature on the Velten procedure and concluded that it mimics the effects of naturally occurring depressed mood. Therefore, the Velten procedure appears to produce a state that is a good analogue of mild, naturally occurring depression.

Inducing negative mood in the laboratory has several important implications. Psychologists can determine the degree to which individual characteristics, such as personality traits or cognitive styles, predispose subjects to respond to mood inductions. Researchers can also test the degree to which interventions prevent or reverse mood changes. Such research may help to identify people who are at greater risk for developing depression or who may be appropriate candidates for cognitive therapy for depression (Rexford & Wierzbicki, 1989; Wierzbicki, Westerholm, & McHugh, 1994).

limitation, analogue studies enable researchers to determine whether their ideas have sufficient support to warrant more costly and extensive research in actual clinical populations.

Genetic Research   In recent decades, psychologists have become extremely interested in the extent to which genetic factors may influence psychological characteristics. Clinical psychologists have examined the role of genetic factors on psychological disorders, such as schizophrenia, as well as on "normal" psychological characteristics, such as intelligence and personality traits.

Three major genetic research methods are used to investigate possible genetic influences on psychological characteristics: the family study, the adoption study, and the twin study.

The *family study* simply determines whether a characteristic runs in families. That is, the researcher tests whether there is an association between genetic similarity and similarity with respect to a trait. This can be done whether the trait is continuous (varying along a continuum, such as intelligence or severity of depressive symptoms) or categorical (all-or-nothing, such as the presence/absence of schizophrenia).

The family study is the simplest of the three genetic research methods. However, it is also the weakest. The family study can demonstrate that a trait runs in families. However, it fails to prove *why* the trait runs in families.

Family studies fail to prove that a trait runs in families for genetic reasons because most people share their genes with the very same people with whom they share their environment—namely their families. That is, genetic and environmental influences are *confounded*. They co-vary in the general population.

Traits can run in families for both genetic and environmental reasons. After all, speaking English, voting democratic, and practicing Judaism all run in families. Few biologically oriented psychologists would claim that language, voting pattern, and religious preference have a genetic influence. These traits are accepted as resulting from environmental influences.

If family studies cannot prove a genetic influence, why use them? Family studies are simpler than the other genetic research methods—less expensive, less time consuming, and less effortful. If a family study shows that a trait runs in families, then the researcher may have sufficient evidence to warrant conducting a more costly and time-consuming adoption or twin study. If the family study finds that the trait does not run in families, then there is no need to conduct a more elaborate investigation.

The second of the genetic research methods is the adoption study. The *adoption study* determines the relative similarity of adoptees to both their adoptive and biological families. This method relies on the fact that adoptees are reared in environments alongside adoptive family members with whom they share no genes. Thus, adoption separates genes from the environment.

Adoption studies can be conducted in either of two ways. The researcher can identify adopted-away offspring of parents who possess the trait of interest (e.g., schizophrenia). These subjects are then followed to determine how many eventually exhibit the trait of interest themselves; they can be compared to the general population or to the adopted-away offspring of parents who do not possess the trait.

Another way of conducting adoption studies is to begin with adoptees who exhibit the trait of interest. The researcher then determines the degree to which this trait appears in both the adoptive and biological families.

Adoption studies permit the calculation of a *heritability coefficient*, which is an estimate of the degree to which genes influence a trait. Heritability coefficients range from 0 to 1, with a coefficient of 0 meaning that there is no genetic influence and a coefficient of 1 meaning that genetic factors are the only influences on the trait. Intermediate values are interpreted in a way similar to intermediate values of correlation coefficients.

Adoption studies attempt to separate the genetic and environmental influences that are confounded for most people. However, adoption studies do not completely distinguish between these two influences. For example, children are placed for adoption at different ages; those placed for adoption at older ages may have shared a significant amount of early environment with their biological parents. If these adoptees are later found to resemble their biological parents, it may not be easy to determine whether this resemblance is due to genetic or early environmental influences.

Even if the adoption study is limited to children placed for adoption in the first weeks of life, there is still a confounding of genes and environment. After all, newborns have experienced a lengthy prenatal environment that may be confounded with their mother's genetics. An example of this could be mothers who decide to place their children for adoption because they have mental disorders that would interfere with their ability to care for their children. Some mental disorders (such as schizophrenia and certain types of mental retardation) have a genetic influence. Because these disorders significantly affect their self-care behavior, these women may provide poorer prenatal environments than other women. Their nutrition, drug use, prenatal medical care, and general physical health are likely to be poorer than in the general population of pregnant women. Thus, if their adopted-away offspring develop later psychological problems, it may be difficult to distinguish between the effects of genetics and prenatal environment.

Adoption studies are not true experiments. That is, the researcher (for very clear ethical reasons) does not randomly assign children to a group that will be adopted out of their biological families. Rather, the biological parents decide, for reasons of their own, to place the child for adoption. Parents who place a child for adoption generally do so because they believe they will be unable to care properly for the child, often because of familial, medical, psychological, economic, or other problems.

Children of parents with these problems may not be representative of all children in the general population. Adopted children have more medical and psychological problems than nonadopted children (Wierzbicki, 1993b). Their increased rate of problems is likely due to both genetic influences and the environmental factors that often accompany adoption (e.g., poor prenatal health care) (Wierzbicki, 1993b). In addition, some parents may first decide to place a child for adoption after learning that the child has a birth defect or neurological impairment. Thus, adopted children are expected to have a higher rate of psychological problems than nonadopted children.

Because adoption studies are not true experiments, they do not provide conclusive evidence of genetic causation. Thus, their results must be interpreted with caution. However, adoption studies are the nearest thing that ethical researchers can use to try to separate genes and environment. Thus, despite their limitations, they are an extremely useful tool in the armamentarium of researchers who study genetic factors.

The third genetic research method is the twin study. In a *twin study,* the relative similarities of identical and fraternal twins are compared; greater similarity in identical twins is taken as evidence of a genetic influence on the trait of interest.

The twin study is the conceptual opposite of the adoption study. Whereas adoption studies hold an individual's genetic make-up constant and vary the environment, twin studies hold the environment constant and vary genetic similarity.

There are two types of twins: *monozygotic (MZ)* twins are identical twins, who share all of their genes; *dizygotic (DZ)* twins are fraternal twins, who share one-half of their genes. MZ twins develop from a single fertilized egg, whereas DZ twins develop from two separate fertilized eggs. Thus, MZ twins are unique in that they are the only people in the world who have exact genetic doubles. DZ twins are only as much alike genetically as are nontwin siblings.

The twin study involves measuring the similarity, with respect to the trait of interest, of both types of twins. MZ twins are similar for two reasons: a common environment and all of their genes in common. DZ twins are also similar for two reasons: a common environment and half of their genes in common. In other words, the effect of being reared in a common environment should be equal for the two types of twins. Environmental factors (such as socioeconomic status, parental personality, and parental style of interacting with the children) commonly thought to influence children's psychological development should be balanced across the two sets of twins. If so, then any greater similarity of MZ twins over DZ twins is the result of their greater genetic similarity. Heritability coefficients can then be calculated.

The twin study has been used for over 100 years in genetic research, since it was suggested by Francis Galton. It has been especially useful in research on possible genetic influence of psychopathology, intelligence, and personality characteristics.

However, like any research method, the twin study has limitations. The twin study assumes that the environmental similarity of MZ twins is comparable to that for DZ twins. However, it is possible that identical twins are treated more similarly than DZ twins, precisely because they are identical. If so, then heritability estimates from twin studies should be regarded as upper estimates. Similarly, it may be the case that environmental influences on both kinds of twins are unique and are not representative of the types of environmental influences experienced by nontwins; in this case, speculations about environmental influences on twins may not generalize to others.

Finally, it should be noted that there are additional variations and combinations of these genetic research methods. For example, some research has been conducted on twins who have been reared apart—a combination of the twin and adoption study methods. Some research has compared the rates of psychopathology in the offspring of identical twins who are discordant for a disorder—a combination of the twin and family study methods. Other combinations and variants are possible as well.

THE SCIENTIST– PRACTITIONER MODEL OF CLINICAL PSYCHOLOGY

In 1944, the APA decided to train clinical psychologists in existing doctoral programs (Reisman, 1981). An APA committee was established to examine and make recommendations concerning the educational requirements of clinical psychology training programs. The report of this committee (Shakow, Hilgard, Kelly, Luckey, Sanford, & Shaffer, 1947) described the foundations for the scientist–practitioner model of training.

As articulated by Thorne (1947), scientist-practitioners adopt a scientific approach to the treatment of individual cases. Every case is regarded as a single-subject study in which a scientific approach is taken to assessment, conceptualization, treatment selection, and follow-up evaluation. In addition, each client is viewed as a part of a larger sample, so that information about individual clients can later be combined into a systematic group analysis. Thus, the clinical psychologist serves a scientific role even when engaged in clinical practice.

In Chapter 1, three functions of the clinical psychologist were noted: to explain, assess, and treat abnormality. Each of these functions benefits from a scientific approach.

The first major function of the clinical psychologist is to explain abnormality. *Psychopathology* is the study of the nature and causes of psychological disorders. Psychopathologists attempt to identify (1) the defining features of a disorder (i.e., how to distinguish one disorder from others); (2) the immediate cause that is producing the current symptoms of the disorder; (3) the initial cause or development of the disorder; and (4) the future course of the disorder.

It is easy to see how the scientific model is implemented in the study of psychopathology. Stage 1 of science involves the careful description of phenomena. This corresponds to the period when psychopathologists identify the symptoms of a disorder and begin to distinguish between two or more disorders on the basis of their symptoms. Stage 2 of science is the explanation stage. When psychopathologists propose possible explanations of the causes (both initial and immediate) of a disorder, they engage in this activity. Stage 3 is the prediction or test stage. Psychopathologists engage in Stage 3 when they conduct controlled research to test the validity of their initial speculations. Finally, Stage 4 of science is the control or application stage. Psychopathologists reach this stage when they apply their theoretical understanding of a disorder in specific cases to treat or prevent it.

Even when clinical psychologists work in applied clinical settings, they benefit from a scientific approach to the study of psychopathology. Ford and Urban (1963) discussed the benefits of using scientific theories in clinical practice. Clinical psychologists who work within a scientific theoretical framework are assisted by a theory in that the theory directs their attention to pertinent symptoms, pathological processes, and causal factors. This has benefits in terms of the efficiency of assessment and selection of treatment, the other major roles of clinical psychologists.

The second major function of clinical psychologists is assessment. Clinical psychologists must accurately assess abnormal behavior and mental processes.

All assessments can be evaluated using the statistical criteria of reliability and validity. This holds true whether the assessment is a diagnostic classification, a score on a psychological test, or a behavioral observation.

Reliability is the extent to which assessments are stable or consistent. *Validity* is the accuracy of the assessment—the degree to which the assessment is actually measuring what it purports to measure. The various types of reliability and validity that are important to clinical psychologists will be discussed in more detail in Chapter 4. For now, let us consider only briefly the relationship between reliability and validity.

There is an old adage in test and measurement theory that *reliability is a prerequisite for validity*. The reliability of an assessment places an upper limit on its validity. It is easy to understand this relationship. Suppose a measure of a psychological construct (say, depression) is not very reliable. Then, a patient who is diagnosed as depressed by one psychologist may not receive this same diagnosis when evaluated by a second psychologist or even when reassessed by the first psychologist.

What impact does this have on validity? Remember that validity refers to the correctness of the assessment. Is the patient truly "depressed"? The diagnosis of depression has many important implications, such as risk of suicide, probability of relapse, potentially effective treatments, and so on. If the diagnosis is low in reliability, then it also is low in validity, and so statements about the probable cause, future course, and most appropriate treatment are not likely to be very accurate.

Assessment plays an important role throughout all four stages of the science of clinical psychology. Clinical psychologists begin to describe abnormality in Stage 1. If initial observations are unreliable, then progress throughout the remaining stages will be hindered: the hypotheses and theories proposed in Stage 2 will have low validity; The assessments conducted to test theories in Stage 3 will be invalid, and so the research results will be weak; and treatment selections in Stage 4 will be less effective.

Clinical psychologists have long recognized the importance of reliable and valid assessments. After the APA adopted the scientist–practitioner model of training, clinical psychologists examined empirically the reliability and validity of their assessment techniques. Projective personality tests, previously regarded as perhaps the most important method of assessing psychological functioning, were found to have lower reliability and validity than is desired in psychological tests (Wierzbicki, 1993a). As a result, clinical psychologists increasingly turned their attention to alternative methods of assessment, including behavioral observations and structured inventories.

Another issue concerning the reliability of assessment that was debated by clinical psychologists following the adoption of the scientist–practitioner model was the reliability of diagnosis. Numerous studies in the 1950s found that traditional psychiatric diagnosis, especially for specific disorders within general categories, was not very reliable and so could not be valid (Wierzbicki, 1993a). For this reason, much research in the 1960s and 1970s was devoted to the development of diagnostic criteria that would be more reliable and so could be more valid than previous systems. The net result was the publication in 1980 of DSM-III (American Psychiatric Association, 1980) and its subsequent revisions, DSM-III-R (American Psychiatric Association, 1987) and DSM-IV (American Psychiatric Association, 1994). Research has shown that diagnoses made with these new systems are in fact more reliable than previous diagnoses (Wierzbicki, 1993a).

The APA recommends this empirical approach to assessment, not only in the scientist–practitioner training of clinical psychologists, but also in its ethical standards. For example, the ethical principle of assessment techniques requires that developers of psychological tests employ "scientific procedures" and that psychologists use tests "in a manner and for purposes that are appropriate in light of the research" (APA, 1992, p. 1603).

The third major function of clinical psychologists is treatment of abnormal behavior. Chapter 8 discusses in detail the scientific issues underlying psychotherapy. However, it is simple to illustrate the importance of a scientific foundation for the types of treatment provided by clinical psychologists.

The empirical approach to assessment clearly aids treatment. Diagnoses can be made more reliably; hence, decisions regarding treatment selection can be made more validly. In addition, goals of therapy can be stated in observable terms. Thus, both the client and the therapist can monitor progress from week to week. If progress does not occur at a satisfactory rate, then it is a simple matter for either party to request that the treatment contract be renegotiated to select an alternative treatment.

Another benefit of the scientist–practitioner approach is that the clinical psychologist relies upon scientific research. Since 1952 (when Eysenck challenged the field to provide scientific evidence to support claims of the effectiveness of psychotherapy), there have been hundreds of controlled studies of psychotherapy outcome. By using treatments that have been proved empirically to be effective (particularly those identified by the APA Task Force on

Promotion and Dissemination of Psychological Procedures [1995] as empirically validated), clinical psychologists ensure that their interventions are effective. In this way, clinical psychologists also meet ethical standards of accountability.

It should be noted, however, that clinical psychologists have not unanimously endorsed the Boulder Model. According to Frank (1984), the APA committee on graduate training in clinical psychology prior to the Boulder conference had recommended that "clinical training should be grounded *in* and *on* research in psychology," and that Shakow and colleagues (1947) changed this emphasis by recommending that clinical psychologists "should be trained to *do* research" (p. 425) (author's emphasis).

Frank (1984) identified two criticisms of the scientist–practitioner model: (1) there is little evidence to support the assumption that scientific training is important for clinical psychologists; and (2) interest in and the skills necessary to succeed as a researcher are incompatible with those required for applied clinical work. Frank (1984) cited numerous results that supported these arguments.

For example, Levy (1962) examined the publication records of about 800 clinical psychologists who had completed their degrees from 1948 to 1953, the period immediately following the APA's endorsement of the Boulder Model. Their modal number of publications was 0! (The mean was 3.7 and median was 1.6.) The distribution of publications was highly skewed, with only 10 percent of the sample producing 45 percent of the publications. Even though these clinical psychologists had been trained in the scientist–practitioner model, few of them actually engaged in scientific research after receiving their degrees.

Meltzoff's responses to the criticisms of the Boulder Model are well taken. Despite Frank's (1984) argument that scientific and clinical skills are distinct, many clinicians today recognize that the two approaches go hand in hand. For example, Beutler, Williams, Wakefield, and Entwistle (1995) surveyed 325 clinical psychologists, dividing them into academics and practitioners, and found, as expected, that academic clinicians read and value research articles more than do practitioners; however, they also found that clinical practitioners value scientific research and consider their clinical practice to be augmented by scientific findings. This result has been reported in other research (e.g., Beutler, Williams, & Wakefield, 1993; Dent & Ormiston, 1979; Kazdin, Siegel, & Bass, 1990) and suggests that clinicians are not as unreceptive to research results as Frank (1984) believed.

However, even though the Vail (or practitioner) Model has been endorsed by the APA, the scientific foundation for clinical practice remains widely accepted. All the major conferences on graduate training—even those that endorsed the practitioner model of training—affirmed the importance of the scientific foundations of clinical psychology (Kendall & Norton-Ford, 1982). For example, the participants of the Salt Lake City conference recommended that "research and scientific inquiry be an essential part of every psychologist's training" (Strickland, 1988, p. 107).

In addition, current professional and ethical standards of psychologists clearly document the scientific foundations of clinical psychology. For example, the most recent version of the ethical standards of psychologists appeared in 1992. Here, the principle of competence states that psychologists "maintain knowledge of relevant scientific and professional information related to the services they render" (APA, 1992, p. 1599).

The APA has also published ethical standards for providers of psychological services (APA, 1987). Under the principle of accountability, psychologists are instructed: "There are periodic, systematic, and effective evaluations of psychological services" (APA, 1987, p. 8). Under another guideline, psychotherapists are reminded that their field is "rooted in a science" (p. 4) and that they should conduct ongoing evaluations of their services and disseminate this information to others.

Thus, the scientific foundations of clinical psychology remain firmly in place, in the ethical standards of clinical practice and in the training of clinical psychologists. As presented above, recognition and implementation of the scientific bases of clinical psychology should enhance the clinical psychologist's functions as assessor, therapist, and psychopathologist.

SUMMARY

Philosophy of science is a branch of epistemology, the philosophy of knowledge, which examines the assumptions and methods of science. Science operates under the assumptions of determinism, empiricism, and order.

Science advances through a four-stage process in which scientists describe, explain, make predictions about, and then control their subject matter. Scientists use operational definitions to specify how their constructs are measured. Scientists generate hypotheses and theories in the second stage of science. Hypotheses and theories are, by definition, tentative. Scientific theories are evaluated in terms of the criteria of comprehensiveness, parsimony, heuristic value, internal consistency, and falsifiability.

Karl Popper regarded falsifiability as the defining characteristic of science. Popper described science as a process of conjectures and refutations. Because there is an asymmetry between proof and disproof, Popper held that science advances more rapidly by refuting an inadequate theory and replacing it with a better one than by simply gathering evidence to support a theory.

Thomas Kuhn, a historian of science, described a more realistic view of science. According to Kuhn, a paradigm is the predominant theory in a science. Scientists do not act to disprove the paradigm, but rather simply to extend the paradigm. Scientists hold to a paradigm as though it were a religious belief and so react emotionally to criticism of the paradigm. When problems with the paradigm are discovered, scientists ignore them. However, if a problem cannot be ignored, then a scientific crisis occurs, in which multiple competing theories are proposed. Ultimately, one new theory prevails and becomes the new paradigm.

Clinical psychologists employ a variety of research designs to study abnormal behavior. Each design should be evaluated according to the criteria of internal and external validity.

The case study is an intensive study of an individual subject. This was perhaps the most commonly used design in clinical psychology up to the 1950s. Although case studies are useful in the first two stages of science, they are weak in the third stage because they are low in both internal and external validity. Several improved single-subject designs have been developed (e.g., the ABAB design, multiple baseline design) that are more powerful than the traditional case study.

In a correlational study, the investigator measures two or more naturally occurring variables. Correlational studies permit the measurement of the strength of the relation between variables, but do not allow causal interpretations. Several elaborations on the correlational study, including multiple correlation, cross-lag correlation, and factor analysis, enable researchers to investigate complex interrelationships among variables.

In an experiment, the investigator randomly assigns subjects to groups and manipulates the level of the independent variable to which groups are exposed, while controlling other variables. Differences between groups on the dependent variable indicate that the independent variable caused the difference.

Placebo studies are used to test the effectiveness of an experimental treatment. Analogue studies involve the study of a group of subjects who only resemble in some way the population to which one wishes to generalize the results. Genetic research methods (family, adoption, and twin studies) are used to investigate possible genetic influences on a trait.

Scientist-practitioners adopt a scientific approach to clinical work. This enhances the clinical psychologist's functions of explaining, assessing, and treating abnormal behavior. Adopting a scientific approach to explaining abnormality benefits clinical psychologists because a scientific theory of psychopathology suggests which symptoms, pathological processes, and causal factors to consider.

A scientific approach to assessment is also important. Two criteria that can be used to evaluate any measurement technique are reliability and validity. Reliability is the stability or consistency of measurement; validity is the accuracy of measurement. If reliability is low, then validity will also be low. If clinical assessments are low in reliability, then all of the statements concerning the disorder's cause, pathology, future course, and treatment will be low in validity.

A scientific approach to treatment is also important. Scientist-practitioners base their treatment selections on empirical research results. Scientist-practitioners also specify treatment goals in measurable terms, so that progress can be monitored and ineffective treatments replaced. In these ways, scientist-practitioners meet ethical standards of accountability in providing for the best interests of their clients.

Several criticisms have been directed against the scientist–practitioner model of training. The APA has adopted an alternative model that emphasizes training in clinical practice more than research. However, even the groups that have endorsed this alternative model of training continue to recognize the scientific foundations of clinical practice.

S T U D Y   Q U E S T I O N S

1. What is the philosophy of science?
2. What are the assumptions and stages of science? How do these apply to a science of clinical psychology?
3. Compare and contrast Popper's and Kuhn's views of the nature of scientific progress. Use examples from psychology to illustrate your answer.
4. What are the two basic criteria used to evaluate research designs?
5. Evaluate the case study methodology using the criteria of internal and external validity. What are the practical advantages of case studies?
6. Contrast correlational and experimental studies in terms of both their methods and conclusions.

7. Describe and evaluate one special research method (e.g., placebo, analogue, family, twin, adoption study) that is used in clinical psychological research.
8. Discuss how the scientist–practitioner approach can be applied to the three major functions of clinical psychologists (i.e., to explain, assess, and treat abnormality).
9. Discuss how a clinical psychologist in an applied setting may benefit from adopting the scientist–practitioner approach.
10. What are the major criticisms of the scientist–practitioner model of clinical training?

3

Theories of Personality and Psychopathology

I. Psychoanalysis
   A. Structure of Personality
   B. Development of Personality
   C. Dynamics of Personality
   D. Psychopathology
   E. Treatment
   F. Evaluation
II. Behaviorism
   A. Structure of Personality
   B. Development of Personality
   C. Dynamics of Personality
   D. Psychopathology
   E. Treatment
   F. Evaluation
III. Humanism
   A. Structure of Personality
   B. Development of Personality
   C. Dynamics of Personality

   D. Psychopathology
   E. Treatment
   F. Evaluation
IV. Cognitive Theories
   A. Structure of Personality
   B. Development of Personality
   C. Dynamics of Personality
   D. Psychopathology
   E. Treatment
   F. Evaluation
V. Biological Theories
   A. Structure of Personality
   B. Development of Personality
   C. Dynamics of Personality
   D. Psychopathology
   E. Treatment
   F. Evaluation
VI. Summary

The previous chapter discussed scientific theories and the nature of scientific progress. Recall that a theory is a set of laws used to explain observations. Theoretical laws are systematic and logically connected, and should enable scientists to generate testable predictions about future possible observations. This chapter will introduce the major psychological theories of personality and psychopathology that have been influential in clinical psychology.

Personality is a construct that is familiar to everyone, yet is difficult to define precisely. There are many possible ways of thinking about personality. Gordon Allport, a leading humanistic personality theorist, reviewed the psychological literature in 1937 and found that psychologists use the term personality in almost 50 distinct ways. From his review of the different meanings of personality, Allport (1937) developed his own definition: "Personality is the dynamic organization within the individual of those psychophysical systems that determine his unique adjustments to his environment" (p. 48).

Although this definition may sound somewhat obscure, it is actually quite useful. Allport's definition includes references to each of the following: (1) organization, or the basic elements of personality; (2) dynamics, or one's motivations and how the basic elements of personality interact; and (3) unique adjustments, or how one develops in a unique way. Included in a person's adjustment is the issue of psychological health or the effectiveness with which the person interacts with others.

A good personality theory should address each of these areas. As an organizational aid, each theory in this chapter will be presented according to four features: structure, dynamics, development, and psychopathology. In addition, the discussion of each theory's approach to psychopathology will be presented according to the medical model.

The *medical model* assumes that patients with common symptomatology are responding to a common pathology that developed through a common etiology and will continue to progress through a common prognosis, including a common response to treatment. In its original form, the medical model focused exclusively on physiological factors. As presented below, the medical model can be generalized to include psychological and environmental factors.

Symptomatology refers to the client's presenting symptoms: behavioral, emotional, cognitive, and physiological. *Pathology* refers to the immediate cause that is currently producing the symptoms; the pathology is that which is wrong and should be corrected in order to alleviate the symptoms. *Etiology* refers to the initial cause of the disorder; how the pathology developed in the first place. *Prognosis* refers to the future course of the condition; how the condition is likely to progress, whether or not the client receives treatment.

The medical model presented here is a generalized version of the original model. The original medical model focused exclusively on physiological pathologies, etiologies, and treatments. Although there is a biological school of clinical psychology that uses the original medical model, many psychologists object to the claim that all psychological problems have a physiological foundation that is best treated with a biological intervention.

Freud extended the medical model to what has been called a *metaphorical* medical model, wherein he suggested that unconscious psychological processes produce the patient's symptoms. However, Freud's metaphorical medical model has been criticized, especially by behavioral psychologists, who do not believe that symptomatic behaviors necessarily reflect the action of an underlying physiological or psychological process.

For these reasons, I have presented the medical model in a still broader sense. A psychological disorder may reflect biological, psychological, or environmental factors. This is a *descriptive* medical model, wherein pathology and etiology are used only to describe the immediate and initial cause and are not restricted to a specific type of cause. Similarly, the treatment of choice for a disorder may be biological, psychological, or environmental in nature.

This flexible approach to the explaining and treating of psychological disorders is consistent with the approach of *eclecticism*. Eclecticism holds that different theoretical approaches may be most appropriate for different cases. It suggests that a variety of approaches is more effective in the long run than a single theoretical approach.

This chapter presents the major theories of personality and psychopathology in clinical psychology, including the psychoanalytic, behavioral, humanistic, cognitive, and biological approaches. These approaches will be presented in the order in which they have exerted most influence on clinical psychology.

PSYCHOANALYSIS

Psychoanalysis, perhaps the most influential theory in clinical psychology during the first half of the twentieth century, was developed by Sigmund Freud. Freud was born in Moravia in 1856, but lived most of his life in Vienna. Trained as a physician at the University of Vienna, his early clinical experiences were in the field of neurology.

Neurology is the medical specialty that studies and treats disorders of the nervous system. Physicians initially attempt to determine whether there are local or peripheral causes of a patient's symptoms. For example, if a patient reports loss of feeling in the arm, the doctor first tries to identify a problem with the muscles, tendons, or nerves in the arm itself. If there does not seem to be such a peripheral problem, the doctor then refers the patient to a neurologist. Perhaps the symptom results from a nervous system disorder in the part of the brain that controls feeling in the arm or in the nervous system pathways leading from the arm to the brain and back again. Thus, neurologists often see clients who report physical symptoms for which there is no obvious physical cause.

As Freud and his contemporaries worked with such patients, they discovered that, in some cases, the actual cause of the symptom was psychological and not physical. Jean Charcot observed that the symptoms of such patients occasionally disappeared when they were hypnotized. Similarly, Josef Breuer introduced what he called the *talking cure* for such clients. He engaged these patients in discussions of their experiences when the symptoms first developed, what they were thinking and feeling when the

symptoms appeared, and what meaning the symptom has for them now. Breuer reported that some clients, such as Anna O., experienced improvements in their apparently physical symptoms after simply talking about the symptoms.

Because truly physical disorders ought not respond so dramatically to psychological interventions, Freud and others concluded that the cause of the symptoms in such cases was psychological and not physical. In Freud's day, these clients were labeled as having *hysterical conversion disorder*. Today, the term *hysterical* has been dropped, and such patients are diagnosed simply as having *conversion disorder*.

Following such observations, Freud became interested in the role of psychological influences on physical disorders. In addition, Freud also became interested in the role of unconscious psychological influences. The influences on conversion disorders were not simply psychological, they were also *unconscious*, or outside the awareness of the individual. Conversion disorder patients believe they are suffering from physical maladies; they do not realize that they actually have a psychological disorder.

Freud (1895/1950) initially attempted to account for conversion disorders in purely physiological terms (in an unfinished work entitled "Project for a Scientific Psychology"). However, he soon abandoned this effort and devoted his attention to the role of unconscious psychological influences on physical symptoms and, later, on psychological symptoms as well.

Structure of Personality

According to Freud, there are three basic elements or components of personality: id, ego, and superego.

The *id* is the primitive side of man, influenced by biological, animalistic instincts. These instincts —sex and aggression—are the basic motivating forces of human behavior.

The id operates under what Freud called the *pleasure principle*. This states that the id seeks to maximize immediate gratification. Thus, the id is greedy, demanding, unable to delay gratification, and altogether rather unsavory. Freud (1930/1961, p.

111) quoted Plautus to describe his view of human nature: "homo homini lupus" ("man is a wolf to man").

The ego is the second component of personality. The *ego* is the realistic component of personality, which can identify and consider the realistic consequences of one's actions. The ego operates under the *reality principle*, which states that the ego seeks to maximize gratification given the constraints of reality.

The superego is the third component of personality. The *superego* is the repository of one's abstract morals and values. Thus, religious, social, artistic, and other abstract values are part of the superego. Freud discussed two important aspects of the superego: the ego ideal and the conscience. These are the moral "do's and don'ts" of personality. The *ego ideal* contains the values and ideals to which one aspires. The *conscience* is that part of personality that causes one to feel guilty after the violation of a moral principle.

Freud described these three elements of personality as engaged in a constant struggle, each seeking to influence the person to act in accordance with its own tenets. For example, suppose you are walking down the street and see an advertisement for an ice cream sundae. According to Freud, the id, demanding immediate gratification, tempts the person to "pig out." The superego, operating on the level of abstract morals and values, notes that *gluttony is one of the seven deadly sins*. The ego, attempting to balance the biological drives of the id with the abstract values of the superego, identifies the realistic consequences of "pigging out" (i.e., the effects on one's waistline, pocketbook, dental bill, and so on). After this exchange, the ego strikes some type of compromise—have a treat now, but make up for it by skipping dessert tonight.

Similarly, when one walks down the street and sees an attractive member of the opposite sex, the id says "attack," seeking immediate gratification of sexual and aggressive urges. The superego counters with abstract moralistic statements, such as *sex outside of the bonds of holy matrimony is a sin*. Finally, the ego evaluates the realistic costs and benefits of the various options: rape (immediate gratification but risk of imprisonment); coming on so strongly that the person recognizes that one is seeking nothing but sexual gratification (little chance of success unless the other person is also seeking sexual gratification); and other strategies. Ultimately, the ego may lead the individual to approach and strike up a conversation with the other person. The ego may suggest that the most cost-effective approach is to "play it cool" so as to appear attractive to the other person, and see where the relationship leads.

Critics of Freud claim that they do not engage in this sort of internal struggle—that their psychological functioning is not characterized by such conflicts. Freud responds by saying that these conflicts occur unconsciously—they occur without awareness.

Because of the importance of such internal psychological struggles and compromises, Freud's theory is often described as a dynamic, intrapsychic, or conflict model.

Development of Personality

Freud described the development of personality as occurring through a sequence of five stages. Because each stage is defined by how the individual gratifies sexual instincts, Freud referred to these as psychosexual stages.

The first stage of development is the oral stage. The *oral stage* is the stage of infancy and persists through about the age of 18 to 24 months. The oral stage is characterized by one's receiving gratification through oral means: suckling, crying, exploring objects with the mouth. Children in the oral stage have only the id, according to Freud. Therefore, the oral stage is characterized by selfish and demanding behavior and by the inability to delay gratification.

The second stage of psychosexual development is the anal stage. The *anal stage* is the stage of toddlerhood, from the end of the oral stage to about the age of 42 to 48 months. According to Freud, children in this stage achieve gratification of basic drives through anal means. A major developmental milestone in this stage is mastery over one's elimination functions—toilet training. Freud believed that when children are toilet trained, they become able to satisfy their own wants and needs. They are no longer completely dependent on others to gratify their urges; they can achieve satisfaction independently.

Another important aspect of toilet training is that Freud believed that the ego developed as a result of toilet training. Freud believed that toilet training is the first time that parents make demands of a child. The child must now consider the realistic consequences of its actions. If the child satisfies the parents' demands, then the child receives praise and approval. However, if the child has an accident, then the child experiences parental disapproval. Freud argued that, as the child begins to consider realistic consequences, the ego begins to develop.

The third stage of psychosexual development is the phallic stage. The *phallic stage* begins at the end of the anal stage and persists through about the age of five to six years. The phallic stage is especially important in Freudian theory because it is in this stage that the child's superego begins to develop.

Freud thought that, in this stage, children learn that there are two sexes in the world, that they are a member of one sex or the other, and that boys and girls grow up to marry one another. Freud thought that children in this stage develop incestuous wishes for the opposite-sexed parent.

According to Freud, a little boy develops his superego in the following way. The boy experiences incestuous wishes for his mother, stemming from the sexual urges of the id. However, by this age, the boy has an ego, which can judge the realistic consequences of his actions. The ego recognizes that the boy faces a rival for the hand of his mother, namely his father. If the boy enters into an open rivalry with father for the hand of mother, the boy will be defeated, since the father is larger and stronger than the boy. The boy begins to fear that the father will castrate him so he will never be a future rival for the mother. Thus, the id's incestuous wishes conflict with the ego's *castration anxiety*. The boy resolves this dilemma by identifying with his father. Now, when father makes love to mother, the boy also, at least symbolically, makes love to mother. Because mother has fallen in love with and married father, the boy will make himself more loveable to mother if he models himself after father.

When the boy identifies with his father, he begins to take on the father's attributes. This includes adopting the father's beliefs and values. Thus, if the father professes certain moral or social values, then the boy imitates the father and professes those same values.

The process through which the superego develops is called the *Oedipal conflict* (*neurosis*, or *complex*), after the character in ancient Greek literature, Oedipus, who unwittingly killed his father and married his mother.

The little girl develops her superego in a similar way. According to Freud, when a girl enters the phallic stage, she begins to recognize that she is different from little boys. She experiences what Freud called *penis envy*, the feeling that she is somehow incomplete or inadequate because she lacks a penis. This leads her to develop incestuous wishes for her father. If she makes love with her father, then she will "possess," at least temporarily, her father's penis. Also, if the girl is impregnated by her father, then she may bring a penis into the world by giving birth to a boy. Thus, the girl's basic sense of inferiority leads her to develop incestuous desires for her father.

The girl resolves her incestuous feelings by identifying with her mother. Now, the girl is able to make love with her father, at least symbolically, when her mother makes love with father. By identifying with her mother, the girl begins to take on her mother's abstract morals and values.

There are two important differences between the boy's and girl's superego, according to Freud. The first concerns the idea that girls somehow experience a sense of inferiority to males. This concept has been severely criticized by contemporary psychologists, including both followers and critics of Freud.

The second difference concerns the strength of the superego. Freud thought that, for boys, id functioning (incestuous desire) was followed by ego functioning (castration anxiety) before the boy identified with father. Because ego functioning is more realistic and so is "higher" functioning than id functioning, the boy may be able to resolve his Oedipal conflict satisfactorily. However, in the case of a girl, id functioning (incestuous desire) is not followed by a comparable stage of ego functioning. Thus, when the girl identifies with her mother, she does so without using as high a level of functioning as the little boy.

According to Freud, this means that girls tend to resolve their Oedipal conflicts less successfully and completely than do boys. In other words, Freud believed that the superegos of males are stronger than those of females. This notion has also been strongly criticized by contemporary psychologists, by both proponents as well as opponents of Freudian theory.

The fourth stage of development is the latency stage. The *latency stage* occurs following the phallic stage and persists through puberty. Freud did not discuss the latency stage at any length. He thought that, although sexual and aggressive urges continue to operate in this stage, the individual tends to channel them into age-appropriate interests and activities such as academics, sports, and hobbies.

The final stage of psychosexual development is the genital stage. The *genital stage* begins at puberty and continues throughout the rest of life. In the genital stage, the individual experiences gratification of sexual urges through appropriate means, that is, through intercourse with mature members of the opposite sex. As with the latency stage, Freud devoted relatively little attention to this stage, directing most of his attention to problems that occur in the first three stages.

Dynamics of Personality

Freud stated that there are two basic motivating forces for human behavior, both of which stem from biological instincts: sex and aggression. According to Freud, because we are human, our bodies constantly generate both sexual energy (*libido*) and aggressive energy (*mortido*). These are products of our evolutionary heritage and so there is no avoiding them.

People act to discharge both types of energy. Freud thought that healthy individuals find appropriate and prosocial channels for discharging psychic energy, such as engaging in competitive sports to discharge aggressive energy or engaging in sexual intercourse with one's spouse to discharge sexual energy. However, some people fail to find such outlets. In these cases, the energy builds to such an in-tensity that it can no longer be contained. The energy is then released in an uncontrolled fashion, guided by unconscious influences.

Another important concept in Freud's description of personality dynamics is the intrapsychic struggle that occurs among the id, ego, and superego. Remember that each component of personality attempts to influence the person to act in accordance with its own preferences: the id's animal instincts, the superego's abstract morals and values, and the ego's recognition of the constraints of reality.

Freud used the concept of defense to explain how sexual and aggressive instincts can be channeled into other, even prosocial, behaviors. A *defense mechanism* is an unconscious ego process that serves to protect the individual from threatening material. Sexual and aggressive instincts lead one to experience desires that conflict with the superego's moral precepts. If recognizing these desires would cause pain or embarrassment, then the ego uses defense mechanisms to prevent one from facing such unpleasantness.

The most basic Freudian defense mechanism is *repression*, through which threatening material is simply blocked from awareness. In this way, the individual does not have to face the threatening material. For example, suppose a student must write a term paper for a class. If the assignment is especially hard, then the student may find that thinking about it causes anxiety: the student dreads starting and feels guilty when not working on the project. To deal with this anxiety, the student may repress the material, blocking it from consciousness. Now, the student no longer experiences the anxiety that would otherwise occur when thinking about it.

This example also illustrates the maladaptive consequences of defenses. In the short run, defense mechanisms are adaptive in that they avoid threat. However, their use becomes maladaptive in the long run. Although the student has succeeded in avoiding anxiety by repressing the assignment, the student will face severe long-term consequences if the assignment is not completed.

Freud and his followers described a large number of defense mechanisms, including *denial, projection, displacement, reaction formation, sublimation,*

EXHIBIT 3.1   Freudian Defense Mechanisms

Defense	Definition	Example
Repression	Blocking threatening material from consciousness	An adult who cannot recall being abused as a child
Denial	Preventing threatening material from entering consciousness	A parent who cannot accept the death of a child
Projection	Attributing one's unacceptable impulse or action to another	A person with homosexual desires who believes that homosexuals are constantly making sexual overtures toward him or her
Displacement	Changing the target of an unacceptable impulse	A man who takes out his frustration with his boss on his wife
Reaction Formation	Expressing the exact opposite of one's unacceptable impulse	A mother who, resentful of the demands of her child, "smothers" it with kindness
Sublimation	Expressing an unacceptable impulse in a symbolic manner	A child who, unable to satisfy a desire to handle fecal matter in the anal stage, becomes a gardener
Rationalization	Providing an implausible excuse to justify one's unacceptable impulse or actions	A student who gives a long series of weak excuses for failing to meet a deadline
Intellectualization	Recognizing the cognitive but not the emotional component of one's unacceptable actions	A child molester who talks in detail about his actions yet fails to appreciate the emotional trauma he caused
Conversion	Expressing painful psychic material through symbolic physiological symptoms	A soldier who, frightened and guilty about having to shoot others, develops paralysis in his hands
Undoing	Engaging in a repetitive action that symbolically atones for some unacceptable impulse	Lady Macbeth who, after the murder of Macduff, feels guilty and repeatedly washes her hands

rationalization, undoing, and *intellectualization.* Definitions and examples of these defense mechanisms appear in Exhibit 3.1.

In general, Freud regarded defense mechanisms as normal psychological processes. Defenses are employed even by the healthiest individuals. They serve an adaptive function in that they help one avoid anxiety that would be experienced if the threatening material is acknowledged directly.

Freud wrote at length of how defense mechanisms influence normal behavior. In *The Psychopathology of Everyday Life* (Freud, 1901/1960), Freud suggested that common accidents of daily living (such as forgetting an appointment, writing the wrong word in a note, misspeaking) are not true accidents but are caused by the same unconscious forces that produce psychopathological symptoms. For example, meaning to say you "love" your mother-in-law but actually saying you "loathe" her is a Freudian slip that carries an underlying meaning that is not difficult to discern.

In *Jokes and Their Relation to the Unconscious,* Freud (1905/1960) examined the meaning of humor. According to Freud, much humor (slapstick, puns, insults, double entendres, and so on) expresses underlying sexual and aggressive themes. By channeling these drives into socially acceptable forms of expression, people avoid the build-up of psychic energy to uncontrollable levels, which could lead to behavior that violates societal constraints.

However, even though Freud regarded defenses as a normal part of living, they are self-defeating and maladaptive when overused. By failing to face the threatening material, one does not resolve the problem, and so it persists, continuing to exert an unconscious influence on one's behavior.

Psychopathology

As described above, defense mechanisms play an important role in Freud's explanation of psychopathology. Another aspect of Freud's theory of pathology is the concept of *fixation*. Fixation occurs when, because of some disturbing event in childhood, one's psychosexual development ceases. Although one continues to grow intellectually and physically, psychosexual development—how the individual gratifies basic sexual and aggressive urges—remains at the early stage of development. Fixation can occur as the result of trauma, such as sexual abuse or the death of a family member. However, Freud also stated that fixation could occur as the result of either undergratification or overgratification.

A related Freudian concept is *regression*, which is a return to the psychosexual functioning associated with a previously completed stage of development. According to Freud, regression occurs when one undergoes stress. The specific stage to which one regresses is influenced by (1) the severity of the current stressor; (2) the similarity of the current stressor to problems experienced in previous stages; and (3) the success with which one has completed the developmental milestones in previous stages.

Freud described several personality or character types that he believed were caused by fixation at or regression to early stages of psychosexual development. The *oral character* exhibits traits associated with the oral stage. In the oral stage, infants are demanding and selfish and achieve gratification through oral means. Freud considered adults who exhibit such characteristics (selfish, demanding, seeking oral gratification through smoking, drinking alcohol, and overeating) as having oral characters.

EXHIBIT 3.2   Emotional and Behavioral Characteristics Associated with Freud's Developmental Stages

Stage	Associated Problems
Oral	Depression; Narcissism; Dependency
Anal	Obstinacy; Obsessive-compulsive disorder; Sadomasochism
Phallic	Sexual immaturity; Gender identity problems; Antisocial personality
Latent	Inadequate or excessive self-control
Genital	Identity diffusion

The *anal character* results from fixation in or regression to the second stage. Toddlers in the anal stage are concerned with being neat and clean, obeying the rules, and satisfying parental demands. Freud considered such traits in adults (excessive neatness, cleanliness, orderliness, stinginess, and deference to authority) as part of the anal character.

Fixation in the phallic stage can result in two types of problems. The child may fail to identify properly with the same-sexed parent, leading to later problems in gender identity or sexual preference. On the other hand, the child may fail to develop a satisfactory superego, growing up with a weak set of morals. In either case, the individual will have significant problems in later social behavior.

Exhibit 3.2 summarizes the emotional and behavioral characteristics that Freud believed to be associated with problems in the various stages of psychological development.

Freud stressed early experiences in explaining the development of psychopathology. For example, he stated explicitly that "neuroses are acquired only in early childhood (up to the age of six)" (Freud, 1940/1964, p. 185). This statement illustrates Freud's principle of *psychic determinism* (the concept that all events are caused, often by unconscious influences that stem from early childhood), which so clearly characterizes Freud's theory.

Freud's explanation of the development of most psychological disorders is modeled after his concep-

EXHIBIT 3.3   Alternative Views of the Case of Anna O.

Ernest Jones, the psychoanalytic biographer of Freud, revealed the true identity of Anna O. in 1953. Anna O. was the pseudonym used by Freud and Breuer for Bertha Pappenheim, a woman who, following her treatment for conversion disorder, became well known in her own right as a feminist and a social worker.

Ellenberger (1970, 1972) tracked down the hospital records of Bertha Pappenheim. He found that she continued to have problems long after Breuer and Freud claimed she had been cured. In addition, Ellenberger found that she exhibited many symptoms not typically associated with conversion disorder, such as mutism, neologisms, hallucinations, and dual personality. The facts that she continued to have significant difficulties and

that she exhibited such severe symptoms suggest that her true condition may have been something other than conversion disorder.

Thornton (1983) published a highly critical account of the development of Freudian theory. She argued that Anna O.'s severe symptoms are consistent with the diagnosis of tuberculous meningitis, a neurological condition resulting from infection. Thornton supported this claim by noting that Anna O. helped to nurse her father in his final illness, a subpleuristic abscess, which was a frequent complication of tuberculosis. In addition, Thornton noted that the course of Anna O's condition, as detailed by Ellenberger, is consistent with this neurological disorder.

tualization of the case of Anna O., a case he and Breuer described in their *Studies on Hysteria*. Anna O. exhibited a variety of physical symptoms, including weakness and loss of feeling in her limbs, visual difficulties, and even "hysterical" pregnancy and labor. These symptoms appeared around the time of the death of her father, to whom she had been very close.

Breuer and Freud diagnosed Anna O. as having hysterical conversion disorder. They suggested that she had experienced some traumatic childhood event, related to her father, which she repressed and was unable to recall. The death of her father increased the painfulness of this material so that it could no longer be repressed; it required some outlet. Freud and Breuer suggested that Anna O. used the defense of *conversion*, which transformed the painful psychological material into physiological symptoms. In this way, they believed that Anna O.'s physical symptoms were somehow symbolic manifestations of the underlying psychological disorder. (For alternative views of the case of Anna O., see Exhibit 3.3.)

This is the basic psychoanalytic model for explaining psychopathology. The presenting symptoms do not necessarily indicate the true nature of the patient's disorder, but rather are only outward manifestations of an underlying problem.

The pathology in the Freudian model is some unconscious troubling material. This material has been repressed because it is so painful. However, it remains active because there is so much energy bound up with the material. The ego employs defense mechanisms to permit the controlled release of this energy. The underlying problem is transformed, through defenses, and is expressed through the individual's presenting symptoms.

The etiology, or initial cause of the disorder, is some painful experience from early childhood. This painful childhood material, often of a sexual or aggressive nature, persists in the unconscious until it leads to the symptoms that the individual later exhibits. Freud used this model to account for the entire range of psychopathology, from obsessions through depression, from phobias to sexual disorders. See Exhibit 3.4 for a summary of the Freudian explanation of a variety of forms of psychopathology.

Treatment

It is an old adage that the aim of Freudian therapy, or *psychoanalysis*, is insight. Since the pathology in Freud's model is some unconscious troubling material, the goal of Freudian therapy is to identify this material and then cope with it using conscious rational processes. Freud used techniques such as free association, dream analysis, and interpretation of the

EXHIBIT 3.4   Examples of Freudian Explanations of Psychopathology

Phobia   Little Hans was a young boy who had an extreme fear of horses. Freud suggested that Hans was truly afraid of his father (i.e., experiencing castration anxiety), and was displacing the fear of father to a more acceptable target. Horses are large and strong, like Hans's father, and so they were symbolic representations of the true fear.

Obsessive-Compulsive Disorder   Lady MacBeth experienced a handwashing compulsion. Freud suggested that such repetitive thoughts and actions occur as the result of underlying guilt. The individual employs the defense of *undoing,* in which a repetitive thought or action becomes a symbolic form of atoning for one's unacceptable impulses or behaviors.

Paranoid Delusions   Freud suggested that paranoid delusions (e.g., that one is Napoleon) are the result of underlying homosexuality. The unacceptable impulse (*I am attracted to him/her*) is transformed through the defense of projection (*He/She is attracted to me*). If this

remains too painful to bear, then it is further transformed through reaction formation (*He/She hates me*). If this is still not acceptable to the person, then it is further transformed through the defense of rationalization (*He/She hates me because Napoleon was hated, so I must be Napoleon*).

Anorexia Nervosa   Psychoanalytic theorists suggest that this condition, in adolescent females, represents a denial of sexuality. By starving oneself, the girl becomes unattractive (and so less likely to attract the attentions of males). If the female is prepubescent, malnutrition can interfere with the development of the secondary sexual characteristics that develop at puberty. Also, through becoming malnourished, menstruation, an important feature of femininity, ceases.

Nocturnal Enuresis   Freud thought that bedwetting in boys, if not due to epilepsy, was a symbolic form of masturbation. The boys expressed underlying sexual urges by converting them to a more acceptable physical symptom.

---

client–therapist relationship to identify the unconscious troubling material. The techniques and effectiveness of Freudian therapy will be discussed in detail in Chapter 9. Chapter 9 will also present material on later variants of Freudian therapy.

Evaluation

Chapter 2 introduced five criteria that are used to evaluate scientific theories. These criteria are readily applied to Freud's theory.

Comprehensiveness   Freud's theory is very comprehensive. It addresses a wide range of issues, from development, through motivation, to psychopathology and psychotherapy. Many diverse topics such as dreaming, interpretation of artwork, and the bases of religion are discussed by Freud. Psychoanalytic theory is one of the most comprehensive approaches in clinical psychology.

Parsimony   On the other hand, Freud's theory suffers from a lack of parsimony. Parsimony, as you re-

call, means simplicity. Freud's model is extremely complicated, introducing many novel theoretical constructs and invoking numerous laws and principles. Because of its complexity, it is difficult to apply Freudian theory in given circumstances to make testable predictions.

Applied or Heuristic Value   Freud's theory stands well on this criterion. Over the years, Freudian theory has been found to have many useful applications. It has been used in research and applied settings. It has been applied in developmental research. It has been employed in the humanities—for example, psychoanalysis is a major school of literary criticism, film criticism, art interpretation, and historical analysis. Many clinical psychologists and other professionals have found psychoanalytic theory to be rich, stimulating, and useful.

Internal Consistency   This is a second criterion along which Freudian theory can be evaluated negatively. Because Freudian theory invokes so many principles and because the theory explains outward behaviors as indirect indicators of underlying processes, Freudian theory risks becoming internally inconsistent.

For example, suppose a psychoanalyst is given a detailed history of a male client. The psychoanalyst may conclude from the facts of the case that the client hates his father. However, if observations then reveal that the client exhibits loving behavior toward his father, the theory has not necessarily been disconfirmed. After all, the client may be using the defense of reaction formation to express unconscious hatred of father in the form of outward caring. Now, this is not a completely fair indictment of psychoanalysis, since it may be possible to predict, on independent grounds, that the client would use the defense mechanism of reaction formation. Still, it illustrates the potential problem of internal inconsistency in Freudian theory.

Freud himself recognized that this criticism had been directed against his system. He noted that analysts had been accused of engaging in a "heads I win, tails you lose" enterprise when making psychoanalytic interpretations: "If the patient agrees with us, then it is right; but if he contradicts us, then that is only a sign of his resistance, which again puts us in the right" (Freud, 1937/1964, p. 257). However, Freud did not regard this as a valid criticism, noting that analysts should be as skeptical when clients accept interpretations as when they reject them (Gay, 1988). Still, internal inconsistency must be recognized as a potential threat to the scientific viability of psychoanalytic theory.

Falsifiability   It is on this criterion that Freudian theory has been criticized most strongly. It is extremely difficult to use psychoanalytic theory to generate testable predictions. Its concepts are vague and difficult to measure; for example, how does one obtain reliable and valid measures of the degree to which one has successfully resolved the Oedipal conflict or the defense mechanism that one is most likely to employ?

In addition to the vagueness of its constructs, Freudian theory contains so many complex and imprecise laws that it is difficult to use them to generate

testable predictions. The discussion in the previous section about the possible internal inconsistency of psychoanalytic theory illustrates the difficulty faced by psychologists who try to test Freudian theory.

Popper introduced the criterion of falsifiability to distinguish between science and nonscience. If a field claimed to be a science but was in fact nonfalsifiable, then Popper labeled the system a pseudoscience. Popper (1963) identified three systems that he considered, alongside astrology, as pseudosciences: the Marxist theory of history, Adler's system of individual psychology, and Freudian psychoanalysis.

Sidney Hook, another eminent philosopher of science, arrived at a similar conclusion. Hook (1959) related how he often asked psychoanalysts to specify the facts of a case that would be inconsistent with the Oedipal conflict. That is, what personal features are so incompatible with the Oedipal conflict that, if such a person were found, psychoanalysts would have to give up the concept of the Oedipal conflict? According to Hook, he never received a satisfactory response to the question, even from noted members of the psychoanalytic community. Hook agreed with Popper that, if no conceivable set of facts would falsify the concept of the Oedipal conflict, then the concept is a pseudoscientific one.

More recently, Adolph Grunbaum has taken up the mantle of philosophers of science in evaluating the scientific status of psychoanalysis. In a detailed critique of the scientific foundations of psychoanalysis, Grunbaum (1984) disagreed with Popper's evaluation. Grunbaum concluded that it is possible for aspects of psychoanalytic theory to be falsified, and so the system meets Popper's criterion for science. However, Grunbaum also concluded that, to date, psychoanalysts have not done a very good job of evaluating their system. Thus, Grunbaum suggested that psychoanalysts improve the quality of their scientific evaluations of the theory.

The lack of empirical evidence has plagued psychoanalytic theory from its beginnings. For example, Sears (1943) reviewed the research to date that attempted to verify some aspect of Freudian theory. He concluded that there is little empirical support for the theory, calling psychoanalysis "bad science."

Sears thought that the evidence that seemed to support Freudian theory could be explained as well or better by other theories.

Scientifically oriented psychologists have been extremely critical of psychoanalysis because of the difficulties faced in subjecting it to empirical test. Thus, scientist-practitioners increasingly turned away from psychoanalytic theory to alternatives, such as the cognitive, behavioral, and biological models, which will be discussed later in the chapter.

Still, it should be recognized that some empirically oriented psychologists have found support for Freudian theory. For example, Kline (1972) reviewed what he regarded as the methodologically strongest tests of Freudian theory. Although Kline found that some aspects of the theory do not have scientific support (e.g., claims of the efficacy of psychoanalytic therapy) he concluded that other aspects of Freudian theory (e.g., the origins of homosexuality, the existence of basic oral and anal personality types) are supported by research. Similarly, Fisher and Greenberg (1977) published a review of research that generally supported several aspects of Freudian theory.

Still, despite the lack of scientific evidence for psychoanalysis, it remains an extremely important approach in psychology, both because of its historical impact and because of its continued use in applied settings and in the humanities.

BEHAVIORISM

A second major theoretical approach in clinical psychology is behaviorism. John Watson introduced this term in his 1913 paper, "Psychology as a Behaviorist Views It." Watson intended to make psychology more scientific. In his opinion, science restricted its attention only to observables. Because mental processes cannot be observed by others, Watson did not consider them to be appropriate concerns for a scientific psychology, but instead the focus of philosophy or other fields. Hence, he limited the attention of psychology to that which can be observed—behavior.

Watson criticized Freudian theory as unscientific. Freud relied on introspection to examine mental functioning. Freud relied on case studies rather than controlled group studies to examine his ideas. Freud utilized constructs, such as the unconscious, that are vague and difficult to measure.

Because Freudian theory relies on subjective methods of interpretation, it is difficult to apply objective scientific standards to determine whether a Freudian interpretation is correct. For example, a psychoanalyst might explain a client's phobia by suggesting that the client has an unconscious fear of sexuality. However, there may not be an objective method of independently verifying this underlying problem. If the psychoanalyst uses the same evidence both to infer the underlying problem and to validate its inference, then the psychoanalyst has committed the logical fallacy of *nominalism*. This is circular reasoning in which a label is first introduced to describe a phenomenon but is later used to explain it. The fallacy, of course, is that one does not explain a phenomenon by naming it.

It should be recalled that (as discussed in Chapter 2) philosophers of science now recognize that science includes nonobservables (hypothetical constructs), as long as claims about the nonobservables can be tested through their relationships with observables. Thus, many contemporary philosophers of science regard Watson's view of science as rigid and outdated.

The major emphases of behaviorism follow directly from Watson's insistence on a scientific approach to psychology. Remember that science operates under the assumptions of determinism, empiricism, and order. Behaviorists adopt these assumptions as well. They regard behavior as determined, not by unconscious influences as Freud assumed, but by external environmental influences. They suggest that behavior is the result of antecedent stimuli that precede the behavior and consequent stimuli that follow the behavior.

Behaviorists are empiricists, as was evident in the very name Watson attached to his movement. In general, behaviorists emphasize the observation and measurement of behavior.

Finally, behaviorists assume that behavior is ordered. They assume that behavior follows a set of basic principles that hold across species of animals. Thus, they adopt a scientific approach to the conduct of research on laboratory animals as well as on humans in efforts to identify the fundamental laws of behavior.

Structure of Personality

Because behaviorists ignore mental entities, they spend little time on traditional concerns of personality theorists such as the structural components of personality. Rather than discuss parts of the personality (such as Freud's id, ego, and superego), behaviorists simply refer to one's *behavior repertoire*. This is the set of behaviors that an individual is capable of exhibiting.

Occasionally, behaviorists may use the terminology of traditional personality theories, referring to an individual as having a *personality trait* of aggression or dependency. It is important to note that, in such cases, behaviorists use the concept of *trait* quite differently from Freudian theorists.

Freudian theory considers a personality trait as a hypothetical construct. As defined in Chapter 2, a hypothetical construct is an unseen entity that is presumed to exist and that can be detected through its lawful relationships with observables. When Freud referred to an individual as having the trait of *aggression*, he believed that aggression existed somehow within the personality and that this underlying aggression was lawfully related to the individual's outward behavior.

However, when a behaviorist says that an individual has the personality trait of aggression, the behaviorist is simply describing the person's behavior. Instead of presuming that aggression exists somewhere within the person, the behaviorist uses the label of aggression as a convenient way of summarizing aggressive behavior. Thus, behaviorists use personality traits as intervening variables rather than as hypothetical constructs. An *intervening variable*

EXHIBIT 3.5   Hypothetical Constructs versus Intervening Variables

Hypothetical constructs are presumed to exist, even though they are unseen. They are considered to be real entities or processes. They contain meaning beyond that included in empirical observations. Hypothetical constructs cannot be quantified or measured exactly through observations, because they are not reducible to observations.

Intervening variables are constructs that merely summarize empirical observations. They are not presumed to exist apart from the observations. They are wholly reducible to empirical observations. Intervening variables do not convey any meaning apart from that already present in the empirical observations. For these reasons, exact quantifications or measurements of intervening variables are possible.

For example, consider a client who behaves aggressively across a variety of settings: driving, working at the office, playing sports, and so on. These observed behaviors lead both psychoanalysts and behaviorists to say that the individual has the trait of aggression. However, psychoanalysts and behaviorists mean two very different things by this term.

Psychoanalysts consider the trait of aggression as a hypothetical construct. For psychoanalysts, the observed

aggressive behaviors are outward expressions of underlying aggression. The underlying aggression is real even though it cannot be seen. In addition, the observed aggressive behaviors do not convey all that can be known about the underlying aggression. After all, the underlying aggression may be expressed in some settings but not others, may be directed toward some targets more than others, may change in intensity over time, and so on. Further observations may lead to additional inferences about the aggression, although even additional observations will not exhaust what can be discovered about the underlying trait.

Behaviorists, on the other hand, consider the trait of aggression as an intervening variable. For behaviorists, the aggressive trait *is* the set of observed aggressive behaviors, and nothing more. The client's aggression is completely understood in terms of the observed aggressive behaviors. When behaviorists say that the client has the trait of aggression, they mean simply that the client behaves aggressively. It is simpler to speak of an aggressive trait than it is to list all of the aggressive behaviors observed to date.

is a label that is used to summarize a set of observable phenomena. The differences between hypothetical constructs and intervening variables were discussed by MacCorquodale and Meehl (1948) and are summarized in Exhibit 3.5.

Development of Personality

Behaviorists are concerned with behavior: how it is acquired, how it changes, and so on. For this reason, behaviorists have devoted much attention to the principles of learning or conditioning. Behaviorists have traditionally discussed two forms of conditioning: classical and instrumental. More recently, behaviorists have considered a third type of conditioning—social learning—as another basic form of learning.

Classical conditioning (also known as respondent and Pavlovian conditioning) is the type of conditioning associated with Pavlov. Through classical conditioning, a response that originally was automatically or reflexively elicited by one stimulus is trained to occur following another, previously neutral stimulus. Responses that are initially elicited automatically by a stimulus are called *respondents*. In the original work by Pavlov, meat powder elicited the automatic response of salivation in dogs. Pavlov repeatedly paired a bell with the meat powder. Originally, the bell was neutral with respect to salivation. However, after repeated pairings of the bell and meat powder, the dogs began to salivate in response to the bell alone. The bell, through repeated associations with the meat, acquired "meat-like" properties and elicited salivation.

In this example, meat powder is called the *unconditioned stimulus (UCS)* and salivation in response to the meat powder is the *unconditioned response (UCR)*. These are unconditioned because no conditioning is necessary for the dog to salivate in response to meat. It is a reflexive response, programmed into the dog's nervous system. When the dog salivates in response to the bell, the bell is the *conditioned stimulus (CS)* and salivation in response to the bell is the *conditioned response (CR)*.

The second basic type of conditioning is instrumental conditioning. This is the type of conditioning most associated with B. F. Skinner, perhaps the most influential leader of the school of behaviorism following Watson. *Instrumental conditioning* is the conditioning of voluntary responses through their consequences. A desirable consequence, or *reinforcement*, increases the future probability of the response; an undesirable consequence, or *punishment*, decreases the future probability of the response. Reinforcement may involve either the presentation of a pleasant stimulus (i.e., positive reinforcement), such as food or money, or the cessation of an aversive stimulus (i.e., negative reinforcement), such as the removal of pain. Similarly, punishment may either involve the presentation of an aversive stimulus (i.e., positive punishment), such as a spanking or scolding, or the cessation of a pleasant stimulus (i.e., negative punishment), such as loss of TV privileges.

In instrumental conditioning, one's behaviors operate on the environment to receive desirable or undesirable consequences. Because these consequences influence the future probability of the behavior's recurrence, this type of conditioning is also called *operant conditioning*.

Instrumental conditioning is more flexible than classical conditioning. Only responses that are initially reflexive can be classically conditioned; however, any voluntary responses, no matter how simple or complex, can be instrumentally conditioned. For example, behaviorists have discussed the operant conditioning of behaviors ranging from barpresses by rats through speech in young children to towel-hoarding by psychiatric patients.

Even though these two forms of conditioning are simple and may appear to be limited in scope, they have several variants that increase the complexity and variety of behaviors they produce.

In *generalization*, a response that was originally learned in one situation (CS in classical conditioning, antecedent stimuli in instrumental conditioning) is trained to occur in other similar situations. For example, if a dog is trained to salivate in response to a particular bell, it is likely that the dog will also salivate in response to other bells. In general, the closer in pitch the other bells are to the initial bell, the greater the salivation response. The tendency for a conditioned response to be greater for situations that more closely resemble the training situation is termed a *generalization gradient*. An example of generalization in instrumental conditioning is the verbal behavior of a child who has learned the word *ball* in the context of a specific ball. The child will then say *ball* when seeing other balls as well.

In *discrimination*, a response is conditioned so that it occurs in response to a specific stimulus and not to other similar stimuli. A dog that repeatedly experiences the pairing of one bell with food and another bell with no food will eventually learn to discriminate between them, salivating in response to one but not the other. A child who learns to say *mama* may mistakenly use the word in the context of all adult females. Through discrimination training, in which the word is reinforced only in the presence of mother, the child learns to say the word in the correct context.

Shaping and chaining are methods of hastening the process of instrumental conditioning. *Shaping* is the systematic reinforcement of successive approximations to a behavior. *Chaining* is the training of separate behaviors that are then combined to form a complex behavior.

Skinner demonstrated how both shaping and chaining can be used to train animals to perform complex behaviors. Suppose a trainer wants to teach a dog to climb a wooden ladder, cross a plank, and then jump through a hoop. It would be hard to use instrumental conditioning in its most basic form, because one would have to wait for a long time (perhaps forever) for the animal to engage in the behavior so one can reinforce it.

However, by using shaping and chaining, one can quickly instill the behavior. The trainer shapes the dog to climb a ladder by breaking the act into small segments, which are reinforced successively. The dog is first reinforced for approaching the ladder. After this is mastered, a bit more is required before the dog receives reinforcement—it must touch the ladder. After the dog learns to spend its time touching the ladder, the dog is then required to touch the ladder with its front paws, to touch the first step of the ladder with its paws, to climb onto the first

step, and so on. After each segment is mastered, the dog is required to exhibit a slightly more complex behavior in order to be reinforced. The dog is trained to walk along a plank and to jump through a hoop in a similar way. After each behavior is established separately, they are chained, so that the dog climbs the ladder, walks the plank, and jumps through the hoop in sequence.

Human behavior can be established in similar ways. People learn piano pieces by practicing the melody with the right hand and the bass with the left hand before combining them. Similarly, piano students may learn to play the first measure, then the first and second measure combined, and then the first three measures, and so on. It is easier to learn small behaviors that are then combined than it is to learn a complex behavior as a whole.

Skinner described how different schedules of reinforcement influence instrumental conditioning. Some behavior is conditioned on a *continuous schedule,* in which every instance of the behavior is reinforced or punished, whereas other behavior is conditioned on a *partial* or *intermittent schedule,* in which not every instance of the behavior is followed by a consequence. Continuous and partial schedules of reinforcement differ in two respects. Continuous schedules lead to more rapid learning than partial schedules. However, behavior acquired on continuous schedules extinguish (or discontinue upon termination of the consequence) more rapidly than behavior acquired on partial schedules.

Skinner also distinguished between two types of partial reinforcement schedules. On a *ratio schedule*, a target behavior must occur a certain number of times before the next instance of the behavior is reinforced. On an *interval schedule*, a certain amount of time must elapse following a reinforcement before the next instance of the target behavior will be reinforced. In general, ratio schedules produce rapid and steady rates of responding, such as when people play video games that provide steady reinforcement (points, noises, explosions). On the other hand, interval schedules produce a pattern of responding in which the target behavior is followed by a pause, with an increased rate of responding after a rest period. For example, some hospitals use a device to administer pain medication on interval schedules. When in pain, the patient pushes a button that causes a dose of morphine to be administered intravenously. However, the device is programmed so that, following a dose of morphine, further button pushes have no effect until after a certain amount of time has passed. This ensures that the patient receives morphine only when in pain and prevents the patient from being overmedicated.

A third type of conditioning, associated with the work of Albert Bandura, is *social learning*. Social learning (also called modeling or observational learning) is learning through observation.

Social learning is a simple and common-sensical notion. We all have seen children who, to their parents' chagrin, imitate their parents' four-letter words. Bandura has shown, in lab research, how children imitate a model's aggressive behavior (Bandura, 1973).

Although social learning may not appear to be a novel or "earth-shaking" concept, its incorporation into behavioral psychology actually has profound consequences. Social learning differs from classical and instrumental conditioning in two ways: (1) the learner does not have to engage in the behavior; and (2) the learner does not have to experience directly the consequences of the behavior (the UCS in classical conditioning and the punishment or reinforcement in instrumental conditioning). For example, consider a 5-year-old child who hears an older boy curse after falling on the school playground. The kindergartner may learn some new and colorful language from this event. Now, if a teacher also hears this language and scolds the offender, the 5-year-old also learns that such language is not acceptable at school, and that its use is likely to be followed by punishment.

In social learning, the *learning* takes place at the cognitive level. Instead of learning a series of muscular contractions, one learns a cognitive representation of behavior and its consequences. In other words, by adding social learning to the basic principles of conditioning, behaviorists have restored cognitions to behavioral theory. The significance of this

will be discussed later in the chapter, and in Chapter 11, Cognitive and Behavior Therapy.

Dynamics of Personality

The behavioral view of the dynamics of personality is straightforward. Behaviorists view people as acting to receive reinforcement and avoid punishment. People repeat behaviors that have been successful and avoid behaviors that have been unsuccessful.

This view of motivation is quite different from that of Freudian and humanistic psychology. Freud, you remember, viewed people as motivated primarily by the animal instincts of sex and aggression. Humanistic psychologists (as will be discussed later in the chapter) viewed humans as motivated to fulfill their potential. These different views regarding the basic motivating forces of human behavior form one of the major distinctions among these three schools of thought. Psychoanalysts view people as having a base, animalistic nature; humanists view people as having a basically good nature; behaviorists, on the other hand, view human nature as neutral. Behaviorists believe that people are neither basically good nor evil; rather, they are conditioned to become whatever they become.

This neutral view regarding human nature is illustrated perhaps most strongly in a quotation from John Watson (1924, p. 104): "Give me a dozen healthy infants, well-formed, and my own specified world to bring them up in and I'll guarantee to take any one at random and train him to become any type of specialist I might select—doctor, lawyer, artist, merchant-chief and, yes, even beggar-man and thief, regardless of his talents, penchants, tendencies, abilities, vocations, and race of his ancestors."

Psychopathology

The behavioral view of psychopathology is the same as its view of normal behavior. Abnormal behavior, like normal behavior, develops through conditioning.

Behaviorally oriented clinical psychologists view their clients' behavioral symptoms as the major focus of treatment. Unlike Freudian psychoanalysts who explain each presenting symptom as due to some underlying pathology, behavior therapists equate the behavioral symptoms with the pathology: the presenting behavioral symptom *is* the disorder.

This also demonstrates the focus of behavior therapists on behavioral symptoms. Instead of concentrating on underlying emotions or cognitions, behavior therapists focus on the client's behavioral symptoms—what the client does or how the client acts.

The etiology of such behavioral symptoms is conditioning. Behavior therapists suggest that the same laws of learning that produce normal behavior also produce abnormal behavior. Thus, the client's disordered behavior is conceptualized as the result of some deviant conditioning process: the client has either been conditioned to exhibit a problem behavior not found in others (*overconditioning*) or has not been conditioned to engage in a desirable behavior exhibited by most others (*underconditioning*).

For example, behaviorists have used classical conditioning to explain the development of emotional problems. Watson and Rayner (1920) conditioned an infant ("Little Albert") to fear a white rat by repeatedly pairing a loud sudden noise, which human infants instinctively fear, with a white lab rat. After repeated pairings, the infant then exhibited fear in response to the white rat. This response then generalized to other stimuli, such as a man with a white beard and a toy stuffed animal.

Physiological reactions are a fundamental aspect of emotional responses. Behaviorists suggest that, through classical conditioning, such physiological reactions become associated with previously neutral stimuli. Fear, anxiety, and pain responses may be classically conditioned as in the case of Little Albert. Other reflexive responses, including allergic reactions, vomiting, and even sexual arousal, may similarly be classically conditioned.

Behaviorists also explain the development of abnormal behavior through instrumental conditioning. A behavior that is followed by positive consequences increases in frequency. Thus, a parent who uses corporal punishment to stop a child's misbehavior is reinforced by the fact that the misbehavior stopped. In the future, the parent's use of corporal punishment will increase. An adolescent who defies authority, vandalizes the school grounds, and engages in other antisocial activities may receive several types of reinforcement for these actions: approval and attention from peers, financial rewards from stealing, and physiological pleasure when engaging in risky behavior. Such reinforcement may outweigh the social disapproval of parents, teachers, and legal authorities. Thus, delinquent behavior may be initiated and maintained by instrumental conditioning.

Behaviorists also suggest that abnormal behavior may result from failure to learn appropriate behaviors that most other people have learned. An example of such underconditioning is lack of assertiveness. Being assertive means being able to express one's wants and feelings in a socially appropriate way. For example, if one cannot enjoy a movie because a person seated nearby is smoking, the assertive response is to request that the person stop smoking. If this does not work, then another assertive response is to ask the manager to put a stop to the smoking. However, some individuals are too inhibited to take these steps and so feel frustrated and unable to enjoy the film. Behaviorists interpret unassertiveness, not as due to underlying psychological problems, but rather as due to a lack of training. Behavior therapists provide assertiveness training for this problem, using conditioning techniques to teach individuals to be more assertive.

Another example of underconditioning is nocturnal enuresis (or bedwetting). When this occurs in an older child whose muscular and neurological development should permit the child to control urinary release, and when purely physical causes for enuresis (such as urinary tract infections, epilepsy, and diabetes) have been ruled out, the behavior therapist views the problem simply as the result of a lack of proper training. Unlike psychoanalysts, who perceive nocturnal enuresis as the result of some underlying psychological difficulty (Yates [1970] summarized psychoanalytic views of nocturnal enuresis, including that it is a symbolic form of masturbating or weeping, a way of expressing homosexual tendencies, a way of attempting to stifle one's sexuality, and a way of expressing aggression), behavior therapists view enuresis simply as due to a lack of training.

Treatment

According to behaviorists, psychopathology develops through conditioning. If this is correct, then an appropriate method of treating abnormal behavior is to modify the problem behavior through further conditioning. *Behavior therapy* is the application of conditioning principles in efforts to modify problem behaviors. Conditioning techniques are used first to remove deviant behaviors and then to replace them with more appropriate alternatives. Behavior therapy will be presented in detail in Chapter 11.

Evaluation

Since its introduction by Watson in 1913, behaviorism has become one of the major theoretical approaches in psychology. Its influence in clinical psychology increased during the 1950s and 1960s, when the field increasingly attended to the scientific foundations of practice and found that many of its traditional assumptions and practices had difficulty meeting scientific criteria (Wierzbicki, 1993a). The criteria used to evaluate scientific theories can also be applied to behaviorism.

Comprehensiveness   Behaviorism, like Freudian psychoanalysis, is remarkably comprehensive. Skinner applied behaviorism to about as wide a range of topics as Freud had for psychoanalysis. Behaviorism has been applied to art, creativity, motivation, development, psychopathology, psychotherapy, and on and on. For sheer range of application, behaviorism approaches psychoanalysis in terms of comprehensiveness.

Parsimony   Behaviorism is a remarkably parsimonious theory. It introduces relatively few constructs and laws. For this reason, behaviorism is easier to understand, apply, and test than psychoanalysis.

However, it is possible that behaviorism is overly simple, or simplistic. Critics of behaviorism have suggested that the basic principles of conditioning do not satisfactorily account for the range and complexity of human behavior. Critics have also contended that, by ignoring mental processes, behaviorism has limited itself to less important and useful topics than other psychological theories. In this way, behaviorism may even be trivial in comparison to other theories.

Applied or Heuristic Value   Behaviorism stands well according to this criterion. Behaviorism has many applications. It has been used in educational, penal, and hospital settings. It has been used to develop educational materials (such as workbooks and computer software). Behavior therapy is now one of the most well-established approaches to treating psychological disorders.

Internal Consistency   Behaviorism also stands well along this criterion. Because the model is relatively simple, it is easy to understand and apply consistently.

Occasionally, minor criticisms have been directed against behaviorism on these grounds. For example, it is possible that a verbal reprimand may actually have different effects on two children; for one, it may be an effective punishment whereas, for another, it may serve as the only attention that the child receives from a teacher and so be a reinforcement.

A related criticism is that behaviorism defines *punishment* and *reinforcement* in circular terms: if a stimulus increases the frequency of a behavior, then it is a reinforcement, but if it decreases the frequency of a behavior, then it is a punishment. Because one cannot determine whether the stimulus will increase or decrease the probability of a behavior until after one has administered the consequence, then critics have argued that the concepts are tautological, or circular.

Behaviorists respond to these criticisms, however, by noting that one stimulus may have different values for different individuals, as a function of their different conditioning histories. If these histories are known, then one can predict accurately whether a stimulus will have reinforcing or punishing properties. In addition, the stimulus value can be determined empirically, and then used to generate testable consistent predictions about an individual's future behavior.

Falsifiability Perhaps the major strength of behaviorism has been its ability to generate testable predictions. Many clinical psychologists were won over to the behavioral model in the 1950s and 1960s when the field began to apply the scientific model to the evaluation of clinical psychology's assumptions and practices (Wierzbicki, 1993a). Behaviorism stresses a scientific approach to psychology; as such, its use has been associated with ongoing research to evaluate behavioral applications.

In clinical psychology, behaviorism has especially had an impact in the area of treatment. There have been numerous studies of the effectiveness of behavioral therapies. Clinical psychologists who insist that therapy have an empirical foundation have been especially receptive to behavior therapies.

The effectiveness of behavior therapy will be discussed in more detail in Chapter 11. At this point, it only needs to be said that contemporary research on the effectiveness of behavior therapy has shown that it is more effective than control conditions and compares well to other forms of treatment.

HUMANISM

The humanistic school of psychology rose in the 1950s. The major figures in the development of humanism included Carl Rogers, Abraham Maslow, and Gordon Allport. Maslow (1962) referred to humanism as *Third Force Psychology* (p. iii), meaning that humanism was the third major approach (or paradigm) in psychology, after psychoanalytic and behavioral theory.

Humanistic psychology developed largely as a reaction against both psychoanalysis and behaviorism. Humanists disliked what they regarded as negative features of both approaches. Humanists considered psychoanalysis too *pessimistic*. Freud emphasized the pathological, the irrational, the unconscious, the fragmentation of personality, and biological motivations. Humanistic psychologists wanted a psychology that focused, instead, on the

healthy, the rational, the conscious, the integrated self, and transcendent or "higher" motivations.

Similarly, humanists disliked behaviorism's rigid scientific approach. By only considering what can be measured in behavioral terms, behaviorists treated people as "objects" and reduced meaningful behavior to trivialities; by insisting on a scientific approach, behaviorists lost the essence of meaningful human experiences such as art, love, and creativity. Humanists wished to develop a psychology that considered subjective experience and examined experience in a meaningful, holistic way.

Humanism has several important philosophical roots. Perhaps the most significant of these is phenomenology. Immanuel Kant (1724–1804) used the term *noumena* to refer to the objective world that exists in itself, independent of human sensation; he used the term *phenomena* to refer to humans' sensory knowledge of the external world (Rychlak, 1981).

Edmund Husserl (1859–1938), the "father of phenomenology," developed an important philosophical system based on this distinction. *Phenomenology* is the philosophical approach that holds that the only way to understand a person is through his or her subjective experience. According to phenomenology, the only way for psychology to derive an adequate science of behavior is to examine people's subjective points of view (Rychlak, 1981).

Humanists retain this phenomenological emphasis. They suggest that psychology should examine subjective experience—how human beings experience the world. If we consider any experience, such as love, humanists argue that psychologists should examine how people actually experience it. This differs from the psychoanalytic view, which stresses unconscious determinants from early childhood, and the traditional behavioral view, which ignores entirely the subjective component and focuses exclusively on the individual's behavior.

Unlike psychoanalysis, humanism is not associated with only a single founder and so it is not characterized by a single model of personality. Different humanists, including Rogers, Maslow, and Allport, offered different theories of personality. What follows is only a summary of several significant elements of the theories of Rogers, Maslow, and Allport.

Structure of Personality

In general, humanists attempted to account for the integrity of personality (Maslow, 1962). Humanists disliked Freud's characterization of personality as a constant struggle among id, ego, and superego. The simplest humanistic view of the structure of personality is perhaps that of Rogers (1959). Rogers suggested that there is one major component of personality: the *self*. Rogers used this term to refer to the person's subjective view of self, and so it may be closer to what lay people call self-image. As one's subjective view of oneself, the self includes both one's strengths and weaknesses and both accuracies and inaccuracies. In general, Rogers suggested that psychological health is associated with a more accurate view of self.

One component of the self is the *self-ideal*: the self (or self-image) one would most like to have. According to Rogers, one index of psychological health is the congruence between one's self and self-ideal, that is, the greater the congruence, the healthier the person.

Development of Personality

Rogers (1959, 1961) thought that both the self and the self-ideal develop through the individual's interpretations of his or her experiences. However, the self and self-ideal also form in response to other people's evaluations of the person. For example, if a young girl's friends tell her that she is funny, then she is likely to incorporate this trait in her view of self.

Rogers described two types of reactions by others that influence healthy and unhealthy psychological development. According to Rogers, conditional positive regard fosters unhealthy development. *Conditional positive regard* means that the person receives positive regard conditionally; that is, the person is cared for and accepted as a worthwhile person only when meeting the conditions of others. For ex-

ample, parents who withhold love from their child when the child does not behave according to their expectations are providing conditional positive regard.

Conditional positive regard affects the child's self and self-ideal. If parents withhold love from a child when the child misbehaves, then the child is likely to develop a self-image consistent with this treatment: *I am not lovable unless I behave correctly*. In this way, conditional positive regard leads to *conditions of worth* that affect the child's self and self-ideal. The child comes to think of self as lovable only when meeting others' standards. This leads to inaccurate and negative perceptions of self and to an overly idealistic self-ideal.

Conversely, Rogers thought that unconditional positive regard fosters healthy development. *Unconditional positive regard* means that the person is regarded positively unconditionally; that is, the person is accepted and respected without having conditions placed upon one in order to receive such treatment. Parents who care for their child regardless of what the child says or does are providing unconditional positive regard.

According to Rogers, children who receive unconditional positive regard receive the message that they are worthy of respect. This message is consistent with their own perception of their experience. Hence, they do not develop conditions of worth, and their self-image is congruent with their actual self.

Another influential humanistic view of personality development is that of Allport (1955, 1961). Allport viewed development—indeed, all of human existence—as a process of *becoming*. For Allport, the individual is never in a static condition but is constantly changing. To reflect this dynamic view, Allport used the term *proprium* rather than *self*. According to Allport, *self* implies a fixed being—something that *is* rather than *is developing*.

Dynamics of Personality

Most humanists agree that people are motivated to develop their potential—to develop in a positive way. Humanists use several terms to reflect this concept of motivation. *Self-actualization, fulfillment of potential, enrichment,* and *becoming* are all terms used by humanists to describe motivation.

Rogers (1959), for example, considered self-actualization as the basic motivation of human behavior. Rogers thought that people are motivated to develop their potential—to strive to become more than they were. Being reared in an environment of conditional positive regard is harmful, according to Rogers, because it leads people to strive, not to fulfill their own nature, but to meet others' conditions of worth.

Maslow (1962) is another humanistic theorist who addressed at length the issue of human motivation. Maslow suggested that there are two classes of motivators: basic needs and metaneeds.

Basic needs (also called *deficiency* or *d-needs*) are needs that must be met, in order, or else the individual suffers from their lack of fulfillment. The basic needs, in order, are physiological needs (food, water, sleep), safety needs (shelter from the environment, physical security), belongingness needs (social contacts, friends), and esteem needs (self-esteem, esteem from others). If any basic need is unfulfilled, then the person is unable to move to the next higher level of needs. Also, if any of the basic needs is unfulfilled, then the individual experiences distress and is likely to develop psychological problems.

After all of the basic needs are met, the individual can move on to the level of *metaneeds* (also called *growth, being,* and *b-needs*). According to Maslow, metaneeds differ from basic needs in two ways. First, metaneeds do not have to be met in any particular order. Second, the failure to fulfill metaneeds does not lead to psychological problems; instead, this simply results in the individual's being less fully actualized.

Metaneeds lead the person to become enriched or fulfilled, and include self-actualization, artistic and aesthetic needs, and intellectual curiosity. For example, consider the metaneed of intellectual curiosity. According to Maslow, many students take a class only to earn a grade, obtain a degree, get a job, and receive a paycheck. However, self-actualized students enjoy learning simply for the sake of learning—for the very joy of learning. Grades, test scores, and others' evaluations of them are unimportant; they learn simply for learning's sake.

This can be generalized to other metaneeds. For Maslow, people fulfill metaneeds when they receive satisfaction in the very act of experience. This can occur in almost any arena: athletics, friendship, religious worship, art. What is important for Maslow is that the individual experiences the activity fully, in the moment. The act in itself is its own justification.

Psychopathology

Humanists view people as basically good and as motivated to self-actualize. Pathology results when this developmental process is stifled and people fail to develop their good nature.

Rogers (1959, 1961), for example, said that psychopathology is related to incongruence between: (1) one's subjective view of the world and the world in reality; (2) one's subjective view of self and the self in reality; and (3) the self (as perceived) and the self-ideal. As discrepancy increases, one has more difficulty behaving effectively and so experiences greater emotional turmoil.

As described above, Rogers stated that such discrepancies result from experiences of conditional positive regard. The more a person receives such treatment, the less accurately the person perceives the world and the self, and the greater the discrepancy becomes between the self (as perceived) and the self-ideal.

Humanists have devoted more effort to describing healthy than unhealthy people. Rogers (1961) and Maslow (1962) described self-actualized people in glowing terms. Self-actualizers are creative, open to experience, existential (i.e., able to "live in the moment"), humorous, and so on. Conversely, Rogers and Maslow held that maladjusted individuals lack such characteristics.

Treatment

The most influential humanistic approach to psychotherapy is clearly the work of Rogers (1942, 1951, 1959). Rogers suggested that psychotherapy is a replay of the environmental conditions that fostered healthy development. For Rogers, the *active ingredient* in psychotherapy is unconditional positive regard. The Rogerian therapist provides unconditional positive regard, caring for and respecting the client regardless of what the client says or does. It is this atmosphere of acceptance that leads to improvement. Once the client learns that the therapist accepts him, regardless of what he says or does, the client eventually comes to accept himself as he is. He no longer tries to meet the conditions of worth adopted from others; instead, he can live to fulfill his own good nature.

Rogers and his colleagues (e.g., Truax & Carkhuff, 1967) articulated the elements of unconditional positive regard: genuineness, warmth, and empathy. The Rogerian therapist is open and honest with the client, cares for the client, and accurately identifies what the client is thinking and feeling.

According to Rogers, it is this unconditional caring that produces therapeutic change. The client need not attain insights into childhood problems as in psychoanalysis. The client need not alter a problem behavior as in behavior therapy. Rather, the therapist must simply establish this open and caring relationship.

Because the client–therapist relationship is so important, Rogerian therapy is sometimes called relationship oriented. Also, because the therapist cares for the client and because the therapist does not dictate the course or the methods of therapy, but instead simply accepts the client, Rogerian therapy is also called *nondirective* and *client-centered therapy*. The techniques and effectiveness of Rogerian and other forms of humanistic therapy will be presented in more detail in Chapter 10.

Evaluation

Humanistic psychology arose in the 1950s as a reaction against the pathological focus of psychoanalysis and the rigid scientific methodology of behaviorism. By providing a positive alternative to psychoanalysis, humanism won over many followers, particularly those who wished to address "normal" and even transcendent types of experience. However, by rejecting the scientific methodology of behaviorism,

humanism falls short on the criteria used to evaluate scientific theories.

Comprehensiveness   The humanistic approach is somewhat less comprehensive than other psychological theories. Humanists focus on positive or healthy aspects of experience; hence, they devote more attention to personality and "normal" experiences (e.g., art, creativity, religion) than to psychopathology and its treatment. Still, within the realm of normal behavior, humanistic psychology has had a major impact, providing an important alternative to psychoanalytic and other theories.

Parsimony   The humanistic view is extremely parsimonious, introducing relatively few novel constructs and principles. However, some critics argue that humanism is overly simple, providing too few principles to account for the complexity of human behavior.

Applied or Heuristic Value   Humanism has good heuristic value, especially in dealing with normal or healthy kinds of functioning. For example, humanism has provided an important alternative to psychoanalytic theory for explaining such human experiences as art, creativity, love, and religiosity. Humanism provides an account that has attracted many followers, from philosophers and theologians, artists and literature critics, to psychologists.

Internal Consistency and Falsifiability   The weakness of humanism, like psychoanalysis, lies in the degree to which it generates testable predictions. Humanistic theory uses constructs that are vague and difficult to measure. For example, how do you assess the degree to which a person's artistic productions are the result of metaneeds versus deficiency needs? How do you measure the degree to which a person has become self-actualized? Measures of humanistic concepts tend to be subjective, and so the reliability and validity of such concepts are limited.

Similarly, the principles of humanistic psychology tend not to lend themselves to exact predictions. For example, Rogers stated that conditional positive regard was the cause of later psychological problems. This statement, however, is imprecise, and questions arise (e.g., How much? From whom? In what contexts? During what developmental period?) that must be addressed before one can generate testable predictions.

Still, despite the difficulty in testing humanistic theory, two features of Rogerian theory have received significant empirical attention and support. As described above, Rogers believed that psychological health is associated with congruence between a person's self and self-ideal. During the 1950s and 1960s, many studies examined this hypothesis. This research often employed the *Q-sort* methodology. In this technique, subjects sort a large number of statements, printed on cards, into piles, according to the degree to which they accurately describe the self. After describing the self, subjects then perform a Q-sort to describe the self-ideal. Researchers then determine the congruence (measured in terms of a Q coefficient, interpreted like a correlation coefficient) between the self and self-ideal.

Butler and Haigh (1954) found that self/self-ideal congruence in 25 patients was smaller before therapy (-0.01) than after therapy (0.34), and was smaller than that in 16 nonpatients (0.58). This supported Rogers's proposal than self/self-ideal congruence is associated with psychological health.

Many other studies also supported this suggestion. For example, Turner and Vanderlippe (1958) reported that self/self-ideal congruence is associated with several indices of adjustment in a large sample of students, including general health, length of hospitalizations, number of visits to a clinic, temperament, and peer acceptance. Similarly, Rosenberg (1962) found that self/self-ideal congruence is significantly correlated with 15 of the 18 scales of the California Personality Inventory.

However, despite such support, problems in this research were soon discovered. For example, some individuals exhibit high self/self-ideal congruence despite their being seriously disturbed (Butler & Haigh, 1954). This suggests that self/self-ideal congruence, although related to psychological health, should not be regarded as the only measure or even

as a linear measure of health. Other indices of adjustment must also be considered.

Another aspect of Rogerian theory that has been researched extensively is his claim that therapeutic effectiveness is associated with therapist genuineness, warmth, and empathy. Chapter 10 will discuss this research in more detail. For now, let it suffice to say that there have been dozens of studies on this topic, many of which have supported Rogers; when therapists express higher levels of unconditional positive regard, therapeutic effectiveness tends to be higher (Truax & Carkhuff, 1967). Of course, this research has not been entirely consistent or free of methodological problems (Parloff, Waskow, & Wolfe, 1978). Still, many clinical psychologists today regard genuineness, warmth, and empathy as fundamental qualities necessary (if not sufficient) for successful therapy.

Humanism has also generated much research on the topic of values. Both Allport (1961) and Maslow (1962) discussed human values and their relation to personality and behavior. Humanists developed several tests to measures basic values (e.g., Shostrom, 1963). Although values are abstract concepts that are difficult to measure reliably (and so this research is easy to criticize on scientific grounds), it is notable that humanists directed the attention of psychologists to such a fundamental issue.

With the exception of the topics above, the humanistic theory of personality and psychopathology tends to have a weaker empirical foundation than the cognitive, behavioral, and physiological approaches. However, this is acknowledged by humanists. Because one of their goals was to develop an alternative to behaviorism, whose rigid scientific focus led psychologists to neglect important aspects of experience, humanists may not consider themselves to be scientists. Thus, failure to conform to these scientific criteria is neither a surprise nor a disappointment to humanists.

COGNITIVE THEORIES

The cognitive theory of personality and psychopathology has an interesting history. Cognitions (thought processes) have always been a concern to psychologists. William James, Wilhelm Wundt, and other early psychologists considered people's mental processes as one of the basic topics of psychology.

The influence of psychoanalysis and behaviorism, however, limited clinical psychology's use of cognitive models during the early 1900s. Freud stressed unconscious influences and was critical of approaches that focused primarily on conscious processes. On the other hand, early behaviorists opposed the intrusion of *mental* processes in a scientific psychology.

Still, despite the popularity of psychoanalysis and behaviorism, psychological attention to cognitions continued in experimental psychology. Cognitive psychologists investigated thought processes in laboratory settings, examining such processes as attention, concept formation, and hypothesis testing. From the 1930s to the 1950s, Tolman attempted to reintroduce cognitions into the psychology of learning (Hill, 1971). Social psychologists employed cognitive models (e.g., dissonance theory, attribution theory) to help explain human social behavior.

Some clinical psychologists also attended to cognitive processes during that period. For example, George Kelly (1955), Albert Ellis (1962), and Julian Rotter (1954) developed systems to explain personality and/or psychopathology in cognitive terms. However, cognitive theories were much less influential in the 1950s than psychoanalytic, behavioral, and humanistic approaches.

In the 1970s, there was a cognitive "revolution" in psychology (Baars, 1986). Albert Bandura (1971) emerged as a leader of this movement, showing that modeling is a basic form of conditioning in which the learning can best be regarded as occurring at the cognitive level. Similarly, Walter Mischel (1973) proposed a "cognitive social learning" model as a more effective way of explaining and predicting behavior than traditional personality or behavioral theories.

Dismayed by traditional behaviorism's elimination of mental processes but attracted by behaviorism's empirical success and therapeutic efficacy, clinical psychologists increasingly reintroduced cognitions into their systems. Contemporary cognitive theories in clinical psychology share with behaviorism an emphasis on scientific methodology

and empirical foundations. Some writers refer to the contemporary cognitive approach in clinical psychology as *cognitive behaviorism* because of the shared scientific foundation of both systems.

Cognitive behaviorism rests on two assumptions:

1. *Cognitions are a form of behavior.* Although cognitions are not observable to others, they are observable to an audience of one—the individual experiencing the cognition.

2. *Cognitions follow the laws of behaviorism.* Indeed, Lloyd Homme (1965) referred to thoughts as *coverants* (covert operants), which, like other operants, follow basic principles of learning. Thus, they can be conditioned, punished, reinforced, shaped, and chained.

One of the basic principles of conditioning is that, in a behavior chain, the most effective place to intervene, to prevent the final step in the sequence, is at the beginning of the chain. After many steps in the chain have occurred, it is difficult to prevent the remaining steps. Clinical psychologists want to help their clients eliminate problem behaviors. If it is assumed that a problem behavior is the final step in a sequence, with thinking of and intending to engage in the behavior as early steps in the chain, then it follows that the most effective place to intervene is at the cognitive level: at the beginning of the chain.

For these reasons, cognitive and cognitive–behavioral models became very influential in clinical psychology from the 1970s to the 1990s. As this book is being written, cognitive and cognitive–behavioral therapies stand among those treatments that are most popular and judged to be most effective.

It is important to recognize that cognitive-behaviorists consider cognitions in a way that is consistent with the assumptions of science. Remember the concept of a hypothetical construct: a nonobservable construct that is presumed to exist and that can be assessed indirectly through its relationships with observables. In cognitive behaviorism, cognitive processes are considered as hypothetical constructs. They are not directly observable, yet statements about their nature can be tested, at least indirectly.

For example, Teasdale and Bancroft (1977) measured facial muscle tension in subjects who had been instructed to think happy or sad thoughts. They found significant differences in muscle tension between the periods in which subjects had been instructed to think happy and sad thoughts. Although there is no way to "read minds" to determine whether subjects had followed instructions and were actually thinking sad and happy events, statements about the presumed type of thoughts could be tested by comparing the physiological responses between the two periods. Thus, happy and sad thoughts, in this study, can be regarded as hypothetical constructs. Statements about the nature of thoughts were testable, at least indirectly.

In this way, cognitive psychologists restored cognitions to scientific psychology. As long as there are at least indirect ways of testing statements about the nature of cognitive processes, cognitive psychologists conform to the scientific principle of empiricism.

Structure of Personality

Cognitive psychologists regard cognitive states and processes as the fundamental structural components of personality. One cognitive structure that plays an important role in cognitive theories is the schema. A *schema* is a set of cognitive statements that an individual uses to help organize and interpret experience. An example of a schema is the set of stereotyped beliefs that some prejudiced persons hold about a minority group. These beliefs are inaccurate, assigning negative characteristics to minority group members that are not in fact characteristic of them. A prejudiced person continues to hold such beliefs even though they are not consistently supported by experience. Why? Experiences are interpreted in a biased way, attending to evidence that supports the beliefs and ignoring evidence that disconfirms the beliefs.

Schema theory has proved to be important in social psychology, where it is used to help understand how an individual forms impressions of and evaluates others. For example, Bem (1984) has explained subjects' sex-role stereotypes using schema theory.

Schema theory has also proved useful in cognitive psychology in helping explain how an individual attends to and interprets evidence that may confirm or disconfirm hypotheses.

Clinical psychologists have also used schema theory in recent decades to help explain why individuals misperceive experience and behave ineffectively. Beck (1976), for example, suggested that depressed individuals have a negative schema that leads them to interpret experience in a negative way so as to support negative views of themselves and the world.

Cognitively oriented clinicians have also addressed many specific types of cognitive constructs and processes. For example, Kelly (1955) described the individual's personality in terms of a personal construct system. *Constructs*, according to Kelly, are the cognitive dimensions along which people interpret, classify, and evaluate experience. Kelly explained emotional and behavioral problems as the result of a system of personal constructs that are inaccurate, so that they do not account for the individual's experiences, and inflexible, so that the individual cannot revise the system to become more accurate.

Albert Ellis (1962) introduced a cognitive theory of psychopathology and therapy, suggesting that emotional difficulties result from extreme and inflexible cognitions. Beck's (1976) cognitive theory proposed that emotional disorders result from irrational negative cognitions that lead the person to interpret experiences inaccurately and to behave ineffectively.

These are only a few of the major cognitive approaches in contemporary clinical psychology; other cognitive models, along with their associated treatments, will be presented in more detail in Chapter 11. Although cognitive approaches have typically been developed to account for psychological disorders, it is easy to see how they can be used to explain normal psychological functioning as well. In general, as one's cognitive processes become more accurate, flexible, and effective, one experiences fewer emotional and behavioral problems; as cognitive processes become less accurate, flexible, and effective, one experiences more difficulties.

Development of Personality

Cognitive theorists have typically devoted less attention to the issue of personality development than they have to treatment. In general, cognitive theorists approach developmental issues in a way similar to that of behaviorists; they assume that one's cognitive structures and processes are the result of learning.

Bandura (1977) introduced the concept of *self-efficacy*, which is the perception of one's ability to perform effectively in a situation. Bandura noted the following influences on self-efficacy: (1) previous conditioning history, (2) observations of others, (3) direct instruction or persuasion by others, and (4) emotional responses and motivations. It is simple to see how each of these factors may influence a person's perception of his or her ability to succeed at a task.

Beck suggested that a depressed client's negative cognitive schema and the irrational patterns of thinking that support this schema may result from early experience. Parents model for their children how to perceive the world, interpret their experiences, and select courses of action to resolve problems. Parents may also influence their children's cognitive styles through direct instruction or shaping. Seligman, Peterson, Kaslow, Tanenbaum, Alloy, and Abramson (1984) assessed cognitive processes that are correlated with depression and found a significant correlation between the cognitive styles of parents and children. This result is consistent with the interpretation that parents teach their own cognitive styles to their children, through modeling or operant conditioning (or both).

In general, cognitive theorists hold that psychological problems are associated with inflexible thinking. It is interesting to note that Jean Piaget, perhaps the most noted theorist of cognitive development, associated inflexible thinking with young children, particularly age seven years and under. According to Piaget (1952), preschool and early elementary school children exhibit egocentricity (have difficulty adopting the viewpoints of others) and centration (focus on only a single dimension of a problem). Although clinical psychologists have not generally made wide use of Piaget's ideas, those interested in investigating the development of the cognitive processes that influence later personality and psychopathology might consider Piaget's work on the inflexibility of early childhood cognitions.

Dynamics of Personality

Cognitive theorists of personality suggest that people are motivated by the principle of cognitive consistency (Maddi, 1996). That is, one's cognitive perceptions of the world should be consistent with one's (perceived) experiences in the world. If one perceives the world accurately, then one's expectations are consistently fulfilled and one can behave effectively. However, if cognitive expectations are not consistent with experience, then one will experience negative affect (surprise, disappointment, anger) and cope less effectively.

Cognitive dissonance theory (Festinger, 1958) is an early cognitive model developed to explain social behavior. According to this model, *cognitive dissonance* is an aversive state that occurs when important cognitions (beliefs, perceptions, expectations) are in conflict. Dissonance theory further assumes that people are motivated to reduce dissonance. Thus, we modify our cognitions to maintain cognitive consonance, or consistency.

For example, an individual who smokes cigarettes may experience dissonance when reading research results on the dangers of smoking. The person's many positive associations with smoking are now inconsistent with the research evidence. Dissonance theory posits that the individual will act to reduce dissonance. In this example, the person may reduce dissonance in several ways: (1) quit smoking and change one's perception of smoking to be consistent with its dangers; (2) disregard the research evidence and maintain one's positive views of smoking (e.g., *Researchers can show that anything produces cancer in rats; such results don't mean a thing for people*); or (3) add new cognitions to the system to resolve the inconsistency between the old beliefs and new evidence (e.g., *You've got to go somehow, so you might as well go out doing something you enjoy*).

Other cognitive models suggest similar motivational approaches. Cognitive processes are reinforced or punished by the consequences of one's actions. If one correctly predicts how the world will be, then one acts accordingly and so one's cognitions are reinforced; if one's anticipations are incorrect, then one behaves ineffectively and the cognitive processes are punished.

Psychopathology

The cognitive explanation of psychopathology has already been introduced. In general, cognitive processes that lead one to perceive the world accurately and to select effective coping behaviors are healthy. Psychological problems are associated with inaccurate and inflexible methods of perceiving the world and with ineffective attempts to cope with the world.

The pathology in the cognitive model is the ineffective thought process. Ineffective thinking leads clients to experience emotional distress or to behave inappropriately.

The etiology is some conditioning process. Children may learn their ineffective cognitive processes from the parents, through modeling or operant conditioning. However, the ineffective thinking need not develop in early childhood. It is possible that some conditioning occurs later, in adolescence or early adulthood, which now produces the client's symptomatology.

Treatment

Because the pathology according to the cognitive model is inaccurate or ineffective thinking, the cognitive approach to therapy is to identify and then modify this cognitive process. Chapter 11 presents in more detail the cognitive approach to treating psychological disorders. For now, it suffices to say that cognitive therapists use problem-focused assessment techniques such as self-report, role-play, and self-monitoring of emotions, cognitions, and behaviors.

After the inaccurate or ineffective cognitions have been identified, cognitive therapists help the client to revise or replace them. In general, cognitive therapy resembles behavior therapy in that it is short term and directive. Like behavior therapy, cognitive therapy employs modeling, rehearsal, graduated homework assignments, and other problem-focused techniques. Also like behavior therapy, cognitive therapy has amassed an impressive list of successful empirical evaluations in recent decades.

Although cognitive theorists hold that cognitive processes are learned, they do not emphasize early childhood development of these processes as did Freud. Remember that, in psychoanalysis, it is necessary to identify the childhood origins of one's present problem. In cognitive therapy, it is not necessary to identify the origins of the pathological cognitive processes in order to change them. Although some clients may benefit from identifying the origins of their problematic thought processes, it is not essential in cognitive therapy that they do so.

Cognitive theorists also do not stress, as do Freudian psychoanalysts, that one's underlying pathology can arise only during early childhood. Cognitive theorists recognize that the conditioning processes that produce problematic cognitions may occur at any time in life.

Evaluation

The cognitive approach to clinical psychology experienced a remarkable increase in emphasis from the 1960s to the 1990s. This occurred for many reasons: the success of cognitive models in social and experimental cognitive psychology; dissatisfaction with traditional behaviorism's ignoring cognitive and other internal processes; the success of the empirical emphasis of behaviorism; the rise of the computer as an information processor, which can be used as a model of human cognitive processing. For reasons like these, clinical psychologists increasingly turned to cognitive theories.

When the criteria for evaluating any scientific theory are applied to cognitive theories, one finds that cognitive theories of clinical psychology stand very well.

Comprehensiveness Cognitive theories in clinical psychology are somewhat less comprehensive than psychoanalytic and behavioral theories. Cognitive theories are used primarily to explain the development and maintenance of psychopathology and to treat psychological disorders. Thus, cognitive models have not, to date, been applied as extensively to the range of topics (e.g., art, creativity, religiosity) that have been addressed by other personality theories. Still, because the cognitive approach is a rather new approach, it is possible that it will eventually be applied to a wider range of topics.

Still, within the area of psychopathology and psychotherapy, cognitive theories are quite extensive. Cognitive theories have been applied to many psychological disorders and their treatment, including emotional disorders, interpersonal problems, physical symptoms resulting from stress, and others. Thus, although cognitive theory may not be as comprehensive as other personality theories, it is quite comprehensive within its defined areas of interest of psychopathology and psychotherapy.

Parsimony   Cognitive theory is parsimonious. It uses the basic conditioning principles of behaviorism. It introduces the idea that cognitions can be regarded as a form of behavior that follows behavioral principles. Thus, cognitive theory is based on relatively few laws and introduces relatively few new constructs.

Heuristic or Applied Value   Cognitive theory has proved very useful in the field of psychotherapy. Although cognitive therapy was first widely employed by Ellis and Beck to treat emotional problems, other cognitive therapists have generalized these ideas so that they are now used to treat other disorders. Current issues of research journals (e.g., *Cognitive Therapy and Research, Journal of Consulting and Clinical Psychology*) routinely publish articles that examine the efficacy of cognitive therapy when applied to different disorders. In terms of applied value, the cognitive approach to clinical psychology stands very well.

Internal Consistency and Falsifiability   Traditional behaviorists criticized psychoanalytic theory

for using mental constructs that could not be measured. For this reason, early behaviorists omitted internal or mental processes from psychology.

Cognitive theory has reintroduced cognitive processes into scientific psychology. This is done by treating cognitions as hypothetical constructs. Statements about cognitions can be tested, at least indirectly, through their relationship to observables, such as overt behaviors or physiological states. Thus, cognitive theory includes nonobservables, but in a much narrower way than traditional psychoanalysis.

Cognitive models of clinical psychology have been tested extensively. Cognitive clinical psychologists, like behavioral psychologists, have operated under rigorous scientific standards, conducting empirical tests of their hypotheses regarding the causes of and effective treatment for psychological disorders.

Much of the research on cognitive models in clinical psychology concerns the effectiveness of cognitive therapy. Empirical evaluations of the efficacy of cognitive therapy will be discussed in Chapter 11. For now, it suffices to say that cognitive therapy has consistently been found to be effective and that several evaluations of the relative efficacies of therapy have determined that cognitive therapy is among the more effective treatments. As this text is written, cognitive (and cognitive–behavioral) therapy is one of the most popular and strongly supported approaches to psychotherapy.

BIOLOGICAL THEORIES

The physiological approach in clinical psychology experienced a remarkable increase in emphasis from the 1970s to the 1990s. Advances in biochemistry, neurology, and genetics contributed to an increased recognition by clinical psychologists of physiological influences on behavior. Before examining the biological approach to personality and psychopathology, it is important to introduce some basic concepts in these areas.

The cells of the nervous system are called *neurons*. Neurons are separated by a minute gap called a *synapse.* When a nerve impulse reaches the end (terminal node) of the presynaptic cell, chemical substances are released into the synapse. These chemicals, called *neurotransmitters*, diffuse across the synapse and can be taken up at *receptor sites* on the postsynaptic cell. Neurotransmitters and receptor sites work in a "lock-and-key" manner. That is, a specific neurotransmitter can only be taken up at specific receptor sites. Excess neurotransmitters in the synaptic gap that are not taken up at receptor sites are returned to the presynaptic cell through a process called *reuptake.*

When a neurotransmitter is taken up at a receptor site, there is a small effect on the postsynaptic cell. This effect is additive so that, after a sufficient amount has been taken up, a new nerve impulse is generated. (It should be noted that some neurotransmitters have an inhibitory effect so that, the more that is taken up, the more difficult it is for other neurotransmitters to initiate a nerve impulse in that cell.)

At this time, over 60 different neurotransmitters have been identified, although only a subset of them have been well investigated. Among the more thoroughly investigated neurotransmitters that are important in clinical psychology are norepinephrine, acetylcholine, dopamine, serotonin, and gamma-aminobutyric acid (GABA).

The nervous system is divided into the central nervous system and the peripheral nervous system. The *central nervous system* consists of the brain and spinal cord, and is the major communication system within the body. The *peripheral nervous system* contains the nerves that connect the central nervous system to the rest of the body, and includes the somatic and autonomic systems. The *somatic system* includes the nerves connecting the central nervous system to the muscles and nerves throughout the body. The *autonomic system* includes the nerves connecting the central nervous system to the organs and glands throughout the body. Whereas the somatic system largely governs voluntary activity (such as turning the pages of this book), the autonomic system primarily governs involuntary psychophysiological activity, such as the changes in heart rate and digestion that occur when one experiences and then

recovers from a stressful event. Many problems treated by clinical psychologists (including stress-related physical symptoms, such as headache and insomnia, and emotional disorders, such as fear and anxiety) are associated with heightened autonomic arousal.

The brain is commonly divided into three sections: hindbrain, midbrain, and forebrain. The *hindbrain* is that part of the brain that lies immediately above and is connected to the spinal cord; it is the oldest structure of the human brain, in an evolutionary sense, and so governs the most basic body functions, such as breathing and swallowing. Because these are fundamental physical functions, damage to the hindbrain is likely to cause severe if not lethal consequences. However, few behavior disorders are thought to be associated with hindbrain disorders.

The *midbrain* lies above the hindbrain; it evolved more recently and so generally governs more advanced functions than the hindbrain. The midbrain contains the *hypothalamus*, which regulates drive-related behavior, such as hunger and sexual activity; some physiological theorists have suggested that the hypothalamus is involved with conditions such as anorexia and homosexuality. The midbrain also includes the *limbic system*, which is important in regulating emotion; damage to the limbic system has been associated with aggression. The midbrain (along with parts of the hindbrain) also includes the *reticular activating system*, which regulates alertness; damage to this system can lead to sleep disorders.

The *forebrain* is the most recently evolved part of the human brain and lies above and around the midbrain; it is considered to control the highest mental functions, including perception, cognition, and memory.

Much of the forebrain is the *cerebral cortex*, or the highly wrinkled surface of the brain beneath the skull. The cerebral cortex is divided into two hemispheres (left and right), which exert contralateral control over most body functions; that is, the left brain hemisphere controls the right side of the body, and vice versa. In addition, the left hemisphere is thought to control functions that require the sequential performance of operations, such as counting or speaking, whereas the right brain hemisphere is considered to control configural operations (that is, functions in which data are processed simultaneously with the goal of recognizing a pattern, such as identifying a face or naming a geometric shape).

The cerebral cortex is also divided into four lobes that regulate different functions. The *occipital lobe* governs vision, the *temporal lobe* controls audition, the *parietal lobe* governs motor functions, and the *frontal lobe* governs somatosensory functions (such as touch and temperature). Of course, there are many interconnections among brain structures, and so this listing of brain structures and their associated functions should be recognized as an oversimplification. Still, it is often possible, using neuropsychological tests, to determine the location and extent of brain damage from a patient's functional impairment. Neuropsychological tests will be discussed at length in Chapter 5.

Technological advances (such as the CAT scan and Magnetic Resonance Imaging (MRI)) have permitted the noninvasive examination of central nervous system structures. These brain scan techniques have assisted researchers in identifying the structural anomalies associated with a number of disorders.

Another field that has contributed to the increased emphasis on physiological influences is genetics. Geneticists have improved their methods of identifying genes that are related to physical traits. This has led to the identification of the genes that cause certain medical and, in some cases, psychiatric conditions. In addition, there has been a "boom" in the field of *behavior genetics,* the specialty area in psychology that studies genetic influences on both normal and abnormal behavior. Almost every psychological disorder has been examined by behavior geneticists, using twin, adoption, and family studies, to determine whether it may have a genetic influence.

Whereas many clinical psychologists in the 1950s and 1960s only paid lip service to the possibility of biological influences on psychological disorders, the physiological model of psychopathology has grown in influence so that, by the 1990s, it is one of the major schools of thought.

Structure of Personality

Physiological approaches to explaining personality and psychopathology do not address internal mental constructs as do traditional personality theories. Whereas psychoanalysts discuss the intrapsychic struggle among the id, ego, and superego, and whereas Rogerian humanists discuss the discrepancy between the self and self-ideal, physiological theorists focus on biological rather than mental influences.

It is somewhat difficult to present the basic structural elements of physiological approaches to clinical psychology because there is no single dominant theory in this area. In addition, physiological theories are often narrowly focused, so that a leading physiological theory of one type of disorder may have little relation to physiological theories of other disorders.

For this reason, this section of the chapter will present two distinct views of physiological influences on personality. Later sections of the chapter will summarize leading physiological theories of psychopathology.

Eysenck's Physiological Theory   Hans Eysenck (1947) proposed an interesting theory of personality. Based on factor analyses of personality test data, Eysenck identified two basic dimensions of personality: *introversion–extraversion* and *neuroticism.* Introverts are individuals who prefer quiet, introspective, and less externally stimulating activities; extraverts are more sociable and impulsive individuals who prefer more active and stimulating activities. Eysenck used the term neuroticism in a somewhat less familiar way. For Eysenck, neurotic individuals exhibit stronger and more labile emotional responses than other people.

Eysenck (1967) reviewed the genetic evidence on these traits and concluded that both neuroticism and introversion have genetic influences. Because these traits have a genetic influence, they must have a physiological basis that is inherited.

Initially, Eysenck suggested that introversion is related to the ease with which one's nervous system is classically conditioned: introverts classically condition rapidly and extinguish slowly whereas extroverts classically condition slowly and extinguish more rapidly. However, when research proved this to be incorrect, Eysenck revised the model, suggesting that introversion is related to increased cortical arousal, whereas extroversion is associated with decreased cortical arousal.

Eysenck also suggested that neuroticism is related to the "arousability" or reactivity of the autonomic nervous system: individuals who exhibit rapid and strong autonomic responses to stress (e.g., increased heart rate, Galvanic skin response (GSR), respiration rate) are more likely than others to develop neurotic personality traits.

It is important to note that Eysenck's theory, although presented here as a biological model, combines physiological and psychological processes. The physical foundation predisposes one to be conditioned, classically and instrumentally, to develop behavioral and emotional responses associated with personality traits.

Consider a person who is high in physical emotional reactivity. This person is more likely than other people to be conditioned to develop neurotic symptoms such as phobias and phobic avoidance behaviors. Similarly, one with the physical foundation underlying extraversion is more likely than others to be reinforced by highly stimulating activities, and so be conditioned to repeat the behaviors associated with extraversion. In this way, Eysenck's theory represents an interaction between physiological and behavioral concepts.

Eysenck (1952) elaborated upon his theory, adding a third dimension, psychoticism. *Psychoticism* is related to eccentric thinking and social indifference. At high levels, psychoticism is associated with severe thought disorder, such as that found in schizophrenia; at moderate levels, however, psychoticism is associated with eccentric thinking and may actually enhance creativity.

Eysenck's theory of personality is important for several reasons. Because it proposed specific physiological mechanisms underlying basic personality traits, it generated a large number of testable predictions and so has been the subject of numerous empirical tests. Although the theory has been found to have several weaknesses and inaccuracies (such as

Eysenck's initial suggestion that introversion is related to conditionability), Eysenck has modeled how scientific psychologists should revise a theory in the face of negative results. In addition, Eysenck has shown how to use factor analysis to identify basic dimensions of personality and how to integrate physiological and environmental factors in a theory of personality.

Eysenck's theory also is related to more recent theories of personality and psychopathology. For example, current personality theories have considered *sensation seeking* as an important trait (Zuckerman, 1989). One proposed explanation of this trait is that sensation seekers are low in internal (cortical) arousal and so seek high levels of environmental stimulation (Zuckerman, 1989).

Similarly, current biological theories of attention deficit hyperactivity disorder (ADHD) suggest that these individuals have a deficit in cortical arousal (Anastopoulos & Barkley, 1988); hence, "hyperactive" children are treated with stimulant medication to increase their alertness. Other physiological research has shown that psychopaths are low in autonomic reactivity (Hare, 1970). One interpretation of this (e.g., Quay, 1965) is that psychopaths' illegal and violent behavior may result from attempts to seek an optimal level of stimulation. Although these are not the only theories of ADHD and psychopathy, it should be clear that they are related to Eysenck's theory.

Temperament   A second important physiological model of personality is temperament theory. *Temperament* refers to the physiological aspects of behavioral and emotional responding. Temperament can be thought of as the part of personality that is built into the person.

Contemporary psychological study of temperament was stimulated by the research of Stella Chess and Alexander Thomas (1977). Chess and Thomas followed a sample of infants from birth through adolescence (and are continuing to monitor the subjects throughout adulthood). Chess and Thomas began by measuring, in early infancy, a set of basic behavioral and emotional responses (such as activity level, quality of mood, regularity, irritability, and so on).

They found that, even in the first few months of life, infants exhibit stability in these areas. That is, the most active infants at several weeks of age continue to be the most active infants at several months of age. What parents have known for ages—that babies are not "blank slates" but instead have their own personalities from birth—Chess and Thomas demonstrated empirically.

Chess and Thomas also observed that these early behavioral and emotional characteristics tend to cluster together. They identified three clusters of behaviors, which they termed temperament types. The *difficult* temperament is characterized by having more negative general mood and by being more easily irritated, less regular, and noisier. The *easy* temperament is characterized by the opposite traits; these infants have a more positive general mood and are less easily irritated, more regular, and less noisy. Chess and Thomas also identified the *slow-to-warm-up* temperament, which is characterized by an initial tendency to withdraw from new stimuli; when faced with an unfamiliar stimulus, these infants tend to withdraw, exhibit distress, and so resemble difficult infants. However, after gaining experience with the new stimulus, these infants adjust and then resemble more closely easy infants.

Chess and Thomas followed these children into adolescence and observed a modest but detectable relationship between infant temperament and later behavior. For example, difficult infants were more than twice as likely as easy infants to develop behavioral or emotional problems in childhood (Chess & Thomas, 1984). Even when considering normal behavior, Chess and Thomas found a significant relation between infant and later behavior. The most active, noisy, and irritable infants tended to become the most active, noisy, and irritable children and adolescents.

Because infant behavioral and emotional responses were stable when measured in the first weeks and months of life, and because these responses were stable even into adolescence, Chess and Thomas argued that these characteristics are temperamental, or part of the individual's physiological make-up. If these traits were purely the result of environmental conditioning, one would not expect them to be present so early in life and to persist over so many years of life.

In addition to the temperament types described by Chess and Thomas, there are alternative systems of classifying temperamental characteristics. Buss and Plomin (1975, 1984) provided a competing model of temperament. Instead of classifying temperament types according to clusters of responses, Buss and Plomin suggested that temperament can best be described in terms of three basic dimensions: *emotionality, activity,* and *sociability*. Buss and Plomin (1975, 1984) regarded these as temperamental dimensions because they (1) are present by and stable in early infancy; (2) have a genetic influence; and (3) are stable from infancy to later life.

These characteristics are already familiar to readers. Emotionality refers to physiological reactivity, which Eysenck termed neuroticism. Activity refers to motility level, one of the stable infant behaviors observed by Chess and Thomas. Sociability refers to the degree to which one approaches or withdraws from others (approach–withdrawal was another of the stable infant behaviors observed by Chess and Thomas), or prefers to engage in activities with others or by oneself (the introversion–extraversion dimension of Eysenck).

Still another model of temperament is that of Kagan (1992; Kagan & Snidman, 1991). Kagan classified infants as *inhibited* or *uninhibited,* based on their responses to novel stimuli. Inhibited infants show more distress (crying, activity) in response to new sights and sounds than uninhibited infants. Kagan has shown that the (un)inhibited response pattern is stable over several years of infancy. He has also begun to examine the underlying biological foundations of this response style. For example, Kagan reported that the physiological variable that best distinguishes between the two response patterns is heart-rate acceleration after tasting a sour fluid: inhibited infants showed much greater acceleration in heart rate than uninhibited infants. From this, Kagan suggested that the (un)inhibited temperament may be mediated by limbic system mechanisms associated with emotional arousability.

Development of Personality

As described above, physiological theorists of personality and psychopathology emphasize biological influences on behavior. Although such biological foundations often have a genetic influence, it should be stressed that physiological theories also recognize the role of the environment. Although there may be a significant genetic influence on a biological trait (e.g., high autonomic reactivity), the individual's environment will influence the way in which this biological trait becomes expressed behaviorally. The physiological characteristic should be regarded as a predisposing, and not a predetermining, influence.

This is clear in both of the physiological personality theories described above. Eysenck emphasized inherited physiological characteristics. However, these physiological characteristics only predispose the individual to be conditioned to exhibit the types of behaviors associated with personality traits. The physiological characteristic interacts with environmental conditioning to produce the trait-related behaviors.

Temperament theorists describe a similar process. They have used the term, *goodness-of-fit* (Thomas & Chess, 1977) to describe the interaction of temperament and environment in influencing a child's personality. According to this idea, development is optimal when there is a match between the child's temperament and environment. Because infants with different temperaments may respond differently to the same environment, it is important that parents try to provide that environment that will optimize each child's development. For example, consider the temperamental trait of activity level. Mothers who provide much stimulation to their infants have been found to increase the activity of low-active infants but to decrease the activity of high-active infants (Gandour, 1989).

Thus, even though physiological theories of personality and psychopathology stress biological factors, they also recognize the role of the environment. Most biological models of personality and psychopathology are really biopsychological theories.

Dynamics of Personality

Biological theorists have not devoted much attention to the basic motivating forces of personality. Like behaviorism, the biological approach assumes that people engage in behaviors to earn positive consequences, such as food, drink, or sexual gratification, and to avoid aversive consequence, such as pain and nausea. In addition, the biological school provides an explanation for these motivations: evolution.

Biological theorists have examined the physiological influences on such biological drives as hunger and thirst. However, this information, although an important part of general psychology, has not had much impact on the study of personality.

Psychopathology

The biological approach, like the original medical model, holds that the pathology and etiology of mental disorders reflect biological processes and so the most appropriate treatment is also biological.

The pathology of mental illness, according to this model, is the immediate biological condition that causes the patient's symptoms. This pathology may consist of problems in neurological structures (e.g., atrophy of neural pathways), neurological functioning (e.g., excess or deficit in neurotransmission), or other physiological features (e.g., excessive autonomic activity). The physiological model recognizes several etiologies, including genetic predisposition, illness, trauma, and physiological reactions to stress. Physiological treatments aim at controlling or reversing the pathology. Treatments here include medication, stress reduction, and other medical techniques (such as surgery or electroconvulsive therapy). Because the physiological approach has become so widespread in contemporary psychopathology, it cannot be presented completely here. Interested readers should consult abnormal psychology texts that discuss this model more fully (e.g., Davison & Neale, 1994; Willerman & Cohen, 1990).

One example of the biological approach to psychopathology will be presented here. Schizophrenia is a mental disorder that is so severe that the patient is said to be out of touch with reality. Schizophrenic patients often experience symptoms such as hallucinations (sense impressions in the absence of sensory stimulation, e.g., "hearing" voices) and delusions (irrational belief systems, e.g., believing that the voices they hear are commands from alien beings).

Since early in the century, family, twin, and adoption studies have shown that schizophrenia has a genetic influence. For example, the lifetime risk for schizophrenia in the general population is about 1 percent. However, the risk in schizophrenic patients' first-degree relatives (i.e., those who share one-half of their genes with one another, such as parent-child and siblings), even when they are adopted out of the biological family, is about 5 to 15 percent (Willerman & Cohen, 1990).

There was no effective treatment for schizophrenia until the 1950s, when antipsychotic medications were discovered. Research showed that these medications lower the activity of dopamine, a neurotransmitter. Thus, it was suggested that schizophrenia is associated with an excess amount (or activity) of dopamine (Willerman & Cohen, 1990). (See Chapter 12 for a more complete discussion of medications used in the treatment of schizophrenia.)

In the 1980s, improved brain scanning techniques permitted noninvasive examination of neurological structures. This research found that the brains of schizophrenic patients are characterized by enlarged ventricles, suggesting the atrophy or incomplete development of neural pathways (Willerman & Cohen, 1990).

This brief overview illustrates the variety of biological factors implicated in schizophrenia. Genetic, biochemical, and neurological factors are all thought to play a role. The pathology can be regarded as excess dopamine activity and/or atrophied neural pathways; the etiology can be regarded as a genetic predisposition, combined with physiological stress (such as that which may affect prenatal neurological development). The treatment is to provide medication that blocks dopamine receptors and so reduces dopamine activity.

Similar biological models have been developed to account for many other forms of psychopathology. For example, much research has examined the neurotransmitters involved in depression. A strong genetic influence has been found on bipolar disorder. Recent studies have suggested genetic influences on autism, obsessive-compulsive disorder, and panic disorder. For these and many other problems, clinical psychologists must seriously consider the biological theory of psychopathology.

Treatment

The biological treatment of psychopathology has also increased dramatically in recent decades. Biological treatments include medications, which have successfully been used to treat a wide range of disorders, including schizophrenia, bipolar disorder, obsessive-compulsive disorder, and anxiety disorders. Chapter 12 presents the medications used to treat these disorders in more detail. Biological treatments of psychopathology also include medical treatments, such as surgery and electroconvulsive therapy, which are used less commonly than medication.

In should be noted that biological treatments also include psychological techniques that have as their goal the alteration of some physiological state. For example, many psychologists use biofeedback, muscle relaxation, or breathing exercises to help clients reduce states of physiological arousal that are thought to be associated with the client's symptoms. Chapter 12 will discuss such psychological methods for reducing physiological arousal.

In addition, a new specialty in clinical psychology, called behavioral medicine, has recently emerged. In behavioral medicine, clinical psychologists employ psychological principles to assist in the treatment of patients who have medical disorders. For example, following a heart attack, it is important for patients to lose weight and exercise regularly. Because attaining these goals requires behavior change, psychologists may contribute significantly to the treatment of these patients, using psychological techniques designed to produce behavioral change. Chapter 12 will also describe behavioral medicine.

Evaluation

At present, the physiological approach to explaining personality and psychopathology is very popular. It holds up well when evaluated using the basic criteria for scientific theories.

Comprehensiveness   The physiological approach is fairly comprehensive. It has been used to explain many (if not most) mental disorders. It has also been used successfully to treat many different disorders.

The physiological model accounts less well for normal than abnormal behavior. However, even in the realm of personality, both Eysenck's personality theory and temperament theory provide useful physiological explanations of normal behavior.

Parsimony   The physiological model of personality and psychopathology is moderately parsimonious. Biological constructs are numerous and complex, and so understanding this approach requires a solid background in biology. The biological models used to explain one disorder (e.g., schizophrenia) may be quite different from those used to explain other disorders (e.g., obsessive-compulsive disorder).

Still, this approach does not introduce novel constructs that are unfamiliar to scientists. Genetic, biochemical, and neurological constructs may be numerous and difficult to understand, but they have already been established as useful constructs in science. Hence, the physiological approach to explaining personality and psychopathology satisfies the requirement of parsimony.

Applied or Heuristic Value   The physiological approach has remarkable applied or heuristic value. Since the 1950s, medications have been found that are helpful in treating a wide range of mental disorders. The biological model is being applied successfully today to disorders that, only two decades ago, had only been interpreted using traditional psychological models.

Internal Consistency and Falsifiability   The biological approach also has excellent internal consistency and falsifiability. This approach leads readily to testable predictions and it has a strong research tradition. Chapter 12 will present in more detail research concerning the effectiveness of various physiological treatments for mental disorders.

SUMMARY

Clinical psychology offers several major theories for explaining personality and psychopathology. These include the psychoanalytic, behavioral, humanistic, cognitive, and physiological approaches. Each theory addresses the structure, dynamics, and development of personality. In addition, each theory presents a view of the nature of psychopathology. A complete model of psychopathology should address the symptomatology, etiology, pathology, prognosis, and treatment of psychological disorders, terms that have been borrowed from the medical model.

Freudian psychoanalysis emphasizes unconscious determinants of behavior, often of a sexual or aggressive nature, stemming back to early childhood. Freud describes psychological processes in a dynamic way, stressing the conflict among the animalistic (id), realistic (ego), and moralistic (superego) aspects of personality.

Freud described development as occurring in a series of five stages (oral, anal, phallic, latent, genital), with each stage defined according to the way in which the person gratifies basic drives. The ego develops in the anal stage, as a result of toilet training, whereas the superego develops in the phallic stage, following resolution of the Oedipal conflict.

Freud thought that behavior was motivated by two instincts: sex and aggression. People use defense mechanisms to protect themselves from the pain that would otherwise be experienced by acknowledging such motivations. Defense mechanisms are also used to channel sexual and aggressive energy into other activities. Freud thought that all people use defense mechanisms. However, their overuse is maladaptive.

Freud explained psychopathology as due to threatening sexual or aggressive material, from childhood experiences, that have been repressed and are being expressed through defense mechanisms in a symbolic way. The goal of Freudian therapy, psychoanalysis, is to bring this troubling material to consciousness. Various insight-oriented techniques are used to achieve this goal, such as free association and dream interpretation.

Psychoanalytic theory is extremely comprehensive. Clinical psychologists and others (e.g., literary critics) have found its ideas to be useful. However, psychoanalytic theory is neither parsimonious nor easily testable. Many research-oriented clinical psychologists have turned to alternatives to psychoanalysis because of its limited empirical support.

Watson founded behaviorism to make psychology more scientific by only considering observable behavior. Behaviorism has long been associated with a scientific approach to psychology.

Behaviorists use basic principles of learning—classical conditioning, instrumental conditioning, and social learning—to explain behavior. Behaviorists do not assume that abnormal behavior reflects an underlying psychological problem; instead they think that abnormal behavior, like normal behavior, is the product of conditioning. Behaviorists view therapy as a process of reconditioning. They apply conditioning principles to remove maladaptive behavior and to replace it with adaptive behavior.

Behaviorism, like psychoanalysis, is comprehensive and has good applied value. However, behaviorism is parsimonious and has strong research support.

Humanistic psychology assumes that people are motivated to actualize their good natures. Psychological problems result when external forces stifle the tendency to self-actualize. Rogers held that being treated with conditional positive regard leads people to adopt conditions of worth that distort their self and self-ideal.

Humanistic psychologists view therapy as a means of restoring the individual to the path of self-actualization. In Rogerian client-centered therapy, the therapist provides the client with unconditional positive regard.

The humanistic approach is very parsimonious. Its optimistic approach has attracted many followers, particularly those who wish to explain healthy and transcendent aspects of experience. However, the humanistic model is not as comprehensive as other models; it does not address psychopathology to the extent that other models do. In addition, humanistic concepts tend to be difficult to measure and to test scientifically. Although several Rogerian ideas have been extensively researched, many aspects of humanistic theory do not have empirical support.

Cognitive theory shares the scientific emphases of behaviorism. However, cognitive theory regards cognitions as a type of behavior. Thus, unlike traditional behaviorism, cognitive theory attends to mental processes such as motivations, expectations, and subjective interpretations of experience.

Cognitive theory assumes that cognitive processes are learned, often in childhood through modeling one's parents. Cognitions are chained to and occur prior to overt behavior. Cognitive theory explains abnormal behavior, then, as the result of inaccurate or ineffective cognitive processes. Cognitive therapy revises these cognitive processes, often using conditioning techniques derived from behavior therapy.

Like behaviorism, cognitive theory is parsimonious and has strong research support. Although cognitive theory has not been applied to as many topics as other theories of personality, it has proved very effective in the treatment of many psychological disorders. For these reasons, cognitive theory experienced a tremendous increase in influence from the 1970s to the 1990s.

The physiological approach to clinical psychology, like cognitive theory, experienced a significant increase in influence from the 1970s to the present. The biological approach gained support in the 1950s when it produced medications that enabled mental health professionals to treat schizophrenia and other disorders. Since that time, advances in biochemistry, neurology, and genetics have contributed to the rise of this movement.

The biological approach has had its greatest impact in the treatment of abnormal behavior. It assumes that the underlying pathology, initial etiology, and most effective treatment of disorders all have a biological basis.

However, the biological approach has also had a significant influence in explaining normal behavior. For example, Eysenck's theory of personality suggests that basic personality dimensions (introversion and neuroticism) have biological foundations that predispose people to be conditioned to exhibit trait-related behaviors. Similarly, temperament research has shown that infants exhibit stable emotional and behavioral responses that persist, at least modestly, through childhood and adolescence. That temperamental characteristics are present so early and persist so long suggests that they are *built into* the person.

The biological model meets scientific standards of internal consistency and falsifiability. Biological approaches are complex; however, because they do not introduce concepts that have not already been accepted by science, they meet the standard of parsi-mony. The biological approach has had more success in treating abnormal behavior than in explaining normal behavior, and so it is somewhat less comprehensive than other models. However, its empirical success and its ability to account for a wide range of disorders has led clinical psychologists to regard the biological approach very highly.

S T U D Y   Q U E S T I O N S

1. Summarize the major components of the medical model. How have psychologists modified the original medical model?

2. Select one of the major theories of personality and psychopathology. Discuss the influences on its development and its rise in influence in clinical psychology.

3. For any of the major theories, describe the structure, dynamics, and development of personality.

4. For any of the major theories, describe the etiology, pathology, and treatment of psychopathology.

5. Select two of the major theories. Compare and contrast their views regarding the structure, dynamics, and development of personality.

6. Select two of the major theories. Compare and contrast their views regarding the etiology, pathology, and treatment of psychopathology.

7. Using the criteria for judging scientific theories, evaluate one of the major theories of personality and psychopathology.

8. Select two of the major theories. Compare and contrast them using the five criteria for evaluating scientific theories.

9. Which theories have experienced an increased influence in the last 30 years? Discuss the reasons for their increased influence.

10. Compare and contrast theories in clinical psychology at the beginning and end of the twentieth century.

C H A P T E R

4

Clinical Assessment
An Introduction

I. *Brief History*
II. *Role and Types of Assessment in Clinical Psychology*
III. *Scientific Issues*
   A. *Criteria for Evaluating Tests*
   B. *Test Theory*

IV. *Applied Issues*
   A. *Standardized Test Administration and Interpretation*
   B. *Test Construction*
   C. *Ethical Issues*
V. *Summary*

The history of psychological testing is as old as civilization itself. From ancient times, educators assessed students' knowledge and abilities and physicians evaluated patients' behavioral functioning. Early methods of assessing ability and personality are addressed in Chapters 5 through 7. Although there were many forerunners to contemporary tests, of greatest concern here is the rise of formal psychological testing after psychology developed as a distinct discipline.

BRIEF HISTORY

Contemporary clinical assessment has its roots in both experimental and clinical methods of the nineteenth century. After Wundt founded the first laboratory devoted to the exclusive study of psychology in 1879 (Boring, 1950), he developed methods for as-

sessing basic psychological processes such as reaction time, sensation, and attention. In this respect, Wundt was following the footsteps of psychophysicists such as Ernst Weber and Gustav Fechner who, in the mid-1800s, had shown that it is possible to measure and develop quantitative laws of human experience. Of course, Wundt and other psychologists shifted attention away from simple sensation toward more complex mental processes.

Other psychologists soon followed Wundt's lead to develop methods of assessing behavior. Most significant for this discussion are James McKeen Cattell and Francis Galton. In 1867, Galton published *Hereditary Genius,* a work in which he speculated that human intelligence has a genetic component. In 1884, Galton opened a laboratory in which he attempted to measure abilities that he thought are related to intelligence. His measures included sensory acuity, memory, reaction time, and anthropocentric measures (i.e., measures of body characteristics, such as height, weight, and arm length) (Rogers, 1995).

Cattell studied under both Wundt and Galton, and helped popularize quantitative psychology in America. Cattell used tests like Galton's to assess individual differences. In fact, in 1890, Galton coined the term *mental test* (Rogers, 1995), which continues to be used by psychologists a century later.

Although the measures of Galton and Cattell were a far cry from the tests used by contemporary clinical psychologists, they helped focus the attention of the field on the need for precise and standardized measurements. Alfred Binet, who later developed the first modern intelligence test (which will be discussed in Chapter 5), initially conducted research using Cattell's measures. However, his research suggested that Cattell's approach was not very accurate and so he ultimately turned his attention to measures of more complex mental processes (Gregory, 1996). For example, in 1895, Binet and Henry used inkblots to study visual imagination (Rabin, 1968); in 1905 Binet and Simon used children's verbal responses to pictures as a test of cognitive abilities (Rabin, 1968). Thus, even though he is most known for developing the first modern intelligence test, Binet also conducted studies with methods that later were used as projective personality tests, which assess personality through interpreting a person's unique responses to vague stimuli.

Contemporary psychological assessment also has roots in the methods used by early clinical practitioners. The clinical case study has been used throughout the history of medicine. Case studies often incorporate assessment techniques such as interviewing and behavioral observation. These methods will be discussed in detail in Chapter 6.

Following Witmer's introduction of clinical psychology as a distinct specialty in the 1890s, clinical psychologists' primary role was considered to be assessment. As psychologists, clinical psychologists were presumed to bring a scientific approach to their evaluations of mental patients. Hence, clinical psychologists were presumed to be more attuned than psychiatrists to specific and abstract mental processes—memory, emotional control, reasoning, general intelligence—that may be impaired by a client's disorder. Because of their scientific training, clinical psychologists were also presumed to be better able than psychiatrists to develop tests to assess specific mental processes affected by a patient's disorder.

Throughout the first half of the 1900s, assessment was the major role of the clinical psychologist. Working in a treatment team with other mental health professionals, the psychologist conducted intellectual, personality, psychodiagnostic, and neuropsychological assessments that contributed to the conceptualization and treatment formulation of clients. However, other mental health professionals—primarily psychiatrists—then used the assessment results to prescribe and deliver treatment.

As discussed in Chapter 8, clinical psychologists became more involved in the direct delivery of mental health services around the mid-1900s. By the 1980s, surveys found that clinical psychologists spent more time providing psychotherapy than conducting assessments (e.g., Norcross & Prochaska, 1982).

Still, assessment remains a significant specialty of the psychologist. Whereas many mental health professionals, including psychologists, psychiatrists, and clinical social workers, can provide psychotherapy, only psychologists are trained to develop, administer, and interpret psychological tests. Hence, it is important for students in clinical psychology to recognize and value their unique contribution to the care of mental patients. I have often advised students in clinical psychology who interview for jobs as a *psychotherapist* (and so may be competing with other mental health professionals such as social workers) to stress the importance of psychological testing in the care of mental health patients and their ability to provide this service.

ROLE AND TYPES OF ASSESSMENT IN CLINICAL PSYCHOLOGY

This textbook stresses the scientific foundations of clinical psychology. As described in previous chapters, scientific progress occurs through a four-stage process. The progress that occurs in later stages of science depends on the accuracy of observations in the initial stage. The validity of hypotheses and theories generated in the second stage, the validity of research conducted in the third stage, and the utility of applications in the fourth stage are all influenced by the accuracy of the observations. It is easy to see that progress in each subsequent stage of science will be slowed if one's observation or assessment methods are inaccurate.

The reliance of progress on accurate assessment is true of clinical psychology as well as for other sciences. Progress in clinical psychology has been closely tied to the development of effective assessment instruments. As clinical psychologists have learned how to assess abnormal behavior and mental processes more accurately, the theories for explaining and the methods for treating abnormal behavior have improved.

An example of the influence of accurate assessment on subsequent progress in clinical psychology is the diagnostic distinction between conversion and somatization disorder. As defined in previous chapters, conversion disorder is a condition in which a client experiences a physical symptom that has no apparent physical foundation but instead has a psychological cause (e.g., a patient who, after seeing her family killed in an automobile accident, is struck blind even though she suffered no physical injury herself). Freud worked with conversion disorder patients early in his career and his psychoanalytic theory was initially developed to account for such conditions. *Somatization disorder,* on the other hand, is a condition characterized by multiple conversion-like symptoms; that is, the client reports one physical symptom after another, each without a physical basis. Somatization disorder patients often acquire medical files that are inches thick and filled with reports of dozens of physical symptoms, none of which has a medical basis.

Before 1980, somatization and conversion disorder were considered as the same condition and were both diagnosed simply as conversion disorder. However, the two conditions were formally distinguished in DSM-III (American Psychiatric Association, 1980).

Once the two conditions were considered as distinct entities, psychologists could conduct research to examine correlates of each. Lo and behold, within a short time, psychologists learned that conversion and somatization disorder had many significant differences: somatization disorder tends to have an earlier onset, a more chronic course, a greater genetic influence, and more severe associated psychological problems than conversion disorder (Willerman & Cohen, 1990). Thus, conversion and somatization disorder are truly distinct conditions. Ultimately, this research may identify distinct causes and develop effective treatments for both disorders.

Even when engaged in applied clinical work, rather than formal scientific research, clinical psychologists must conduct accurate and effective assessments. After all, if one has not accurately identified the nature of a client's problem, then one will not be able to provide the most effective treatment.

Clinical psychologists conduct assessments across several realms of functioning that may be related to abnormal functioning: intellectual, behavioral, and personality/emotional. In addition, clinical psychologists employ several methods of conducting assessments, including standardized tests, clinical interviewing, and observation.

One of the most important types of clinical assessment is the measurement of intelligence. A child's intelligence must be assessed whenever the referral question concerns poor academic performance, which may be due to mental retardation or learning disabilities. In addition, intellectual assessment is important when a client has a neurological condition that may be causing deterioration in functioning. Intellectual assessment also is important in cases in which knowing the client's intellectual level would be helpful in selecting the most appropriate form of treatment (e.g., insight-oriented therapy may be less appropriate with a client who has a low average IQ than with another who has a superior IQ). Chapter 5 will discuss the major intelligence tests used by clinical psychologists, such as the Stanford-Binet and Wechsler Adult Intelligence Scale–Revised (WAIS–R), as well as many other tests of specific psychological abilities.

Another important part of clinical assessment is behavioral assessment. Clinical psychologists are trained to observe and evaluate behavior. When psychologists interview a client, they not only ask a se-

ries of questions, they also observe the client's behavior. Behavioral assessment instruments have
been developed to help clinical psychologists to
monitor and evaluate a client's behavior in its natural
surroundings, such as a classroom, hospital ward, or
the family home. Finally, methods have been developed that allow a client or someone close to the client
(such as a parent or teacher) to rate the client's behavior. The information sought in clinical interviews
and examples of important behavioral assessment
instruments, such as the Child Behavior Checklist
(CBCL), will be presented in Chapter 6.

Personality testing is another important type of
clinical assessment. Before treating a client, clinical
psychologists develop a clinical conceptualization,
or a theoretical explanation of the cause and maintenance of the problem. Personality assessment is a basic part of determining a client's diagnosis and understanding the dynamics involved in the initiation
and maintenance of the problem. Chapter 7 will examine the major personality tests used by clinical
psychologists, including structured tests (such as the
Minnesota Multiphasic Personality Inventory [2nd
ed.]—MMPI-2) and projective tests (such as the
Rorschach Inkblot Test and Thematic Apperception
Test).

Clinical psychologists use several forms of assessment, including standardized tests, clinical interviewing, and observation. Standardized tests are
instruments that are administered to all clients in the
same way. Standardized tests have been developed
across all realms of functioning, including intelligence, personality, and behavior. For example, the
WAIS-R is a standardized test of intelligence, which
requires that clients answer verbal questions (including arithmetic problems and questions about general
information, such as the length of a year) and perform various visual-motor tasks (such as copy designs with blocks or construct objects using puzzle
pieces). The MMPI-2 is a standardized personality
test, which consists of over 500 self-statements that
clients endorse as true or false as descriptions of
themselves. The CBCL is a standardized test of behavior, which consists of almost 100 behavioral
symptoms that a parent or teacher rates as typical of a
child.

Clinical interviewing is a form of assessment in
which the psychologist assesses functioning by asking questions and then attending to and interpreting
the client's verbal responses and nonverbal behavior. Clinical interviews can be structured or unstructured, depending on the degrees to which the wording and order of questions are scripted and to which
there are norms available for interpreting clients' responses. Interviewing is generally used in diagnostic
assessments, to obtain the history and a current description of the client's problem.

Direct observation is another important aspect
of clinical assessment. As noted above, methods
have been developed that permit clinical psychologists to rate a client's behavior in many settings.
However, clinical psychologists continually monitor
client behavior even when they do not use such formal rating scales. For example, clinical psychologists observe client's behavior throughout their therapeutic contacts with a client. They attend to the
client's emotional expressions and nonverbal behaviors. They assess the quality and nature of the client's
verbal and interpersonal behaviors. They note the
ways in which the client's in-session behavior
changes over the course of therapy. Thus, in these
ways, all clinical psychologists—even those who do
not identify themselves as behaviorally oriented—
attend to and assess client behavior.

The next three chapters will discuss in detail the
major types of assessment conducted by clinical psychologists. Each chapter will present a brief history
of and an overview of the scientific and applied issues concerning a form of assessment. The remainder of this chapter will address the major scientific
and applied issues regarding psychological tests in
general.

SCIENTIFIC ISSUES

Criteria for Evaluating Tests
The most fundamental scientific issue concerning
clinical assessment techniques is whether they work.
Clinical psychologists must address several basic
questions about their tests: (1) Are they accurate? (2)
Do they truly measure the abnormal behaviors and
mental processes they were designed to measure?

The criteria of reliability and validity are used to evaluate these questions empirically.

Reliability   Reliability is the extent to which assessments are stable or consistent. In order for a test to be useful, it must yield measures that are stable.

There are four basic types of reliability. *Test–retest reliability* is consistency across time or situations. For a test to be useful, it must demonstrate consistency across time. For example, many clients must be evaluated on two or more occasions (say, before and after therapy, or during different episodes of a recurring disorder). In order for the clinical psychologist's diagnoses, measures of psychological traits, and behavioral observations to be useful, they must be stable across time.

Test–retest reliability must be evaluated, of course, with the understanding that an individual's condition can actually change over time. Thus, test–retest reliability must be interpreted in light of the interval between assessments (the greater the interval, the more likely that the individual's condition actually changed); the persistence of the characteristic in question (some disorders such as schizophrenia and personality disorders have a persistent course whereas others such as adjustment disorders have a time-limited course); and other factors related to the duration of the patient's condition (for example, many behavior disorders in children have a relatively brief course, possibly due to maturational effects).

A second kind of reliability is *inter-rater reliability*. This is the degree to which two judges who use the test agree with one another. When considering any evaluation by a clinical psychologist, inter-rater reliability is crucial. For example, psychological diagnoses must demonstrate inter-rater reliability in order to be useful. If two or more diagnosticians cannot consistently agree on a diagnosis, then it will be difficult to conduct research to identify the causes, correlates, and effective treatments of the disorder. Similarly, when using a test to measure a psychological trait, it is essential that two evaluators agree on the presence and magnitude of the trait. If inter-rater reliability cannot be established, it will be impossible to demonstrate that the trait is related to other constructs.

The third type of reliability is *internal consistency*, or the degree to which subsections of a test agree with one another. This type of reliability is especially important in psychological tests that have subscales to assess different aspects of the trait in question. If the various sections of the test yield inconsistent results, then this demonstrates that the test is not a stable measure of the construct in question.

The fourth type of reliability is *alternate form reliability*. This is the degree to which two versions of the test agree with one another. For alternate form reliability to be assessed, there must be two (or more) *parallel forms* of the test. Forms are considered to be parallel when they have the same statistical characteristics (such as the mean score and measures of reliability and validity). Alternate form reliability is especially important when a test will be given repeatedly. If subjects can recall their previous responses to test items, then later administrations of the test would assess, not only current functioning, but also subjects' recollections of their previous responses. To avoid this problem, some psychologists develop parallel forms of the test. Of course, this demands additional time and expense for test development.

It is clear from the presentation above that reliability is influenced by several factors: (1) as test–retest interval increases, test–retest reliability decreases; (2) as test conditions vary across administrations, reliability decreases; (3) as procedures for scoring and interpreting test results vary, test reliability decreases; and (4) as the construct measured by the test becomes more unstable, test reliability decreases.

What may be less clear from the presentation above are some statistical influences on test reliability. For example, test reliability is related to test length; as a test becomes longer (by adding items with statistical properties equivalent to the original items), it becomes more reliable. Given the reliability of a test with known length, psychologists can determine by how much the test must be lengthened to increase its reliability to a desired level (Kuder & Richardson, 1937).

Another statistical influence on test reliability is the homogeneity of the subject population. In general, as subjects become more homogeneous (and so the range of test scores becomes restricted), estimates of a test's reliability decrease. For example, an intelligence test that is reliable in the general population may be unreliable when used in a sample with a restricted range of scores, such as a group of college students.

Validity   The second criterion used to evaluate the utility of any assessment is validity. Validity is the accuracy of the assessment—the degree to which the test actually measures what it purports to measure. Like reliability, there are several important types of validity: content validity, criterion-related validity, and construct validity.

Content validity is the extent to which the test has sampled from the entire domain of interest. For example, suppose a psychological test claims to measure social skills, but only asks questions concerning the ability to interact with members of the opposite sex. This test has neglected other information concerning social skills, and so lacks content validity.

Criterion-related validity is the extent to which a test agrees with other measures of the construct and is associated with measures of other theoretically related constructs. For example, suppose a clinical psychologist develops a new measure of intelligence. Before using the measure in clinical settings, the psychologist should evaluate its criterion-related validity by determining the degree to which it agrees with other previously developed and validated tests of intelligence.

Criterion-related validity is often further divided into concurrent validity and predictive validity. *Concurrent validity* is the extent to which a test agrees with other measures of the construct that are administered concurrently—at the same time. For example, if a newly developed measure of anxiety is highly correlated with previously validated measures of anxiety, when both are administered at the same time, then the new test has concurrent validity.

Predictive validity, on the other hand, is the degree to which a test agrees with future measures of the construct. For example, one's present intelligence level ought to be related to one's future intelligence level and to future correlates of intelligence

(such as how far one goes in school). If a clinical psychologist develops a new measure of intelligence, then the predictive validity of the test can be evaluated by measuring the degree to which the test is related to future tests of intelligence and related variables.

The third major type of validity is *construct validity.* Construct validity is the extent to which the theoretical relationships between the psychological construct, as measured by the test, and other constructs are supported. Construct validity is by far the most abstract and difficult type of validity to demonstrate. In fact, construct validity is never demonstrated by just a single study. Rather, construct validity is a function of the degree to which the entire body of research using the test supports theoretical statements concerning the construct.

For example, intelligence is thought to be related to many other factors: quality of the home, academic achievement, ability to adapt to new situations, ability to solve problems rapidly, and so on. Demonstrating the construct validity of an intelligence test means that these theoretical relationships to intelligence, as measured by the test, have been supported throughout an entire body of research.

Validity, like reliability, is influenced by statistical factors. For example, test validity is related to the homogeneity (range) of scores. If a test is examined in a population with a restricted range of scores, then test validity decreases.

Test validity also is influenced by the population *base rate*—the percentage of individuals in the group who exhibit the trait of interest. In general, when base rates approach extreme levels (100 or 0 percent), test validity decreases. In addition, if the base rates differ between the populations in which the test was originally developed and is later used, then test validity in the second population is unknown—it can differ dramatically from its validity in the first population. These statistical problems are illustrated in Exhibit 4.1.

Relation between Reliability and Validity   It is an old adage in test and measurement theory that reliability is a prerequisite for validity. The reliability of a test places an upper limit on test validity.

EXHIBIT 4.1   The Base Rate Problem for Test Validity

It is important to recognize that population base rates affect test validity. Extreme base rates decrease test validity. In addition, when base rates differ between populations, then a test's validity will also likely differ between groups. These problems can be illustrated with examples of a test designed to detect a clinical disorder.

Suppose a psychologist administers the test to a sample and identifies individuals with *positive* and *negative* test results. Positive results indicate that an individual has the disorder in question. Some of these individuals are *true positives* who actually have the trait of interest; others are *false positives* who do not have the trait of interest but were mistakenly identified as such by the test. Negative results suggest that an individual does not have the disorder. Some of these individuals are *true negatives* who in fact do not have the disorder; others are *false negatives* who do have the trait of interest but were not identified as such by the test.

It is useful to chart these groups as below:

Test Results

Trait	Positive	Negative
Present	A	B
Absent	C	D

A = True Positive   B = False Negative
C = False Positive   D = True Negative

Now, clinical psychologists distinguish between test sensitivity and specificity. *Sensitivity* is the ability of a test to correctly identify people who have the trait of interest. In the chart above, sensitivity is calculated as follows: A/ (A + C). As the false positive rate decreases, test sensitivity increases.

On the other hand, *specificity* is the ability of a test to correctly identify individuals who do not have the trait of interest. In the chart above, specificity is calculated as follows: D/(C + D). As the false positive rate decreases, specificity increases.

Sensitivity and specificity are both useful ways of evaluating a test. In some cases, the cost of a false positive is low relative to that of a false negative. For example, mistakenly identifying some people as having a brain tumor or being at risk for suicide may far outweigh the cost of failing to identify individuals who actually have these problems. In this case, psychologists should adopt a strategy of increasing test sensitivity relative to specificity.

All of the information in the chart above is used when calculating the diagnostic efficiency of a test. *Diagnostic efficiency* refers to the percentage of individuals who are correctly classified by the test. In the chart above, diagnostic efficiency is calculated as follows: (A + D)/ (A + B + C + D).

With this as background, one can consider the problem of base rates. Suppose a psychologist wants to develop a test to identify who, in the general population, will commit suicide. Unfortunately, this effort is unlikely to be unsuccessful. Suicide is statistically rare. The annual suicide rate is the United States is about 12 per 100,000 (or 0.012 percent).

Suppose the psychologist administers the test to a random sample of 10,000 people. Of these, only about one will commit suicide in the next year; the remaining 9,999 people will not commit suicide. Without using any test, we can predict that no one will commit suicide; the diagnostic efficiency of this base rate prediction is 9,999/ 10,000, or .999. For the new test to be as efficient as the base rate prediction, the test must identify the one true positive, without making any false positive errors! This is highly unlikely.

In this example, the cost of false negatives is much greater than that of false positives and so the psychologist may be willing to use a test with a diagnostic efficiency lower than that of the base rate prediction. It may be worth identifying five, ten, or even fifty false positives for every false negative. Still, it is easy to see how, when dealing with such extremely low base rates, the number of false positives may quickly overwhelm a psychologist and so lower the utility of a test.

Comparable problems occur when base rates differ between populations. It is possible for a test to have good reliability and validity in a population. However, when the test is used in a new population with a different base rate, the test's reliability and validity may change dramatically (Carey & Gottesman, 1978).

For example, suppose a clinical psychologist works in a psychiatric hospital and only sees inpatients who have severe disorders, such as schizophrenia, depression, and manic depression. In this setting, the suicide rates of patients with different diagnoses may be substantial (from 1 to 10 percent). It may be possible to develop a test that is useful for identifying patients at the hospital who are at risk for suicide. However, even though this test may be useful within the hospital setting, it is not likely to be very useful in the general public.

It is easy to understand this relationship using the example of psychological diagnosis. Suppose that there are two equally prevalent psychological disorders. Suppose further that each disorder has a single necessary and sufficient cause. Finally, suppose that the differential diagnosis of the two disorders is not very reliable, with each disorder being mislabeled as the other in 50 percent of the cases.

Now assume that a clinical psychologist conducts a study of the relationship between the causal factors and the two disorders. Because diagnosticians misclassify one disorder as the other about half the time, it will be impossible for the researcher to determine that each disorder is related to only a single factor. The low reliability of the diagnoses makes it impossible for the clinical psychologist to identify the causes of the disorders.

The limit of the reliability on validity extends to every type of psychological assessment. If a trait cannot be measured reliably across occasions, then psychologists can never validly show that the trait is caused by or correlated with other traits. If two psychologists cannot agree on the existence and level of a disorder, then they will never be able to validly demonstrate a cause or an effective treatment of the condition.

Test Theory

Introduction   Clinical psychologists are trained, not only in how to administer and interpret tests, but also to develop psychological tests. They learn how to select items that are superior to others. They learn how to measure the reliability and validity of tests.

To accomplish these goals, clinical psychologists must be trained in *psychometrics*—the statistical foundation of psychological measurement. Students who go on to doctoral training programs in clinical psychology may take an entire course in psychometric theory. What follows is only an introduction to classical test theory and generalizability theory. Students who would like additional information should consult works on test theory such as Lord and Novick (1968), Cronbach, Rajaratnam, and Gleser (1963), and Rozeboom (1966).

Classical Test Theory   Suppose a psychologist administers a test to an individual in order to measure

a trait. Classical test theory assumes that there is a true score for the individual; that is, the individual is presumed to have some actual value for the trait that the test attempts to measure.

Now, even though the true score is presumed to exist, it is not possible to measure with perfect accuracy. Every measurement contains at least some error variance. *Error variance* refers to the contribution of factors such as fatigue, distraction, idiosyncratic misunderstanding of a test item, and other factors that vary unpredictably across subjects and test occasions. Thus, the obtained measure (or observed score) of the trait is only an estimate of the true score. If the error component of an observed score is assumed to be random (that is, there is no systematic bias that causes an overestimate or underestimate of the true score), then the best estimate of the true score is the expected value or the mean of the observed scores. That is, we can estimate the true score by administering the test repeatedly and determining the mean of the observed values.

Now, assume that the error variance for an individual's observed scores is the same as the error variance for the entire population. This means that error factors are distributed randomly throughout the population—that no one person is assessed more or less accurately than other persons. When we administer the test repeatedly to a subject to obtain the mean observed score (the best estimate of the person's true score), we can calculate the standard deviation of the observed scores. This is called the *standard error of measurement (SEM)*. Like any other standard deviation, this statistic is a measure of the spread of observed scores around a mean, and so is a useful statistic in judging the accuracy of the estimate of the mean.

For example, in your statistics class, you calculated a confidence interval for an estimate of a population mean. A *confidence interval* is a range of scores within which one can state, with a certain degree of probability, that a true score lies. Just as you can calculate a confidence interval for a population mean, given the standard deviation for the sample, you can calculate a confidence interval for an estimate of an individual's true score, given observed score *(0)* and the SEM, using the formula: $0 \pm (z_{.95/2})\text{SEM}$.

For example, suppose that the standard error of measurement for an intelligence test is 2.5 and that an individual's score on the test is 108. Remember that 95 percent of a normal distribution falls between ±1.96 standard deviations from the mean (i.e., $z_{.95/2} = 1.96$) and 90 percent of the distribution falls between ±1.645 standard deviations from the mean (i.e., $z_{.90/2} = 1.645$). So, the 95 percent confidence interval for the person's true score is 108 ± 1.96(2.5), or approximately from 103 to 113. The 90 percent confidence interval is 108 ± 1.645(2.5), or approximately from 104 to 112. In other words, when an individual obtains an IQ score of 108 on this test, then we can state, with 95 percent confidence, that the true score is in the 103 to 113 range, and with 90 percent confidence that the true score is in the 104 to 112 range.

Classical test theory also provides formulas for measuring test reliability and validity. Although there is not room to develop these formulas here, clinical psychology students should become intimately familiar with the following basic results (Lord & Novick, 1968):

1. Test reliability is defined as the square of the correlation between observed scores and true scores.
2. Test reliability is estimated as the correlation between observed scores on parallel forms of the test.
3. Test validity, with respect to a second measure, is defined as the correlation between scores on the two tests.
4. Test validity, with respect to any criterion, cannot exceed its reliability.
5. Test reliability, as measured in terms of internal consistency, becomes greater as the length of the test increases.

Generalizability Theory   Generalizability theory was introduced by Rajaratnam (1960) and his associates (Cronbach et al., 1963) and is an important extension of classical test theory. Generalizability theory defines a person's true score, not as an abstract or Platonic value that exists and that one tries to measure by administering a specific test, but rather as the mean score obtained by all possible tests of a certain type. Thus, whereas classical test theory is concerned with a subject's true score for a given test, generalizability theory addresses the subject's mean score on tests of a particular type.

Although this distinction may seem minor, it is actually quite significant. Generalizability theory defines true score relative to the specific test used; if a different test (set of questions; set of conditions in which a test is administered) is introduced, then one must reconceptualize a person's true score in terms of this new type of test.

Generalizability theory permits psychologists to calculate the percentage of variance in test scores that is associated with the class of tests employed. Thus, when a new test is introduced (say, by adding items or modifying the items of the old test), then generalizability theory determines the degree to which the new test shares variance with the old test and so enables psychologists to estimate the degree to which the new test will be related to the old.

APPLIED ISSUES

Standardized Test Administration and Interpretation

One of the major functions of clinical psychologists is to administer psychological tests. For this reason, an essential aspect of clinical training is the use of tests. The clinical psychologist must learn how to establish and maintain rapport with a client, how to use a test manual for asking questions and administering test items, and how to score a test according to standardized procedures.

Of course, the specifics of test administration and interpretation vary widely across tests. For example, the Rorschach Inkblot Test and the MMPI-2 are both personality tests (which will be discussed in detail in Chapter 7), yet the procedures for administering and interpreting these tests are quite different. The Rorschach Inkblot Test has ten items, each consisting of an inkblot and requiring that subjects say what they see in each picture. The scoring and interpretation of responses are very complex, requiring a high level of training. On the other hand, the MMPI-2 has over 500 true–false items. Scoring of the MMPI-2 is objective and can be performed by a computer. Interpretation of MMPI-2 profiles also requires extensive training, but is assisted by quantitative rules derived from empirical research.

What follows is an overview of the procedures to be followed in using the major psychological tests, emphasizing the importance of following standardized procedures. Important aspects of the administration and scoring of specific tests will be addressed in later chapters, when those tests are discussed in more detail.

Establishing and Maintaining Rapport   The purpose of psychological testing is to determine an individual's *true score*. That is, the clinical psychologist wishes to assess the client's actual level of functioning in some area—intellectual, symptomatic, behavioral. In order to do this, the clinical psychologist needs to ensure that the client is functioning, during testing, at the appropriate level.

For example, the purpose of intellectual assessment is to determine intellectual potential—how well a person is capable of functioning intellectually. To this end, it is essential that clients function optimally during testing. Clients who are not motivated to comply with testing are unlikely to function at their best. Similarly, if clients are nervous about being tested, then their test performance may not be an accurate reflection of their abilities.

For these reasons, the clinical psychologist should attempt to prepare clients for testing. By engaging the client in simple conversation for several minutes, the psychologist may "break the ice" and help clients overcome their initial hesitancy. By explaining the nature and purpose of testing and by answering questions about how the test results may be used, the psychologist can enhance clients' compliance. By attending to signs of fatigue and then taking breaks or rest periods as appropriate, the psychologist ensures that clients' effort and alertness remain high. In these ways, the clinical psychologist establishes and maintains rapport to elicit the clients' optimal or true performance.

Of course, there will always be cases in which, despite the psychologist's best efforts, the client's test performance does not represent the true level of functioning. For example, some individuals are nonvoluntary participants and resist the psychologist's efforts to establish rapport. Some clients, due to their psychopathology, will not function during testing at their "normal" level. In such cases, the factors suspected of biasing the client's test performance should be noted, and the overall test results should be reported as having limited validity.

Following Standardized Procedures   Psychological tests are published with the understanding that they will be used only according to standardized procedures. Administrative procedures are standardized and presented in a test manual (or other publications concerning the development and use of the test). Administrative procedures address basic procedural questions such as whether the test can be used with individuals or groups, what materials (e.g., stopwatch) the examiner must have on hand, in what order the questions must be presented, and whether the questions are to be read aloud by the examiner or silently by the client.

Test manuals also provide standardized procedures for scoring and interpreting tests. Thus, general principles for judging the quality or correctness of responses (say on the Rorschach Inkblot Test) as well as examples of specific responses and scoring keys are available.

It is essential that a psychologist follow the standardized administrative and scoring procedures carefully. After all, a test is useful only to the degree that it is reliable and valid. The research originally conducted to demonstrate reliability and validity used the test in a standardized way. If a psychologist deviates from the standardized procedures, the psychologist is in essence using a new test and so it is unclear whether the test remains reliable and valid.

Occasionally, situations dictate that the psychologist must deviate from standardized administrative procedures. For example, I have tested clients who were so suspicious of me (due to their psychopathology) that I tested them in the presence of friends or family members whom they trusted, rather than test them alone as dictated by administrative norms. In such cases, conditions that may affect the reliability and validity of the test should be included in the test report, and the test results should be reported as tentative.

After a test has been administered, it must then be scored and interpreted in a standardized fashion. Scoring and interpretive rules vary from test to test. For example, some personality tests use a true–false or multiple choice format; scoring such tests is a simple matter of using an objective scoring key. Everyone who scores these tests will obtain the same scores, with the exception of the occasional clerical error. Similarly, the interpretation of some tests is assisted by the use of clear and readily applied formulas. For example, every psychologist who scores a WAIS-R knows that a Full Scale IQ score below 70 is in the mentally retarded range. Every psychologist who scores the MMPI-2 knows that validity scale scores above 65 are indicative of a test protocol with doubtful validity.

On the other hand, other tests require substantial judgment to determine the presence or nature of certain qualities in test responses; clinical psychologists must receive extensive training and experience before they can score and interpret them reliably. For example, the Exner Scoring System for the Rorschach Inkblot Test requires raters to make numerous judgments about the form quality and determinants of responses. The test then yields dozens of scores that require extensive analysis in order to arrive at an appropriate interpretation.

Every test is published with the understanding that psychologists will score and interpret them in standardized ways. The research conducted to document the reliability and validity of the test has employed a specific set of scoring and interpretative rules. Any deviation from these norms, say by a psychologist whose clinical experience has suggested an alternative approach to scoring and interpreting a test, means that the test is no longer the same as that which has been published. Hence, the reliability and validity of the test become questionable.

Test Construction

In addition to learning how to administer, score, and interpret psychological tests, clinical psychologists also receive training in test construction. Even clinical psychologists who are not directly engaged in developing new instruments should have a basic understanding of how they are developed. Understanding the methods used to develop tests may influence a psychologist's decision to select one test over another, as well as the psychologist's general evaluation of the usefulness of a test.

Selection of Items   Test items may be selected on rational or empirical grounds. For example, if a psychologist wants to develop a test to measure the presence and severity of panic disorder, the psychologist may initially introduce items using suggestions from traditional clinical lore, his or her own clinical experience, and the major theoretical views of the condition. These are regarded as rational methods of item selection. Clinical experience, tradition, and theory all suggest symptoms and associated features that may be useful indicators of a condition.

Rational methods may also be used to develop scoring and interpretative criteria. For example, traditional clinical wisdom may hold that a certain symptom is *pathognomonic*—both a necessary and sufficient criterion—for a condition. In this case, a psychologist interprets the presence of the symptom on the test, on rational grounds, as evidence for the clinical syndrome.

However, despite the reasonableness of such methods of test development, they are not error free. Traditional clinical lore may be wrong. One's own clinical impressions may be biased or incomplete. The major theoretical explanations of a disorder may be incorrect. Thus, although rational methods of item development must be respected, they should not be relied on completely. Most developers of psychological tests supplement rational methods of item development with empirical methods.

Test items can also be developed empirically. Here, statistical methods are used to develop and select those items that are most useful in measuring the construct in question. For example, suppose a clinical psychologist wishes to develop a test to determine the presence of depression. An empirical technique called the *method of contrasted groups* can be used to select items that distinguish depressives from others. In this method, a large number of items is administered to groups of depressed and nondepressed people. Statistical methods are then used to identify items that subjects in the two groups answer differently.

For example, one such statistical technique is *discriminant analysis.* Discriminant analysis identifies those variables that significantly discriminate between two or more groups of subjects. This subset of discriminating variables enables a psychologist to successfully identify to which group a person belongs. Thus, the items identified by discriminant analysis comprise a new test that distinguish depressed from nondepressed people.

Interpretative norms for a test can also be developed empirically. For example, a psychologist can administer a test of depression to individuals who have different levels of depression (as determined by some independent criterion, such as a clinician's judgment). In this way, the psychologist obtains mean scores for people who have high, low, and intermediate levels of depression. When one administers this test to a client, it is a simple matter to compare the obtained score to the norms and determine to which group of individuals the client is most likely to belong.

In addition, development of a valid and reliable test may require repeated looping through the procedures described so far. For example, after empirical methods are used to select the initial list of test items, it is important to cross-validate the test. In *cross-validation,* the psychologist administers a test to a new sample and determines whether each item continues to discriminate between the contrasted groups. This is important because the statistical procedures used to select items that discriminate between groups capitalize on the random variation and chance effects present in the initial sample. If many items are selected that discriminate between two groups, it is likely that some of those items do not truly discriminate between the groups, but were selected on the basis of chance alone. Cross-validation should remove such items.

Various *item analysis* techniques are also used to evaluate and select items for the final version of a test. For example, an *item-total correlation* measures the association between one's score on a single item and one's score on the sum of the remaining

items of a test. Items that are substantially correlated with the rest of the scale are retained, whereas items that are not significantly associated with the rest of the items are excluded.

Of course, rational and empirical methods are often used jointly in test development. For example, one may use rational methods to generate an initial large list of items, and then use empirical methods to select those items that distinguish between groups. Similarly, one may employ statistical methods to select items that discriminate between groups, and then use rational methods to interpret and label the dimensions represented by these items.

A common method of combining rational and empirical methods in test development is factor analysis. Recall that factor analysis is a statistical technique that examines the interrelationships among a large set of items and identifies subsets of items to which subjects respond in related ways. These subsets of items represent the dimensions that underlie the original set of items. By examining the items in a factor, the psychologist can judge why they are related and in this way interpret or label the factors. The subsets of items can then be used as tests of the factors or as subscales of the original test. In this way, factor analysis empirically identifies item subsets, while the psychologist rationally interprets the factors.

Development of Norms   An essential part of test development is the publication of statistical norms that permit test users to interpret test scores. It is important that these norms are obtained from samples that are representative of the population in which the test was designed for use. For this reason, test developers must first identify the population in which a test will be used—psychiatric inpatients, elementary school children, adults in the general population—and then derive norms from a representative sample of this population.

There are several methods of obtaining a representative sample of a larger population. Random sampling is a method of selecting subjects so that every member of the population has an equal chance of being included. For example, psychologists who wish to develop an instrument for use with formerly hospitalized psychiatric patients may select every tenth name from an alphabetical listing of former patients.

Now, when the population of interest is large (such as children in elementary school), it may be prohibitively expensive to obtain a sample using truly random procedures. In these cases, *quasi-random sampling* may be used. Here, subjects are selected, not from the entire population of interest, but from preselected segments of the population. For example, rather than sample from the entire population of elementary school children, the psychologist may sample children from selected schools. Similarly, rather than draw a sample from the entire population of college students, a psychologist may obtain subjects from the subset of students in introductory psychology classes who volunteer to participate in research projects.

A potential problem with quasi-random sampling is that the sample may not be representative of the larger population. For example, if students in the preselected schools differ from students at other schools (in family income, ethnic background, etc.), then the quasi-random sample would not be an appropriate group for use in developing norms. Thus, before continuing, the psychologist should ensure the representativeness of the sample, comparing the sample to the general population on relevant variables: age, gender, income, racial background, intelligence, and other potentially confounding variables. If the sample differs significantly from the general population on some important factor, then the sample should be discarded and a new sample obtained.

A method of ensuring the representativeness of a sample is *stratified random sampling*. This procedure randomly selects previously specified numbers of subjects from various groups, to ensure that the groups are represented proportionally in the sample. The groups (or strata) are typically defined by level of variables that may be confounds of the trait to be assessed. For example, intelligence is known to be associated with socioeconomic status and geographic region. Psychologists who develop intelligence tests have typically employed stratified sampling to ensure that their normative groups are representative of the general population along these variables.

After a representative sample has been obtained, the psychologist administers the test and calculates appropriate descriptive statistics for the group—means, standard deviations, standard errors of measurement, and so on. These statistics should be provided in the test manual. In addition, descriptive statistics should be provided for important subgroups that are relevant to the trait being assessed.

For example, tests of cognitive abilities in children should provide norms for different age groups; when psychologists administer the test, they can then determine whether their client's score is age-appropriate. Another example is the Depression Scale of MMPI-2, which was developed using the method of contrasted groups, discriminating between depressed patients and nonpatients. MMPI-2 norms enable psychologists to determine whether an individual's Depression Scale score is high or low—more like the typical score of depressed patients or nonpatients.

Test developers should be especially sensitive to the representativeness of their normative groups with respect to gender and minority group membership. Historically, these factors were relatively neglected by researchers and led some segments of the population to be oppressed through the misuse of tests. APA standards for the use of psychological tests (APA, 1985) state explicitly that test developers should include representative proportions of minorities in normative samples and, whenever appropriate, should publish norms for both males and females. In addition, if a test's normative sample did not have adequate minority representation, then the developer must indicate so explicitly and caution users about the possible limits of using the test with minority groups.

Ethical Issues

A second class of applied issues concerns the ethics of testing. In 1954, a joint committee of the American Psychological Association, American Educational Research Association, and National Council on Measurements Used in Education published the first set of formal recommendations for psychological and educational tests (American Psychological Association, 1954). Over the years, several revised versions of these standards have been published by the American Psychological Association (1966, 1974, 1985). In addition, the ethical standards of psychologists (American Psychological Association, 1992), guidelines for providers of psychological services (American Psychological Association, 1987) and guidelines for industrial/organizational psychologists (American Psychological Association, 1981) provide guidelines for the ethical use of psychological tests. These guidelines can be divided into those concerning either the developer or the user of psychological tests.

Guidelines for Developers of Psychological Tests   Developers of psychological tests should provide the following information:

1. Standardized instructions for administering the test
2. Data to demonstrate the reliability of the test
3. Data to document the validity of the test
4. Uses for which the test has been validated
5. Limitations of the test

Most of this material is straightforward and follows from earlier discussion of the importance of standardization and the psychometric criteria of reliability and validity. That is, unless a test is administered in a standardized fashion and has both reliability and validity, it cannot be useful.

It is also important for developers of tests to state explicitly the purposes for which the test had been developed and validated. For example, if a test was developed and validated as a measure of cognitive ability, then it should not be used to assess personality. Test developers should articulate in the test manual the purposes for which the test was developed and for which there are data to support its validity.

It is also important for the test developer to identify significant limitations of the test. For example, if the validation sample did not include an adequate

representation of minority group members, then the test developer should state this explicitly so that test users know that the test has not been validated in minority populations. Similarly, if the developer has validated the test in a sample of nonpatients, but the test may be used by some psychologists within clinical samples, then the test developer should state explicitly that the test has not been validated for use in clinical samples.

Guidelines for Users of Psychological Tests   Psychologists and other users of psychological tests should:

1. Use tests for which they have been trained appropriately.
2. Use tests for the purposes for which the tests have been developed and validated.
3. Be familiar with the evidence for the reliability and validity of tests.
4. Be aware of specific limitations of tests that may affect their validity for a particular client.
5. Note any specific problems that may affect a test's validity in a particular case.

Again, these guidelines are straightforward and require little elaboration. Many tests (especially intelligence tests and personality tests) require professional psychological training to administer and interpret; hence, undergraduate research assistants, social workers, psychologists whose specialty did not require training in the administration of psychological tests, and psychiatrists do not have the expertise to use such tests.

Psychologists should use tests for the purposes for which they have been developed and validated. Students should be aware that some psychologists may, through personal experience rather than empirical evidence, start to use tests for purposes for which they have not been validated. Also, psychological practice in general may eventually lead to a test being used for purposes other than its original purpose. For example, the Rorschach Inkblot Test was not originally intended to be used as a diagnostic instrument (Piotrowski, 1965); the Draw-a-Person Test was originally introduced as an intelligence test but is today used more as a personality test than as an intelligence test. In such cases, such new purposes are acceptable only so far as empirical findings validate the new purposes. Other new uses of tests should be regarded with suspicion. For example, I know of psychologists who have used responses to questions on an intelligence test as a projective personality test, even though there is no published evidence to support this practice.

Psychologists should also be familiar with the reliability and validity of their instruments. Common sense, along with the scientist–practitioner model of clinical training, dictate that a psychologist selects that test (or test battery) that has the best documented reliability and validity for the purpose at hand. In addition, the test user should be aware of the specific limitations of a test that may decrease its reliability and validity for the case at hand. For example, if a test has been well validated in a nonclinical sample, but not with clinical patients, then the test should be used only cautiously with actual clients. If the test is used with clients, then any report of the test results should acknowledge the limitations of the test with this client. Similarly, if there are idiosyncratic factors that may limit a test's validity in a particular case, such factors must also be indicated explicitly in the psychological report.

For example, I have administered intelligence tests that have been interrupted by fire alarms requiring the evacuation of the building; even though the test was completed later, a child's test protocol may have been affected by the excitement of the interruption. Similarly, I have tested clients whose psychopathology has been so severe that they had to be tested in the presence of a family member; even though the family member was silent, it is possible that they may have communicated subtle messages that provided assistance to the client. In such cases, the factors that may limit the validity of the test result need to be identified explicitly in the test report.

SUMMARY

Psychologists, like other scientists, have devoted much attention to the development of useful assessment tools. Clinical psychologists have developed methods to assess a client's intelligence, personality, and behavior, all of which are important in determining the client's problem and implementing appropriate interventions.

Modern clinical assessment techniques have their roots in both the scientific laboratory and the clinical ward of the nineteenth century. Although other mental health professionals can, like psychologists, provide psychotherapy, psychologists are the only mental health professionals who are trained to develop, administer, and interpret psychological tests.

Psychological tests are evaluated according to the psychometric properties of reliability and validity. Of these, reliability is the more fundamental, and so reliability is a prerequisite for validity.

Reliability refers to the consistency or stability of test scores and can be assessed across judges (inter-rater reliability), across time (test–retest reliability), across subsections of the test (internal consistency), and across parallel forms of the test (alternate form reliability).

Validity refers to the degree to which a test actually measures what it purports to measure. Validity can be determined by the degree to which a test samples the entire domain of interest (content validity), agrees with other measures of the construct (criterion-related validity), and is associated with related theoretical constructs (construct validity). In addition, criterion-related validity can be further divided into demonstrations that the test is associated with other tests of the construct administered at the same time (concurrent validity) or with future tests of the construct (predictive validity).

Psychometrics is the statistical theory of assessment. Classical test theory assumes that an obtained test score reflects both a subject's true score and a random error factor. If the subject could be administered the test repeatedly, then the mean observed score approaches the true score, and the standard deviation of the observed scores is called the standard error of measurement. These figures permit the calculation of confidence intervals for a subject's true score.

Generalizability theory is an extension of classical test theory that defines a subject's true score as the mean score obtained by all possible tests of a certain type. This permits psychologists to calculate the percentage of variance in test scores associated with the class of tests. In this way, psychologists can estimate the reliability (or generalizability) of tests across classes, such as item type or rater.

Clinical psychologists should administer and interpret psychological tests in standardized ways, otherwise published reports of their reliability and validity no longer hold. Clinical psychologists should also establish and maintain rapport with examinees, else the subjects' performance may not be adequate for obtaining a valid result. Part of the professional training of clinical psychologists is in how to establish and maintain rapport with test subjects.

Psychological tests are developed using both rational and empirical methods. Rational test development involves selecting items on the basis of clinical experience, tradition, and theory. Empirical item development involves the use of statistical methods (e.g., contrasted groups, discriminant analysis) to select items that are empirically shown to be related to the construct of interest. When using empirical item selection, it is important to cross-validate items, by testing them in an independent sample before including them in the final version of the test. Empirical techniques can also be used to select individual items that are related to an entire test (e.g.,

item–total correlation). In actual practice, rational and empirical methods of test construction are often used jointly.

Developers of tests should publish norms that enable psychologists to interpret a client's test score. Normative samples can be obtained using random sampling, quasi-random sampling, and stratified random sampling. They must be representative of the population within which the test will be used. It is especially important that normative samples include appropriate numbers of minority group members and females, groups that have historically been neglected by research and have sometimes been oppressed through the misuse of tests.

Since 1954, the American Psychological Association has published guidelines for the development and use of psychological tests. Test developers should provide instructions for the standardized administration of tests, should provide sufficient evidence to document the reliability and validity of the test, and identify the uses and limitations of the test. Psychological test users should use tests that they have been trained to use and that have appropriate reliability and validity for the purpose and population at hand. If circumstances arise that may limit the validity of the test for a client, psychologists must acknowledge these factors when interpreting and reporting the test results.

STUDY QUESTIONS

1. Identify and discuss the major types of assessment instruments used by clinical psychologists.
2. Discuss the function of assessment within the scientist–practitioner model of clinical psychology.
3. Define reliability and validity. Describe how reliability and validity can be measured.
4. Discuss the relationship between reliability and validity. Explain how reliability is a prerequisite for validity.
5. Identify the basic assumptions of classical test theory. How does classical test theory permit psychologists to construct confidence intervals for a subject's true score?
6. How does generalizability theory extend classical test theory?
7. Discuss the importance of using standardized procedures of administration and interpretation.
8. Contrast rational and empirical methods of item selection and test development. Discuss how the two approaches can be used jointly.
9. Identify guidelines for the ethical development and use of psychological tests.
10. Discuss the scientific foundations for the ethical guidelines for the development and use of psychological tests.

5

Assessment of Psychological Ability

I. *History of Ability Testing*
II. *Intellectual Assessment*
   A. *Intelligence Tests*
III. *Academic Assessment*
   A. *Achievement Tests*
   B. *Aptitude Tests*
IV. *Neuropsychological Assessment*
   A. *Neuropsychological Tests*
V. *Scientific Issues*

A. *Reliability of Intelligence Tests*
B. *Validity of Intelligence Tests*
VI. *Applied Issues*
   A. *Ability Testing in Diagnosis and Treatment Planning*
   B. *Labeling*
   C. *Test Bias*
VII. *Summary*

One of the most important types of psychological assessment is the measurement of ability. Clinical psychologists assess many types of psychological ability, including intellectual, academic, occupational, and other special abilities (such as visual–motor ability, language, and so on).

Clinical psychologists assess ability both for scientific and applied clinical reasons. Some clinical psychologists conduct basic research to determine the fundamental dimensions, causes, and correlates of psychological ability. This research should ultimately have applications for psychologists in the fourth stage of science—applied science.

In applied settings, clinical psychologists assess ability for two major reasons: diagnosis and intervention. It is easy to see how the assessment of intelligence plays an important role in diagnosing many clinical problems. For example, suppose a child has been referred for evaluation because the child is experiencing academic difficulty. Among the many hypotheses the psychologist must consider are that the child has an intellectual limitation, learning disorder, attention deficit, or emotional problem. It is essential that the child's intellectual potential and academic achievement be established to help distinguish among these possibilities. The diagnostic criteria for mental retardation and learning disorder, along with some of the applied issues in diagnosing these conditions, are presented later in the chapter.

Clinical psychologists also assess many specific cognitive abilities, such as memory and abstract reasoning. Such cognitive processes are often impaired in clients who have neurological disorders. For this reason, many clinical psychologists use neuropsychological tests with clients suspected of neurological impairment. Neuropsychological testing determines the level of cognitive functioning across many domains and may help determine the presence, extent, and even the location of brain damage.

Another type of ability assessed through psychological testing is occupational aptitude (or interest). Clinical psychologists occasionally use these kinds of tests with adolescents and adults for whom career planning becomes an issue over the course of psychotherapy.

The second reason why clinical psychologists use ability tests is to help plan clinical interventions. Ability tests indicate the client's level of functioning in many domains (language, intellectual, academic) that may influence the psychologist's recommended intervention. For example, different forms of psychotherapy may be recommended for clients who have similar clinical disorders but have markedly different intellectual abilities. The type of special educational programming recommended for a child with academic problems will vary as a function of the child's intellectual and academic ability. Whether the recommended intervention is a clinical, educational, or vocational training program, ability tests provide useful information in determining the appropriate course of action and the likely result of each intervention.

This chapter introduces readers to the ability tests used by clinical psychologists. Most attention will be devoted to tests of intelligence and academic functioning. For the purposes of this chapter, neuropsychological tests will be considered as a cognitive ability test and will be addressed at length. Tests of vocational abilities and interests will be considered only briefly.

HISTORY OF ABILITY TESTING

Throughout history, societies have performed evaluations of their members' abilities. Anthropologists have described the *rites of passage* that both ancient and contemporary cultures have used to determine whether adolescents are ready to adopt adult roles

(Fried & Fried, 1980). Often, such tests require that adolescents demonstrate that they can provide for self and family, and so are capable of performing the skills (e.g., hunting, fishing, sewing) essential in the culture (Fried & Fried, 1980).

As societies introduced more formal educational programs, they developed more structured methods for evaluating student progress. Doyle (1974), for example, discussed the forms of assessment used in ancient Greece. Although standardized tests were not used, Athenian boys were tested in a sequence of physical accomplishments (such as running and wrestling), Spartan children were tested for endurance and self-sufficiency, and military cadets were assessed for proficiency in military skills (Doyle, 1974). Of course, such evaluations consisted of behavioral demonstrations of capability and did not involve standardized or written exams such as are commonly used in contemporary education.

Perhaps the earliest use of standardized testing was the civil service examination of ancient China. According to DuBois (1970), by 2200 B. C., Chinese officials were tested every three years to ensure that only the most capable individuals held office. By about 200 B. C., the exam was administered in written form and covered subjects such as law, geography, and agriculture. Indeed, DuBois (1970) wrote that, as Europe increased its contacts with China from the 1500s on, the Chinese civil service examinations became widely admired by Europeans and were considered a model system by Voltaire and other notable figures. By the early 1800s, British diplomats, familiar with the Chinese civil service exams, used them as a model for the first British civil service exams in 1833 (DuBois, 1970).

In the 1700s and 1800s, several movements developed that held that psychological characteristics—both character and abilities—were related to physical characteristics. Chapter 7 will briefly present two of these views, *phrenology* and *physiognomy,* as early physiological systems for assessing character or personality. *Craniology* was the view that cranial capacity is related to brain size; *craniometry,* or the measurement of cranial capacity (brain size), was used as an index of intelligence. Leading scientists of the 1800s, including Louis Agassiz and Paul Broca, were advocates of this position.

Of course, this view was eventually recognized as invalid and has long been discarded by psychologists and other scientists. Still, it is important to recognize that this position was based on a scientific hypothesis that seemed reasonable at the time. It made some sense in the 1800s, in the face of evidence of human evolution, to hold that increases in cranial capacity from primitive to contemporary humans are associated with increases in intelligence; if comparable differences in cranial capacity existed between contemporary groups, then perhaps they represented different levels of evolution and intelligence. Of course, we know today that this hypothesis was incorrect.

Perhaps the definitive criticism of such biological approaches to assessing intelligence and other psychological abilities is Stephen Jay Gould's (1981) *The Mismeasure of Man.* As Gould forcefully argued, early demonstrations of different cranial capacities across races were flawed by experimenter bias and mismeasurement. Also, brain size is not the physical feature of the brain most strongly related to intelligence (if it were, then elephants and whales would be vastly more intelligent than humans); rather, the number of synaptic connections (related to the convolutions or wrinkling of the brain) and the ratio between brain mass and body mass are more closely related to intelligence than mere brain size.

By the late-1800s, psychologists had developed systematic methods for assessing psychological abilities. As noted in the previous chapter, Francis Galton, Wilhelm Wundt, and James McKeen Cattell had established laboratories by this time in which they measured basic abilities such as reaction time, memory, and sensory acuity. Although their success in generalizing from such basic abilities to more complex psychological processes was limited, their efforts were important in stimulating the modern scientific psychological approach to using standardized procedures and accurate assessment.

INTELLECTUAL ASSESSMENT

Intelligence is a psychological concept that is understood by everyone, from the ancient Greeks to contemporary laypersons (Eysenck & Kamin, 1981). Jensen (1980) suggested that the concept of intelligence has probably been recognized by every culture on earth and that, if the term were included in a vocabulary test, it would be one of the easier items for people to define correctly.

Even though the concept of intelligence is familiar to everyone, it is quite difficult to define. Gregory (1996) listed 13 definitions of intelligence proposed by noted psychologists. For our purposes, we can adopt Gregory's (1996) definition of intelligence, derived from his observation of two features of intelligence upon which most psychologists agree, namely, that intelligence is both: (1) the capacity to learn from experience and (2) the capacity to adapt to one's environment.

Just as psychologists have suggested various definitions of intelligence, so have they offered many views of its fundamental nature and dimensions. Most psychologists have recognized that intelligence includes multiple dimensions. In the early decades of the twentieth century, Charles Spearman and L. L. Thurstone developed factor analysis to identify the basic or underlying dimensions that contribute to performance on a set of test items. Spearman conducted factor analyses of various tests and concluded that intelligence consists of a *general factor* (g), which contributes to performance across tests, and *specific factors* (s_1, s_2, and so on), which contribute to performance on individual tests (e.g., verbal, memory, mechanical).

Other psychologists also have attempted to identify the fundamental dimensions of intelligence. Exhibit 5.1 lists several of the more influential views concerning the basic dimensions of intelligence.

This overview of the major approaches taken by psychologist to describe intelligence suggests several related issues. For example, psychologists have long debated whether intelligence is a general capacity for future learning or whether intelligence reflects what one has already learned. Cattell's distinction between *fluid* and *crystallized intelligence* addresses this distinction directly. However, other dimensional models of intelligence, such as those of Spearman and Sternberg, also recognize this distinction. No matter how great one's *capacity for future*

EXHIBIT 5.1   Psychological Models of the Dimensions of Intelligence

1. *Charles Spearman*—Two types of factors:
   a. *General (g) factor:* Influences performance across tasks
   b. *Specific (s) factors:* Influence performance on a single, specific task
2. *L. L. Thurstone*—Seven primary mental abilities:
   a. *Verbal comprehension*
   b. *Verbal fluency*
   c. *Number*
   d. *Visual-Spatial*
   e. *Associative memory*
   f. *Perceptual speed*
   g. *Inductive reasoning*
3. *Raymond McKeen Cattell*—Two factors:
   a. *Fluid intelligence:* The general capacity to learn, which enables one to adapt to novel situations
   b. *Crystallized intelligence:* Specific abilities one has already learned, which enable the person to solve familiar problems.
4. *J. P. Guilford*—A dimensional model, comprised of 150 basic abilities, representing all possible combinations of:

   a. *Five contents:* Visual, auditory, symbolic, semantic, behavioral
   b. *Five operations:* Cognition, memory, divergent thinking, convergent thinking, evaluation
   c. *Six products:* Unit, class, relation, system, transformation, implication
5. *Howard Gardner*—Six types of intelligence:
   a. *Linguistic*
   b. *Musical*
   c. *Spatial*
   d. *Mathematical*
   e. *Bodily Kinesthetic (i.e., motor skills)*
   f. *Personal (i.e., introspection, empathy)*
6. *Robert J. Sternberg*—Three forms of intelligence:
   a. *Componential:* Executive processes (such as defining the problem and planning how to solve it) and abstract reasoning
   b. *Experiential:* Ability to deal with novel situations and learn quickly from experience
   c. *Contextual:* Ability to cope with real-world problems; involves adaptation to, selection of, and shaping of one's environment

learning, one's ability to solve present problems has been influenced by previous training and experience. A person with high potential but little experience in an area may only perform at the level of another person who has lower potential but more experience. Thus, even psychologists who stress the aptitude component of intelligence recognize that experience is an important influence on intelligence.

Another debate related to the nature of intelligence concerns the degree to which intelligence is unchanging. Once one recognizes that intelligence includes both capacity for future learning and ability to solve present problems (which has been influenced by previous experience), one must admit that intelligence is malleable. After all, two children who have equivalent capacities for future learning may receive different levels of training and experience.

Over time, their potential may remain equivalent but their ability to solve present problems will differ because of the differences in training. Thus, psychologists recognize that, over extended periods of time, one's intelligence can increase or decrease relative to that of others, as a result of experience and training.

A related issue concerns the degree to which intelligence is inherited or learned—the nature–nurture debate. Perhaps no other topic in psychology has generated as much public criticism as the claim that intelligence has a genetic influence.

Remember that questions about a genetic influence on a trait can be examined using family, twin, and adoption studies. Scores of such studies have been conducted concerning the heritability of intelligence. Although an exhaustive review of this literature is beyond the scope of this text, it is fair to say that these studies show significant influences of both genes and environment.

For example, in a review of the genetic studies of intelligence, Bouchard and McGue (1981) found that the correlations between intelligence test scores for pairs of individuals with different genetic and environmental similarity were as follows: MZ twins reared together (0.86); MZ twins reared apart (0.72); fraternal twins reared together (0.60); biological siblings reared together (0.47); biological siblings reared apart (0.24); biological parent–child living together (0.42); biological parent–child living apart (0.22); adoptive siblings living together (0.34); adoptive parent–child (0.19).

In other words, as environmental relationship is held constant (e.g., parent–child living together; twins living together) but genetic similarity increases (e.g., from adoptive to biological parent–child relationship; from DZ to MZ twins), there is an increase in similarity in intelligence. Conversely, when genetic relationship is held constant (e.g., MZ twins; biological parent–child) but environmental similarity increases (e.g., from living apart to living together), there is an increase in similarity in intelligence. Thus, such studies support both environmental and genetic influences on intelligence.

Of course, debates on genetic influences on intelligence often address the relative influences of genes and environment. Some people misunderstand these results, thinking that, if there is a genetic influence on intelligence, then this means that genes are the only (or the most important) influence on intelligence. I have heard students say, incorrectly, that if genes influence intelligence, then there cannot be a role for the environment, say through education or enrichment programs. Such positions are based on a simplistic view of genetic influence.

Psychologists who have estimated the heritability of intelligence have not suggested that intelligence is solely determined by genes. In studies from the first half of the twentieth century, heritability of intelligence was generally estimated to be from 0.7 to 0.8 (Jensen, 1969), suggesting that intelligence is more important than environment in influencing intelligence. However, later studies (using better mea-

sures of intelligence and procedures for selecting adoption and twin samples) have obtained more modest heritability estimates, with a median of about 0.5 (Scarr & Kidd, 1983). This figure indicates that genes and environmental factors are about equally important in influencing intelligence. Exhibit 5.2 presents a case that illustrates the influence of environment on and the malleability of intelligence.

Intelligence Tests

There are several types of intelligence tests. The most reliable and valid intelligence tests, as will be argued later in the chapter, are those that are administered individually and require at least one hour to administer. There are also group tests and quick tests that can be administered in under 30 minutes. Although such quick and group intelligence tests are not as reliable or valid as individual tests, there are some clinical situations in which they can be used appropriately. This next section of the chapter will address both individual intelligence tests and the short and group intelligence tests.

Binet   Alfred Binet developed the first modern intelligence test. As noted in the previous chapter, Binet was a French psychologist who originally conducted research using Cattell's measures of simple motor and mental processes. However, Binet found that such measures were not sufficiently reliable and so he turned his attention to other assessment techniques. According to Thorndike and Lohman (1990), Binet developed a reputation as a strong empiricist in the assessment of individual differences.

By 1900, Binet was collaborating with Theodore Simon, a psychiatrist who worked at a facility for people with mental retardation, on methods of measuring intellectual functioning in people with mental retardation. This work led to Binet being asked by the Ministry for Public Education in 1904 to develop a method for identifying children who would not benefit from education in the regular classroom due to retardation (Thorndike & Lohman, 1990).

In 1905, Binet and Simon published their initial test, consisting of 30 scales. These scales included both simple sensory tasks (such as following a mov-

---

EXHIBIT 5.2   Case Illustrating the Influence of Environment on and the Malleability of Intelligence

Joey was evaluated at age 6 after failing the first grade. His intelligence was found to be in the low average range (IQ of 89) but his academic skills, particularly in reading and spelling, were at the pre-kindergarten level. Thus, he was diagnosed as having a learning disability and it was recommended that he receive special education for learning disabled children.

Joey lived in a farming community that had only modest educational resources. The boy's parents had limited educations themselves and did not provide much intellectual stimulation at home. Joey's school system did not have a classroom for children with learning disability. Rather than transport him to a neighboring county so that he could be in a learning disability classroom, the system placed Joey in a classroom for children who are mentally retarded and tried to provide him with an individualized educational program in that setting.

I first met and evaluated Joey two years later, when he was 8 years old. I found that his intelligence was in the retarded range (IQ of 67) and that his academic skills were at the kindergarten level. In other words, Joey's cognitive skills had remained almost constant in the two years since his previous assessment. Because his mental level remained at about the level of a 5-year-old but he was now almost 9, his intellectual level was considered to be in the retardation range.

This case did have a happy ending. Following my assessment, the school recognized that it had not provided an adequate program to meet Joey's educational needs. The school responded by sending the boy by taxi to a neighboring county, where he spent the entire day in a more appropriate classroom. Within a year, the Joey's intellectual functioning had improved to the point where he no longer tested in the retardation range and, after two years, his academic functioning had improved enough so that he spent only a half-day in the special education classroom.

---

ing object with one's eyes) and more complex mental tasks (such as forming a sentence using three words, finding rhymes, saying how two objects are alike).

The Binet-Simon Intelligence Test differed from previous methods of measuring intelligence in four ways:(1) it purported to assess general mental development rather than any single mental ability; (2) it was short and practical, requiring only about an hour to administer; (3) it was based on Binet's view that intelligence involves the ability to solve applied problems; and (4) items were arranged according to difficulty level, as determined by the performance of a small normative sample (Goodenough, 1949).

In 1908, Binet and Simon published a revised test consisting of 54 scales, grouped according to the ages at which nondisabled children passed them (Thorndike & Lohman, 1990). Thus, a child's test performance could be reported in terms of *mental age* (or *mental level*), the age of a standardization sample of nondisabled children who perform at the same level as the child being examined. The intro-

duction of the concept of mental age was an advantage over the 1905 scale, which had simply categorized children as retarded or nonretarded. With the measure of mental age, Binet and Simon could classify children along a continuum within both retarded and nondisabled populations.

Binet continued to revise his test, publishing a third version in 1911 just a few months before his death (Thorndike & Lohman, 1990). After Binet died, other psychologists took up the mantle of refining the test, the most important of whom was Lewis Terman at Stanford University. Terman translated Binet's test into English, revised items, increased the number of scales to 90, and obtained norms for U.S. samples of retarded and nondisabled children and of nondisabled and gifted adults (Gregory, 1996). In 1916, Terman published an English version of the test, originally called the Stanford Revision of the Binet Simon Scale but soon referred to as the Stanford-Binet (Thorndike & Lohman, 1990).

An important advance in the Stanford-Binet was the report of intellectual level in the form of an *intel-*

ligence quotient or *IQ*. This statistic, originally proposed in a slightly different form by Stern (1912/1914), is calculated according to the formula: IQ = 100 × [(mental age)/(chronological age)]. If a child's mental and chronological age are the same, then the child's IQ is 100 (and so the mean IQ for any age group of children is 100). If mental age exceeds chronological age, IQ is above 100; if mental age lags behind chronological age, IQ is below 100.

IQ scores allow the intellectual levels of children of different ages to be expressed on a common scale. For this reason, IQ is a more useful measure than mental age. From hearing a child's IQ, one knows immediately how the child functions relative to age-peers, regardless of the child's age.

Because IQ is such a simple and readily understood measure, it became widely used to report intelligence test scores. Most other intelligence tests followed Terman's lead in reporting intelligence test scores in terms of IQ scores with a mean of 100 and a standard deviation of about 15.

Like the original Binet-Simon Test, the Stanford-Binet was revised and refined, with later editions published in 1937 and 1960. The fourth edition of the test was published in 1986 and is the current form of the test. This version includes 15 scales. Although the meaning of the IQ score has been revised (to conform to the use of the IQ in Wechsler's tests described below), the Stanford-Binet (4th ed.) continues to conceptualize intelligence as an ability that enables one to solve practical and real-life problems (Thorndike, Hagen, & Sattler, 1986). The Stanford-Binet can be administered in under 90 minutes to children, adolescents, and adults. It provides IQ scores from the retarded through the superior ranges. Like the Wechsler Scales described below, the Stanford-Binet remains one of the more widely used and well validated individual tests of intelligence.

Wechsler David Wechsler introduced the next major individual intelligence test. Wechsler worked with adults, first as an army psychologist during World War I and later as a staff psychologist at Bellevue Hospital in New York (Thorndike & Lohman, 1990). Although Wechsler recognized the Stanford-Binet as a useful test of intelligence for children, he questioned its applicability to adults. After all, the Stanford-Binet reported intelligence in the form of an IQ score, which reflects one's chronological and mental ages. Although everyone accepted Binet's assumption that a child's mental age increases with chronological age, Wechsler questioned whether this assumption holds for adults. After all, it is not clear that the average 34-year, 6-month-old adult has greater mental abilities than the average 28-year, 9-month-old adult. If adults do not continue to experience a consistent increase in mental abilities with increasing age, then the concept of the IQ becomes meaningless for adults.

Wechsler suggested that the original IQ be replaced by the *deviation IQ*. This is a statistical measure in which one's intelligence test score is determined relative to a group of age-peers. Wechsler assumed that intelligence follows a normal distribution within each age group in the general population. Wechsler transformed these distributions to have a mean of 100 and a standard deviation of 15. Remember that, if a variable is distributed normally with a known mean and standard deviation, then one can determine the percentage of scores that fall above or below any given score. For example, given a normal distribution with a mean of 100 and a standard deviation of 15, approximately 16 percent of the population falls below a score of 85; about 2.3 percent of the population lies above the score of 130. Thus, by knowing where a person stands relative to a normative sample of age-peers, one can assign the person a deviation IQ score.

Wechsler published the Wechsler-Bellevue Test in 1939. This test was suited for use with adults and reflected Wechsler's views of intelligence. Like Binet, Wechsler designed an intelligence test consisting of numerous subscales, with items arranged in order of increasing difficulty. Also like Binet, Wechsler viewed intelligence as largely involving the ability to deal effectively with the environment (Thorndike & Lohman, 1990).

However, unlike Binet, Wechsler conceptualized intelligence as consisting of two major types of abilities: nonverbal (which he termed performance) and verbal. The Wechsler-Bellevue consisted of 11 scales in two sections: six Verbal scales (Informa-

EXHIBIT 5.3   Scales of the Wechsler Intelligence Tests

Verbal Scales

Information: General knowledge; e.g., What is the length of a year in days and months?

Comprehension: Judgment, ability to solve problems in daily living, abstract reasoning; e.g., What is the thing to do if . . . ? Interpretation of proverbs.

Digit Span: Short-term memory; e.g., Repeat a sequence of digits in order, first forward and later backward.

Similarities: Ability to perceive relationships between objects; e.g., How are two objects alike?

Arithmetic: Ability to perform mental arithmetic; e.g., Simple arithmetic operations with 1- and 2-digit numbers; sequences of two arithmetic operations; complex word problems.

Vocabulary: Ability to understand and explain the meaning of words; e.g., What does _____ mean?

Performance Scales

Picture Arrangement: Ability to perceive ordinal (cause–effect, means–end) relationships; e.g., Arrange these pictures so that they tell a story.

Picture Completion: Attention to visual detail, familiarity with common objects; e.g., Find what is missing in this picture.

Block Design: Ability to perceive visual relationships; ability to synthesize an abstract design from its components; e.g., Use blocks to copy designs.

Object Assembly: Ability to recognize and synthesize a concrete object from its visual components; e.g., Use pieces of a puzzle to make an object.

Digit Symbol: Ability to rapidly pair-associate two sets of symbols; ability to rapidly switch between two sets of symbols; e.g., Each number from 1 to 9 is paired with a symbol; draw the symbol that goes with each number in a list of numbers.

---

tion, Comprehension, Digit Span, Similarities, Arithmetic, and Vocabulary) and five Performance scales (Picture Arrangement, Picture Completion, Block Design, Object Assembly, and Digit Symbol). Descriptions of these scales are in Exhibit 5.3.

The Wechsler-Bellevue provided a Full Scale IQ score (considering information from all scales), both Verbal and Performance IQs (reflecting the scales in each section), and scores on each separate scale. Psychologists use all of this information to describe an individual's intellectual functioning on both general and specific abilities.

Wechsler later revised the test, refining individual items and improving the normative sample. In 1955, he published the Wechsler Adult Intelligence Scale (WAIS), which he again revised in 1981 (the WAIS-R). Wechsler also extended his test downward for use with children. In 1949, Wechsler published the Wechsler Intelligence Scale for Children (WISC) for use with children from ages 5 to 15, which he revised in 1974 (WISC-R) for children

ages 6 to 16 and again in 1991 (WISC-III). In 1967, he published the Wechsler Preschool and Primary Scale of Intelligence (WPPSI) for use with children ages 4 to 6, which he later revised in 1989 (WPPSI-R) for children ages 3 to 7.

In all of Wechsler's intelligence tests, he retained the basic format of the Wechsler-Bellevue. That is, about a dozen scales are administered, divided into verbal and performance sections. The tests yield Full Scale, Verbal, and Performance IQs, as well as scores on individual scales. Although a few different scales are used with preschool children than with older children and adults, most scales across the three Wechsler tests have the same names and are designed to assess the same abilities.

Other Intelligence Tests   There are many other intelligence tests. For example, two individually administered intelligence tests that can be used with children are presented in Exhibit 5.4.

EXHIBIT 5.4   Other Individually Administered Intelligence Tests

Kaufman Assessment Battery for Children   The Kaufman Assessment Battery for Children (K-ABC; Kaufman & Kaufman, 1983a) is an individually administered test designed for children from 2. 5 to 12. 5 years of age. It requires about an hour to administer and provides measures of both general ability and academic achievement.

The K-ABC was developed in the early 1980s. Kaufman and Kaufman attempted to avoid the problems of sex and racial bias that have often been raised as criticisms of the Binet and Wechsler tests (and are discussed in the applied issues section of this chapter).

Kaufman and Kaufman also incorporated findings from cognitive psychology's information processing model. The K-ABC yields a Mental Processing Composite score, which is based on two scales: Sequential Processing and Simultaneous Processing. The Sequential Processing scale contains three subtests: Hand Movements (repeat a sequence of hand movements and taps on the table); Number Recall (repeat a sequence of digits); and Word Order (point to a series of objects in the same order that they are named by the examiner). The Simultaneous Processing scale contains seven subtests: Magic Window (identify an object that is shown behind a rotating slotted window that allows only a portion of the object to be seen at a time); Face Recognition (attend to one or two faces in a photograph and then identify these faces in a group picture); Gestalt Closure (recognize a partially completed drawing); Triangles (use blue and yellow triangles to reproduce a series of abstract designs); Matrix Analogies (select that picture that best completes an analogy presented in picture form); Spatial Memory (recall the location of pictures arranged randomly on a page and presented only briefly); and Photo Series (arrange a series of pictures so that they are in chronological order, as in the Picture Arrangement subtest of the Wechsler tests).

The K-ABC provides scores on each subtest as well as on the Sequential and Simultaneous Processing Scales, which are then combined to yield the Mental Processing Composite. This Composite score is interpreted like an IQ score and has been shown to correlate highly with IQ

scores from other individually administered intelligence tests (Kaufman & Kaufman, 1983b).

The K-ABC also has an Achievement scale consisting of six subtests: Expressive Vocabulary (name objects presented in pictures); Faces and Places (identify well-known people, fictional characters, or places from pictures); Arithmetic (mentally solve problems requiring computation and understanding of mathematical concepts); Riddles (use inductive reasoning to identify an object or concept represented by a series of items read by the examiner); Reading/Decoding (identify letters and read individual words); and Reading/Understanding (act out a set of written commands).

Although the test–retest reliability of the K-ABC Achievement scale is over 0.90 for both preschool and school-aged children (Kaufman & Kaufman, 1983a), some question has been raised about its validity. Anastasi (1988) noted that the term *achievement scale* is an "unfortunate choice" (p. 269) for the K-ABC since the term implies that examinees have mastered a specific set of material; however, Kaufman and Kaufman (1983b) attempted to make their test independent of the specific information presented in the classroom. Thus, Anastasi regards the K-ABC Achievement Scale more as an aptitude than an achievement test.

McCarthy Scales of Children's Abilities   The McCarthy Scales of Children's Abilities (MSCA; McCarthy, 1972) is an individually administered intelligence test for children ages 2. 5 to 8. 5 years. The MSCA has 18 subtests, divided into five scales, and requires about an hour to administer. The five scales and their associated subtests are: Verbal (Pictorial Memory, Word Knowledge, Verbal Memory, Verbal Fluency, and Opposite Analogies); Perceptual-Performance (Block Building, Puzzle Solving, Tapping Sequence, Right-Left Orientation, Draw-a-Design, Draw-a-Child, Conceptual Grouping), Quantitative Scale (Number Questions, Numerical Memory, Counting and Sorting), Memory Scale (Pictorial Memory, Tapping Sequence, Verbal Memory, and Numerical Memory), and Motor (Leg Coordination, Arm Coordination, Imitative Action).

(continued)

EXHIBIT 5.4   *Continued*

The MSCA provides a General Cognitive Index (GCI) (rather than an intelligence quotient) with a mean of 100 and a standard deviation of 16. McCarthy (1972) noted that the concept of IQ has become associated with many inaccurate connotations and so preferred to use the GCI as an alternative to the traditional IQ. Still, many psychologists interpret the GCI as an IQ score.

Although the MSCA has good reliability, some questions have been raised concerning its validity. The MSCA tends to yield lower scores than the Stanford-Binet and the WISC (Sattler, 1992). In addition, factor analytic studies have not consistently supported the five dimensions assessed by the MSCA (Kaufman & Kaufman, 1977). For these reasons, many practitioners prefer to use the Stanford-Binet or Wechsler scales when assessing the general intelligence of young children. However, when clinicians have special interests in assessing one or more dimensions of the MSCA, such as motor skills or memory, then the MSCA may be a useful supplement to other instruments.

In addition to the individually administered tests of intelligence, several brief and group tests of intelligence are widely used. Although they are not as psychometrically sound as the Stanford-Binet and Wechsler tests and should not be used to assign formal diagnoses, clinical psychologists frequently find them to be helpful.

For example, when working with a client for whom a formal diagnosis of mental retardation or learning disability is not an issue but for whom an estimate of intelligence would be helpful in formulating a treatment plan, a quick test of intelligence may suffice. In some cases, the clinical psychologist may use a quick test as a screen to determine whether it would be useful to administer a longer and more expensive individual intelligence test. Finally, some school systems use group or quick tests, not to diagnose children with learning problems or to assign them to special education programs, but as a screen to identify those children who should be individually assessed. An overview of several quick intelligence tests is presented in Exhibit 5.5.

ACADEMIC ASSESSMENT

Schools in ancient Greece and Rome and in medieval Europe did not use formal examinations (DuBois, 1970). However, by the early Renaissance, European universities had begun to standardize the requirements for eligibility for a degree and for teaching. Early examinations were conducted orally. Mulhern (1959) compared exams of the 1500s to the work required of an apprentice craftsman before he or she could be admitted to a guild. According to Mulhern, early candidates for a bachelor degree were examined through a disputation with a supervisor, a test on books by an examining board, and an oral defense of a thesis. Those who earned the bachelor's degree were then eligible to teach as an apprentice-professor. After two or three years of apprentice teaching, they were examined by a chancellor and a board of faculty, who determined whether candidates would become *master* or full professors.

Written examinations were used by major European universities by the early 1800s (Cordasco, 1976; DuBois, 1970). However, standardized examinations based on a common curriculum were not introduced until the end of the nineteenth century.

Binet's intelligence test pioneered the use of standardized testing. In developing a test to identify children who could not learn in the regular classroom, Binet articulated a set of basic information that school children should be expected to know.

Soon after Binet introduced his test, standardized tests of educational achievement were used at higher levels. For example, the College Entrance Examination Board (CEEB) was founded in 1900 with the purpose of providing standardized examinations to be used by colleges (DuBois, 1970). In 1947, the

EXHIBIT 5.5   Quick Intelligence Tests

Slosson Intelligence Test   The Slosson Intelligence Test (SIT; Slosson, 1961, 1983) is a brief intelligence test that can be administered to either children or adults in under 30 minutes. Its items resemble those of the Stanford-Binet and, like the Stanford-Binet, the SIT yields mental age scores that can be converted into IQ scores.

Sattler and Covin (1986) reviewed 27 studies of the validity of the SIT. In general, the correlation of the SIT with individually administered intelligence tests was satisfactory (median *r* of 0.74 with the WISC and 0.55 with the WISC-R). However, the SIT tends to yield higher IQ scores than the WISC-R when used with children with learning disability (Sattler & Covin, 1986). Thus, the SIT is not sufficient for formally assigning diagnoses of learning disability or mental retardation to children. In addition, Sattler (1982) noted that the SIT places heavy emphasis on language skills and so may not be appropriate for young children who are experiencing language delays.

Peabody Picture Vocabulary Test   The Peabody Picture Vocabulary Test (PPVT) was developed by Dunn in 1959 and later revised in 1981 (PPVT-R; Dunn & Dunn, 1981). The PPVT-R consists of 175 cards containing four line drawings. The examiner presents the card, says the stimulus word, and asks the client to point to the picture that best represents the stimulus word. The PPVT-R can be administered in 10 to 15 minutes to clients ranging in age from 2.5 years to adults. In addition, because the PPVT-R makes few demands on the examinee's verbal ability, it is useful for individuals who have limited verbal abilities, such as clients who are hearing or speech impaired.

According to Sattler (1992), studies of the psychometric properties of the PPVT-R have generally found it to have good reliability. In addition, the PPVT-R correlates relatively well (median *r* = 0.68) with measures of verbal intelligence (Sattler, 1992). However,

the PPVT-R is limited to tapping into the examinee's vocabulary and related constructs (receptive language, verbal intelligence). Thus, although it is at least moderately correlated with other measures of intelligence, the PPVT-R should be regarded primarily as an index of vocabulary rather than intelligence. This caution was stated explicitly in the PPVT-R manual, which now reports results, not as IQ scores, but as *standard scores* with a mean of 100 and a standard deviation of 15 (Dunn & Dunn, 1981).

Human Figure Drawings   The Goodenough-Harris Drawing Test (Harris, 1963) (also called the Draw-a-Man or DAM Test) is a brief nonverbal test of intelligence. The client is given a pencil and blank sheet of paper and told simply to "make a picture of a man; make the very best picture that you can." Goodenough introduced this method in 1926, arguing that children's observation of detail and conceptual ability were associated with their intellectual ability and could be assessed through their drawings. Harris's (1963) revision generalizes the instructions so that examinees are also asked to draw a picture of a woman and of themselves.

Goodenough (1926) and Harris (1963) developed scoring methods based on assessing aspects of the drawing such as inclusion of specific body parts, detail of clothing, and proportion. They also provided norms that allow children's drawings to be converted into standard scores with a mean of 100 and standard deviation of 15.

Studies of the validity of the Draw-a-Man Test have found that it is only moderately associated with other measures of intelligence (e.g., Abell, Heiberger, & Johnson, 1994). However, the Draw-a-Man test may be useful when clinicians need a brief nonverbal estimate of intelligence or when assessing adolescents who resist more lengthy or formalized testing (Horkheimer, Abell, & Nguyen, 1995).

Educational Testing Service (ETS) was established by three educational groups: the American Council on Education, the Carnegie Foundation for the Advancement of Teaching, and the CEEB (DuBois, 1970). The ETS quickly became a leading influence

in the development of nationally standardized educational achievement tests.

Educational tests fall into two categories, achievement and aptitude tests, which serve two major purposes. *Achievement tests* assess what one has learned in a formal educational program. If a psychologist wishes to know whether a child or adolescent has learned what others of the same age have learned, then an achievement test is appropriate. Achievement tests are useful in assessing current level of academic functioning and in identifying one's relative academic strengths and weaknesses. This information may be helpful in determining why a student has difficulty in the classroom (say, in diagnosing learning disability) and identifying an individual's weaknesses so that he or she may receive remedial or additional training.

Aptitude tests assess more general abilities than achievement tests and are used to predict future learning. In a sense, intelligence tests are aptitude tests because they can be used to predict future learning. However, aptitude tests that are used to predict performance in future training programs, such as college and graduate school, have been developed.

Achievement Tests

Individual tests of educational achievement are most frequently used by clinical psychologists when assessing individuals who are experiencing academic problems. If a child has difficulty in the classroom, it is possible that the child has limited intelligence, an emotional problem, an attention deficit, a learning disability, or some other problem that interferes with learning. Distinguishing among these possibilities often requires assessment of intellectual level and academic achievement. For example, diagnosing and assigning a child to a special education program for a learning disability requires that an individual achievement test be administered. Several widely used individual tests of educational achievement are presented briefly below.

The Woodcock-Johnson Psycho-Educational Battery was published in 1977 (Woodcock, 1977) and revised in 1989 (WJ-R; Woodcock & Mather, 1989). It can be administered in about two hours to subjects from ages two years through adulthood. The WJ-R has three sections: Cognitive Ability, Achievement, and Interest. Although some have interpreted the Cognitive Ability score as a measure of general intelligence, Sattler (1992) and others have noted problems with the validity of this index. Still,

the WJ-R Achievement Tests are quite useful. The Achievement section includes nine subtests that are combined into five clusters: Reading, Mathematics, Written Language, Knowledge, and Skills. According to Spreen and Strauss (1991), the WJ-R Achievement scales are well validated and useful in clinical practice.

The Peabody Individual Achievement Test (PIAT; Dunn & Markwardt, 1970) and the revised test (PIAT-R; Markwardt, 1989) were developed for children from 5 to 18 years old. It takes under an hour to administer. The PIAT provides both achievement levels for several subjects (Reading, Mathematics, Spelling, General Information, and Written Expression) as well as diagnostic information about weaknesses in specific skills.

The Wechsler Individual Achievement Test (WIAT) was published in 1992 (Psychological Corporation, 1992). It can be administered to children and adolescents (ages 5 to 19 years) in 60 to 90 minutes. The WIAT assesses both basic academic skills (Spelling, Reading Vocabulary, Arithmetic) and more complex academic skills (Reading Comprehension, Listening Comprehension, Mathematical Reasoning, Oral Expression, and Written Expression).

The WIAT was developed for use with the WISC-III (or WAIS-R) and was co-normed with the WISC-III. One of the advantages of the WIAT over other individually administered tests of academic achievement is that, because it was co-normed with the WISC-III, the WIAT provides scores for expected level of academic achievement given the individual's general intelligence. Thus, the WIAT provides information, not only about the examinee's academic functioning relative to age-peers, but also indicates whether the individual's academic skills are significantly below the level expected of one with the examinee's intelligence.

The Wide Range Achievement Test—Revised (WRAT-3; Jastak & Wilkinson, 1984) is a brief achievement test that contains three subtests: Reading, Spelling, and Arithmetic. The WRAT-3 takes about 30 minutes to administer and can be used with both children (age 5 and up) and adults. The WRAT-3 assesses basic skills (such as word recognition and ability to perform mathematical computations) rather than more advanced skills. For this reason, it is not used to assign children to special education programs. Still, it is a useful screening tool that may suggest whether further individual assessment of higher academic skills is needed.

Other individual tests of achievement are also available. For example, the KeyMath Diagnostic Arithmetic Test (KMDAT; Connolly, Nachtman, & Pritchett, 1976) is widely used in school systems to assess children's math skills. The Kaufman Test of Academic Achievement (K-TEA; Kaufman & Kaufman, 1985) is an untimed test of five academic skills (Reading Decoding, Reading Comprehension, Mathematics Application, Mathematics Computation, and Spelling) that can be given to children ages 6 to 18 years. The Illinois Test of Psycholinguistic Abilities (ITPA; Kirk, McCarthy, & Kirk, 1968) assesses verbal and nonverbal language abilities in children from ages 2 to 10 years. These and other achievement tests are often used when clinical psychologists must assess particular academic skills.

Just as there are both individual and group tests of intelligence, so are there both group and individual tests of academic achievement. As with intelligence tests, decisions involving diagnosis of learning disorders and placement in special education programs should be made using individually administered achievement tests. However, group tests may be used as screening tools to identify children who require individual testing. In my experience, group academic achievement tests are rarely administered by clinical psychologists; instead, such tests tend to be administered by school systems for institutional reasons. However, when working with children who are referred for academic problems, I have often found it useful to obtain the results of group academic achievement tests—not to use as a basis for a diagnosis or treatment plan, but to supplement the individual tests I use. For this reason, it is important for clinical psychologists to have some familiarity with group achievement tests. Exhibit 5.6 describes several widely used group academic achievement tests.

EXHIBIT 5.6 Group Academic Achievement Tests

Iowa Tests of Basic Skills   The Iowa Tests of Basic Skills (ITBS) are used to measure basic academic skills (reading, language, mathematics, work-study skills) from kindergarten through grade 9. The tests have been well normed, and provide information that is useful to teachers regarding both the grade level of a child's functioning as well as more specific information such as specific skills that may be problems.

Iowa Tests of Educational Development   The Iowa Tests of Educational Development (ITED) constitute a set of tests that are related to the ITBS and are used with children in grades 9 through 12. The ITED has seven subtests that measure more advanced skills than the ITBS: Correctness and Appropriateness of Expression, Vocabulary, Quantitative Thinking, Analysis of Social Science Materials, Analysis of Science Materials, Ability to Interpret Library Materials, and Uses of Sources of

Information. The ITED provides indices on each subtest as well as a composite score and a reading score. Like the ITBS, the ITED has been well normed and correlates highly with scholastic performance (Feldt, Forsyth, Ansler, & Alnot, 1994).

Metropolitan Achievement Tests   The Metropolitan Achievement Tests (MAT) measure academic achievement from grades Kindergarten through 12. The tests come in two forms: a Survey Battery, which provides age and grade norms, and a Diagnostics Battery, which provides information regarding the child's mastery of different skills. The Survey Tests assess the following academic areas: Reading, Mathematics, Language, Science, and Social Studies. In addition, a Research Skills score is provided by items across the five subject areas.

Aptitude Tests

In addition to achievement tests that are designed to assess mastery of particular subject areas, psychologists also have developed aptitude tests that assess more general abilities and are used to predict learning in future training programs. Perhaps of most concern to readers of this book are the group-administered tests of scholastic aptitude that are frequently used in helping admissions committees select applicants to college and graduate school. The most widely used tests of this type are the Scholastic Aptitude Test (SAT), taken by high school seniors who are applying to college, and the Graduate Record Examination (GRE), taken by college seniors who are applying to graduate school. Of course, there are many additional such tests, including the LSAT (for law school admissions), MCAT (for medical school admissions), MBAT (for business administration admissions), and others. Because these tests are generally used in admissions decisions and not in general clinical practice, these tests will not be addressed at length in the text. Instead, Exhibit 5.7 briefly discusses several of the more widely used aptitude tests.

Another kind of aptitude that psychologists assess is vocational aptitude. Since early in the twentieth century, psychologists have tried to develop methods for determining which people will be successful in occupational training programs or successful in or satisfied with different professions.

Vocational aptitude and interest tests are frequently used by counseling psychologists in high school and university settings to help adolescents and young adults identify career goals and training paths. They are also commonly used by I/O (industrial/organizational) psychologists in large businesses or institutions to guide personnel selections and to assign personnel to appropriate tasks.

Clinical psychologists do not typically use vocational aptitude tests as often as do counseling and I/O psychologists. Still, the assessment of career interests and aptitude occasionally arises in clinical work. For example, I have worked with clients whose presenting problem (such as depression or anxiety) was ultimately determined to be related to uncertainty about their occupational future or to dissatisfaction with their current occupation. In these cases, it became appropriate for me to assess their vocational interest and aptitude. Selecting appropriate occupational goals became part of the clinical intervention.

Because career planning sometimes becomes part of clinical management, clinical psychologists should have some familiarity with the available vocational tests. Several vocational aptitude and interest tests are presented briefly in Exhibit 5.8.

NEUROPSYCHOLOGICAL ASSESSMENT

Clinical neuropsychology has its origins in the medical field, initially practiced by physicians such as Paul Broca and Karl Wernicke, who attempted to associate psychological functions with damage to specific brain sites (Franzen, 1989). Neuropsychological assessment, in which psychologists use standardized procedures to determine the extent and possible location of neurological impairment, arose in the 1930s and 1940s.

Kurt Goldstein performed studies from the 1920s through the 1940s on brain-damaged soldiers, reporting that the effects of brain damage include a decrease in abstract thinking and a tendency to respond to extraneous stimuli (Anastasi, 1988). As standardized intelligence and personality tests became widespread, psychologists also sought to standardize neuropsychological assessments. Goldstein (1992) noted that the early neuropsychological tests drew heavily from existing psychological tests, such as the Wechsler-Bellevue test and human figure drawing test, as well as from the standard neuropsychological and mental status exams used by physicians.

Goldstein (1992) wrote that neuropsychological tests have most frequently been thought of as "tests for brain damage." That is, neuropsychological tests can be used to estimate the extent and location of suspected brain damage. However, there are many other uses of neuropsychological tests (Goldstein, 1992):

1. Assessing development of brain function across the life span
2. Evaluating competence in forensic settings and judging extent of disability

EXHIBIT 5.7   Aptitude Tests

SAT   The SAT was introduced by the CEEB in 1926. Since then, the SAT has become part of a large-scale testing program administered by ETS for the CEEB. The SAT is administered to high school seniors and juniors. The SAT is administered to approximately 1.2 million high school students annually and is the most widely used standardized college entrance examination (*New York Times*, 1994).

The SAT yields scores for both Verbal (V) and Mathematical (M) Reasoning. These scores are on a scale with a mean of 500 and standard deviation of 100. However, it should be noted that these scales were based, for decades, on the performance of about 11,000 students who took the SAT in 1941. That is, scores after 1941 reflected the student's performance relative to a small group of prospective college students in 1941 (Donlon, 1984). SAT scores had been dropping consistently from the 1960s on (perhaps due at least in part to an increasing percentage of high school students who intended to go to college), and so the SAT was renormed in 1992 to reflect the distribution of contemporary students.

The SAT can be used by students and their counselors to help make choices about whether to attend college and, if so, to what type of college to apply. The SAT also is widely used by colleges to help select applicants for admission. It should be stressed, however, that the SAT should not be used by itself to make admissions decisions. A student's academic performance reflects many things in addition to academic aptitude, including motivation, personality, work habits, opportunity, and other personal characteristics.

Research has shown that the SAT tends to be highly reliable. For example, internal consistency and parallel form measures of reliability for the SAT typically are in the 0.90s (Donlon, 1984). In addition, test-retest measures of reliability are quite high; in fact, a study of students who took the SAT in both their junior and senior years of high school found that, on average, students obtain scores only about 20 points higher on both the Verbal and Mathematical sections of the second administration of the SAT (College Entrance Examination Board, 1987).

Research on the validity of the SAT has generally shown it to be significantly correlated with college performance. For example, Donlon (1984) noted that

over 2,000 studies had been conducted to evaluate the validity of the SAT. The mean correlation between the SAT V + M score and college freshman GPA was 0.42. College freshman GPA had a mean correlation of 0.48 with high school GPA; thus, the SAT is about as good as the student's entire high school record in predicting college performance. (Some readers may interpret these results as a significant criticism of the SAT and question why colleges use SAT scores in admissions decisions. I view these results as strong evidence for the validity of the SAT. Remember that the SAT takes only several hours to administer. On the other hand, one's high school GPA is based on many thousands of hours of work over four years, and that high school performance is also influenced by factors such as motivation and encouragement from parents. For a test administered over several hours to be able to predict college GPA about as well as high school GPA means that the test is quite good.) When both the SAT and high school performance were used, the multiple correlation with college freshman GPA was 0.55. Thus, although the SAT and the student's high school record are about equally effective in predicting college performance, use of both indicators increases the ability to predict college performance.

ACT   The American College Testing Program (ACT) is a widely used alternative to the SAT. The ACT was introduced in 1959 as part of the University of Iowa Testing Research Program. Since its introduction, the ACT has grown to the level where it is administered to high school juniors and seniors at over 4,000 testing centers throughout the country. According to a representative from the ACT National Office, the ACT was administered 1.5 million times during the 1994–1995 academic year (K. Hayden, personal communication, November 10, 1995).

Whereas the SAT is presented as an aptitude test, the ACT attempts to assess achievement in particular subjects (English Usage, Mathematics Usage, Social Studies Reading, and Natural Sciences Reading). However, the ACT also yields a composite score that is interpreted by many as an index of the student's aptitude for college work. For this reason the ACT is discussed here.

The ACT is scored on a 36-point scale, with a mean of 18 and a standard deviation of about 7. The ACT is extremely well normed, with norms based on scores of

(continued)

EXHIBIT 5.7   *Continued*

well over 100,000 students throughout the country. Reviews of the ACT (Aiken, 1985; Kifer, 1985) have reported that correlations between the ACT Composite score and college GPA tend to fall in the range from 0.40 to 0.50; hence, the ACT is about as effective a predictor of college performance as are the SAT and high school performance.

GRE   The Graduate Record Examination (GRE) was introduced by the Carnegie Foundation for the Advancement of Teaching in 1936. It has expanded to the point where it is administered annually to over 300,000 students in the United States who plan to apply to graduate school (ETS, 1994). The GRE is offered at selected sites five times per year. However, in 1993, the GRE became available in a computerized form that could be taken almost daily at 226 sites around the country. In 1995, the computerized version of the GRE was temporarily discontinued because of the possibility that a group of students could, by working together, piece together most of the items of the test (Kiernan, 1995). However, computerized versions of the GRE were reintroduced in 1996 and are intended to become the primary administrative format.

The GRE consists of a General Test (of graduate school aptitude) and 20 Subject Tests (such as psychology and biology). The GRE General Test includes three major subscales: Verbal, Quantitative, and Analytical.

The General and Subject Tests of the GRE, like the SAT, are scored on a scale with a mean of approximately 500 and a standard deviation of about 100. The Subject Tests are anchored to the scores of a group of college seniors who took the GRE in 1952. Thus, a Quantitative score of 500 means that the student scored at the mean level of the normative sample in 1952; a Psychology score of 500 means that the student's Psychology Test performance is at the level obtained by students who obtained mean scores on the General Test in 1952. Because some fields are more selective than others, scores on different subject tests are not directly comparable. For example, physics is a highly selective and demanding undergraduate major; for this reason, a student who receives a Physics score of 600 is likely to

earn higher General Test scores than a student who gets a 600 on a Subject Test in a less demanding field.

The GRE has high reliability (usually in the 0.90s). In addition, the GRE significantly predicts graduate school performance (correlations typically range from about 0.20 to 0.40). For example, Goldberg and Alliger (1992) reviewed studies of the ability of the GRE to predict various performance criteria in graduate psychology programs. They reported a mean predictive validity coefficient of 0.18. It should be noted, however, that these correlations, though modest, do not mean that the GRE is less effective than the SAT and ACT in predicting future scholastic performance. Remember from your statistics classes that when the range (variability) of a variable is restricted, the correlation between that variable and any other variable is attenuated. Because graduate schools tend to admit students with the highest aptitude, students with low GRE scores tend to be screened out of validity studies. Because students with a narrow range of GRE scores are admitted to graduate school, the correlation between GRE score and any other variable, such as graduate school GPA, must be limited.

An interesting demonstration of this effect is available from a study of the GRE scores of students admitted to the graduate program in psychology at Western Michigan University (Huitema & Stein, 1993). According to Huitema and Stein, the graduate program in psychology at Western Michigan University stopped using GRE scores for admissions decisions because of the view that use of such scores was elitist and biased. After more than 10 years, the program examined the relationships between students' GRE scores and various outcome measures (such as grades in specific courses and an overall evaluation of students). Huitema and Stein reported that these correlations ranged from 0.60 to 0.73, indicating that GRE scores do significantly predict graduate school performance. In addition, they noted that, if the program had restricted admissions only to those students who attained a combined score on the V and Q scales of at least 1200, then the correlation between GRE scores and outcome would have been reduced to 0.24.

EXHIBIT 5.8   Vocational Aptitude and Interest Tests

Strong Interest Inventory The Strong Interest Inventory (SII; Hansen & Campbell, 1985) is the current version of the Strong Vocational Interest Blank (SVIB; Strong, 1927), one of the first published tests of vocational interest. The SVIB consisted of various educational, occupational, and recreational activities that are rated for the degree to which subjects like or dislike them. The SVIB was constructed empirically, with scale items selected on the basis of their ability to differentiate among individuals in selected occupations, such as accounting. The SVIB has been revised to include norms for women, improve the standardization samples, and update the occupational scales.

The SII has 317 items. It provides six General Occupational Theme scores (Realistic, Investigative, Artistic, Social, Enterprising, and Conventional) and 211 Occupation scores. The Occupation scales were constructed empirically, contrasting members of a given occupation with members of the general population. Analysis of the General Occupation Theme scores and individual Occupation scores may help identify the kind of work environment and specific occupations that a client would most prefer.

The manuals of the various versions of the test show that it has good internal consistency and test–retest reliability over short intervals (Campbell, 1971; Hansen & Campbell, 1985). In addition, research shows that the test has at least moderate validity (e.g., Worthen & Sailor, 1995). It should be noted that it is difficult to demonstrate the predictive validity of vocational aptitude tests because occupational interests may change over time and because many practical influences (including opportunity) determine the jobs one finds. Still, Strong (1955) presented predictive data showing that, 18 years after testing, there is about a 66 percent chance that subjects will be in an occupation with a high interest score and only about a 20 percent chance of being in an occupation with a low interest score.

Kuder General Interest Survey The Kuder General Interest Survey (KGIS; Kuder, 1975) is a version of the Kuder Preference Record, which was originally published in 1939. Like the Strong Inventory, the Kuder test has undergone several revisions since its introduction. It is also available in different forms for adolescents (KGIS) and young adults (the Kuder Occupational Interest Survey—Revised [KOIS-R; Kuder & Diamond, 1979]).

The KGIS contains 168 items, each of which contains three activities to be ranked in order of preference. It yields scores on ten scales of Occupational Interest: Outdoor, Mechanical, Computational, Scientific, Persuasive, Artistic, Literary, Musical, Social Service, and Clerical. The KGIS also has one validity scale to check the accuracy of subjects' responses.

According to its manuals, the various versions of the Kuder inventory have high internal consistency and test–retest reliability over short intervals (Kuder, 1975; Kuder & Diamond, 1979). However, test–retest reliability over periods as long as four years is lower; similarly, reliability coefficients for the KGIS tend to be lower than those of the KOIS-R (Williams & Williams, 1985). This is to be expected, because occupational interests may change over years and because occupational interests of adolescents are less stable than those of older subjects.

The validity of the Kuder test is mixed. Williams and Williams (1985) considered it to be an excellent measure of vocational ability and interest. However, because opportunity plays such a significant role in determining the jobs one obtains, the Kuder test, like the SII predicts future vocational status only modestly.

Jackson Vocational Interest Survey The Jackson Vocational Interest Survey (JVIS; Jackson, 1977, 1991) has 289 items, each consisting of a pair of activities from which subjects select the one they prefer. The JVIS provides scores on 34 scales: 26 Work Roles (e.g., life science, business, adventure) and 8 Work Styles (e.g., accountability, job security). It was designed for use with older adolescents and adults and is primarily used in counseling high school and college students.

The JVIS has good psychometric properties, with high test–retest reliability and internal consistency (Jackson, 1977, 1991). The JVIS was validated against the SVIB (Jackson, 1977, 1991). In addition, Jackson (1977, 1991) provided data from several studies that suggested that the JVIS has at least moderate validity. However, as with other tests of vocational aptitude and interest, predictive validity is difficult to demonstrate.

Reviewers of the JVIS have judged it to be a sound alternative to other tests of vocational interest and aptitude (Brown, 1989) and to have the potential to be one of the best measures of occupational interest (Shepard, 1989).

3. Evaluating students in educational settings for learning disability

4. Assessing functioning in medical patients who have been exposed to toxic substances or who have degenerative conditions

5. Assessing functioning in educational and vocational rehabilitation settings

6. Assessing functioning in disorders with known or suspected neurological influences, such as autism and schizophrenia

7. Evaluating the effects of drugs in clinical trials

The next section of the chapter will introduce several of the batteries as well as individual scales that have been used in neuropsychological assessments.

Neuropsychological Tests

The Halstead-Reitan was the first major neuropsychological test battery. It originated with a set of tests used by Ward Halstead (1947) that was later revised and expanded by Ralph Reitan (Reitan & Davison, 1974). The original battery consisted of seven tests:

1. *Category Test,* which measures abstracting ability by having clients identify the organizing principle used to group objects

2. *Tactual Performance Test,* which assesses tactile memory by having subjects use one hand to put a set of blocks of assorted shapes into the appropriate holes in a board

3. *Rhythm Test,* which tests nonverbal auditory memory by having the client judge whether two recordings of musical beats are the same or different

4. *Speech Sounds Perception Test,* which tests auditory acuity by having the client judge whether similar sounding consonants are the same or different

5. *Finger Oscillation Test,* which tests finger agility by having the subject rapidly tap a key, using one finger on each hand

6. *Critical Flicker Fusion Test,* which measures the frequency at which a flashing light appeared to be fused or steady

7. *Time Sense Test,* which measures visual-motor reaction time and ability to estimate a just-elapsed time span

Halstead later added several additional tests to the battery, including (1) the WAIS; (2) an Aphasia Exam, which assesses the client's ability to name and recognize the functions of a series of objects; (3) the Trail Making Test, which tests the ability of the client to track a series of objects and to alternate between two conceptual systems (the client first draws a line to connect a series of consecutively numbered circles, and then draws a line to connect a set of circles containing both letters and numbers, by alternating between numbers and letters, (i.e., 1-A-2-B-3-C, and so on); and (4) Grip Strength (Franzen & Robbins, 1989). The Halstead Battery comes in three forms used with subjects of different ages: young children (ages 5 to 9 years), older children (ages 9 to 15 years), and adult (ages 15 years and older).

The entire battery takes from 6 to 8 hours to administer, and so many neuropsychologists use only a portion of the tests in their evaluations (Lezak, 1976). Franzen and Robbins (1989) noted that the Critical Flicker Fusion Test and Time Sense Test are not typically used, because research has failed to support their ability to discriminate neurologically impaired from nonimpaired subjects. The remaining subtests can be scored to calculate the Impairment Index, which represents the proportion of the subject's scores that are in the impairment range.

Because few psychologists routinely use the entire battery, the reliability and validity of the Halstead-Reitan are usually reported for separate subtests or sets of subtests. Franzen and Robbins (1989) summarized the validity data for the Halstead-Reitan and concluded that it can accurately determine the following: right- versus left-hemisphere involvement; focal versus diffuse damage; static versus growing lesions; and the nature of the disease process (cerebrovascular, neoplasm, trauma, or degenerative).

The Luria Nebraska Neuropsychological Battery (LNNB; Golden, Purisch, & Hammeke, 1985) is the major alternative to the Halstead-Reitan Test.

The LNNB is based on Alexandr Luria's theory of brain organization and function and bases its items on Luria's procedures to assess brain impairment (Franzen, 1989).

The LNNB (Form I) contains 269 items and can be administered in about 2. 5 to 3 hours. Items are scored along several dimensions (such as accuracy, quality, and speed). The entire test yields 11 scale scores: Motor Functions, Rhythm, Tactile Functions, Visual Functions, Receptive Speech, Expressive Speech, Writing, Reading, Arithmetic, Memory, and Intellectual Processes. An alternative version (Form II) is available, permitting clinicians to obtain additional information using a parallel form. Although both Forms I and II are used with individuals ages 15 years and older, a version of the

---

EXHIBIT 5.9   Selected Neuropsychological Tests of Specific Cognitive Abilities

Boston Naming Test   The Boston Naming Test (BNT; Kaplan, Goodglass, & Weintraub, 1983) assesses the ability to recognize and name objects. It is a widely used instrument because aphasia is a common neuropsychological disorder. The BNT consists of 60 items, each containing a line drawing. Items range from simple, familiar objects (e.g., tree) to uncommon objects (e.g., abacus). Clients are asked to identify the item on each card; if the client is unable to do so, then two standardized prompts (a phonemic prompt and a stimulus cue) are provided.

Research has shown that the BNT has sufficient internal consistency and alternate form reliability (Thompson & Heaton, 1989). Although Franzen (1989) judged the reliability of the BNT to have been demonstrated more than its validity, recent research has found that the BNT discriminates between patients with organic disorders (such as Alzheimer's disease) and normal controls (e.g., Williams, Mack, & Henderson, 1989).

Wisconsin Card Sorting Test   The Wisconsin Card Sorting Test (WCST) was originally introduced by Berg (1948) as a measure of abstractive ability. The current version of the test was published by Heaton (1981). The WCST consists of two sets of 64 cards. Each card has one or more figures that vary in color and geometric shape. Subjects are given the two sets of cards along with four target stimuli, consisting of a red triangle, two green stars, three yellow crosses, and four blue circles. Subjects are asked to sort the two sets of 64 cards into piles, matching each card with one of the four target stimuli. Subjects are instructed to try to get as many right as possible, and are given feedback after each trial. Unknown to the subject, the "correct" principle for sorting cards changes after the subject obtains 10 consecutive correct responses.

Performance is scored for whether the subject apparently identifies the correct sorting principle, as well as for flexibility of thinking as evidenced by discovering the correct principle as it changes. Continuing to respond according to the previously correct principle after it has been changed indicates errors of perseveration, which suggest organic impairment.

Although Franzen (1989) criticized the WCST for lack of information about its reliability, both Franzen (1989) and Spreen and Strauss (1991) regarded the WCST as having been demonstrated to have good validity. For example, Spreen and Strauss cited several studies that found that the WCST is sensitive to frontal lobe functioning and discriminates well between patients with neurological impairment and normal controls.

Wechsler Memory Scale—Revised   The Wechsler Memory Scale (WMS; Wechsler & Stone, 1973) and the Wechsler Memory Scale—Revised (WMS-R; Wechsler, 1987) are widely used measures of memory and so are useful when assessing clients for whom memory loss or neurological impairment that may be affecting memory are issues. The WMS-R consists of 13 subscales (e.g., Information and Orientation, Digit Span, Logical Memory, Mental Control), which yield scores on five factors: General Memory, Attention/Concentration, Verbal Memory, Visual Memory, and Delayed Memory.

Franzen (1989) noted that the original WMS, although widely used, had significant problems in its standardization sample and validity. However, Franzen considered the revised version of the test to be much more carefully normed than the original. Both Franzen (1989) and Spreen and Strauss (1991) judged the WMS-R to have adequate reliability and good validity.

LNNB is being developed for use with children (Anastasi, 1988).

Each of the 11 clinical scales is normed on a scale with a mean of 50 and a standard deviation of 10. The test manual contains explicit instructions for scoring items and for obtaining clinical scale scores. In addition, there are localization and other factor scores that have been derived empirically.

Interpretation of the LNNB is done in five stages (Franzen, 1989):

1. The 11 clinical scales are examined to determine which, if any, fall above a critical level that suggests neurological impairment.
2. The scatter among clinical scales is then examined.
3. The localization and factor scale scores are examined to determine whether they meet critical values.
4. Performance on items across scales is examined to determine whether there are patterns suggesting particular types of neurological impairment.
5. Qualitative aspects of the client's responses are reviewed.

Franzen (1989) summarized the research on the reliability and validity of the LNNB. Studies of the split-half, internal consistency, test-retest reliability, and interscorer reliability typically have found reliability coefficients above 0.75. The validity of the LNNB also tends to be quite good. Franzen (1989) noted that the LNNB discriminates neurological patients from normal subjects, shows high agreement with ratings of neurological impairment from the Halstead-Reitan, and is generally accurate in identifying the site of a brain lesion.

Still, Franzen (1989) noted several limitations of the LNNB. For example, it is not as comprehensive as other tests since it does not assess reading comprehension or memory (other than short-term verbal memory). The LNNB cannot distinguish between average and superior performance and so is not appropriate when assessing normal subjects. Still, in clinical populations for which it has been normed, the LNNB is more readily administered and interpreted than the Halstead-Reitan, and is a useful clinical tool.

There are many other neurological tests besides the Halstead-Reitan and the LNNB. Many tests measure a specific cognitive function that may be affected by a neurological disorder. For example, Spreen and Strauss (1991) described several scores of neuropsychological instruments, categorizing them according to the cognitive ability assessed, including attention and memory, language, visuomotor, auditory, tactile, and motor.

These neuropsychological tests are too numerous to address here. Still, clinical psychologists should become familiar with these tests, since they are likely to encounter clients who exhibit deficits in specific abilities that may have a neuropsychological cause. Exhibit 5.9 summarizes several of the more widely used neuropsychological tests of specific abilities.

In addition to the Halstead-Reitan and the LNNB, there are numerous tests that can be used as screens for assessment of psychoneurological impairment. Franzen (1989) discussed such neuropsychological screening instruments, arguing that they are useful for determining which clients may require more extensive neuropsychological testing. Even though many clinical psychologists are not trained to administer complete neuropsychological batteries, such as the Halstead-Reitan and the LNNB, they should become familiar with such screening instruments so that they can more effectively refer clients for neuropsychological assessment.

Perhaps the most well-known screen for visual–motor impairment is the Bender Visual Motor Gestalt Test (commonly known as the Bender-Gestalt Test). Lauretta Bender (1938) introduced this test in 1938. The test consists of nine line drawings of geometric designs. The examinee is given a set of blank sheets of paper and a pencil and is asked simply to copy each design. No further instructions are given about how to organize the drawings on the page. A copy of the drawings of the Bender-Gestalt test are in Figure 5.1.

Deviations from the basic designs are scored. For example, rotations, distortions of shape, disproportion, lack of integration, and perseveration are counted as errors. Pascal and Suttell (1951) published scoring criteria and norms for interpretation in an adult population. Koppitz (1963) published scor-

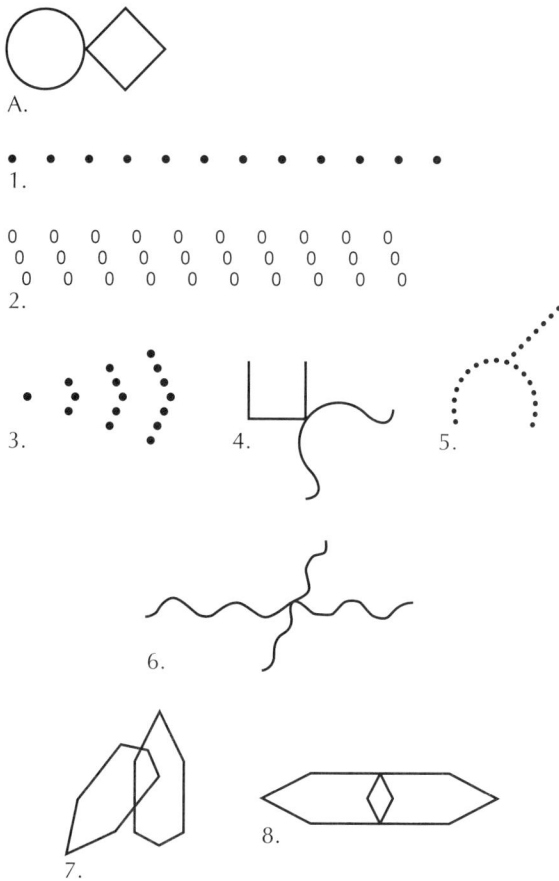

FIGURE 5.1   Designs on the Bender-Gestalt Test

Source: Published and distributed by the American Orthopsychiatric Association, 330 Seventh Avenue, New York NY 10001. © 1938 by Lauretta Bender, M.D., and American Orthopsychiatric Association, Inc. All rights reserved. "Bender" is a trademark registered in the U.S. Patent & Trademark Office.

ing criteria and interpretive norms for use with children.

Since its introduction, the Bender-Gestalt Test has become one of the most widely used tests by clinical psychologists. Surveys of psychologists (Lubin, Wallis, & Paine, 1971; Wade & Baker, 1977) and neuropsychologists (Craig, 1979; Hartlage & Telzrow, 1980) have consistently found the Bender-Gestalt to be among the most widely used psychological tests. It is quick (15 to 20 minutes) and easy to administer and score. Although Franzen (1989)

judged the validity research on the Bender-Gestalt Test to be "sadly deficient" (p. 241), Heaton, Baade, and Johnson (1978) summarized the results of almost 100 studies of adult psychiatric patients and reported that the median percentage of correct classifications (of brain-injured and non-brain-injured patients) by the Bender-Gestalt Test was about 75 percent. Therefore, although the Bender Gestalt does not have the precision and the validity of the neuropsychological batteries described above, it is useful as a quick screen of possible neurological impairment.

In addition to the Bender-Gestalt Test, there are many other neuropsychological screening instruments. Exhibit 5.10 briefly presents two of them.

SCIENTIFIC ISSUES

Reliability of Intelligence Tests

The most important scientific issue concerning ability tests is their psychometric worth. How reliable and valid are ability tests? By far, more criticisms have been directed against intelligence tests than other measures of ability. For this reason, this section of the chapter will address the psychometric properties of intelligence tests. The reliability and validity of achievement, vocational aptitude, and neuropsychological tests were mentioned in passing as these tests were introduced.

The research literature on intelligence tests is too vast to be exhaustively reviewed here. For this reason, only several general conclusions concerning the reliability of intelligence tests will be drawn. Readers who would like to read more detailed examinations of the reliability of intelligence tests should consult works devoted to this subject (e.g., Eysenck & Kamin, 1981; Jensen, 1980; Sattler, 1992).

The first general conclusion about intelligence tests is that individually administered tests are highly reliable. The manuals for the WAIS-R (Wechsler, 1991), WISC-III (Wechsler, 1991), WPPSI-R (Wechsler, 1989), and Stanford-Binet (4th ed.) (Thorndike et al., 1986) indicate that the reliability coefficients of these tests routinely fall above 0.90. This is true for measures of internal consistency, interscorer reliability, and test-retest reliability. These reliability coefficients tend to be higher than those of the quick and group intelligence tests and as high as

EXHIBIT 5.10   Neuropsychological Screening Instruments

Clinical Tests of the Sensorium   The Clinical Tests of the Sensorium (CTS; Withers & Hinton, 1971) consist of a series of nine tasks designed to discriminate between psychiatric and neurological disorders: Orientation, Days of Week Reversed, Serial Sevens, Recall of Address and Telephone Number, Babcock Sentence, Logical Memory Test, General Information, Digit Span, and Story Recall. According to Withers and Hinton (1971), the CTS is available in three forms, has adequate parallel form reliability, and significantly discriminates between groups of psychiatric and organic patients.

Neuropsychological Impairment Scale   The Neuropsychological Impairment Scale (NIS; O'Donnell & Reynolds, 1983). The NIS is a self-report questionnaire consisting of 45 symptom-related items and 5 response style items. O'Donnell and Reynolds (1983) reported that the internal consistency and test–retest reliability coefficients for the NIS are adequate. In addition, O'Donnell, Reynolds, and DeSoto (1983) found that the NIS shows substantial agreement with other brief measures used to discriminate among neurological patients and both psychiatric and normal controls.

or higher than those of other types of psychological measures, such as personality and behavior tests. In short, individually administered intelligence tests are about as reliable as any psychological instrument yet developed.

A second general conclusion about the psychometric properties of intelligence tests is that reliability tends to be lower in younger samples. For example, WISC-III Verbal, Performance, and Full Scale IQ scores have slightly larger standard errors of measurement (indicating lower reliability) for 5- and 6-year-olds than for 15- and 16-year-olds (Wechsler, 1991). Similarly, the Full Scale IQ standard error of measurement is somewhat greater for the WPPSI-R (Wechsler, 1989) than for the WAIS-R (Wechsler, 1981). This result is not surprising. Inattention, lack of familiarity with test procedures, distractibility, and situational factors are more likely to influence the performance of younger than older examinees.

Validity of Intelligence Tests

The general conclusions above concerning intelligence test reliability also hold for validity: (1) intelligence tests are generally valid; (2) individually administered intelligence tests tend to have greater validity than brief and group tests; and (3) intelligence tests tend to be more valid with older adolescents and adults than with younger adolescents and children.

For example, the manuals of the WPPSI-R, WISC-III, WAIS-R, and Stanford-Binet (4th ed.) report the results of numerous validity studies. These include concurrent validity studies, in which IQ test scores are demonstrated to be significantly correlated with other measures of intelligence, and predictive validity studies, in which children's IQ test scores are shown to predict future test scores and academic achievement (Thorndike et al., 1986; Wechsler, 1981, 1989, 1991). This research generally supports the validity of the individually administered intelligence tests.

In addition, many hundreds of studies have been conducted on the influences on and correlates of intelligence test scores. Although the results of these studies are by no means entirely consistent, the body of evidence provides support for the construct validity of individually administered intelligence tests. That is, these tests measure *something* that is related to the capacity to learn and the ability to adapt to and solve problems in the environment.

Still, critics have frequently attacked the validity of intelligence tests. Remember that validity is the degree to which a test measures what it was designed to measure. Critics have argued that IQ tests do not truly measure intelligence but instead assess other variables, such as exposure to the mainstream culture or socioeconomic status.

As noted at the beginning of the chapter, intelligence is a broad concept that can be defined in many different ways and can be expected to be associated with many behaviors and environmental variables. It is precisely because of the broadness of the construct of intelligence that opens the validity of intelligence tests to attack.

For example, a commonly heard criticism of intelligence tests is that they do not truly measure *intelligence* but instead simply measure *what they measure.* This has led some psychologists to propose a tongue-in-cheek definition of intelligence: intelligence is what intelligence tests measure (Boring, 1923).

Of course, this definition of intelligence does not further the field's understanding of intelligence. Still, it highlights the point that intelligence is a broad concept that can be defined in different ways and can be validated against many real-world variables. If one wishes to develop an intelligence test, one must first define intelligence and then specify the behaviors or variables that should be related to it. It is a straightforward matter to construct a test that predicts the criterion variables. However, if one then adopts a different definition of intelligence and investigates whether the test is associated with other criteria, then one may find that test lacks validity.

This problem can be illustrated by the criticism that intelligence tests are biased. Perhaps IQ score is confounded with exposure to the general culture. If so, then people who receive less exposure to the mainstream culture (such as members of minority groups and those of lower socioeconomic status) may score low, not because their intelligence is low, but because their exposure to the majority culture is limited.

The problem of IQ test bias will be addressed at length in the section on applied issues later in the chapter. However, one response to the criticism of IQ test bias is pertinent to this discussion of test validity. Remember that intelligence includes both the capacity to learn from experience and the ability to adapt to the environment. The first of these dimensions is the potential to learn. Almost all psychologists assume that different ethnic and racial groups have the same general potential to learn. Thus, if one stresses this aspect of intelligence, then one is likely to find that IQ tests are biased since different ethnic and racial groups with the same presumed potential are often found to have different mean IQ scores (Sattler, 1992).

However, if one emphasizes the second aspect of intelligence—the ability to adapt to the environment—then the criticism of test bias becomes less significant. This dimension of intelligence reflects one's actual ability to adapt to new situations and solve problems, an ability that has been influenced by previous experiences. Persons with a more limited range of previous experiences are likely to be less adaptable and to have fewer problem-solving skills than those with a greater range of experiences. Hence, individuals with more limited experiences, whether because of minority group membership, lower socioeconomic status, or other reasons, are likely to have lower adaptability and problem-solving ability than others. This says nothing about the potential of different racial or ethnic groups to learn, and does not disparage any group's innate intelligence.

Another common criticism of intelligence tests is found in the ability of IQ scores to predict academic performance. Brody (1992) summarized numerous investigations of the relation between IQ score and academic achievement. According to Brody, these correlations generally fall in the range from 0.40 to 0.70, with a typical correlation of about 0.50. Children's IQ scores are not only associated with current academic performance but also significantly predict future academic attainment (McCall, 1977) and even adult occupational status (Terman & Oden, 1959). Many psychologists point to these results as evidence of the concurrent and predictive validity of intelligence tests.

However, some critics of intelligence tests have used these studies to attack the validity of intelligence tests. After all, IQ score is not a perfect predictor of academic attainment. Other factors, including motivation and personality (Zigler & Seitz, 1982), family environment (Grotevant & Cooper, 1988), and social class (Grotevant & Cooper, 1988) also predict academic success. If these factors predict academic success, then is this not evidence of weakness of the predictive validity of IQ scores?

Absolutely not! Intelligence test developers have not claimed that IQ is the only (nor necessarily even the strongest) predictor of future academic success. They also have not claimed that IQ is fixed throughout one's lifetime. They recognize that IQ may change over time and that many factors other than intelligence influence academic performance. To criticize the validity of an intelligence test because its correlation with educational attainment is only about 0.50 is to attack the test based on a definition of intelligence that is quite different from that of the test developers (as well as most psychologists).

The facts that IQ score is not a perfect indicator of academic performance, and that it predicts educational attainment only about as well as family and social class variables, do not invalidate the test. Remember that an individually administered intelligence test takes about 90 minutes to complete. Family and social class influences operate throughout the child's entire life. That a single 90-minute test in childhood predicts academic performance about as well as such environmental variables should be regarded as substantial support for the validity of the test.

When considering criticisms of the validity of intelligence tests, one must consider how the test developer defined intelligence and the purposes for which the test was developed. After all, a test may be valid for some purposes (such as selection of individuals who are mentally retarded for placement in special education classes) but not others.

APPLIED ISSUES

Ability Testing in Diagnosis and Treatment Planning

Clinical psychologists frequently administer ability tests to assist in the diagnosis of clinical disorders. Several disorders are associated with intellectual functioning, and so the proper diagnosis of these conditions requires administration of IQ tests. These conditions include mental retardation, learning disabilities, and various neurological disorders. In addi-

tion, when a child experiences academic difficulty, even though it may be due to emotional or personality problems, clinical psychologists may administer an intelligence test to understand the level of academic performance of which the child is capable; this may clarify the severity of the emotional or personality problem. Finally, questions concerning legal competency may also require information about intellectual functioning.

When a child is referred because of academic difficulty, the psychologist must consider many possible explanations. The child may have limited intelligence or a learning disability (see Exhibit 5.11 for a summary of the criteria necessary for the diagnosis of these conditions). However, it is also possible that the child has an emotional problem (such as depression) that interferes with learning. The child may also be responding to situational stress (such as parents fighting and threatening to divorce). Intelligence tests are necessary in the diagnosis of mental retardation and learning disabilities and are important in judging the severity of an emotional problem that may be detracting from the child's academic performance.

Clinical psychologists may also use intelligence tests when diagnosing adults. For example, adults who have not previously been diagnosed as mentally retarded, but who have a neurological condition (e.g., Alzheimer's, neurological damage caused by chronic alcoholism, brain tumors), may experience significant losses in mental capacity. When judging the severity of their conditions and determining whether they are capable of caring for themselves, intelligence tests are important. Also, when judging whether a defendant is competent to stand trial (i.e., capable of understanding the charges and of assisting in their defense) or whether an individual should be committed because they are not capable of caring for themselves, IQ tests are again useful.

Intelligence tests are also used by clinical psychologists in developing treatment plans. I have known psychologists who are classical psychoanalysts, seeing clients several times weekly for up to several years. They prefer to work with highly verbal and insightful clients, who also happen to be highly intelligent. Such psychologists may use intelligence

---

EXHIBIT 5.11   Diagnostic Criteria for Mental Retardation and Learning Disorder

According to DSM-IV (American Psychiatric Association, 1994), mental retardation is diagnosed when a client meets the following criteria: (1) score of 70 or lower on an individually administered intelligence test; (2) evidence of concurrent deficits in adaptive functioning; and (3) onset before age 17 years.

Students should note that these criteria help limit the possible problems that may arise from the use of biased tests. Criterion (1) requires the use of an individually administered test; thus, quick and group tests, which have lower reliability and validity than the individually administered tests, are not sufficient for diagnosing mental retardation. Criterion (2) requires that the individual exhibit deficits in adaptive functioning (e.g., social, self-care) in daily behavior; thus, the diagnosis of mental retardation is not based on a test score alone. There must also be evidence of deficient functioning in daily living.

Learning disorder (or learning disability) is diagnosed in a comparable way. Diagnostic criteria for this condition include: (1) score on an individually administered test of achievement that is substantially below the level expected given one's age, intellectual

level, and education; (2) evidence that the academic deficit interferes significantly with actual academic functioning or daily living; and (3) the deficit is not due solely to a sensory or motor handicapping condition.

Again, these criteria help avoid possible problems with biased evaluations. An individually administered test of achievement, which has greater reliability and validity than group-administered tests, is required. The academic deficit must be substantially below the level expected given the person's age, intelligence and education. Thus, a child whose IQ is 80 should be expected to have below-average academic achievement. However, if a child with an IQ of 80 has academic functioning with a standard score of 50, then there is a substantial deficit in academic functioning relative to the child's intellectual potential. As with the diagnosis of retardation, the diagnosis of learning disorder is only made when there is evidence from the person's daily functioning of a significant deficit in a particular area. Thus, if the child's academic performance in the classroom is not deficient relative to others of the same age, then the child is not diagnosed as having a learning disorder.

---

tests to help decide whether classical psychoanalysis is appropriate for their clients.

Psychologists may also use intelligence tests to decide between verbal, insight-oriented therapies and more directive, behavioral therapies. For example, I have used cognitive–behavioral self-control training with bright 10-year-olds. However, I have found more concrete methods, such as parent training and behavior modification, to be more effective with less gifted children.

Clinical psychologists who work with adolescents or young adults for whom career planning becomes an issue may also find it helpful to administer intelligence tests. I have seen clients who are depressed because of their dissatisfaction with their job. Even though the primary focus of therapy was depression, career planning (such as deciding whether to return to school and, if so, identifying an appropriate level of training) became a significant

part of treatment. In these cases, intelligence testing was conducted to help set appropriate educational and career goals.

Finally, psychologists often use intelligence tests in follow-up evaluations of clients who have chronic disorders. Although this is not an issue for many cases, it is important for clients whose chronic conditions are degenerative. For example, patients who have chronic alcoholism are likely, if they do not decrease their drinking, to experience a gradual reduction in mental functioning. Similarly, patients who have chronic schizophrenia, even if they respond favorably to medication, often experience a lessening of mental functioning. Patients who have ongoing and degenerative neurological disorders (e.g., Alzheimer's Disease, Huntington's Chorea) gradually experience diminished mental capabilities. In such cases, it is helpful to conduct periodic cognitive evaluations to ensure that the clients are competent to care for themselves and that they receive training or assistance in areas in which they are having difficulty.

Labeling

A frequent criticism of ability testing of children is the possibility of a damaging *labeling* effect. That is, perhaps the very act of being labelled as a *slow learner* or having a learning disorder may lead children to experience lowered self-esteem or to be treated by others as though they have some stigmatizing condition.

Rosenthal conducted the classic studies of the influence of experimenter expectations on subject performance (e.g., Rosenthal, 1966) and reported that experimenters tended to find the results they expected to find, whether their subjects were animals or people. Rosenthal and Jacobson (1968) went on to claim that the experimenter expectancy effect was powerful enough to influence children's performance in the classroom. For example, after learning that certain children designated as *late bloomers* were likely to improve their performance relative to other children, teachers in fact found that these children improved their academic performance and achievement test performance during the semester, even though the label had been assigned randomly (Rosenthal & Jacobson, 1968). This finding was referred to as the *Pygmalion in the Classroom* effect and received wide attention in the 1960s and 1970s. The result was interpreted as evidence against the practice of labeling children, lest the very act of labeling lead to the expected result.

Current psychological opinion is that the Pygmalion in the Classroom effect is weaker and less consistent than was first thought. Barber (1976) detailed the methodological flaws of Rosenthal's research; the flaws were so severe that the early studies should not be regarded as having proved the phenomenon. Independent replications were necessary.

However, much of the work stimulated by Rosenthal's research has not supported his results. For example, Barber and Silver (1968) reviewed a series of studies that failed to demonstrate the experimenter expectancy effect; Barber (1976) later cited

an additional 40 studies that failed to demonstrate the effect. A meta-analysis of 47 studies by Smith (1980) found that the teacher expectation effect is marginal (mean effect size = 0.16). Thus, it is not clear that simply labeling a child as having an educational problem is itself a factor in leading to reduced performance.

Still, psychologists are aware that labeling may occur and so take steps to minimize the impact of a hasty and possibly inaccurate label. For example, since 1980, the criteria used to diagnose mental retardation and learning disability include deficient daily functioning as well as substandard performance on ability tests (American Psychiatric Association, 1980). Thus, a child who obtains low scores on an IQ test will not be diagnosed as mentally retarded unless there is concurrent evidence of deficits and adaptive functioning. Similarly, a child who obtains low scores on a measure of academic achievement is not diagnosed with a learning disability unless there is also evidence of substandard performance in academic functioning in the classroom.

Another criticism of ability tests is that, by labeling children as having a disorder, children are subsequently segregated and may receive inadequate education. In evaluating this criticism, one must weigh the benefits against the risks of labeling. Of course, labeling children incorrectly and assigning them to special programs, when they do not have handicapping conditions, is undesirable and possibly harmful. On the other hand, failing to identify children who do have a handicapping condition and failing to obtain the appropriate special educational services for them also is harmful. One must judge the potential advantages from properly labeling a child against the disadvantages of inaccurately labeling the child. Exhibit 5.12 presents a case in which a child was unable to receive the help he needed because of a school system's well-intentioned policy to reduce the labeling of minority group children.

Test Bias

By far, the most widely raised criticism of ability tests is the possibility that they may be biased against members of minority groups. Sattler (1992) discussed five ways in which intelligence tests may be biased against minorities:

1. *Intelligence tests are culturally biased in that their content largely draws from a White, Anglo-Saxon, middle-class background.* For example, "Who wrote Hamlet?" is more likely to be answered correctly by a European American with an upper-middle-class income who attends the theater than by an African American with a low income who cannot afford to attend plays.

As the major IQ tests have been revised, efforts have been made to remove or revise items that were clear examples of culturally loaded questions. For example, early editions of the Stanford-Binet had an item in which children were shown cartoon pictures of people and asked to point to the one that is "prettier." Although the incorrect picture did not portray a member of a minority racial group, the person had large lips and a large nose and so might be considered to have facial features associated more with African Americans than European Americans. This item was removed from the Stanford-Binet long ago.

Thus, revisions of the major IQ tests have attempted to reduce the "cultural loading" of questions. Still, it is not possible to eliminate such cultural loading altogether. One response to the criticism of culturally loaded items concerns the meaning of intelligence. If the ability to cope with applied problems is included in one's definition of intelligence, then questions with cultural content may be appropriate. After all, one's ability to cope with problems commonly faced in a culture should

---

EXHIBIT 5.12   Case Illustrating How a Well-Intentioned Effort to Reduce Labeling of Minority Children Led a Child to be Unable to Receive the Help He Needed

Jimmy was an 8-year-old boy who was referred to me for a psychological evaluation because of aggression and other conduct problems in the classroom. Jimmy had failed and repeated first grade and was now near the end of the second grade. However, Jimmy was failing second grade and was likely to be held back a second time.

I administered the WISC-III and found that Jimmy's Full Scale IQ was 55; I administered tests of academic achievement and found that Jimmy's academic functioning was at the kindergarten to pre-kindergarten level. I diagnosed Jimmy as mentally retarded and recommended that he be placed in a classroom for children who are mentally retarded.

I was soon contacted, however, by the school system's Director of Special Education Services. Jimmy was African American. In order to protect minority children from being overrepresented in special education classes, the school system had established an upper limit on the percentage of minority children who could be placed in special education classes. This limit had been met, so the school could not place Jimmy in a classroom for children with mental retardation, even though he was clearly mentally retarded and probably should have been in such a classroom since he failed the first grade. I then suggested that Jimmy be placed in a classroom for children who are emotionally disturbed (ED), since he was exhibiting significant misconduct in the classroom, but was informed that the ED classes also had reached their upper limit for minority children and so were closed to Jimmy. Although Jimmy did not meet the criteria for learning disability, I asked whether there was room for him in an LD class and learned that there was no room in an LD class for him.

Eventually, the school system decided to remove Jimmy from the school (due to his significant misconduct) and to assign him a home tutor for the final two months of the school year; the following school year, Jimmy would be placed in a class for children with mental retardation. Although school systems generally prefer to mainstream children (that is, use the least restrictive intervention possible to provide the required special educational services), the school in this case was forced to exclude Jimmy from the very classes designed specifically for him due to a well-intentioned policy of preventing minority children from being overrepresented in special education classes.

be related to one's experience with the culture. If so, then one's ability to answer culturally loaded questions is likely to be related to one's exposure to the culture and will significantly predict one's ability to cope with daily problems.

Another response to the criticism of culture bias is a statistical one. Jensen (1980) discussed how test bias can be measured statistically. In general, Jensen argued that an item is biased if it predicts a criterion (such as the total score on a test or some external measure of intellectual ability) differentially across groups. That is, if an item is easier relative to other items for one racial group than another or if an item is more closely correlated with the total score for one gender than another, then the item can be considered to be biased.

However, according to the research reviewed by Jensen (1980) and Sattler (1992), there is little evidence that IQ tests show such statistical bias. For example, IQ tests tend to predict academic performance for African American and Hispanic American children as well as they do for European American children (Sattler, 1992).

Even when individual items that have been singled out by critics are examined statistically, little empirical evidence has been found to support the criticism of culture bias. For example, the WISC Comprehension subtest item, "What should you do if a child much smaller than you starts to fight with you?" was identified in a documentary on IQ tests as being biased against black children (Sattler, 1992). Yet, Miele (1979) found that this item was actually easier for black than for white children.

2. *National norms are not appropriate when interpreting the scores of minority group members.* This criticism is an important one. Early IQ test developers did not use normative samples that sufficiently represented the various ethnic, racial, and other minority groups in the country. For example, Terman's normative sample for the Stanford-Binet consisted of Californians. Wechsler's initial normative sample for the Wechsler-Bellevue consisted primarily of Caucasian New Yorkers. If the normative sample does not include representative numbers of various geographic and socioeconomic groups, including racial, ethnic, and cultural minority groups,

then national norms may not be appropriate for use with members of minority groups.

One of the major improvements in the major IQ tests since their introduction in the first half of the 20th century has been to improve the representativeness of normative samples. Revised editions of the Stanford-Binet and Wechsler tests have made concerted efforts to employ national samples and to ensure that various geographic, socioeconomic, and minority groups are represented appropriately.

Of course, no normative sample can be perfect. The proportions of various minority groups in the population vary across time and localities. For example, Vietnamese and Hmong children are more heavily represented in U. S. schools in the 1990s than in the 1950s. Hispanic Americans are more prevalent in Southern California and the American Southwest than in the upper Midwest. For this reason, a normative sample, no matter how carefully selected to represent the national population, may not accurately reflect the population at a later time or in a specific region.

In addition, a national sample, even though it may include appropriate proportions of minority group members, may still be limited in its applications in a community with a different make-up. For example, suppose the national normative sample includes 12 percent African Americans—approximately the proportion of African Americans in the country. Suppose further that a psychologist plans to use the test in an inner city school system in a large urban area, where as many as 60 percent of the children are African American. In this case, use of the national norms may lead to a significantly high number of children being assessed in the mentally retarded range—more than the 3 percent figure that is found nationally.

For these reasons, tests that will be used to make important decisions concerning the treatment and education of clients should be well normed. Test developers should describe the characteristics of the normative sample and the populations for which the test is appropriate; test developers also should identify groups for which the test has not been normed and so may not be useful. Finally, intelligence tests, because they are used to help make such important decisions, such as diagnosing individuals as mentally retarded and placing children in special education programs, should report the norms for significant minority groups that may have received biased treatment from IQ tests in the past. Thus, many contemporary tests report norms for minority group children and many sources discuss how intelligence tests should be administered and interpreted with members of minority groups (e.g., Dana, 1993; Sattler, 1992).

3. *Minority group children may have less experience in taking standardized tests and so may not have the same motivation or test-taking skills as majority group members.* This argument suggests that members of minority groups have limited experience with standardized test situations, perhaps because of different interactions with their parents (such as less emphasis on word games or puzzle-solving) or fewer opportunities (say in preschool groups). If this occurs, then minority group members may perform more poorly than others on standardized tests, not because of lower intellectual levels, but because of poorer test-taking attitudes and skills.

According to Sattler (1992), there is little empirical evidence that either supports or refutes this argument, and so he suggested that psychologists conduct research on this topic.

4. *Minority group members who are tested by majority group examiners may experience difficulty due to problems in rapport and communication.* This criticism has been raised frequently since the 1960s. Most psychologists (just as most physicians, lawyers, and other professionals) are members of the majority group. Minorities are underrepresented in the professions. Thus, when a client from a minority group is assessed, it is probable that the client will be assessed by a member of the majority group. When differences occur in the race, ethnicity, or socioeconomic status between client and psychologist, the client is much more likely than the psychologist to be a member of a minority group.

Children have most of their social experiences with people who share their backgrounds—family, neighbors, friends. If a child comes from a minority group with its own dialect, slang, speech patterns, and other idiosyncracies, then the child is most likely to be able to interact successfully with someone from the same background. Thus, children are likely to perform more successfully when tested by someone from their own cultural background. Because minority group children are more likely than majority group children to be tested by an examiner from a different cultural background, the argument suggests that minority group children are discriminated against.

This argument, though compelling, has not typically been found to occur. Sattler and Gwynne (1982) examined research on the effect of examiner race on children's IQ test scores and found that most (25 of 29) studies did not find a relation between race of examiner and children's performance. In addition, research has shown that African American children do not perform better when tested by a black examiner using a black dialect than when they are tested by a white examiner (e.g., Quay, 1974).

Thus, although clinical psychologists should be sensitive to possible problems in rapport and communication that may occur when testing a client of a different racial or cultural background, there is little scientific reason to expect that such an occurrence necessarily leads to lowered test scores.

5. *Intelligence tests lead to the segregation of minority group members by placement in special classes that provide less adequate training than the regular classroom.* Since the 1954 Supreme Court Decision, *Brown* v. *Topeka Board of Education,* the country has recognized that the historical "separate but equal" model of educating racial minorities is a myth. Children who are placed in separate programs tend to experience lower self-esteem and decreased performance expectations (Kluger, 1975). Thus, placing minority children in separate educational programs because they are members of a minority group is likely to have harmful psychological and education consequences and is illegal.

However, placing children in a special educational program because they have a condition (such as mental retardation or a learning disability) that interferes with their ability to learn in the regular classroom is permissible and, indeed, is required by law! If children with handicapping conditions are placed in special educational programs, then they are likely to receive training that is superior to that available in the regular classroom.

The key issue is the efficacy of the intervention program. If children are placed in inadequate special education programs as a result of intelligence testing, the problem is not with the test but with the educational program. Psychologists should be sensitive to the possibility that a special education program may be inadequate and therefore arrange for follow-up evaluations to ensure that such placements have been effective.

SUMMARY

Clinical psychologists assess intellectual, academic, occupational, and other abilities for both scientific and applied reasons. Basic scientific research attempts to determine the dimensions, causes, and correlates of psychological abilities. In applied clinical settings, ability tests are used to assist both in diagnosing disorders and in planning clinical interventions.

Every society has evaluated its members' abilities. Ancient cultures often had "rites of passage" in which adolescents demonstrated their readiness to perform adult roles. Standardized tests were used in ancient China to ensure that civil servants were capable. In the 1700s and 1800s, some European scientists used cranial capacity (head size) as a measure of intelligence. By the late-1800s, psychologists had started to develop systematic methods for assessing psychological abilities.

Intelligence is one of the most important abilities assessed by clinical psychologists. Intelligence is the capacity both to learn from experience and to adapt to the environment. It includes both the general capacity for future learning and the ability to apply what one has already learned. Research shows that intelligence has both genetic and environmental influences. Hence, intelligence is malleable and can change over time as a function of training and experience.

The most reliable and valid intelligence tests are those that are administered individually and require at least one hour to complete, such as the Binet and Wechsler tests. Group and quick tests of intelligence (such as the Peabody Picture Vocabulary Test, Slosson Intelligence Test, and Draw-a-Man Test) are sometimes used as screening instruments to determine whether more extensive testing is required. However, they are not as reliable or valid as the individually administered tests, and should not be used to assign a formal diagnosis or to assign a client to a special education program.

In 1905, Alfred Binet developed the first modern intelligence test to distinguish between children who are retarded and nonretarded. The test was based on Binet's view that intelligence involves the ability to solve applied problems. Binet revised the test in 1908, reporting scores in the form of a mental age, which permitted the classification of children within both retarded and normal populations. Lewis Terman revised the test in 1916, translating it into English and reporting scores in terms of an intelligence quotient (IQ), which reflects the relation between a child's mental and chronological ages. Terman's version of the test, the Stanford-Binet, has been revised several times, and currently can be used with children or adults.

In 1939, David Wechsler published the next major individual intelligence test, the Wechsler-Bellevue Test. Wechsler argued that the concept of mental age does not apply to adults. For this reason, he measured adult intelligence in terms of a deviation IQ, a statistical measure in which intelligence is determined relative to one's age-peers. Unlike Binet, Wechsler conceptualized intelligence as consisting of two major types of abilities: nonverbal (performance) and verbal. The Wechsler-Bellevue consisted of six Verbal scales and five Performance scales. It provided a Full Scale IQ score, Verbal and Performance IQs, and scores on each separate scale. Wechsler has revised the test several times and extended it downward for use with children. The current versions of the Wechsler tests are the WAIS-R for adults, the WISC-III for children and adolescents, and the WPPSI-R for preschoolers. All of these tests follow the basic format of the Wechsler-Bellevue, with about a dozen subscales divided into verbal and performance sections.

Clinical psychologists also use several other individually administered intelligence tests. These include the Kaufman Assessment Battery for Children (K-ABC) and the McCarthy Scales of Children's Abilities (MSCA). The K-ABC is used with children from 2. 5 to 12. 5 years of age. It yields a Mental Processing Composite score, based on measures of both sequential and simultaneous processing, and an Achievement Score. The MSCA is used with children ages 2. 5 to 8. 5 years. It has 18 subtests, divided into five scales: Verbal, Perceptual-Performance, Quantitative, Memory, and Motor.

Clinical psychologists also frequently assess academic ability. Achievement tests assess current level of academic functioning and are useful in identifying academic strengths and weaknesses. Aptitude tests assess more general abilities and are used to predict future learning.

Individual tests of academic achievement are most frequently used by clinical psychologists when assessing clients who are experiencing academic problems. Individually administered tests of academic achievement include the Woodcock-Johnson Psycho-Educational Battery, the Peabody Individual Achievement Test, the Wechsler Individual Achievement Test, and the Wide Range Achievement Test—Revised.

Group tests of academic achievement are commonly used by schools for institutional reasons. Although clinical psychologists typically do not administer group tests of achievement, they should be familiar with such tests as the Iowa Tests of Basic Skills, Iowa Tests of Educational Development, and Metropolitan Achievement Tests.

Several academic aptitude tests are widely used by institutions to help guide admissions decisions. Although clinical psychologists do not typically administer these tests, they should be familiar with them. The major academic aptitude tests used are the ACT and SAT, which are used in college admissions decisions, and the GRE, which is used in graduate school admissions decisions.

Another kind of aptitude that psychologists assess is vocational aptitude. Vocational aptitude and interest tests are frequently used by counseling psychologists to help high school and college students identify career goals and training paths. They are also commonly used by industrial/organizational (I/O)

psychologists in large businesses or institutions to guide personnel selection decisions and to assign personnel to appropriate tasks. The assessment of career interests and aptitude occasionally arises in clinical work. Several of the more widely used tests of career interests and aptitude include the Strong Interest Inventory, the Kuder General Interest Survey, and the Jackson Vocational Interest Survey.

Neuropsychological testing is another important type of clinical assessment. Neuropsychological testing involves the assessment of cognitive and motor functioning in an effort to determine the extent and location of neurological impairment.

The two major neuropsychological assessment batteries are the Halstead-Reitan and the Luria Nebraska Neuropsychological Battery. Both have multiple subtests, require at least several hours to administer, and must be interpreted by a psychologist with specialized training. Research suggests that both of these batteries have at least moderate validity or ability to identify patients with neurological impairment.

In addition to these lengthy batteries, there are many scales that assess a single cognitive ability that may be affected by a neurological disorder and so are useful in neuropsychological assessment. Among these are the Boston Naming Test, which screens for aphasia; the Wisconsin Card Sorting Test, which assesses abstractive ability and cognitive perseveration; and the Wechsler Memory Scale, which assesses memory.

In addition to the lengthy batteries, there are also several widely used screens for neuropsychological impairment. These require less time and training to administer, and may be used by a clinical psychologist to determine whether more extensive neuropsychological testing is necessary. Perhaps the most well-known screen for visual–motor impairment is the Bender-Gestalt Test, which consists of nine simple line drawings that a client is asked to reproduce. Deviations from the designs, such as rotations, disproportion, and perseveration, are errors that suggest neurological impairment. Two other neurological screening instruments, which are newer and have somewhat better psychometric properties than the Bender-Gestalt Test, are the Clinical Tests of the

Sensorium and the Neuropsychological Impairment Scale.

The most important scientific issue concerning ability tests is the psychometric value of intelligence tests. In general, individually administered tests are highly reliable, with measures of internal consistency, interscorer reliability, and test-retest reliability in the 0.80s and 0.90s. These reliability coefficients tend to be higher than those of the quick and group intelligence tests. In addition, the reliability of intelligence tests tends to be lower in younger samples.

The general conclusions concerning the reliability of intelligence tests also hold for validity: (1) intelligence tests are generally valid; (2) individually administered intelligence tests tend to have greater validity than brief and group tests; and (3) intelligence tests tend to be more valid with older adolescents and adults than with younger adolescents and children.

Still, the validity of intelligence tests has often been criticized. It is important, when evaluating intelligence tests, to consider the way in which the test developer defined intelligence and intended the test to be used. Because intelligence can be defined in different ways, it is possible for an intelligence test to be a valid index of one definition of intelligence but not for another.

Ability tests are used in diagnosis and treatment planning. The diagnosis of mental retardation requires that one receives an IQ score at or below 70 on an individually administered test and that there be concurrent deficits in adaptive functioning. Similarly, the diagnosis of learning disability requires that the individual scores significantly below average on an individually administered test of achievement and that there be evidence of substandard performance in this subject in daily functioning. Quick and group tests, which have limited validity, are not sufficient for diagnosing retardation and learning disability. In addition, low test scores alone are not sufficient for diagnosing mental retardation and learning disability. The individual must also show significant deficits in daily functioning.

Ability tests are most often used in diagnosing mental retardation, learning disability, and other conditions that affect academic performance. They help ensure that children receive appropriate educational and clinical interventions. In addition, ability testing is often used with adult clients when there are questions about competence or deteriorative neurological condition. Finally, ability tests are sometimes used to help select forms of psychotherapy. For example, verbal and insight-oriented therapies are sometimes used with more intelligent clients, whereas more directive and concrete interventions are used with less capable clients.

A frequent criticism of ability testing of children is the possibility of a harmful labeling effect. Rosenthal's initial research suggested that labeling is powerful enough to influence children's performance in the classroom. However, more recent research has shown that the labeling effect is weaker and less consistent than was first thought. Still, clinical psychologists should be aware that labeling may occur and so take steps to minimize the impact of a hasty and possibly inaccurate label.

Perhaps the most widely raised criticism of ability tests is that they may be biased against members of minority groups. Intelligence tests have been criticized as biased against minorities in five ways: (1) culture bias; (2) inadequate norms; (3) different test-taking skills and attitudes across groups; (4) examiner–examinee racial effect; and (5) use of test scores to segregate minorities. Psychologists have responded to these criticisms by eliminating culturally loaded items, improving the representation of minorities in standardization samples, examining the extent to which minority groups exhibit different test-taking skills and obtain lower scores when tested by a majority group member, and ensuring that special education placement is done for the purpose of improving the educational quality of children with handicapping conditions. Still, test bias cannot be eliminated altogether, and so clinical psychologists should be aware of and attempt to limit these problems when using ability tests with minority group members.

1. Discuss early forms and examples of ability assessment. How were they similar to and different from contemporary methods of ability assessment?
2. Discuss the development of the modern intelligence test.
3. Compare and contrast the Binet and Wechsler intelligence tests.
4. Compare and contrast academic achievement and aptitude tests.
5. With what types of cases might a clinical psychologist administer tests of vocational aptitude and interest? Neuropsychological tests?
6. Summarize the psychometric value of individual versus group intelligence tests.

7. Discuss the importance of one's definition of intelligence when evaluating the validity of an intelligence test.
8. Discuss how contemporary diagnostic criteria for mental retardation and learning disability have addressed the criticisms of the validity of intelligence and academic achievement tests.
9. Discuss the problem of labeling. How have psychologists attempted to limit the influence of the labeling effect?
10. How have intelligence tests been criticized for being biased? What steps have psychologists taken to respond to these criticisms?

6

Behavioral Assessment

I. *History*
II. *Theory*
III. *The Interview*
   A. *The Clinical Interview*
   B. *The Structured Interview*
IV. *Behavioral Observation*
   A. *Naturalistic Observation*
   B. *Standardized Behavioral Assessment*
   C. *Behavior Checklists*
   D. *Self-Monitoring*
V. *Cognitive Assessment*

A. *Think Aloud*
B. *Cognitive Skills Assessment*
C. *Cognitive Self-Assessment*
VI. *Applied Issues*
   A. *Reactivity to Measurement*
   B. *Selection and Training of Observers*
VII. *Scientific Issues*
   A. *Assumptions of Behavioral Assessment*
   B. *Reliability and Validity of Behavioral*
     Assessment
VIII. *Summary*

Every society—even ancient cultures—developed methods of assessing their members' characters and abilities.

HISTORY

Before the development of formal personality testing at the beginning of the 1900s, many societies used informal methods of assessing behavior. For example, many cultures developed *rites of passage* in which adolescents proved their ability to perform adult tasks, such as hunting or sewing (Fried & Fried, 1980). Artistic guilds in the Renaissance required that apprentices exhibit their skill by completion of a major project. Universities since the 1600s required that students demonstrate their knowledge by writing and orally defending a thesis. In all of these cases, behavioral competency was being assessed

and so these represent early examples of behavioral assessment.

In the 1700s and 1800s, physicians formalized the assessment of patients through interviews and examinations. Clinical interviews are a form of behavioral assessment, since clinicians consider not only the client's verbal responses but also the client's nonverbal behavior to be important. For example, when physicians ask clients to track a moving object or move their arm in a circle, they are assessing behavior.

In the late 1800s, psychologists such as Galton, Wundt, and Cattell developed methods for measuring simple psychological processes. Although some of their methods tapped into mental processes (e.g., memory), other methods addressed behaviors (e.g., reaction time). As researchers such as Thorndike and

Pavlov began to systematically study basic learning processes in animals, they focused their attention on behaviors. By the time that Watson introduced the term *behaviorism* in 1913, it was clear that the assessment of behavior was a fundamental task of psychologists.

This chapter discusses behavioral assessment. It will present the theory of behavioral assessment and the distinctions between behavioral and other forms of assessment. In addition, the chapter discusses the major forms of behavioral assessment, including the interview and cognitive assessment.

THEORY
When John Watson introduced behaviorism in the second decade of the 1900s, he intended to make psychology more scientific by restricting its attention to the study of that which can be observed directly, namely behavior. This approach was welcomed by scientifically oriented psychologists who found the introspective techniques of Wundt's structuralists and Freud's psychoanalysts to be too subjective. Behaviorism rapidly became a major force among experimental psychologists because of its scientific rigor.

B. F. Skinner (1953) described the basic model of behavioral assessment, which he called *functional analysis.* According to Skinner, psychologists should explain behavior as a function of the environmental forces that act on the organism. These include the antecedent stimuli that occur prior to and serve as cues for the behavior and the consequent stimuli that occur after the behavior and serve to punish or reinforce it.

Skinner conceived of the organism as a *black box.* This term describes a complex mechanism whose internal workings are unseen. Observers can see the input entering and the output exiting the mechanism; however, what goes on within the mechanism is unknown. According to Skinner, people can be considered as black boxes. Psychologists observe the antecedent and consequent stimuli that act on the person (the input), and the behavior exhibited by the person (the output); however, what goes on within the person is unseen. According to Skinner, our inner processes are not a proper subject for study by psychologists. However, less radical behaviorists, such as the cognitive behaviorists, are very interested in these inner processes.

Behavioral assessment typically involves a *baseline period* during which a target behavior is monitored prior to an intervention. The baseline period sets a standard against which later behavior is compared and change is measured. In addition, the baseline period is used in conducting a Skinnerian functional analysis. The baseline may help the psychologist understand the characteristics of the problem behavior as well as identify the environmental stimuli associated with it.

A "user-friendly" way of conceptualizing the elements of a functional analysis was offered by Goldfried and Sprafkin (1976). They introduced the acronym, *SORC,* which stands for *S*ituational influences, *O*rganismic variables, *R*esponse characteristics, and *C*onsequences. In a behavioral assessment, the clinical psychologist gathers information concerning each of these areas.

For example, suppose a client presents with the problems of anger and aggression. Situational influences on the problem behaviors must be addressed. In what situations does the person lose his temper? With which people? At what times? Following what events?

Similarly, the organismic variables must be examined. This refers to physiological or internal conditions that are related to the problem behaviors. For example, does the loss of temper occur when the client is fatigued? Intoxicated? Sexually aroused? Emotionally upset?

Response characteristics refer to the dimensions of the problem behavior itself, such as its frequency, duration, intensity, and latency. How frequently does the client lose his temper? How soon does the person become angry after a provocation? How long does the anger outburst last? How severe is the aggressive behavior? Later in this chapter, methods of observing such features of the problem behavior will be described.

Finally, behavioral assessment also requires a description of the consequences of the problem behavior. What happens after the client loses his temper and becomes violent? How does the client feel?

How do others react? What does the client gain or lose? All of these speak to what Skinner referred to as the consequent variables that maintain the behavior.

Lazarus (1973) presented another way of organizing this material. Lazarus introduced the acronym BASIC ID to summarize the information gathered in a behavioral assessment. BASIC ID stands for *Be*haviors, *A*ffective processes, *S*ensations (such as emotional arousal and physiological conditions), *I*mages (such as painful memories), *C*ognitions, *In*terpersonal processes, and *D*rugs (by which Lazarus referred to biological factors—he substituted the word drugs simply to obtain a more memorable acronym). It is easy to see that Lazarus, by including cognitions and images, is a cognitive behaviorist rather than a radical behaviorist.

In some respects, behavioral assessment, as described so far, sounds similar to other types of assessment. After all, psychoanalytically and humanistically oriented psychologists will likely address most of these issues in their assessments.

However, behavioral assessment differs from other theoretical approaches to assessment in its concreteness and specificity. This has several advantages over other approaches to assessment. First, because behavioral assessment directly addresses the client's problem behaviors, it often has more face validity than traditional assessment; that is, it makes sense to the client to examine the problem behaviors directly. Second, because behavioral assessment attempts to identify factors that contribute to and maintain the problem behavior, it has direct treatment implications; once the factors that appear to be controlling the problem behavior are identified, it is a simple matter to target them for change in therapy. Third, because behavioral assessment addresses the client's overt behavior, it is easy to monitor change over the course of treatment; because behavioral changes can be observed by the client as well as the therapist, the client is in a better position to monitor the course of behavior therapy than in other forms of therapy.

For these reasons, behavioral assessment became popular and rapidly grew in influence from the 1950s on, the period when clinical psychologists in-

creased their use of empirically validated procedures (Wierzbicki, 1993a). One index of its rise in influence is the appearance of journals devoted to behavior assessment (*Behavioral Assessment, Journal of Behavioral Assessment*) and other journals (such as *Behavior Modification*) that address both behavior therapy and behavioral assessment. Today, behavioral assessment represents a major approach to assessment, with many behavioral assessment instruments. For example, Hersen and Bellack (1988) included almost 300 instruments in their *Dictionary of Behavioral Assessment Techniques*. The rest of this chapter discusses the major forms of behavioral assessment, including behavioral interviews, cognitive–behavioral methods, and more traditional behavioral assessment.

THE INTERVIEW

All clinicians, regardless of their theoretical orientation, conduct interviews. The interview has been characterized as the *main tool* used by psychiatrists to gain knowledge about their clients' problems (Freedman, Kaplan, & Sadock, 1976). I have included interviewing in this chapter as a form of behavioral assessment for two reasons. First, interviews comprise an active interaction between psychologist and client, in which the interviewer directs the session and gathers information about specific aspects of the client's functioning. Such an active and directive process is clearly in line with other behavioral techniques. Even though some psychologists may seek information that is not considered important by behaviorists (such as the content of one's dreams), the basic interview can be interpreted as a behavioral interaction. Second, all clinical psychologists, regardless of their theoretical orientation, consider the observations made of the client's nonverbal behaviors (e.g., interpersonal skill) as an important component of the interview.

Shea (1988) identified six goals of interviews: (1) establish an alliance (or rapport) with the client; (2) collect basic facts about the client; (3) develop an understanding of the client; (4) arrive at a tentative diagnosis; (5) develop a disposition–treatment plan; and (6) decrease the client's anxiety.

Shea's goals can be compressed into three major headings: (1) information gathering (both history and current functioning); (2) clinical conceptualization (including the symptomatology, etiology, pathology, prognosis, and recommended course of treatment); and (3) rapport building.

Of course, some situations require that more attention be paid to one or another of these areas. For example, in some cases, the interviewer's goal is to formulate a diagnosis and treatment recommendation, with treatment to be provided at another setting. In other cases, the goal of the interview is to establish a foundation for later psychotherapy with the same clinician. In the latter case, the psychologist may defer questions about certain topics or may not "push" the client to provide information about issues that are especially troubling, since the clinician will have many later sessions with the client when such information can be obtained.

The Clinical Interview

As noted above, clinical psychologists conduct interviews to gather information about the client's history and current problem. In practice, these two types of information are often obtained simultaneously. However, it is useful, for didactic purposes, to present them separately. Exhibit 6.1 presents an outline of the initial clinical interview.

The outline is straightforward and requires little elaboration. When first meeting a client, the clinical psychologist should spend a few minutes in basic introductions, both personal and professional. That is, the interviewer should introduce himself or herself, greet the client by name, engage the client in several minutes of conversation to initiate rapport and help make the client feel more at ease, and cover the purposes and guidelines under which the interview will be conducted. For example, the purpose of the interview (e.g, diagnosis and recommendations only, assessment as a preliminary step toward ongoing psychotherapy, evaluation of competency for a court, etc.) should be clarified beforehand. Similarly, the guidelines (cost, length, future relationship, ethical principles) should also be discussed. In my experience, these introductory matters usually take about 10 minutes.

It is then useful for the psychologist to begin with a general question concerning the client's presenting problem. What does the client perceive to be the problem? What is the client seeking from the psychologist? Although some clients may be unable to articulate their problem, most have at least some idea (even if it is not clearly developed or accurate) of what is bothering them. By spending a few minutes on the presenting problem, the clinical psychologist has the opportunity to form initial judgments about the client's verbal ability, insight, and psychological mindedness as well as get a preliminary idea of what to focus on in the remainder of the interview.

In addition, this preliminary stage of the interview permits the psychologist to make initial judg-

---

EXHIBIT 6.1   Outline of the Initial Clinical Interview

I. Introduction
   A. Personal Introductions
   B. Review of the Purpose and Guidelines of the Interview

II. Presenting Problem

III. History of the Problem
   A. Symptoms
   B. Onset, Course
   C. Previous Episodes (including treatment, outcome)
   D. Impact on Current Functioning (including social, family, and work)
   E. Methods Used to Cope

IV. Social History
   A. Family Background, Relationships
   B. Education/Work
   C. Social Relationships
   D. Legal Problems
   E. Substance Use
   F. Medical

V. Other
   A. Client's Strengths
   B. Client's Goals

VI. Summary
   A. Assessment Results and Recommendations
   B. Future Relationship with the Psychologist

ments as to whether the client is in crisis and requires immediate intervention. For example, clients who are psychotic, assaultive, suicidal, or experiencing drug withdrawal may be identified in the first few minutes of an interview. In such emergencies, the psychologist may have to discontinue the interview to obtain immediate treatment, such as admission to a hospital emergency room.

After hearing the client's perception of the major problem and ruling out the possibility of an emergency that requires immediate intervention, the psychologist then gathers information about the nature and history of the problem. When did the problem first develop? What were the circumstances in the client's life when the problem first appeared (e.g., did any stressful events occur at about the time the problem developed)? Has the problem followed a particular course (such as episodic, or gradual deterioration)? Has the problem worsened in the last few months? If so, did any changes occur in the client's life that coincided with the worsening of the condition? How does the problem affect the client's current functioning (including social, family, work/school, and other areas)? Has the problem affected the client's physical health? Has the client received any previous treatment for the presenting problem or other psychological problems? If so, with what result? How else has the client attempted to cope with the problem? Through these questions, the clinical psychologist should obtain a thorough picture of the client's view of the problem.

At this stage in the interview, the clinical psychologist then attends to the client's history. Of course, when reviewing the history of the presenting problem, the clinician may already have obtained information concerning social history (such as family background and work history); however, certain areas of the client's life may not have been covered. These blanks need to be filled in. As listed in Exhibit 6.1, the clinician should obtain information concerning several major topics in the client's history, including family, social, education/work, substance use, legal problems, and medical condition.

The order of topics covered should be considered flexible and can be modified as necessary to fit the flow of the session. In addition, different topics may be given more or less emphasis as dictated by the nature of the client's problems. For example, a client with a substance dependence disorder may have experienced legal and medical problems that must be addressed fully in the interview; a child with attention deficit hyperactivity disorder (ADHD) may have experienced birth complications and early developmental problems; a woman who is depressed because of a long history of physical abuse by her husband may have to be queried about her parents' marriage and her relationship with her parents. Thus, the clinician must be sensitive to the needs of the client and attend to research findings that indicate which factors may be associated with the client's disorder.

In addition to covering the client's problems, interviews should also attend to the client's strengths. What resources does the client have? What are the client's good points? What social support does the client receive? After discussing one's problems with a stranger, it is easy for a client to feel down toward the end of the interview. Focusing attention on the client's strengths is often helpful in overturning the negative affect that may develop following a lengthy discussion of problems. It is also useful, at this point, to ask the client about his or her goals. What would the client like to change? What does the client expect from the contact with the psychologist? Addressing the client's goals can provide closure to the interview and again set a positive tone for the end of the session.

Finally, before the end of the initial interview, the psychologist should clarify once more the relationship with the client. The client should be reminded how the information from the interview will be used and what the nature of the relationship with the psychologist will be. For example, in many cases, the interview will lead to a set of treatment recommendations; the client needs to know when the assessment results and treatment recommendations will be provided. If the recommended treatment will be provided by the psychologist, the client should know what the relationship with the psychologist will be (e.g., weekly one-hour individual psychotherapy sessions for 10 to 15 sessions). Exhibit 6.2 provides several segments from a clinical interview.

EXHIBIT 6.2   Segments of a Clinical Interview

Ms. R was a 50-year-old Caucasian woman who was referred for a diagnostic evaluation. She was dressed casually, wearing slacks and a large and poorly fitting t-shirt. Her hygiene was poor—her hair was mussed and she had a distinct body odor. After entering the examiner's office, she asked if she could keep the door propped open, saying she has "claustrophobia." Ms. R was obviously tense. She sat stiffly, leaning forward and gripping her knees with her hands. Periodically, she closed her eyes and took a few slow breaths before continuing. Several segments of the initial interview with Ms. R appear below.

INTERVIEWER (I):   The first thing I'd like to know is what you see as your major problem. What is it that brought you to a psychologist?
MS. R (R):   I can't get along with people. I don't like being around people. I have a short attention span. And I have claustrophobia.
I: What do you mean by you "can't get along with people"?
R: I have a lot of depression and nervousness. I withdraw from people. I don't answer the phone or go out. And when people talk to me, I get irritated and snap at them.
I: So when you say you don't get along with people, you mean that you get nervous around them?
R: Uh-huh.
I: What happens when you get irritated with people?
R: Huh?
I: What do you do when you get irritated? Do you have fistfights or yell?
R: No, I just get quiet and get away from them.
I: You said that you have a short attention span. What did you mean by that?
R: I have trouble remembering things.
I: Could you give me an example of your forgetting something?
R: Yeah. I went to the store and I got nervous. I couldn't remember the prices of the stuff I was getting.

In this opening segment, Ms. R reported that she is highly anxious, which was consistent with her evident physical tension. In addition, she reported

problems in interpersonal behavior that might be related to her anxiety. Note that Ms. R's language often was imprecise, requiring that the interviewer ask follow-up questions to clarify her meaning.

In the next part of the interview, Ms. R related the history of her problem. After being married, raising three children, and running a small business for many years, Ms. R's husband divorced her seven years ago. Since then, she gradually limited her social and recreational activities so that she no longer sees old friends. She also is no longer on good terms with her children and so sees them only infrequently. Ms. R reported that she has become increasingly reclusive over the past three years.

In the next segment of the interview, Ms. R described her daily activities.

I: What is a typical day like for you?
R: I stay at home and do my chores.
I: How exactly do you spend your time?
R: I do the laundry, clean house. I also play with my dogs.

[Several minutes followed during which the examiner asked about Ms. R's dogs—their breed, names, games, etc. It is sometimes useful to break the tension of an interview by addressing nonthreatening positive topics.]

I: What kinds of things do you do with other people?
R: I don't do anything with other people. I don't have any friends. My children won't visit.
I: Do you get out of the house?
R: No, I don't go anywhere.
I: What about shopping and other errands?
R: I shop about twice a month. I go at night to a store that's open 24 hours so it won't be crowded.
I: Do you go out for any social activities? To church? To walk your dogs?
R: I don't go to church. There's too many people there. I walk my dogs at night so I don't have to see anybody.
I: How do you get to the store? Do you drive?
R: Yeah, I don't mind driving. I feel safe in my car.

EXHIBIT 6.2   *Continued*

But I get nervous and sometimes have to pull over and stop. I was in an accident last month and am more worried about driving than I used to be.

In this part of the interview, Ms. R described some of the ways in which her daily activity is affected. She continues to care for herself, although her hygiene is evidently poor. However, her interpersonal behavior is clearly limited. It appears that her inability to get along with people, which she identified as her major problem, is a consequence of her anxiety. Ms. R's description of her social avoidance behavior sounds like agoraphobia, a disorder in which the individual experiences fear of panicking in unfamiliar surroundings and so limits one's activity outside the home. Because agoraphobia usually is associated with a history of panic episodes, in which the person experiences discrete periods of intense anxiety, the interviewer addressed the possible occurrence of panic episodes.

I: Do you know what it means to have a panic attack?
R: Oh, yeah. I have those all the time.

I: What happens to you when you have a panic attack?
R: My heart races. I sweat. I feel cold and faint. I feel like I'm gonna die.
I: How often do you have panic attacks?
R: Oh, pretty often.
I: When was the last one?
R: Three days ago, when I tried to eat dinner at a restaurant. I don't like crowds. I panicked. After a few minutes, I had to leave.
I: When do you have panic attacks? Is there a pattern you've noticed for when they occur?
R: I get them whenever I'm out. I don't like being around more than two people. I also get them in small rooms, like an elevator.

Ms. R acknowledged that she suffers panic attacks and that her social avoidance is the result of her effort to limit the occurrence of panic. This confirmed the diagnosis of Panic Disorder with Agoraphobia. As a result of the this diagnostic interview, it was recommended that Ms. R receive treatment for Panic Disorder with Agoraphobia.

In addition to asking about the client's presenting problem and history, the interviewer also must observe several important aspects of the client's behavior. Exhibit 6.3 summarizes the major areas in which the psychologist needs to observe the client's functioning. This assessment of the client's in-session functioning is sometimes called a *mental status examination.*

From the opening moments of the interview, the psychologist makes useful observations of the client's appearance. The psychologist should note the basic features of the client's appearance, such as height, weight, and phyiscal condition. Although these observations are not always relevant to the client's mental state, they are often helpful. For example, clients with eating disorders, neglected children, chronic substance abusers, and psychotic clients are frequently thin. Abused children frequently have bruises and other outward signs of repeated injuries. Neglected children, depressed clients, chronic substance abusers, and psychotic patients may exhibit poor hygiene and a disheveled appearance. Individuals with gender identity disorders may cross-dress. Psychotic individuals may exhibit other forms of odd appearance (I knew one schizophrenic individual who used cellophane tape to keep his eyes, ears, and nostrils wide open—his odd appearance was apparent from the moment I saw him).

The psychologist also should attend to the client's attitude and manner during the interview. Was the client compliant and cooperative? If not, why not? Clients may be uncooperative for many reasons. I have interviewed clients who were hostile and who openly refused to cooperate. I have seen clients who were depressed and could not answer questions because they could not stop crying. I have seen schizo-

---

EXHIBIT 6.3   Observations during the Interview

I. Appearance
   A. Physical Description (height, weight, age)
   B. Dress (neatness, cleanliness, age- and gender-appropriateness, neglect)
   C. Hygiene (hair, nails, teeth, odor)
II. Behavior and Attitude
   A. Compliance, Cooperativeness
   B. Activity Level
   C. Appropriateness of Activity
III. Verbal Behavior
   A. Expressive Language (clarity, vocabulary, appropriateness, ability to make self understood)

   B. Receptive Language
   C. Bizarre Language (loose associations, neologisms, echolalia, perseveration)
IV. Expressed Affect
   A. Range
   B. Intensity
   C. Appropriateness
V. Cognitive Processes
   A. Mental Stream (ability to follow a flow of ideas, remain on a subject)
   B. Reality Contact (e.g., delusions, hallucinations)
   C. Preoccupations
VI. Other

---

phrenic patients who were hallucinating and who responded more to their visions than to me. In each case, the nature of their noncompliant behavior was useful in conceptualizing their problem.

Also related to manner and attitude are the client's interpersonal skills. Does the client look the interviewer in the eye? Is the client friendly? Does the client follow the interviewer's lead, going from topic to topic and elaborating on responses when asked? These questions may help identify problems, such as schizophrenia or certain personality disorders, which are characterized by poor interpersonal skills. In addition, evaluating the client's cooperativeness can serve as a check on the validity of the client's verbal responses; just as structured personality inventories have scales that check the validity of test responses, the client's interpersonal behavior and manner can be used as a check on the validity of the information provided.

Other aspects of the client's behavior should also be addressed. For example, activity level and rate should be noted. Clients who are depressed, have certain neurological disorders, or are under the influence of certain drugs respond more slowly than other people. On the other hand, individuals who are in manic episodes, who are under the influence of stimulants, or who are experiencing marked distress

are more active and respond more rapidly than others. Children with ADHD may also spend much of an interview session out of their chair, looking around the room, or generally fidgeting; for example, I have seen children with ADHD who, within the first 20 seconds of the session, were out of their chair, playing with the light switch or pulling books off the shelf. Observations of such behaviors may help interviewers identify the type and severity of the client's problem.

The client's verbal behavior should also be evaluated. What vocabulary level does the client use and understand? Is this consistent with the client's age and education? Does the client understand questions? Can the client express thoughts clearly? Is the client's speech so loose or disconnected that it cannot be understood? Does the client speak in odd ways (such as vague metaphors)? Does the client use *neologisms* (i.e., words that a person makes up or uses in idiosyncratically)? The client's vocabulary level and receptive and expressive language abilities are useful indicators of one's general ability to function. If these verbal skills are deficient, the client may have mental retardation or a neurological condition that limits functioning. If a client's language abilities are inconsistent with his or her educational attainment or with previous assessments of these abilities, then this may suggest that a disorder is interfering significantly with the client's cognitive functioning; if language abilities are so affected, then it is likely that other cognitive abilities are also being disrupted. Other forms of language problems, such as *aphasia* (inability to identify objects) or *perseveration* (non-purposive repetition of words or phrases), suggest neurological problems.

Another important area observed by the interviewer is expressed affect. During the interview, has the client exhibited any strong emotions? How intense were these emotions? Were they appropriate to the situation? All of these questions may yield useful information. For example, clients who are depressed may have a sad facial expression or cry during the interview. Depressed clients, as well some schizophrenic and organic disorder patients, may exhibit flat or blunted affect, showing little or no emotional responsiveness even when such a response is appropriate. I have interviewed clients who have impulse control problems and histories of violent and illegal activity; such individuals may be quick to exhibit intense anger. Individuals who are intoxicated, manic, or schizophrenic may be silly, giggling frequently and inappropriately. Again, observation of the client's emotion, its severity, and its appropriateness may often help clarify the nature and severity of the client's disorder.

Finally, the psychologist should evaluate the client's thought processes. For example, does the client exhibit a problem in his or her mental stream? Can the client follow the flow of conversation? Does the client become distracted? Is the client's mental stream disconnected, jumping from topic to topic? Is the client's thinking tangential? Does the client recognize cause–effect relationships? Are the client's perceptions of the world accurate? Does the client exhibit bizarre thought processes, such as delusions? The psychologist should also assess the client's abstractive abilities. Is the client's use of abstract concepts appropriate for his or her age and education? Is the client's speech circumstantial? Problems with abstractive abilities are often associated with neurological disorders and with other severe forms of psychopathology, including schizophrenia.

Exhibit 6.4 provides several examples from clinical practice of how observations made during an initial interview helped to understand a client's disorder.

The Structured Interview

Clinical interviews involve both information gathering and behavioral observations. As with any form of assessment, the reliability and validity of both aspects of interviews must be examined. It is possible that the client's report is inaccurate or that the psychologist's observations are unreliable. Thus, information obtained through clinical interviews should be regarded like any other information obtained during assessment—as data of uncertain validity. As with other forms of psychological assessment, the psychologist should attempt to verify the information gathered through the clinical interview via independent sources, such as the client's family members or through standardized testing.

A recent development to enhance the reliability and validity of interviews is the *structured interview*. A structured interview is one in which the interviewer follows a script that determines, not only the wording of questions, but also the sequence of questions, depending on the client's responses. In this way, interviewers ask the same questions in the same order, and ask the same follow-up questions given a particular response.

One of the first structured interviews was the Schedule for Affective Disorders and Schizophrenia (SADS; Endicott & Spitzer, 1978). The SADS was based on the Research Diagnostic Criteria (RDC; Spitzer, Endicott, & Robins, 1978), an experimental set of criteria used to diagnose psychopathology that was widely investigated in the 1970s as an alternative to the existing diagnostic system. The SADS is divided into two parts that address current and prior problems. Clients are asked a series of questions about the occurrence and severity of various symptoms. Each response is rated, generally on a 5- or 6-point scale. The SADS usually takes from 90 minutes to 2 hours to administer. Based on the SADS, the psychologist can determine whether the client meets the criteria for more than 20 diagnostic categories.

EXHIBIT 6.4   Examples of Useful Observations Made in Initial Interviews

About one week before writing this chapter, I interviewed a 30-year-old woman who presented to a clinic because of sleep difficulties and panic episodes, subsequent to her recent move to a new city. In the opening minutes of the interview, I observed that she was perspiring profusely, even though the room was not overly warm. From this, I inferred that she was experiencing significant distress and, perhaps, even physical discomfort. It turned out that the woman had recently discontinued using drugs following a 10-year history of daily intoxication and was experiencing significant distress due to her craving.

In another interview conducted about one week before writing this chapter, I saw a 10-year-old boy who was referred by his parents (and the school system) for academic problems and possible ADHD. The boy reportedly had difficulty attending to school lessons and had suffered a decline in academic performance in the last year. When I asked the boy's mother to summarize the presenting problem, the boy started crying—not at all a common response for 10-year-old boys. The boy continued to cry, on and off, throughout the rest of the session. During an extended period in which I worked individually with the boy, attempting to test his intellectual and academic skills, the boy cried and refused to comply. Although formal results from IQ and

achievement testing could not be obtained during the initial session, the boy's affective response suggested that the problem was depression rather than an academic or intellectual problem.

Several years ago, I saw a 27-year-old woman college student who presented at the psychology department's clinic for problems with depression. My opening question was "What brings you to the clinic?" She responded, "A car." Although this is a legitimate answer to the question, it is a highly concrete response indicating that she had not understood the more abstract question implied, "*why* are you coming to the clinic?" Such concrete thinking is uncommon among college students and suggested that she may have a problem with her thought processes. I eventually learned that the client had experienced a schizophrenic episode about eight months previously and had been treated successfully with medication. The woman had stopped taking the medication when she moved to a new city to attend college, and was beginning to experience a worsening of her symptoms. I brought the woman to the student health center to obtain a prescription for antipsychotic medication, and continued to see her in therapy to address issues of coping with the daily problems of being a college student in a new city.

Spitzer and colleagues (1978) reported the results of several studies of the reliability of the SADS. In two studies of inter-rater reliability, Spitzer and colleagues found that *Kappa coefficients* (measures of agreement, independent of chance, on assignment to categories) for diagnoses ranged from 0.68 to 1.00. In a study of test–retest reliability for diagnoses assigned by different diagnosticians over a 1- to 2-day interval, Spitzer and colleagues found that Kappa coefficients ranged from 0.40 to 1.00.

The SADS is also available in a format designed to assess an individual's lifetime history of mental disorders (the SADS-L). Spitzer and colleagues (1978) reported that the inter-rater reliability of diag-

nosis was high (Kappas ranging from 0.46 to 1.00) when the SADS-L was administered to first-degree relatives of patients.

In summary, the reliability of the SADS was significantly higher than that of the formal diagnostic system. For this reason, Spitzer and colleagues (1978) concluded that basing psychiatric diagnoses on operational criteria is "an idea whose time has come."

Because of the success of the SADS, psychologists soon introduced other structured diagnostic interviews. For example, a version of the SADS was developed for children and adolescents, referred to as the *Kiddie-SADS* (or K-SADS; Chambers et al.,

1985). Using the K-SADS, the psychologist interviews the parent(s) first and then the child or adolescent. According to Chambers et al. (1985), affective disorders can be reliably diagnosed in children and adolescents using the K-SADS.

Another widely used structured interview is the Structured Clinical Interview for DSM-III-R (SCID; Spitzer, Williams, Gibbon, & First, 1990). The SCID is an elaboration of the SADS and RDC, and was originally designed to elicit sufficient information to establish diagnoses according to DSM-III criteria (American Psychiatric Association, 1980). The SCID has since been revised along with the diagnostic system. The SCID is currently available in a nonpatient edition (as a screen for psychological disorders or for use in general populations in epidemiological research) and in a form for evaluation of personality disorders. In addition, responses on the SCID can be recorded on a form that can be scored by machine, enhancing the speed and accuracy of interpretation. Currently, the SCID is perhaps the most widely used structured interview in both research and applied clinical settings.

Other structured interviews are available for the diagnosis of a range of disorders, such as the Diagnostic Interview Schedule (DIS; Robins, Helzer, Croughan, & Ratcliff, 1981) and the Diagnostic Interview Schedule for Children (DISC; Costello, Edelbrock, Dulcan, & Kalas, 1984). In addition, other structured interviews are available that assess specific forms of psychopathology. For example, Morrison (1988) listed structured interviews for diagnosing anxiety disorders, depression, and personality disorders, among others.

Structured interviews ensure that the same topics are covered and that certain responses are followed up in the same way. Because structured interviews are more standardized than traditional interviews, they should yield more reliable results. This is exactly what research to date has found. In a review of the research on the reliability of psychiatric diagnosis, Wierzbicki (1993a) noted that structured interviews, such as the SADS, yielded higher reliability coefficients than was found in most previous studies of diagnosis based on traditional assessment methods. In addition, the success of the SADS

(and the RDC) led to its being incorporated to a substantial degree in DSM-III (American Psychiatric Association, 1980) and its subsequent revisions (Wierzbicki, 1993a).

BEHAVIORAL OBSERVATION

Since the 1950s, behavioral observation has become an important clinical assessment technique. As will be discussed in Chapter 11, behavior modification was widely recognized as an effective form of intervention in the 1960s and 1970s. An essential step in effective behavior modification is behavioral observation. Thus, with the rise of behavior therapy (Goldfried & Davison, 1976; Rimm & Masters, 1974; Yates, 1970), behavioral observation methods became a crucial part of the training of clinical psychologists.

Foster, Bell-Dolan, and Burge (1988) discussed five elements of effective behavioral observation: (1) selecting, (2) defining, (3) recording, (4) training judges to observe, and (5) evaluating the reliability of observations of the observed behavior.

It should be clear that the first step in behavioral observation is to select the behavior to be observed. However, what may be less clear is that sound clinical judgment plays a key role in this selection. Early critics of behavior therapy attacked behavioral assessment for focusing on trivial behaviors unrelated to actual clinical disorders.

For example, suppose a couple seeks treatment for a sexual dysfunction such as premature ejaculation. Suppose further that, during the course of the initial interview, the couple expresses significant hostility toward each other, making numerous derogatory remarks about one another. If a behavior therapist is not attuned to the quality of the relationship, ignores the possibility that the poor relationship may be contributing to the sexual dysfunction, and simply attempts to identify environmental stimuli that occur before and after the sexual dysfunction, any therapy based on the behavioral assessment is likely to be ineffective.

Thus, the first step in behavioral observation is to select the target behavior. The target behavior should be relevant to the client's problem. Often, this relevance will be clear from the client's own presentation of the problem; that is, the target behavior has face validity (e.g., number of cigarettes smoked for a client who wishes to stop smoking). However, in other cases, the relevance may not be based on the client's presentation of the problem but through empirical research on the client's disorder (e.g., assessing couple communication when their presenting problem is a sexual dysfunction).

The next step in behavioral observation is to define the target behavior. The behavior must be defined so that it is measurable and clinically relevant. For example, a depressed college student may complain that he "does not know who he is anymore." This complaint is vague and hard to define in measurable terms. However, other symptoms of depression are readily observed and can be targeted for behavioral assessment; for example, the number of mornings the student oversleeps, the number of classes skipped, the number of times late to class, the number and kind of social contacts, and so on.

An important issue in defining the target behavior is to determine the context in which the behavior will be observed. Some problems occur in private settings (e.g., sexual dysfunctions, nightmares) or involve mental processes (e.g., obsessive thoughts) and so are not readily accessible to an outside observer. Some problems occur relatively infrequently (e.g., binge drinking), making it impractical for an outside observer to monitor the client continually until the target behavior occurs. Some problem behaviors show high *reactivity* to observation, meaning that they occur less frequently in the presence of others or when clients know they are being observed. In such cases, the psychologist must determine the context in which observations will be made (natural environment, structured clinical setting, simulation) and the person who will serve as the observer (psychologist, client, significant other).

After the target behavior has been selected and defined, the next step is to record it. The target behavior should be recorded along a relevant clinical dimension. In this way, the recording may consist of frequency (number of occurrences), rate (number of occurrences in a time period), duration (length of occurrence), intensity (strength of occurrence), nature (type of response), latency (delay between a stimulus and the problem response), or other dimension. For example, a client who wishes to stop smoking cigarettes may record the number of cigarettes smoked during an assessment period; the relevant dimension in this case is frequency. However, for a child who has difficulty attending in the classroom, the most relevant behavioral dimension is time engaged in on-task behavior; here, the observer records how much time the child spends attending versus not attending.

In some cases, the behavior may be recorded mechanically. For example, psychophysiological recording equipment has been used to monitor a variety of physical responses, such as heart rate, blood pressure, and muscle tension. Other devices have been used to measure specific behaviors, such as overactivity in a child with ADHD (e.g., Tryon, 1984) or the number of steps taken by one who is trying to lose weight. Such devices simplify data collection, eliminating the need for an observer. Still, such devices must be tested for reliability and selected following a judgment that they are valid instruments for the client's problem.

The context in which the problem behavior occurs may influence the choice of observer. For many cases, the problem behavior will be observed by a trained professional; for example, it is routine in many clinical training programs to have graduate students observe a child's behavior in the classroom. I have occasionally observed a family's interaction in their home. However, depending on the nature of the problem, it is sometimes more appropriate to have an observer other than a psychologist. For example, for many childhood problems, the child's parents or teachers may serve as observers. For many habit disorders in adults (e.g., smoking, overeating), it may be appropriate to have the client or a significant other (e.g., spouse, roommate) serve as the observer.

The final step in making behavioral observations is to ensure that the observations are reliable. In some cases, behavioral assessment techniques are used that have already been shown to have adequate reliability. In such cases, judges must follow the published training procedures to ensure that they use the observation system in the way it was intended.

In other cases, it may be necessary to conduct a reliability check on the raters. Two or more raters can independently observe the target behavior so that inter-rater reliability coefficients can be calculated. In some cases, it may be necessary to train judges in use of the technique until they demonstrate sufficiently high reliability so that their ratings can be useful.

Naturalistic Observation

Naturalistic observation involves observation of the target behavior in its natural setting. For example, psychologists may observe a family interaction in the home, children's behavior in the classroom, children's social behavior on the playground, or inpatients' social behavior in the dayroom of a psychiatric ward.

Naturalistic observation is feasible when the problem behavior occurs frequently, in the presence of others, and is not so reactive to observation that an observer would significantly alter the occurrence of the behavior. Many instruments have been developed to help psychologists make naturalistic observations.

For example, the Observational Record of Inpatient Behavior (ORIB; Rosen, Tureff, Daruna, Johnson, Lyons, & Davis, 1980) assesses eight ward behaviors of psychiatric inpatients. It was designed for use in studies of the effects of medication on inpatients and includes measures of simple motor activity (e.g., body activity, extremity activity, scanning), social activity (e.g., proximity to others, social interaction, laughing/smiling, group activity), and idiosyncratic behavior (e.g., bizarre behavior or talking to oneself). The observer monitors a patient for 5 seconds, noting the occurrence or nonoccurrence of each behavior during the next 20 seconds, and then repeats this process nine times. According to Rosen (1988), the ORIB has good inter-rater reliability (mean $r = 0.87$) following a 3-week training period. In addition, Rosen (1988) also noted that the ORIB has good validity; for example, the ORIB can distinguish normals from patients, various patient groups, drug classes administered to patients, and responders versus nonresponders to medication.

Perhaps the most well-known behavioral method for assessing family interactions is the Family Interaction Coding System (FICS; Patterson, Ray, Shaw, & Cobb, 1969). The FICS was originally developed to assess interactions in families with children with conduct disorders. It is a system of coding 29 types of behavior, including common childhood problem behaviors (such as crying) and both positive and negative parental responses (such as approval and disapproval). The observer typically goes to the family's home and observes each family member for at least five minutes. Every six seconds, the observer records the behaviors exhibited by the targeted family member and the response of the other family members. With training, observers can achieve better than 80 percent agreement on coding most categories (Jones, Reid, & Patterson, 1975). In addition, FICS ratings discriminate between children with and without conduct problems, are correlated with parents' ratings of children's problems, and are associated with independent ratings of clinical improvement (Moore, 1988).

Several methods are available for assessing children's behavior in the classroom. For example, Abikoff, Gittelman-Klein, and Klein (1977) published a system for assessing the classroom behavior of children with ADHD. The observer monitors the child's behavior during predetermined time periods and codes the behaviors in 14 categories (such as moving around the classroom). Abikoff et al. reported that 12 of the 14 categories of behavior significantly discriminated between children with ADHD and children without ADHD.

Other naturalistic observation methods are used to assess specific clinical disorders, including agoraphobia (Williams, 1985), acrophobia (Williams & Watson, 1985), and self-injurious behavior in inpatients (Schroeder, Rojahn, & Mulick, 1978).

Standardized Behavioral Assessment

Another type of behavioral assessment is *standardized behavioral assessment*. Here, the psychologist observes the client's behavior in a standardized setting rather than its natural setting. This approach is more convenient than naturalistic observation because assessment can be conducted in a clinic or laboratory, rather than in the client's home or school.

The standardized setting can take several forms. First, it is possible for the psychologist to simulate the natural environment as closely as possible in the treatment setting. Perhaps the most well-known example of such a simulated environment is the work of Sobell, Schaefer, and Mills (1972), who observed the drinking behavior of males who are alcoholic and nonalcoholic in a simulated cocktail bar. They showed that, compared to the control group, alcoholics drink more, sip larger amounts, drink more rapidly, and select more straight drinks. Although few clinical psychologists in private practice have the resources to simulate the natural environment as realistically as did Sobell and colleagues (1972), their work is notable for its effort to observe a problem behavior in a standardized environment.

A more frequently used method of observing behavior in a standardized setting is role playing. Here, the client is presented with a problem situation and must show how he or she would behave in the situation. The problem situation may be presented orally (the psychologist reads a vignette), visually (the client observes a film or videotape), or behaviorally (the psychologist enacts the role of another person). In each case, the client responds to the problem situation while the psychologist observes the client's behavior.

An example of this is the Behavioral Assertiveness Test–Revised (BAT–R; Eisler, Hersen, Miller, & Blanchard, 1975), which consists of 32 items that describe situations in which nonassertive individuals often experience difficulty. Each situation is read by the psychologist (or presented by audiotape) and the client demonstrates how he or she would respond. The client's behaviors are videotaped for later scoring along several dimensions: nonverbal assertive behaviors, positive and negative assertive content, and global assertiveness. BAT-R scores are related to clinical judgments of assertiveness, clinical improvement following assertiveness training, and skills deficits in patient populations (Eisler, 1988).

Role-play assessment techniques have been developed to assess many other target behaviors, in-

cluding children's assertiveness (Bornstein, Bellack, & Hersen, 1977), children's fears (Esveldt-Dawson, Wisner, Unis, Matson, & Kazdin, 1982), children's social skills (Williamson, Moody, Granberry, Letherman, & Blouin, 1983), and adults' social skills (Rehm & Marston, 1968; Twentyman & McFall, 1975).

Another type of behavioral assessment involves giving the client a standardized task and then observing the client's behavior. This can readily be done in a clinic or laboratory. The standardized task may consist of solving a problem, interacting with others, delivering a monologue describing oneself, or other common tasks.

For example, the Marital Interaction Coding System (MICS; Weiss & Summers, 1983) was modeled after the FICS and is used to assess the behavioral interaction of married couples. The observer directs a couple to resolve a series of problems and then monitors the couple's discussion, coding each response in 32 categories (such as blame, facilitation). Although the MICS requires that observers be highly trained, once judges attain proficiency in coding, the MICS can distinguish between distressed and nondistressed couples and is sensitive to improvements over the course of marital therapy (Tennenbaum, 1988).

Hetherington, Stouwie, and Ridberg (1971) introduced a similar method for assessing family interactions, the Family Conflict and Dominance Code (FCDC). A family is presented with a problem to solve. After each member provides an individual response, the family is then brought together to discuss the problem until it achieves a mutually agreeable solution. The interaction is audiotaped and later scored along several scales for conflict (e.g., interruptions, simultaneous speech, disagreements) and dominance (e.g., speaking first, speaking last, passive acceptance of solution). Hetherington and colleagues reported that the FCDC significantly distinguished among nondelinquent and delinquent families, including several subtypes of delinquents.

Behavior Checklists

In addition to direct observation of a client's behavior, another widely used form of behavioral assessment is the *behavior checklist.* A behavior checklist consists of a list of behavioral symptoms that are marked as present or absent. Behavior checklists are sometimes referred to as *behavior rating scales,* when target behaviors are rated for severity or frequency, along a scale with clearly defined anchors (e.g., 1 = never; 5 = always).

Behavior checklists are completed by someone who knows the client well and can judge whether the client exhibits each symptom, such as a parent, teacher, clinician, or hospital ward staff member. In some cases, checklists are completed by the client as a form of self-assessment.

Behavior checklists are easy to administer and so are usually less time-consuming, expensive, and labor-intensive than direct behavioral observation (Aiken, 1996). Also, because behavior checklists have many items with only a small number of possible answers, it is relatively simple to develop checklists that have sound psychometric properties.

The disadvantage of behavior checklists is that they are often completed by nonprofessionals who are less skilled observers than trained psychologists. Thus, when using behavior checklists, it is important to make sure that raters have sufficient contacts with the clients so as to be able to evaluate them and that raters receive the standardized instructions to ensure that published reliability and validity information apply.

Behavior checklists have been widely used in the assessment of children. Children are usually referred by adults (parents, teachers) who have observed the children's problems. In addition, children's problem behaviors are often situation specific (e.g., conflicts with siblings, inattention in the classroom) and so are difficult for the clinical psychologist to observe directly.

Perhaps the most widely used and best documented checklist for assessing childhood problems is the Child Behavior Checklist (CBCL; Achenbach, 1978; Achenbach & Edelbrock, 1979). The CBCL lists over 100 behaviors to be rated on a 3-point scale for frequency of occurrence. It is now available in teacher-, parent-, and self-report forms. The CBCL yields scores on two general dimensions of childhood problems (Internalizing and Externalizing)

along with nine specific problems. Internalizing problems are those in which the child experiences emotional, cognitive, or somatic symptoms. Externalizing problems are those in which the child's behavioral symptoms cause problems for those around the child (such as aggression, overactivity, delinquency). Since its introduction, the CBCL has become widely used in both clinical and research settings. It provides scores of both general and specific childhood problems with high reliability. In addition, validity studies have consistently found that CBCL scores are meaningfully related to children's clinical problems.

Another commonly used behavior checklist for childhood problems is the Revised Behavior Problem Checklist (RBPC; Quay & Peterson, 1987). The RBPC consists of 89 items to be rated by parents or teachers. The RBPC yields scores on six factors: Conduct Disorder, Socialized Aggression, Anxiety Withdrawal, Psychotic Behavior, Motor Excess, and Attention Problem. Lahey and Piacentini (1985) judged the RBPC to have good psychometric properties and considered the RBPC to be one of the most widely researched and used behavior rating scales.

In addition to the CBCL and RBPC, which were developed to assess a broad range of childhood problems, many behavior checklists have been developed to assess a single problem or a narrow range of problems. Of these, perhaps the most commonly used are several rating scales developed by Conners (1969, 1970, 1973; Goyette, Conners, & Ulrich, 1978). These scales were developed primarily for the purpose of discriminating between children with ADHD and nondisabled children and have been widely used in drug studies of the effects of stimulant medication for children with ADHD. They can be completed by parents or teachers in only a few minutes. Reliability and validity of these scales are generally good.

Other child behavior checklists that assess single problems or narrower ranges of problems include: the Devereux Child Behavior Rating Scale (DCBRS; Spivack & Spotts, 1965), to evaluate children in a residential treatment center; the Eyberg Child Behavior Inventory (ECBI; Eyberg, 1980), to assess conduct disorders; and the Childhood Autism

Rating Scale (CARS; Schopler, Reichler, DeVellis, & Daly, 1980), to evaluate preschool-aged children in 15 areas associated with autism.

Behavior checklists and rating scales are also widely used to assess problem behavior in adult clients. For example, the Nurse's Observational Scale for Inpatient Evaluation (NOSIE-30; Honigfeld, Gillis, & Klett, 1966) is a 32-item checklist designed to assess ward behavior of psychiatric inpatients. Nurses and other ward staff rate patients on 32 behaviors (e.g., shows interest in activities around him, refuses to speak) on a 5-point scale. The NOSIE-30 yields scores on several scales, such as Social Competence, Psychosis, and Total Assets. Honigfeld et al. showed that the NOSIE-30 was useful in monitoring inpatients' improvement over the course of hospitalization. Aiken (1996) also judged the NOSIE-30 to be useful for assessing inpatients' aggressive, communicative, and cooperative behaviors.

Many other behavior checklists have been developed so that adult clients can rate themselves. These are addressed in the next section of the chapter.

Self-Monitoring

Self-evaluation has several advantages over observation by others. Some problem behaviors occur privately or so infrequently that it is not practical to have another person serve as observer. Even if another person can serve as observer, there may be practical advantages to having clients monitor their own behavior; for example, self-monitoring may increase clients' awareness of the problem behavior and so enhance later interventions.

There are two main approaches to behavioral self-assessment. First, clients can monitor their behavior as it occurs. Second, they can complete a behavioral checklist or rating scale.

I have used behavioral self-monitoring in several treatment contexts. For example, one symptom of depression is decreased activity level. Both cognitive–behavioral (e.g., Beck, Rush, Shaw, & Emery, 1979) and behavioral (e.g., Lewinsohn, Biglan, & Zeiss, 1976) therapy for depression recognize that it is important to increase activity. This is generally done following a baseline recording period in which clients monitor their daily activities.

For example, clients can use a form like that in Exhibit 6.5 to record their activities during the week. The major activity in every hourly period is recorded, along with ratings of the mastery and pleasure afforded by the activity. If it is inconvenient to record this information hourly, then clients can schedule a few periods during the day (such as a morning coffee break) to record several hours at a time. Clients should use only a word or phrase to summarize each activity, lest the writing become so cumbersome that the task is not completed.

After two weeks of self-monitoring, it may become clear to the therapist (and often to the client as well), that activities are related to mood. For example, some depressed clients feel fulfilled at work but are lonely and sad when alone at home in the evenings and on weekends; other depressed clients are happy at home with family but dread being at work during the day. I have seen clients who recognized such patterns after completing an activity schedule for two weeks. These patterns can then be used to target specific behaviors for intervention. For example, the client may be encouraged to initiate more social activities, more recreational activities at home, more pleasant social encounters at work, more activities that will give a sense of accomplishment at home, and so on.

Another form of behavioral self-monitoring is used in weight loss programs. Research has repeatedly shown that the most effective psychological treatment for obesity is behavior therapy in which clients learn to modify their eating and activity behaviors (Yates, 1975). One of the more effective behavioral treatment programs for obesity is that of Stuart (1971; Stuart & Davis, 1973). Stuart's treatment program includes self-monitoring of daily calory intake and activity. Following a baseline period, patterns in the client's eating and exercise behaviors may become apparent and are targeted for change. The focus is on gradual weight loss (from 1 to 2 pounds per week) produced by moderate changes in eating and exercise. The hope is that, by training the client to lose weight through eating and exercising in moderation (rather than through drastic measures,

EXHIBIT 6.5 Example of a Daily Activity Self-Monitoring Form

Activity Record

	Sunday	Monday	Tuesday	Wednesday	Thursday	Friday	Saturday
8:00 A.M.							
9:00 A.M.							
10:00 A.M.							
11:00 A.M.							
12:00 Noon							
1:00 P.M.							
2:00 P.M.							
3:00 P.M.							
4:00 P.M.							
5:00 P.M.							
6:00 P.M.							
7:00 P.M.							
8:00 P.M.							
9:00 P.M.– Bedtime							

Use a word or phrase to indicate your major activity in each time period. Then, rate the activity on a 5-point scale for both Pleasure (1 = Not at all pleasurable, 5 = Very pleasurable); and Mastery (1 = No sense of master accomplishment, 5 = Very high sense of mastery, accomplishment).

such as fasting or vigorous exercise programs), it will be easier for the client to continue engaging in these modified behaviors and maintain the weight loss after meeting the original goal.

Many other self-monitoring techniques have been used, including counting cigarettes smoked, recording symptoms of fear and panic, assertiveness, and countless other behaviors.

Another form of behavioral self-assessment uses behavior checklists or rating scales. Because checklists are quick, practical, and frequently have good psychometric properties, they have experienced a large increase in popularity since the 1950s.

One checklist that I have found useful in psychotherapy research is the Symptom Checklist (SCL-90; Derogatis, 1977). The SCL-90 consists of 90 items, each reflecting a symptom to be rated on a 5-point scale for severity in the last week. The SCL-90 yields scores on nine scales (Somatization, Obsessive-Compulsive, Interpersonal Sensitivity, Depression, Anxiety, Hostility, Phobic Anxiety, Paranoid Ideation, and Psychoticism). In addition, the SCL-90 yields an overall score that can be used as an index of general distress or symptomatic severity.

Perhaps the most widely used self-rating forms today are symptom checklists designed to assess specific sets of symptoms. For example, a widely used instrument in both clinical and research settings is the Beck Depression Inventory (BDI; Beck et al., 1979; Beck, Ward, Mendelson, Mock, & Erbaugh, 1961). The BDI consists of 21 items, each concerning a symptom of depression (e.g., suicidal thinking, appetite loss, sleep difficulty, crying). BDI items are multiple-choice, with statements reflecting different levels of severity of a symptom (absence, mild, moderate, severe). Clients select the statement that best reflects the severity of the symptom.

Beck, Steer, and Garbin (1988) reviewed 25 years of research using the BDI and concluded that its psychometric properties—internal consistency, test–retest reliability, and criterion-related validity—are high. Thus, when it is clear that a client's problem is in the area of depression, the BDI is a useful tool for determining the severity of depression and for assessing changes in severity of depression over the course of treatment.

Many other self-rating symptom or behavior checklists are now widely used by clinical psychologists. Exhibit 6.6 lists several of the more commonly used instruments.

EXHIBIT 6.6   Commonly Used Self-Rating Symptom or Behavior Checklists

Problem	Instrument	Reference
Anger	State-Trait Anger Scale	Spielberger, Jacobs, Russel, & Crane (1983)
Alcoholism	Michigan Alcoholism Screening Test	Selzer (1971)
Anxiety	State-Trait Anxiety Inventory	Spielberger, Gorsuch, & Lushene (1970)
Bulimia	Bulimia Test	Smith & Thelen (1984)
Depression	Beck Depression Inventory	Beck et al. (1961)
Fear	Fear Survey Schedule—II	Geer (1965)
Marital Problems	Marital Happiness Scale	Azrin, Naster, & Jones (1973)
Sexual Behavior	Sexual Behavior Inventory	Bentler (1968a, 1968b)

COGNITIVE ASSESSMENT

As presented in Chapter 3, an important contemporary variant of behaviorism is cognitive–behaviorism. Cognitive-behaviorists have adapted many behavioral assessment techniques for assessing cognitions. Because cognitive assessment techniques are often derived from behavioral methods, it is appropriate to consider cognitive assessment in this chapter on behavioral assessment.

Think Aloud

Cognitive processes are not directly observable by an outsider. However, the clinical psychologist can present the client with a problematic situation and ask the client to think aloud: "What would go through your mind if you faced this problem? What would you say to yourself while contemplating what you should do?" This is a cognitive counterpart to standardized behavioral assessment methods discussed above.

An early nonclinical application of the think aloud technique was the work of de Groot (1965). de Groot presented a series of chess positions to chessplayers of different playing strengths and asked them to analyze the position aloud. de Groot identified both similarities and differences between the thought processes of master-level and weaker players. The characteristic thought processes of strong chessplayers are now used as models in training chessplayers and in artificial intelligence research designed to simulate human chessplaying.

This same technique was used by Schwartz and Gottman (1976) in a clinical context. They had dating-anxious and non-dating-anxious male college students think aloud, demonstrating what they would think when faced with situations involving interactions with women. Schwartz and Gottman identified several differences between the two groups. Dating-anxious males exhibited more negative and self-derogatory thoughts and anticipated more negative outcomes than other males. Schwartz and Gottman used this information in assertiveness training. Treatment consisted of training dating-anxious males to model the cognitive processes characteristic of non-dating-anxious males. Following treatment, dating-anxious males experienced a significant increase in the number of and satisfaction from contacts with women.

Similar methods have been used to assess the cognitive processes of clients with social anxiety (Smye & Wine, 1980), test anxiety (Hollandsworth, Glazeski, Kirkland, Jones, & Van Norman, 1979), and other clinical problems (Genest & Turk, 1981).

Cognitive Skills Assessment

Another cognitive counterpart to standardized behavioral assessment is assessment of cognitive skills. This can be done using the think aloud or self-report methods. Many cognitive theories of psychopathology assume that the accuracy of cognitive functioning is related to behavioral effectiveness. Hence, identifying cognitive errors or weaknesses is helpful when using cognitive therapy to treat clinical disorders.

For example, several psychologists have developed measures of problem-solving ability. The rationale for this is clear. The more able one is to solve interpersonal and other problems in daily living, the more successful one will be.

An early effort to assess problem-solving ability is the Means-Ends Problem Solving Procedure (MEPS; Platt & Spivack, 1975). The MEPS consists of 10 problematic situations (e.g., getting along with one's boss, finding a lost watch), describing the problem and a successful conclusion. The examinee fills in the middle of the story, giving the means by which the successful outcome is attained. Trained judges evaluate the story, rating the response for relevant means, irrelevant means, obstacles, and other factors. Using the MEPS, Spivack and his colleagues have shown that, compared to normal controls, psychiatric patients have poorer problem-solving skills (Platt & Spivack, 1972, 1974).

Although the MEPS was the first instrument developed to assess problem solving, it has been surpassed by two newer tests. One problem with the MEPS is that it requires trained judges to score a test protocol. Another problem is that the 10 situations include unrealistic problems (e.g., stealing a diamond). For these reasons, Heppner and Peterson

(1982) developed the Problem Solving Inventory (PSI). The PSI consists of 35 items that provide various responses to problems. Each response is rated for the degree to which the subject is likely to respond to a problem in this way. Items represent the five steps of problem solving, described by D'Zurilla and Goldfried (1971): orientation, problem definition, generation of alternative courses of action, decision making, and evaluation. Several studies have shown that the PSI is associated with clinical disorders, improvement over the course of therapy, and behavioral evaluations of problem-solving ability (Nezu, Nezu, & Perri, 1989).

A related and somewhat newer instrument is the Social Problem-Solving Inventory (SPSI) of D'Zurilla and Nezu (1990). This instrument consists of 70 items, each concerning a method of dealing with a problem (e.g., "When I have a problem, I often doubt that there is a solution to it," "Difficult problems make me very upset"). Subjects rate the degree to which they would respond to a problem in the way described by items. Although the SPSI is relatively new, preliminary research has suggested that it is reliable and is associated with a variety of clinical problems such as stress (D'Zurilla & Nezu, 1990).

Another set of cognitive assessment instruments measure the degree to which one exhibits general irrational beliefs. The rationale for this is that, as irrational thinking increases, the effectiveness of one's daily functioning is likely to decrease.

Albert Ellis (1962) introduced a popular approach to psychotherapy that rests on the assumption that emotional problems often result from irrational thinking. According to Ellis, if an individual operates using absolutistic thinking (e.g., "I must be successful in everything I try, or else I am a failure"), then one is likely to experience frequent emotional problems. Several instruments have been developed to assess the degree to which subjects subscribe to Ellis's irrational cognitions.

For example, the Irrational Beliefs Inventory (IBI; Alden & Safran, 1978) consists of 11 common irrational beliefs listed by Ellis (1962). Subjects rate each statement on a 9-point scale for the degree to which they agree with it. Alden (Alden & Safran, 1978; Alden, Safran, & Weideman, 1978) has shown

that the IBI is related to social anxiety and lack of assertiveness and is sensitive to improvements in these problems over a course of therapy.

Other instruments that assess endorsement of Ellis's irrational cognitions include the Rational Behavior Inventory (RBI; Shorkey & Whiteman, 1977) and the Common Belief Inventory for Students (CBIS; Hooper & Layne, 1983).

Cognitive Self-Assessment

Several forms of cognitive self-assessment have also been developed. These include thought sampling, self-monitoring, and self-statement inventories.

Thought sampling is a technique in which the client is cued, at random intervals, to record the thoughts one is experiencing at the moment. Hurlburt (1979) described an application of this technique. Hurlburt gave clients a beeper to carry at all times. The beeper sounded at random intervals throughout the day, at which time clients recorded the time of day and their thoughts and activities. Thought sampling has several advantages over the think aloud approach: it takes place in the client's natural setting; it yields a representative sample of the client's thoughts; and it is less likely to have reactive effects due to the artificiality of role-playing or responding to artificial vignettes in the therapist's office. On the other hand, it has the disadvantage that it requires that the client carry the beeper at all times; in addition, some clinical problems occur relatively infrequently and so the thought sampling method may not be appropriate for them.

Another and more commonly used cognitive self-assessment technique is self-monitoring. *Self-monitoring* requires that clients attend to and record their thoughts at certain times between sessions. For example, in Beck's cognitive therapy of depression, clients maintain a thought diary in which they jot down their thoughts, activities, and time of day when they are feeling sad. After a baseline period, the therapist (and the client as well) may recognize relations among thoughts, feelings, and activities. These patterns are then discussed and targeted for change in therapy. An example of a client's thought diary in cognitive–behavioral treatment for depression is in Exhibit 6.7.

EXHIBIT 6.7   Example of a Thought Diary Used in Cognitive-Behavioral Therapy for Depression

Thought Record

Date	Situation What were you doing when you started to feel sad?	Feelings What emotions did you experience (e.g., sadness, anger)? How bad did you feel? Rate your feeling on a scale from 1 = fine to 100 = terrible.	Automatic Thoughts What were you thinking when you started to feel bad?	Counters How might you counter the automatic negative thoughts? Use realistic counters. How might you test whether your negative thoughts are correct or incorrect?	Outcome How do you feel now that you have countered the automatic negative thoughts? Rate your feeling on a scale from 1 = fine to 100 = terrible.

The thought diary has several advantages over thought sampling. It is face valid—it is relevant to the client's disorder and so may be more readily accepted by the client. It addresses the client's problem as it occurs naturally, and so the information obtained may be more representative of the client's actual problem than that obtained by other methods, such as simple recall. Because the client must attend to the problem more now than in the past, it may be easier in therapy for the client to understand the connection among them and to change them.

However, these advantages also point out the weaknesses of cognitive self-monitoring. Because clients must record their thoughts following an occurrence of the problem, they may become distracted or too upset to complete the assessment. If the problem episodes are frequent, it may become too cumbersome for clients to record the required information regarding every event. Another problem with thought diaries is that they may be reactive; that is, because clients attend to their thoughts, feelings, and activities more than in the past, they may actually experience fewer episodes of the problem behavior. If this happens, then the information obtained is not representative of their typical functioning, and so may not be useful in therapy.

A third form of cognitive self-assessment that has become popular is the thought checklist. Like a behavior checklist or rating scale, a cognitive checklist provides a set of problematic cognitions that are rated for frequency and/or severity.

Many of the advantages of behavior checklists apply to thought checklists. They are easy to administer, easy to develop, and have good reliability. Because they frequently have good reliability, they often have good validity. They have clinical relevance and can be used to further clients' understanding of the relation between cognitive functioning and their clinical disorders. Exhibit 6.8 lists several of the more commonly used cognitive checklists.

APPLIED ISSUES

Reactivity to Measurement

One of the most significant threats to the utility of behavioral assessment is the possibility of reactivity to measurement. *Reactivity* occurs when individuals respond differently when they are being observed than at other times. In a review of the research on reactivity to measurement, Haynes and Horn (1982) noted that reactivity can occur both when clients know that they are being observed and when they are engaged in self-observation. For example, if a psychologist monitors a family interaction in the family's home, the presence of the observer may lead the family to be "on its best behavior," which may not be representative of its typical interaction. Similarly, if a client monitors a problem behavior (say, counting the number of cigarettes smoked), the very act of self-monitoring may lead the person to alter his behavior. After all, the client must not only attend to the act of smoking, but must also anticipate how to record the observations.

Foster and colleagues (1988) summarized several recommendations for limiting the effects of reactivity. These include minimizing the intrusiveness of the observation (e.g., having the observer out of sight), using participant observers (such as teachers or parents) who are already familiar figures in the client's environment, using an extended observation period so that the client has a chance to become acclimated to the observation, informing clients of the rationale for and importance of accurate observations, and establishing rapport with the client so that the client is more willing to comply with the psychologist's recommendations.

I have found that clients are unlikely to exhibit reactivity to observation if the observation procedure is presented as routine. For example, in our training clinic, all psychotherapy and assessment sessions are audiotaped or videotaped (with the client's written permission) so that supervisors can later review students' contacts with clients. Although graduate students often express uneasiness about taping their sessions, clients almost never question the procedure. Usually, within a few minutes into the opening session, clients seem to forget that the session is being recorded and do not appear to be affected by the procedure.

Even if clients continue to exhibit reactivity to observation, this is not necessarily a problem. Of course, the baseline data become of doubtful valid-

EXHIBIT 6.8   Commonly Used Cognitive Checklists

Problem	Instrument	Reference
Agoraphobia	Agoraphobic Cognitions Questionnaire	Chambless, Caputo, Bright, & Gallagher (1984)
Anxiety	Cognitive-Somatic Anxiety Questionnaire	Schwartz, Davidson, & Goleman (1978)
Assertiveness	Assertiveness Self-Statement Test	Schwartz & Gottman (1976)
Depression	Attribution Style Questionnaire	Seligman, Abramson, Semmel, & von Baeyer (1979)
	Automatic Thoughts Questionnaire	Hollon & Kendall (1980)
	Dysfunctional Attitude Scale	Weissman & Beck (1978)
Eating Disorders	Eating Attitudes Test	Garner & Garfinkel (1979)
Social Anxiety	Social Anxiety Thoughts Questionnaire	Hartman (1984)
	Social Interaction Self-Statement Test	Glass, Merluzzi, Biever, & Larsen (1982)

ity. However, if clients' increased awareness of the problem behavior leads it to occur less frequently, then clients benefit, albeit in an unintended way, from the assessment.

Lynn Rehm has shown that self-monitoring, in and of itself, has a therapeutic effect on depression (Rehm, Kornblith, O'Hara, Lamparski, Romano, & Volkin, 1981). I have found, in treating depression as well as other problems, that clients who perform self-monitoring at the start of therapy often experience a reduction in symptoms. The client's heightened awareness of the target behavior reduces its occurrence. Although some clients interpret this as a failure (since they are not able to complete the monitoring assignment), the therapist can help them reinterpret it positively, as an indication that they in fact have control over their problem.

Selection and Training of Observers

Another practical issue concerning behavioral assessment is the selection and training of observers.

Three types of observers are possible: the client himself or herself, a participant observer, or a nonparticipant observer. A *participant observer* is someone, such as a spouse, parent, or teacher, who is already in the client's natural environment and who records the client's problem behavior. A *nonparticipant observer* is a person, such as the psychologist or a clinic assistant, who is not generally in the client's natural environment and who records the client's problem behavior.

Participant observers are often selected to record problem behaviors that are infrequent or when the observation period will persist for an extended period (Foster et al., 1988). In these cases, the cost of using a nonparticipant observer becomes prohibitive. Participant observers also have the advantage of eliciting less reactivity than nonparticipant observers. Finally, the choice of an observer should also be influenced by the nature of the behavior to be observed. If the target behavior is concrete (e.g., smoking a cigarette), then a participant observer may be appropriate; however, if the target problem is subtle and requires judgment to detect (e.g., type of communication, such as sarcasm), then a trained nonparticipant observer should be used. Foster and colleagues (1988) also noted several requirements for participant observers: promptness, honesty, dependability, ability to maintain a good relationship with the client, and ability to keep the collected information confidential.

Use of self-observation is possible when the client is motivated to comply with the assessment; is capable of performing the assessment; and the target behavior is concrete and readily judged by a nonprofessional. When the client is uncooperative, then self-assessment is unlikely to be successful. If the client is cognitively limited (say, due to young age, limited intellectual ability, or intense distress), then self-assessment is not feasible. If the target behavior is subtle and not readily noted by the client (such as verbal sarcasm), then self-assessment is not likely to be effective.

Regardless of who records the observations, it is important that observers receive sufficient training. Training should include issues such as when and where to make the observations, how to identify and rate the target behavior, and how to record the observations. Often, training is followed by a demonstration, in the psychologist's presence, that the judge can observe and record the behavior accurately. In some instances, training continues until the judge can demonstrate that the ratings are sufficiently reliable.

Studies of the accuracy of self-monitoring and participant observers have reported mixed results. For example, self-monitoring has been shown to be more accurate with impersonal behaviors than with more complex interpersonal behaviors such as parenting (Lipinski & Nelson, 1974). Similarly, studies of participant observers have found that agreement between participant and nonparticipant observers often is quite substantial (over 80 percent), although occasional lapses in agreement have occurred (Foster et al., 1988).

Another potential problem in behavioral assessment is observer drift. *Observer drift* occurs when the accuracy of behavioral observations decreases when observers, following training, introduce idio-

syncratic modifications of the recording system. For example, consider a group of psychology graduate students who are trained to use Patterson and colleagues' FICS with sufficient inter-rater reliability. Now consider what could happen if some students monitor families in crisis while other students observe nondistressed families. It is possible that the students who observe only distressed families will come to use the coding system differently from those who observe nondistressed families. After all, judgments concerning positive, negative, and neutral interactions may be influenced by the intensity of the observed interactions. Following experience with only a limited sample of families, the two groups of students may experience observer drift, and therefore use different criteria than presented in the original training.

Interestingly, if observers discuss their ratings, they may experience *consensual drift* (Foster et al., 1988), wherein they no longer use the original criteria but continue to show good inter-rater reliability with one another. It is not hard to understand why this occurs. If observers have questions about how to code a particular behavior, they may seek guidance from one another. Over time, they may come to share the same idiosyncratic criteria that differ from the original criteria they were trained to use.

Several times, I have seen an interesting clinical example of consensual drift in which psychologists at different agencies develop local diagnostic customs. That is, diagnosticians in some agencies show good inter-rater reliability on a diagnosis, even though the diagnosis would not be assigned by psychologists at other agencies. The diagnosticians may think that their diagnoses are sound, given that there is high inter-reliability within the setting. However, because they have drifted away from the formal diagnostic system, through consultations and discussions at case conferences, their diagnoses are no longer valid. Differences in diagnostic practice were reported cross-nationally in a series of studies in the 1960s and 1970s (e.g., Kendall, Cooper, Gourlay, & Copeland, 1971; Sandifer, Hordern, Timbury, & Green, 1968). I suspect that there are many local examples of observer drift in which diagnosticians at agencies use diagnostic labels in idiosyncratic ways that are quite different from the formal diagnostic criteria of the DSM.

Observer drift can be reduced in several ways. Random surreptitious checks improve observer reliability (Kent & Foster, 1977). Continued practice and ongoing training maintain reliability (DeMaster, Reid, & Twentyman, 1977). Foster and colleagues (1988) also suggested other methods of limiting observer drift, including rotating pairs of observers, videotaping sessions for later scoring, using independent reliability checks, and discussing the coding system only in the presence of the trainer.

SCIENTIFIC ISSUES

Assumptions of Behavioral Assessment

There are significant theoretical differences between behavioral assessment and more traditional personality assessment (usually associated with psychodynamic or humanistic theories). Goodenough (1949) distinguished between traditional and behavioral assessment by their use of the *sign* versus *sample* approach. Traditional assessment considers test responses as signs of underlying psychological characteristics; test behavior, whether on a multiple-choice test, inkblot test, or interview, is interpreted in terms of underlying mental constructs, such as personality traits, motivations, and defense mechanisms.

On the other hand, behavioral assessment considers test behaviors simply as samples of one's behavior in general. The client's behavior during an interview or observation period is not interpreted in terms of mental constructs, but is regarded as typical of that person's behavior in other settings.

Chapter 3 presented the distinction, clarified by MacCorquodale and Meehl (1948), between hypothetical constructs and intervening variables. As you recall, hypothetical constructs are unseen entities that are presumed to exist and are detected only through their relationships with observable constructs; intervening variables are constructs that are used simply to summarize a set of empirical observations. The distinction between hypothetical constructs and intervening variables is exactly the same distinction as that between traditional and behavioral

assessment. Traditional assessment uses observable test behaviors to infer the nature of underlying mental entities, such as personality traits, which are hypothetical constructs. Behavioral assessment, on the other hand, does not make inferences from test behaviors to unseen entities; instead, test behaviors are regarded purely on their own terms, as a sample of other behaviors that the person may exhibit. When a behavioral assessment generates a descriptive term such as *aggressive personality,* the term is used as an intervening variable—the label aggression does not represent an unseen mental entity but simply summarizes the observed behavior.

Goldfried and Kent (1972) published an important paper in which they highlighted the different assumptions of traditional and behavioral assessment. Both forms of assessment make methodological assumptions (concerning the accuracy of observed test responses) and sampling assumptions (concerning the degree to which observed test responses are representative of the examinee's responses in general). However, traditional assessment differs from behavioral assessment in that it has a third level of theoretical assumptions, concerning the degree to which an underlying construct is correctly inferred from test behavior. Because these assumptions are made both when drawing the inference and when validating the inference by making predictions about subsequent behavior, Goldfried and Kent observed that traditional assessment makes two more inferences than behavioral assessment. Although this does not ensure that traditional assessment is less accurate than behavioral assessment, it does mean that traditional assessment has two more opportunities to make mistakes than behavioral assessment.

Reliability and Validity of Behavioral Assessment

Because behavioral assessment is conceptually simpler and makes fewer inferences (and so has fewer opportunities to make a mistake) than traditional assessment, many clinical psychologists in the 1950s and 1960s welcomed behavioral assessment as an approach that would be more reliable than traditional assessment.

Interestingly, some proponents of behavioral assessment have questioned whether the traditional psychometric criteria of reliability and validity are appropriate for evaluating their methods. For example, Barrett, Johnston, and Pennypacker (1986) and Hayes, Nelson, and Jarrett (1986) noted that psychometric concepts (such as test–retest reliability and internal consistency) were developed for use with group data and that, since behavior analysts often assess the situation-specific behavior of individuals, these psychometric criteria may not be applicable to behavioral assessment.

This argument is not convincing. It is reminiscent of the argument made in the 1950s that empirical measures of psychometric properties are not appropriate for projective tests since projective tests examine unique psychological processes (Wierzbicki, 1993a). This argument was not accepted as valid for projective tests (Wierzbicki, 1993a) and it is not generally accepted for behavioral assessment either. Mash and Hunsley (1990) noted that most behavioral assessors recognize the need for psychometrically sound instruments and apply psychometric concepts rigorously in evaluating their methods.

As with any broad category of assessment techniques, it is not possible to state categorically whether the reliability of behavioral assessment is or is not sufficient. Any sweeping generalization will have many counterexamples. Still, it is a fair summary to say that behavioral assessment, as a general approach to psychological assessment, has adequate reliability.

Behaviorism stresses the measurement of observables. Hence, behavioral assessment addresses specific, discrete, and operationally defined constructs. For this reason, behavioral assessment tends to have good inter-rater reliability. After all, it is much easier for two observers to agree on the occurrence/ nonoccurrence of a problem behavior than a mental process.

Behaviorism also emphasizes the scientific method. For this reason, behaviorally oriented psychologists have, as a group, tended to conduct empirical evaluations of their techniques more than other schools of psychologists. Thus, as behavioral assessment techniques have been introduced, they have typically been accompanied by more demonstra-

tions of their empirical reliability than was the case for traditional personality tests.

It should be noted that, of the various forms of reliability, test–retest reliability may be least appropriate for evaluating behavioral assessment (Hayes et al., 1986). After all, behaviors are modifiable and change over time, perhaps more rapidly than traditional personality constructs. In addition, Hayes and colleagues noted Mischel's (1968) well-known conclusion that behavior is not consistent across dissimilar situations. Thus, if behavior is assessed in one situation, it should not be expected to be highly related to behaviors in dissimilar situations. Although Mischel's issue of the stability of personality and behavior is too extensive to be discussed here (see Wierzbicki [1993a] for a review and discussion of this issue), students should recognize that, due to the malleability of behavior, test–retest reliability assessments may be less appropriate with behavioral assessment than other forms of reliability.

As noted in Chapter 4, a crucial factor used to judge the utility of an assessment instrument is validity. Does it accurately identify the construct in question? Can it successfully identify individuals who are likely to respond more to one form of treatment or another?

One of the early criticisms of behavioral assessment was its lack of clinical validity. Ford and Urban (1963), in a classic overview of systems of psychotherapy, criticized early behavioral models of personality and psychotherapy for inadequately representing "the content or substance of behavior" (p. 272). That is, early behaviorists stressed the method of observing behavior and the theory underlying learning and the change of behavior, but failed to concern themselves with the kinds of behaviors that other psychologists, and many laypersons, would consider as important behaviors to be addressed by psychologists. Similarly, Goldfried and Davison (1976) noted that one of the frequent criticisms of behavior therapy was that the behaviors it targeted for change were not meaningfully related to the problems treated by clinical psychologists in actual practice.

Behaviorally oriented clinical psychologists acknowledged this criticism. For example, behaviorists were at the forefront of the anti-diagnosis movement of the 1960s because of a lack of scientific evidence that psychiatric labels provided useful information about the etiology or effective treatment of disorders (Wierzbicki, 1993a). Indeed, the development of behavioral assessment in the 1960s was largely influenced by behavior therapists' attempts to develop assessment methods that are directly related to the client's symptomatic behavior. Although early behavior therapists may have erred on the side of using behavioral assessments that were not always clinically meaningful, this problem has largely been corrected. For example, Bellack and Hersen (1985) observed that one of the most significant changes in behavior therapy since the early 1970s was an increased focus on clinically relevant problems.

SUMMARY

Although standardized psychological assessment is a relatively modern development, all societies have evaluated their members' behavioral competencies. Since the 1910s, when Watson introduced the school of psychological behaviorism, behavioral assessment has been a basic tool of psychologists.

Skinner introduced the term functional analysis to describe behavioral assessment. According to Skinner, psychologists should attempt to explain behavior as a result of the environmental stimuli that act on the person. The acronyms, SORC (Situation, Organism, Response, Consequences) and BASIC-ID (Behavior, Affect, Sensation, Images, Cognitions, Interpersonal processes, and Drugs), have been used to summarize the important aspects of functioning to be addressed in clinical behavioral assessment.

As clinical psychologists in the 1950s started to examine their assessment practices empirically, behavioral assessment grew in influence. By the 1960s, behavioral assessment was recognized as an important adjunct to other forms of clinical assessment.

Interviews can be considered a form of behavioral assessment. Interviewers attend to many aspects of behavior, including self-care behavior (appearance), interpersonal behavior, verbal behavior, affective responding, and behavioral indicators of cognitive processes. Interviewers also gather information about the nature and history of the presenting problem and the client's social history. In addition to traditional clinical interviews, psychologists now also perform structured interviews, in which they ask the same questions, in the same order, and with the same follow-up questions of everyone. Diagnostic structured interviews have been found to have good reliability and validity.

Behavioral observation has become a basic form of clinical assessment. Effective behavioral observation requires that the psychologist selects and defines the target behavior, determines how best to record it, trains judges to observe it, and then evaluates the reliability of the recording technique. Problem behaviors should be recorded along relevant clinical dimensions by observers who are capable of recording them accurately.

Behavioral observation can take place in the client's natural setting (naturalistic observation) or in a standardized setting. In standardized behavioral assessment, the client's behavior is assessed following presentation of a standardized stimulus or task (such as a role play or simulation).

Another widely used form of behavioral assessment is the behavior checklist, which consists of many specific behavioral symptoms that are rated for their presence or severity. Behavior checklists are widely used in assessing children's behavior, with teachers or parents rating children's problem behaviors. Behavior checklists have become popular because they are easy to administer and to develop so that they have sound psychometric properties.

Self-monitoring is another widely used form of behavioral assessment. Clients may monitor their behavior as it occurs or describe their behavior using behavior checklists.

Cognitive assessment is another popular form of assessment. Because cognitive approaches to explaining and treating disorders often share behaviorism's theoretical emphases and empirical methods, many clinical psychologists consider cognitive assessment to be a form of behavioral assessment. There are cognitive analogues to most of the measurement techniques designed to assess behavior. For example, the think-aloud technique is one in which clients role-play a problematic situation, demonstrating their cognitive processes by speaking aloud what they would think when faced with the problem.

Cognitive skills that are associated with behavioral effectiveness can also be assessed. For example, rational thinking and effective problem solving are two cognitive skills that are thought to be related to emotional and behavioral functioning. Several measures of rational thinking and problem-solving ability are widely used.

Clients also monitor their cognitive processes using thought sampling, thought diaries, and cognitive checklists and rating scales.

Several practical problems must be addressed when performing behavioral assessment. Some clients exhibit behavioral reactivity to measurement, altering their problem behavior when they know it is being observed. Reactivity to measurement can be minimized by using observers who are already in the client's environment, using extended periods of observation so that the client can become accustomed to observation, educating the client about the importance of accurate assessment, and establishing rapport with the client to enhance compliance.

Behavioral assessors also must address the issue of the selection and training of judges. Participant observers are individuals, such as parents or teachers, who are in the client's environment and so are already familiar to the client. Nonparticipant observers are not already in the client's environment, such as the psychologist or a psychological assistant. Participant observers are appropriate when the target behavior is infrequent, reactive to observation, or concrete. Nonparticipant observers may be more useful when the target behavior is frequent, nonreactive to observation, and subtle. In some cases, clients may monitor their own behavior. Regardless of who serves as observer, observers should be trained so that they are able to record the target behavior reliably.

A potential problem in behavioral observation is observer drift, which occurs when, following training, observers introduce idiosyncratic modifications of the recording system. In some cases where observers work in teams, consensual drift can occur, in which the team of observers continue to agree with one another but drift away from the original recording criteria.

Behavioral assessment has been described as a sample approach, whereas traditional personality assessment is a sign approach. In traditional personality assessment, observed test behaviors are considered as signs of underlying personality traits that must be inferred; in behavioral assessment, observed behaviors are considered only as a sample of one's behavior in general. Because behavioral assessment does not make inferences concerning underlying personality constructs, it makes fewer inferences than traditional assessment and so has fewer opportunities to make errors.

As a general rule, behavioral assessment has good reliability. Behaviorism emphasizes a scientific approach to psychology. Hence, many of the features of science—observation, measurement, empirical testing—are characteristic of behavioral assessment. Such emphases enhance the operationalism of behavioral assessment and so enhance its reliability.

With good reliability, behavioral assessment has the possibility of attaining good validity. Early behavioral clinical psychologists were criticized for examining behaviors that have little clinical utility. Such behavioral assessment may have been reliable but not valid. Since the 1960s, behavior therapists have increased their attention to clinically relevant problems, which has increased the validity of behavioral assessment.

STUDY QUESTIONS

1. Discuss Skinner's concept of functional analysis. How has Skinner's model of behavioral assessment been modified for use in clinical assessment?
2. How can a clinical interview be conceptualized as a form of behavioral assessment?
3. Discuss the information gathered in the different types of clinical interviews.
4. Describe the steps taken as part of behavioral assessment. What judgments must the clinical psychologist make at each step?
5. Describe two forms of making behavioral observations in standardized situations. Discuss the application of such observations in clinical practice.
6. Discuss self-monitoring as a form of behavioral assessment. What types of self-assessment techniques are available? When is self-assessment appropriate?
7. Describe two forms of cognitive assessment. Why do many clinical psychologists now consider cognitive assessment as a form of behavioral assessment?
8. Discuss the problem of reactivity to measurement. How can psychologists try to minimize the impact of reactivity?
9. Discuss the use of participant versus nonparticipant observers in behavioral assessment.
10. Discuss the different theoretical assumptions underlying behavioral and traditional personality assessment.

7

Personality Assessment

I. *Meaning of Personality*
II. *Uses of Personality Testing*
III. *History of Personality Assessment*
   A. *Classical Approaches*
   B. *Pre-Modern Approaches*
IV. *Projective Personality Assessment*
   A. *Projective Tests*
V. *Structured Personality Assessment*
   A. *Structured Personality Inventories*

VI. *Scientific Issues*
   A. *Evaluation of Projective Tests*
   B. *Evaluation of Structured Tests*
VII. *Applied Issues*
   A. *Detection of Faking*
   B. *Response Sets*
   C. *Use of Computerized Interpretations*
VIII. *Summary*

Previous chapters discussed clinical psychologists' use of ability tests and behavioral assessment. This chapter addresses a third major type of clinical assessment—personality testing.

MEANING OF PERSONALITY

Chapter 3 introduced Gordon Allport as an influential personality theorist who is known for his efforts to clarify the meaning of personality. Allport (1937) reviewed the literature and found that psychologists use the term *personality* in almost 50 conceptually distinct ways. He then provided his own definition of personality, which was used in Chapter 3 as the organizing schema for the major theories of personality and psychopathology: "personality is the dynamic organization within the individual of those psychophysical systems that determine his unique adjustments to his environment" (Allport, 1937, p. 48). A more user-friendly way of thinking about personality is an individual's most striking or dominant characteristics that are relatively consistent over time and across situations.

This notion of personality is based on the concept of *personality trait*. Evaluation of personality often concerns individual personality traits. Lay persons commonly discuss personality in terms of traits such as dependency, aggressiveness, or friendliness. Allport and Odbert (1936) illustrated the extent to which personality traits are used in everyday conversations; they examined an unabridged dictionary and found about 18,000 terms that could be used to describe personality characteristics.

Major theories of personality address such traits. Again, Allport is known for his examination of the meaning of traits. Allport (1961) defined a *personality trait* as a "neuropsychic structure having the capacity to render many stimuli functionally equivalent, and to initiate and guide equivalent (meaningfully consistent) forms of adaptive and expressive behavior" (p. 347).

Although this formal definition may sound obscure, it is actually quite useful. Key in Allport's definition is the notion of *functional equivalence*. For example, suppose a person has a highly aggressive personality. The person exhibits aggression across situations—driving aggressively, playing basketball aggressively, enjoying aggressive films and jokes, and so on. Now, driving aggressively is a very different behavior from playing basketball aggressively or attending violent movies; the actual behaviors exhibited by the person are extremely different from one another. The settings in which these behaviors occur (car, basketball court, theater) are certainly distinct. Yet, in each instance, the person acts in a way that expresses a common theme. It is the *functional equivalence* of these behaviors—in this example, exhibiting aggression—that lead Allport to consider them as manifestations of a single personality trait.

Personality traits vary in strength. One person may exhibit extreme aggression across all settings whereas another person may exhibit moderate aggression in only a few settings. Thus, assessment of personality requires not only the identification of significant traits but also the quantification of traits.

In some cases, personality traits become so extreme that they interfere significantly with a person's ability to function. It is such extreme and maladaptive traits that are considered *personality disorders*. DSM-IV (APA, 1994) describes personality disorders as "personality traits [that] are inflexible and maladaptive and cause significant functional impairment or subjective distress" (p. 630). Exhibit 7.1 lists the personality disorders in the current diagnostic system.

USES OF PERSONALITY TESTING

Clinical psychologists use personality tests in both clinical and research settings. In applied clinical work, personality tests are used for two reasons: diagnosis and treatment selection. These two purposes

---

EXHIBIT 7.1 Personality Disorders

DSM-IV (American Psychiatric Association, 1994) lists 10 personality disorders in three clusters. Each personality disorder is characterized by early onset and an enduring pattern of inflexible and maladaptive behavior that causes significant distress or interferes significantly with adaptive functioning.

Cluster A

Paranoid Personality Disorder: Distrust, suspiciousness.

Schizoid Personality Disorder: Detachment from social relationships and restricted range of expressed affect.

Schizotypal Personality Disorder: Acute discomfort with close relationships; eccentric perceptions and behaviors.

Cluster B

Antisocial Personality Disorder: Disregard for and violation of the rights of others.

Borderline Personality Disorder: Unstable interpersonal relationships, self-image, and affect; marked impulsivity.

Histrionic Personality Disorder: Excessive emotionality and attention-seeking.

Narcissistic Personality Disorder: Grandiosity, need for admiration, lack of empathy.

Cluster C

Avoidant Personality Disorder: Social inhibition, feelings of inadequacy.

Dependent Personality Disorder: Need to be taken care of; submissive and clinging behavior.

Obsessive-Compulsive Personality Disorder: Preoccupation with orderliness, perfectionism, and interpersonal control.

---

were discussed in previous chapters on assessment and should be familiar to readers.

Personality tests are commonly used in clinical practice to assist diagnosis. Some settings routinely administer a structured test (such as the MMPI-2) to all new admissions as a cost-effective way of gathering information that may help determine a client's problem. Personality tests are also useful when clients present multiple symptoms (e.g., affective and cognitive) or problems that may exacerbate one another (such as depression and alcohol abuse); in such cases, personality tests may help determine which is the primary or initial problem.

Personality tests also help in treatment selection. Clients with the same clinical disorder may require different treatments depending on their personalities. For example, depression is often associated with dependent personality disorder and borderline personality disorder. Dependent personalities tend to be reliant on others for help; they are likely to form ties with a therapist and to comply with treatment. Borderline personalities, on the other hand, are characterized by unstable interpersonal relationships. They tend to form uneasy relationships with therapists and often drop out of therapy. Psychotherapy is likely to take two very different courses depending on the depressed client's personality.

Personality tests are also used in basic research. Many clinical psychologists engage in the scientific study of personality. They attempt to identify fundamental dimensions of personality, along with the influences on and the correlates and consequences of these dimensions. Identifying the basic personality dimensions and developing valid measures of these traits should enable clinical psychologists to better explain and predict both normal and abnormal behavior. This should ultimately lead to more effective interventions for clinical disorders in the fourth or applied stage of science.

HISTORY OF PERSONALITY ASSESSMENT

Classical Approaches

All societies have employed strategies for "knowing" people (McReynolds, 1975). Even primitive and ancient cultures developed methods for determining who is honest and reliable. Of course, such methods were not very accurate by contemporary standards. Still, it is worth taking some time to note briefly the early precursors to contemporary personality assessment.

One of the earliest systems for classifying and explaining personality was that of Hippocrates and Galen. The ancient Greeks held that there are four basic elements: fire, earth, air, and water. Hippocrates and Galen also suggested that there are four basic bodily fluids (humors), each of which is associated with an element and a personality type: yellow bile is related to fire and a choleric or irritable personality; black bile (*melancholia*) is related to earth and a melancholic or depressed personality; blood is related to air and a sanguine or optimistic personality; phlegm is associated with water and a phlegmatic or calm personality. In this model, personality and emotional problems were thought to be due to imbalances in bodily fluids.

This model, though influential throughout the Middle Ages, has no impact today and is regarded only as a humorous footnote in the history of personality theories. Still, the terms *melancholic, phlegmatic, sanguine,* and *choleric* remain in our vocabulary as descriptions of personality.

The body fluid model established a precedent for later models of personality based on body type. For example, in the early 1900s, Ernst Kretschmer (cited in Hall & Lindzey, 1978), a German psychiatrist, suggested that there are three basic body types: (1) *pyknic,* the round soft physique; (2) *athletic,* the hard, muscular physique; and (3) *asthenic,* the thin, frail physique. Kretschmer reported an association between body type and diagnosis: manic-depressive patients more frequently had the pyknic body type whereas schizophrenic patients more frequently had the asthenic and the athletic types.

An American psychologist, William Sheldon, subsequently extended Kretschmer's work. Sheldon (Sheldon & Stevens, 1942; Sheldon, Stevens, & Tucker, 1940) also suggested that there are three basic body types (though he later considered these to be dimensional rather than categorical), each of which he considered to be associated with a particular temperament type: (1) *endomorphy,* the round, soft body type, was related to *viscerotonia,* the temperament type characterized by love of comfort and sociability; (2) *mesomorphy,* the hard, muscular body type was related to *somatotonia,* the temperament type characterized by love of vigorous activity and risk-taking; (3) ectomorphy, the thin, frail body type was associated with *cerebrotonia,* the temperament type characterized by inhibition and restraint.

Kretschmer's and Sheldon's models represented a step above the Greek system, since body types are more readily observed and tested than imbalances in bodily fluids. However, research has not generally supported Kretschmer's and Sheldon's ideas (Hall & Lindzey, 1978), and so their models deserve little more than a brief note in a historical review of personality assessment.

McReynolds (1975) discussed two ancient methods of personality assessment: astrology and physiognomy. According to McReynolds, the practice of astrology to make statements and predictions about an individual probably arose in Greece in about the fifth century B.C. McReynolds noted that a work commonly attributed to Ptolemy in the second century A.D. summarized the procedures that astrologists used to cast an individual's horoscope and describe the individual's personality, generating descriptions such as "unstable, versatile, lazy, and acquisitive."

Of course, although astrology was widespread throughout much of the ancient world (and continues to remain popular today), it is not valid. No scientific explanation is provided for how a planet or constellation produces its alleged effect. A further problem is that the characteristics associated with heavenly bodies vary across cultures, and so there is little reliability across cultures in astrological interpretations. In addition, empirical studies have consistently failed to support the claims of astrology (Campbell & Beets, 1978; Culver & Ianna, 1979; Jerome, 1977). For these reasons, few scientifically oriented clinical psychologists take astrology seriously today.

The other ancient method of personality assessment noted by McReynolds (1975) is *physiognomy,* the practice of determining character from physical appearance. McReynolds attributed physiognomy to the ancient Greeks, including Hippocrates, Aristotle, Plato, and Galen among the notables who practiced it. Even the Old Testament refers to physiognomy,

e.g., "the shew of their countenance doth witness against them" (Isaiah 3.9).

Physiognomy remained popular throughout Western history. McReynolds (1975) noted that Medieval and Renaissance scientists continued to promote it. Even into the 1800s, prominent scientists practiced physiognomy. For example, Cesare Lombroso (1910), an influential psychiatrist and criminologist, wrote that genius is associated with elevated foreheads, long noses, and large heads, whereas mental retardation, criminality, and insanity are associated with the opposite characteristics.

In the 1700s and 1800s, other influential movements held that psychological and physical characteristics are related. For example, *phrenology,* introduced and popularized by Franz Joseph Gall, is the practice of judging one's faculties and personality through reading the bumps on the head.

Of course, these views were eventually recognized as invalid and have long been discarded by scientists (although one phrenological journal continues to publish research to support its views). Still, it is important to recognize that these positions were based on scientific positions that seemed reasonable at the time. For example, scientists in the 1700s and 1800s were beginning to demonstrate that brain structures are related to psychological and motor functions; it made sense to propose that people with advanced abilities have more fully developed (i.e., larger) brain areas that, over time, press against the skull and produce the phrenological bump.

Of course, we know today that these early hypotheses were inaccurate. Except in the case of certain chromosome anomalies (e.g., Down Syndrome, Fragile-X Syndrome) or other developmental neurological disorders (e.g., microencephaly), there is no relationship between facial features and psychological characteristics such as intelligence or personality.

Another approach to assessing personality used throughout much of recorded history is *graphology,* or the practice of interpreting personality from handwriting. Nickell (1992) noted historical references to graphology in the works of Romans and Hebrews of 2,000 years ago. According to Nickell, Abbe Jean-Hippolyte Michon introduced the term graphology and founded the Society of Graphology in 1871. Even though empirical research has shown that graphology lacks sufficient reliability and validity to be useful (Dean, 1992), many people continue to accept its validity.

Pre-Modern Approaches

As indicated in previous chapters, psychology evolved as a distinct discipline in the mid- to late-1800s. Psychology distinguished itself from philosophy in its emphasis on empirical methods; it distinguished itself from biology and physiology in its focus on behavior and mental processes. By the late-1800s, laboratories had been established by Galton, Wundt, and others to study psychological processes scientifically.

Much of this early psychological research addressed simple behaviors, such as reaction time and sensory acuity. However, psychological research quickly broadened to include more complex mental processes, such as Galton's early efforts to study mental ability. Eventually, this research broadened still further to the point that it addressed what is considered today as part of one's personality.

For example, Bell (1948) observed that word association tests were used by Galton in 1879 and by Wundt in 1880. Gregory (1996) noted that Galton classified responses to a target word as "parrot-like," "image-mediated," and "histrionic," and believed that mental operations "below the level of consciousness" influence the subject's response. In fact, some historians have suggested that Freud's use of free association in psychoanalysis was influenced by Galton's work (Gregory, 1996).

Emil Kraepelin used word association tests in clinical studies with schizophrenic patients in 1892 (Ben-Porath & Butcher, 1991). Jung went on to refine the word association test. In 1910, Jung published a paper in which he reported that certain types of responses (e.g., long response times, repetitions of the word, providing multiple associations) indicate that the stimulus word is associated with troubling material.

In fact, Jung (1910) described an incident in which he used word associations to determine which of three suspects was guilty of a crime. At Jung's

hospital, a nurse's purse had been stolen from a cupboard to which only three other people had access. The purse was red leather and contained, among other things, a silver watch chain. Jung constructed a list that included both critical words (words pertaining to the theft, such as leather, chain, and silver) and neutral words. Jung administered the word lists to the three suspects and recorded their reactions. He found that one person had substantially longer reaction times to critical words, had a greater difference in reaction time between critical and neutral words, and provided more "imperfect reproductions" (such as multiple associations) to critical words than the other two suspects. This individual later confessed to the theft.

Other precursors to contemporary personality tests also appeared around the turn of the century. For example, in 1896, Binet and Henri used inkblots in a study of imagination (DuBois, 1970); in 1905, Binet and Simon used children's verbal responses to pictures as tests of their cognitive abilities (Rabin, 1968). These efforts resemble, respectively, the Rorschach Inkblot Test and the Thematic Apperception Test (TAT), two of the most widely used projective personality tests. Still, in a review of psychological tests that appeared in 1910, Whipple (1910) did not even include "personality" as a category of psychological tests.

In the early 1900s, Freud's psychoanalytic theory of personality became influential. Freud stressed the concept of *psychic determinism*—the notion that one's actions are caused, usually by unconscious factors beyond awareness. As psychoanalytic theory grew in popularity, many psychologists adopted the view that such unconscious influences can be inferred from one's responses to a set of unfamiliar stimuli. Tests in which the examinee's personality is interpreted from responses to inkblots, pictures, drawings, or other ambiguous material are now called projective personality tests and form the first major class of modern personality tests.

PROJECTIVE PERSONALITY ASSESSMENT

A projective test is a measure of personality that consists of vague or unstructured stimuli to be interpreted or organized by the examinee and that enables each person to respond to items in a unique way, yielding an unlimited number of possible answers.

Projective tests are based on the assumption that one's personality influences how one organizes or interprets ambiguous test items. Hence, a skilled psychologist may be able to glean the subject's underlying personality from the test responses.

Freud (1895/1962) introduced *projection* as a neurotic mechanism in which an individual, unable to control his or her sexual energy, directs it outward. Later, Freud (1896/1962) revised his view of projection, coming to regard it as a defense mechanism in which an individual attributes his or her own threatening thoughts or impulses to others.

The term *projective method* is generally attributed to L. K. Frank. Frank (1948) wrote that he first used the term publicly in 1939 in a paper he presented to the New York Academy of Sciences. It should be noted, however, that Murray (1938) had previously used the term projective test. Frank (1939) compared projective tests to X-rays. Both are indirect methods of assessing one's internal state by passing a stimulus through the person, yielding a picture that only dimly reflects the internal state and so must be interpreted by a trained professional.

Interestingly, some psychologists have objected to the term projective test. For example, Anderson (1951) and Zubin, Eron, and Schumer (1965) noted that projective tests do not invoke the defense mechanism of projection, because responses to test items are neither unconscious nor defensive. Projective test responses may be influenced by many factors—conscious and unconscious—other than unconscious defenses. For these reasons, some psychologists have proposed other terms for projective tests, such as "misperception test" (Cattell, 1951) and "apperception test" (Bellak, 1950). However, these alternatives have not received wide support, and so the conventional term for this class of instruments continues to be projective test.

Projective testing is largely based on Freud's assumption of psychic determinism. Just as Freud held that a person's slip of the tongue are meaningful and can help a psychoanalyst understand the inner workings of a client's psyche, so do projective test users hold that an examinee's responses to projective test items yield information about one's personality. Thus, as Freudian personality theory became popular in the first half of the twentieth century, projective personality testing became the predominant type of personality testing used by clinical psychologists.

The major projective tests were introduced in the first half of the century. The Rorschach Inkblot Test (Rorschach, 1921/1942), TAT (Morgan & Murray, 1935), Draw-a-Person (Machover, 1949), Incomplete Sentences Blank (Rotter & Rafferty, 1950) and other projective tests appeared in this period.

Clinical psychologists originally responded favorably to projective tests. For example, Aronow and Reznikoff (1973) reviewed 275 reviews of the Rorschach Inkblot Test from 1938 to 1965 and reported that the early reviews were predominantly positive, expressing optimism and enthusiasm about the test.

The rise of projective tests can also be shown empirically. Louttit and Browne (1947) surveyed clinics regarding their use of psychological tests and found that a major change from the 1930s to the 1940s was the appearance of projective tests, especially the Rorschach and the TAT, among the most commonly used tests. Similarly, Sundberg (1954) examined the citations in the Buros (1951) *Mental Measurements Yearbook* and found that, from 1937 to 1951, the Rorschach Inkblot Test became the psychological test most often cited in the professional literature.

The next section of the chapter discusses four widely used projective tests: the Rorschach Inkblot Test, TAT, human figure drawings, and incomplete sentences tests. However, students should note that there are many other projective tests. Several are described briefly in Exhibit 7.2.

Projective Tests

Rorschach Inkblot Test   As early as 1896, Binet and Henri suggested that responses to inkblots be used to study imagination (DuBois, 1970). However, the most influential figure who used inkblots to assess psychological functioning was Hermann Rorschach.

EXHIBIT 7.2   Other Projective Personality Techniques

Free Association   Freud's "fundamental rule" of psychoanalysis. Clients say whatever comes to mind, without making a conscious effort to inhibit their speech. Unconscious troubling material is interpreted from slips of the tongue, blocking, and other verbal expressions.

Word Association Test   Items consist of single words read aloud by the examiner and to which subjects provide the first word that comes to mind. Jung (1910) claimed that long pauses, infrequent associates, and other unusual responses suggest that the stimulus word is related to one's underlying problem.

Projective Play   Erik Erikson's (1951) suggestion that play is a child's natural mode of expression and serves the same purpose with children as free association does with adults. The child's emotions, concerns, and other psychological processes are thought to be expressed in free play.

Handwriting Analysis   Frank (1939) and Allport (1953), among others, suggested that personality can be interpreted from handwriting as well as from any other form of expression.

Rorschach was a Swiss psychiatrist who worked at the Burgholzi Hospital. This was the same site where Jung had worked previously, and so Rorschach was likely familiar with Jung's use of projective word association (DuBois, 1970). Rorschach observed patients playing a game, popular in the region at the time, in which they gave interpretations of inkblots (Ben-Porath & Butcher, 1991). Based on his observation that patients and nonpatients provided different types of responses, Rorschach began to experiment with inkblots as a means of distinguishing schizophrenics from nonschizophrenics (Ben-Porath & Butcher, 1991). After 10 years, Rorschach (1921/1942) published a set of 10 inkblots that he considered most useful for this purpose. Although psychologists occasionally administer other sets of inkblots, such as the Holtzman Inkblot Technique (Holtzman, 1961), Rorschach's original 10 inkblots remain the most frequently used.

Administration of the Rorschach Inkblot Test consists of two phases and usually takes from one to

two hours. In the free association phase, the examiner shows each of the 10 inkblots to the subject and asks, "What might this be?" The subject takes as much time and provides as many responses for each card as he or she wishes.

The inquiry phase is the second and longer part of the test. Here, the examiner again shows the subject each card and asks about each response. The subject must identify the exact part of the blot used in the response and indicate what aspect of the blot (e.g., the form, color, or texture) made it "look like" the response. Based on this information, the examiner codes the location, determinant, form quality, and content of each response.

Rorschach died shortly after publishing his test, and so he did not have much time to investigate it. Interestingly, Rorschach's interpretations of the test were not based on psychoanalytic theory but were instead founded on the cognitive functioning of schizophrenic patients (Ben-Porath & Butcher, 1991). However, following Rorschach's death, several colleagues (such as Walter Morganthaler) and followers (including Bruno Klopfer, Zygmunt Piotrowski, and David Rapaport) continued to use the inkblot test and developed formal scoring and interpretative procedures. It is the work of these individuals that led to the largely psychoanalytic interpretation and use of the test.

Unlike what many members of the general public think, interpretation of the Rorschach does not rely primarily on response content. Although I have had clients who provided multiple responses of sexual mutilation, explosions, gunfights, and bizarre monsters (which were in fact related to their disorders), most interpretations of Rorschach protocols are based on other aspects of the responses, such as location, form quality, color and texture, and so on. In their assessment courses, graduate students in clinical psychology learn to score and interpret Rorschach protocols. Today, the most widely used method of scoring the Rorschach is the Exner system (Exner, 1993, 1995).

Despite the popularity of the Rorschach, the test has met with significant criticism. After the scientist–practitioner model of training was adopted in the late 1940s, clinical psychologists began to examine their assumptions and practices empirically. As research in the 1950s examined the reliability and validity of the test, many psychologists concluded that the Rorschach was neither as reliable nor as valid as is required in order for a test to be useful (Wierzbicki, 1993a). Whereas clinical psychologists had viewed the Rorschach with enthusiasm in the 1930s and 1940s, they became more wary of the test from the 1950s on (Aronow & Reznikoff, 1973).

The Rorschach has problems with reliability. Inter-rater reliability and test–retest reliability tend to be low (Wierzbicki, 1993a). With low reliability, validity must be poor. Such results have led psychologists to question the continued use of the Rorschach (Peterson, 1978). Although Exner's (1993, 1995) scoring system yields higher reliability coefficients than previous Rorschach scoring systems, much research remains to be done to demonstrate the validity of Exner's interpretations (Gregory, 1996). Wood, Nezworski, and Stejskal (1996) reviewed the research on the Exner scoring system and identified several problems with it: (1) the inter-rater reliability of most scores in the system has not been demonstrated empirically; (2) several important scores and indices in the system are of doubtful validity; and (3) the research base for the system consists mainly of unpublished studies that often are unavailable for critical examination. Hence, the status of the Rorschach Inkblot Test remains questionable, at least for scientifically oriented clinical psychologists.

The problem with the reliability and validity of the Rorschach can be illustrated by a study by Miale and Selzer (1975). Miale and Selzer had experienced clinicians interpret the original Rorschach protocols of 17 Nazi war criminals. These protocols, along with several additional Rorschach protocols from Nazi war criminals who were evaluated and tried later, were reproduced in Zillmer, Harrower, Ritzler, and Archer (1995). One of the protocols is presented in Exhibit 7.3.

Miale and Selzer reported that the test interpretations consistently showed that the subjects were characterized by psychopathy, lack of responsibility, and other failings. As an undergraduate, I was impressed by Miale's and Selzer's book and considered this research as supportive of the Rorschach.

However, two later studies of these same Rorschach protocols were conducted, using judges who were blind with respect to the subjects' identities. Harrower (1976) presented four sets of Rorschach protocols (two sets of four Nazi war criminals, one set of four clergy, and one set of four mental patients), to ten Rorschach experts. Harrower asked judges to determine whether each set of protocols shared any trait in common and, if so, to identify the characteristic. Harrower also provided judges with 10 possible traits that the sets of protocols may share (including war criminal, facing the death sentence, clergy, and patients). Harrower found that only 25 percent of the judges believed that the sets of Nazi Rorschach protocols shared a common characteristic; of these, only once did a judge suggest that they shared a characteristic that was close to correct (i.e., military men); the other judges suggested that the Nazi protocols were produced by patients, clergy, superior adults, or a cross-section of middle-class individuals. Thus, Rorschach experts, blind with respect to the identity of Nazi war criminals, were unable to determine that they shared any psychological trait and were unable to distinguish between Rorschach protocols of Nazis and controls.

Ritzler (1978) compared 16 of the Nazi Rorschach protocols with those of age-matched normal controls and schizophrenic, depressed, and anxious patients. Ritzler then scored all test protocols according to a standard scoring system and assessed several Rorschach indicators of psychopathy. Ritzler found that the Nazi protocols differed slightly from those of normal controls, but not by as much as had been reported by Miale and Selzer (1975). In addition, the Nazi protocols were distinct from those of the patient groups, although they did not fit the Nazi stereotype that had been reported previously.

Thus, these follow-up studies suggest that Miale's and Selzer's (1975) findings were due to their use of nonblind judges. That is, if a psychologist knows that the subject is a Nazi war criminal, the psychologist may inadvertently tailor the test interpretation to accommodate what is already known about the subject. The psychologist can look for and find evidence to support the previously known information.

EXHIBIT 7.3   Herman Goering's Rorschach Test Protocol

I. 1. A bat.
The entire card is a flying animal, but it looks more like a bat.

2. A June bug because of the feelers.
The entire card. You can see the claws. It is alive and spread out.

II. 1. Two dancing men. A fantastic dance.
Two men, here are their heads, their hands together, like whirling dervishes. Here are their bodies, their feet.

III. 1. Two men.
Usual men. Are seen in very close detail with eyes, forehead, legs, beard, etc. During inquiry he mentions the red center which means nothing to him. On testing states it might indicate the hearts of the two men.

2. Skeletons.
This is the center gray detail and is seen as the chest cavity. Form used, not shading.

IV. 1. Fantastic fish.
Card was turned several times before answer was given. Fish is seen as a flat fish, prehistoric type such as is found in deep ocean bed. The eyes, feelers, fins are pointed out. The fish is alive.

V. 1. Bat.
Card is turned for some twenty seconds and he then adds, "a night bat." He states bat is fantastic, not entirely true to detail; but the main parts, head, wings, legs are there. He calls it a night bat for no particular reason. Color not used. It is seen as the whole card and is alive.

VI. 1. Comments: "Interesting." A flying or crawling night animal.
Card was turned many times and the animal is seen as a whole. He calls attention to the head and the feelers, and states that it is "one of the things that come out of the night." It is seen alive.

2. Fur or skin.
This is the blot without the top detail. It is seen with the fur side out.

VII. 1. Fantastic figures.
He sees the usual two figures and indicates the faces and jaws sticking out. They seem to be in movement and are covered with capes.

2. Hands.
These are the top two details which look like hands waving.

VIII. 1. Two animals climbing up a plant.
The plant is of a fantastic form but the animals are good. The entire center area is the plant. The plant is seen primarily for its form with some effect because of its color. The rats are not fantastic. He has seen big rats like this before.

IX. 1. Before giving this response, the card is turned repeatedly, moved backward and forward and he holds his two fists over his eyes and peers through them muttering "fantastic." Finally, he says "Plants and dwarfs."
Plants are the pink and green areas; dwarfs the top details. Plants are described as being colored with the form of bushes and dwarfs are seen as spooks with fat stomachs and are alive.

X. 1. This is the prettiest card. "Witches Sabbath." Whole card is used with sense of motion and he builds this response into his second response.

2. Two figures.
These are fantastic figures, half man and half animal and are the upper gray details. They are seen alive and are what made him think of witches using the rest of the blot as figures in motion.

3. Two more figures.
Top part of pink detail. Usual faces. He points out nose, etc. These two figures are also alive.

4. Scorpions.
Lateral blue seen as scorpions crawling.

5. Two caterpillars.
Center green details. Caterpillars are seen alive and crawling.

End of record

Source: Rorschach test protocol adapted from *The Quest for the Nazi Personality* (pp. 202–204) by E. A. Zillmer, M. Harrower, B. A. Ritzler, and R. Archer, 1995, Mahwah, NJ: Lawrence Erlbaum Associates. Used by permission.

EXHIBIT 7.4   Examples of TAT Responses

Michael was a 13-year-old boy who had a history of severe misconduct, including fighting, truancy, and possible gang-related activity. He was referred for a complete psychological evaluation, including intellectual, neuropsychological, behavioral, and personality assessment. As part of the personality assessment, Michael was administered the TAT. Two of his test responses follow.

Card 8 (a picture of a boy and what is possibly a rifle in the foreground, with two men who may be surgeons holding a knife over a patient in the background): "Once there was a man that got bit by a snake. No, he got shot with a gun. And then he went to the hospital and the doctor told him he might not be able walk again. He was very nervous, didn't feel too good. And then when he finally came to the doctor, the doctor said all you got to do is practice to learn how to walk again. Then he was feeling OK. Then he got shot again, got shot in the

stomach this time. They had to get the bullet out of his stomach with them doctor tools. He was scared about that. He said next time I get shot I might not live again. Then he got better. Then he felt good. Then he learned never to come to another place without a weapon. That's that. The end."

Card 14 (a picture, in silhouette, of a boy looking out a window): "One night it was a dark and stormy night. Guy was looking out the window, being nosy as usual. Got shot up in the nose. Learned never to be nosy again. That's how it ends."

These responses are typical of Michael's TAT protocol. Most of his stories included conflict and violence, often involving guns. Interpersonal relationships were almost entirely absent. Emotions, except for hostility, were infrequent. These stories are consistent with Michael's significant misconduct. Ultimately, Michael was diagnosed as having Conduct Disorder, along with several learning disorders.

TAT   Shortly after the turn of the century, Binet and Simon used children's verbal responses to pictures as tests of their cognitive abilities (Rabin, 1968). This approach to studying psychological functioning was formalized by Morgan and Murray (1935) in their publication of the TAT.

The TAT consists of a set of 20 pictures, which generally have human figures of recognizable age and gender (although different pictures are used for males and females). A subset of pictures is selected on the basis of the nature of the client's problems, since different pictures may tap into different psychological themes. The examinee is shown a picture and asked to tell a story about it, including four components: (1) what is going on in the picture; (2) what led up to the picture; (3) what is going to happen next; and (4) what are the people in the picture thinking and feeling. The psychologist records the stories verbatim for later analysis.

The TAT is based on Murray's (1938) theory of personality. According to Murray, there are many psychological needs that influence how we perceive

and respond to our environment (e.g., dominance, aggression, achievement, exhibition, and deference). Hence, such needs will be evident in people's responses to TAT cards. Exhibit 7.4 provides examples of TAT responses.

Since its introduction in 1938, the TAT has been a popular and widely used psychological test. For example, when Louttit and Browne (1947) surveyed 43 clinics about their use of tests, they found that the TAT ranked as the fifth most widely used test (following only two IQ tests, the Rorschach, and human figure drawing tests). More recently, Piotrowski and Keller (1989) and Watkins, Campbell, Nieberding, and Hallmark (1995) found that the TAT was in the top 10 most frequently used psychological tests.

Because of the popularity of the TAT, other story-telling tests have been introduced. For example, the Children's Apperception Test (CAT; Bellak, 1986) ranks among the 20 most frequently used psychological tests (Piotrowski & Keller, 1989; Watkins et al., 1995). In addition, other story-telling tests, such as the Blacky Pictures Test (Blum, 1950), for use with children as young as 5 years, and the Senior Apperception Technique (Bellak, 1986) have been used.

Murray (1938, 1943) described a method for scoring and interpreting the TAT, which involves rating the degree to which 36 psychological needs are expressed in the examinee's stories. However, many other scoring systems have been developed by others. Unfortunately, no one scoring system prevailed. In practice, few clinical psychologists use objective scoring systems for interpreting the TAT (Klopfer & Taulbee, 1976). As a result, there is little empirical evidence to document the reliability or validity of the TAT (Swartz, 1978).

For example, Jensen (1959) observed that, although more than 700 studies had been published using the TAT, only a handful addressed its empirical reliability. Lindzey (1952) reviewed the empirical evidence regarding 10 assumptions of the TAT and found little support for their validity. Because of the lack of empirical support, Swartz (1978) questioned "the ultimate usefulness of an instrument that yields such mixed results after 40 years of investigation" (p. 1130).

Still, the TAT remains popular among psychologists. Because of its continued popularity, some effort has been made recently to develop a more reliable TAT scoring system (e.g., McGrew & Teglasi, 1990). However, it remains to be seen whether independent research can substantiate the validity of such systems.

Human Figure Drawing Tests   Goodenough (1926) originally introduced the Draw-a-Man (DAM) Test to assess developmental level or intelligence in children. However, Karen Machover (1949) considered drawings to be a rich source of clinical information and suggested that human figure drawings, the Draw-a-Person Test (DAP), be used as a projective test of personality.

Interpretation of human figure drawings is largely based on psychoanalytic theory. Features of drawings are thought to represent the artist's psychological make-up. For example, drawing figures with large eyes indicates a concern that others are watching, suggesting suspiciousness or even paranoia. Ex-

aminees who draw figures with wide hips may have a preoccupation with sex; such drawings by males may suggest latent homosexuality. Drawings of hands with conspicuous fingers and thumbs may suggest a preoccupation with masturbation.

Machover's use of projective drawing tests quickly became popular. For example, Lubin, Wallis, and Paine (1971) surveyed outpatient psychological clinics regarding their test use and found that Machover's DAP had become the fifth most widely used psychological test. More recently, both Piotrowski and Keller (1989) and Watkins et al., (1995) found that projective drawings rank among the 10 most frequently used tests.

In addition, several variations of the DAP have been developed, such as the House-Tree-Person Technique (HTP; Buck, 1948, 1981), the Draw-a-Family Test (Hulse, 1951), and the Kinetic Family Drawing (Burns & Kaufman, 1970). Of these, the most widely used is the HTP. For example, Piotrowski and Keller (1989) found that the HTP is the seventh most frequently used psychological test.

The HTP requires that the examinee produce three drawings—a tree, a house, and a person. Few restrictions are made, and so the subject can make the drawings of various sizes, using different drawing materials, and so on. The HTP is interpreted psychoanalytically, like the DAP, with features of the drawings representing aspects of the examinee's psyche. According to Buck (1981), each drawing taps into different aspects of the individual: the house yields information about home life, the tree provides information about the environment, and the person reflects interpersonal relationships.

Unfortunately, empirical research on human figure drawings has consistently failed to support their reliabilty and validity. In her book that introduced the DAP as a projective personality test, Machover (1949) did not explicitly address the reliability of the DAP. She thought that the validity of the test had been demonstrated in "thousands of drawings" in clinical settings.

Swensen (1957, 1968), Roback (1968), and Harris (1972) reviewed the empirical research on projective human figure drawings and concluded that there is little support for their personality interpretations. Although the quality of a drawing may be used as a "rough screening device, and as a gross indicator of adjustment" (Swensen, 1957, p. 463), there is little evidence to support Machover's specific personality interpretations.

Similarly, there is a clear lack of empirical support for the reliability and validity of other projective drawing tests. For example, reviews of the HTP (e.g., Haworth, 1970; Killian, 1984) have concluded that the test has little empirical support. In fact, Buck (1981) noted that it is not even possible to conduct research to validate the HTP. For these reasons, scientifically minded clinical psychologists are skeptical about the HTP, despite its popularity in applied clinical settings.

Sentence Completion Tests Goldberg (1965) noted that incomplete sentences tests were used as early as 1897 by Ebbinghaus. As with several of the projective tests discussed so far, sentence completion tests were originally used to measure intellectual or other cognitive abilities (Goldberg, 1965). However, once projective tests became popular in the mid-1900s, incomplete sentences became widely used to assess personality. For example, Lubin and colleagues (1971) found that sentence completion tests ranked as the ninth most frequently used psychological test. More recently, Piotrowski and Keller (1989) and Watkins and colleagues (1995) found that sentence completion methods ranked sixth and fourth, respectively, in terms of frequency.

Sentence completion tests are straightforward. Items consist of sentence stems (e.g., "I feel _____," "If only _____," "My mother _____," "My greatest fear is _____"). They are presented in written form to examinees, who simply complete each sentence, writing their answer in the space provided.

Several sentence completion tests are available. Sets of standardized sentences have been developed for use with college students, psychiatric patients, and military recruits (Goldberg, 1965). In addition, clinical psychologists may develop their own sentences for use with specialized populations.

The most widely used and well documented sentence completion test is Julian Rotter's Incomplete Sentences Blank (ISB; Rotter & Rafferty, 1950). The ISB consists of 40 sentence stems. Each response is scored along a 7-point continuum, with a neutral midpoint and three degrees of conflict (unhealthy) and positive (healthy) responses. The sum score over 40 items is used as an index of general adjustment. According to Rotter and Rafferty (1950), the ISB has high reliability (inter-rater reliability over 0.90 and internal consistency over 0.80). In addition, Rotter and Rafferty reported that the ISB had adequate validity, as determined by significant correlations with other measures of personality traits and emotional problems.

Although Rotter's ISB has substantial reliability, the test is limited by its reliance on a single score (Goldberg, 1965). In addition, the test has been criticized as being a self-report test, rather than a true projective test (Goldberg, 1965). As such, the factors that limit self-report tests (which will be addressed later in the chapter) may also apply to the ISB.

STRUCTURED PERSONALITY ASSESSMENT

Structured personality inventories are tests consisting of self-report items that have a limited number of possible responses. That is, structured tests typically have true–false items, multiple-choice items, or rating scales.

This is a major difference between structured inventories and projective tests. Remember that projective test items are vague or ambiguous (such as inkblots) and can be answered in an infinite number of ways. Every person provides a unique response to projective test items. Structured inventories, on the other hand, limit examinees to a small number of possible responses.

According to Ben-Porath and Butcher (1991), Galton was the first to use questionnaires in the scientific study of mental functioning. As early as 1883, Galton described the use of a questionnaire in a study of visual images (DuBois, 1970). Although such basic perceptual processes are far removed from personality, other psychologists soon followed Galton's lead in using structured instruments to assess personality.

Ben-Porath and Butcher (1991) identified Heymans and Wiersma as the first psychologists to use a structured scale to assess character. In 1906, Heymans and Wiersma had 3,000 physicians rate people whom they knew well on a 90-item scale (Ben-Porath & Butcher, 1991). From these data, Heymans and Wiersma identified three fundamental dimensions of personality: Activity, Emotionality, and Primary/Secondary Functioning. According to Ben-Porath and Butcher (1991), these dimensions are similar to those of Eysenck's contemporary theory of personality: Extraversion, Neuroticism, and Psychoticism.

The first widely used and empirically developed structured personality inventory was that of Robert S. Woodworth (1920). Woodworth attempted to develop a test to identify soldiers in World War I who were susceptible to *shell shock* or *war neurosis* (terms for what today is called *Post-traumatic Stress Syndrome*). Woodworth amassed hundreds of symptoms that had been identified by psychiatrists and neurologists as early symptoms of neurosis. He put them in a questionnaire that he refined empirically, eliminating items that were frequently endorsed by normal subjects. The final questionnaire, the Woodworth Personal Data Sheet, had 116 items, each considered a symptom of neurosis. Although the war had ended by the time Woodworth published the instrument, it became widely used by psychologists in both clinical and research settings. It also set a standard for how psychologists could empirically develop and validate a structured inventory. For example, Woodworth's procedure of writing items that had clinical relevance and then selecting items on empirical grounds was the model followed in the development of the MMPI.

Following the development of Woodworth's Personal Data Sheet, psychologists published many similar tests in the next two decades. Among those considered by DuBois (1970) to be the most significant were Allport's Ascendance-Submission Test, Thurstone's Personality Schedule, the Allport-Ver-

non Study of Values, and Bernreuter's Personality Inventory (regarded by Ben-Porath & Butcher [1991] as the most commonly used structured personality test in the first half of the century).

By the 1940s, structured personality inventories had become a major tool of psychologists especially when screening large numbers of people (say, in the military) and in research. However, in clinical settings, projective tests remained more popular than structured inventories (Louttit & Browne, 1947).

An important influence on the rise of the clinical use of structured inventories came in the late-1940s, with the APA's endorsement of the scientist–practitioner model of training clinical psychologists. As clinical psychologists in the late-1940s and 1950s empirically tested their traditional assumptions and practices, projective personality tests were consistently found to have lower reliability and validity than is necessary for a test to be useful (Wierzbicki, 1993a). For this reason, clinical psychologists in the 1950s and 1960s looked for alternatives to projective tests and increasingly turned to structured inventories and behavioral assessment.

The next section of the chapter describes two widely used and influential structured personality inventories: the MMPI-2 and the MCMI. However, there are many additional structured tests that are commonly used by clinical psychologists. Several of these structured inventories are described briefly in Exhibit 7.5.

Structured Personality Inventories

MMPI-2 In 1939, Starke Hathaway and J. C. McKinley (1940, 1943) began the research to develop the MMPI with the purpose of developing a screening instrument for use in psychiatric settings to assist in differential diagnosis. They modeled their work after that of Woodworth, writing a large number of self-report items that had clinical relevance and then using empirical methods to select the most useful items. Hathaway and McKinley started with over 1,000 items that covered a wide range of topics—psychiatric symptoms, social history, medical conditions, attitudes—and administered them

EXHIBIT 7.5   Common Structured Personality Tests

California Psychological Inventory (CPI)   The CPI (Gough, 1957, 1957, 1987) was designed to assess normal personality characteristics. The current version of the CPI has 462 true–false items and yields scores on 20 scales: 17 personality dimensions and 3 validity scales. The personality dimensions include many familiar and face valid traits, such as dominance, sociability, social presence, self-acceptance, and empathy. Most scales were developed using the empirical method of contrasted groups; however, several scales were developed rationally. Cross-validation and restandardization studies have been conducted periodically to ensure that CPI scales remain high in reliability; however, several scales have only modest validity (which may be due at least in part to instability in the traits themselves). Since its publication, the CPI has been used in numerous studies. The CPI has generally been found to be a useful measure of personality in nonpatient adolescents and adults (Bolton, 1992; van Hutton, 1990; Wegner, 1992).

Personality Inventory for Children (PIC)   The PIC (Wirt, Lachar, Klinedinst, & Seat, 1984) is a 600-item true–false test completed by a parent or adult who lives with a child. The test, revised from earlier forms dating back to 1958, was developed using a combination of empirical and rational methods. The PIC yields scores on 3 validity, 1 general screening, 12 clinical (e.g., depression, family relations, delinquency, withdrawal, and anxiety), and 17 experimental or supplementary scales. The clinical scales yield four broad factor scores: poor self-control, social incompetence, internalization, and cognitive development. Although Knoff (1989) criticized the PIC's norms for being dated and geographically limited, both Knoff (1989) and Rothermel and Lovell (1985) regarded it as a useful adjunctive instrument in assessing children's problems.

Jackson Personality Inventory (JPI)   The JPI (Jackson, 1976) is a 320-item true–false test that can be used with adolescents and adults. The JPI has 15 scales of normal personality traits (such as anxiety, conformity, organization, responsibility, self-esteem, and risk taking) and 1 validity scale. Scale items were carefully selected through a sequence of carefully defining the trait to be measured by a scale and then empirically selecting the

most reliable and valid items. Though the JPI has been criticized for its brief manual (Dyer, 1985; Goldberg, 1978), it has shown promise for use with adolescents and young adults in academic and career counseling (Dyer, 1985).

Eysenck Personality Questionnaire-Revised (EPQ-R)   The EPQ-R (Eysenck, Eysenck, & Barrett, 1985) is a 100-item true–false test used to measure personality in adults (there is an alternative form of the EPQ for adolescents). The EPQ-R was designed to measure the three basic dimensions in Eysenck's personality theory: Introversion–Extroversion, Neuroticism, and Psychoticism. It also has a Lie scale to assess the validity of the subject's responding. The EPQ-R (and earlier versions from the previous three decades) have been used in numerous studies of Eysenck's theory. Studies generally have found that the EPQ-R and its previous versions have high reliability and relatively high validity (Corulla, 1987; Friedman, 1984). In general, the EPQ-R is a good instrument that assesses Eysenck's fundamental dimensions of personality.

Revised NEO Personality Inventory (NEO-PI-R)   The NEO-PI-R (Costa & McCrae, 1992) has 240 items, each rated on a 5-point scale for the degree to which the item describes the examinee. There are two forms of the NEO-PI-R: a self-report and an other-report form. The NEO-PI-R is based on a five-factor model of personality, incorporating five dimensions identified by various researchers as fundamental dimensions of personality: neuroticism, extraversion, openness to experience, agreeableness, and conscientiousness. Thus, like the EPQR, the NEO-PI-R attempts to describe the fundamental dimensions of personality. Currently, the NEO-PI-R is more popular than the EPQR, perhaps because it includes a broader range of constructs and because the personality dimensions are not as closely tied to biological foundations as in Eysenck's personality theory. Reviews of the NEO-PI-R have generally evaluated its psychometric characteristics favorably (e.g., Botwin, 1995). Even more critical reviewers (e.g., Juni, 1995) have acknowledged that the NEO-PI-R is well constructed and validated, and is a good instrument for assessing the five-factor model of personality.

EXHIBIT 7.6   Clinical Scales of the MMPI and MMPI-2

Scale Number	Scale Name (and Abbreviation)	Type of Symptoms
1.	Hypochondriasis (Hs)	Concern with physical symptoms
2.	Depression (D)	Sadness, hopelessness
3.	Hysteria (Hy)	Immaturity, denial
4.	Psychopathic Deviate (Pd)	Conflict with authority, illegal activity
5.	Masculinity-Femininity (Mf)	Cross-gender interests
6.	Paranoia (Pa)	Suspiciousness
7.	Psychasthenia (Pt)	Anxiety
8.	Schizophrenia (Sc)	Hallucinations, delusions, unusual thoughts
9.	Hypomania (Ma)	High energy/activity
10.	Social Introversion (Si)	Shyness, introversion

both to patients with known psychiatric disorders and to normal controls. In this way, they identified items that significantly discriminated among patient groups and between patient and nonpatient groups.

The MMPI consisted of 550 true–false items and yielded scores on 10 clinical scales, which are listed in Exhibit 7.6. Each scale received a T-score (a normally distributed variable with a mean of 50 and standard deviation of 10). Thus, scores greater than 70 (i.e., two standard deviations above the mean) were considered significantly elevated and so suggested the presence of a clinical disorder.

The MMPI has become the most thoroughly investigated and widely used personality inventory (Lubin, Larsen, & Matarazzo, 1984). Research on the test has flourished. For example, the MMPI has been translated into 115 languages, has been examined in over 12,000 books and articles, and has been used to develop 455 special scales beyond the original 10 clinical scales (Ben-Porath & Butcher, 1991). Much of this research concerns the interpretation of MMPI profiles. A large literature is available that suggests possible interpretations of MMPI profiles with one, two, and three clinical elevations (e.g., Gilberstadt & Duker, 1965; Lachar, 1974).

For example, clients with significantly elevated scores on Scales 1 and 3 (Hypochondriasis and Hysteria) and a lower score on Scale 2 (Depression) are sometimes described as exhibiting a conversion V profile (due to the shape of the line connecting the T-scores on the first three scales). Such clients are concerned with somatic symptoms and lack insight into and even deny the significance of their psychological problems (hence the low depression score). When clients obtain such a profile, clinical psychologists should consider possible diagnoses such as conversion disorder, chronic mild physical disorders, and hypochondriasis. Because such individuals tend to lack insight into and even deny the significance of their psychological symptoms, they tend to be poor candidates for psychotherapy.

Another common MMPI profile is the 2-7 (Depression and Psychasthenia) combination. These scales reflect affective distress (sadness and anxiety) and are commonly elevated in clients who seek outpatient therapy due to situational problems or long-term dissatisfaction with their life circumstances. The traditional term of *neurosis* was often associated with clients who had 2-7 MMPI profiles.

The rise in popularity of the MMPI in the 1940s and 1950s led many psychologists to adopt a "cookbook" approach to test interpretation, in which they relied on actuarial tables and empirically supported rules of interpretation. Paul Meehl (1954, 1957) was a leading figure in recommending that clinical psychologists base test interpretations on scientifically validated methods. Wierzbicki (1993a) outlined the history of the debate over whether statistical or subjective clinical methods make more accurate clinical predictions.

The use of actuarial cookbooks and statistical interpretation of personality tests also led to the practice of using computers to assist on the interpretation of personality tests. The issue of computerized test interpretation will be discussed later in the chapter in the section on applied issues in personality testing.

Despite the fact that the MMPI was the most widely used and well validated personality test (Lubin et al., 1984), clinical psychologists raised several significant criticisms of the test (Butcher, 1972). First, the normative sample in the original development of the MMPI consisted primarily of white midwesterners (most were family members of patients or staff members at a Minnesota hospital). It is possible that midwesterners may differ from other members of the general population in education, income, and other important demographic variables. Thus, the use of MMPI norms with minority group members and even with individuals from other parts of the country could be problematic.

A second problem with the MMPI is that its norms became dated. Diagnostic standards were revised substantially since the 1940s; hence, it is possible that patients in the 1940s differ from those in the 1990s, even if they share a common diagnostic label. Similarly, there have been many significant cultural changes since the 1940s: greater education, improved physical health, increased divorce rate, and so on. Many of these issues are addressed in MMPI items. Hence, it is possible that the normal controls of the 1940s differ significantly from normal controls of the 1990s.

A third criticism of the MMPI is that some of its items were dated (e.g., referring to "streetcars" and "sleeping powder"). Contemporary examinees may not be familiar with these terms. If examinees do not understand items, then their test scores have increased error variance and reduced reliability. In addition, use of such outdated terminology could reduce the face validity of the test, possibly affecting subjects' motivation to comply with the psychologist and respond honestly.

For these reasons, researchers at the University of Minnesota initiated a research project in 1982 to revise the MMPI (Ben-Porath & Butcher, 1991). MMPI items were revised by altering dated references, sexist language, and other objectionable material; in this way, 14 percent of the items were rewritten (Ben-Porath & Butcher, 1991). In addition, MMPI items were also selected and normed separately for adolescents and adults. The new standardization sample was large and carefully selected to match 1980 U.S. census data demographic characteristics.

The researchers published the revised MMPI (the MMPI-2) in 1989 (Butcher, Dahlstrom, Graham, Tellegen, & Kaemmer, 1989). The MMPI-2 has 567 items. Like the MMPI, the MMPI-2 yields scores on 10 clinical scales that have means of 50 and standard deviations of 10 (although one modification from the original test is that MMPI-2 T-scores above 65 rather than 70 are considered clinically significant). Like the original MMPI, preliminary research has shown that MMPI-2 scores are both reliable and valid. For example, Ben-Porath and Butcher (1989) showed that the rewritten MMPI items are about as reliable as the original items. Also, from preliminary studies by the Minnesota researchers, the MMPI-2 is about as highly correlated with clinical criteria as was the MMPI (Graham, 1990). Since the two versions of the test have substantial item overlap, much of the validity data gathered for the original MMPI should hold for the MMPI-2. For example, Archer, Griffin, and Aiduk (1995) examined the clinical correlates of 10 frequently obtained 2-point MMPI-2 codes and found that they were generally similar to those of the original MMPI codes.

The Minnesota researchers also developed a version of the test for use with adolescents, the MMPI—Adolescent form (MMPI-A; Butcher et al., 1992). According to Archer (1992), the MMPI has been used with adolescents since the early 1940s. However, it soon became clear that the original MMPI norms, obtained primarily with young adults, were not suitable for use with adolescents. For this reason, several psychologists had published MMPI norms for use with adolescents, the most frequently used of which were those of Philip Marks (Marks, Seaman, & Haller, 1974).

The MMPI-A was developed by administering the original 550 MMPI (with items revised as noted above) along with 154 new items to a group of 2,500 adolescents around the country. The standardization sample was selected to be representative of the U.S. in terms of race and to represent a wide range of geographic regions and educational backgrounds. Thus, the MMPI-A standardization sample was more representative of the general population of adolescents than the original MMPI standardization sample. From these data, Butcher and colleagues (1992) developed the 478-item MMPI-A. The MMPI-A, like the MMPI and MMPI-2, provides scores on 10 clinical scales. In addition, the MMPI-A yields scores on scales reflecting problem areas common in adolescence (e.g., school problems, family problems, low aspirations).

To date, there has been less research published on the clinical utility of the MMPI-A than either the MMPI or the MMPI-2. However, the MMPI-A overlaps substantially with both the MMPI and MMPI-2 and so much of the clinical utility of those instruments can be expected to generalize to the MMPI-A (Archer, 1992). In addition, the high quality of the MMPI-A standardization sample suggests that the test will be more useful than previously used adolescent norms for the MMPI. Still, continuing research is needed to demonstrate that the 10 clinical scales are as useful on the MMPI-A as on the MMPI and MMPI-2.

MCMI-III   Another structured personality inventory that became popular in the 1980s is the Millon Clinical Multiaxial Inventory (MCMI; Millon, 1977) and its subsequent revisions: the MCMI-II (Millon, 1987) and the current MCMI-III (Millon, 1994). Whereas the MMPI was designed to assess clinical syndromes, such as schizophrenia and depression, the MCMI was designed to assess personality disorders.

Remember that personality disorders are personality traits that are inflexible, maladaptive, and cause significant impairment or distress. As such, personality disorders are long-standing patterns of behavior that tend to be resistant to change.

Personality disorders are commonly seen in clinical settings, often as an adjunct to clinical syndromes. Because personality disorders cause significant impairment and distress, may trigger or exacerbate clinical syndromes, and may influence the treatment of clinical syndromes, clinical psychologists have become increasingly interested in the assessment, explanation, and treatment of personality disorders (Millon, 1984, 1990).

All versions of the MCMI have 175 self-statements that examinees mark as true or false descriptions of themselves. The current version of the test yields scores on 10 scales, which generally correspond to DSM-IV personality disorders, and 14 clinical syndromes (such as depression and substance abuse).

The MCMI clinical scales were constructed like those on the MMPI. A large number of clinically relevant items were written (largely based on Millon's [1981] theory of personality disorders) and then selected on the basis of their empirical ability to discriminate between patient and comparison groups. Revisions of the test were based both on modifications in DSM criteria and on research conducted by Millon and others to improve the reliability and validity of MCMI scales.

The MCMI has been demonstrated to have good reliability, with test–retest reliability coefficients hovering in the upper .80s to low .90s and internal consistency coefficients ranging from 0.66 to 0.95 (Millon, 1994). In addition, the MCMI has also been shown to have adequate validity, especially for the personality disorder scales (Wetzler, 1990; Widiger, 1985). For these reasons, Widiger (1985) judged the MCMI as one of the best instruments available for the assessment of personality disorders.

The MCMI has several advantages over the MMPI. First, because it is shorter than the MMPI, it is easier to administer, especially to clients who have difficulty reading or sustaining attention. Second, it provides scores on measures of personality disorders, which are not addressed by the MMPI but are often important in clinical management. Third, unlike the MMPI, which reports scores as T-scores, the MCMI provides *Base Rate (BR) scores,* which reflect the prevalence of a problem within the population. Base Rate scores are interpreted somewhat differently from other types of scores. According to Millon, various BR cutoff scores can be interpreted as indicating the "presence of a trait," the "presence of a problem," and the "prominence [i.e., most significant problem for an individual] of a syndrome." Although BR scores are relatively new to psychologists, they appeal to many clinicians because of their simplicity and face validity.

On the other hand, the MCMI also has several problems. Because its 175 items yield over 20 clinical scale scores, there is significant item overlap across scales. Endorsing an item adds to scores on some scales but failing to endorse the item adds to scores on other scales. This may lead to the artificial inflation of scores, especially when the MCMI is used with nonclinical or only minimally disturbed subjects (Holliman & Guthrie, 1989; Wierzbicki & Gorman, 1995). Another problem with the MCMI is that the reliability and validity coefficients of its clinical syndrome scales tend to be lower than those for its personality disorder scales (e.g., Bonato, Cyr, Kalpin, Prendergast, & Sanhueza, 1988). Thus, the MCMI is likely not as effective as the MMPI when diagnosing clinical syndromes.

Still, despite these problems, the MCMI is respected for its clinical relevance and is widely used. For example, both Keller and Piotrowski (1989) and Watkins and colleagues (1995) found that the MCMI is among the 20 most frequently used psychological tests.

SCIENTIFIC ISSUES

Evaluation of Projective Tests

Projective tests were the predominant form of personality test used by clinical psychologists prior to 1950. Louttit and Browne (1947) examined the frequency of test usage and found that human figure drawings, the TAT, and the Rorschach were the most commonly used personality tests, following only individually administered IQ tests. Similarly, Sundberg (1954) reviewed the 1936 to 1951 editions of the *Mental Measurements Yearbook* and observed that the Rorschach ranked either first or second among all psychological tests in the frequency with which it was cited in the professional literature.

The status of projective tests was quite high at that time. Projective tests are based on Freudian psychoanalytic theory, the most widely held theory of personality and psychopathology among clinical psychologists during that period. Evaluations of projective tests were predominantly favorable, with only a minority opinion dissenting. For example, Frank's (1939, 1948) discussion of the theory underlying and utility of projective methods was very enthusiastic. Aronow and Reznikoff (1973) noted that the reviews of the Rorschach at this time were overwhelmingly positive, endorsing the test in glowing terms.

However, although projective tests were widely used and held in high esteem at that time, relatively little empirical research had been conducted to evaluate their psychometric properties. For example, Machover's (1949) book, which introduced the use of human figure drawings as a projective personality test, did not even include the term *reliability* in the index; although Machover considered the validity of the test to have been demonstrated by her clinical examination of "thousands of drawings," she did not report any empirical data to support her hypotheses. Similarly, Macfarlane and Tuddenham (1951) observed that, in Bell's (1948) book on projective tests, only 15 of 748 references on the Rorschach and only 14 of 91 references on the TAT had as their primary focus the empirical validation of the tests.

Following the APA's endorsement of the scientist–practitioner model of clinical training, clinical psychologists began to evaluate empirically their assumptions and practices. Reliability and validity were recognized as essential features of any useful test. Proponents of projective tests, such as Bell (1948) and Tomkins (1947), acknowledged that the psychometric properties of projectives needed to be demonstrated to ensure that they are useful. It was at that time that the field began to conduct empirical evaluations of the reliability and validity of projective tests. For example, Schofield (1950) reviewed the research published in four professional journals from 1946 to 1948 and found that only 7.1 percent of empirical clinical studies addressed the validation of projective techniques; however, when he repeated this review in 1951 (Schofield, 1952), he found that the figure jumped to 21.0 percent.

The research literature on projective tests is too large to be exhaustively reviewed here; for example, the *Ninth Mental Measurements Yearbook* (Buros, 1985) indicated that 4,644 works had been published to date on the Rorschach. Still, it is possible to summarize this research, granting that such a brief overview may carry some exceptions.

Anastasi (1988) identified five significant limitations of projective tests: (1) inadequate standardization of administration and scoring; (2) inadequate norms; (3) limited reliability; (4) questionable validity; and (5) doubtful theoretical basis. Although she recognized that projective tests vary in terms of their research support, Anastasi's overall evaluation of projectives is gloomy.

Wierzbicki (1993a) summarized the major reviews of projective tests in general and of several major projective tests. Among his conclusions was that the reliability and validity of projective tests have not been demonstrated to be as high as is needed for tests to be considered useful. He also doc-

umented the changing status of projective test within the professional community. For example, whereas over 21 percent of the references in the *Fifth Mental Measurements Yearbook* (Buros, 1959) cited the Rorschach, TAT, or DAP, fewer than 2.5 percent of the references in the *Ninth Mental Measurements Yearbook* (Buros, 1985) cited these tests; thus, there has been a substantial decrease in the degree to which projective tests are used in research and cited in professional publications. Another piece of evidence to demonstrate the reduced status of projective tests is that the Society for Projective Techniques and Personality Assessment voted in 1970 to remove the term "Projective Techniques" from its name and journal title (Ames, 1970).

Still, despite the relative lack of empirical support for the reliability and validity of projective tests, clinical psychologists continue to use them. For example, Piotrowski and Keller (1989) surveyed 413 outpatient mental health facilities across the U.S. and found that projective tests continue to be widely used; following the MMPI, Wechsler IQ tests, and Bender-Gestalt, five projectives ranked from fifth to ninth in frequency of use (human figure drawings, sentence completion, House-Tree-Person, Rorschach, and TAT, respectively). Similarly, Watkins and colleagues (1995) surveyed 412 clinical psychologists who perform assessments and found that, following the interview, WAIS-R, and MMPI-2, four of the next five most frequently used tests are projectives (sentence completion, TAT, Rorschach, and projective drawings). Watkins and colleagues (1995) concluded that "Projective techniques have long been, are, and, we suspect, will always be among the assessment procedures most frequently used by clinical psychologists. Whatever negative opinions some academics may hold about projectives, they are clearly here to stay, wishing will not make them go away . . . , and their place in clinical assessment now seems as strong as, if not stronger than, ever" (p. 59).

Thus, despite the relative lack of empirical support for their reliability and validity, many clinicians find projective techniques valuable and continue to use them. Although this may at first seem contrary to the scientist–practitioner training of most clinical psychologists, there are several practical reasons why projective techniques may be used along with or prior to other assessment methods.

First, clinical tradition has held that clients who intend to fake their appearance during testing may find it easier to fake on structured tests than on projective tests. After all, structured tests are limited to true–false, multiple-choice, or rating scale items that permit only a limited number of possible responses. Most structured test items require that examinees rate themselves, and so the construct being assessed

by the item may be relatively easy to identify. For these reasons, clients who intend to manipulate their appearance may find it easy to do so on structured tests. For this reason, the issue of faking and how to detect it on structured tests is an important issue that will be discussed later in the chapter.

On the other hand, projective tests have an unlimited number of possible responses. In addition, the constructs assessed by projectives, as well as the way in which test responses are interpreted, are rather ambiguous and unclear to untrained subjects. For these reasons, individuals who intend to fake

---

EXHIBIT 7.7   A Case in Which a Projective Test Provided Information Not Obtained by Interview and Structured Personality Assessment

Mr. S. was a 31-year-old male who was referred by his family for evaluation at a state mental hospital. The family reported that Mr. S. had, for the last three months, isolated himself in his apartment, closing the curtains and refusing to go to work or answer the phone. They said that Mr. S. was fearful because he heard voices and complained that people were trying to harm him. Thus, from the family's report, it sounded as though Mr. S. was experiencing a severe mental disorder, such as schizophrenia.

On interview, Mr. S. did not appear to have any disorder. He was dressed neatly in a three-piece suit. He was polite and soft-spoken. His speech was articulate and relevant. He appeared embarrassed by his family's description of his behavior. He sheepishly admitted that he had been under stress at work and so had taken some time off, but he denied experiencing hallucinations or delusions. He denied that he had shut the curtains and refused to answer the phone.

Mr. S. was administered the MMPI. His test profile did not indicate any psychopathology. His validity scales were all within the normal range, suggesting that his profile was valid, and none of his clinical scale scores were significantly elevated.

The author then administered Mr. S. the Rorschach. Mr. S. seemed taken aback by the test, taking longer than average to respond. His first several responses were popular responses, reported by many people and so providing relatively little information about his own functioning. However, in his next seven responses, he

reported three scenes of sexual mutilation and two perceptions of genitalia. Also, his protocol included three *confabulations,* responses in which the examinee identifies two distinct percepts and then combines them inappropriately, a type of response long held by Rorschachers as a sign of psychosis.

After Mr. S. completed the Rorschach, he appeared pleased with himself. It seemed as though, despite his clearly pathological protocol, he believed that he had managed to present himself in a favorable way.

Mr. S. spent three days at the hospital, under observation. In that time, he appeared extremely tense and he exhibited withdrawn social behavior, staying mostly to himself. On several occasions, he became visibly upset by other patients. On one occasion, he started yelling at another patient, telling him to stay away and not cut his genitals.

The clinical conceptualization based on the entire assessment was that Mr. S. was beginning to experience symptoms of paranoid schizophrenia; however, since he had not yet experienced these symptoms for six months, the interim diagnosis of schizophreniform disorder, rather than schizophrenia, was assigned. The reason why this case is pertinent to the text discussion is that, although Mr. S.'s thought processes remained sufficiently intact so that he could successfully manipulate his appearance during a brief (90-minute) interview and on a structured test, he was unable to hide his disturbed thought processes on the projective test.

their test appearance may find it more difficult to do on projectives than on structured personality tests. Exhibit 7.7 presents a case that illustrates the way in which projective tests may be more helpful than other forms of assessment when examinees attempt to manipulate their appearance.

A second advantage of projective tests over structured tests is that they may foster the interpersonal relationship between examiner and examinee. This is important when the client is young or highly anxious. For example, 6-year-olds have little experience being interviewed by adults or completing self-report inventories. When working with a young child, it may be helpful to have the child draw or play while the psychologist observes, interacts with, and questions the child. Similarly, if an anxious client feels too inhibited to discuss his or her problem, it may be helpful for the psychologist to use a less direct method, such as a projective test (say, the TAT or an incomplete sentences test) to help the client open up. In this way, projective tests can be used as "ice-breakers" to help establish rapport.

Third, despite their limited reliability and validity, projective tests may be rich sources of hypotheses about an examinee's psychological makeup. Although the interpretations drawn from projective test protocols have limited validity, some psychologists regard the potential value of such insights into the client's dynamics as outweighing the limited validity of the test. Of course, if projective tests are used as sources of hypotheses about client functioning, the psychologist should regard these hypotheses as tentative or unproved and so seek independent evidence to confirm or disconfirm them.

Finally, it is possible to use projective tests, not for their original purpose, but rather as structured interviews. Zubin (1954) reviewed the research on the reliability and validity of the Rorschach and concluded that the test had failed in both respects. However, rather than stop using the test altogether, Zubin suggested that clinical psychologists use it as a structured interview. In this way, psychologists observe their clients' behavior in unfamiliar, standardized situations. Rather than rely on the traditional determinants of the Rorschach, clinical psychologists at-

tend to the test behavior, including response to a new task, performance in an ambiguous situation, interpersonal behavior, motivation, and effort. Thus, projective tests can be treated along behavioral rather than psychodynamic lines.

It should also be noted that projective tests may be used, not for the legitimate purposes listed above, but for invalid reasons. Some psychologists may think that projective tests are valid even though empirical evaluations show the opposite. Since the APA adopted the scientist–practitioner model of training clinical psychologists, much research has been directed toward studying how clinicians make judgments about projective tests and other clinical techniques.

For example, Forer (1949) conducted a classic study in which subjects completed a personality test and received a personality description based on the test. Subjects rated the accuracy of each statement in the personality description, the accuracy of the description in general, and the validity of the test. Forer found that most subjects rated the personality descriptions as "good" or "excellent" and the personality test as a valid instrument.

What Forer's subjects did not know was that all subjects received identical feedback. The personality description consisted of truisms that could be interpreted as true of most people (e.g., "You have a tendency to be critical of yourself," "At times you are introverted, affable, and sociable, while at other times you are introverted, wary, and reserved"). Forer showed that subjective evaluation of the accuracy of a personality test is inadequate; subjects may judge test results to be accurate and a test to be valid, even though the test provides descriptions that are meaningless as applied to an individual.

Following Forer's (1949) study, vague statements that can be interpreted as true of almost everyone have been termed *Barnum statements* and the tendency for people to accept Barnum statements as true about themselves is called the *Barnum effect*. The Barnum effect may help explain why invalid assessment techniques (e.g., palm reading, tea leaf reading, and astrology) have devoted followings. It also is not hard to see that, if clients enthusiastically endorse such personality descriptions, well-intentioned providers of such assessments may also be convinced of the validity of the technique.

Many subsequent studies have examined the Barnum effect. For example, Snyder, Shenkel, and Lowery (1977) reviewed over 25 studies of the Barnum effect and found that Barnum statements are most likely to be accepted as accurate when the following are true: the statements are global and ambiguous; clients believe that the personality description has been prepared especially for them; the personality description is more favorable than unfavorable; the personality description is derived from an assessment technique that is ambiguous (i.e., the rules of interpretation are unknown to the client); and the examiner has high status. Because most of these features apply to projective testing, the Barnum effect may help explain why some psychologists continue to view projectives as valid in the face of empirical evidence to the contrary.

Chapman (1967) proposed another reason why some clinical psychologists may continue to regard a test as valid despite evidence to the contrary. Chapman presented word pairs to subjects so that all words on a list were paired equally frequently with all words on another list. However, subjects reported that certain word pairs were paired more often than had actually occurred. This mistakenly perceived association occurred for word pairs that were meaningfully connected or that had a prior association (such as table and chair). Chapman introduced the term *illusory correlation* to refer to a mistakenly perceived association between apparently associated events that in fact have no statistical association.

Chapman and Chapman (1967) investigated the possibility that illusory correlations may explain why some psychologists perceive an association between projective test responses and personality characteristics when there is in fact no association between them. They presented to college students a series of DAP drawings along with the symptoms of the person who produced the drawings. They found that subjects mistakenly perceived associations between features of the drawing that seemed to be meaningfully related to the artist's symptoms. Interestingly, the illusory correlations of college students were similar to traditional psychoanalytic interpretations of the DAP (Chapman & Chapman, 1967). Chapman and Chapman (1969) reported a similar result, with subjects who were professional diagnosticians trained in using the Rorschach test.

Evaluation of Structured Tests

As was the case with projective tests, the research literature on structured personality inventories is too vast to be exhaustively reviewed here. Still, several general conclusions about structured tests can be drawn.

First, structured personality inventories are widely used. Following the introduction of the MMPI, it soon became one of the most widely used tests by psychologists. For example, Sundberg (1954) noted that the MMPI ranked third (behind only the Rorschach and the Wechsler-Bellevue) in terms of number of citations in the 1951 edition of the *Mental Measurements Yearbook*. Surveys by Lubin (Lubin et al., 1984; Lubin et al., 1971) showed that the MMPI is one of the most widely used psychological tests and has increased in use, from the sixth most frequently used test in 1971 to the most frequently used test in 1984. More recent surveys of psychologists have found that the MMPI is either the most widely used test (Piotrowski & Keller, 1989) or the third most frequently used technique, after only the clinical interview and the WAIS-R (Watkins et al., 1995).

Although the MMPI has been by far the most frequently used structured personality inventory, other objective personality tests are also widely used. For example, both Piotrowski and Keller (1989) and Watkins and colleagues (1995) found that the MCMI/MCMI-II and other structured inventories (including the CPI and PIC) are among the 20 most widely used psychological tests.

A second general conclusion about structured inventories is that, as a group, they tend to have higher reliability and validity than projective tests. There are, of course, many exceptions to this generalization and so this conclusion must quickly be qualified. Some structured inventories are poorly constructed and so have limited reliability and validity; some projective tests have higher reliability than some structured inventories. However, after granting such exceptions, the generalization remains fair.

It is not hard to see why structured personality inventories are more reliable than projective tests. Administration of a paper-and-pencil test is much simpler than administration of a projective test, such as the Rorschach. Thus, fewer factors that may influence test results will vary across administrations. Thus, administrative procedures tend to be better standardized for structured tests than for projective tests.

Structured tests are also easier to score than projective tests. It takes little judgment to score a true–false, multiple-choice, or rating scale item. With fewer judgments to make, clinical psychologists will attain greater inter-rater reliability when scoring structured tests than they will scoring projective tests.

It is also easier to construct internally consistent structured tests than projective tests. Because structured test items have limited possible responses, it is an easy matter to write many items and then select for further use those that meet certain statistical criteria, such as high item-total correlation. Although projective tests could be constructed in the same way using empirical methods to select items, this has not typically been done. Projective test proponents (e.g., Piotrowski, 1937) have argued that projective test items tap into different aspects of personality and so are not equivalent. If this is so, then it is difficult to develop internally consistent projective tests.

Thus, structured tests tend to be superior to projective tests in their standardization of administration, internal consistency, and inter-rater reliability. All of these contribute to greater reliability.

With greater reliability, structured tests are likely to have greater validity than projective tests. Because of the limited number of possible responses to structured test items, it is easier to obtain interpretative norms for structured tests than with projective tests. Similarly, if a particular interpretation of test results is invalid, it is easier to demonstrate this with

structured tests than with projective tests. The greater ease in administration, scoring, and interpretation of structured tests make it easier for clinical psychologists to investigate their validity. This leads both to greater empirical support for their validity and to more frequent revisions to improve their validity.

A third general conclusion about structured tests is that they are easier to use than projective tests. Thus, even if they were not more reliable and valid, many clinical psychologists would prefer them over projective tests for practical reasons. It takes less time to administer, score, and interpret structured tests than projective tests. Administering and scoring structured tests require less professional training. This means that structured tests are more cost efficient than projective tests.

For example, in my experience, it takes from 60 to 90 minutes to administer a Rorschach, another 60 minutes to score it using the Exner system, and another 30 minutes to interpret the protocol. This entire 2.5- to 3.5-hour task must be completed by a master's or doctoral level psychologist. On the other hand, it only takes about 5 minutes to instruct a client how to complete the MMPI (and these instructions can be given by someone other than a psychologist, such as a secretary or psychiatric nurse). Scoring the basic scales takes about 15 minutes by hand (virtually no time at all if a computer scores the test); this scoring does not require a professional psychologist but can be done by a clerk or unit secretary. Finally, it requires from 10 to 20 minutes to interpret an MMPI profile; this cannot be done by a secretary and so demands the attention of a professional psychologist. However, interpretation may be assisted by a computer-generated report that highlights important test results. Thus, administering, scoring, and interpreting the MMPI requires about 30 minutes of staff time, not all of which requires a psychologist. This frees the psychologist to perform other activities, either seeing additional clients or spending more time in delivering treatment.

I once worked at a hospital where nurses administered the MMPI to all patients who were admitted to the psychiatric unit. A secretary then scored the basic scales. Thus, the psychologist usually had in hand the patient's MMPI profile before meeting the patient. When I was a graduate student, clients who made appointments to be seen in our training clinic were routinely given the MMPI (along with a personal history questionnaire) by a secretary; before student therapists saw a client for the first time, they had in hand an MMPI profile and other important background information. In these ways, structured personality tests provided a quick and practical assessment that assisted the clinician's initial interview and would not have been possible using projective tests.

Although structured tests have these clear advantages over projective tests, several notable criticisms have been directed against them. First, because structured test items have only a limited number of possible responses, it may be easier for people to determine what the test is supposed to measure and then provide a response that presents them in the way that they want to appear; that is, structured tests have been criticized as being easier to fake than projective tests. Second, examinees may select their responses on structured test items, not because of the personality trait that the test is designed to measure, but because of *response sets* that lead them to answer questions according to certain patterns; thus, the occurrence of response sets has been more of a problem to structured tests than to projective tests. Third, because of the ease with which structured tests can be scored and interpreted by computers, structured tests have been criticized for opening the possibility that clinical psychologists may rely exclusively on computerized interpretations and so fail to use appropriate clinical judgment with clients. These three criticisms are each important enough to warrant a substantial discussion. Each of these issues is discussed at length in the section below on applied issues concerning personality testing.

APPLIED ISSUES

Detection of Faking

As noted above, structured personality inventories have been criticized for the possibility that people may be able to deliberately manipulate their appearance. If a true–false question reads, "I have often heard voices when no one is there," you do not have to be Freud to figure out which response signifies a "problem." If a person intends to portray himself or herself in a particular way (e.g., "healthy," "sick," etc.) it may not be difficult to do on this item and throughout the entire test. For this reason, clinical psychologists who develop structured tests have devoted much effort to detecting faking. Several types of scales are commonly used to determine whether examinees may be attempting to manipulate their appearance. These scales are *validity scales,* which help determine whether the examinee is responding accurately on the test.

Among the earliest and most well-known validity scales are those on the MMPI (and MMPI-2). Along with its 10 clinical scales, the MMPI has 3 validity scales: L, F, and K. Each was designed to detect a different sort of faking.

The L (or Lie) scale consists of 15 rationally derived items. Each item describes a slightly negative behavior or character flaw that virtually everyone has experienced (e.g., telling a lie, not liking everyone). People who deny ever having experienced these activities are probably not responding truthfully, and so their scores on other MMPI scales are suspect.

The MMPI-2 F scale consists of 60 items that are only infrequently endorsed by nonpatients. Most F scale items reflect significant problems, such as paranoid thinking, poor health, and antisocial behavior. Thus, F scale scores are elevated when subjects are truly experiencing severe forms of psychopathology, such as schizophrenia. However, F scores are also elevated when examinees report high levels of symptoms in general. This may occur because they are indeliberately exaggerating their symptoms (say, because they are in distress or are making a "cry for help") or because they are deliberately trying to present themselves as sick (i.e., faking bad). Thus, elevated F scores reflect the examinee's endorsing more unusual and severe symptoms than is typical. If the client is judged to have a severe disorder, then the F scale is not taken as invalidating the profile; however, if the client is judged not to have a severe disorder, then the elevated F score is interpreted as suggesting either a deliberate or indeliberate exaggeration of symptoms. Other evidence, such as the client's history, presentation during interview, and so on will help distinguish among these possibilities.

The K scale includes 30 items that were empirically identified through a contrast of groups of nonpatients and clearly abnormal patients who produced normal MMPI profiles (Meehl & Hathaway, 1946). Thus, high K scale scores suggest that the examinee has failed to endorse items that accurately describe problems he or she is experiencing.

Of course, high K scores, in and of themselves, do not say *why* the person has failed to report symptoms accurately. High K scores may occur for several reasons. For example, people who are deliberately trying to present themselves as healthier than they actually are to obtain high K scores. However, people who are defensive or who generally try to present themselves in a socially desirable manner may also obtain elevated K scores; these response sets (which are discussed in more detail in the next section of the chapter) may lead people to understate their symptoms, even if they are not making a deliberate or conscious effort to fake good. Graham (1990) noted that elevated K scores also have been associated with higher education and income levels, and with higher ego strength and psychological resources. That is, successful individuals may cope with their symptoms effectively, do not perceive them as problems, and so deny them on the MMPI. In this way, such persons may indeliberately underreport their problems.

Because the K scale is associated with underreporting of symptoms, it is used to adjust scores on several clinical scales. That is, examinees have points added to their clinical scales, depending on their K scale score. In this way, people who obtain very high K scores (and so who are likely underreporting many symptoms) have more points added to their clinical scales than people who obtain lower K scores.

Validity scales comparable to the MMPI L, F, and K scales have also been developed for other structured personality inventories. For example, the MCMI-III (Millon, 1994) has validity scales called

Validity, Debasement, and Desirability, which roughly correspond to the MMPI validity scales. The MCMI-III Validity scale has four items that are endorsed only very rarely by most people; endorsement of two or more of these items leads the entire profile to be regarded as suspect. The MCMI-III Debasement and Desirability scales reflect self-presentations in more negative or more positive terms than other people. Such scores may reflect either a deliberate effort to fake (bad or good) or an indeliberate response set to present oneself in a generally negative or positive way.

Another MMPI Validity scale is the Cannot Say (or ?) scale. This scale simply reflects the number of items that are skipped or are answered as both true and false. Although the MMPI instructions direct examinees to answer every question and to provide only one response per question, some people may be unable to answer a question or may inadvertently skip an item or provide both answers. Research has shown that skipped or double-marked items are rare. If a few items are skipped or double-marked, the examinee's profile should not be significantly affected, because the MMPI has over 500 items with many items per scale. However, if many items are skipped or double-marked, then the entire test profile becomes suspect. High ? scale scores may reflect extreme carelessness, defensiveness, or confusion, any of which invalidates the rest of the profile. According to Graham (1990), MMPI profiles with ? scale scores above 10 should be regarded as suspect and above 30 should not even be interpreted.

Two additional Validity scales were developed for the MMPI-2. The Variable Response Inconsistency (VRIN) scale consists of 67 pairs of items with either similar or opposite content. High VRIN scores reflect inconsistent responding, which may occur for reasons such as carelessness, poor reading ability, or confusion.

Graham (1990) suggested that the VRIN scale is most useful when interpreted along with the F scale. For example, if a person scores high on F and on VRIN, this may mean that the person is confused or has responded randomly across the test; however, if F is high but VRIN is low, then this may mean that the individual has responded consistently to test items, and so is likely to be experiencing severe problems or to be trying to present self as more seriously disturbed than is actually the case.

It should be noted that consistency scales have been used previously on structured personality inventories. For example, the Edwards Personal Preference Schedule (EPPS; Edwards, 1959) was developed as a test of 15 psychological needs from Henry Murray's theory of personality. The EPPS consisted of 210 pairs of statements, with each statement in a pair reflecting a different need. Subjects select that statement in each pair that best describes themselves. The EPPS has a consistency scale, consisting of 15 pairs of statements that are presented twice. A low score indicates that the examinee has not responded consistently to identical items and suggests that the subject was careless or confused during testing.

Another validity scale developed for the MMPI-2 is the True Response Inconsistency (TRIN) scale. This consists of 23 pairs of items that have opposite content. Thus, responding true or false to both items represents inconsistent responding. The TRIN score reflects the relative number of times the examinee responds inconsistently to these pairs of items by responding true versus false to both items. High TRIN responses suggest that the individual has responded true indiscriminately to test items; low TRIN scores suggest that the individual has responded false indiscriminately. Thus, the TRIN scale can be used to identify subjects who have responded positively or negatively to items regardless of their content.

Another approach to identifying invalid MMPI test profiles was introduced by Wiener (1948). Wiener recognized that the content of some MMPI items is so obvious that untrained examinees can determine what the item is measuring; for example, an item that reflects suicidal thinking is obviously pathological and related to depression. On the other hand, the content of other items is subtle and less clearly related to a specific form of pathology; for example, the MMPI Depression scale has items based on religious beliefs and being thirsty, which are not obviously related to depression. Wiener identified subtle and obvious subscales for five clinical scales (for some scales, virtually all items are obvious and so he could not identify subtle items for

them). There are now norms for subtle and obvious subscales of five MMPI clinical scales. When clinical psychologists suspect that examinees have attempted to fake their appearance (by attempting to fake either good or bad), they can examine the differential responding to subtle and obvious subscales. People who consistently obtain higher obvious subscale scores than subtle subscale scores may be attempting to fake bad; those who consistently obtain higher subtle scores than obvious scores may be attempting to fake good. For an example of the use of subtle and obvious subscale scores in interpreting MMPI profiles, see Exhibit 7.8.

Although subtle and obvious subscales have long been used by clinical psychologists to help identify invalid MMPI profiles, they do have some significant limitations. Schretlen (1990) noted that MMPI item subtlety is confounded with severity; the most obvious items also tend to be the most severely pathological. Hence, differential responding to MMPI subtle–obvious items may reflect the severity of an honest examinee's disorder rather than a deliberate attempt to manipulate one's profile. A second limitation of Wiener's subtle–obvious scales is that they were developed rationally and so may not have as high validity as a set of empirically developed subscales. Graham (1990) also noted that examinees' actual behavior is more highly correlated with their score on obvious than on subtle subscales. Thus, MMPI subtle–obvious subscales should be used cautiously.

Wierzbicki (1993d, 1995a; Wierzbicki & Howard, 1992) used empirical methods to develop subtle and obvious subscales for the MCMI and MCMI-II and showed that both college students and prisoners respond differentially to subtle and obvious subscales. Wierzbicki (1993c) also showed that subtlety and severity are less closely associated on the MCMI than on the MMPI. For this reason, Wierzbicki has argued that the subtle–obvious distinction may be as useful or more useful with the MCMI than the MMPI.

Response Sets

Another widely discussed limitation of structured personality tests concerns response sets. A *response*

EXHIBIT 7.8   A Case Illustrating the Use of Differential Responding to Subtle–Obvious MMPI Subscales

Mr. O. was a 46-year-old male who was referred for assessment of possible depression. Mr. O. was a college graduate and had worked as a business executive. However, he had recently completed a three-year prison sentence for commission of a white-collar crime and was currently on parole. Prior to his arrest and imprisonment, he had been treated for about one year for major depression, which may have been due, at least in part, to his concern that his criminal activity would be detected. When Mr. O. was evaluated, he was requesting that his parole restrictions be relaxed so that he could move to another state where he had made arrangements to get a job. However, he was concerned that a finding of depression might lead his parole officer to recommend against allowing him to leave the state. Thus, Mr. O. had a clear motive for attempting to present himself in a healthy way.

Mr. O. was given a complete psychological evaluation, including a lengthy interview and assessment of his intelligence, academic achievement, and personality. Intelligence testing showed that Mr. O. had an IQ in the high average range, consistent with his academic and professional attainment. Personality testing included both structured instruments (the MMPI-2 and Beck Depression Inventory) and projective tests (Rorschach, TAT). Throughout the personality testing, Mr. O. gave short and relatively uninformative responses. He denied experiencing significant problems. For example, he scored a zero on the Beck Depression Inventory, which is very low given his prior history of major depression

and his recent life circumstances. His MMPI-2 profile was completely flat, with the K scale moderately elevated but with no clinical scales significantly elevated. Because Mr. O. was above average in intelligence, the examiner thought that Mr. O. may have been successful in manipulating his MMPI-2 profile without causing the validity scales to be elevated. For this reason, Mr. O.'s differential responding to the Subtle and Obvious MMPI-2 scales was examined.

On the Obvious subscales, Mr. O. received low scores, consistent with his overall MMPI-2 profile. However, on all of the Subtle scales, he received significantly elevated scores, the highest of which was his score on the Subtle Depression subscale. The mean difference in the Subtle and Obvious T scores was over 40 points. Thus, it appeared that Mr. O. had systematically presented himself in a healthy way and had done so effectively without being detected on the MMPI-2 validity scales.

The final evaluation report noted that Mr. O. was not currently exhibiting symptoms of a major depression. In addition, the facts that he seemed to be experiencing mild distress (perhaps due to the circumstances surrounding his recent imprisonment) and that he denied these symptoms were also noted. Although Mr. O. did not meet diagnostic criteria for a current mood disorder, his distress and tendency to deny these symptoms were noted, with a recommendation that he continue counseling to help him better manage stress.

---

set is a tendency to respond to test items, not because of the content of the item, but for some other reason. For example, some individuals tend to agree rather than disagree with self-statements, regardless of item content. This response set is called *acquiescence* (or *"yea-saying"*). The converse also occurs, with some individuals tending to disagree rather than agree with self-statements, regardless of content; this response set is called *nonacquiescence* (or *"nay-saying"*).

Yea-saying and nay-saying can pose problems for structured personality inventories if items measuring a construct are worded consistently; that is, if most items that assess depression are worded so that agreement indicates the presence of depression, then yea-saying and nay-saying will be confounded with depression.

Acquiescence and nonacquiescence are easy to cope with. Test developers should include items worded in both directions so that agreement with items does not consistently add to a single scale score. Historically, psychologists have been diligent, including comparable numbers of items worded in both directions and ensuring that the severity and content of items are not confounded with the direction of scoring.

As noted above, psychologists have also developed scales to detect yea-saying and nay-saying. For example, the TRIN scale of the MMPI-2 detects inconsistencies in an examinee's protocol and determines whether the inconsistencies are due to agreeing or disagreeing with pairs of items with opposite meanings.

Perhaps the most important and commonly discussed response set is *social desirability,* or the tendency to respond to test items by selecting the most socially desirable option. From early childhood, people are taught to make a good impression, to get along with others, not to "make waves." Many people have learned to present themselves in a socially desirable way, so that they do so without deliberately intending to falsify their appearance.

Edwards recognized the potential problem of social desirability and tried to minimize it in his development of the EPPS (Edwards, 1959). EPPS items consist of a pair of statements representing two of Henry Murray's psychological needs. Subjects select that statement in the pair that best describes them. Edwards constructed the test so that pairs of statements are about equal in social desirability. Thus, it is not possible for the social desirability response set to bias the subject's protocol.

Interestingly, although psychologists initially viewed social desirability as a significant threat to the validity of structured personality tests, they later came to see social desirability as an important personality characteristic in its own right. An example of this is the MMPI K scale, originally viewed as a means of determining the degree to which subjects deliberately attempt to present themselves in an overly positive way. However, it later became recognized as a more general tendency to present oneself favorably—a tendency related to positive characteristics, such as education and income, as well as negative characteristics.

Much research has been conducted on social desirability. For example, the Marlowe-Crowne Social Desirability Scale (MCS; Crowne & Marlowe, 1960) was developed to assess social desirability as a normal personality characteristic. Reviews of scores of studies of the MCS (e.g., Evans, 1982; Strickland, 1977) have noted that the MCS is related to overt behaviors associated with social desirability, such as seeking approval and responding to experimental demand characteristics

In summary, although response sets were initially seen as a significant threat to the validity of structured inventories, psychologists soon developed methods to assess and limit their impact. In addition, psychologists also came to appreciate that the tendency to respond according to such response sets is itself a stable trait and so worthy of inclusion in personality tests. Rather than a major impediment to the use of structured inventories, response sets have contributed to the refinement of structured inventories and to the understanding of personality.

Use of Computerized Interpretations

Another common criticism of structured personality tests concerns the possible misuse of computerized test interpretation. Structured personality tests are easily scored by machine. In addition, computers can quickly generate possible interpretations of test protocols. The concern is that, because computerized interpretation is so simple, some clinical psychologists may rely solely on the computerized interpretation and so fail to properly consider other information known about the client.

Computers have been used in psychological assessment for four purposes: (1) test administration; (2) test scoring; (3) suggesting possible interpretations for consideration by the psychologist; and (4) generation of a psychological interpretation. It is easy to understand how computers make each of these tasks simpler. However, it is also easy to see how the incautious use of computers may lead to problems in each area.

Mechanical administration of psychological tests began shortly after computers became generally available to psychologists. In 1961, the Mayo

Clinic initiated a policy of having all patients who came to the clinic for evaluation complete the MMPI on computer cards, which were then scored by computer (Butcher, 1994). More recently, the MMPI and other structured tests have been programmed so that they can be administered on PCs in a clinic office. For example, in the early 1970s, an online testing program was initiated at the Veterans Administration Hospital in Salt Lake City, Utah, which included the MMPI, a test of intelligence and memory, a social history and problem checklist, a structured depression inventory, and a structured mental status exam (Honaker & Fowler, 1990). Empirical evaluations of this assessment system found that it was more internally consistent, quicker, and less expensive than traditional assessments (Honaker & Fowler, 1990).

It is easy to see the benefits of computerized test administration. Paperwork is reduced, staff time is saved, and test protocols are immediately ready for computer scoring. For these reasons, many additional structured tests are now available in online form, including the CPI, MCMI, PIC, and others.

Of course, the advantages of computerized test administration must be balanced against their possible problems. Some individuals have physical or psychological problems that limit their ability to take computerized tests. For example, I have evaluated clients who had poor reading ability and so required an oral rather than written presentation of the MMPI. I once saw a client whose conversion disorder led him to have difficulty keeping his eyes open; he was unable to complete the MMPI in written form. I know a psychologist who once conducted a study on computer anxiety. Interestingly, he had subjects complete a questionnaire administered by computer! It is possible that individuals who experienced the very problem he wanted to assess were selectively screened out of the study because of the use of computerized test administration.

The moral of the story is that computers may be very economical for administering tests; however, there should be some mechanism for identifying individuals who are unable to provide valid responses on computer-administered tests.

Another use of computers in psychological assessment is test scoring. Machines have been used to score structured tests since early in the century. According to DuBois (1970), mechanical card-sorting machines were used as early as 1919 to analyze the results of the Army Alpha and other tests. DuBois (1970) also noted that, in 1934, IBM developed a test scoring machine to score multiple-choice tests. In my work as a college professor, I routinely have multiple-choice exams scored by machine.

As with test administration, the use of computers to score tests has clear advantages. Computer scoring is quicker, less expensive, and more accurate than hand scoring. Because less time is required to score tests, professionals have more time available to interpret and make recommendations based on test results.

Computer test scoring has relatively few problems. One potential problem is the possibility that an individual may, through carelessness, skip an item and so record the answers to subsequent items in the wrong spaces. This error might be detected through hand scoring, but is unlikely to be detected by a machine. Such an error would lead the individual's MMPI profile to be evaluated as invalid, since many responses are seemingly random. Another potential problem is the possibility that a subject may not fill in the answers so that they can be detected by the machine. For example, some individuals press down so lightly or fill in so little of the answer space that the machine fails to detect the response. I once taught at a university whose mechanical test-scoring program considered multiple-choice items with two responses to have been skipped. I learned to check by hand any answers that the machine marked as skipped. Students often change their answers to multiple-choice items and sometimes erase their original answer incompletely. A machine scorer may not be able to determine which of the two marked responses was the intended answer, although a human scorer could easily do so. These potential problems exist, but are rather minor and can be addressed through more detailed instructions to subjects and by occasionally hand scoring tests to check machine accuracy.

By far, the strongest criticisms of computers in psychological assessment concern their use in test interpretation. As noted above, the Mayo Clinic developed a program in the early 1960s to score MMPI protocols. This program provided a brief interpretation of the profile, based on the basic scale elevations (Honaker & Fowler, 1990). The purpose of the interpretation was to screen a large number of medical patients for possible psychological problems when there was not sufficient staff to conduct psychological evaluations with each patient (Honaker & Fowler, 1990). Medical patients who obtained clinically elevated scores then received a more thorough evaluation by a psychologist.

This use of computerized test interpretations is quite valuable. The Mayo Clinic program stimulated the development of numerous computerized test interpretative services. For example, in 1963, Fowler initiated the first widespread computerized MMPI interpretative service; after this system became available nationally in 1965, it generated MMPI interpretations for over 1.5 million clients from 1965 to 1982 (Honaker & Fowler, 1990).

By the 1990s, computerized scoring and interpretation of psychological tests has become so widespread that virtually every major psychological test can be interpreted by computer (Gregory, 1996). Even projective tests have been interpreted by computer. For example, Piotrowski (1964) introduced a computer program to interpret Rorschach protocols. This program differed substantially from that of the MMPI computer programs, because the Rorschach test still had to be administered and scored by a clinician. However, after the quantitative information (such as total number of responses, number of responses based on each determinant, and so on) is entered, the computer generates an interpretation of the individual's personality.

Computerized test interpretation has several advantages. First, it is economical, since it demands less time from the professional. Of course, this advantage also carries risks. For example, clinics may come to rely solely on the computer interpretation—what Butcher (1994) described as a "passive" reliance on computers. If so, it is possible that there may

not be sufficient supervision of the evaluation process by a psychologist, so that insufficiently trained staff members use the computer interpretation, or that psychologists do not judge whether the computer interpretation is consistent with other evidence. Clearly, clinical psychologists need to evaluate computer interpretations and judge whether, for the case at hand, the computer interpretation may be invalid.

A second advantage of computerized test interpretations is that they are more reliable than the interpretations generated by people. After all, the computer program will interpret the same configuration of scores identically on every occasion. The computer does not experience the occasional lapses of attention (due to illness, fatigue, time pressures, and other understandable factors) that even the best clinician experiences. Hence, the computer should be more reliable across time than any single clinician. In addition, clinicians have different levels of training, theoretical biases, and types of experiences that may lead them to interpret a single test protocol in different ways. Hence, computerized interpretations should have greater inter-scorer reliability than many pairs of clinical psychologists.

Finally, some have argued that computerized test interpretations are more valid than those of clinicians. This is the rub. Clinical psychologists employ tests in order to gain information about people that is useful in making judgments about clients—assignment to treatment, selection for training, prediction of violence, and so on. If computerized test interpretation is more reliable than human test interpretation, then it follows that computerized test interpretation might be more valid than human test interpretation. Of course, this is a major point of contention that has generated much research.

Paul Meehl (1954) published a book called *Clinical versus Statistical Prediction. Statistical prediction* involves making predictions for a person based on quantitative measures (such as test scores and demographic characteristics), using prediction formulas derived from empirical research with other subjects. In statistical prediction, clinical psychologists use actuarial or statistical methods that have been reported in the research literature. On the other hand, *clinical prediction* is the practice of making predictions about the person based on the clinical psychologist's judgment of the person, from information gained in interviews, observations, tests, and other sources. Clinical predictions are subjective judgments made by clinicians based on their understanding of the individual.

Meehl (1954) discussed the two types of prediction and reviewed about 20 studies that compared their relative accuracies. Meehl observed that statistical prediction almost always equals or surpasses clinical prediction. For this reason, he suggested that clinical psychologists make a greater effort to incorporate statistical findings in their clinical work. He also called for research on clinical judgment, to determine what predictions clinical psychologists make accurately.

Meehl's book touched off a storm of controversy. Wierzbicki (1993a) reviewed the history of the debate on the relative merits of clinical versus statistical prediction, including the many criticisms of the research reviewed by Meehl and the defenses of clinical prediction. Still, after a half-century, the empirical research remains clear. With over 100 empirical studies in the medical and social sciences on the relative accuracies of clinical and statistical prediction, Meehl's conclusion from his 1954 book remains unchanged. Almost all of the studies show that statistical predication equals or surpasses clinical prediction (Wierzbicki, 1993a).

SUMMARY

Personality refers to the consistencies in a person's behavior. Personality traits are tendencies to respond in functionally equivalent ways across situations. Personality disorders are personality traits that are so extreme and inflexible that they lead to significant distress and problems in daily functioning. Clinical psychologists assess personality both to diagnose or understand a client's problem and to assist in selecting appropriate treatments.

All societies have developed methods for assessing its members' psychological characteristics. Ancient methods often relied on the person's physio-

logical characteristics, such as body type and physical appearance. Other ancient assessment methods included astrology and graphology.

As psychology developed as an independent discipline in the late-1800s, psychologists started using scientific approaches to measure behavior and mental processes. Forerunners to today's personality tests appeared at this time and were used by Wundt, Binet, and others.

Two types of personality tests are now widely used. Projective personality tests present stimulus materials that are vague or ambiguous and must be interpreted or organized in some way. Each person provides a unique response to a projective test item. The way the examinee interprets or organizes the material is presumed to yield information about underlying psychological processes. Projective tests are based on Freudian theory and were very popular in the first half of the 1900s. Examples of projective tests include the Rorschach Inkblot Test, the TAT, human figure drawings, and sentence completion tests.

The other major type of personality test is the structured inventory, which consists of items that have a limited number of possible responses (e.g., true–false, multiple-choice items). Subjects use these items to describe themselves. Common structured personality tests include the MMPI-2 and MCMI-III.

Compared to structured personality inventories, projective tests tend to be less well standardized in their administration and scoring. Projective tests also tend to have less adequate interpretative norms than structured tests. Thus, projective tests tend to have lower reliability and validity than structured inventories. Still, projective tests may be useful to test clients who are suspected of trying to fake their test appearance; to serve as "ice-breakers" with anxious or young clients; and to suggest hypotheses about a client's psychological make-up. Projective tests can also be used as opportunities for clinical psychologists to conduct behavioral observations of clients in an unfamiliar and ambiguous situation.

Subjective validation of psychological tests is not a sufficient reason to use them. Research has shown that the Barnum Effect and the illusory correlation may lead people, including psychologists, to accept tests that are invalid.

Structured personality tests are superior to projective tests in standardization of administration, scoring, and interpretation. Thus, they tend to be more reliable and valid than projective tests. For this reason, the use of structured tests has increased relative to that of projectives since the 1950s.

Structured inventories are subject to several criticisms that do not apply to projective tests. Structured inventories may be easier to fake than projective tests. For this reason, psychologists have developed methods of testing the validity of responses on structured tests. Validity scales have been developed to identify subjects who are faking good, faking bad, and answering inconsistently.

Another criticism of structured tests is the possibility that response sets may invalidate the test protocol. Response sets are tendencies to respond to items in a particular way regardless of item content. Common response sets are social desirability, acquiescence, and nay-saying. Psychologists have also developed validity scales to detect these response sets.

A third criticism of structured inventories is the possible misuse of computer interpretation. The structured nature of these tests makes it easy for computers to administer, score, and help interpret them. However, the ease of computer administration and scoring raises the possibility that a psychologist may rely solely on the computer interpretation, without considering information about a client that cannot be considered by the computer.

S T U D Y   Q U E S T I O N S

1. Discuss the difficulties inherent in defining personality.
2. Compare and contrast the concepts of personality trait and personality disorder.
3. Identify three ancient approaches to assessing personality. Discuss the contemporary variants of these approaches.
4. Discuss the theoretical rationale underlying projective and structured personality tests.
5. Describe three major projective tests. What do they have in common?
6. Discuss the relative strengths and weaknesses of projective and structured personality tests.
7. Discuss the history of projective tests. What factors contributed to their rise in the early 1900s and their decline in the mid-1900s?
8. Discuss the importance of validity scales in structured personality inventories. What approaches have psychologists used to detect invalid profiles on structured inventories?
9. What is a response set? How can response sets affect a person's score on a structured personality inventory?
10. Discuss the use of computers in structured personality testing. What are the proper uses of computers in testing? What are the misuses of computers?

CHAPTER

8

Psychological Treatment
An Introduction

I. Brief History
II. Scientific Issues
   A. Psychotherapy Process
   B. Psychotherapy Outcome

III. Applied Issues
   A. Ethical Issues
   B. Case Management
IV. Summary

The preceding four chapters discussed the clinical psychologist's role in assessment. As noted in those chapters, the primary function of the clinical psychologist through the first half of the 1900s was assessment—intellectual, personality, and behavioral. However, from the mid-1900s on, clinical psychologists became increasingly involved in the provision of treatment services.

This chapter introduces the topic of psychotherapy. It begins with a brief history of psychological interventions and then addresses both scientific and applied issues related to therapy. The scientific issues addressed are the processes that make psychotherapy work and the general effectiveness of psychotherapy. Applied issues discussed include the ethical standards that govern the provision of psychological treatment and case management.

This chapter also serves as an introduction to the next five chapters. Chapters 9 through 12 will discuss psychological treatments from the major theoretical perspectives, including the psychoanalytic, humanistic, cognitive–behavioral, and biological models. Chapter 13 will examine psychotherapy as presented in various formats, such as marital, family, and group therapy. The scientific and applied issues in this chapter will be examined repeatedly in the succeeding chapters on specific approaches to psychotherapy.

BRIEF HISTORY

As presented in Chapter 1, the foundations of clinical psychology extend back to ancient times. The ancient Greeks, Romans, and Chinese recognized the occurrence of psychological disorders and advocated their treatment alongside medical disorders. According to Brems, Thevenin, and Routh (1991), the awareness of psychological disorders and their treatment date as far back as 2100 B.C., to the Babylonians in Mesopotamia. Brems and colleagues (1991) suggested that the earliest known hospital devoted expressly to the treatment of mental illness was established in Jerusalem in about A.D. 490. In addition, they identified Johann Weyer (1515–1588) as the first physician who specialized in the treatment of mental illness—the first true *psychiatrist*.

Although physicians from early times recognized the occurrence of mental illness, the treatment of psychological disorders remained a rather minor specialty in medicine until the late 1800s. In the last century, however, psychotherapy experienced a tremendous increase in influence. The number of providers, forms, and receivers of psychotherapy have all increased dramatically since the 1890s.

For example, Freud was one of only a handful of physicians who, in the 1890s, examined the role of psychological influences on physical and behavioral disorders. By 1990, however, there were 100,000 fully trained, highly qualified psychotherapists and, using a broad definition to include therapists and counselors without doctoral degrees, at least 250,000 therapists/counselors in the United States alone (VandenBos, Cummings, & DeLeon, 1992).

As of 1892, psychotherapists provided only a limited range of forms of psychotherapy: from hypnosis and catharsis to directive, supportive, and expressive therapies (Ellenberger, 1970). Less than a century later, Corsini (1981) listed over 250 different forms of psychotherapy. Whereas only a handful of clients can afford the lengthy and expensive psychotherapy available in the 1890s, VandenBos and colleagues (1992) estimated that fully one-third of the U.S. population had, by 1990, used some form of mental health service.

Like psychotherapy, the field of clinical psychology also experienced a tremendous boom in the 1900s. Lightner Witmer introduced the term *clinical psychology* and founded the first psychological clinic in 1896. By 1914, 19 universities in the United States had established psychological clinics (Reisman, 1981). The number of clinical psychologists in this country increased from 800 in 1931 to over 12,000 in 1969 (Reisman, 1981). In fact, the number of psychologists rose so dramatically in the early 1900s that Boring once calculated that if the growth curve of APA membership should keep its shape,

then by the year 2100 there would be ten and a half billion psychologists (Hall, 1967).

Several social factors contributed to the rise of the clinical psychologist as psychotherapist throughout the 1900s. World War II led both the public and the psychological community to recognize the frequency and social impact of mental disorders. For example, VandenBos and colleagues (1992) cited an army estimate that at least 2 million veterans would require treatment for mental problems following the war.

VandenBos and colleagues (1992) discussed economic influences on the rise of clinical psychology. For example, the community mental health center movement, proposed by President Kennedy in the early 1960s, emphasized the need for additional providers and alternative forms of mental health services. In addition, both private and public health insurance providers increasingly covered psychological services from the 1960s to the 1990s (VandenBos et al., 1992). Thus, therapy provided by clinical psychologists was covered by third-party payers more frequently than in the past.

As will be discussed in Chapter 12, the rise of psychiatric medications in the 1950s and 1960s also contributed to the role of the clinical psychologist as therapist. Although psychologists could not prescribe the medications discovered to be helpful in treating psychotic conditions such as schizophrenia and bipolar disorder, medications helped these patients to recover from their psychoses and so enabled them to be responsive to psychological treatments.

Chapter 12 will also discuss the role of the clinical psychologist in treating psychophysiological and medical disorders. In the 1960s, the medical and mental health fields both recognized the influence of stress on somatic disorders. The clinical specialty of behavioral medicine arose in the 1960s and 1970s devoted especially to the treatment of such problems.

Chapters 9 through 13 will discuss in more detail the development and practice of different forms of psychotherapy. Each of these chapters will address theoretical influences on specific therapies. In addition, they will also address social and other influences on the rise of each therapy as practiced by clinical psychologists.

SCIENTIFIC ISSUES

Clinical psychologists must address two fundamental scientific questions regarding psychotherapy: Does psychotherapy work? If so, then how does it work? These are the issues of psychotherapy outcome and process.

Since the introduction of psychotherapy at the turn of the twentieth century, hundreds of studies have investigated these questions. This part of the chapter introduces readers to these issues and the research designs developed to investigate them. This part of the chapter also discusses some of the controversies and issues concerning psychotherapy process and outcome.

Psychotherapy Process

The issue of psychotherapy process addresses the "active ingredients" of therapy. That is, what makes psychotherapy work? Chapters 9 through 12 will examine the proposed explanations of therapeutic effectiveness according to the psychoanalytic, humanistic, cognitive, behavioral, and biological theories. Discussions of the reasons why therapy works, according to these theories, and empirical evaluations of the effectiveness of these approaches to therapy will be presented in these chapters.

This section of the chapter will present several ideas, independent of any theory of therapy, on why psychotherapy works. That is, this section of the chapter will examine proposals concerning the basic elements common to all forms of therapy.

Jerome Frank's Model Jerome Frank (1961) wrote an influential book called *Persuasion and Healing*. In this work, Frank discussed the basic elements of psychotherapy—those factors that are common to all forms of psychotherapy and even to nontraditional forms of therapy, such as Shamanism.

According to Frank, persons who enter psychotherapy are characterized by *demoralization*. That is, they have failed to cope with their life problems and

suffer as a result. Moreover, clients are aware of their failure and no longer have the expectancy that they will be able to cope. For this reason, they turn to a socially sanctioned healer.

Frank identified four elements he believed are common to all forms of psychotherapy: (1) a relationship between the client and therapist; (2) a setting that is socially sanctioned as a place of healing; (3) a theory to explain the development of the problem; and (4) an intervention prescribed by the theory. Frank cited research that showed that each of these factors is related to cognitive and emotional change.

Frank argued that psychotherapies produce positive change because they (1) provide opportunities for learning; (2) enhance the client's hope of relief; (3) provide success experiences that increase the client's sense of mastery; (4) overcome the feeling of alienation from others; and (5) arouse the client emotionally.

Students should consider how these factors may play a role, not just in formal psychotherapy provided by clinical psychologists, but also in other therapeutic relationships, such as may occur with witch doctors, so-called psychic healers, and other providers of services of dubious value. The common elements of psychotherapy are found in Shamanism and psychic healing and may account for the success of such practices.

It was not Frank's intention to suggest that psychotherapy is nothing but a placebo. Rather, he argued that the common elements of therapy may account for the effectiveness of placebos. If therapists recognize such factors, they may be able to incorporate them so as to increase the effectiveness of therapy.

It is also important to recognize that Frank was not claiming that all therapies are equally effective. Therapies differ in the face validity (or reasonableness) of the rationales they provide for their interventions and in the effectiveness with which they provide opportunities for learning. For example, Frank suggested that behavior therapies may be especially effective in providing clients with opportunities to enjoy success experiences. Because therapies differ in the extent to which they help clients attain the common goals, it is possible in Frank's model to observe differences in effectiveness between therapies.

Nonspecific Factors in Therapy   Following Frank's classic description, many other psychologists offered their views on the common elements of therapy. Of course, some writers presented their ideas within a specific theory. Specific theoretical explanations of why psychotherapy works will be postponed until later chapters. This part of the text will summarize more general discussions of the basic elements of psychotherapy.

The basic elements of psychotherapy, independent of the therapist's theoretical orientation or techniques, are sometimes referred to as *nonspecific elements of therapy* (Kazdin, 1986). Numerous discussions of nonspecific factors in therapy have appeared, including some that (with a somewhat comical oxymoron) identify specific nonspecific factors. Nonspecific factors in therapy can be divided into characteristics of the (1) client, (2) therapist, and (3) relationship.

As Frank (1961) observed, individuals who seek therapy are experiencing distress. Virtually every school of psychotherapy, from psychoanalysis to behaviorism, has recognized that clients in distress are motivated to change their condition, and so clinical psychologists interpret distress as a predictor of compliance.

Students should note that social psychological research on attitude change has shown that individuals who are experiencing emotional arousal, such as fear, are more easily persuaded than others, especially when the message purports to provide advice on how to cope with the fear-inducing stimulus (Brehm & Kassin, 1993). Research has also suggested that individuals in distress are more likely than others to respond positively to both medical and psychological placebos (Shapiro & Morris, 1978). For these reasons, clinical psychologists from virtually all theoretical persuasions interpret client distress as a predictor of positive response to therapy.

Another client variable that has received attention as a nonspecific element of therapy is client

expectation. Client expectation has been found to be associated with both length (e.g., Pekarik & Wierzbicki, 1986) and outcome (e.g., Lick & Bootzin, 1975) of therapy. These results have led clinical psychologists to develop methods of informing potential clients as to the length, nature, and potential results of therapy, with the goal of improving retention rates and outcome (Garfield, 1986).

The second group of nonspecific factors in psychotherapy consists of characteristics of the therapist. Beutler, Crago, and Arizmendi (1986) reviewed research on the many therapist variables that have been proposed as possible influences on therapy outcome. Although their results are too complex to present in detail here, Beutler and colleagues did identify several therapist variables that are consistently related to outcome across a significant number of studies. These variables include therapists' well being, social influence attributes, expectation, and competence.

Of course, all theories of psychotherapy provide explanations for why therapist competence and well being are related to therapy outcome. Psychologically healthy and competent therapists should perceive the client's problems more accurately and provide therapeutic interventions more effectively than less healthy or competent therapists. This holds true whether the therapy provided is psychoanalytic or behavioral.

Of perhaps most interest to a discussion of nonspecific factors of therapy are the therapist's social influence attributes. According to Beutler and colleagues (1986), research has repeatedly found that outcome is positively related to therapist credibility. This is consistent with social psychological research on attitude change; social psychologists have often observed that persuasiveness is positively associated with credibility (believability) (Brehm & Kassin, 1993).

Coe (1980) described a series of studies by Gillis in which social influence variables were systematically manipulated in the context of psychotherapy. Coe reported that the same factors associated with persuasion and attitude change in social psychological research (e.g., prestige of the therapist, expectation of success) are related to therapy outcome.

The third class of nonspecific therapy variables concern the client–therapist relationship. The major schools of psychotherapy have all recognized that treatment is more likely to be successful when a good client–therapist relationship, or *rapport,* has been established. Although each theoretical approach to therapy emphasizes a different aspect of the client–therapist relationship and provides a different explanation for why this relationship is important, they all agree that the rapport between client and therapist is an important factor in the success of therapy.

Freudian psychoanalysis stresses the client–therapist relationship. According to Freud, clients develop strong feelings for the therapists over the course of therapy. Psychoanalysts use these feelings in two ways. First, they help the therapist understand the client's dynamics related to early childhood interactions. Second, examining the client–therapist relationship helps the client gain insight into these childhood issues.

Rogerian therapy regards the therapist's acceptance of the client as the active ingredient of therapy. The Rogerian therapist accepts the client unconditionally, as she is, without placing any demands on or making any judgments about her. According to Rogers, after the therapist has accepted the client in this way, the client can then accept herself. Thus, the Rogerian client–therapist relationship helps the client to understand and accept herself.

Cognitive–behavioral therapy places somewhat less emphasis on the client-therapist relationship than the other schools of therapy. Still, even here, the quality of the relationship is important. Cognitive and behavioral therapists regard therapy as a didactic or educational enterprise. They employ training techniques to help clients develop skills that enable them to function more effectively. Research has shown that models are more likely to be imitated when they are warm and nurturing (Grusec & Skubiski, 1970). Virtually any effort to influence another person will be more effective when the persuader is liked or admired (Brehm & Kassin, 1993). Thus, cognitive and behavioral therapy is likely to be more effective when the therapist has established a good rapport with the client.

It should be noted that other health professionals also recognize the importance of client–therapist rapport. For example, it is common for medical students to receive advice on developing a good "bedside manner." The best medical intervention in the world will not be effective if a client dislikes or distrusts the doctor and so does not use the treatment as directed. For this reason, medical health professionals, biologically oriented clinical psychologists, and others also recognize the importance of the client–therapist relationship.

Psychotherapy Outcome

From the turn of the century, when Freud introduced psychoanalytic therapy, to the 1950s, clinical psychologists paid relatively little attention to the question of the effectiveness of psychotherapy. Psychotherapists relied upon the subjective perceptions of their clients, supervisors, and themselves to assess the efficacy of their techniques.

Freud, often regarded as the founder of modern psychotherapy, expressed a lack of interest in empirical evaluations of therapy. For example, Freud (1917/1963) rejected a suggestion that psychoanalysts collect data regarding their successes, because "statistics are worthless if the items assembled in them are too heterogeneous; and the cases of neurotic illness which we had taken into treatment were in fact incomparable in a great variety of respects" (p. 461). Similarly, when presented with the results of cases seen over a 10-year period at the Berlin Psychiatric Institute, Freud (1933/1964, p. 152) said that "statistics of that kind are in general uninstructive; the material worked upon is so heterogeneous that only very large numbers would show anything. It is wiser to examine one's individual experiences."

Freud and other therapists in the early 1900s published a large professional literature, using case studies to illustrate the techniques and outcome of psychotherapy. Unfortunately, case studies, as described in Chapter 2, provide little evidence to prove that a therapy is effective. Although case studies are useful in the first two stages of science, they are weak when it comes to testing hypotheses in the third stage of science.

Research in the 1970s and 1980s showed that clinical psychologists make the same types of perceptual, reasoning, and interpretational errors that people make in general (Wierzbicki, 1993a). Thus, clinicians' subjective perceptions of the effectiveness of therapy may be erroneous and should be verified using more objective methods.

Eysenck's Argument   In 1952, Hans Eysenck published a classic paper in which he attempted to answer the question "Does psychotherapy work?" Eysenck located all the published studies that reported therapy outcome rates with neurotic adults (5 of psychoanalytic therapy and 19 of eclectic therapy). Because these studies did not include control groups of untreated patients, Eysenck estimated the *spontaneous remission rate,* or the percent of neurotics who improve without receiving formal therapy. Based on two earlier studies of neurotics who received minimal treatment, Eysenck suggested that a reasonable estimate of the spontaneous recovery rate for neurotics is 72 percent.

Eysenck found that the overall improvement rate was 44 percent for psychoanalytic therapy and 64 percent for eclectic therapy. When the overall improvement rate of therapy is compared to the spontaneous remission rate, the result is not favorable to psychotherapy. Eysenck concluded that these data "fail to prove that psychotherapy, Freudian or otherwise, facilitates the recovery of neurotic patients" (p. 322).

Clinical psychologists reacted vigorously to Eysenck's paper (e.g., Bergin, 1971; Luborsky, 1954). Critics raised five major arguments with Eysenck's review (Wierzbicki, 1993a):

1. *The "apples and oranges" argument.* The 24 studies varied with respect to disorders treated, training and level of experience of therapists, and methods of assessing outcome. Combining such a heterogeneous group of studies is questionable.

2. *The control group argument.* Eysenck's comparison was not a true experiment in that it compared previously existing groups. The treated and untreated neurotics may have differed in the nature and severity of their disorders.

3. *The spontaneous remission argument.* The studies used to estimate spontaneous remission rate actually provided minimal treatment. Thus, this figure should not be used as an estimate of the *no treatment* success rate but as a *minimal treatment* response rate. For example, Bergin (1971) reviewed 14 studies and concluded that the spontaneous remission rate for neurotics is about 30 percent. If Bergin is correct, then Eysenck's estimates of the recovery rates for psychoanalytic and eclectic therapies actually support claims of the effectiveness of psychotherapy.

4. *The outcome criteria argument.* The studies used different methods to measure outcome. It is possible that the outcome criteria differed between the treatment studies and the studies used to estimate the spontaneous remission rate.

5. *The alternative interpretations argument.* Eysenck made subjective judgments in order to force the results of 24 studies into a uniform classification scheme. Other reviewers could make different judgments that could lead them to draw different conclusions. For example, Bergin (1971) classified outcomes in the 24 studies somewhat differently from Eysenck and estimated that the improvement rates of psychoanalytic and eclectic psychotherapy are, respectively, 83 and 65 percent.

Although these criticisms of Eysenck's review are powerful, readers should note that Eysenck was familiar with them and had even raised several of them himself. Readers should also note that these arguments may invalidate Eysenck's review but they do not prove that psychotherapy is not effective. To show that Eysenck's review was flawed does not substitute for empirical evidence that proves the effectiveness of therapy.

Eysenck's 1952 paper, then, constituted a challenge to clinical psychologists. If psychotherapy works, then therapists should be able to demonstrate this empirically. If existing psychotherapies do not work, then clinical psychologists should develop newer therapies that can be supported empirically.

Research Methods to Examine Therapy Effectiveness   Chapter 2 introduced the research methods used by clinical psychologists. Methods used to examine the effectiveness of therapy include the case study and several single-case designs, such as the ABAB Reversal Design and the Multiple Baseline Design.

In the traditional case study, the investigator describes a client's functioning before and after providing some intervention. The case study permits the clinician to describe the case in detail and to develop ideas concerning the cause and amelioration of the problem.

However, because the case study does not permit the investigator to rule out alternative explanations for the observed changes, it does not have sufficient internal validity to permit causal conclusions. No matter how well trained, careful, and diligent the investigator, it is always possible for the psychologist to fail to observe the variable that causes the client's problem or improvement. Similarly, it is always possible for the psychologist to introduce a bias into the observations so as to support a favored theory. For these reasons, the case study, although important in the first two stages of science (observation, generation of hypotheses), is relatively weak when it comes to the third stage of science.

Chapter 2 also described several single-case designs that are elaborations of the traditional case study. The ABAB Reversal Design and the Multiple Baseline Design are methods of introducing a control or comparison phase even when working with a single subject. In the ABAB Reversal Design, a clinical psychologist assesses the client's functioning during alternating periods in which treatment is and is not provided. If the target symptom is observed to alternate along with treatment, then this is evidence that the treatment may have a causal effect on the symptom.

In the Multiple Baseline Design, the clinician assesses several distinct symptoms and introduces treatments designed to help each symptom in sequence. If targeted symptoms decrease in severity while nontargeted symptoms remain constant, then this is interpreted as support for the effectiveness of treatment.

Although these methods are improvements over the traditional case study, they are not conclusive. After all, it is possible that some variable unknown to the clinician varies along with the treatment. It is also possible that clinicians, while introducing treatment, may provide some therapeutic condition (e.g., attention, interest, empathy) of which they are unaware.

Experimental research is most pertinent to claims of the effectiveness of therapy. As described in Chapter 2, experiments involve the random assignment of subjects to two or more groups that are then exposed to different levels of the independent variable. In experiments on psychotherapy outcome, the independent variable is the type of treatment provided.

In the most basic experimental psychotherapy outcome study, clients with the same disorder are randomly assigned to two groups: the experimental group, which receives the treatment under investigation, and the control group, which receives no treatment. Comparison of the groups at the end of treatment shows whether treated subjects have a better outcome than control subjects. If so, then the psychologist can validly conclude that the treatment caused the improvement.

Now, there are many ethical and practical issues that must be addressed in conducting such research. First, if the condition treated is severe, one may question the ethics of withholding treatment from the control group. Given this concern, clinical researchers often employ variants of the untreated control group, such as a *delayed* (or *wait-list*) *treatment group*. In this case, clients in the control group are assured that they will receive future treatment. Delayed treatment groups are commonly used in therapy outcome studies. Because many facilities do not have the resources to provide immediate treatment to every new client, it is standard practice to place incoming clients on waiting lists. The delayed treatment group is consistent with existing practices at many treatment agencies and addresses both the ethical and practical issues of withholding treatment from clients.

Another alternative to the untreated control group is the *minimal treatment group*. In this case, subjects in the control group receive some minimal intervention, without receiving the experimental treatment. Such minimal treatment may consist of brief contacts with a professional who provides general advice or educational material. In this way, clients receive some of the elements common to all therapy (e.g., contact with a professional, reassurance), but do not receive a formal course of therapy. As in the case of the wait-list control group, subjects in a minimal treatment group may receive the experimental treatment later.

Another alternative to the untreated control group is the placebo treatment group. In this case, clients engage in some structured exercise or activity under the supervision of a professional, but do not receive a formal course of therapy. Psychotherapy placebos have consisted of such activities as filling out questionnaires in the presence of a psychologist, receiving false feedback from a biofeedback device, or reading aloud the parts of a play. As with the delayed treatment control group, clients who receive a placebo treatment can be offered the experimental treatment at the end of the study.

Psychotherapy placebos, if properly presented, introduce expectancies of success. Thus, comparing the outcomes in the treatment and placebo groups will determine the degree to which the treatment produced improvement beyond that caused by simple expectancy. Of course, the catch here is that the placebo must be presented in a manner that has *face validity*. If the placebo does not appear to be a legitimate intervention, then it will not adequately control for expectancy effects.

A final alternative to the untreated control group is to use another treatment already in common use. This older treatment may have been found in previous studies to be at least moderately effective in treating the condition at hand. Even if there is no empirical evidence to support the efficacy of the older treatment, it may be supported by clinical experience and case study evidence. For these reasons, clients who are assigned to receive this older treatment are not receiving a therapy that is less adequate than what they might receive if they approached a clinical psychologist in the community. The experimental outcome study can then determine the degree to

which the experimental treatment is superior to the older treatment already in use.

It should be noted very quickly that, in any study with human subjects, the ethical standards of psychologists require that subjects be fully informed of any potential risk and that they provide their informed consent before the study. In the case of psychotherapy outcome studies, potential clients must be informed that, if they participate in the study, they may receive the experimental treatment or an alternative treatment.

In my experience, clients readily accept the possibility that they may be assigned to wait-list or minimal treatment control groups. Clients are aware of the clinical reality that, if they go to another agency, they may well be placed on a waiting list before starting therapy. For this reason, many clients are willing to enter an experimental program where they may, at least initially, be assigned to a control condition.

Reviews of Psychotherapy Outcome Studies

Clinical psychologists began to conduct psychotherapy outcome studies in the 1950s and 1960s. This occurred in response both to Eysenck's (1952) challenge to the field to demonstrate empirically the effectiveness of psychotherapy and to the APA's adoption of the scientist–practitioner model of training of clinical psychologists. In 1952, Eysenck could locate only 24 studies that reported the outcome of psychotherapy; only three decades later, Smith, Glass, and Miller (1980) identified 475 experimental studies in which one form of psychotherapy had been compared either to no therapy or to another form of therapy.

Because the empirical literature on psychotherapy research has become so large, it is difficult for clinical psychologists to read and evaluate all of the research. For this reason, many psychologists rely on research reviews that examine a portion of the research with the goals of summarizing the results, interpreting the findings, and making recommendations concerning the practice of therapy and the conduct of future studies.

One of the most important sources of reviews of psychotherapy research are the handbooks on psychotherapy research edited by Bergin and Garfield (1971, 1994; Garfield & Bergin, 1978, 1986). These are regarded by empirically oriented clinical psychologists as the "Bibles" of psychotherapy research. They provide reviews of research on virtually every major form of psychotherapy (psychoanalysis, behavior therapy, cognitive therapy, family therapy, crisis intervention, and so on), and so are essential references for clinical psychologists.

Problems It should be recognized that reviews differ in the research they examine, the criteria used to evaluate studies, and the theoretical orientations of their authors. Thus, it is not uncommon for different reviewers to reach different conclusions. This section of the chapter summarizes the results of several major reviews of psychotherapy outcome research.

Bergin (1971) summarized the results of 52 studies on therapy outcome. On the basis of 22 positive, 15 doubtful, and 15 negative findings, he concluded that research supported the claim that therapy has at least a moderately positive effect. Bergin also noted that both design quality and therapist experience are positively related to therapy outcome, but that neither duration nor type of therapy is related to outcome.

Luborsky, Singer, and Luborsky (1975) published an influential review of therapy outcome research. They found that treated subjects had a better outcome than untreated subjects in 20 studies and had an equivalent outcome to untreated subjects in 13 studies. They found few differences in effectiveness between therapy types, supporting the phrase in their title that "everyone has won and all must have prizes." The only differences in effectiveness between types of therapy were that drug treatment was superior to psychotherapy (found primarily in studies of schizophrenics) and that multiple treatments were superior to single treatments. The only matches they found between specific disorders and effective treatments were that behavior therapy was superior to other therapies for phobias and that psychotherapy and medication combined were superior to other therapies for psychosomatic disorders.

These reviews did not stimulate as strong a reaction as Eysenck's (1952) review, probably because they were based on larger and more recent studies and because they drew conclusions that were more consistent with mainstream psychological thought. Still, these reviews were not without fault. The same criticisms of Eysenck's (1952) review can be directed against each of them (Wierzbicki, 1993a).

Smith and Glass (1977) published a research review that, like Eysenck's (1952) paper, become an instant classic. They performed a meta-analysis of 375 experiments in which one form of therapy was compared to a control condition or another form of therapy. *Meta-analysis* refers to a set of statistical techniques developed for the purpose of combining data from a group of studies (Cook & Leviton, 1980). See Exhibit 8.1 for a description of the techniques and characteristics of meta-analysis.

Smith and Glass found that the average effect size of treated patients was 0.68. According to Smith and Glass, this means that "the average client receiving therapy was better off than 75% of the untreated controls" (p. 754).

Perhaps their most well-known results concern the relative efficacies of different forms of therapy. Smith and Glass calculated the average effect size for ten types of therapy and found that the largest effect sizes occurred for the following: systematic desensitization (0.91), rational-emotive therapy (0.77), behavior modification (0.76), Adlerian (0.71), and implosion (0.64). They then created two "superclasses" of therapy—behavioral and nonbehavioral, with average effect sizes, respectively, of 0.8 and 0.6. Although some psychologists might regard this difference as substantial, Smith and Glass did not.

Smith and Glass (1977), then, reached two major conclusions. First, their analyses "demonstrate the beneficial effects of counseling and psychotherapy" (p. 760). Second, "the results of research demonstrate negligible differences in the effects produced by different therapy types" (p. 760).

Smith and Glass (Smith et al., 1980) extended their meta-analysis, examining 475 studies. The average effect size in this meta-analysis was 0.85 or, if placebo treatments are excluded, 0.89. As in their previous review, differences between types of therapy were interesting. Smith and colleagues (1980)

EXHIBIT 8.1   Meta-Analysis: Methods and Characteristics

Meta-analysis is a set of statistical techniques developed for the purpose of integrating data from a set of studies. Meta-analysis first derives measures that are comparable across studies regardless of differences in their procedures. A measure commonly used to summarize the results of a study is *effect size (d)*, which is calculated according to the formula $d = (M_1 - M_2)/sd$. Effect size is generally interpreted as a measure of the difference between two groups (although in studies of the relationship between two variables, another measure of effect size, r, can be calculated). Thus, the effect size (strength of the effect) in one study can be compared to that in another study.

After a common metric is calculated for all studies, the reviewer then examines effect size as a function of the studies' characteristics. In this way, the reviewer can determine the degree to which effect size is related to both subject variables (such as percent male, average age, and diagnosis) and method variables (such as therapy type, self-report versus other-report measures, treatment setting, objectivity of ratings).

Meta-analysis has been characterized both as more precise and as more objective than traditional, qualitative methods of reviewing large bodies of research. Meta-analysis can be regarded as more precise because it considers information that is ignored by simple box-score analyses. For example, suppose a reviewer simply tallies the number of times that significant versus insignificant results have been found. This method is biased in favor of studies that have large samples and so yield statistically significant results with smaller effect sizes. It also ignores

the direction and the magnitude of statistically nonsignificant differences. If a consistent nonsignificant trend occurs across studies, then meta-analysis, by incorporating these results, may reach a different conclusion from that of a traditional review (Cook & Leviton, 1980).

Meta-analysis is also more precise than traditional reviewing methods because it evaluates the degree to which factors of the studies interact (Cook & Leviton, 1980). Meta-analysis can examine simultaneously (say, through multiple regression analysis) the relationships between effect size and multiple treatment factors. Hence, it can provide a more precise description of the relationships between treatment outcome and aspects of therapy.

Meta-analysis has also been described as more objective than traditional methods of reviewing research (Cook & Leviton, 1980). Reviewers who use qualitative methods of evaluating research results can introduce bias in several ways: they may exclude studies whose results differ from their bias on methodological or theoretical grounds, or they may interpret studies in ways favorable to their own position. Although this need not occur, it is a risk of which readers must always be aware.

Now, meta-analysis is not free of the risk of reviewer bias. However, meta-analysis requires that the rules for inclusion and analysis of studies be stated explicitly (Nurius & Yeaton, 1987; Strube & Hartmann, 1983). Thus, both the reviewer and the reader are in better positions than in traditional reviews to detect the occurrence and minimize the influence of reviewer bias.

---

calculated the mean effect size for 18 different types of therapy, the largest of which were found for cognitive therapies (2.38), hypnotherapy (1.82), cognitive–behavioral therapy (1.13), systematic desensitization (1.05), eclectic–dynamic therapies (0.89), eclectic behavioral therapies (0.89), and behavior modification (0.73).

They grouped these 18 therapies into six classes, with the following mean effect sizes: cognitive

(1.31), cognitive–behavioral (1.24), behavioral (0.91), dynamic (0.78), humanistic (0.63), and developmental (0.42). Finally, they grouped these six classes into three major headings: behavioral (0.98), verbal (0.85), and developmental (0.42).

As in their previous review, Smith and colleagues (1980) concluded that there is little difference in the mean effect size of Behavioral and Verbal therapies. However, when examining only those studies that directly compared Behavioral and Verbal therapies, they found that "behavioral therapies produced reliably larger effects" (p. 107).

In their summary, Smith and colleagues (1980) concluded that "the results show unequivocally that psychotherapy is effective" (p. 124) and that the average treated client has an outcome superior to that of 80 percent of untreated patients. In addition, Smith and colleagues suggested that, whereas the issue of the comparative effectiveness of different types of psychotherapy "does not yield a single answer," some therapies such as cognitive, cognitive–behavioral, hypnosis, and systematic desensitization appear to be the most effective. When therapies were divided into major classes, the "behavioral therapies were more effective than the verbal therapies, which were in turn more effective than the developmental therapies" (p. 124).

The Smith and Glass meta-analyses of psychotherapy outcome generated an enormous response. Although their conclusions have often been cited as evidence supporting the effectiveness of psychotherapy (e.g., Lambert, Shapiro, & Bergin, 1986), many criticisms have been directed against their techniques and conclusions (e.g., Eysenck, 1983; Rachman & Wilson, 1980; Searles, 1985). Wierzbicki (1993a) discussed at length the criticisms of the Smith and Glass meta-analyses. For example, many of the criticisms directed against Eysenck's initial review (e.g., comparison of "apples and oranges;" the possibility of alternative interpretations) apply to these meta-analyses as well.

Despite these criticisms, meta-analysis has now become a standard method of evaluating therapy outcome studies (Kazdin, 1986). Since the original Smith and Glass meta-analyses, many other reviewers have conducted meta-analytic reviews to refine the techniques of Smith and Glass or to evaluate a specific form of psychotherapy. Wierzbicki (1993a) discussed the methods and conclusions of eight meta-analytic reviews of psychotherapy outcome, most of which concluded that psychotherapy is effective. In addition, although several reviews concluded that there is little difference in effectiveness across types of therapy, when differences in effec-

tiveness were observed, they tend to favor cognitive and behavioral therapies over other forms of therapy.

In an excellent overview, Lambert and Bergin (1992) summarized 10 major achievements of psychotherapy outcome research:

1. Psychotherapy has a general positive effect.
2. Many therapies are more effective than a placebo.
3. Research has moved in the direction of determining the relative efficacies of different forms of psychotherapy.
4. Behavior therapies are effective for many disorders.
5. Cognitive therapy is effective for depression.
6. Different forms of therapy are often found to be about equally effective.
7. Several common factors (including patient, therapist, and relationship variables) operate in most forms of therapy.
8. Psychotherapy may have negative effects in some clients.
9. Brief therapy has a significant effect on many clients (with about 50 percent showing improvement by the eighth session).
10. The effects of psychotherapy are relatively lasting.

Several of these conclusions will be addressed later in the text in chapters on specific forms of therapy. Lambert and Bergin also noted additional contributions that have resulted from the process of conducting therapy outcome research. These include the operationalization of therapy and the development of methods to assess treatment response and outcome.

Many forms of psychotherapy have been operationalized, or described in such specific terms that it is possible for other clinical psychologists to reproduce the treatment in their own settings. Such operationalization is essential so that therapy outcome studies can be replicated by independent researchers. However, such operationalization is also beneficial in the training and supervision of therapists.

Operationalization of therapy has led to the publication of therapy manuals (e.g., LeCroy, 1994), which describe the procedures followed and the treatment plan over the course of therapy. Thus, therapy can be provided in a standardized format. This helps other clinical psychologists learn how to provide the therapy, train other therapists to provide the therapy, and conduct independent tests of the effectiveness of therapy. The use of such therapy manuals is so widespread that some therapy research journals (e.g., *Cognitive Therapy and Research*) require that authors of therapy studies provide a treatment manual so that other clinical psychologists can duplicate the treatment.

Treatment outcome research has also led to an increase in the quantity and quality of measures that a psychotherapist can use to assess the client's functioning. Therapists from different theoretical schools emphasize different aspects of client functioning. For example, behavior therapists emphasize behavioral changes while cognitive therapists emphasize cognitive changes. Still, the emphasis on therapy outcome research has led to an increase in measures to assess client functioning across a variety of domains. The previous four chapters addressed the various forms of clinical assessment, noting the types of measures that have been introduced and emphasized since APA adopted the scientist–practitioner model of training clinical psychologists.

Wierzbicki (1993a) reviewed the history of the issue of the effectiveness of psychotherapy. He concluded that the increase in quantity and the quality of psychotherapy outcome research has contributed substantially to our understanding of the effects and processes of therapy. He also noted that research on therapy outcome is much more focused than at the time of Eysenck's (1952) review; current therapy research does not merely try to determine whether therapy is effective, but rather whether a specific form of therapy is effective when treating a specific disorder when delivered under specific circumstances. Wierzbicki (1993a) also concluded that the increased emphasis on a scientific foundation for therapy influenced the development of new treatments, such as behavioral and cognitive therapy, that

are more suited to empirical evaluations than previous therapies, and that some have concluded are more effective than traditional therapies.

Finally, Wierzbicki (1993a) noted that the increased emphasis on empirical foundations for therapy has occurred along with increased attention to the ethical principle of accountability. The *General Guidelines for Providers of Psychological Services* (APA, 1987) lists "Accountability" as one of its guidelines. Providers are instructed, "There are periodic, systematic, and effective evaluations of psychological services" (p. 8). Under another guideline, providers "are encouraged to develop and/or apply and evaluate innovative theories and procedures, to provide appropriate theoretical or empirical support for their innovations, and to disseminate their results to others" (p. 4). Furthermore, psychotherapists are informed that their profession is "rooted in a science" (p. 4) and, as such, they must continually explore, study, and evaluate their procedures.

As a result of the increased emphases on the scientific foundations of psychotherapy and the ethical principle of accountability, the client benefits. Today's therapies are more likely than those of the past to have empirical support, and so the client has more assurance than in the past that what is being offered actually works.

APPLIED ISSUES

Ethical Issues

In addition to scientific issues concerning the effectiveness and active ingredients of therapy, clinical psychologists have also considered many applied issues related to the conduct of therapy. This section of the chapter discusses ethical issues concerning confidentiality, informed consent, and accountability.

The last half-century has witnessed an increase in the number of clinical psychologists who provide therapeutic services. As more and more clinical psychologists became involved in the delivery of psychotherapy, the need for professional and ethical guidelines was recognized as essential for the profession. Indeed, Schofield (1982) regarded the development of the ethical principles of psychologists as one of the major indices of the development of psychology as a true profession.

The APA founded a committee in 1938 to consider adopting a code of ethical standards; in 1940, the APA Committee on Scientific and Professional Ethics was established as a standing committee to consider ethical complaints against psychologists (Pryzwansky & Wendt, 1987). In 1948, the APA asked its members to submit reports on ethical problems they had encountered; from over 1,000 reports, the APA developed an initial set of standards that was published in 1953 (APA, 1953). Since then, the APA has revised the general ethical principles of psychologists several times and has developed standards for psychologists engaged in specific professional activities.

A recent version of the ethical standards of psychologists appeared in 1992 (APA, 1992). This set of ethical standards contains six general principles: competence, integrity, professional and scientific responsibility, respect for people's rights and dignity, concern for others' welfare, and social responsibility. It also presents 102 specific standards arranged under eight headings: General Standards; Evaluation, Assessment, or Intervention; Advertising and Other Public Statements; Therapy; Privacy and Confidentiality; Teaching, Training Supervision, Research, and Publishing; Forensic Activities; and Resolving Ethical Issues. Exhibit 8.2 summarizes the specific standards regarding therapy.

In addition to the ethical principles of psychologists, the APA has also developed sets of ethical guidelines for psychologists engaged in specific professional activities. For example, in 1954, the APA published a set of recommendations concerning the development and use of psychological tests (APA,

---

EXHIBIT 8.2   Ethical Standards Regarding Therapy

The ethical principles of psychologists were revised by the American Psychological Association and published in the *American Psychologist* in 1992 (pp. 1597–1611). What follows is a summary of eight specific standards concerning therapy.

1. *Structuring the relationship.* Psychologists must clarify, as early as feasible, the nature of the therapy relationship. This includes issues such as the nature and anticipated course of treatment, fees, and confidentiality.
2. *Informed consent to therapy.* Psychologists must obtain informed consent from clients before providing therapy. In the case of a minor or other person who is incapable of legally consenting, informed consent must be obtained from a parent or guardian.
3. *Couple and family relationships.* Psychologists must clarify which members of a couple or family are clients and the nature of the relationship that the therapist will have with each person. If it becomes apparent that a psychologist may be called on to perform conflicting roles, the psychologist must clarify and resolve this conflict.
4. *Sexual intimacies with current patients or clients.* Psychologists do not engage in sexual intimacies with current patients or clients.
5. *Therapy with former sexual partners.* Psychologists do not accept as clients persons with whom they have engaged in sexual intimacies.
6. *Sexual intimacies with former therapy patients.* Psychologists do not engage in sexual intimacies with former therapy patients for at least two years after the termination of professional services. In unusual circumstances, where it can be shown that no exploitation has occurred, psychologists may engage in sexual intimacies with former patients two years after termination.
7. *Interruption of services.* Psychologists make efforts to plan for their patients' care in the event that services are interrupted.
8. *Terminating the professional relationship.* Psychologists do not abandon clients. Termination of the professional relationship occurs when it becomes clear that the client no longer needs the service, is not benefiting, or is being harmed by continued service.

1954). These guidelines are important for psychologists who develop, standardize, and use psychological tests, and have been discussed in Chapter 4.

The APA has also developed ethical standards concerning the provision of psychological services. These standards initially appeared in 1974 and have since been revised on several occasions (APA, 1977, 1987). These standards are currently presented under three major headings: Providers, Programs, and Accountability. Basically, these guidelines require that psychologists provide services only in areas in which they have been trained, that these services are provided in programs designed appropriately to meet the needs and respect the rights of clients, and that psychologists are accountable for their professional activities. Exhibit 8.3 summarizes the guidelines under each major heading.

Because of their importance in psychotherapy, three ethical issues will be discussed at greater length: confidentiality, informed consent, and accountability.

Confidentiality   The ethical standards of psychologists require that information about their clients be kept confidential. This means that psychologists may not divulge what they learn from their clients to others. To discuss their clients' problems and identities with friends or spouses is a violation, not only of professional ethical standards, but also of the legal statutes governing the practice of psychology in most states.

Of course, students should recognize that the clinical psychologist's office is not a confessional— there are exceptions to the limits of confidentiality. For example, staff members other than the clinical psychologist may have access to at least some of the client's records in order to conduct the business of the agency: clerical staff must know the identity of the client in order to schedule appointments; business personnel must know the identity and diagnosis of the client in order to bill appropriately; other professional staff may learn the identity of the client and the nature of the client's problem through supervision or case staffing meetings. In these contexts, the rules of confidentiality extend from the clinical psychologist who sees the client directly to all of the agency's personnel who learn about the client.

Students should also be aware that psychologists may discuss a client's problem in a professional context without divulging any information that could identify the client. In this way, a psychology professor can describe a case in a classroom, while omitting personal details that would enable students to determine the client's identity. In this way, students can benefit from the clinical psychologist's experiences without the psychologist violating the principle of confidentiality.

Similarly, a clinical psychologist can consult other psychologists so as to gain suggestions about how to help a client. Again, as long as the identity of the client is safeguarded, the clinical psychologist has not violated the ethical standard of confidentiality.

There are additional exceptions to the standard of confidentiality that may be less familiar to students. In Wisconsin (where this book was written), the laws governing the practice of psychology specify three exceptions to the standard of confidentiality: cases of child abuse or neglect; cases in which the client is about to commit actions that are dangerous to self or others; and cases in which there is a legitimate court order requesting a psychologist's records.

Because of increased recognition of the problem of child abuse, most states have passed laws that require psychologists to report cases of child abuse or neglect. Although this law exists for the welfare of children, it should be clear that this law sometimes poses difficult ethical questions for psychologists. I have known clinical psychologists who do not report cases of child abuse when the perpetrator is in therapy and is not currently abusing his or her child. These psychologists argue that the child is better off remaining in an intact family and that the family is better off when the perpetrator receives treatment rather than legal sanctions.

Of course, there are strong arguments against this position. For example, the victim, perpetrator, and family can receive therapy even after the abuse is reported. The perpetrator's being in treatment does

EXHIBIT 8.3   Guidelines for Providers of Psychological Services

Guidelines for providers of psychological services are presented under three major headings: Providers, Programs, and Accountability. Under each heading are specific guidelines concerning the provision of services, followed by one or more paragraphs that illustrate and interpret the guideline. What follows below are the 1987 ethical guidelines (APA, 1987).

Guideline 1: Providers

1.1   Each psychological service unit offering psychological services has available at least one professional psychologist and as many more professional psychologists as are necessary to assure the quality of services offered.

1.2   Providers of psychological services who do not meet the requirements for professional psychologists are supervised, directed, and evaluated by a professional psychologist to the extent required by the tasks assigned.

1.3   Wherever a psychological service unit exists, a professional psychologist is responsible for planning, directing, and reviewing the provision of psychological services.

1.4   When functioning within an organizational setting, professional psychologists seek, whenever appropriate and feasible, to bring their education, training, experience, and skills to bear upon the goals of the organization by participating in the planning and development of overall operations.

1.5   All providers of psychological services attempt to maintain and apply current knowledge of scientific and professional developments that are directly related to the services they render.

1.6   Professional psychologists limit their practice, including supervision, to their demonstrated areas of professional competence.

1.7   Psychologists who change or add a specialty meet the same requirements with respect to subject matter and professional skills that apply to doctoral education, training, and experience in the new specialty.

1.8   Psychologists are encouraged to develop and/or apply and evaluate innovative theories and procedures, to provide appropriate theoretical or empirical support for their innovations, and to disseminate their results to others.

Guideline 2: Programs

2.1.1   The composition and programs of a psychological service unit strive to be responsive to the needs of the people and settings served.

2.1.2   A psychological service unit strives to include sufficient numbers of professional psychologists and support personnel to achieve its goals, objectives, and purposes.

2.2.1   A written description of roles, objectives, and scope of services is developed by multi-provider psychological service units as well as by psychological service units that are a component of an organization, unless the unit has a specific alternative approach. The written description or alternative approach is reviewed annually and is available to the staff of the unit and to users and sanctioners upon request.

2.2.2   Providers of psychological services avoid any action that will violate or diminish the legal and civil rights of users or of others who may be affected by their actions.

2.2.3   Providers of psychological services are familiar with and abide by the APA's *Ethical Principles of Psychologists* and other APA policy statements relevant to guidelines for professional services issued by the APA.

2.2.4   Providers of psychological services seek to conform to relevant statutes established by federal, state, and local governments.

2.2.5   In recognizing the matrix of personal and societal problems, providers make available, when appropriate, information regarding additional human services, such as specialized psychological services, legal aid societies, social services, employment agencies, health resources, and educational and recreational facilities.

2.2.6   In the best interest of the users, providers of psychological services endeavor to consult and collaborate with professional colleagues in the planning and delivery of services when such consultation is deemed appropriate.

2.3.1   Each psychological service unit is guided by a set of procedural guidelines for the delivery of psychological services.

(continued)

EXHIBIT 8.3 *Continued*

2.3.2   Psychologists develop plans for psychological services appropriate to the problems presented by the users.

2.3.3   There is a mutually acceptable understanding between a provider and a user or that user's responsible agent regarding the delivery of service.

2.3.4   Professional psychologists clarify early on to users and sanctioners the exact fee structure or financial arrangements and payment schedule when providing services for a fee.

2.3.5   Accurate, current, and pertinent records of essential psychological services are maintained.

2.3.6   Each psychological service unit follows an established policy for the retention and disposition of records.

2.3.7   Psychologists establish and maintain a system that protects the confidentiality of their users' records.

2.3.8   Providers of psychological services do not use privileged information received in the course of their work for competitive advantage or personal gain.

2.4.1   Providers of psychological services promote the development of a physical, organizational, and social environment in the service setting that facilitates optimal human functioning.

Guideline 3: Accountability

3.1   The promotion of human welfare is the primary principle guiding the professional activities of all members of the psychological service unit.

3.2   Psychologists pursue their activities as members of the independent, autonomous profession of psychology.

3.3   There are periodic, systematic, and effective evaluations of psychological services.

3.4   Professional psychologists are accountable for all aspects of the services they provide and are appropriately responsive to those people who are concerned with these services.

3.5   In the public interest, professional psychologists may wish to provide some services to individuals or organizations for little or no financial return.

---

not ensure the child's safety. A perpetrator in treatment may mislead the therapist as to whether the abuse is continuing. For these reasons, I strongly believe that all such cases should be reported as required by law.

The second legal exception to the bounds of confidentiality is in cases where the client is a dangerous to self or others. This statute stems from a famous case, Tarasoff versus the Regents of the University of California, in 1976. In this case, a man in therapy made threats against the life of a young woman. The therapist judged the client to be dangerous and conveyed this judgment to his supervisor and the police. However, the intended victim was not warned. The client subsequently killed the woman, whose family then sued the therapist. The court ruled that a psychotherapist who treats a potentially dangerous client must take precautions to prevent injury.

Specifically, the threatened person should be warned, or other precautions necessary to prevent injury must be taken (Lakin, 1988).

Of course, it is difficult for clinical psychologists to predict accurately whether their clients are about to commit such violent actions. In general, such actions are difficult to predict because of their low frequency. Whenever an event is extremely rare, it is impossible, for basic mathematical reasons, to identify variables that are statistically useful in predicting the event. The inability of psychologists to predict such extreme behavior is not an indictment of psychologists, but rather a consequence of the laws of probability.

Still, clinical psychologists must occasionally attempt to predict violent behavior in their clients. In these cases, perhaps the best predictors of violent behavior are variables such as previous violent behavior, threats to commit violent acts, whether previous threats were acted upon, exhibited loss of control or violence in the presence of the therapist, possession of or access to weapons, and so on.

The final legal exception to the limits of confidentiality is in cases where there is a legitimate court order. In Wisconsin, clinical psychologists must provide their professional records when such information has been subpoenaed. Of course, some psychologists may attempt to circumvent this by keeping personal notes that are separate from and that contain more potentially sensitive information than their professional records. However, in Wisconsin, psychologists' personal notes as well as their professional records can both be subpoenaed.

I have found that many people are unaware of these limits to the ethical principle of confidentiality. I have had students who believe that a clinical psychologist's office is like a confessional—that the psychologist can *never* reveal the information under any circumstances. It is important to clarify the limits of confidentiality at the beginning of the client–therapist relationship. This avoids instances where the client believes that the information revealed cannot leave the psychologist's office, but where the psychologist is bound by legal statute to divulge the material. I have found it helpful to summarize the exceptions to the principle of confidentiality at the beginning of the first session with a client, and to provide a written summary of the guidelines.

Informed Consent   A second ethical issue that warrants special attention is the principle of informed consent. According to the ethical standards of psychologists, a client must provide informed consent prior to the provision of a psychological service. In normal circumstances, this means that the clinical psychologist provides a potential client with an assessment of the problem and a recommended treatment plan prior to beginning therapy. This treatment plan should include information concerning the goals of treatment, the treatment methods, the likely length and cost of treatment, and any potential adverse effects of treatment. The therapist should also be willing to discuss alternative treatments that

the client may prefer and answer questions about the recommended and alternative treatments. After discussing this information, the client and therapist then agree to a contract for the provision of therapy.

This procedure is simple when the client is an adult, is self-referred, and is capable of understanding the assessment and recommendation. However, the situation becomes more complicated when the client is a minor, is not self-referred, or is not capable of understanding the assessment and treatment plan.

When the client is a minor, the therapist must have the informed consent of a custodial parent (or legal guardian). However, the therapist should also seek to obtain the consent of the minor. Of course, this is not possible with an infant or toddler. It also is difficult when the child is a preschooler. However, with an older child, the therapist should explain the purpose and procedures of therapy in terms that the child can understand and then obtain the child's verbal or written consent.

Wisconsin statutes require only the consent of a parent or guardian and do not require that children provide their consent for therapy. However, my preference is to obtain this consent. I have found that this aids in gaining the child's compliance with treatment. Other ethical issues related to the treatment of children will be addressed in more detail in Chapter 13.

Another troublesome area is the treatment of clients who are not self-referred. Most psychotherapy clients are self-referred, and so they are aware that they have a problem and are motivated to comply with treatment. However, some clients are referred by others. Children and adolescents, marital partners and other family members, court-ordered clients, and others may be in therapy because they have been referred by others. In such cases, they may not think that they have a problem and so may not be motivated to change. It is tricky, both on ethical and on practical grounds, to treat such clients.

Professional ethical standards require that clients provide their informed consent prior to treatment. However, an unwilling client, such as those above, may provide consent while under duress from family or legal authorities. In such cases, it is helpful to address the client's reasons for therapy at the beginning of therapy. It also is helpful to clarify for the referrer the extent to which one can work with an uncooperative client. If the psychologist can gain the cooperation of the client, then therapy can proceed normally. However, if the individual continues to be uncooperative, then the therapist may choose to work with the referrer. In this case, the goal does not become how the referrer can change the uncooperative party, but rather how the referrer can better cope with the other person.

Another type of client who poses a problem for the principle of informed consent is one who is not capable of understanding the psychologist's assessment and recommendation. For example, individuals who are mentally retarded, psychotic, or demented may be unable to provide informed consent for treatment. In these cases, family members may provide consent. In other cases, the family or the mental health professional may have to seek legal commitment for psychiatric treatment.

Most states have statutes governing involuntary commitment for psychiatric treatment. Criteria for involuntary commitment generally include evidence that (1) the individual is a danger to self or others; and (2) the individual is not capable of acting in his or her own best interests, due to a mental condition or state (such as psychosis, retardation, or dementia). Involuntary commitment is generally difficult to accomplish, so as to protect the legal rights of the individual. Still, the family or the mental health professional can commit a person for treatment if sufficient evidence, meeting legal standards, is presented.

Accountability   A fundamental principle governing the professional activity of psychologists is accountability. Clinical psychologists are accountable for their actions. Clinical psychologists are also accountable for the actions of their support staff and personnel. For example, if a secretary or intern violates a client's confidentiality, then the supervising psychologist is held accountable.

Clinical psychologists act in the best interests of their client. This means that they need to clarify, at the start of a therapy relationship, just who is the client and what is the goal to be accomplished. This be-

comes a major concern when there are two or more parties involved. For example, spouses in couples therapy may actually have different goals: one may hope to dissolve the marriage while the other may hope to salvage it. Similarly, the goals that parents have in mind may differ from the best interests of a child.

Clinical psychologists also need to keep current with professional and scientific developments concerning treatment. Principle 1.5 of the *Guidelines for Providers of Psychological Services* (APA, 1987) requires that psychologists keep current with scientific and professional developments in the areas in which they provide services. To offer one form of therapy for a problem when the field has shown that another form of therapy is superior (in terms of probable success, cost effectiveness, or risk of adverse side effects) means that the psychologist is not acting in the best interests of the client.

This review of the ethical standards of clinical psychologists focused on those standards related to the issue of the delivery of psychotherapy, especially the principles of confidentiality, informed consent, and accountability. Of course, many of the other ethical standards also affect the practice of clinical psychologists. Readers should consult other works for more extensive discussions of the history of the development of psychology's ethical standards (Mills, 1982; Pryzwansky & Wendt, 1987) and for discussions of ethical issues in clinical research and practice (Hedberg, 1981).

Case Management

In addition to the ethical issues addressed above, clinical psychologists have also discussed at length practical issues concerning the delivery of psychotherapy. Of course, different theoretical schools offer conflicting suggestions concerning which techniques to use. Such theory-specific techniques will be discussed in detail in Chapters 9 through 13. This section of the chapter will examine practical issues in the management of clients that occur regardless of the type of therapy provided.

Much has been written about how clinical psychologists work with clients over the course of psychotherapy. Regardless of their theoretical orientation, clinical psychologists must be sensitive to several aspects of the client-therapist interaction. Part of the applied training of clinical psychologists is to learn how to interact with and manage the interaction with clients. This section of the chapter will discuss several important aspects of working with clients, including the initial contact, monitoring client progress, and termination.

Initial Contact   Principle 2.2.1 of the *Guidelines for Providers of Psychological Services* (APA, 1987) indicates that agencies that provide psychological services should have a written description of the roles, objectives, and scope of available services. This written description should be available to potential clients upon request.

Thus, in the initial contact with a potential client, sufficient information should be provided to give the client an idea of the services that are available, their length and cost, and the procedures to be followed. This includes the ethical principles of confidentiality and informed consent. Following the initial assessment, a client must again provide informed consent before beginning a course of treatment. The client must understand the treatment goals, methods, and estimated length and cost of treatment.

Although ethical principles demand that this information be provided during initial contacts with clients, there are also practical reasons for doing so. Remember the research on nonspecific factors in therapy. Therapy dropout rates are lower when clients understand what to expect in therapy and when clients' expectations of therapy match therapists' expectations (Garfield, 1986). Thus, clarifying the nature, procedures, and cost of therapy at the start of a therapy relationship should help enhance client satisfaction and reduce dropout from therapy.

Of course, some clinical psychologists find it awkward to discuss such business arrangements with potential clients in the initial contact. I have known clinical psychologists who prefer to leave the discussion of business matters to office staff who perform billing. Although it is understandable that some psychologists are uncomfortable when discussing financial matters with clients (because their training is in therapy and not business and because they may think that such discussions interfere with the client–therapist relationship), I have found it helpful for the clinical psychologist to address such matters. I think that this helps to establish the professionalism of the therapist and the formal nature of the therapy relationship. I think that this also helps avoid misunderstandings that might later interfere with the quality of the client–therapist relationship. For therapists who are uncomfortable discussing such matters during the initial contact, I would recommend that they (or their agencies) make their policies concerning procedures, goals, techniques, and costs available in written form to potential clients.

Monitoring Client Progress   An important aspect of psychotherapy is monitoring progress over the course of treatment. As noted above, the therapist and client should have agreed to a therapy contract that specifies the goals, methods, cost, and length of treatment. It is helpful for the goals of therapy to be described in operational or measurable terms so that both client and therapist can monitor progress from week to week. If unsatisfied, either party can raise this issue in the next session. If progress is slower than expected, then the methods, goals, or expected length of treatment should be renegotiated.

This illustrates the importance of the scientist–practitioner model. Clinical psychologists trained as scientist–practitioners approach individual cases from a scientific perspective. They adopt a scientist's critical eye even when working with individual cases. Thus, they establish treatment goals that are observable; they regularly monitor progress toward the goal; if progress is not satisfactory, then they reevaluate their treatment plan and consider initiating an alternative treatment. In this way, an ineffective course of therapy will be identified early and replaced with a more effective treatment. Thus, both the client and the therapist have greater assurance that the treatment will be effective.

Termination   Another important aspect of the client–therapist interaction is termination. In general, termination requires more preparation when treatment has been more lengthy or has involved more intense emotions. For example, long-term therapy (e.g., weekly sessions for two years) tends to require more elaborate preparation for termination than short-term therapy (twelve or fewer sessions). Similarly, therapy involving more intense and intimate revelations (e.g., therapy for sexual abuse) tends to require more elaborate preparations for termination than less intense therapy (such as cigarette cessation training).

It is important to prepare all clients for termination, regardless of the length or intensity of treatment. Preparation for termination generally involves three features. First, the client's progress over the course of therapy should be reviewed. The client's initial level of functioning, initial treatment goals, and progress toward meeting those goals are reviewed.

Second, an analysis or interpretation of the progress over therapy should be provided. Why did the client make progress? What has the client learned? How did the client overcome obstacles that arose? Such issues need to be discussed so that the client understands how and why life changes occurred.

Third, the client should consider what future problems may arise and how they can be addressed by applying what one has learned throughout therapy. Regardless of how successful therapy has been, the client is likely to experience difficulties at some time in the future. Such difficulties should be anticipated. The client should understand that such difficulties are normal, that occasional failures to function successfully are common, and that it will be possible, despite the occasional failure, to continue to apply the lessons gained from therapy to future problems.

Of course, the specifics of what the client has gained through therapy will vary across therapeutic schools. Similarly, the length of time necessary to complete these steps will vary depending on the length and intensity of therapy. Still, these steps provide a useful guide for preparing clients for termination, whether they have completed a successful course of psychoanalysis or cognitive–behavioral therapy.

Students should note that many therapists prepare a client for termination by gradually increasing the length of time between sessions. As the client approaches termination, the therapist can extend the time between sessions, from once a week to once every other week to once a month. In some cases, clients may be scheduled for brief follow-up sessions up to several months apart. In this way, the client and therapist both have the opportunity to determine whether the client can function successfully without weekly contacts with the therapist.

A final note concerning termination is that it is important to keep the door open to the client's possible return. Even though the client may have met the therapeutic goals, it is possible that future problems may lead to a relapse. If the client cannot cope with the new problems, despite efforts to apply the gains from therapy, then the client can return to treatment. This possibility can be anticipated and the client should be encouraged to view it as something other than a personal failure.

SUMMARY

The field of psychotherapy has experienced a tremendous increase over the last century in terms of the numbers of therapists, forms of therapy, and agencies that provide therapy.

A major scientific issue concerning psychotherapy is what makes it work: What are the elements of psychotherapy that account for its effectiveness? Different theories have proposed different active ingredients. However, Frank (1961) suggested that all therapies have several basic elements in common: a client–therapist relationship, a setting socially sanctioned as a place of healing, a theory that explains the problem, and a treatment based on the theory.

Following Frank, many clinical psychologists have discussed the nonspecific elements that are common to all forms of therapy. Nonspecific elements of therapy generally address characteristics common to clients (e.g., distress, expectations), therapists (e.g., well being, social influence, perceived competency, expectations), and the client–therapist relationship.

The other major scientific issue concerning psychotherapy is its effectiveness: Does psychotherapy work? In 1952, Eysenck reviewed studies that reported the outcome of therapy with adult neurotics.

He found that about two-thirds of patients improve—about the same as the spontaneous remission rate. Eysenck concluded that, to date, there was no scientific evidence that psychotherapy is effective.

Although Eysenck's review was criticized on many grounds, many clinical psychologists regarded it as a challenge to the field to provide evidence from controlled experimental studies that therapy is effective.

Clinical psychologists began to conduct controlled therapy outcome studies in the 1950s and 1960s. This research often compared a psychological treatment to a no treatment (or delayed treatment) control, a placebo treatment, or an alternative treatment. Reviews of these therapy outcome studies in the 1960s and 1970s concluded that psychotherapy is effective.

In 1977, Smith and Glass conducted a meta-analysis of 375 psychotherapy outcome studies. Meta-analysis is a set of statistical techniques that integrate the results of a set of studies. Smith and Glass concluded that the average patient who receives psychotherapy has a better outcome than 75 percent of untreated controls. In addition, they concluded that there is little difference in effectiveness between forms of therapy.

Other meta-analyses of psychotherapy outcome have been conducted. In general, they agree with Smith and Glass that psychotherapy is effective. However, they disagree with one another concerning the relative efficacies of different forms of therapy. When one form of therapy has been found to be more effective than another therapy, these comparisons have tended to favor cognitive and behavioral therapies.

Ethical and case management issues are applied issues important to all forms of therapy. The APA has developed sets of ethical principles that govern the professional activities of psychologists. Of special concern to clinical psychologists who provide psychotherapy are the principles of confidentiality, informed consent, and accountability.

Therapists may not divulge information about their clients, except in cases involving child abuse, imminent danger, and legitimate court orders. Information about clients may be presented to students or to consultants if no identifying information is provided.

Clients must provide informed consent prior to beginning a course of therapy; that is, therapists must present the assessment results and proposed treatment plan, which includes the goals and methods, and expected length and cost of treatment. Special precautions must be followed when clients are minors, when clients are unwilling participants in therapy, or when clients are incapable of providing their informed consent.

Clinical psychologists are accountable for their professional activities. They work for the best interests of their client. Thus, they must clarify issues such as who is their client and what is the client's goal prior to initiating a course of therapy. Clinical psychologists are expected to keep current with scientific and professional developments in their field so that they can provide the treatments that are currently regarded as most effective for their clients' problems.

Psychotherapists of all theoretical orientations must also consider how they manage the client–therapist interaction. In their initial contact, therapists should provide potential clients with information about procedures, ethical guidelines, and costs. Ethical standards require that agencies have such information in written form, which is made available to clients upon request.

Clinical psychologists should monitor client progress over the course of therapy. Setting clearly defined and measurable goals assists both the therapist and client in evaluating progress and determining whether the therapy contract should be renegotiated.

Clients should be prepared for the termination of therapy. More extensive preparation for termination is necessary for longer and more intensive forms of therapy. Preparation for termination involves summarizing therapeutic gains, understanding the reasons for progress, and anticipating how to apply therapeutic gains to future problems.

STUDY QUESTIONS

1. Discuss the elements regarded by Jerome Frank as the common factors of psychotherapy. What other factors have clinical psychologists regarded as nonspecific factors of therapy?

2. Summarize the methods and conclusions of Eysenck's (1952) review of therapy outcome studies. Some people think that Eysenck claimed that therapy is not effective. Why is this a misinterpretation?

3. Discuss the criticisms of Eysenck's (1952) review.

4. What is meta-analysis? Why have some writers described meta-analytic research reviews as more objective and more precise than traditional qualitative research reviews?

5. What were the methods and conclusions of the Smith and Glass meta-analyses? What have more recent meta-analyses of psychotherapy outcome studies concluded?

6. Discuss the ethical principles of psychologists that are especially relevant to the practice of psychotherapy.

7. Discuss how the ethical principle of informed consent, confidentiality, or accountability influences the practice of therapy. What circumstances occasionally arise that pose special problems regarding this ethical principle?

8. What information should be conveyed by a therapist in the initial contact with a potential client?

9. How should a client be prepared for therapy termination?

10. Discuss how the scientist–practitioner model of training assists a clinical psychologist in the management of his or her therapy cases.

9

Psychoanalytic Therapy

I. Freudian Approaches to Psychotherapy
  A. Psychoanalysis
  B. Freudian Contemporaries
  C. Neo-Freudian Therapies
  D. Contemporary Variants
II. Applied Issues
  A. How Long/Expensive Is Psychoanalysis?
  B. Who Benefits from Psychoanalysis?
  C. Who Should Provide Psychoanalysis?
III. Scientific Issues
  A. Difficulty Evaluating Psychoanalytic
     Treatment
  B. Empirical Evaluation of Psychoanalysis
IV. Summary

Freudian psychotherapy, or *psychoanalysis*, may well be the most influential form of psychotherapy in the twentieth century. This chapter will present the goals and techniques of psychoanalysis, introduce historical and contemporary variants of Freudian therapy, and discuss scientific and theoretical issues concerning this form of therapy.

Following his introduction of psychoanalytic theory at the turn of the twentieth century, Freud's approach to explaining and treating psychopathology dominated clinical psychology for the next 50 years. Indeed, Ford and Urban (1963) stated that the "entire field of individual verbal psychotherapy has been built upon his initial work" (p. 109). Clinical psychologists and psychiatrists trained prior to 1960 almost invariably received a heavy exposure to Freudian theory and therapy. For example, Aaron Beck, Albert Ellis, Carl Rogers, and many of the other noted theorists of therapy to be discussed in the next several chapters were all originally trained to provide psychoanalytic therapy.

Torrey (1992), a severe critic of psychoanalysis, discussed the rise of psychoanalytic thinking and its influence on American thought. Torrey noted that, in the first several years following the publication of his theory of sexuality, Freud's name evoked laughs, as though someone had told an off-color joke. However, both professional and popular acceptance of the theory soon skyrocketed. By 1959, sociologist Philip Rieff praised Freud as having had a greater influence than any other thinker on modern Western thought (Torrey, 1992).

In 1946, Benjamin Spock published his famous book on baby and child care, which went on to become one of the best-selling books in the English language. Literally generations of American children have now been reared by parents who consulted Dr. Spock when they had questions about child rearing. According to Torrey (1992), Spock has acknowledged that this book was expressly intended to have a Freudian foundation.

FREUDIAN APPROACHES TO PSYCHOTHERAPY

Psychoanalysis

Theory of Psychopathology   The Freudian theory of the development of psychopathology was presented in Chapter 3. As you recall, Freud held that neuroses are caused by a troubling experience, often of a sexual or aggressive nature, in early childhood. This experience leads the individual to become fixated in an early stage of psychosexual development. The troubling incident leaves a psychological "residue" in the unconscious. Even though one is not aware of the material, it influences the person's responses. The individual continues to function psychologically—in terms of the psychological processes used to obtain gratification—at the level of the stage of fixation.

For example, Little Hans was a young boy who was afraid of horses. According to Freud's analysis, Hans was experiencing the Oedipal conflict and was actually afraid of his father. To avoid this unsettling truth, Hans transferred his fear of father to horses through the defense mechanism of displacement. Other examples of how Freudian defense mechanisms are used to transform unconscious sexual and aggressive material to one's outward symptoms were presented in Chapter 3.

Goal of Psychoanalysis   According to Freud, the client's current psychological problem has its roots in unconscious defensive functioning related to early childhood experiences. To counter this, Freudian therapy aims at uncovering the troubling unconscious material. Once the client recognizes the *true* cause of the problem, the client can then cope with it using conscious rational processes.

There is an old adage that the aim of psychoanalysis is *insight*. Freud illustrated this idea with an oft-quoted statement: "Where id was, there ego shall be" (Freud, 1933/1964, p. 80). The unconscious troubling material had been producing symptoms through unconscious defense mechanisms. There-fore, therapy tries to bring the troubling material to consciousness so that one can cope with the problem using rational conscious processes. By removing the need for the ego to produce symptoms through defensive functioning, one may "cure" the symptoms.

It is important to recognize, however, that insight alone is not sufficient to remove the client's symptoms. Simply recognizing the childhood origin and the defensive function of one's symptom does not mean that the underlying problem has been removed. One must face the problem directly and address it so that it no longer carries the emotional weight it once had.

Thus, a related goal of psychoanalysis is *catharsis*. Catharsis refers to the release of psychic energy. According to Freud, the client's unconscious problem is highly charged with psychic energy. Because the material has been repressed and kept unconscious, its associated psychic energy has not been discharged. Prior to therapy, the client had used defense mechanisms, which permit the gradual release of psychic energy but produce the presenting symptoms. In psychoanalysis, after the client gains awareness of the underlying problem, the psychic energy associated with this material no longer needs to be repressed. It can be expressed outwardly and appropriately, rather than be expressed indirectly through defense mechanisms.

Judith Guest's novel, *Ordinary People*, illustrates insight and catharsis as goals of psychoanalytic therapy. The book tells the story of Conrad, a teenage boy who became depressed and suicidal following the accidental death of his brother. During therapy, Conrad ultimately recognizes the true reason for his depression. Consistent with the traditional psychoanalytic explanation of depression, Conrad was angry at his brother for dying but was unable to express this anger outwardly. He turned the anger inward, blaming himself for his brother's death. After his insight into this dynamic, Conrad experienced a rush of emotions, followed by a period of near exhaustion. He was then able to start resolving his own (and his family's) problems more rationally.

Techniques of Psychoanalysis   Early in his career, Freud experimented with several techniques designed to help bring forth troubling unconscious material. Following Charcot, Freud employed hypnosis, originally regarding it as an important method of accessing unconscious material. However, later in his career, Freud stopped using hypnosis. Not all of his patients could be hypnotized. In addition, he came to believe that the client–therapist relationship had to be well established and addressed in therapy in order for true improvement to occur; in the absence of such a relationship, insights obtained under hypnosis were superficial and would not bring true improvement.

Early in his career, Freud also used a technique developed by Hippolyte Bernheim, a French physician known for his research on hypnosis. Bernheim had shown that a subject could recall what transpired during a hypnotic session, despite hypnotically induced amnesia. Recall occurred following the hypnotist's repeated, insistent, confident urgings (Monte, 1987).

Freud adapted this technique in therapy, calling it *willful concentration*. He sat behind the client, held the client's head in his hands, exerted mild pressure, and suggested that the troubling psychological material would be "released" when he released the physical pressure (Breuer & Freud, 1893/1955). This technique, like hypnosis, is based on enhancing the client's suggestibility, though Freud used it without a formal hypnotic induction.

Through years of clinical experience, Freud ultimately settled on free association as the primary technique of psychoanalysis. In *free association,* the client says aloud whatever comes to mind, making no conscious effort to inhibit or censor the speech. According to Freud, this technique gives unconscious troubling material the opportunity to come forth.

The technique of free association is difficult to master. From early childhood, we have been taught to think before we speak, speak in complete sentences, and not say anything that sounds stupid, rude, or distasteful. Thus, it may take a long time—weeks or even months—before a client can spend an entire therapy session freely associating.

However, Freud thought that free association was essential to therapy, labeling it the "fundamental rule" of psychoanalysis (Freud, 1940/1964). Freud was so insistent that clients' verbalizations be free and uncensored that he had them lie down so that they were unable to see his face. After all, if they saw his facial expressions, they might be influenced by his reactions and so begin to think about what was said.

During the course of the free associations, the client may suddenly recall significant events from early childhood. In addition to such direct insights, free association may yield other information for the psychoanalyst. For example, the client may experience *blocking*, or being unable to think of a word or finish a sentence. The client may suddenly change topics. The client may stutter or stammer. Such responses suggest that the client has touched on a sensitive subject that raised his or her defenses. The psychoanalyst examines the timing and content of these responses in an effort to understand the client's unconscious difficulties.

Psychoanalysts also examine free associations in which the client means to say one thing but actually says something else (a *parapraxis* or "Freudian slip"). For example, if the client means to say that he *loves* his mother-in-law but actually says that he *loathes* her, the analyst would interpret this as conveying some important unconscious feeling.

In addition to analyzing the client's free associations, psychoanalysts also attempt to interpret the underlying meaning in other forms of expression. For example, psychoanalysts analyze the symbolism in the client's dreams. Freud believed that all dreams reflect unconscious wishes. Thus, by proper interpretation of the symbols in dreams, Freud believed that he could begin to understand the client's unconscious psychological processes. Psychoanalysts often ask clients to keep a dream diary so that dreams can be brought in and discussed in therapy. Similarly, psychoanalysts interpret their clients' daydreams and fantasies.

Freud (1900/1953) provided the example of a normal young woman, who dreamt that she was arranging various flowers (lilies, carnations, violets) as table decorations for a birthday party. When Freud asked her to freely associate to the elements in her dream, she associated *violet* with *violate*, a word having both sexual and aggressive connotations. Freud interpreted the flowers as symbols of fertility and the birthday as a symbol of an impending birth or pregnancy. According to Freud, the woman's dream symbolized her desire to become impregnated by her fiance.

Psychoanalysts also interpret the symbolism in a client's artwork—drawings, paintings, poems, stories, and sculptures. As a proponent of psychic determinism, Freud believed that all of one's thoughts and actions are caused and that the most significant of these causes are unconscious. Just as a symptom represents an unconscious problem, so does the client's artistic productions represent underlying psychological processes. Projective personality tests (discussed in Chapter 7), are a basic offshoot of this aspect of Freudian theory.

Finally, psychoanalysts also interpret the client's relationship with the therapist. During the course of Freudian therapy, a client may develop strong positive or negative feelings, or *transference*, for the therapist.

Common forms of positive transference include falling in love with the therapist, becoming so dependent that one has difficulty making decisions without consulting the therapist, and admiring and emulating the therapist. For example, I once knew a psychotic patient who developed a crush on me, writing me poems, giving me gifts, and even coming unannounced to my home (which, of course, was quite unsettling for my wife). I have known many clients who, following a course of psychotherapy, spoke of becoming therapists themselves. I have known many clients who, over the course of therapy, began to imitate their therapist's style of dress, appearance, and speech mannerisms. (Since the time of Freud, many male psychology students have grown beards and started smoking pipes or cigars, which is commonly interpreted as a form of transference with their professors.)

Common forms of negative transference include resentment and anger. Many clients come to resent the psychoanalyst's influence over them. They may become angry when the therapist remains silent, not solving their life problems and insisting that the cli-

ents spend most of the hour freely associating. They may then question the efficacy of the therapist's methods and even belittle the therapist. Negative transference may be expressed passively (such as sitting and fuming silently) or actively (such as yelling at and cursing the therapist).

According to Freud, transference represents feelings the client experienced toward significant others earlier in life. For example, if the client becomes overly dependent on the therapist, this may mean that the client had been excessively dependent on parents during the oral stage. If the client falls in love with the therapist, this may mean that the client failed to resolve the Oedipal conflict during the phallic stage, when the client experienced incestuous wishes for the opposite-sexed parent.

Freud used the transference relationship in two ways. First, he interpreted transference in an attempt to understand the client's problem from early childhood. Then, he used transference to treat the client. As the client examines or "works through" the transference relationship, the client gains insight into and resolves the difficulty from early childhood. Thus, transference serves both diagnostic and treatment functions.

Interestingly, Freud also observed that therapists commonly develop strong feelings for their clients, which he referred to as *countertransference*. Like transference, countertransference represents feelings that one experienced earlier in life toward significant others. However, in the case of countertransference, the feelings are those of the therapist rather than the client.

Therapists find some clients more engaging than others. Some clients are a joy to work with while others are quite challenging. Occasionally, therapists may become physically attracted to clients. I have known therapists who, because of personal prejudices, were unable to work objectively with homosexuals, African Americans, substance abusers, and other clients. I once worked with a severely depressed client who had survived a suicide attempt in which he doused himself with kerosene and set himself on fire (and was now horribly disfigured as well as depressed); I was so moved by his plight that I could not work with him objectively and so transferred him to another therapist at the agency.

It is important that therapists not permit their feelings for clients to affect their professional judgment. Therapists should be aware of their emotional reactions toward clients and deal with the countertransference so that it does not interfere with treatment.

For this reason, Freud and other leaders of the psychoanalytic community thought that personal analysis is an important part of training to become a therapist. Through personal analysis, therapists examine their childhood relations to others, understand their personality dynamics, and learn to recognize and interpret their feelings. The issue of personal analysis for therapists is discussed more fully later in the chapter.

A second aspect of the client–therapist relationship that Freud interprets is called resistance. *Resistance* is anything that the client does to interfere with therapeutic progress.

Remember that the cause of the client's symptomatology is some threatening unconscious material. As the client begins to make progress toward understanding this material, the intensity of the threat looms larger than ever. Even though the client wants to improve, the ego unconsciously raises defenses to prevent the individual from facing the troubling material.

One common form of resistance is for a client to introduce a significant issue at the very end of a session so that there is not sufficient time to deal with the issue. Other forms of resistance include missing appointments, coming late to sessions, talking of trivialities rather than significant issues, and refusing to comply with the treatment regimen. All of these interfere with therapeutic progress and are forms of resistance.

Psychoanalysts use resistance just as they use transference—for both diagnostic and treatment purposes. Remember that resistance prevents the client from becoming aware of the unconscious troubling material. Thus, the occurrence of resistance may suggest the nature of the underlying problem. By being sensitive to the onset and form of resistance, the therapist gains an understanding of the client's true problem. Then, by addressing resistance directly in the therapy session, the client develops insight into the nature of the underlying problem.

After the Freudian therapist is confident of the underlying meaning of the client's responses, the therapist then attempts to communicate this meaning to the client. This may be done through *interpretation*, wherein the therapist "refers to something the patient has said or done in such a way as to identify features of his behavior that he has not been fully aware of" (Weiner, 1975, p. 115). Interpretations therefore help the client gain insight.

For example, after observing that a client has developed a hostile transference relation with the therapist and that this relationship is similar to that between the client and a parent, the therapist may bring this similarity to the attention of the client. The client can then ponder the quality of these relationships, consider whether they are typical of other relations with authority figures, and examine the possible childhood influences on this pattern.

Interpretations should be offered cautiously. The therapist should have observed sufficient evidence to be confident in the accuracy of the interpretation. Thus, the therapist does not make an interpretation the first time some underlying meaning to the client's behavior is suspected, but waits until at least several more instances of the pattern occur.

The therapist should also present interpretations in a tentative rather than authoritative manner. There is always the possibility that an interpretation is incorrect. Making inaccurate interpretations may confuse the client and lower the client's confidence in the therapist. A common mistake by novice therapists is to make interpretations too soon, without sufficient evidence to support them.

Interpretations should also be made only when the client is prepared to accept them. An interpretation made without preparation may simply be ignored by the client. In addition, premature interpretations also risk weakening the transference relationship and raising such strong resistance that the further course of therapy is threatened.

The psychoanalyst can also attempt to convey interpretations in a more indirect way. The therapist can model the process of interpretation, which teaches the client how to analyze the underlying meaning of his or her actions. The therapist then directs the client's attention to the evidence that supports the therapists's interpretation. By asking leading questions and by directing the client's attention to the pertinent evidence, the client may reach the interpretation independently. In this case, the impact of the interpretation is likely to be stronger than if the therapist had simply made the interpretation for the client. Of course, if the client does not reach the interpretation on his or her own, then this process has served to prepare the client to accept the interpretation when made by the therapist.

Freudian Contemporaries

Carl Gustav Jung   Carl Jung was a contemporary of Freud and one of the early leaders in the psychoanalytic movement. After publishing *The Psychology of Dementia Praecox* (1907/1974), a psychoanalytic study of schizophrenia, Jung came to the attention of Freud. Freud and Jung then began a lengthy correspondence, the bulk of which was collected and published by McGuire (1974).

Jung rapidly rose to a position of influence within the psychoanalytic community, becoming the first president of the International Psychoanalytic Association in 1910. One index of his prestige at this time is that Freud himself referred to Jung as his "crown prince," the theorist who would succeed Freud as the leader of the psychoanalytic movement. However, Jung's disagreements with Freud grew until, in 1914, Jung resigned his presidency of and membership in the International Psychoanalytic Association. Jung then developed his own psychoanalytic theory, which he called *analytical psychology.*

Jung's differences from Freud concerned three major points. First, Jung thought that Freud's focus on sex as the major motivation of human behavior was simplistic and reductionistic. Jung emphasized, instead, psychological and even spiritual influences on behavior.

Second, Jung disagreed with Freud's extreme determinism, which held that personality and adult neurosis are set in early childhood; Jung offered a *teleological* alternative, suggesting that people are motivated by future goals rather than determined by past events.

Third, Jung disapproved of Freud's use of free association as the primary technique of therapy. Jung believed that a therapist's remaining silent throughout most of the session and only occasionally making interpretations could lead to a situation in which the client is intimidated by the therapist and so accepts interpretations, not because they are correct, but because they are the only way of making contact with and receiving attention from the therapist.

Jung offered an alternative form of psychoanalytic therapy in which the therapist and client played more nearly equal roles. Jung's therapist is more active than the Freudian therapist. Jung's psychoanalyst offers interpretations, based not only on the possible underlying meaning for the client, but also on the possible meanings for the therapist himself and for society in general. In this way, Jungian therapy has been called *mutual analysis*. Also, Jungian analysts bring in cultural *archetypes*, or universal symbols, from myths, literature, and religion, which may suggest the underlying meanings of the client's actions.

A fictional example of Jungian analysis, which incorporates cultural and mythological symbols in the interpretation of a client's dreams and symptoms, is in Robertson Davies's novel, *The Manticore*. This book tells the story of a man who enters Jungian therapy following the murder of his father. During the course of therapy, many archetypes are discussed with respect to their meaning for the client. Cultural archetypes, such as The Friend, The Deserving Person, and the Orphan of the Storm, as well as Jungian archetypes, such as the Anima and Shadow, are addressed. The title of the book comes from a recurring figure in the client's dreams. The manticore is a mythological creature, which has the head of a man, body of a lion, and tail of a scorpion. According to legend, the manticore can hurl darts from its tail. As therapy progresses, the therapist interprets this creature as a symbol for the client, who does not consider himself to be a whole man. Like the lion, he is touchy and defiant; like the scorpion, he is able to wound others by hurling darts or verbal barbs.

Jung described therapy as proceeding through four stages:

1. *Confession.* In the first stage, clients acknowledge their limitations. By seeking help from a therapist, clients receive comfort from the fact that they are not alone—that there are others who have similar problems. The very act of confessing the problem is cathartic.

2. *Elucidation.* In this stage, clients establish and begin to explore the transference relationship with the therapist. In so doing, they begin to understand aspects of their unconscious and to recognize the origins of their problems.

3. *Education.* Here, clients begin to cope more successfully with current situational problems because of their greater self-understanding.

4. *Transformation.* After beginning to cope more successfully with external demands of the environment, clients move on to the task of greater self-exploration. Self-realization is the ultimate goal of Jungian therapy.

Although Jung has not had as great an impact on the field of clinical psychology as Freud, he remains an important figure. His concept of archetypes has become a popular way for academics to discuss cross-cultural similarities in religion, literature, art, and mythology. Jungian institutes have been established in major cities, and several Jungian journals (e.g., *British Journal of Analytical Psychology, Psychological Perspectives*) are published.

Alfred Adler   Alfred Adler is another of the early leaders in the psychoanalytic movement. Like Jung, Adler initially worked collegially with Freud. Adler joined Freud's group, the Vienna Psychoanalytic Society, when it was founded in 1902. He swiftly rose to a position of leadership within the society, becoming its president in 1910. However, like Jung, Adler had a series of disagreements with Freud. In

1911, Adler resigned his presidency of and membership in the Vienna Psychoanalytic Society and founded his own psychoanalytic school, called *Individual Psychology.*

Adler (1931/1979) identified six major conflicts between his views and those of Freud. These are summarized in Exhibit 9.1.

Despite these differences, Adler's theory of personality clearly reflects its psychoanalytic origin. For example, Adler held that an individual's personality was influenced by experiences in the first five or six years of life. Adler introduced the notion of *sibling rivalry,* which suggests that early conflicts with siblings have an important influence on the development of personality.

Adler also suggested that social experiences related to a child's *birth order* significantly influenced the development of personality. For example, the first-born child is the center of the family's attention until the birth of the second child; being "dethroned" in this way may lead the first-born to resent the younger sibling and to seek to restore his or her favored position. Conversely, the youngest child never loses the position of being the baby of the house; for this reason, last-born children are more likely to be pampered than their older siblings.

Adler considered neurosis to be a *"life lie,"* based on a faulty style of life reflecting a poorly developed social interest. For example, Adler considered selfish, hostile, and isolated individuals to be neurotic, because they do not interact cooperatively with others.

According to Adler, neurotic styles of life stem from early childhood experiences, such as sibling rivalry and pampering. However, neuroses may also stem from an *inferiority complex,* which is a real or perceived inferiority that leads to efforts to compensate for the deficiency. A fictional example of this is the character Laura in *The Glass Menagerie* who is characterized by a sense of inferiority and self-imposed isolation due to her suffering from pleurosis and wearing a leg brace. Attempts to compensate for inferiority are not necessarily unhealthy. Adler noted that his own severe childhood illness led him to compensate by becoming a physician. However,

EXHIBIT 9.1   Theoretical Differences between Alder and Freud

Adler (1931/1979) summarized six major differences between his ideas and those of Freud. These are summarized below.

1. *Ego.* Freud viewed the ego as attempting to satisfy the instinctive needs of, and so as subservient to, the id. Adler viewed the ego as independent from the id.

2. *The Oedipal conflict.* Freud viewed the Oedipal complex as a sexual conflict in which children experience incestuous desires for the opposite-sex parent. Adler perceived the Oedipal conflict as a power struggle, relatively free of sexual tension, wherein a child seeks alliances with one parent in order to gain power in conflicts with the other.

3. *Fragmentation of personality.* Freud stressed the intrapsychic struggle among components of personality. Adler viewed people holistically, as "whole persons." In fact, this is why Adler called his approach *individual psychology.* He wished to study the entire individual, without fragmenting personality into separate components.

4. *Narcissism.* Freud viewed people as narcissistic or selfish. Freud (1930/1961) used the Latin phrase, *Homo homini lupus* ("Man is a wolf to man"), to describe human nature. Adler, however, viewed people as having an innate social drive. Adler viewed narcissism as unhealthy and as a sign of psychological maladjustment.

5. *Human nature.* Related to the previous point, Freud viewed people as animalistic, primarily motivated by the animal instincts of sex and aggression. Adler, however, saw people as cooperative—as having a social drive.

6. *Dreams.* Freud believed that dreams represented unconscious wishes and so the client's underlying problems might be identified through appropriate interpretation of dream symbolism. Adler, on the other hand, described dreams as continuing efforts to solve problems from waking life. Dream analysis may help to identify current problems and to find methods of coping with them. However, Adler did not think that dreams represent unconscious wish fulfillment as they do for Freud.

---

when the compensation interferes with one's social relations, then the inferiority complex can be considered to be neurotic.

Adlerian therapy similarly reflects its psychoanalytic roots. Clients are not aware of their life lie. The Adlerian therapist tries to help clients identify their life lie and to improve their style of life. Often, the faulty life style is identified by examining early family interactions. Adlerian therapists also use the technique of having clients relate their earliest memories, with the idea that such recollections reflect significant early social interactions and emotional experiences that may have influenced the developing style of life.

Adler also developed several approaches to psychoanalytic therapy that differed from those of Freud. Adler did not require that clients lie on the couch facing away from him; they could stand, sit, or move around the room. Also, unlike early Freudian

therapy (but like later Freudian therapy), Adler rejected hypnosis as an artificial and inadequate method of gaining insight.

During the course of therapy, Adler emphasized the client's current problems and behaviors more than Freud; for example, dream interpretation for Adler consists of trying to identify the client's current problems or goals expressed symbolically in dreams. Similarly, Adler monitored the client's nonverbal behavior during therapy more than Freud, to determine whether the client's posture or other motor behaviors might suggest the nature of his underlying problems.

Adler's therapist also plays a more active role than the traditional Freudian therapist. Adlerian therapists use the technique of *comparison*, in which they compare themselves to the client and ask, "What goals would I be seeking if I behaved like the client?" For Adlerian therapists to introduce their

Psychoanalytic Therapy   **223**

own personalities and reactions into the therapy room is a significant departure from classical Freudian psychoanalysis.

Through Adler's emphases on the creative problem-solving aspect of the ego, the role of social rather than sexual influences and the influence of self-directed goals rather than early childhood determinants, he "softened" some of the more extreme elements of classical psychoanalytic theory. In these ways, he anticipated the modifications of Freudian theory made by later theorists and so he has sometimes been referred to as the first "ego psychologist." Adler, like Jung, has had less of an impact on the psychoanalytic community than Freud. However, his ideas remain influential, not only in the ego psychology movement described below, but also in the Adlerian Society of Individual Psychology, which publishes its own journal.

Neo-Freudian Therapies

From the presentation above, it is clear that even early psychoanalysts disagreed with Freud on important theoretical and applied issues. Adler and Jung disagreed with Freud's exclusive emphasis on sexuality as the motivation for human behavior; Jung disagreed with Freud's emphasis on early determinism; Adler emphasized social influences on personality development.

These and other criticisms of classical psychoanalysis led to the establishment of two major schools of Neo-Freudian theories, ego psychology and object relations theory, and to significant modifications of the techniques of psychoanalysis.

Ego Psychology   Freud claimed that all behaviors and psychological processes are derived from the biological instincts of sex and aggression. According to Freud, people develop more complex psychological processes, such as ego functioning, merely to better satisfy these biological instincts.

Followers of Freud soon raised several criticisms of this idea. First, Freud derived the ego from the id. Yet, Freud assigned the ego an executive function, helping the individual to balance the drives

of the id against the constraints of reality. For Freud, the ego functioned autonomously in order to direct id impulses, yet the ego developed to serve the id. This seemed contradictory to many psychologists.

Second, Freud explained human behavior as the result of a struggle or compromise among the three components of personality. Critics argued that this lessened the integrity or unity of personality. They suggested that Freud had difficulty accounting for the synthesis, coordination, and integrity of personality.

These criticisms led a number of theorists to develop a modified version of Freudian psychoanalysis called *ego psychology*. Unlike classical psychoanalysis, ego psychology places a greater emphasis on ego functioning than id functioning. This leads to a relatively greater focus than classical psychoanalysis on conscious motivations for behavior, healthy forms of human functioning (such as creativity, curiosity, and play), and the integrity of personality.

Heinz Hartmann is one of the foremost ego psychologists (and has been called the "father of ego psychology"). Hartmann (1958) suggested that the ego and the id emerge simultaneously in the development of personality. He emphasized the ego's role in promoting a synthesis of personality both within the psyche as well as in behavioral interactions with the outside world.

Robert White is another of the foremost ego psychologists. White (1963) proposed that the ego has inborn motivational properties of its own that, along with instinctive id impulses, influence behavior. These motivational forces of the ego are expressed in healthy outlets such as exploratory play and intellectual curiosity.

Although ego psychology is not closely associated with specific therapy techniques independent of those employed by traditional Freudian therapists, it is easy to see how ego psychology therapists differ from classical psychoanalysts. Compared to classical psychoanalysts, ego psychologists place more emphasis on conscious processes and healthy behavior and less emphasis on intrapsychic conflict and instinctual motivation. Although they employ such traditional Freudian techniques as free association, interpretation, and analysis of family dynamics, they place less emphasis on sex, aggression, and early determinism.

Object Relations Theory Another important modification of psychoanalysis developed in response to similar criticisms of classical psychoanalysis. Freud thought that all human interactions with "objects" (including persons as well as things) serve the function of energy discharge. Freud believed that a relationship with another person originally developed through repeated associations of the person with instinctual gratification. The relationship becomes a "secondary drive" that in itself produces short-term gratification. For example, Freud thought that an infant's bond with its mother resulted from the mother's being paired repeatedly with nursing; later, the infant is gratified by the sight of the mother, even when the mother is not feeding the child.

By the 1960s, research showed that there were several problems with Freud's idea. Harlow and Zimmerman (1959) demonstrated that infant monkeys preferred surrogate mothers that provide "contact comfort" over surrogates that provide food and warmth but are not "cuddly." Later primate studies (e.g., Goy & Goldfoot, 1974) showed that behavioral problems arise, not just from separation from mother, but also from isolation from peers. Thus, these studies showed that primates (and perhaps humans as well) need tactile and social stimulation, from mothers as well as from peers, in order to develop normally.

Berk (1994) noted other problems with Freud's explanation of maternal attachment. Babies form attachments to fathers and others who are not directly involved in feeding. Babies form strong attachments to parents who are abusive or neglectful. If infants bond to mothers only because mothers met their basic nutritional needs, then these results should not occur.

Finally, research by developmental psychologists showed that human infants have innate preferences for certain types of sensory stimulation, including color, brightness, complexity, and novelty (Berk, 1994). From birth, babies act to obtain more over less preferred stimuli. Because babies have these innate preferences, Freud's claim that all human interactions with objects serve the gratification of sexual and aggressive instincts must be modified.

Object relations theory emphasizes the influence of social and other object-related motivations that do not simply serve to gratify sexual and aggressive instincts. This approach suggests that people form relationships with others, not merely to satisfy sexual and aggressive drives, but also because people have a basic social drive. Object relations theory also holds that motives, such as curiosity and desires for complexity and novelty, influence our interactions with both human and nonhuman objects.

Object relations theory has become quite popular in recent decades. However, like psychoanalysis itself, object relations theory has generated numerous variants of its own. For example, some object relations theorists (e.g., Margaret Mahler, Otto Kernberg) maintained the primacy of Freudian drive theory, while acknowledging the existence of object-related motivations as well. Other theorists (e.g., Heinz Kohut in his early writings) suggested that Freudian instincts and object-relatedness are equally important in motivating behavior, with each applied appropriately to its own set of phenomena. Finally, still other theorists (e.g., Ronald Fairbairn, Melanie Klein, Kohut in his later writings) rejected instinct theory altogether and replaced it with object relations theory.

Object relations therapists, like ego psychologists, have not developed their own set of therapeutic techniques distinct from those of traditional psychoanalysis. They use traditional insight-oriented techniques of interpretation, free association, and analysis of family dynamics. However, the emphasis in object relations therapy is on underlying social and cognitive motives, rather than on the instinctive motives of sex and aggression.

Psychoanalytically Oriented Psychotherapy Franz Alexander has been credited with the development of a more flexible form of psychoanalysis (Prochaska, 1984). Alexander proposed that psychoanalysis be modified when the clients' problems are mild or are clearly the result of situational stressors.

In these cases, Alexander adopted a technique he termed *psychoanalytically oriented psychotherapy*.

In this form of therapy, Alexander established more limited goals than are typical of classical psychoanalysis. Instead of extensive personality restructuring, Alexander set goals such as supporting the client's ego or resolving the current life problem.

To reach these goals, the therapist is more active and directive than in classical psychoanalysis. The therapist may engage in direct conversation or direct the client's attention to specific issues rather than rely exclusively on free association.

Such active therapy tends to be briefer than classical psychoanalysis. Whereas Freud preferred to see his clients six times a week, the psychoanalytically oriented therapist schedules appointments once or twice weekly, and then tapers off from this as therapy progresses.

Alexander and French (1946) described the results of this therapy with 600 clients, treated in from 1 to 65 sessions. Their results were better than expected by classical psychoanalysts, who believed that much longer and more extensive therapy was necessary to achieve these results.

More recently, other therapists have suggested that psychoanalytically oriented therapy can be delivered in even briefer formats. For example, Sifneos (1972) has described the techniques of brief psychodynamic therapy, delivered often in fewer than 20 sessions. Sifneos (1979) has also investigated the efficacy of this therapy, judging it to be an effective and appropriate treatment for many psychotherapy outpatients.

Contemporary Variants

The list of variants of Freudian therapy is quite extensive. It would be possible to add literally scores of other theorists and therapists to those already described. This section of the chapter will present two contemporary approaches to therapy that may not always be recognized as having been influenced by Freud. Because space does not permit an exhaustive presentation of Freudian-oriented therapies, interested readers are encouraged to read works devoted exclusively to this topic (e.g., Cooper, Kernberg, & Person, 1989; Hendrick, 1967; Wyss, 1973).

Transactional Analysis   *Transactional Analysis* (TA) was introduced by Eric Berne (1958) and has been popularized in books such as *Games People Play* (Berne, 1964), *Beyond Games and Scripts* (Berne, 1976), and *I'm OK, You're OK* (Harris, 1969).

TA describes personality as consisting of three components: child, parent, and adult. The *child* is the playful side of personality, which is impulsive, emotional, and selfish. The *parent* is the strict overseer of personality; it represents the "voice" of our parents that is constantly reminding us of the "correct" thing to do. The *adult* is the mature side of personality, which balances the impulsive child against the strict parent. It is not too difficult to see that TA's child, parent, and adult are similar to, but are somewhat "softened" versions of, Freud's id, superego, and ego.

TA holds that therapy clients engage in psychological "games" that have some immediate emotional "payoff" for the client, even though the long-term result of the game is maladaptive. Dusay and Dusay (1989) provided the example of a game played by a boss and his secretary. The boss asks the secretary for the time, which she provides. Although this overt interaction is straightforward and on an adult-adult level, there is an underlying communication. The boss's parent is conveying the message to the secretary's child that she is frequently late. According to Dusay and Dusay, the boss is playing the game, "Now I Got You, You SOB." As a result, the boss feels angry and self-righteous. On the other hand, the secretary is playing the game, "Kick Me," and feels angry and picked on. Both parties feel that they are in the right and are being treated badly by the other. Hence, the game is likely to continue.

The TA notion of a psychological game is analogous to the psychoanalytic concept of neurosis. Both are repetitive patterns of behavior that earn some short-term gain but are maladaptive in the long run. Both occur without direct awareness of the gain.

TA therapists employ traditional insight-oriented techniques to help clients identify the games they play and the emotional payoffs they receive. Clients also learn to identify the various sides of their personality and understand how they may be impulsive and selfish at some times but strict and demanding at other times. In general, clients learn, using TA terms, to understand the reasons for their repetitive maladaptive behaviors.

Family Systems Therapy   Chapter 13 will present in detail various approaches to family and marital therapy. However, it should be noted here that at least some forms of family systems therapy have psychoanalytic roots.

Remember that Freud believed that a presenting symptom is only an outward expression of some unconscious problem and that psychoanalytic therapists use insight-oriented techniques to identify the underlying problem. Family systems approaches to therapy similarly assume that a presenting symptom reflects some underlying problem. However, rather than consider an intrapsychic difficulty within the individual client, family systems therapists assume that the problem is one within the family system—some difficulty in the family dynamics or patterns of interaction is thought to be the fundamental cause of the client's disorder.

As will be presented in Chapter 13, family systems therapists differ in how they describe and treat the family problem. For example, family systems therapists may adopt psychoanalytic, humanistic, cognitive, or behavioral approaches. Still, regardless of the specific conceptualization of the family problem and the methods used to correct it, family systems approaches to therapy can be viewed as "psychoanalytic" in terms of the assumption that the presenting symptom is caused by an underlying problem.

Murray Bowen and Nathan Ackerman are two noted family systems therapists whose methods clearly reflect psychoanalytic roots. When individual clients present themselves for therapy, Bowen and Ackerman conceptualize these problems in psychoanalytic fashion, emphasizing early childhood experiences, family interactions, and unconscious dynamics. However, to properly treat psychopathology, Bowen and Ackerman think that it is important to treat the entire family—to address the family dynamics and patterns of interaction.

APPLIED ISSUES

Freudian approaches dominated the field of psychotherapy throughout the first half of the twentieth century. Even after alternative therapies developed and became widespread by the 1960s, Freudian therapy continued to be popular. This part of the chapter will present several practical or applied issues that arise when considering psychoanalytic therapy.

How Long/Expensive Is Psychoanalysis?

One of the strongest criticisms directed against classical psychoanalysis is its extreme length and cost. As originally practiced by Freud, psychoanalysis involved multiple therapy sessions every week. Freud preferred to see patients six times per week; in mild cases or when therapy was close to completion, he scheduled only three sessions per week (Gay, 1988). The cost of a one-hour session of psychotherapy (as this is written, in Milwaukee, Wisconsin) ranges from $75 to $250 per hour, depending upon the profession and degree of the therapist. It is easy to see that, even if one pays the low end of this scale for the minimum three sessions per week, the cost of psychoanalysis quickly becomes very high.

Torrey (1992) discussed the fees of early psychoanalysts. He estimated that, in adjusted dollars, Freud charged his American clients about $200 per hour. Gregory Zilboorg charged $100 per hour in 1940, which Torrey estimated to be about $770 in 1992 dollars.

The cost of psychoanalysis is compounded by the fact that it is extremely lengthy. Because classical psychoanalysis uses free association as its primary technique and because there is no way to hasten the rate at which unconscious material is brought to consciousness using this method, there may be weeks or even months between therapy sessions in which significant insights are attained. It is not unusual for a client to remain in psychoanalysis for three or more years. I know of clients who have been treated by psychoanalytic therapists for up to 30 years.

If one assumes that three years is the average length of classical psychoanalysis and if one assumes an average cost of $75 per hour for three hours per week (which are both conservative assumptions), then one finds that the average psychoanalytic client will be seen for 468 sessions, for a total cost of $35,100. This amount is well beyond the ability of most people and the willingness of most insurance companies to pay.

Another way of illustrating the high cost of classical psychoanalysis is to consider the career of a therapist who only treats clients using this method. Suppose a psychoanalyst completes her training and begins treating clients independently at age 30. Also, suppose that she sees clients four times per week and works a 40-hour week. This means that she has an active caseload of 10 clients. If the average length of psychoanalysis is three years, then the therapist will pick up about three new clients a year. In the course of a 35-year professional career, this therapist will have completed the treatment of about 100 cases. After years of training in medicine or psychology, and after years of specialized training in psychoanalysis, this therapist will have treated fewer cases in her career than most psychotherapists see in one year. If the therapist received any form of public support during her training (say, in the form of assistantships, fellowships, or grants), then critics could easily argue that the societal benefit of this therapist's services is not worth the investment in her training.

This hypothetical example is admittedly extreme, since psychoanalysts may see only some of their clients in classical psychoanalysis and other clients in briefer psychoanalytically oriented psychotherapy. One survey (Rogow, cited in Torrey, 1992) found that the average psychoanalyst treated 28 patients per year (and saw another 23 patients in consultation).

Because of the extreme length and cost of classical psychoanalysis, many psychoanalytically oriented therapists have modified the therapy to make it more accessible to the general public. As discussed previously in the chapter, psychologists have introduced numerous modifications of Freudian therapy since its introduction. Many of these modifications, while retaining the emphasis on insight as the goal of therapy and examination of one's early family dy-

namics, have shortened the overall length of therapy. For example, therapists may hasten the course of therapy by making interpretations, directing the client's attention to specific issues, and by settling for partial rather than complete insight so long as symptom relief has been achieved.

Psychoanalytically oriented or psychodynamic therapy tends to be shorter than classical psychoanalysis. The client may be seen once or twice a week or from several months up to two or more years. The cost of this therapy is therefore substantially less than that of classical psychoanalysis. However, this form of therapy still tends to be longer and more costly than alternative approaches, such as Rogerian, cognitive, and behavioral therapy.

Who Benefits from Psychoanalysis?

As noted above, classical psychoanalysis is a very expensive form of therapy; hence, it has traditionally been offered only to the most affluent members of the community. Clients from lower and even lower-middle income brackets are unlikely to be able to afford or to have insurance that covers psychoanalysis.

It should also be noted that the methods of psychoanalysis make it appropriate only for certain types of clients. The primary technique of psychoanalysis is free association. During a therapy session, clients must spend much of the time talking. Thus, psychoanalysis has traditionally been thought to be most appropriate for clients who are highly verbal.

In addition, psychoanalysis employs insight-oriented techniques, such as dream interpretation and analysis of Freudian slips. The therapist initially interprets this material; later, the client learns how to analyze the symbolic meaning without the assistance of the therapist. Thus, psychoanalysis is most likely to be successful with clients who are psychologically minded—are interested in examining their underlying motivations and are fluent with the abstract concepts pertinent to psychoanalysis. Clients who are verbal and psychologically minded tend also to be intelligent and well educated.

These characteristics describe the ideal psychoanalytic client, sometimes referred to as the YAVIS client (Schofield, 1964), which stands for Young, Attractive, Verbal, Intelligent, and Successful.

Two qualifiers should be recognized immediately. First, most people are not YAVIS clients. Thus, even though psychoanalysis may be quite appropriate for YAVIS clients, it is not likely to be as effective for other people. Second, other verbal therapies, including Rogerian client-centered therapy, cognitive therapy, and others, also are most suited to YAVIS clients. Thus, even though psychoanalysis has been recommended for such ideal clients, it is not alone in this respect. Verbal therapies in general are more effective with bright and verbal clients than with other clients.

Another factor has also been associated with successful outcome in psychoanalysis. As noted above, psychoanalysis is most successful with clients who are bright, verbal, able to examine their motivations, and willing to cooperate in the therapeutic process. From this, it is easy to predict that clients who are less severely disturbed will benefit from psychoanalysis more readily than clients who are more severely disturbed.

For example, Freud did not believe that psychoanalysis is appropriate for patients with psychotic disorders (which he called "narcissistic neuroses"). According to Freud, psychoanalysis is successful only when the client is able to "cathect" or form a relationship with the therapist. He did not think that psychotic individuals were capable of forming such a relationship, and so he did not advise psychoanalysis for them (Freud, 1940/1964). Similarly, Freud did not think that psychopaths and individuals with other severe personality disorders are good candidates for psychoanalysis (Freedman, Kaplan, & Sadock, 1976).

Perhaps the most well-known study that supported the claim that psychoanalysis is most suited to less severely disturbed clients is the Menninger Foundation Psychotherapy Research Study (Kernberg, Burstein, Coyne, Appelbaum, Horwitz, & Voth, 1972). In this study, 21 clients who received an average of 835 hours of psychoanalysis were compared with 21 clients who received an average of 289 hours of psychoanalytically oriented psychotherapy. Numerous measures were obtained before, during,

and after therapy, with many subjects followed over a period of about 20 years.

At the conclusion of therapy, one of the most significant predictors of successful outcome was ego strength. Pre-therapy ego strength was significantly correlated ($r = 0.35$) with an index of global improvement over the course of therapy. High initial ego strength predicted positive change, regardless of the type of therapy received. Thus, the most well adjusted clients at the start of therapy tended to have the best outcomes.

Who Should Provide Psychoanalysis?

Another important practical issue regarding psychoanalysis concerns the therapist: Who should provide psychoanalysis? What professional training is required to conduct psychoanalysis?

Freud and many of the early leaders of the psychoanalytic movement (including Jung and Adler) were physicians. However, Freud did not believe that the practice of psychoanalysis should be limited to those with medical degrees. Certainly, medical training is important in distinguishing between conversion symptoms and symptoms caused by actual physical disorders. However, Freud thought that the theoretical and applied work of psychoanalysis could be provided by non-physicians.

Freud (1926/1959) argued the case for allowing non-physicians to practice psychoanalysis. However, despite Freud's advocacy, the psychoanalytic community resisted "lay" analysis. This was especially true in the United States. For example, the New York Psychoanalytic Society, founded in 1911 by A. A. Brill, was an association of physicians. Although they permitted nonphysicians as associate members, it was clear that they intended to restrict psychoanalytic practice to those with medical training (Torrey, 1992).

Although psychoanalysis continues to be dominated by physicians, nonphysicians can and do become psychoanalysts. Indeed, several prominent figures in the psychoanalytic community (e.g., Erich Fromm, Anna Freud, Melanie Klein, and Otto Rank) did not have medical degrees. Psychoanalysts have come from the ranks of psychology, art history, and even Sanskrit and Indian Studies.

Still, there continues to be resistance to lay analysts. Both the International and the American Psychoanalytic Associations have been sued because of restrictive admission of lay analysts. In an out-of-court settlement in 1989, the American Psychoanalytic Association agreed to admit nonmedical applicants at the same rate as in 1987 (28 percent). Also in 1989, the International Psychoanalytic Association agreed to admit in a fair and timely manner institutes that are not affiliated with the American Psychoanalytic Association. However, dissatisfaction concerning compliance with the settlements has persisted among some psychologists (Youngstrom, 1990).

The debate over the requirement of a medical degree for the practice of psychoanalysis primarily concerns classical psychoanalysis. Psychoanalytically oriented or psychodynamic psychotherapy is commonly provided by all the major mental health professionals, including psychiatrists, social workers, and clinical psychologists.

Another issue related to the practice of psychoanalysis is the requirement that analysts-in-training undergo psychoanalysis themselves. Following World War I, psychoanalytic institutes established the requirement that every prospective psychoanalyst undergo a personal or training analysis (Gay, 1988). This requirement continues today. Masson (1990) described his training as a psychoanalyst. His "training" analysis, required by the Toronto Psychoanalytic Institute, was to last not less than three or four years, including five sessions per week.

However, for therapists who are not going to practice classical psychoanalysis, but who will instead provide psychodynamic or other forms of therapy, most training programs do not list personal psychotherapy as a formal requirement. In a survey of 87 APA-approved clinical training programs, Wampler and Strupp (1976) found that only 4 percent required personal therapy. One of the training programs that currently requires personal therapy is the California School of Professional Psychology (CSPP). The various campuses of the CSPP require that its doctoral students in clinical psychology receive from 40 to 45 hours of individual psychother-

apy, and may also require at least one year of group psychotherapy (CSPP, 1991–1992).

Surveys of clinical psychologists have routinely found that many have received personal therapy. Guy, Stark, and Poelstra (1988) reported that about 70 percent of clinical psychologists have received some form of therapy before completing their training. (Interestingly, a survey of psychologists found that, when behavior therapists obtain therapy, they receive psychoanalytic therapy more frequently than any other type of therapy [Norcross & Prochaska, 1984].)

Wampler and Strupp (1976) found that 67 percent of APA-approved training programs encourage but do not require therapy. Such personal therapy need not be classical psychoanalysis. Formal therapy may be recommended for some candidates while informal counseling may be provided to others through supervisory and advisory sessions. I have had several students who entered therapy for help in coping with stress or family problems that arose during their graduate training. I have also had several graduate students who had difficulty interacting with others (such as homosexuals or assertive women) due to personal issues; they found it helpful to see therapists, outside of our department, to resolve these issues before they completed their training.

SCIENTIFIC ISSUES

Although psychoanalysis has had many proponents since its development, it has also had its critics. Opponents of psychoanalysis have identified the practical problems noted above. However, they have also evaluated psychoanalysis as lacking a sound scientific foundation. This section of the chapter will first address why it is difficult to test psychoanalysis empirically, and then present a brief overview of some of the research efforts to evaluate psychoanalytic therapy.

Difficulty Evaluating
Psychoanalytic Treatment

Several factors make it difficult to evaluate psychoanalysis scientifically. First, there are many variants of psychoanalytic therapy; what holds for one form may not hold for another. Even psychoanalysts themselves have difficulty agreeing on the nature of psychoanalysis. In 1947, the American Psychoanalytic Association established a Committee on Evaluation of Psychoanalytic Therapy. Rangell (1954) later reported that the committee was not able to attain any general agreement as to what constituted psychoanalysis or psychoanalytic therapy.

Second, psychoanalytic theory does not readily lend itself to empirical evaluation. Chapter 3 presented a scientific evaluation of psychoanalytic theory. Although psychoanalytic theory is comprehensive and has many applications, it suffers from an inability to generate testable predictions. Psychoanalytic concepts are vague and difficult to measure. Psychoanalytic laws are numerous and imprecise. These characteristics apply not only to the theory in general, but also to psychoanalytic therapy.

For example, it is difficult to operationalize or measure psychoanalytic concepts of adjustment and maladjustment. It is not easy to identify specific behaviors, emotions, or psychological test responses that clearly indicate the presence and degree of some psychoanalytic construct. What measures should be used to assess the degree to which one has resolved the Oedipal complex? How can we determine the degree to which one has expressed the psychic energy that had previously been repressed and had been influencing unconscious functioning? Because Freudian theory stresses unconscious psychological processes, self-report measures are not very appropriate. In order to identify the nature of such unconscious processes, psychoanalytic researchers often employ projective psychological tests; however, psychologists must interpret projective test responses, a process that increases the subjectivity of scoring and so decreases inter-rater reliability (see Chapter 7).

Third, psychoanalytic therapy was developed and practiced long before clinical psychologists generally agreed that a scientific evaluation of their theories and therapies was required. Remember that the American Psychological Association formally approved the scientist–practitioner model of training of clinical psychologists in 1949. Psychoanalytic therapy had been provided for a half-century before then.

Related to this point is the fact that the criteria used to evaluate scientific claims and the distinction between science and nonscience were clarified only after the development of psychoanalysis. Freud regarded himself as a scientist because his model provided causal explanations, after the fact, of human behavior. Popper introduced falsifiability as the line of demarcation between science and nonscience after Freud developed psychoanalysis (Popper, 1959, 1963). Thus, some of the scientific criticisms of Freud are based on criteria that were only developed and accepted after Freud had developed his theory. Judged in hindsight, all theories and practices can be found lacking.

Finally, Freud himself was uninterested in scientific evaluations of psychoanalysis. As cited in the previous chapter, Freud dismissed statistical evaluations of psychoanalysis as "worthless" and "uninstructive." He preferred case study evidence to group studies.

Many psychoanalysts have shared Freud's indifference toward empirical evaluations of psychoanalysis. For example, Kris (1947) noted that psychoanalysts tend to "look upon rigorous procedures of verification, upon what has come to be called 'experimental psychoanalysis' with a scornful or patronizing eye" (p. 211). Rangell (1954) found that members of the American Psychoanalytic Association exhibited strong resistance to the attempt by his committee to evaluate psychoanalytic therapy.

Various psychoanalysts have interpreted their profession as a philosophy or belief system (e.g., Bettelheim, 1982) rather than as a science, and psychoanalytic therapy as a subjective exercise akin to literary interpretation (Spence, 1982) rather than as a scientifically or medically based treatment. For these reasons, many psychoanalysts have not conducted research to evaluate the efficacy of psychoanalysis, and have not been concerned about the lack of such scientific support for psychoanalysis.

Still, despite these problems, some psychologists have called for increased scientific efforts to evaluate psychoanalysis and psychoanalytically oriented therapy (Luborsky & Spence, 1971, 1978). According to Henry, Strupp, Schacht, and Gaston

(1994), psychodynamic approaches to psychotherapy have been the focus of an increasing number of empirical evaluations, especially with regard to the issues of the client–therapist alliance and the accuracy of interpretation. Although psychodynamic psychotherapy differs from classical psychoanalysis, Henry and colleagues regarded psychodynamic therapy as a topic that is suited to rigorous scientific investigation.

Empirical Evaluation of Psychoanalysis

With these cautions in mind, let us consider several attempts to evaluate empirically the efficacy of psychoanalysis. As noted above, Freud preferred clinical case study evidence, rather than group empirical studies, when evaluating the effectiveness of psychoanalysis. Although many successful case studies are cited as support for psychoanalysis, there are also noted cases that speak against its efficacy.

For example, E. G. Boring, a Harvard professor known for his history of experimental psychology, entered psychoanalysis at a time when he was experiencing depression. After 168 sessions, he felt that he had not experienced the personality change or the increased productivity he had sought. In addition, he was so distressed by the lack of improvement that his professional productivity decreased. Boring postponed work on another volume of the history of experimental psychology while he waited for the personality change to manifest itself. When no change occurred, Boring wrote: "I was sad and distraught, knowing that I had wasted one of the four precious sabbaticals that are due me during my life" (Boring, 1940, p. 10).

Such unsuccessful case reports do not prove that psychoanalysis is ineffective, just as positive case reports do not prove that it is effective. Clinical psychologists today recognize that case studies lack internal validity and so do not provide strong evidence when evaluating claims.

Myerson (1939) conducted an early evaluation of psychoanalysis, surveying 307 psychiatrists, psychologists, and neurologists regarding its scientific support. Myerson reported that the prevailing opinion was that, "as a therapeutic system, psychoanalysis has failed to prove its worth" (p. 64).

Eysenck (1952) published an influential review of early outcome studies of therapy with adult neurotics. He summarized the results of 5 studies of psychoanalytic therapy and 19 studies of other, eclectic therapy, and found that the improvement rates were, respectively, 44 and 64 percent. Because Eysenck's estimate of the spontaneous remission rate was about 70 percent, Eysenck concluded that the research evidence, to date, did not show that psychotherapy, psychoanalytic or otherwise, produced outcomes with adult neurotics that were superior to that of no treatment.

Bergin (1971) reinterpreted the very same studies that Eysenck (1952) reviewed. Using different methods of classifying outcomes (e.g., not counting dropouts as failures), Bergin estimated the improvement rate of psychoanalytic therapy to be 83 percent and of other therapy to be 65 percent. Because Bergin's recalculation of the spontaneous remission rate was about 30 percent, he concluded that there was evidence, even from the very studies examined by Eysenck (1952), that therapy with adult neurotics is superior to no therapy.

Weinstock (cited in Salter, 1963) chaired a Fact Gathering Committee of the American Psychoanalytic Association regarding the outcome of psychoanalysis. After examining outcome statistics, Weinstock stated that the Association made no claims of therapeutic usefulness of psychoanalytic methods.

Kline (1972) reviewed evidence concerning Freudian theory. He recognized that many studies of Freudian concepts were poorly designed, and so he limited his attention to the best designed and strongest tests of the theory. Kline concluded that, although some aspects of Freudian theory had empirical support, there was no scientific evidence that Freudian therapy is effective.

Luborsky and Spence (1971) reviewed the quantitative studies of Freudian psychoanalysis and concluded: "Quantitative research on psychoanalytic therapy presents itself, so far, as an unreliable support for clinical practice. Far more is known through clinical wisdom than is known through quantitative, objective studies" (p. 358). Luborsky and Spence (1978) later updated their review but reached the same conclusion. When the handbook in which their reviews was revised in 1986, the editors chose to omit the chapter on psychoanalytic therapy because "there was insufficient *new* material" to warrant an entire chapter (Garfield & Bergin, 1986, p. ix) (authors' emphasis).

Fisher and Greenberg (1977) published a generally favorable review of the scientific research on psychoanalytic theory. However, with regard to psychoanalytic therapy, they concluded that, although psychoanalysis is superior to no treatment with chronic neurotics, it has not been shown to be more effective than any other type of therapy for any specific type of disorder.

Thus, empirical evaluations of classical psychoanalytic therapy, even by proponents such as Kline and Fisher and Greenberg, have not provided clear support for its effectiveness.

Since 1977, reviews of the research on the effectiveness of psychotherapy have typically employed meta-analytic procedures. As you recall from Chapter 8, meta-analysis is a set of statistical techniques that enables a reviewer to combine and compare the results of different studies, using the common metric of effect size. Numerous meta-analyses have now appeared that address the issues of the effectiveness of and relative efficacies of various forms of therapy. Chapter 8 also summarized the results of major meta-analytic reviews of the effectiveness of psychotherapy in general. What follows is a summary of several meta-analytic reviews of the effectiveness of psychoanalytically oriented (i.e., psychodynamic) therapy.

In the initial meta-analytic review of 375 studies of therapy outcome, Smith and Glass (1977) found that the average effect size of nonbehavioral treatments (including dynamic therapy) was 0.6 whereas the average effect size of behavioral treatments was 0.8. When they extended their review to include 475 studies, Smith, Glass, and Miller (1980) found that the mean effect sizes for behavioral and verbal (including psychodynamic) therapy were, respectively, 0.98 and 0.85. Thus, Smith and Glass noted that psychodynamic therapy is effective, though behavioral therapy is slightly more effective than verbal (including dynamic) therapy.

Following the publication of the Smith and Glass meta-analyses, several other meta-analytic reviews addressed the issues of the effectiveness of psychodynamic therapy and the relative efficacies of psychodynamic and other therapies. Searles (1985) refined an earlier meta-analysis by Andrews and Harvey (1981), by excluding conditions (e.g., homosexuality, underachievement) not commonly considered as neurotic, and by including only those studies that compared treatment to a control condition. In 16 studies, 8 on each of behavioral and psychodynamic therapy, Searles found that the mean effect size of psychodynamic therapy (0.32) is substantially less than that of behavior therapy (0.88).

Searles (1985) also refined an earlier meta-analysis by Landman and Dawes (1982), by eliminating studies of the efficacy of undifferentiated "counseling." Searles identified 19 behavioral studies and two psychodynamic studies and found that the average effect size of behavioral therapy (1.22) is substantially higher than that of psychodynamic therapy (0.27). Although Searles noted that this result may not be interpretable due to the small number of studies of psychodynamic therapy, he argued that the Landman and Dawes review was based on a sample that virtually excludes psychodynamic therapy, and so its conclusion (that psychotherapy is effective) cannot be generalized to psychodynamic therapy.

Shapiro and Shapiro (1982) refined the meta-analysis of Smith and colleagues (1980). Shapiro and Shapiro identified 143 studies that compared two therapies to one another and to a control condition. They found that dynamic–humanistic therapy (0.40) has a lower mean effect size than mixed behavioral (1.42), behavioral (1.06), cognitive (1.00), unclassified behavioral (0.78), and minimal (placebo) treatment (0.71).

Svartberg and Stiles (1991) examined the efficacy of short-term psychodynamic psychotherapy (STPP). They identified 19 studies that compared STPP to either no treatment or to an alternative treatment. At post-treatment, they found that STPP is significantly more effective than no treatment but significantly less effective than alternative treatment. At 6-month follow-up, these differences diminished and were no longer significant. However, at 12-month follow-up, STPP was not more effective than no treatment, but was significantly less effective than alternative treatment.

Crits-Christoph (1992), however, performed a meta-analysis of 11 studies of brief dynamic psychotherapy and reached a more favorable conclusion. Crits-Christoph reported that, compared to wait-list control groups, brief dynamic therapy has effect sizes of from 0.81 to 1.10, depending on the type of outcome assessed. When dynamic therapy was compared to other psychotherapies, Crits-Christoph found no difference in effectiveness.

Most of the meta-analytic reviews found that psychodynamic therapy, although superior to no treatment, is less effective than behavioral and cognitive therapies. It should be quickly noted that many of these reviewers have argued that these differences are not meaningful because studies of behavioral therapy have several advantages over studies of other therapies such as treatment of less severe disorders, shorter follow-up, and outcome measures administered by the therapist or patient. Thus, the reviews are about evenly divided between concluding that psychodynamic therapy is as effective as cognitive and/or behavioral therapies and concluding that psychodynamic therapy is less effective than these alternative forms of therapy. Interestingly, no major meta-analysis to date has concluded that psychodynamic therapy is more effective than cognitive and/or behavioral therapy.

SUMMARY

Freudian psychotherapy, or psychoanalysis, was perhaps the most influential form of psychotherapy during the first half of the 1900s. Freudian therapy served as a model for the other schools of psychotherapy that developed later.

Freud assumed that the cause of psychopathology is troubling unconscious material, usually of a sexual or aggressive nature, which stems from early childhood experiences. The goal of Freudian therapy is for the client to gain insight into this troubling material.

Freudian therapy uses a variety of insight-oriented techniques. The fundamental technique of psychoanalysis is free association. Psychoanalysts interpret dreams, Freudian slips, and other forms of expression. They also interpret the transference and resistance that occurs during therapy.

Jung and Adler were contemporaries of Freud who founded their own schools of psychoanalytic therapy. Jung's theory, *analytical psychology,* did not regard sexual motives and early childhood experiences as important as Freud's. In addition, Jungian therapists are more active and interactive than Freudian therapists. Adler called his approach *individual psychology.* Adler also disagreed with Freud's emphasis on sex and early determinism. Adlerian therapists are also more active than Freudian therapists.

Neo-Freudian schools developed in the mid-1900s. Ego psychologists emphasize the ego over the id. Thus, they stress conscious, rational, and healthy functioning more than Freud. Object relations theory suggests that there are important motivations for human behavior other than sex and aggression, such as social bonding. Alexander introduced psychoanalytically oriented psychotherapy, a briefer and more flexible form of psychoanalysis.

There are many contemporary variants of psychoanalytic therapy. Transactional analysis and certain forms of family systems therapy retain Freud's emphasis on the influence of unconscious motivations and the goal of insight in therapy.

Psychoanalysis has several practical problems. It is lengthy and expensive, and so it is generally restricted only to the most affluent. Such lengthy insight-oriented therapy tends to be most effective for YAVIS patients; however, most individuals do not fit into this category. Psychoanalytic theory also suggests that this therapy is most effective for patients who have high ego strength—that is, who are functioning well prior to therapy. Psychoanalysts must undergo analysis as part of their training. Although psychoanalysts do not have to be physicians, most practicing psychoanalysts in the United States do have medical degrees.

It is very difficult to evaluate scientifically the effectiveness of psychoanalytic therapy. Psychoanalytic concepts are difficult to measure; psychoanalytic theory does not generate precise, testable predictions. Freud was indifferent to empirical evaluations of psychoanalysis, preferring case study evidence.

Attempts to evaluate psychoanalysis scientifically have produced mixed to negative results. Recent reviews of research on the effectiveness of psychotherapy have reported that clients who receive psychotherapy (including psychodynamic therapy) have a superior outcome to untreated individuals. However, these reviews also tend to find that cognitive and behavioral therapies are at least as effective, if not more effective than other therapies.

STUDY QUESTIONS

1. What is Freud's view of the etiology and pathology of abnormal behavior?
2. What are the goals of Freudian therapy? What techniques does Freud use to achieve these goals?
3. Explain the importance of the client–therapist relationship in Freudian therapy.
4. What theoretical differences did Freud have with both Jung and Adler? How do these differences affect the goals and techniques of their forms of therapy?
5. Describe the theoretical differences between classical psychoanalytic theory and ego psychology or object relations theory.
6. How does Alexander's psychoanalytically oriented psychotherapy differ from classical psychoanalysis?
7. Describe one contemporary variant of Freudian psychoanalysis. How is this therapy similar to classical psychoanalysis?
8. Discuss the practical problems of classical psychoanalysis.
9. Why is it difficult to evaluate the effectiveness of psychoanalytic therapy?
10. Discuss the empirical evidence presented to attempt to evaluate the effectiveness of psychoanalytic therapy.

10

Humanistic Therapy

I. Humanistic Approaches to Psychotherapy
   A. Theory of Psychopathology
   B. Goal of Psychotherapy
   C. Techniques of Psychotherapy
   D. Variants of Humanistic Therapy
II. Applied Issues
   A. Selection and Training of
      Psychotherapists

   B. Providing Psychotherapy to the
      Healthy
III. Scientific Issues
   A. Effectiveness of Humanistic
      Psychotherapy
   B. Influence of Rogerian Therapeutic
      Qualities
IV. Summary

H umanistic psychotherapy is an important alternative to psychoanalysis. By far, the most important figure in the development of humanistic therapy is Carl Rogers. Like most of his contemporaries, Rogers was originally trained to conduct psychoanalytic therapy. However, after years of clinical practice and supervision, Rogers found himself developing a novel approach to therapy.

On December 11, 1940, Rogers presented a paper entitled "Some Newer Concepts in Psychotherapy," which he identified as the birth of Rogerian therapy (Raskin & Rogers, 1989). The response to this paper was enthusiastic, and so Rogers expanded it and published his classic work, *Counseling and Psychotherapy: Newer Concepts in Practice* (Rogers, 1942). In this book, Rogers summarized his ideas on psychopathology and psychotherapy. In addition, he suggested that empirical research be conducted to evaluate the effectiveness of therapy and its components.

A few years later, Rogers (1957) published another classic paper in which he identified the "necessary and sufficient" conditions for therapeutic personality change to occur. These conditions are characteristics of the therapist and the client–therapist relationship. Rogers's list of the fundamental elements of therapy stimulated the field to conduct research on therapy process and outcome. It also had significant implications for applied issues such as selecting and training future therapists.

This chapter introduces students to humanistic psychotherapy. Emphasis will be given to the theory and techniques of Rogerian therapy. In addition, several variants of humanistic therapy will be described briefly, including Gestalt therapy, existential therapy, and transpersonal therapy. Following the presentation of these treatments, this chapter will examine several applied issues concerning humanistic therapy, including the selection and training of therapists and provision of therapy to the healthy. Finally, this chapter will summarize empirical evidence concerning the effectiveness of humanistic therapy and the influence of the elements of Rogerian therapy.

HUMANISTIC APPROACHES TO PSYCHOTHERAPY

Theory of Psychopathology

The humanistic theory of personality and psychopathology was introduced in Chapter 3. As you recall, humanistic psychology was influenced by phenomenology, which holds that one's subjective perception of the world is more important than the world in actuality. Humanists also opposed the determinism of behaviorism and psychoanalysis, stressing instead that people are free to choose their actions. They focus on the here and now, rather than on past experiences and influences. In addition, humanists generally believe that people are basically good and are motivated to self-actualize—to develop their potential; psychological problems occur as the result of a failure in the process of self-actualization.

Rogers thought that psychopathology is associated with psychological incongruence—discrepancies between one's self-image and ideal self-image, one's self-image and one's actual self, and one's subjective perception of the world and the actual world. The greater the discrepancy, the more emotional and real-world problems one experiences.

Rogers believed that such incongruences stem from the experience of conditional positive regard—being treated with respect and caring only when meeting the conditions of others. As a result, the person develops conditions of worth, perceiving self as worthy only when meeting the standards of others. In this way, the person develops a self-image that is inaccurate and overly negative or an ideal self that is overly demanding. The result is psychological incongruence and emotional or behavioral problems.

For example, suppose a young boy consistently receives the message that his parents approve of him only when he receives straight "A"s in school. If the boy adopts this condition of worth, then he will ac-

cept himself only when he attains this high standard. If so, he is likely to continue to set extremely high academic and vocational goals throughout life. When he fails to meet this standard of excellence, even though his performance may be above average, he experiences a sense of failure and rejection.

According to Rogers, this person's condition of worth may lead to emotional problems. For example, he may feel like a failure and become depressed. He may experience constant stress as he tries to meet his standards of excellence. He may become angry at the world because he is not able to reach his goal. The person may also develop behavior problems; for example, because the person feels that he is not worthy of acceptance by others, his social relationships may suffer.

In other words, Rogers believed that psychological incongruence is associated with psychopathology. As one's self-image becomes inaccurate or negative and when one's ideal self becomes unrealistic and overly demanding, the discrepancy between self and ideal self leads to emotional and behavioral problems.

Goal of Psychotherapy

The goal of Rogerian therapy is to restore psychological congruence. Although Rogers identified several types of incongruence that cause psychological problems, he attended primarily to incongruence between the self and ideal self. Rogerian therapy largely aims at helping clients increase the congruence between their self as perceived and ideal self-image. Through Rogerian therapy, clients come to perceive themselves more accurately. They then develop more positive self-images and more appropriate ideal self-images. As a result, incongruence between clients' self- and ideal self-images is reduced.

Rogers (1957, p. 96) proposed six conditions that are both necessary and sufficient for therapeutic personality change:

1. Two persons are in psychological contact.
2. The client is in a state of incongruence, being vulnerable or anxious.
3. The therapist is congruent or integrated in the relationship.

4. The therapist experiences unconditional positive regard for the client.

5. The therapist experiences an empathic understanding of the client's internal frame of reference and endeavors to communicate this experience to the client.

6. The communication to the client of the therapist's empathic understanding and unconditional positive regard is to a minimal degree achieved.

Thus, according to Rogers, the "active ingredient" in psychotherapy is *unconditional positive regard.* This means that the client-centered therapist cares for and accepts clients regardless of what they say or do. After clients learn that the therapist accepts them, they come to accept themselves. They no longer live to meet the conditions of worth they adopted from others; instead, they live to fulfill their own good natures.

Techniques of Psychotherapy

Carl Rogers would not approve of an attempt to reduce humanistic therapy to a set of techniques. He viewed therapy as involving much more than simple techniques (such as biofeedback or the behavioral technique of systematic desensitization). Rather, he thought that therapy demands a close relationship between client and therapist. It is only in an atmosphere of caring and understanding that the client ultimately puts aside conditions of worth and comes to perceive the self more accurately.

Still, despite Rogers's aversion to discussing techniques of client-centered therapy, it is possible to summarize the methods that Rogers used to establish and maintain the therapeutic relationship. Rogers discussed at length the elements of unconditional positive regard. Of these, three have received the most attention: warmth, genuineness, and empathy. According to Rogers, therapy is more effective when these elements are present; if any of them is absent, then therapy will be less effective.

The client-centered therapist expresses *warmth.* This simply means that the therapist creates an atmosphere in which clients feels safe, accepted, and cared for. Rogerian therapists give permission to cli-

ents to express their innermost thoughts and feelings. When clients reveal their emotions and behaviors, Rogerian therapists do not judge them. Instead, they accept clients for who they are.

There are many ways in which therapists express warmth. For example, they speak in a gentle, calming voice. They lean forward to get near the client. They mirror the client's posture, leaning forward when the client leans forward and relaxing when the client relaxes; such mirroring demonstrates that the therapist is "connecting with" the client. If the client tears up, the therapist offers the client a box of tissues, giving the client permission to express the sadness more openly.

It is important for Rogerian therapists to avoid judging their clients' emotional reactions. For example, if a client starts to cry over a minor setback at work, Rogerian therapists do not try to convince the client that the incident was insignificant and not worth their tears. This would show a clear lack of acceptance of the client's feelings.

It is also important that Rogerian therapists avoid imposing their own evaluations of the client's experiences. For example, if a client describes a traumatic life event, the therapist should not say, "That's terrible" or "I'm sorry to hear that." These responses, though expressing some caring, stress the therapist's judgment of and reaction to the event. Rogerian therapists should keep the focus on the client's emotions and experiences. Hence, more appropriate responses would be: "That was very upsetting for you" or "It must have been hard for you to cope with that."

A second component of unconditional positive regard is *empathy.* This means that client-centered therapists understand what the client is experiencing and communicate this understanding to the client. Therapists know how the client thinks and feels, and may actually think and feel the same way, along with the client. In accurately understanding the client's feelings, therapists come to know the client's true self. This is helpful in assisting the client to understand his or her true nature.

To be empathic, the Rogerian therapist must listen carefully to what clients say. Because clients may not use the same terms that a psychologist would use to describe their reactions and because clients may not express themselves clearly when in distress, it is crucial that Rogerian therapists attend to clients' spoken as well as unspoken messages. Nonverbal behavior (e.g., high muscle tension, fidgeting), facial expressions, vocal characteristics (e.g., speech rate, pitch), and inconsistencies between verbal and nonverbal communications all are useful in understanding clients' emotional reactions.

A third component of unconditional positive regard is *genuineness*. Rogerian therapists should be open and honest. They should not wear a forced smile that clients will perceive as phony. They should not express confidence in the outcome of therapy that they do not truly believe.

Rogerian therapists should "be themselves." Rogers believed that therapists should themselves be congruent, that is, have an accurate understanding of self. When therapists experience strong feelings in response to what their clients say or do, congruent therapists recognize these feelings and express them. Now, client-centered therapists do not judge or impose their own standards on their clients and so they do not express shock or disappointment at clients' revelations. Still, they may experience joy at their clients' successes and so should express this openly. If they are accurately understanding the clients' experiences, they may actually feel these emotions along with the clients. These emotions are genuine and should be expressed.

Client-centered therapists use a variety of methods to establish and maintain a relation characterized by unconditional positive regard. Rogers (1942) identified the most commonly used types of verbalizations by client-centered therapists: open-ended statements, reflection, interpretation, and paraphrasing.

An important Rogerian technique is the *open-ended statement*. Open-ended statements indicate the topic of conversation but leave the development of the topic to the client. They do not set limits on how the client may respond.

Consider the question, *Did you have a good week?* This question is closed-ended because the proper response is "yes" or "no." An open-ended alternative is *Tell me about your week.* This leaves it up to the client to choose what weekly events to re-

late and to judge whether to label the week as good or bad.

Suppose a client describes a fight with her spouse. The Rogerian therapist should not ask *Did that make you feel angry?* This closed-ended question implies the therapist's reaction to the event and limits the client's response. Instead, an open-ended question (How did that make you feel?) allows the client to identify her own reaction, anger or otherwise.

Open-ended comments ensure that the therapist does not determine the course of the conversation. It is up to the client to introduce topics and determine the depth to which topics are addressed. Rogers viewed his therapy as client-centered precisely because the therapist does not determine the direction of therapy. For this reason, open-ended comments are crucial to client- centered or nondirective therapy.

During a client's presentation, Rogers frequently made noncommittal comments such as *uh-huh, hmmm, yes,* and *go on.* When made skillfully, punctuating the client's presentation, these verbalizations serve as open-ended statements, encouraging the client to continue.

Open-ended statements are also especially useful at the beginning of the client–therapist relationship. Many therapists start the first session with a client by saying, "Tell me why you are here." This allows clients to express in their own words what they see as their problem and what they are seeking from the therapist. As noted in Chapter 8, one of the important tasks at the start of therapy is to ensure that clients know what to expect from therapy. Because one of the ground rules of therapy is for clients to be self-disclosing, it is helpful to use open-ended questions early in therapy to "shape" the client to be disclosing.

Another important Rogerian technique is *reflection*, which is the technique of recognizing in some way a feeling or attitude that the client has just expressed. If a client says, "I am so upset, I don't know where to begin," the Rogerian therapist reflects this feeling by saying, "You are upset. It is difficult to know how to start." If the client begins to cry when talking about her relationship with her father, the Rogerian therapist reflects this by saying, "It is upsetting to talk about your father." If a client resents being in therapy, sitting and fuming silently, the therapist reflects this by saying, "You seem to be angry." (A psychologist I know once saw a delinquent male who, in the first therapy session, pulled a knife. As a good Rogerian therapist, the psychologist reflected this behavior, saying, "I see you have a knife.")

Reflection expresses empathy. It also expresses warmth—a therapist who is interested in understanding what the client is feeling must care for the client.

Interpretation is the technique of recognizing feelings or attitudes expressed by the client's general demeanor, behavior, or previous statements. Rather than simply repeating a feeling that the client has just openly expressed, the therapist who employs interpretation provides a new way of thinking about the client's experiences—one that the client may not yet have perceived.

Consider a client who begins to examine his fingernails during a discussion of his relationship with his wife. This behavior may distract the client so that his attention wanders. If the therapist believes that this behavior is a way for the client to avoid discussing his marriage, then the therapist may make the interpretation: "You seem to be distracted. I am wondering if this means you do not want to talk about your wife."

Therapeutic interpretations were discussed in the previous chapter. The same cautions about interpretation raised in Chapter 9 should be reiterated here. Interpretations should only be made when the therapist has evidence, perhaps from several incidents, that the interpretation is accurate. The interpretation should be made tentatively, so that the client has the opportunity to respond to and correct the interpretation.

Although both Rogerian and Freudian therapists make interpretations, it is important to recognize that they differ in the type of insight that they are helping the client to attain. Freudian therapists use interpretations to bring to awareness some previously unconscious material, often of a sexual or aggressive nature going back to childhood. Rogerian therapists,

on the other hand, use interpretations to help clients recognize some aspect of their true self, usually a current emotion or motivation.

Interpretations, like reflections, express empathy. However, they also express genuineness—the therapist is striving to understand the client. When the therapist develops a hypothesis to explain some of the client's behavior, it is a sign of openness for the therapist to introduce the interpretation, rather than postpone it.

A final Rogerian technique is *paraphrasing*. Here, the therapist summarizes what the client said. For example, after a client describes a troubling interaction with a friend, the therapist summarizes it to highlight the major elements of the event: "I hear you saying that you become angry when your friend ignores your feelings and doesn't listen to you." After the client talks about a complex issue, it is helpful for the therapist to summarize what was said. "Let me make sure I understand this. You are feeling _____because of _____." The therapist highlights the major features in the account, including significant details of the events and the client's reactions.

Paraphrasing is a very useful technique. Clients often experience emotional distress, which interferes with their ability to describe their problem clearly. Clients may not have the insight or psychological mindedness to distinguish among troubling emotional states. Also, clients may use terms with several possible meanings and it may not be clear which meaning they intended. For these reasons, clients' accounts of their problems are often less clear than their therapists would like to hear. Paraphrasing gives therapists the opportunity to check the accuracy of their understanding of the client and gives the client the chance to correct any of the therapists' misperceptions.

Paraphrasing, like reflection, expresses understanding. Because paraphrasing also indicates that the therapist wants to understand the client, it also expresses caring.

I have often recommended the use of paraphrasing to graduate student therapists, even when they are not providing Rogerian therapy. Novice therapists are sometimes unsure of what to do next in a session. Paraphrasing the content of the previous segment of the session may help therapists, as well as clients, understand the issue previously discussed and see which issue should be tackled next.

Exhibit 10.1 presents an excerpt from a session between a student and a nondirective counselor (Rogers, 1942). It illustrates how the Rogerian therapist interacts with a client in a nondirective, accepting manner.

Students who are first introduced to Rogerian techniques may underestimate their significance. Reading a transcript of a nondirective therapy session may make therapy sound impersonal or mechanical. After all, whenever the client expresses a feeling or attitude, the therapist reflects it. To keep the discussion of a topic alive, the therapist makes frequent open-ended comments, such as *Uh-huh* and *Tell me more.* After an extended presentation, the therapist summarizes the material. The student may mistakenly think that such comments are automatic and that Rogerian therapy is nothing but a set of simple techniques.

However, students should recognize that Rogerian therapists do not use such techniques in an impersonal or mechanical manner. When Rogerian therapists reflect their clients' feelings, they do so in a warm and caring manner. They speak in gentle tones, lean forward to get near to the client, and make eye contact; although Rogerian techniques may sound mechanical, when read in a transcript, it is clear from observing experienced client-centered therapists that the techniques are anything but mechanical.

Students should also be aware of how Rogerian therapy is related to classical psychoanalytic therapy. Both forms of therapy are nondirective: psychoanalysis relies on free association whereas Rogerian therapy emphasizes open-ended and reflective interactions. Both forms of therapy employ interpretation: the psychoanalyst makes interpretations to bring the client's unconscious conflicts to the fore, whereas the Rogerian therapist uses them to express understanding and caring.

However, the similarity stops here. Classical psychoanalysts are rather passive in their interactions with clients. They do not take notes so as not to distract the clients' free associations. Their clients lie down, unable to see the therapists' facial expressions, which might interfere with the clients' free associations.

The Rogerian therapist is quite different from the psychoanalyst. Client-centered therapists interact actively with the client, constantly expressing both understanding and caring. The goal is to establish a warm, accepting relationship. This is very different from the classical psychoanalyst who is a "blank slate" on whom clients project their own transference needs.

Variants of Humanistic Therapy

Following Rogers's (1942, 1951, 1957) introduction of client-centered therapy, it became one of the leading schools of psychotherapy in the 1960s. It generated a large following, not only because of its theoretical foundation and clinical applications, but also because of its empirical support (which will be examined below). By the 1970s, many clinical psychologists considered Rogerian techniques to be among the most fundamental for psychotherapists to master. In fact, some psychotherapy textbooks present the Rogerian therapeutic qualities (genuineness, warmth, empathy) and techniques (open-ended statements, paraphrasing, interpretation, reflection) as *active listening skills* that are necessary for the conduct of any type of psychotherapy.

For example, suppose a behavior therapy technique has been shown to be an effective treatment for a disorder (such as systematic desensitization for phobias). Before starting treatment, the behavior therapist should try to establish a good relationship with the client. After all, if the client does not trust the therapist, stops attending therapy sessions, or fails to comply with the treatment regimen, then therapy will not work. If the therapist has not succeeded in establishing a good rapport with the client, then even the most effective behavior therapy technique will not work. Thus, behavior therapists employ Rogerian techniques to establish rapport prior to implementing a behavioral technique (Goldfried & Davison, 1976).

EXHIBIT 10.1   Excerpt from a Client-Centered Therapy Session

Rogers (1942) described the foundations of client-centered therapy. In this book, Rogers provided many transcripts of nondirective therapy sessions. The following is a selection that illustrates the basic techniques used by Rogerian therapists to provide unconditional positive regard. The interaction occurred between a student (S) and a counselor (C).

S: I haven't written to my parents about this at all. In the past they haven't been of any help to me in this respect, and if I can keep it away from them as much as possible, I'll do so. But there's a slight matter of grades to explain and they're not good, and I don't know how I'm going to explain without telling them about this [the client's emotional problems]. Would you advise me to tell them about it?
C: Suppose you tell me a little more about what you had thought about it. **[Open-ended statement]**
S: Well, I think I'm compelled to, because—
C: It's a situation you've really got to face.
[Reflection]
S: Yes, there's no use getting around it, even if they can't take it the way they should, because I've already flunked my gym course. Now, they'll know that you can't flunk in gym without being negligent about it. They'll ask me.
C: It will be fairly hard for you to tell them.
[Reflection]
S: Yes. Oh, I don't know if they're going to sort of condemn me. I think so, because that's what they've done in the past. They've said "It's your fault. You don't have enough will power, you're not interested." That's the experience I've had in the past. I've been telling them that I improved in this respect. I was—I was all right in the first quarter. Well, I wasn't entirely all right, but I just got worse.
C: You feel that they'll be unsympathetic and they'll condemn you for your failures.
[Paraphrasing]

S: Well, my—I'm pretty sure my father will. My mother might not. He hasn't been—he doesn't experience these things; he just doesn't know what it's like. "Lack of ambition" is what he'll say.
C: You feel that he could never understand you?
[Paraphrasing]
S: No, I don't think he is—is capable of that, because I don't get along with him, don't at all!
C: You dislike him a good deal? **[Reflection]**
S: Yes, I—I did feel bitter toward him for a while and I've gone out of that stage, and now I don't feel bitter against him but I—I'm sort of ashamed. I think that that's it more than anything else, an experience of failure of shame that he is my father.
C: You feel he isn't much good. **[Reflection]**
S: Well, he's putting me through school but [unintelligible]. I'm sorry to say that, but that's my opinion about it. I think he had a lot to do in forming it, too.
C: This has been something on which you have felt pretty deeply, for a long while. **[Reflection]**
S: I have.
C: Have you worried a lot about this matter of writing home?
S: About this? Well, yes, because it's going to be a pretty difficult proposition to put it across. I haven't got any idea of what action they're going to take.
C: You sound as though you feel a little bit like a prisoner before the bar. **[Interpretation]**
S: [laughs] That's just about it. I—I don't know, I feel sort of strangled; that's how I feel.
C: Strangled? **[Reflection]**
S: By the world. I feel licked.
C: It's kind of tough to feel that you can't fight back. [long pause] You feel more licked now than you did awhile ago? **[Reflection]**
S: I do.

In this way, even nonhumanistically oriented therapists may view Rogerian therapy techniques as necessary, if not sufficient, conditions for effective treatment. Thus, many contemporary psychotherapists incorporate Rogerian principles in psychotherapy, regardless of their primary therapeutic orientation.

In addition to such applications of Rogerian techniques by nonhumanistically oriented therapists, there are several other approaches to therapy that have clear humanistic leanings. The next section of the chapter will briefly summarize several of the major variants of humanistic therapy.

Existential Therapy Existential psychology arose in the 1940s and 1950s. It is based on the ideas of existential philosophers, such as Martin Heidegger, Jean-Paul Sartre, and Paul Tillich. *Existentialism* is a school of philosophy that examines problems of human existence, including issues such as the meaning of life, the inevitability of pain, isolation, and death, and the responsibility of self-determination.

In the 1940s and 1950s, some mental health professionals began to interpret psychological problems from the vantage point of existentialism. Medard Boss and Ludwig Binswanger are perhaps the first psychiatrists who explicitly applied existential principles to psychotherapy. More recently, Rollo May and Irvin Yalom have furthered the existential therapy movement.

Several common psychological problems have been interpreted as existential dilemmas. For example, following the Women's Movement of the 1960s, some women experienced doubt about their proper social roles—mother and homemaker versus career-woman. Some adolescents and young adults have experienced depression and anxiety related to a sense of alienation from society. Given modern society's changes (e.g., increased divorce rate, increased mobility), many people have reported feeling lonely and isolated.

Some psychologists interpret these problems as existential, related to issues such as the meaning of life and the pain of loneliness. In these cases, the psy-

chologist may adopt a form of existential therapy to treat them.

It is difficult to enumerate the techniques of existential therapy. As a general rule, existential therapists have neither provided explicit descriptions of their methods nor articulated how their methods are distinct from those of other schools of therapy. It is possible to see existential therapy as more of a philosophy than a science of therapy.

Norcross (1987) provided one description of the methods of existential therapy. Norcross surveyed clinical psychologists and identified several differences in the methods employed by existential, behavioral, and psychodynamic therapists. Compared to therapists of other orientations, existential therapists employed less psychometric testing and more physical contact, self-disclosure, and nonverbal evaluation. In addition, existential therapists occupied a middle position between behavior therapists and psychodynamic therapists in their use of psychodynamic techniques and education. Thus, Norcross showed that existential therapists resemble humanistic therapists more than behavioral and psychodynamic therapists.

Existential psychology shares other similarities with humanistic psychology. Both approaches are phenomenological, stressing the individual's subjective perception of the world over objective reality. Both approaches view people as free to determine their own actions; people are not determined by their past nor by their environmental circumstances. Both approaches are present-oriented.

Existential psychologists may consider their approach to be distinct from humanism. Indeed, just as humanistic psychology was labelled the *third force* in psychology, I have heard some psychologists refer to existential psychology as the fourth force. However, the similarities are sufficient for existential therapy to be considered, for the purposes of this book, as a variant of humanistic therapy.

Although existential therapists have not developed treatment techniques unique to their approach, it is possible to list several basic principles of existential therapy. First, existential therapy stresses the here and now. What is important in existentialism is *being* or current functioning. Although a client may attribute the presenting problem to a troubling past, the existential therapist continually refocuses the client's attention on the present. What is important is what the client thinks, feels, and does now. The therapist directs the client's attention to current functioning, especially within the therapy session. Discussing the client's interactions with the therapist is a useful way of helping the client learn how to interact more effectively with others outside of therapy.

A second emphasis of existential therapy is self-determination. Existentialists believe that people are free to choose their own actions. Existential therapists help clients recognize that they are free and responsible for their actions. It is important for clients to learn that choosing not to act is itself a choice and one for which they must take responsibility.

Norcross (1987) listed other related themes emphasized in existential therapy, including individuality, authenticity, and potentiality. However, because these are closely related to the other emphases in existential or humanistic psychology, they will not be addressed further here.

One psychiatrist who has written at length about existential therapy is Viktor Frankl (1963, 1965, 1969). Frankl developed a form of existential therapy called *logotherapy* ("meaning therapy"). Frankl thought that a major motivation of human behavior is to find meaning in life. When people have not found a meaning to their lives, they experience existential problems.

Frankl believed that there are three ways to find meaning in life. First, some people find meaning through their contributions to the world (say through becoming a healer, artist, or loving parent). Others find meaning through what they experience or "take" from the world (say, by enjoying great works of art or communing with nature).

However, some people are not fortunate enough to find meaning in these ways. They may not have the talent or opportunity to make meaningful contributions to the world and their circumstances may not allow them to enjoy such uplifting experiences. For example, people who have terminal illnesses, who

are in prison, or who have lost a loved one may have trouble finding meaning in their lives.

For these people, Frankl suggested a third way to find meaning: through the attitude they take in facing a difficult (and unchangeable) situation. It is primarily for this group of people that Frankl developed logotherapy. In logotherapy, Frankl adopted a philosophical—even spiritual—approach to help clients find meaning. (Students may be interested to learn that Frankl was a prisoner in the German concentration camps during World War II and developed his approach to therapy as a way of helping individuals in such dreadful circumstances find meaning in life.)

For example, Frankl (1963) described a case in which he saw an elderly man, distraught following the death of his wife. Frankl asked whether he would have preferred dying before his wife, so that she would be the one coping with his loss. The client admitted that he would have done anything to spare her this suffering—including bearing the pain himself. Even though the man continued to miss his wife terribly, he found meaning in his life by seeing that his suffering had spared her.

In addition to helping clients find global meaning in their lives, Frankl also described two interesting therapy techniques that are useful with more circumscribed problems: paradoxical intention and dereflection. In *paradoxical intention,* the therapist encourages the client to exhibit a problem behavior or symptom that he fears and has been trying to avoid. Frankl used paradoxical intention in the short-term treatment of clients with anxiety disorders, such as phobias and obsessive-compulsive disorder. Frankl considered paradoxical intention to be appropriate when the client fears that the symptom will occur, and it is this very anticipatory anxiety that leads to the symptom.

For example, suppose a client is anxious about speaking in public because he frequently stammers when addressing an audience. Frankl believed that fear of stammering is a major factor that causes stammering. To disrupt this chain, Frankl used paradoxical intention. The therapist prescribes stammering, having the client practice the symptom, even exaggerating it comically. This allows the client to distance himself from the symptom. The client stammers, not because he has a flaw but because the therapist has prescribed the symptom. The client need not worry about whether or not the symptom will occur. By ridiculing the symptom, the client may no longer see it as a threat. In this way, Frankl enables the client to live "in the moment," without concerning himself about the consequence of one's actions.

Frankl introduced another technique to treat conditions associated with hyper-reflection, or excessive self-observation. For example, consider a client who has insomnia. She may dread going to bed because she fears that she will not fall asleep. She lies in bed, monitoring her mental state to see if she is getting sleepy. However, the very act of attending to her state of alertness interferes with the relaxation needed to fall asleep! (Remember the fable of the centipede who walks without difficulty until another insect asks him about the order in which he moves his legs. As the centipede ponders this question, his ruminations interfere with his walking, so that he is left stranded, unable to walk.) Frankl listed other disorders that are caused by hyper-reflection, such as sexual dysfunction and fear of swallowing.

Frankl treated symptoms associated with hyper-reflection with *dereflection*. Using dereflection, the therapist helps the client focus attention outside of the self, so that excessive self-observation no longer interferes with functioning. For example, in the case of insomnia, the therapist may have the client focus on a spot on the ceiling, count sheep, or think about getting out of bed to shovel snow or perform some other difficult task. In treating a sexual dysfunction, the therapist may have the client focus on the partner's body rather than his or her own physiological reactions.

According to Frankl, dereflection, like paradoxical intention, helps the client "get outside of the self." The client no longer is concerned about the occurrence or consequence of the symptom. Instead, the client functions more *existentially*—in the moment.

Because the techniques of existential therapy are not clearly defined, it is difficult to assess its effectiveness. Research reviews have found few studies that evaluated existential therapy (Bergin, 1971;

Prochaska, 1984). Also, because existential therapists employ Rogerian and psychodynamic techniques, case study evidence presented to support existential therapy could be explained within other theoretical frameworks.

Still, despite the lack of empirical support, students should recognize that existential therapy is popular among several groups of therapists. Therapists who work with terminally ill patients and their families, with the recently bereaved, and with individuals who have spiritual crises (such as clergy who provide pastoral counseling) may find the philosophical—even spiritual—aspects of existential therapy to be helpful.

Gestalt Therapy   *Gestalt therapy* is a form of therapy developed by Frederick ("Fritz") Perls (1897–1970). Gestalt therapy represents an interesting blend of humanistic, existential, and psychoanalytic principles. Because Gestalt therapy shares several features with humanistic therapy, such as a strong here-and-now orientation and an emphasis on individual freedom and responsibility, I have included it in this chapter as a variant of humanistic therapy.

Yontef and Simkin (1989) identified several influences on the development of Gestalt therapy. Perls originally trained as a psychoanalyst. His training analysis was conducted by Wilhelm Reich, who is known both for his application of Freudian theory to personality disorders and for his emphasis of biological/sexual functioning. Perls also trained in the laboratory of Kurt Goldstein, a neurologist who worked with brain-injured patients and who developed a holistic model of conceptualizing and treating patients. Perls was also influenced by existential philosophers.

Like humanism, Gestalt therapy adopts a holistic approach. *Gestalt* is the German word for pattern or whole. Perls called his approach Gestalt therapy because he was interested in treating the "whole" person—in dealing with the person as an integrated entity. He thought that a major cause of pathology is the lack of awareness of some major aspect of self—behavioral, emotional, or cognitive. Perls used the term *polarity* to refer to a false distinction drawn by a person between different aspects of self (e.g., past/present, conscious/unconscious). Perls believed that such distinctions are artificial and only hindered acceptance of self as an entity.

Another humanistic emphasis of Gestalt therapy is relatedness to the world. Perls used the term *contact* to refer to one's relation to the world (including other people). Psychological health, for Perls, is associated with the degree to which one is aware of one's contact with the world. Perls considered individuals who have only superficial relations or who are not fully aware of their contact with others to be neurotic. People who avoid intimate relations, holding others at arm's length, have limited contact with the world. On the other hand, those who are not aware of their relationships (e.g., are not aware of the nonverbal messages they send to others or do not understand the verbal and nonverbal messages that others send to them) lack understanding of much of their behavior. A major goal of Gestalt therapy is to help clients to become more aware of their contact with others.

Another humanistic emphasis of Gestalt therapy is the here and now. Perls adopted an extremely active and present-oriented approach to treatment. He focused the client's attention on the present. He refused to discuss the client's childhood or other past experiences. Instead, he forced the client to focus on current functioning.

Gestalt therapy reflects Perls's psychoanalytic heritage in several ways. Both systems view lack of awareness as a major cause of psychopathology. Both systems have insight as a major goal of treatment. Like Freud, Perls viewed biological forces (such as emotional reactions and sexual drives) as important aspects of human experience.

However, unlike psychoanalysis, Perls did not view childhood trauma as the cause of pathology, nor did he think that clients must become aware of unconscious conflicts that are the source of psychological problems. Instead, the awareness sought by Perls is of the client's emotional, behavioral, and cognitive functioning in the here and now!

Gestalt therapists employ techniques that force clients to attend to their current functioning. For example, Gestalt therapists often use confrontation.

Confrontation is the technique of directly pointing out some aspect of the client's functioning of which the client is unaware or has been denying.

For example, if a client's nonverbal behavior (frowning, crossing the arms) suggests that the client is dissatisfied with the therapist, the Gestalt therapist confronts this directly: "Are you aware of your facial expression?" "Look at your arms." "What are you doing?" "What do these mean to you?"

The Gestalt technique of confrontation is often used in drug and alcohol abuse treatment programs, since substance abusers frequently deny that they have a problem. It is not uncommon in such programs for group Gestalt therapy to lead clients to admit that they have a problem. The confrontation may be quite forceful, as the therapist and other group members confront the client directly: "Don't give me that garbage," "Look at yourself," " We have all been through the same thing you're going through," "You don't fool us," " You don't fool your family," "Stop trying to fool yourself."

Gestalt therapists also frequently employ body awareness exercises that stimulate physical reactions and focus the client's attention on these experiences. For example, if a client has difficulty trusting others, a Gestalt therapist may have the client stand up, close his eyes, and fall backwards, trusting that the therapist will catch him. This exercise forces the client to trust others. If a couple has difficulty communicating, a Gestalt therapist may have them try to communicate nonverbally. This forces them to be aware of how they are acting and how their spouse interprets their signals.

Like Rogers, Perls disapproved of attempting to reduce Gestalt therapy to a set of simple techniques. Perls thought that Gestalt therapists should be spontaneous and creative, and so should not be bound by a limited set of methods. Perls and other Gestalt therapists (e.g., Polster & Polster, 1973) have described dozens of Gestalt exercises designed to enhance awareness. However, Perls (Levitsky & Perls, 1970) has listed the most commonly used Gestalt techniques. These include the following:

1. *Games of dialogue.* When clients fail to recognize some aspect of their functioning because they have adopted a polarity (e.g., body–mind, past–present), Gestalt therapists have clients engage in a conversation in which they play both sides of the polarity. In this way, clients become aware of the polarity and of the false distinction between the two poles.

For example, suppose a client blames his current problems on the way his parents reared him. Perls would consider the distinction between present and past selves a polarity—a false dichotomy that hinders awareness of self as an integrated whole. For this reason, Perls would have the client role-play his past and present selves, discussing his current problem. In this way, the client may come to see that the two sides of self are not disparate.

2. *Playing the projection.* When clients report that they cannot behave in a certain way because of how other people would react, Perls perceives such excuses as the client's projections, which he has them role-play. This helps clients become aware that their perceptions of others' reactions are actually their own.

For example, suppose a woman says that she cannot ask a man out for a date because she is embarrassed about what people would think of her. Perls would have this client play the roles of both self and others, discussing her asking a man out. This exercise should help her to see that the perceived reactions of others are truly her own fears.

3. *I take responsibility.* When clients have difficulty accepting or admitting responsibility, Perls has them say, "I take responsibility," for every statement they make about themselves, their actions, or their feelings. This highlights the existential aspect of Gestalt therapy that people are self-determined.

4. *Rehearsals.* Here, clients talk aloud, revealing their thinking prior to playing certain social roles. This helps them develop an awareness of their thoughts and feelings when in certain situations. This technique resembles the role-play methods of assessing cognitions that are commonly employed in cognitive-behavioral approaches to therapy.

5. *May I feed you a sentence?* This technique involves having the Gestalt therapist ask permission to instruct the client to repeat some statement that the therapist thinks is significant for the client. This resembles the psychoanalytic and Rogerian techniques of making interpretations. However, the Gestalt approach is to use the technique in a more casual, even game-like, manner. The client then actively "tries on for size" the statement, determining whether it "feels" right and may be an accurate way of characterizing one's experience.

Gestalt therapy became very popular in the 1960s and 1970s. Perls (1969a, 1969b) wrote in an informal, nonacademic, and entertaining style that appealed to many during this period of anti-establishment thinking.

However, Gestalt therapy suffers from the lack of a firm scientific foundation. Perls's ideas on the development of personality and psychopathology have generally not been evaluated empirically. In fact, Gestalt therapy as a school has been very slow in generating empirical research to support either its theoretical foundation or its therapeutic effectiveness.

For example, Prochaska (1984) could locate only a handle of studies that examined the effectiveness of Gestalt techniques. These studies primarily addressed normal individuals seeking growth experiences rather than clients seeking treatment for psychological disorders, and they provided only mixed results for Gestalt techniques.

Prochaska located only one controlled study of Gestalt therapy as treatment for a troubled population. Gannon (cited in Prochaska, 1984) randomly assigned 60 high school students who were experiencing behavioral problems to one of three conditions: Gestalt group therapy, placebo group therapy, or a no treatment control group. Gannon found that subjects in the Gestalt therapy group experienced improved openness and contact, relative to subjects in the control conditions. However, Prochaska noted that this study did not include outcome measures for the problem behaviors that led subjects to be included in the study; hence, even this controlled study does not provide much support for Gestalt therapy. Because of the lack of empirical evidence for its theory of psychopathology and for the effectiveness of its treatment techniques, scientifically oriented clinical psychologists have been critical of Gestalt therapy.

There is another, practical problem with Gestalt therapy. One of the major techniques of Gestalt therapy is confrontation. I have observed Gestalt therapists place too much emphasis (in my opinion) on confrontation and too little emphasis on emotional support or cognitive understanding. For example, I have seen Gestalt therapy groups in substance abuse treatment centers use confrontation to force abusers to stop denying that they have a problem. However, on occasion, the confrontation became so extreme that, to a non-Gestalt therapist, the experience could be perceived as a form of emotional battering. Of course, this is not a necessary outcome of confrontation. Still, my experience has been to encourage students not to use Gestalt confrontational techniques until they have had at least several years of experience in other, less confrontational forms of therapy.

Transpersonal Therapy Another approach to therapy that has become popular in recent years is transpersonal psychotherapy. This term applies to treatments based on Asian philosophies or religions. Even though some psychologists have called transpersonal therapy the *fourth force* of psychology, I have classified such treatments as humanistic because, like Rogerian therapy, they have a strong existential focus, emphasizing the here and now and self-determination. In addition, they suggest that existential problems may be overcome through transforming one's consciousness and sense of identity (Walsh, 1989).

Walsh (1989) described two influential approaches to transpersonal therapy: meditation and yoga. *Meditation* combines physical and psychological exercises designed to heighten attention and enhance mental functioning. Physical meditative exercises include deep breathing and muscle relaxation; psychological meditative exercises include mental imagery and repetition of a phrase or prayer.

Research on the physiological effects of meditation have somewhat mixed results. Wallace and Benson (1972) showed that meditation leads to significant changes in physiological measures of arousal. However, in a review of such research, Holmes (1984) found that the physiological changes associated with meditation are neither greater than nor different from the changes caused by other forms of relaxation, such as simple resting. Still, such relaxation in and of itself may be beneficial in the treatment of stress-related disorders, and is a major goal of treatments such as biofeedback and muscle relaxation, which will be discussed in Chapter 12.

Yoga is a more global discipline in which one combines meditation with study, ethical training, and changes in lifestyle in order to increase one's mental discipline and consciousness. For example, many practitioners of yoga are vegetarians. They avoid eating meat for ethical rather than dietary reasons—to avoid inflicting pain on sensate animals. Similarly, many practitioners of yoga are pacifists, both in their daily lives and in the social and political movements that they support.

Another Asian approach to therapy that has received recent attention is Morita therapy. Shoma Morita, a Japanese therapist, introduced this approach in the 1910s, about the same time that Freud was popularizing psychoanalysis. Morita therapy is based on Zen Buddhism, which emphasizes one's relatedness to the world and existence in the moment. For these reasons, it fits nicely into this chapter's discussion of humanistic therapies.

Morita therapy was developed primarily for patients with anxiety disorders, especially those who exhibit excessive self-consciousness, self-preoccupation, and hypersensitivity to threats (Ishiyama, 1986). Morita helped clients overcome anxiety by having them embrace it as a normal part of existence and recognizing that their concerns are unnecessary.

To accomplish this, Morita first had clients rest in bed for about one week (Reynolds & Kiefer, 1977). They were isolated and permitted no distractions, such as music or visitors. Clients were encouraged to contemplate their anxieties—not to fight them but to accept them as a part of themselves.

After several days, clients usually experience a period of heightened anxiety and so want to discontinue the bedrest (Suzuki, 1989). Morita did not permit them to escape the anxiety through physical activity or other distractions. Instead, clients had to cope internally with their emotions. Eventually, Morita found that clients recognize that their anxieties are not catastrophic consequences to be avoided at all costs but are normal reactions that can be dealt with successfully.

At this point, Morita had clients return to their daily routines. Morita used homework assignments to show clients that their emotions need not interfere with their daily work. Morita's goal was to help clients accept their emotional arousal as a part of themselves that need not deter them from ongoing functioning (Suzuki, 1989).

Like psychoanalysis, Morita therapy is primarily used to treat anxiety disorders (Ishiyama, 1986). However, unlike psychoanalysis, Morita therapy does not explain anxiety disorders as resulting from a client's childhood experiences. Instead, Morita emphasizes the client's current interpretation of events.

In this respect, Morita therapy shares some similarities with cognitive–behavioral therapy. For example, Morita stressed the client's rationality and attempted to modify the client's negative beliefs so that they become more self-enhancing. Morita therapy also resembles cognitive–behavioral therapy in its use of homework assignments and exposure to heightened anxiety.

Still, Morita therapy differs from cognitive–behavioral therapy in its rootedness in Asian philosophy. Morita therapy is clearly based on Zen Buddhism. It has an existential focus and stresses that the client should direct attention beyond self to the outside world. In this respect, Morita therapy resembles Frankl's existential treatment of anxiety disorders.

Despite their popularity, transpersonal therapies suffer from a lack of empirical support. They combine philosophical, spiritual, and mystical elements in psychotherapy. However, these nonscientific features make transpersonal therapy difficult to evaluate. For example, research has shown that meditation is effective in producing physiological relaxation (Wallace & Benson, 1972). Training in relaxation techniques can then produce significant psychological benefits. However, the effectiveness of such techniques can be explained entirely in terms of physiological or cognitive theories (Holmes, 1984). It is difficult for a transpersonal therapist to demonstrate that the effectiveness of such interventions is in fact related to its philosophical or spiritual elements.

Ellis and Yeager (1989) wrote a very pointed criticism of transpersonal therapy. They argued that transpersonal therapy lacks an empirical foundation for its theory of psychopathology and psychotherapy. In addition, they stated that the principles and techniques of transpersonal therapy actually contradict those of therapies that have received extensive empirical support (such as cognitive and behavioral therapy). For these reasons, transpersonal therapy requires a more extensive empirical foundation before it will be adopted by a larger segment of the professional community.

APPLIED ISSUES

Selection and Training of Psychotherapists

Rogers's theory of therapy has had a significant impact on the selection and training of therapists. After Rogers identified the fundamental therapeutic qualities of genuineness, warmth, and empathy, he recommended that psychotherapy training programs use these qualities as criteria for selecting applicants. Rogers also made recommendations about how to train student- therapists to express these qualities.

Rogers (1957) recommended that training in client-centered therapy should consist of a series of graduated steps in which students (1) listen to audiotaped therapy sessions of experienced therapists; (2) role-play client–therapist interactions with other trainees; (3) observe live demonstrations of therapy by experienced clinicians; (4) participate in group or co-therapy sessions with other therapists; (5) conduct individual therapy sessions with clients, recording their sessions for later supervision; and (6) receive personal therapy. These training steps are graduated, progressing from least to most demanding. Students should note that Rogers, like Freud, recommended personal therapy as a part of the training of psychotherapists.

Truax and Carkhuff (1967) developed a similar series of graduated exercises, wherein trainees (1) interact in a therapeutic context with supervisors who provide high levels of genuineness, warmth, and empathy; (2) receive didactic training in methods of implementing Rogerian conditions; and (3) participate in a quasi-group therapy format in which they have the opportunity to explore their own "selves."

Although much has been written since the 1960s on the training of psychotherapists, most clinical psychology training programs—even those that do not describe themselves as having a humanistic orientation—provide students with training experiences comparable to those described by Rogers (1957). Of course, programs differ in the degree to which they emphasize Rogerian versus non-Rogerian treatment methods and in terms of their relative emphases on training in psychotherapy versus other activities, such as assessment and clinical research. Still, most clinical psychology programs train their students in basic Rogerian techniques and introduce their students to psychotherapy through graduated training exercises.

A related applied issue is the selection of students for training in psychotherapy. Rogers's theory of therapy provides clear predictions as to which individuals are most likely to become effective therapists—those who express high levels of genuineness, warmth, and empathy.

Psychotherapy training programs have adopted several methods for selecting applicants. Of course, given the current large applicant-to-opening ratio in doctoral programs in clinical psychology, admissions committees often initially rely on simple quantitative information, such as undergraduate grade-point average and performance on the Graduate Record Examination. However, after using such information to cull a large pool of applicants down to a more manageable number, admissions committees then attend to more qualitative information such as the applicant's personal statement, letters of recommendation, and experience in both research and applied clinical settings.

Many doctoral programs in clinical psychology also require an interview, at which time the applicant's therapeutic potential is evaluated. Although the applicant has not yet received formal training in expressing Rogerian therapeutic qualities, the presumption is that applicants who exhibit superior verbal and interpersonal skills are more likely than others to develop effective therapeutic skills.

For example, I know of one doctoral training program that requires that applicants, during an interview, participate in a group discussion akin to a group therapy session. Observation of applicants in such a context gives the admissions committee the opportunity to assess applicants' poise, psychological-mindedness, and interpersonal and verbal skills.

Some institutions require other information about the applicant's potential for becoming a psychotherapist. For example, I know of one program that requires that applicants submit the MMPI-2. As described in Chapter 7, the MMPI-2 is a structured personality inventory designed to measure several clinical disorders. As part of an application to a clinical psychology training program, the MMPI-2 may be used to screen out applicants who exhibit evidence of severe psychological problems (such as schizophrenia or drug abuse) that may interfere with success as a therapist.

Although clinical lore on the selection and training of psychotherapists is extensive, relatively little empirical evidence exists to validate selection and training techniques. Early studies on methods of selecting applicants for training in psychotherapy or predicting effectiveness as a psychotherapist were relatively unsuccessful. For example, Holt and Luborsky (1958) found little difference between the personalities of psychiatrists and successful individuals in other professions. Similarly, Kelly and Goldberg (1959) studied the personalities of psychologists and failed to find variables that correlated with performance and specialization in psychology; they did not observe differences between the personalities of clinical psychologists and other psychologists.

Matarazzo (1971, 1978; Matarazzo & Patterson, 1986) has written extensively on research evaluating the success of programs designed to select and train psychotherapists. Although many methods have been tried, clinical psychologists still have a long way to go before they can accurately identify candidates who will become successful therapists. For example, Matarazzo (1978) wrote that "selection programs so far have been disappointing, however, and no well-defined personality variables have been satisfactorily measured and related to performance" (p. 959). Even the APA has acknowledged the difficulty of selecting and training psychotherapists. For example, an APA task force concluded that there was no scientific evidence that either professional training or experience is related to professional competence (APA, 1982).

Some evidence on the prediction of effective therapists comes from research on selecting and training paraprofessionals. A *paraprofessional* is an individual who does not have formal training in a profession, but who receives specialized training and then works alongside professionals. In the mental health field, paraprofessionals may serve as hotline counselors, volunteers who interact with inpatients in recreational ward activities, or in other roles.

Matarazzo (1971) described several studies that selected individuals to be trained as mental health paraprofessionals and found that therapy provided by paraprofessionals is about as effective as that provided by professionally trained therapists (a conclusion also reached by Durlak [1979] in a review of 42 studies of the effectiveness of paraprofessionals). Matarazzo (1971) concluded that paraprofessionals can be trained to provide effective therapeutic services when applicants (1) are mature, well adjusted, and socially skilled; and (2) are trained to function in specific interpersonal roles. Although these results were obtained in studies of paraprofessionals, they can easily by generalized to the training of clinical psychologists.

Matarazzo and Patterson (1986) examined later research on the training of therapists and reached the following conclusions: (1) when studies have found that variables predict the ease with which students can be trained to become effective therapists, they tend to support Rogers's basic therapeutic qualities; (2) evaluation of progress in training should be based on assessment of specific skills; (3) therapy training should identify and then practice clearly defined behaviors; (4) methods that seem to be effective in conveying such clearly defined therapeutic behaviors include programmed texts, specific cuing, and role-play.

Providing Psychotherapy to the Healthy

Another applied issue stemming from the rise of humanistic therapy is whether psychotherapy should be provided to nonpatients. As noted in Chapter 3, humanistic psychology emphasizes psychological health rather than pathology; it identifies growth or self-actualization as a basic motive for human behavior. For these reasons, many humanistic psychologists have suggested that therapy ought to be available to healthy individuals, not to "treat" a disorder but instead to foster further growth. Polster and Polster (1973), for example, noted that one of the major themes of Gestalt therapy is that "therapy is too good to be limited to the sick" (p. 23).

The 1960s saw the rise of group interventions designed to provide healthy individuals with growth experiences. Because participants in such groups are nonpatients, it is not completely appropriate to call them treatment programs; instead, they are typically referred to as *T-groups* or *training groups*; other terms for them include sensitivity, growth, and encounter groups. Yalom (1975) estimated that, in 1974 alone, over 5,300 individuals participated in Esalen-sponsored encounter groups; in 1969, at least 75 other centers ran encounter groups.

The most detailed discussion and evaluation of encounter groups was provided by Lieberman, Yalom, and Miles (1973). Lieberman and colleagues evaluated the outcome of 18 encounter groups. The subjects were 210 undergraduate students who participated in order to receive course credit. The subjects were randomly assigned to one of 18 groups, which met for 30 hours over a 12-week period. Groups included many therapeutic approaches, such as Gestalt, TA, and psychoanalytically oriented therapy. Lieberman and colleagues assessed subjects' functioning before and after training, and they examined the relation to outcome of group process variables.

Lieberman and colleagues reported many interesting and important results. First, they identified the relation to outcome of four leadership functions. Positive outcome was associated with therapists who provided caring and who fostered meaning attribution (the basic goals, respectively, of client-centered and cognitive therapy). However, positive outcome was curvilinearly related to emotional stimulation and executive functioning (i.e., setting limits, managing time, suggesting procedures); that is, both too much and too little of these leadership functions were associated with negative outcomes.

A second important result from this study was that the majority of subjects evaluated their experience as therapeutic (from 50 percent to 90 percent, depending on the question asked). However, objective outcome measures demonstrated that subjects overestimated the effectiveness of training. Whereas more than half of the subjects judged the experience to be therapeutic, objective assessments indicated that only about one-third had experienced actual growth.

Another important result from the study was that encounter group participation is not without risk. Objective assessments of outcome showed that about 10 percent of subjects experienced a decrease in adjustment. Although some of this decline may have been due simply to test error, this result suggests that a sizable minority of individuals respond negatively to T-groups.

This result corresponds to research on psychotherapy with patients. For example, Bergin (1971) reviewed over 30 studies of therapy outcome, which found that a modest proportion of patients deteriorate over the course of therapy. Bergin estimated that about 10 percent of therapy patients deteriorate, whereas only about 5 percent of control subjects deteriorate. Bergin interpreted this result as further evidence of the potency of psychotherapy.

Later reviews have not been consistent in recognizing the therapy deterioration effect. For example, in their meta-analysis of therapy outcome, Smith, Glass, and Miller (1980) reported that "little evidence was found for the alleged negative effects of psychotherapy. Only 9 percent of the effect-size measures were negative. . . . Nor was there convincing evidence in the dispersions of the treatment groups that some members became better and some worse as a result of psychotherapy" (p. 88).

On the other hand, Lambert, Shapiro, and Bergin (1986) concluded that there is evidence of a psychotherapy deterioration effect. Surveys of clinical psychologists and several outcome studies have indicated that a small number of patients—from 5 to 10 percent—worsen over the course of therapy.

Students should recognize that psychotherapy, like medications and other forms of treatment, is not risk-free; there is the risk that harmful side effects may occur in at least some patients. Ethical use of any treatment requires that the potential benefits outweigh its potential risks.

When an individual is suffering from a psychological problem, the potential benefits of psychotherapy may well outweigh the potential risks. However, when an individual is already "normal," the potential benefits of therapy are likely to be less than in the case of a patient with a clinical disorder. Thus, the cost–benefit ratio is greater in nonpatients than patients. The decision to provide a "growth" experience to a nonpatient should not be taken lightly.

Since the advent of humanistic psychology, several works have criticized the extent to which humanistic therapy techniques have been applied to nonpatients. Rosen (1975) and Gross (1978) published interesting and entertaining criticisms of the spread of this movement, from the perspective of journalists rather than mental health professionals. Ellis and Yeager (1989) have written what may be the strongest criticism of this movement from within the profession.

Of course, students should be aware that these criticisms apply to the misuse of humanistic techniques, especially with nonpatients who do not require treatment. This is not to say that healthy individuals cannot benefit from humanistic training experiences. I am simply cautioning against the uncritical acceptance of such programs or the use of such programs by nonprofessionals. Such growth experiences should be provided, like other forms of treatment, by trained psychotherapists. They should have the training and expertise to identify individuals who have actual clinical disorders and so require other forms of treatment and to recognize when individuals are beginning to experience adverse effects of therapy.

SCIENTIFIC ISSUES

There are two major scientific issues concerning humanistic therapy. First, is it effective? Second, what are the components that contribute to its effectiveness?

Both issues have generated significant amounts of empirical research, largely stemming from the work of Rogers. Rogers developed his form of therapy with the express intention of meeting scientific standards of evaluation. In fact, because of his initial research in this area, Rogers has been regarded as the "father" of therapy process research. For example, Matarazzo (1978) judged Rogers and his school of client-centered therapy as having made "the strongest influence toward making psychotherapy observable, its practice and training techniques specifiable, and its results measurable" (p. 943).

Interestingly, many humanistically oriented psychologists have not continued the Rogerian research tradition. For example, when Wertheimer (1978) requested information from humanistic psychologists concerning the effectiveness of therapy, he was dismayed by their response. Wertheimer observed that, to many humanists, "it is almost heretical, 'dehumanizing,' to raise a question about the effectiveness of these procedures.... But there is no documentation that any of these forms of treatment—'humanistic' or otherwise—produces results that cannot readily be explained as due to self-fulfilling prophecies" (p. 744).

As presented above, clinical psychologists have not conducted much empirical research to evaluate the effectiveness of Gestalt therapy, existential therapy, and transpersonal therapy. Still, despite the relative lack of empirical evidence on these variants of humanistic therapy, there is a large body of evidence on Rogerian client-centered therapy.

Effectiveness of Humanistic Psychotherapy

Rogers (1951; Rogers & Dymond, 1954) reported the results of early studies of the effectiveness of client-centered therapy. Although the research methodologies and assessment instruments in these studies are somewhat primitive by today's standards, they were extremely influential. They marked the first time that a major theorist of therapy attempted to systematically and empirically evaluate a specific form of psychotherapy.

Perhaps the most well-known study from this period is that of Butler and Haigh (1954). They evaluated the congruence between self and ideal self in patients (pre- and post-therapy) and nonpatients. They found that, pre-treatment, patients have a significantly lower mean level of congruence (-0.01) than nonpatients (0.58). In addition, over the course of therapy, patients' mean level of congruence increased significantly (0.34), although it remained below that of the control group.

Although this study was limited in that it did not determine the degree to which congruence in patients is related to non-Rogerian measures of adjustment (such as behavioral outcome ratings), it showed that Rogerian therapy is associated with increased patient congruence—a fundamental component of Rogers's theory of pathology and therapy.

In their seminal meta-analysis of psychotherapy outcome studies, Smith and Glass (1977) summarized the results of 375 studies. They calculated the mean effect size of both client-centered therapy and Gestalt therapy to be 0.63, significantly greater than zero. Thus, the original Smith and Glass meta-analysis suggested that client-centered therapy is effective.

Smith and colleagues (1980) updated their meta-analysis, including 475 studies. The mean effect size of both client-centered and Gestalt therapy was 0.64. In addition, the mean effect size of the entire class of humanistic therapies was 0.63. These estimates again suggested that humanistic therapies are more effective than no treatment. However, these figures were lower than the mean effect sizes of cognitive and behavioral treatments, and were not much greater than the mean effect size of placebo treatments (0.56). Thus, the Smith and colleagues (1980) meta-analysis suggested that, although humanistic therapies are more effective than no treatment, they may be less effective than alternative treatments.

Influence of Rogerian Therapeutic Qualities

Students may find the meta-analytic evaluations of the effectiveness of Rogerian therapy somewhat disappointing. However, Rogers also initiated a large body of research on the influence of the therapeutic qualities of genuineness, warmth, and empathy.

Much of this research supports Rogers's view that these qualities are associated with successful therapy outcome.

Among the earliest studies on the components of psychotherapy is that of Fiedler (1950). Fiedler reported that both therapists from different schools of psychotherapy and nontherapists describe the *ideal* client-therapist relationship in similar terms. Moreover, when Fiedler assessed the degree to which *expert* and *inexpert* therapists succeeded in establishing this relationship, he found that expert (experienced) therapists from different theoretical schools exhibit greater similarity to one another than to inexpert (less experienced) therapists within their same school.

Rogers (1951) cited this result to support his claim that the active ingredient in therapy is the client–therapist relationship. Perhaps experienced therapists—regardless of theoretical orientation—are successful in therapy because they have learned to establish the ideal client–therapist relationship, rather than because they provide treatment techniques associated with their school.

Following Rogers's (1957) statement of the necessary and sufficient conditions for therapeutic personality change, Rogers and his colleagues began to evaluate these elements empirically. Perhaps the most significant contributions in research on the Rogerian components of therapy were made by Truax and Carkhuff (1967). Truax and Carkhuff developed scales for assessing a therapist's genuineness, warmth, and empathy. Judges listen to segments of audiotaped therapy sessions and rate the therapist for Rogerian qualities. With training, judges can use these scales with sufficient inter-rater reliability so that the ratings are suitable for research. Truax and Carkhuff employed these ratings in a series of studies that demonstrated that, when Rogerian therapeutic qualities are high, therapy is more successful.

Other clinical psychologists adopted the Truax and Carkhuff scales, both for their own research and for use in training therapists. Truax and Mitchell (1971) summarized the research on the relation between levels of Rogerian qualities and therapy outcome. Nine of 14 studies on empathy, 4 of 8 studies on genuineness, and 5 of 13 studies on warmth supported Rogers. In addition, Truax and Mitchell observed that "low levels of accurate empathy, nonpossessive warmth, and genuineness are important factors leading to deterioration" (p. 313).

Although their initial research was favorable, other researchers soon noted problems with the Truax and Carkhuff measures (Parloff, Waskow, & Wolfe, 1978). For example, ratings of Rogerian qualities are based on judges' perceptions of therapist qualities, even though Rogers stressed that it is the *client's* perception of these qualities that is important. Another problem is that ratings of genuineness, warmth, and empathy were so highly intercorrelated that they may not be measuring distinct constructs, but instead a single dimension.

Later studies attempted to address these problems, assessing the client's perception of the relationship and refining the measures of the client–therapist relationship. Orlinsky and Howard (1986) reviewed this research and came to a very favorable conclusion regarding Rogerian therapist characteristics. They identified about 1,100 research findings over a 35-year period on the relation between therapy outcome and various aspects of the client-therapist relationship. In general, Orlinsky and Howard observed that from 50 to 80 percent of the studies yielded results that supported Rogers. Specifically, 20 of 53 studies on genuineness, 41 of 86 studies on empathy, and 19 of 31 studies on warmth/affirmation yielded results showing a positive relation between high levels of the Rogerian quality and therapy outcome.

In summary, then, a very large body of research has supported Rogers's claim that genuineness, warmth, and empathy are related to positive outcome in therapy. However, as noted in the previous section, meta-analytic reviews of therapy outcome studies have not found client-centered therapy to be as or more effective than other forms of therapy.

These results can be integrated by interpreting Rogerian therapeutic qualities as necessary, but not sufficient, conditions for therapeutic growth. That is, Rogerian therapist qualities appear to be associated with superior outcome, regardless of the form of therapy provided. However, Rogerian therapist characteristics do not seem to be sufficient to account for all of the changes that occur in some forms of psychotherapy.

SUMMARY

Humanistic psychologists emphasize psychological health rather than pathology. They view self-actualization as the fundamental motive for human behavior. Humanistic psychotherapy aims at helping clients to grow or to actualize their potential.

Carl Rogers is the most influential theorist of humanistic therapy. Rogers viewed pathology as the result of psychological incongruence, especially between one's self and ideal self, which results from having experienced conditional positive regard.

Rogerian therapy aims at enhancing the client's congruence. This is done by providing unconditional positive regard—accepting the client regardless of what the client says or does. Because the therapist accepts the client unconditionally, the client eventually comes to accept himself or herself. Rogerian therapy is client-centered, in that the focus of therapy is the client's perception of self.

Rogers identified what he regarded as the necessary and sufficient conditions for therapeutic personality change to occur. These include three components of unconditional positive regard: genuineness, warmth, and empathy. Rogers also identified four basic techniques used by client-centered therapists: open-ended statement, reflection of feeling, paraphrasing, and interpretation. These techniques demonstrate empathy and caring, and help to establish a relationship of unconditional acceptance.

There are many variants of humanistic therapy. Gestalt therapy, founded by Fritz Perls, stresses the client's awareness of self. Gestalt therapy employs body awareness exercises and confrontation to help the client develop awareness of current functioning.

Existential therapy is based on existential philosophy. It interprets psychological problems as the result of existential dilemmas, such as struggling with the meaning of life, the inevitability of death, or the burden of responsibility of self-determination. Existential therapy adopts a philosophical approach to assisting clients cope with such problems. Viktor Frankl introduced logotherapy as an existential therapy designed to help clients find meaning in their lives.

Transpersonal therapies are based on Asian philosophies or religions. They use a combination of psychological (e.g., contemplation, imagery) and physiological (e.g., relaxation, breathing) exercises designed to enhance self-awareness and self-control. Transpersonal therapies include yoga, meditation, and Morita therapy.

Some proponents of Gestalt, existential, and trans-personal therapy consider these therapies to be distinct from humanistic therapy. However, they share with humanistic therapy emphases on the present, the integrated self, and self-determination. For these reasons, these therapies may be considered as variants of humanistic therapy.

Rogers suggested how students should be trained to express genuineness, warmth, and empathy. Clinical psychology training programs may select students who already exhibit these qualities and then train students to develop them further. Even programs that do not have a humanistic orientation frequently emphasize Rogerian qualities and techniques as the fundamentals of therapy. However, research has not always supported the effectiveness of these selection and training procedures. Clinical psychologists should continue to examine the effectiveness of their methods for selecting and training psychotherapists.

Some humanistic psychologists suggest that therapy is appropriate for healthy persons as well as for those with problems. In the 1960s, several approaches to providing treatment for healthy persons became popular, including encounter groups and sensitivity training. Although most nonpatients report such experiences to be beneficial, a minority of individuals are casualties who experience a decline in functioning. For this reason, the decision to provide encounter group experiences to nonpatients should not be taken lightly. In addition, encounter groups should be led by trained professionals who can detect and intervene appropriately when casualties occur.

Rogers was the first major theorist of psychotherapy to conduct systematic empirical research to evaluate the process and outcome of therapy. Meta-analytic reviews of psychotherapy outcome studies have suggested that client-centered therapy is more effective than no treatment. However, these reviews have also reported that client-centered therapy may be less effective than alternative treatments, such as cognitive and behavioral therapy. Humanistic therapies other than Rogerian therapy have not been evaluated systematically in empirical research.

Much research has been done on the influence of the components of Rogerian therapy. Truax and Carkhuff developed scales for assessing a therapist's genuineness, warmth, and empathy. They conducted a series of studies that demonstrated that therapy outcome is positively related to these qualities. More recent research has generally supported Rogers's claim that these therapeutic qualities are positively related to therapy outcome. From the empirical research on therapy process and psychotherapy outcome, the Rogerian therapeutic qualities can be interpreted as necessary but not sufficient conditions for therapeutic change to occur.

S T U D Y   Q U E S T I O N S

1. Describe the Rogerian theory of the development and treatment of psychopathology.
2. Summarize the conditions that Rogers believed are the necessary and sufficient causes of therapeutic change.
3. Identify and describe the techniques used by client-centered therapists to establish these conditions.
4. Compare and contrast the roles of Rogerian and Freudian therapists.
5. Summarize the basic principles underlying one of the following: Gestalt therapy, existential therapy, or transpersonal therapy. How is this approach related to Rogerian therapy?
6. How did Rogers influence the field's thinking about the selection and training of psychotherapists?
7. Summarize the research on the effectiveness of programs for selecting and training psychotherapists.
8. Why do humanistic therapists place more emphasis on *treating* nonpatients than other therapists? Discuss the arguments for and against this practice.
9. Describe Rogers's influence on research in psychotherapy process and outcome.
10. Summarize and integrate the empirical evidence concerning the effectiveness of client-centered therapy and the relation of Rogerian therapist qualities to therapy outcome.

11

Cognitive and Behavioral Therapies

I. Behavior Therapy
   A. Theory of Pathology and Nature of
      Behavior Therapy
   B. Techniques of Behavior Therapy
II. Cognitive Therapy
   A. Nature of Psychopathology
   B. Techniques of Cognitive Therapy
III. Applied Issues
   A. Symptom Substitution

B. Problem Relapse
C. Use of Analogue Subjects
D. Ethical Problems
IV. Scientific Issues
   A. Early Reviews of the Effectiveness of
      Behavior Therapy
   B. Meta-Analytic Reviews
V. Summary

Following its introduction in 1913 by Watson, behaviorism soon became one of the leading approaches to psychology among academic and experimental psychologists. However, it remained until the 1950s for behaviorism to begin to become accepted by clinical psychologists as an effective approach to treating abnormal behavior. By the 1960s, behavior therapy was widely accepted as an important form of therapy. In the 1970s, behavioral techniques were applied to the modification of cognitive processes. By the late-1970s to 1980s, cognitive (and cognitive–behavioral) therapies were among the most influential types of therapy.

This chapter discusses the development and techniques of behavior and cognitive therapy. After presenting the techniques of these therapies, this chapter will also discuss practical and scientific issues concerning these treatments.

BEHAVIOR THERAPY

Although behaviorism became popular among academic and experimental psychologists shortly after its introduction by Watson in 1913, it had relatively little impact on clinical psychology prior to the 1950s. Yates (1970), for example, found only 28 articles published before 1940 that concerned the application of conditioning principles to treat clinical disorders. Still, there were several notable efforts from this period that set the stage for the rise of behavior therapy.

Although Pavlov is most known for his research on the conditioned reflex in dogs, he discussed the application of classical conditioning principles to specific disorders such as obsessive-compulsive disorder and paranoia (Pavlov, 1934) as well as to psychiatric disorders in general (Pavlov, 1941).

Perhaps the most well-known early application of classical conditioning to the treatment of abnormal behavior is the work of Mary Cover Jones (1924a). Following a suggestion of Watson and Rayner (1920), who had instilled a fear in an infant using classical conditioning, Jones successfully treated children's fears by pairing the feared object with food when the children were hungry. Jones (1924b) described in detail the case of Peter, a 3-year-old boy who was one of her "most serious" cases. Peter recovered after two months of daily treatment.

Andrew Salter (1949) applied Pavlov's ideas to the treatment of disorders. His approach, called *conditioned reflex therapy,* was perhaps the first systematic effort to treat a range of clinical disorders with behavioral methods.

Joseph Wolpe (1958) applied classical conditioning to the treatment of phobias. Wolpe's method, which he called *reciprocal inhibition,* involved pairing the feared object with muscle relaxation, a state that is incompatible with the physiological arousal accompanying fear.

Clinical applications of instrumental conditioning appeared somewhat later than applications of classical conditioning. B. F. Skinner (1953) suggested that instrumental conditioning principles could be applied in clinical treatment. However, it remained for his student, Ogden Lindsley, to be the first psychologist to systematically use instrumental conditioning with psychiatric patients (Spiegler & Guevremont, 1993). Lindsley showed that adult psychiatric patients respond to reinforcement as do other subjects, by increasing the frequency of behavior.

By the early 1960s, Teodoro Ayllon and Nathan Azrin (1968) used operant techniques to manage the behavior of patients in hospital settings. Ivar Lovaas (1966) employed operant techniques to teach psychotic and retarded children speech and social behaviors. By this time, Hans Eysenck, Arnold Lazarus, and many others were using operant and classical conditioning techniques to treat both inpatients and outpatients.

By the 1960s, behavior therapy had become established as a major school of therapy. Professional organizations devoted to behavior therapy (e.g., Association for the Advancement of Behavior Therapy) were founded during this period (Rimm & Masters, 1974). Although behavior therapy met with resistance from other theoretical schools, behavior therapy developed into an active and influential approach to treatment. Spiegler and Guevremont (1993) listed 20 professional journals (e.g., *Behaviour Research and Therapy, Journal of Applied Behavior Analysis*) devoted to behavior therapy that were founded from 1963 to the present.

Theory of Pathology and Nature of Behavior Therapy

As presented in Chapter 3, behaviorists hold that abnormal behavior, like normal behavior, results from three basic conditioning processes: classical conditioning, instrumental conditioning, and modeling. Behaviorists assume that, just as it was produced by conditioning, so abnormal behavior can be altered through conditioning. Eysenck (1964) defined *behavior therapy* as "the attempt to alter human behavior and emotion in a beneficial manner according to the laws of modern learning theory" (p. 1).

Behavior therapists classify abnormal behavior as behavioral excesses or deficits. A *behavioral excess* is a maladaptive behavior that occurs more frequently or more strongly than desired and that causes problems for a person. For example, aggression, panic disorders, and sexual fetishes are problems in which the individual responds more strongly than usual or in ways that do not typically occur at all in other people. Therapy for behavior excesses consists of decreasing the level of the maladaptive behavior.

Behavioral excesses are treated using the conditioning principles of punishment, extinction, and aversive conditioning, which reduce the frequency of behaviors.

A *behavioral deficit* is an adaptive behavior that does not occur frequently or strongly enough, so that a person experiences problems as a result. For example, individuals may experience problems because they failed to acquire certain types of social skills (e.g., assertiveness) or self-control skills (e.g., dietary regulation, time management). Behavioral deficits can be treated using the conditioning principles of reinforcement, shaping, and social learning, which increase the frequency of behaviors.

The goal of behavior therapy is to change problem behavior. Behavior therapists do not assume that a presenting symptom is due to some underlying psychological problem, nor do they assume that self-understanding or insight is essential to therapy. Behavior therapists aim simply at modifying the problem behavior. Undesirable behaviors are *unconditioned* and more desirable alternative behaviors are *conditioned*.

This goal means that behavior therapy differs from humanistic and psychoanalytic therapy in several ways. First, behavior therapy is more directive than these other forms of therapy. The behavior therapist sets behavior change as the goal of therapy. The therapist knows the conditioning principles that alter the frequency of behavior and suggests the course of treatment to the client.

Second, the goal of behavior therapy is more limited than the goals of psychoanalytic and humanistic therapy. Because behavior therapists aim at behavior change rather than personality reconstruction, behavior therapy tends to be shorter than other forms of therapy.

Third, behavior therapy has more of a scientific foundation than both psychoanalytic and humanistic therapy. Whereas psychoanalytic and humanistic therapy were developed in clinical settings, behavior therapy derives from conditioning principles established in the laboratory. When psychologists began to apply behaviorism to clinical treatment, they retained Watson's scientific emphasis. Thus, behavior therapy is associated with a strong research tradition. Behavior therapy, from its inception, has generated a very large number of controlled investigations.

Techniques of Behavior Therapy

It is convenient to present behavior therapy techniques according to the conditioning principle used: classical conditioning, instrumental conditioning, or social learning. Note, however, that treatment may combine two or more types of conditioning.

Classical Conditioning The classical conditioning technique most commonly employed in therapy is systematic desensitization, which was developed and investigated by Joseph Wolpe. *Systematic desensitization* is a treatment in which a phobic client is gradually exposed to the feared object, while remaining relaxed. The theory underlying desensitization is simple. Behaviorists assume that the phobia was produced through classical conditioning—by the phobic object being paired with a stimulus that elicited fear. If the phobic response was conditioned in this way, then it can be "de-conditioned" in the same way, by pairing the phobic object with relaxation, a state that interferes with the physiological arousal of fear. Indeed, desensitization is also referred to as *counterconditioning*.

For example, suppose a client has a fear of heights. The client and therapist first construct a hierarchy of stimuli that vary in terms of their resemblance to the feared situation (e.g., from standing on the first step of a footstool through standing in an observation tower overlooking the city). The therapist then trains the client in muscle relaxation. Muscle relaxation counters the physiological arousal that occurs when afraid. The client is then introduced to the first step of the hierarchy while relaxed. If the client experiences no anxiety, then the client proceeds to the next step. Any time the client experiences fear, the fear-inducing stimulus is removed and the client is given the opportunity to relax. Following relaxation, a lower object on the hierarchy is reintroduced and treatment continues. Eventually, the client can face the highest object on the hierarchy without experiencing fear.

It should be noted that relaxation is not the only state, incompatible with fear, that can be used in desensitization. Exercise, fatigue, sexual arousal, tranquilization, and other states can also be used. However, clinical practice has shown that relaxation is more convenient than the alternatives, and so relaxation is typically used.

Desensitization has been thoroughly studied. In their meta-analytic review of 375 controlled studies of psychotherapy outcome, Smith and Glass (1977) found that desensitization had the highest effect size of any form of therapy. Other reviews (e.g., Emmelkamp, 1986; Marks, 1978; Ollendick, 1986) have consistently found that desensitization is effective in treating fears and anxieties. Desensitization can also be used to treat clients who have other difficulties secondary to fear or anxiety. For example, Emmelkamp (1986) concluded that desensitization is effective in treating sexual dysfunctions that occur as the result of sexual anxiety.

However, it should be noted that desensitization is limited to clients who experience fear or anxiety in a specific situation. If there is no clearly identifiable phobic object (as in generalized anxiety disorder), then desensitization is not appropriate.

Two behavioral techniques, similar to desensitization, are flooding and implosive therapy. In *flooding,* the client is exposed directly to the feared object without being allowed to escape. For example, a client who is afraid of being in enclosed spaces, such as elevators, would stand in a closet. This leads the client to experience intense fear. However, in flooding unlike desensitization, the client is not permitted to leave the closet. Eventually, perhaps through sheer exhaustion, the client experiences a reduction in anxiety while in the closet. At this point, the closet is no longer being paired with anxiety (or escape responses), and so the client should experience decreased fear of closed spaces in the future.

Flooding is based on the principle of extinction. After a fear response has been classically conditioned to a CS, the response can be extinguished by presenting the CS without further pairings of the CS with the UCS.

According to Wolpe (1982), the first reported case in which flooding was successfully used to treat a phobia appeared in 1938. Since then, flooding has been evaluated in many controlled studies and has been found to be effective (Marks, 1975; Wolpe, 1982).

A closely related treatment is implosive therapy, which was popularized and investigated by Thomas Stampfl (Stampfl & Levis, 1967). Like flooding, *implosive therapy* exposes a phobic client directly to the feared object; however, implosive therapy also includes visual imagery of the feared object along with images related to psychodynamic issues. For example, psychodynamic concerns related to childhood traumas, conflicts with parents, low self-esteem, and troubling social relationships can be brought into the implosive therapy session. In addition, images based on symbolic representations of psychodynamic concerns are also introduced.

For example, consider the client above whose fear of enclosed spaces was treated with flooding. To use implosive therapy with this client, the therapist should first discuss with the client the meaning and origins of the fear. Perhaps the fear goes back to childhood, when an older sibling locked the client in a dark room. As a child, the client may have had fears of being unable to escape from monsters in a locked room. If so, then these images should be used in implosive therapy. The client is exposed, not only to an enclosed space, but also to images of being helpless and unable to escape from monsters. In addition, psychodynamic material, such as sibling rivalry and fear of abandonment by parents, may also be introduced.

Since its introduction, there has been a good deal of research on the effectiveness of implosive therapy. Reviews of this research (e.g., Rimm & Masters, 1974; Wolpe, 1982) have been cautious and mixed. Although early reports tended to support implosive therapy, later studies showed that it was not as effective as was first thought. In addition, these studies have not shown that psychodynamic content adds to the effectiveness of exposure alone (i.e., flooding), nor that implosive therapy is as effective as desensitization.

Despite the research support for flooding and the mixed support for implosive therapy, many clinical psychologists prefer to use desensitization. Desensitization does not produce the extreme distress experienced in flooding and implosive therapy. In addition, in order for implosive therapy and flooding to be effective, the client must be exposed to the feared object for prolonged periods, without opportunity for escape. This requirement leads to practical problems. For example, it may not be possible to conduct these therapies during the course of a "50-minute hour." Some clients may require more than one hour to experience the diminished fear response necessary for flooding and implosive therapy to be effective. In addition, if the session is interrupted or if the client insists on leaving before the extinction of the fear, then the treatment may backfire by reinforcing escape responses.

Aversive conditioning is another treatment based on classical conditioning. In *aversive conditioning,* a stimulus, previously associated with an undesired behavior, is paired with an aversive stimulus. The goal is to condition the client to respond with discomfort to the previously tempting stimulus. This leads the client to avoid the temptation altogether or to experience discomfort in the presence of the temptation, and so decreases the probability of engaging in the undesired behavior.

Aversive conditioning has been used most often in the treatment of substance abuse and sexual disorders. These behaviors are immediately reinforcing; however, their punishing social and physical consequences occur only much later. For these reasons, substance abuse and sexual disorders have traditionally been among the most difficult problems to treat.

Voegtlin and colleagues pioneered the use of aversive conditioning in the treatment of alcoholism (Voegtlin, 1940). Voegtlin administered a drug that induces vomiting within about a minute. Before vomiting, the client was given an alcoholic drink. Voegtlin repeated this process several times per session, for five inpatient sessions, followed by several additional sessions on an outpatient basis. According to Voegtlin, this led to a classically conditioned aversive response, with the client becoming nauseated by the taste and smell of alcohol.

Miller and Hester (1980) summarized various outcome studies by Voegtlin from the 1940s. In general, Voegtlin found about a 60 percent abstinence rate over a 1-year follow-up, a very high success rate

compared to other treatments. More recent studies of aversive conditioning treatment for alcoholism have reported somewhat lower success rates than reported by Voegtlin (Miller & Hester, 1980). Still, it is an interesting approach that may be used if other treatment options have been unsuccessful.

Another application of aversive conditioning is rapid smoking, a treatment designed to help people stop smoking cigarettes. In *rapid smoking,* the client sits in an enclosed cubical, inhaling smoke from a cigarette every six to eight seconds. In a short time, even a veteran smoker will become physically ill from the toxins in the smoke. When this is repeated for six to eight sessions, the taste, smell, and even the sight of cigarettes become classically conditioned to elicit an aversive response. Lichtenstein and colleagues have reported that this method produces at least a 50 percent abstinence rate over 3- to 6-month follow-ups (Lichtenstein & Brown, 1980). In a review of controlled outcome studies, Danaher (1977) concluded that rapid smoking is the single most effective psychological method for producing smoking cessation.

Aversive conditioning has been criticized on both ethical and practical grounds. There are ethical concerns over the use of aversive techniques with clients. Clients must provide their informed consent for any treatment. If treatment includes potential negative side effects or unpleasant experiences, these must be presented to clients who then have the opportunity to decline treatment. With aversive conditioning, the criticism has been raised that clients may not appreciate the extent of the negative experience, and so not be in a position to be able to truly give their informed consent.

There are cases from the 1950s and 1960s where this criticism is appropriate. For example, Sanderson, Campbell, and Laverty (1963) used succinylcholine (a drug that inhibits respiration by inducing temporary paralysis) in the aversive conditioning treatment of alcoholics. Sanderson and colleagues found that this treatment produced about a 50 percent abstinence rate.

However, Campbell, Sanderson, and Laverty (1964) later discussed the ethical problems with their treatment. Patients described the temporary paralysis as "horrific," leading them to feel as though they were dying. Even though the patients had volunteered for treatment, they did not realize how painful and disturbing the treatment would be. Thus, the original study by Sanderson and colleagues did not meet contemporary ethical standards of informed consent.

Today, therapists who use aversive conditioning do so very carefully. Clients are informed of the nature and severity of the experience. Clients are able to discontinue the unpleasant experience if it becomes too painful or intense. In addition, aversive techniques tend to be used after alternative treatments have already been used without success. In these circumstances, many therapists believe that the ethical questions raised above are addressed satisfactorily.

In addition to ethical concerns regarding aversive conditioning, there are also several practical ones. To induce vomiting is a messy business that many therapists and clients prefer to avoid. Also, inducing vomiting requires that the client has been evaluated by a physician and judged to be healthy enough to withstand its effects. Finally, any therapy is most likely to be effective when clients are willing to comply with the treatment regimen. In general, the more unpleasant the treatment, the less willing clients are to complete treatment. Thus, because aversive conditioning is so unpleasant, many clients will discontinue treatment before it has been completed.

Still, despite the potential problems, aversive conditioning remains an option for clients whose problem behaviors are immediately reinforcing, punishing only in the long run, and do not respond to other treatments.

Another technique based on classical conditioning is the bell-and-pad treatment of nocturnal enuresis. Mowrer and Mowrer (1938) described and investigated this method of treating bedwetting. The *bell-and-pad* is an alarm device that wakes the child when it is triggered by urine. It can be built into a bed pad or sewn into the child's clothes. The bell-and-pad treatment is thought to work through classical conditioning. The alarm (unconditioned stimulus—UCS) leads to awakening (unconditioned response—UCR). The alarm is repeatedly paired with physical stimuli associated with the release of urine (say, the

pressure of a full bladder). Ultimately, these sensations become a CS that lead to the CR of waking.

Research on the bell-and-pad method has found that, over a 5- to 12-week period, from 70 to 90 percent of enuretic children develop urinary continence (Doleys, 1989). Although some children relapse when the bell-and-pad device is removed, techniques such as overlearning, scheduling the alarm device on an intermittent schedule, and combining the bell-and-pad method with other training techniques (such as retention control training) reduce relapse rates (Doleys, 1989). Such methods of preventing relapse are discussed later in the chapter.

Instrumental Conditioning Instrumental (operant) conditioning is learning through reinforcement and punishment. When such consequences follow behavior, the frequency of the behavior increases or decreases. Because reinforcement and punishment can follow virtually any behavior, instrumental conditioning can be used to modify a wide range of behaviors. Instrumental conditioning techniques have therefore been used to treat many more clinical disorders than classical conditioning treatments.

For example, one of the most well known applications of operant conditioning is the token economy. A *token economy* is a method of influencing the behavior of people in institutional settings, wherein desirable behaviors are rewarded with the presentation of tokens and undesirable behaviors are punished by the loss of tokens (Ayllon & Azrin, 1968). A token is anything that can be administered immediately—poker chips, points on a merit card, gold stars, and so on. Tokens can be saved and later cashed in for other forms of reinforcement.

Tokens are used rather then other reinforcers for several reasons: tokens are convenient (it would be disruptive to have students in a classroom stop to eat a snack after every correct answer); tokens can be administered immediately (unlike the larger reinforcement that clients work for, such as extra TV time or special outings); and clients do not become satiated on tokens (as they would if snacks such as small candies were used).

Research has shown that token economies are effective in managing the behavior of groups of individuals in institutional settings, such as classrooms, hospital wards, and penal institutions (Ayllon & Azrin, 1968). For example, I once served as a consultant to a youth shelter that housed adolescents who were nonviolent offenders or who were awaiting placement by Social Services (e.g., runaways, abused teenagers). The shelter used a token economy. Clients earned tokens by making their beds, behaving on the bus ride to and from school, doing homework, and performing assigned chores at the shelter, such as cooking or laundering. Clients lost tokens by violating rules at the shelter, such as fighting or destroying property. Tokens were used to earn midweek and weekend outings (movies, sporting events, dances). (Interestingly, the staff at the shelter discovered that the reward that the adolescents would pay the most tokens for was cigarettes.)

I once worked at an inpatient psychiatric setting for children. Clients had a variety of problems, including depression, severe learning disability and attention-deficit disorder, autism, and conduct disorder. The children's schedule was highly structured, with closely supervised educational, therapeutic, and recreational activities throughout the day. Every 15 minutes, children had the opportunity to earn three points. The supervising staff member assigned points for attitude, following the direction of the adult staff member, and interacting with the other children. Every two hours, children who received enough points could receive a treat: a midmorning cup of juice, extra playtime after lunch, a midafternoon cookie, extra TV time in the evening, and so on. In this structured environment, even children who were out of control in other settings soon learned the rules and complied with the staff.

Another well-known example of therapy based on operant conditioning was developed by Lovaas (1977). Lovaas used the technique of shaping to instill speech in autistic children. *Shaping* is the systematic reinforcement of successive approximations to a desired behavior. Training speech is especially important in autistic children because their long-term prognosis is extremely poor—they may be institutionalized for most of their lives—if they do not develop communicative speech (Prior & Werry, 1986).

Lovaas adapted Skinner's (1957) theory of the development of verbal behavior to the treatment of children with autism who were mute or who did not use speech to communicate (e.g., some were echolalic: they repeated the speech they heard, without using speech to interact with others). The therapist begins by reinforcing a distant approximation to the desired word. Suppose the first word to be taught is *mama*. The therapist reinforces any vocalization, including grunts, with a small candy. Then, after the child vocalizes regularly, the child is then reinforced only for saying the consonant *m* sound. If the child does not imitate this sound voluntarily, the therapist guides the child by holding the child's lips shut while vocalizing, producing the desired sound. After the child produces the *m* sound voluntarily, the therapist demands a bit more, continuing the vocalization of *m* while opening the mouth—an m-vowel combination. In this way, the child ultimately learns to say *mama*.

After learning to say a word, the child is then taught its meaning. Lovaas continued to use basic conditioning techniques such as discrimination training. When the child says the word in the correct context (seeing, looking at, touching mother), then the child receives reinforcement. However, when the child says the word in an inappropriate context, there is no reinforcement. In this way, the child is taught both to say a word and to use the word in the correct context.

Lovaas also reinforced the autistic child to imitate entire words spoken by the therapist. Although this is difficult at first, it becomes easier after the child has learned the meaning of several words. At this point, the child imitates complete words and the training proceeds at an accelerated pace.

Lovaas (1966, 1977) showed that behavior therapy is an effective way to teach basic language skills to autistic children. He also used similar operant techniques to train social skills other than language and to eliminate self-stimulatory behaviors in children who are psychotic or retarded (e.g., Lovaas, Koegel, Simmons, & Long, 1973; Lovaas & Simmons, 1969). Lovaas has also recently suggested that behavior therapy may actually "cure" some autistic children. Lovaas (1987) provided intensive treatment (40 hours per week) with very young autistic children (younger than age 46 months) and trained parents to continue treatment at home. Follow-up studies found that about half of the autistic children treated in this fashion were functioning at age level on social and academic measures (Lovaas, Smith, & McEachin, 1989).

These results are extraordinary, given the limited successes found in other studies, and have been questioned (e.g., Schopler, Short, & Mesibov, 1989). Certainly, Lovaas's work requires replication and close examination. Still, it provides optimism in a field where treatment successes tend to be only modest at best. Even if such behavior therapy does not "cure" autism, Lovaas's techniques have become what many regard as the treatment of choice for autism. Behavior therapy for autism is now a very influential and widely used approach; by 1986, over 1,500 papers had been published on the behavioral treatment of autism (Richards, 1986).

Instrumental conditioning is also widely used to treat less severe problems in outpatient settings. For example, stimulus control is often used to treat habit disorders in outpatients. In *stimulus control,* a functional analysis is conducted to identify the stimuli that immediately precede and follow a problem behavior. These stimuli exert significant control over the behavior by triggering or reinforcing it. After identifying the stimuli that control the problem behavior, the client and therapist change them. This then leads to a change in the occurrence of the problem behavior.

Stimulus control is often used to treat habit disorders in individuals who are free of severe disturbances, such as clients who want to control overeating or smoking, improve study skills or time management, or maintain a regular exercise program.

For example, I have used stimulus control with overweight clients. Before suggesting any changes in eating or exercise, it is important to know the stimuli associated with the problem—when and where the client overeats. For this reason, several weeks are devoted to self-monitoring the clients' eating. I remember one woman who swore that she did not overeat and could not understand why she was gaining weight. Self-monitoring revealed that she routinely finished her three young children's meals after they said they were full, rather than let the food "go to waste." In this way, even though her extra portions were so small that she had not considered them to be significant, she was actually ingesting the equivalent of several extra meals per week. Stimulus control in this case was straightforward. She served smaller first helpings to her children and then provided small second and third helpings to them until they had eaten enough.

In another case, a woman's self-monitoring showed that she snacked much of the afternoon when she was in the kitchen preparing dinner for her family. She had several teenagers who were always hungry and so the family kept snack foods, such as potato chips and cookies, in the kitchen. Unfortunately, this woman had developed the habit of snacking whenever she walked by the kitchen cupboard with the goodies. In this case, the woman was unwilling to get rid of the snacks altogether—she did not think that her teenagers would stand for elimination of the chips. However, it helped to store the snacks for the teenagers in a rec room in the basement. In this way, the snacks were not such a temptation when the woman was in the kitchen to prepare dinner. By making a simple change in the client's environment, it was possible to modify a problem behavior.

Another common treatment application of instrumental conditioning is *contracting.* In this technique, as its name suggests, a client and therapist form a contract, wherein the client earns small reinforcements for making progress toward a goal. Reinforcements and punishments may be administered by the therapist, client, or others in the client's environment, such as a spouse or roommate.

Contracting, like stimulus control, is often used with clients who are generally well functioning, but who have a problem in a single area. For example, as a professor I have suggested contracting to students as a way of increasing study time. Start a "kitty" that you will use to pay for social events. Pay a half-dollar to the kitty for every 15 minutes you study and one dollar for every written assignment you complete. If you want to go out, you must "earn" enough money to pay for it.

Contracting has occasionally been used with more severe conditions. I once read about a treatment program that used contracting with affluent substance abusers. Clients set up a large bank account to be controlled by the therapist and they earned their money back by maintaining their abstinence. If clients failed to meet a goal, they lost money. In this case, a donation was made in their name to an organization of which they disapproved (such as the American Nazi Party).

Another widely used application of instrumental conditioning is *child management*. Here, parents are trained in the principles of instrumental conditioning so that they manage their child's behavior more successfully. For example, parents learn to use punishment and reinforcement effectively. Punishment and reinforcement are administered immediately after the child's behavior; they are used in small doses so that they can be used repeatedly. In addition, the child is clearly told why the behavior is being punished and reinforced. Much of what is presented in self-help books for parents on how to manage their child's behavior clearly represents an instrumental conditioning orientation. I have used this approach to help parents who had trouble with their children picking up toys, performing chores, swearing, and fighting.

Social Learning   Social learning is the third major type of conditioning discussed by behaviorists. *Social learning* (also called modeling, imitative learning, vicarious conditioning, and observational learning) is learning through observation of other people's behavior. Clinical psychologists use social learning to treat many disorders. However, it is especially helpful in training social skills (e.g., assertiveness) and cognitive coping skills (e.g., self-talk to cope with emotional arousal).

To be assertive means that one can express one's desires and feelings appropriately. Suppose you are in the No Smoking section of a restaurant and a person at a nearby table lights a pipe. One assertive behavior is to ask the person to stop smoking. Other assertive responses include asking the restaurant staff to deal with the smoker and requesting to be moved to another table. Of course, there is no guarantee that

assertive behaviors will gain the desired results. Still, even if one does not achieve the desired result, one has some small satisfaction that one has tried to set things right.

Unassertive people, however, sit silently, feeling imposed upon, frustrated, and unable to enjoy their meal. (Of course, assertiveness needs to be distinguished from aggression. For example, some people would yell or curse at the smoker, which might obtain the desired results but violates the rights of the smoker and of other people seated nearby. Such threatening behaviors are aggressive rather than assertive.) These individuals would benefit from assertiveness training.

Assertiveness training generally involves a significant modeling component. The therapist and client identify the situations in which the client has trouble being assertive (e.g., turning down unreasonable requests from family members; being imposed upon by one's employer). The therapist then models appropriate assertive behaviors.

Of course, other conditioning techniques, in addition to social learning, may also be used to train assertiveness. For example, the client rehearses assertive behaviors; the therapist shapes the behavior by reinforcing partial successes; the client practices the behavior between therapy sessions; the client engages in graduated homework assignments between sessions. Although assertiveness training has been conceptualized both as simple behavioral rehearsal (e.g., Rimm & Masters, 1974) and as cognitive therapy (e.g., Hollon & Beck, 1986), it is clear that social learning is an important component in this treatment.

There is a large body of research evidence demonstrating the effectiveness of assertiveness training (e.g., Schroeder & Black, 1985). In addition, assertiveness training can be used as an adjunctive therapy for other problems. For example, Hersen, Bellack, Himmelhoch, and Thase (1984) found that assertiveness training is about as effective as antidepressant medication for the treatment of unipolar depression.

Social learning is also widely used to train cognitive coping skills. One of the most widely cited applications of social learning therapy is Meichenbaum's (1971) study of the treatment of phobias using coping versus mastery models. In one condition, clients observed a *mastery model,* a model who successfully faced the feared object successfully from the outset. In another condition, clients observed a *coping model,* one who initially experienced the same problem as the clients but who "talked himself through" and so managed to cope with the problem. Meichenbaum found that, although exposure to both models reduced fear more than a control condition, the coping model was significantly more effective than the mastery model.

For example, I once knew a preschool girl who was terrified of dogs. She would run into her house, crying and screaming, even if a dog was being walked on a leash on the sidewalk in front of her house. A coping model was helpful in reducing her fear. The model said things like: "Take a deep breath," "I shouldn't run because the dog might think I am playing and chase me, " "If I scream, I might scare him," "I am bigger than the dog, so I don't want to move too fast or I might scare him," "Let's move slowly." Later, as the girl's fear of dogs was lowered, the model demonstrated other coping skills: "I will never go near a strange dog," "But if the owner is there and if the owner says it is alright, then maybe I can pet the dog," "But I still have to go slow, because I don't want to scare the dog," "Take a deep breath," "Pet the dog gently."

Since Meichenbaum's (1971) study, many others have shown that coping models are more effective than mastery models for clients who are fearful and anxious (Bandura, 1986). Apparently, clients identify with coping models (who are similar to themselves) more than mastery models, and they learn the specific techniques, demonstrated by the coping model, for coping with fears, doubts, and other obstacles to effective performance.

Social learning has been used to train clients in other cognitive coping skills. For example, modeling is a part of treatment designed to enhance interpersonal problem-solving skills (e.g., Spivack & Shure, 1974). Many of these applications involve modeling of thought processes (i.e., what to say to oneself in order to solve problems more effectively). These treatments can be labelled cognitive–behavioral, because they apply basic conditioning processes to

cognitions, and will be described in more detail later in the chapter.

It is clear that social learning is a widely used and effective treatment. In addition to the large body of research support to document its effectiveness, social learning also has several practical advantages. Modeling has a simple and intuitive appeal. Clients have observed parents, teachers, and others demonstrate appropriate behavior through modeling and so they are familiar with the technique. Modeling sessions are easy to conduct. It is easy for clients to remember and to practice the trained behaviors between therapy sessions.

Because social learning is so simple, it is often used even by clinical psychologists who do not consider themselves behavior therapists. For example, psychoanalytic and humanistic therapists hope that, by demonstrating how to attend to and interpret clients' psychological processes, clients will learn how to do this on their own. Clients in virtually all forms of group therapy benefit from the model of other group members; similarly, self-help groups provide multiple models who demonstrate how to cope with a shared problem. Therapists who recommend books for their clients are providing symbolic models.

COGNITIVE THERAPY

Social learning serves as a useful transition from behavioral to cognitive therapies. As presented in Chapter 3, social learning differs from the other two forms of conditioning in two ways: in social learning, the learner does not personally engage in the behavior and does not directly experience the consequences of the behavior; rather, it is the model who behaves and is punished or reinforced.

Although this sounds quite basic, it has profound consequences. Social learning is cognitive by its very nature. Social learning does not take place at the muscular level; instead, it occurs at the cognitive level. The individual develops a cognitive representation of the behavior along with a cognitive expectation concerning the behavior's likely consequences. In considering modeling as a basic form of learning, behavioral theory is incorporating a form of cognitive processing.

Cognitive models of psychopathology and psychotherapy developed during the 1950s and 1960s. Cognitive processes had certainly been acknowledged as important by other schools of therapy. For example, the goal of classical psychoanalysis—insight—is a cognitive goal. However, psychoanalysis emphasized unconscious processes and instinctive motivations more heavily than conscious cognitive processes.

As you recall from Chapter 3, George Kelly (1955) developed a cognitive theory of personality, which provided a cognitive foundation for psychotherapy. Kelly's theory, however, did not have a major immediate impact on the field. The traditional psychodynamic approach to therapy, along with the rise of both behavioral and humanistic therapies, carried more weight with clinical psychologists than Kelly's cognitive model in the 1950s.

By the 1960s, clinical psychologists recognized that behavior therapy is effective. Behavior therapy is relatively short-term and inexpensive, is simple to conduct and teach to therapists-in-training, and, most important, has a firm scientific foundation. Although these strengths impressed many clinical psychologists, others remained unconvinced. They did not want to adopt a rigid behavioral theory that ignored mental processes.

Cognitive theory provides an alternative to traditional behaviorism. Cognitive theory combines the strengths of behavioral and mentalistic approaches. Cognitive theory employs the scientific orientation of behaviorism (theoretical foundation, research tradition, use of short-term effective therapies) while including mental processes (motivation, self-control, emotional experience, subjective world view) that many regard as the very core of psychology.

Albert Ellis (1962) and Aaron Beck (1967, 1976) are two of the earliest and most influential proponents of cognitive therapy. Both were originally trained to conduct psychoanalytically oriented psychotherapy but developed cognitive alternatives in the 1960s as a result of their clinical experiences.

By the late-1960s to early-1970s, cognitive behaviorism had been introduced as a legitimate alternative to traditional behaviorism. Homme's (1965) suggestion (that cognitions are a type of operant behavior that follow the principles of behaviorism) was being incorporated into several treatment approaches. Albert Bandura (1969, 1971) and Walter Mischel (1968, 1973) were among the most influential theorists who advocated cognitive–behavioral approaches to personality, psychopathology, and psychotherapy. George Spivack (Spivack & Shure, 1974; Spivack, Platt, & Shure, 1976) and Donald Meichenbaum (1977) were among the first clinical psychologists to study systematically the effectiveness of cognitive–behavioral therapies.

From the late-1970s through the present, cognitive–behavioral therapy has been among (if not) the most influential approaches to psychotherapy. By the late-1980s, Kendall (1987) judged cognitive behaviorism to be at the forefront of behaviorism.

In fact, cognitive factors have been purported to be the "active ingredient" in *all* forms of therapy. For example, Bandura (1977) introduced the concept of self-efficacy to explain the effectiveness of psychotherapy. *Self-efficacy* is an individual's perception of his ability to perform effectively in a situation. Bandura (1977) suggested that all therapies are effective to the extent that they help improve a client's self-efficacy. Therapies differ in how they accomplish this—for example, self-examination, behavior change, or relief from troubling feelings. Still, regardless of their different goals and techniques, all therapies ultimately improve clients' perceptions of their ability to behave successfully.

Nature of Psychopathology

As presented in Chapter 3, cognitive theories of personality and psychopathology hold that the immediate cause of psychological disorders is some inaccurate or ineffective cognitive process. Clients experience emotional or behavioral symptoms because of the way they think. Since this is the cause of psychopathology, the cognitive approach to therapy is to identify and then modify this faulty cognitive process.

For example, consider a person who is dissatisfied unless he is the best at everything he tries—academics, sports, business, or hobby. This person is likely to be highly motivated and may actually enjoy high success in many areas. However, if the person thinks that he must be the best in everything or else he is a failure, then he is also likely to feel like a failure much of the time. After all, no matter how capable the person, it is impossible for him to be the best at everything. By thinking that he must excel in all areas, he is setting himself up for major disappointments.

Cognitive therapy first attempts to identify the underlying cognitive process that is the core of the problem. Cognitive therapists use several assessment techniques to identify the cognitive problem. For example, clients may keep thought diaries, recording the thoughts that accompany their troubling emotions. Clients may complete cognitive checklists that list typical maladaptive cognitions, indicating which of these thoughts they experience, how frequently they occur, and how significant they are with regard to their emotional and behavioral problems. Another cognitive assessment technique is to have a client talk aloud, demonstrating typical thought processes when facing a problematic situation. In this way, the therapist can "observe" the client's thought processes and evaluate their accuracy and effectiveness. These and other cognitive assessment techniques were described in Chapter 6.

After identifying the inaccurate or ineffective cognitions, cognitive therapists then try to help the client to modify them. In some instances, minor revisions of the thought processes may be sufficient to help the client view the world more accurately. However, in other cases, the client may have to experience significant revisions or replacements of his cognitive processes.

Techniques of Cognitive Therapy

Cognitive therapists use a variety of techniques to help clients recognize and modify their ineffective or inaccurate patterns of thinking. Some of these techniques have been adapted from insight-oriented or behavior therapy. For example, cognitive therapists use interpretation and discussion of the client's experiences, using leading questions to guide the client's introspection until the client attains some significant insight. Of course, when cognitive therapists

employ these techniques, they are not seeking the same type of insight sought by a Freudian or Rogerian therapist; cognitive therapists help the client to gain insight into the ineffective or inaccurate thought processes that are currently affecting the client's behavior or feelings. Still, these traditional insight-oriented techniques are often helpful in gaining such understanding.

Because it is relatively straightforward to see how cognitive therapists can use the insight-oriented and Rogerian techniques introduced in the previous chapters, the rest of this section of the chapter will address at more length the cognitive analogues of behavior therapy techniques.

Cognitive Analogues of Behavior Therapy   An important aspect of cognitive therapy is training the client to think more accurately or effectively. For this reason, cognitive therapy uses many teaching or conditioning techniques. Mahoney (1974) described how the three basic types of conditioning can be applied to cognitive processes. He termed these *covert techniques.*

Remember the behavior therapy techniques based on classical conditioning. Systematic desensitization is a treatment for phobias in which the client is gradually exposed to the feared object. Desensitization can be applied in a cognitive format, in which the client is exposed to *images* of the feared object, rather than to the object in vivo (i.e., in actuality).

Reviewers of research comparisons of the relative efficacies of imaginal and in vivo desensitization have generally found that in vivo desensitization is the more effective (e.g., Marks, 1978). However, imaginal exposure remains an important component of desensitization. The desensitization hierarchy may include imaginal presentations as the least stressful stimuli. Consider, for example, implosive therapy, which combines images and psychodynamic symbols along with direct presentations of the feared object. The client may find it easier to practice imaginal than in vivo exposure between therapy sessions. In addition, in vivo desensitization is often impractical. Consider, for example, a client who fears flying on airplanes. It would be difficult (and expensive) to treat this case using only in vivo exposure.

A second classical conditioning therapy is aversive conditioning. Cautela (1966, 1967) introduced a cognitive analogue of aversive conditioning called covert sensitization. In *covert sensitization,* thinking of engaging in a problem behavior is paired with an extremely aversive imagined consequence.

The goal of covert sensitization is to establish an automatic connection between the images of the undesired behavior and the aversive consequence. To accomplish this, the imagined aversive consequence should be extremely detailed. If successful, when the client is tempted to engage in the desired behavior, thinking of the aversive consequence should follow automatically. This then helps the client keep from engaging in the behavior.

For example, Cautela and others have used covert sensitization to treat alcohol abuse. The client first forms a vivid image of his favorite alcoholic beverage. After imagining in detail the sight, smell, and feel of the glass, the client imagines taking a sip. Immediately, the client is instructed to imagine a rumbling in his stomach, followed by a bitter taste in his mouth—a sign that he is about to vomit. The aversive scene continues, with the client imagining himself becoming violently and disgustingly ill. According to Cautela, the more graphic and explicit the aversive consequence, the more effective the conditioning.

Several public service commercials are based on covert sensitization. One commercial shows a group of rowdy teenagers, drinking and getting into a car. As the driver turns the key in the ignition, there is a flash of lightning, followed by a view of four skeletons in the car. I find this commercial to be quite effective, as I cannot think of drinking and driving without experiencing a mental flash of this image.

The relatively few controlled studies of covert sensitization have yielded mixed to negative results (Mahoney & Arnkoff, 1978; Miller & Hester, 1980). As was the case with systematic desensitization, the research suggests that in vivo aversive conditioning is more effective than its cognitive analogue (Miller & Hester, 1980).

Still, covert sensitization has several advantages over in vivo aversion. Covert sensitization avoids the practical and ethical problems of aversive conditioning. The client is in complete control of the procedure; there is no pain or mess; the client can practice the procedure repeatedly between sessions. For these reasons, many clients and therapists use covert sensitization as a supplement or alternative to aversive conditioning.

There are also cognitive analogues of instrumental conditioning therapies. Remember that instrumental conditioning uses reinforcement and punishment. *Covert reinforcement* consists of the client imagining himself engaging in an adaptive behavior followed by social approval. For example, as part of assertiveness training, a client may imagine herself being more assertive when a friend requests too great a favor, followed by the friend apologizing for imposing. Conversely, *covert punishment* consists of the client imagining himself engaging in a maladaptive behavior followed by social disapproval. For example, suppose a college student has contracted with a counselor to help increase his study time; along with this contract, the student may imagine how unhappy and left out he would feel if he did not earn enough money by studying to enable him to attend a concert with his friends.

According to Mahoney (1974), other analogues of overt instrumental techniques are possible as well. For example, *covert rehearsal* consists of the client's repeatedly imagining himself engaged in the target behavior. For example, suppose you have to present a paper to your class and then lead a class discussion of the material. You should first use overt rehearsal, practicing the presentation aloud. However, there are many situations in which covert rehearsal is more practical than overt rehearsal (say, when sitting in the library or walking through campus); in addition, covert rehearsal is quicker than overt rehearsal and may be more suited than overt rehearsal to unstructured situations in which many possible outcomes may occur, such as leading the class discussion. For these reasons, you may find covert rehearsal helpful. As vividly as possible, imagine yourself making the presentation. Try to "hear" yourself speaking. When will you pause? What words will you stress? Try to anticipate the possible reactions to the presentation and prepare "ad libs" to the most likely questions.

(I used covert rehearsal countless times when I was a member of the Society of American Magicians. In addition to practicing the physical moves and verbal patter of tricks, I would also rehearse routines mentally, anticipating possible audience reactions and appropriate ad libs.)

These cognitive analogues of instrumental conditioning techniques are similar to covert modeling. In modeling, the individual learns from observing another person engaged in a behavior and experiences the consequences. In *covert modeling,* the client imagines someone engaging in an adaptive behavior. The model could be the therapist, a friend, a public figure, a fictional hero, or anyone whom the client is likely to imitate.

For example, in the movie, *Play It Again, Sam,* Woody Allen plays a character who aspires to be like Humphrey Bogart. Throughout the movie, Woody Allen's character imagines how "Bogie" would handle a situation and then tries to imitate the behavior.

I once treated a 9-year-old boy who had problems with aggression, attention deficit hyperactivity disorder, and severe learning disabilities. Over an extended course of treatment, the boy began to experience anxiety at bedtime. The boy had a set of cowboy figures on his dresser. We discussed how his cowboy heroes might handle their bedtime fears. I then suggested that, when he begins to feel uneasy at night, he imagine how the cowboys coped with their fears and then try to imitate them. After only a single session, the bedtime fears abated. Although the boy continued in therapy for other problems, the bedtime anxiety did not recur.

Cognitive Restructuring   Although most cognitive therapists employ one or more of the cognitive conditioning techniques presented above, there are several influential approaches to cognitive therapy that warrant individual attention. *Cognitive restructuring* refers to cognitive therapy that is designed to correct a set of faulty or maladaptive beliefs. There are several major approaches to cognitive restructuring.

Personal Construct Psychology   George Kelly (1955) introduced what may be the earliest cognitive

theory of psychopathology and psychotherapy. Kelly described the individual's personality in terms of a personal construct system. *Constructs* are the cognitive dimensions along which people interpret, classify, and evaluate experience.

Kelly compared a person in daily life to a scientist. Just as a scientist has a theory that she uses to generate predictions, so does a person use her personal construct system to develop expectations. A scientist conducts experiments to test predictions; a person has daily experiences that are informal tests of her expectations. A scientist revises or replaces her theory as indicated by empirical results; a person similarly revises or replaces her personal construct system as necessary.

Continuing the analogy, Kelly suggested that psychological problems are associated with "inadequate" theories and "closed-minded" scientists. That is, if a construct system does not generate accurate predictions, then the person behaves ineffectively. If the construct system is inflexible, then the person has difficulty revising it to make it more accurate.

For example, Kelly would consider a person with strong racial prejudices to have a rigid and closed construct system. This person expects others to behave according to certain stereotypes; when these expectations are not met, the person cannot account for the behavior. Hence, the person must ignore the behavior and so does not have an accurate view of the world.

Psychotherapy, for Kelly, is a process of "reconstruction." The therapist identifies those constructs that are ineffective and inflexible, and then helps the client modify them. Kelly generally employed techniques that were already familiar to therapists. For example, Kelly used interpretation to help clients understand their reactions in terms of alternative *theories* or constructs. He used the Socratic method of asking leading questions to guide the client's introspection until the client attained some insight into his construct system. He also used role-play to give the client an opportunity to experiment with new construct systems.

Kelly occasionally used an interesting variant of role-play called fixed-role therapy. In *fixed-role therapy,* the client plays from one therapy session to the next the role of a fictional character, whose construct system was scripted by the client and therapist. This gives the client the opportunity to experiment with a different construct system; however, because this new construct system belongs to a fictional character, the client has a "buffer" if the experiment is unsuccessful. That is, it is not the client who fails, but the scripted character.

For example, suppose a shy male is seeking to become more self-assured around women. Kelly and the client would discuss how the client would like to be—less self-conscious, less concerned about embarrassing himself, more self-confident, and so on. In fixed role therapy, Kelly and the client write a description of an alter ego for the client. This new character is not tied up in knots by self-doubts. He anticipates pleasant outcomes from his interactions with women. He is not concerned that women are judging him negatively. If one woman does turn him down, this does not mean that all other women will reject him. Kelly has the client practice these new ways of thinking in the session and then throughout the entire week.

Although Kelly's therapy is similar to the cognitive therapies of today, his approach did not gain a wide following in the 1950s. The time simply was not ripe for cognitive therapy; psychodynamic, humanistic, and behavioral therapies were all more influential in the 1950s than cognitive therapy. In addition, Kelly conducted relatively little research on the effectiveness of cognitive therapy. Because the 1950s was a time when clinical psychologists were examining the empirical foundations of their practices, the lack of research on cognitive therapy contributed to Kelly's therapy being surpassed by behavioral and Rogerian therapy.

However, the lack of an immediate impact does not diminish Kelly's importance. Kelly's cognitive theory helped set the stage for later cognitive approaches. Also, Kelly's students (Leon Levy, Julian Rotter, and many others) went on to become leading clinical psychologists in their own right, thereby spreading Kelly's influence.

Rational-Emotive Therapy (RET).   Albert Ellis is another early proponent of cognitive therapy. Ellis

(1962) developed a cognitive approach to psychotherapy, which he termed *rational-emotive therapy (RET)*. Ellis assumed that troubling emotions result from irrational cognitions. Although a client might explain her depression as the result of a situational problem, Ellis argued that the true cause of emotional difficulties is the way she perceives her situation—what she says to herself regarding the situation.

Ellis identified a set of common irrational beliefs that he thought are the source of many emotional problems. These beliefs tend to be examples of "all-or-none" thinking and catastrophizing. For example, according to Ellis (1962), people who think that they must be loved by everyone or be thoroughly competent in everything are likely to feel miserable much of the time. They have set impossibly high goals for themselves and so they will experience constant frustration and disappointment.

RET identifies the client's underlying irrational cognitions and then employs a variety of techniques to modify them. Ellis was eclectic in his methods, using any technique that had the effect of altering the client's irrational cognitions. For example, he used nontraditional therapy techniques, such as argument, confrontation, humor, and even ridicule in attempts to change clients' thinking. Although Ellis has been criticized for using these methods, he has also advocated more traditional techniques from other schools of therapy. For example, Ellis frequently used the behavioral techniques of graduated homework assignments, role-play, and rehearsal. Ellis also used cognitive methods, such as keeping a thought diary. Ellis even used traditional insight-oriented techniques, such as interpretation.

In general, RET is a short-term, directive therapy that is appropriate for outpatient emotional problems. RET has also been evaluated favorably in several outcome studies. For example, in the initial meta-analysis of psychotherapy outcome by Smith and Glass (1977), RET was found to have the second largest effect size of any form of therapy, second only to systematic desensitization.

Beck's Cognitive Therapy of Depression   Aaron Beck (1967, 1976; Beck, Rush, Shaw, & Emery,

1979) has developed an extremely influential form of cognitive therapy. Beck's therapy was originally developed to explain depression; however, Beck (Beck & Emery, 1985) later applied his treatment to anxiety and other emotional problems.

Beck assumed that depression is actually a cognitive disorder. According to Beck, depressed individuals have negative views of self, world, and future. In addition, depressed people have a negative schema, or set of beliefs, which leads them to misinterpret experiences so as to support their negative views. Beck identified a variety of thinking errors that lead depressed individuals to distort their perceptions of the world. These thinking errors are illustrated in Exhibit 11.1.

In Beck's cognitive therapy, the therapist first conducts an assessment to identify the client's thinking errors and negative views. The client keeps a diary, recording the thoughts and situations that are associated with periods of depression. The client records daily activities and associated moods. The client also rates the frequency of depressogenic thoughts, using the Dysfunctional Attitude Scale (Weissman, 1979). Analysis of the situations in which the client is depressed, the client's thoughts in

these situations, and the relation between thoughts and emotions should identify the problems in the client's cognitions.

Like Ellis, Beck uses a variety of techniques to modify the client's negative patterns of thinking. He begins treatment by increasing the client's pleasant activities. This is a behavioral technique, primarily associated with Lewinsohn's (1974) reinforcement model of depression. However, Beck finds it helpful in cognitive therapy of depression. Increasing pleasant activities leads quickly to increased energy and mood. Although simply increasing social and recreational activities does not solve life problems or modify a depressing style of thinking, it may help the client feel better so that he can work at the subtle changes in thinking essential in cognitive therapy.

Increasing pleasant activities is common-sensical. Ask your grandmother (my "common sense test"), "Grandma, when someone is depressed, is it better to go out and be active or to stay home and not do anything"? She will almost certainly say that it is better for the depressed person to keep active.

Of course, this is easier said than done. One of the problems in depression is that the client has little energy to be active and little motivation to do any-

EXHIBIT 11.1   Depressogenic Thinking Errors

1. *Maximization/minimization.* Exaggerating the impact of negative experiences while understating the impact of positive experiences; for example, becoming extremely upset finding that a roommate borrowed your favorite sweater.
2. *Absolutistic thinking.* Thinking in "all-or-none" terms; for example, thinking that, unless you are the top student in class, then you are a failure.
3. *Overgeneralization.* Drawing a general conclusion on the basis of a single incident; for example, after earning a low grade on an exam, concluding that you will never be able to receive a higher grade in the class.
4. *Personalization.* Interpreting events as personal affronts or obstacles; for example, after a teacher

announces a change in the exam schedule, dwelling on how the change will adversely affect you.
5. *Arbitrary inference.* Drawing a conclusion without sufficient evidence to support it; for example, during a stern lecture on the evils of plagiarism, interpreting the instructor's making eye contact with you as evidence that he suspects you of cheating.
6. *Selective abstraction.* Focusing on an insignificant detail taken out of context; for example, despite receiving mostly favorable feedback on a term paper, you dwell on the instructor's few criticisms and think that the evaluation was largely negative.

thing. For these reasons, increasing activities should be done gradually. Goals must be realistic. Activities must be selected with the client and therapist working collaboratively.

After the client has experienced some improvement in energy and mood, Beck then addresses the depressing style of thinking. Beck uses straightforward didactic methods, informing the client about the relationship between thinking and feeling and how certain thinking errors can affect mood. However, much of the change in cognitive therapy comes from training in new ways of thinking. Beck teaches the client alternative ways of interpreting experience. The cognitive therapist frequently asks questions such as: What evidence did you use to draw your negative conclusion? Was there any evidence that you overlooked? How else might you have interpreted this experience? How might you have interpreted the event at a time when you were not depressed? Are you making an overgeneralization (or any of the other thinking errors)?

During the session, the client and therapist apply such questions to the client's experiences. The goal is to help the client develop a less pessimistic way of interpreting events. Over the course of therapy, the client learns to recognize depressing thinking when it occurs and to replace it with more effective and realistic thinking.

Beck, like other cognitive and behavior therapists, also relies heavily on homework between therapy sessions. Homework assignments are given after every session, wherein the client attends to his or her cognitions, moods, and activities, and practices these alternative ways of thinking when in troubling situations.

Beck's cognitive therapy of depression is perhaps the single most widely investigated and empirically supported approach to cognitive restructuring. Beck's cognitive therapy has been the focus of scores of empirical investigations. These studies have generally been supportive, indicating that it is more effective than no treatment and placebos, and at least as effective as other treatments, including insight-oriented, relationship-oriented, behavioral, and even pharmacological therapy (Sacco & Back, 1985).

Perhaps the most extensive investigation of Beck's cognitive therapy of depression was the National Institute of Mental Health (NIMH) Collaborative Research Project on the Treatment of Depression (Elkin et al., 1989). This study provided antidepressant medication, cognitive therapy, or interpersonal therapy to a large number of depressed patients at several treatment centers. In general, this study found that cognitive therapy is an effective therapy for depression, although it also found that antidepressant medication is somewhat more effective then cognitive therapy. Still, this result is significant because of the size of the sample and the variety of treatment centers in which the treatment was investigated.

Cognitive Skills Training   In addition to cognitive restructuring therapy, which is designed to modify a faulty set of general beliefs, there are several important approaches to cognitive therapy that aim at improving a specific type of cognitive functioning. By mastering this cognitive skill, the client can function more effectively.

Problem-Solving Therapy   D'Zurilla and Goldfried (1971) conceptualized problem-solving as a set of specific cognitive skills. Effective problem solving requires that people (1) define the problem clearly; (2) generate alternative possible courses of action; (3) evaluate the likely consequences of each alternative, and act on the most attractive option; and (4) reevaluate the situation to determine whether additional problem solving is warranted. D'Zurilla and Goldfried suggested that these skills can be assessed independently and that deficiencies in any of them can be overcome through behavioral training.

Spivack pioneered the use of problem-solving therapy, in which clients are taught to improve their problem-solving skills. Spivack developed the Means-Ends Problem-Solving Test (MEPS) to assess social problem-solving skills. Spivack and colleagues (e.g., Spivack et al., 1976; Spivack & Shure, 1974) showed that youths who are aggressive, impulsive, and overactive have problem-solving deficits relative to others. Following therapy that included training in problem-solving skills, Spivack and colleagues found, not only that clients' problem-solving skills improved, but also that their clinical disorders had decreased in severity.

Following Spivack, other clinical psychologists have used problem-solving therapy. Mahoney (1974) discussed problem solving as a general method of treating clinical problems. More recently, Nezu, Nezu, and Perri (1989) described problem-solving therapy as a general technique that can be employed with depression and other disorders.

Self-Instruction Training Meichenbaum (1977) popularized self-instruction as a form of therapy. Here, clients are taught to *talk to themselves* to provide effective instructions for coping with troubling situations. Clearly, self-instruction training overlaps with other cognitive therapy techniques discussed so far. For example, in problem-solving training, clients learn to *instruct themselves* to solve problems more effectively. Problem-solving training could well be considered an example of self-instruction training.

Meichenbaum has used self-instruction training extensively in the treatment of anxiety disorders. For example, Meichenbaum (1985) described *stress inoculation,* in which clients are taught how to give themselves effective instructions for (1) preparing to encounter a stressor; (2) confronting and coping with a stressor; (3) coping with the feeling of being over-whelmed by the stressor; and (4) evaluating one's performance afterward.

This inoculation model has been employed in the treatment of other distressing states, such as pain management (Turk, 1978) and anger control (Novaco, 1978). Meichenbaum and Turk (1976) illustrated how the four stages of stress inoculation can be adapted to these other problems. Examples of the self-statements in each stage of the inoculation model for coping with stress, anger, and pain are presented in Exhibit 11.2.

A very large body of research supports the effectiveness of self-instruction training (Meichenbaum, 1985). Because of this research foundation, self-instruction training is currently regarded as one of the most effective methods for helping clients cope with troubling emotions.

APPLIED ISSUES

When the popularity of behavior therapy increased in the 1950s and 1960s, several issues were raised concerning its practice. This section of the chapter examines several of these issues, including the problem of symptom substitution, the issue of problem relapse, the use of analogue subjects, and the ethics of behavior therapy.

Symptom Substitution

As behavior therapy became increasingly widespread in the 1950s and 1960s, psychoanalysts raised the issue of symptom substitution (Bookbinder, 1962; Yates, 1958). *Symptom substitution* is the criticism that, by treating only the symptomatic behavior, behavior therapy ignores the underlying problem; hence, the true problem persists and may manifest itself in a new symptom.

This criticism is based on psychoanalytic theory, which assumes that a presenting symptomatic behavior is only an outward manifestation of the "real" problem in the client's unconscious. According to psychoanalysis, behavior therapy is superficial—it may change symptomatic behavior, but it ignores the underlying problem.

If this is the case, then behavior therapy provides only a brief respite for the client. The immediate symptom may be relieved, but the underlying problem persists and will ultimately manifest itself in other symptoms. The new symptom may be more severe than the old symptom. Even if the new symptom is not more severe than the old, it is unfamiliar and so the client has not learned how to cope with it. Thus, according to psychoanalysts, behavior therapy is not merely ineffective, it actually exacerbates the client's problems!

The problem of symptom substitution, although originally raised as a criticism of behavior therapy, can also be directed against cognitive therapy. If cognitive symptoms are only an outward manifestation of an unconscious problem, then cognitive therapy, designed to alter conscious cognitive processes, also leaves the "real" problem untouched.

Behavior therapists respond to this criticism in two ways. First, they agree that any therapy that targets an inappropriate symptom is unlikely to be ef-

EXHIBIT 11.2   Self-Statements Used in Inoculation Training

Stage	Self-Statements
1. Prepare for the Stressor	What is it I should do?
	Remember what the therapist and I talked about. I'll be able to handle it.
	Don't worry. Worrying doesn't help.
2. Confront and Handle the Stressor	Relax, take a deep breath.
	Don't think about how bad I feel.
	Use the tension as a cue to start coping.
	Use one of the relaxation techniques I learned in therapy.
3. Cope with the Feeling of Being Overwhelmed	It will be over soon.
	Think of something else.
	Keep thinking of what the therapist and I talked about. Keep coping.
	Don't try to eliminate the pain entirely;
	just keep it under control.
	If it gets too bad, try another coping technique.
4. Reinforcement	I did it.
	The coping techniques worked.
	It wasn't so bad. I was able to handle the stress.
	Wait until I tell this to my therapist.

fective. For example, suppose a couple seeks treatment for the sexual dysfunction of premature ejaculation, when the "real" problem is that they have severe discord exacerbated by poor communication. A behavior therapist who conducts an inadequate assessment may not recognize the "real" problem and in fact treat the sexual dysfunction. In this case, behavior therapy is not likely to be successful. Although the sexual dysfunction may no longer trouble the couple, other sexual dysfunctions or problems in the couple's interactions may arise.

However, the problem here is not behavior therapy, but rather inadequate assessment. A behavior therapist who conducts a proper assessment will set appropriate target behaviors for the couple, such as communication and problem-solving skills. Behav-

ior therapists are not the only therapists who may be guilty of conducting inadequate assessments and treating an inappropriate problem. This problem may occur in any type of therapy. (For example, I know of a psychoanalytic therapist who treated an 8-year-old boy with enuresis. The therapist assumed that bedwetting was a symptom of underlying depression and initiated a lengthy course of insight-oriented therapy. After eight months of unsuccessful treatment, it was found that the boy was suffering from juvenile diabetes, which caused the enuresis. By delaying proper medical treatment, the boy's life had become endangered. Inadequate assessment led to inappropriate psychoanalytic treatment.) What is needed is accurate assessment so that the primary problem can be addressed in therapy.

Of course, behavior therapists strongly disagree with psychoanalysts on the nature of the "real" problem. Whereas psychoanalysts believe that the true pathology is always some underlying psychological problem, behavior therapists think that behavioral problems are true problems in and of themselves.

A second response by behavior therapists to the criticism of symptom substitution is an empirical one. Since the rise of behavior therapy, there have been literally hundreds of controlled studies of behavioral treatments with clinical and analogue subjects. These studies often include at least brief follow-ups, and so they provide empirical evidence to address the occurrence of symptom substitution.

To date, reviews of empirical studies of behavior therapy have repeatedly concluded that symptom substitution is not a major problem (e.g., Bandura, 1969; Lazarus, 1971). These reviews have found that symptom substitution occurs in only a small portion (from 5 to 10 percent) of clients who receive behavior therapy. Because this figure is smaller than that expected by psychoanalytic critics and because little evidence exists to show that this figure is greater than the occurrence of symptom substitution in clients treated with psychoanalysis or other forms of psychotherapy, reviewers of this research have generally concluded that symptom substitution is not a significant threat to the effectiveness of behavior therapy.

Erwin (1978), in an illuminating philosophical critique of behavior therapy, noted that contemporary psychoanalysts have conceded that symptom substitution is not the problem they once thought it to be. In fact, some Freudians (e.g., Rhoads & Feather, 1974) have now provided psychoanalytic explanations for the fact that symptom substitution does not occur.

Problem Relapse

A second practical problem with behavior therapy, raised soon after its rise in the 1950s and 1960s, is the issue of problem relapse. Target behaviors certainly change when reinforced or punished by a therapist. However, what happens when the client is in the "real world" and there is no therapist to monitor the client's behavior and deliver such consequences?

This criticism was directed perhaps most pointedly at token economies. Two early reviews of research on token economies (Carlson, Hersen, & Eisler, 1972; Kazdin & Bootzin, 1972) concluded that, although the effectiveness of token economies had been demonstrated, a major problem in many studies was their failure to provide evidence that treatment gains were maintained after the client left the token economy.

The problem of symptom relapse was also observed with other behavior therapies. For example, Lovaas and colleagues (1973) found that, following inpatient behavior therapy, children with autism regressed when later hospitalized at a facility that did not continue behavior therapy.

Behavior therapists soon recognized relapse as a significant problem. They incorporated several techniques to enhance the maintenance of improvements following treatment, including (1) overlearning, (2) booster sessions, (3) fading, (4) use of social reinforcers, (5) use of intermittent reinforcement schedules, and (6) combining behavioral with cognitive techniques.

Overlearning consists of continuing training after initial criteria for success are attained. For example, overlearning has been used to reduce relapse rates in the bell-and-pad treatment of enuresis (Doleys, 1989; Siegel & Smith, 1991).

Booster sessions consist of additional training sessions scheduled several months after the end of the regular treatment. For example, Vogler, Lunde, Johnson, and Martin (1970) reported that periodic booster sessions enhanced the effectiveness of aversive conditioning treatment of alcoholics.

Fading is the gradual removal of concrete or salient cues used in behavior therapy. Fading attempts to bring the behavior under the control of cues that are available in the client's natural environment. This will enhance the maintenance of improvement.

For example, Lovaas described how, in training a child who is autistic to sit on command, he used both a verbal command (*sit*) and a physical prompt (a light tap on the child's shoulders). After the child learned to sit in response to these cues, Lovaas then used only the verbal command, fading out the shoulder tap. Individuals in the child's natural environment are more likely to use verbal commands than physical prompts such as shoulder taps.

Fading is related to the two other methods used to reduce relapse rates. For example, behavior therapists may initially employ concrete reinforcements (such as candy) to produce improvements in a child's behavior. However, this is a rather artificial method that will not occur naturally in the child's environment. For this reason, behavior therapists then pair the candy with social reinforcement. *Social reinforcement* is reinforcement that occurs naturally in social interactions, such as smiles and verbal praise. After the desired behavior is being maintained by both candy and the social reinforcement, the candy can be faded out.

Similarly, behaviorists use intermittent reinforcement schedules to enhance the maintenance of improvements following the end of formal training. Recall from Chapter 3 that a continuous reinforcement schedule is one in which every instance of the desired behavior is reinforced; continuous reinforcement schedules produce rapid initial learning, but produce behaviors that extinguish quickly once reinforcement is discontinued. Conversely, an intermittent (partial) reinforcement schedule is one in which not every instance of the desired behavior is reinforced; compared to continuous schedules of reinforcement, intermittent schedules produce behaviors that are learned more slowly but are more resistant to extinction.

To increase the maintenance of behavioral gains, behavior therapists may start with continuous reinforcement schedules—this produces rapid learning of the desired behavior. However, after the adaptive behavior has been learned, then the therapist gradually fades to an intermittent schedule. In this way, the behavior becomes resistant to extinction, and so is more likely to be maintained after the client returns to his home environment. I know of a state correctional facility for delinquent youths that follows this procedure. New arrivals are assigned to one cottage, which operates very strictly, using concrete cues and reinforcements administered on a continuous schedule. After demonstrating appropriate behavior here, youths graduate to another cottage, in which there is more flexibility—fewer cues, more

social reinforcers. If resident behave appropriately in this setting, they move on to a third cottage that operates as a halfway home—as near to a noncorrectional residence as can be arranged.

A final way of increasing the generalizability of behavioral gains is to combine behavioral with cognitive procedures. Behavior therapy is provided by the therapist in the treatment setting. However, cognitive methods are then used to supplement the treatment, so that the client can use the cognitive techniques at home. For example, in vivo desensitization can be conducted in the therapist's office, with the therapist gradually introducing the feared object. The client can then practice this procedure at home, utilizing imaginal exposure to the feared object.

Thus, clinical psychologists have recognized that failure to maintain improvements is a common problem in behavior therapy. However, they have also learned that, by incorporating the principles listed above, which had been developed in the learning laboratory, they are able to significantly lower the risk of problem relapse.

Use of Analogue Subjects

Another criticism of behavior therapy, raised soon after its rise, concerns its use of clinical analogues. Many studies on behavior therapy employed subclinical analogues as subjects, rather than actual clients. For example, the literature on systematic desensitization includes scores of controlled studies of college students who score above average on measures of fears. Although relatively few people seek clinical help for fear of snakes, snake-phobic analogues are among the most extensively studied subjects in controlled research on desensitization.

This criticism also applies to cognitive therapy. For example, although Smith and Glass (1977) identified RET as the therapy with the second largest mean effect size, examination of the studies on RET shows that many were conducted in university settings with student analogues as subjects. Similarly, much of the early experimental research on cognitive models of depression was conducted with depressive analogues in student populations.

Behavior therapists respond to this criticism in the following way. Behavior therapy has a strong research tradition. Prior to using a new treatment in an applied setting, scientific (and, arguably, ethical standards as well) require that initial research be conducted in analogue settings. After a new therapy has received initial support in analogue studies, then it can be applied with more confidence to clinical subjects.

History has shown that, after behavioral and cognitive therapies have been tested and applied in analogue research, they are later generalized to clinical populations. For example, although many early desensitization studies were conducted with phobia analogues (Rachman, 1971), later research examined its use with clinical disorders such as agoraphobia (Chambless, 1985).

The same is true for cognitive therapy. Whereas many early studies of cognitive therapy used depressive analogues, recent research has been conducted with patients who meet DSM-IV criteria for mood disorders. Similarly, cognitive–behavioral therapy has recently been applied to disorders such as post-traumatic stress disorder (Deblinger, McLeer, & Henry, 1990) and personality disorders (Turkat & Maisto, 1985).

Ethical Problems

Following the rise of behavior therapies in the 1950s and 1960s, numerous criticisms were directed against the ethics of behavior therapy. The ethical issues concerning behaviorism and behavior therapy are so extensive that a complete discussion of them is not possible here. Still, several ethical criticisms will be presented here to introduce the reader to this issue.

Consider the ethical criticisms of behavior therapy by Allen Wheelis (1973, p. 104), a noted psychoanalytic writer:

> *We are in no position to comment on the efficacy of behavior therapy as generally practiced, but in principle we know it works. People may indeed be treated as objects and may be profoundly affected thereby. Kick a dog often enough and he will become cowardly or vicious. People who are kicked undergo similar changes; their view of the world and of themselves is transformed. The survivors of Hitler's concentration camps testify that the treatment received did have an effect. Nor find we reason to doubt the alleged results of Chinese thought-control methods. People may indeed be brainwashed, for benign or exploitative reasons.*

In the space of a few sentences, Wheelis compared behavior therapy to kicking a dog, Nazi concentration camps, and brainwashing! Of course, Wheelis's views of behavior therapy are extreme; still, they illustrate the negative opinion that many have of behaviorism and behavior therapy.

Ethical criticisms of behavior therapy include the following: (1) the use of aversive or painful techniques is unethical; (2) the use of positive reinforcement is simply bribery; and (3) that the use of reinforcement and punishment is manipulative.

Use of Aversive Techniques   Behavior therapists have been criticized for using punishment and other aversive techniques. For example, Lovaas was criticized for using punishment to decrease the frequency of self-stimulatory behavior in children with autism. There are isolated cases where parents, educators, or even psychologists have, in the name of "behavior therapy," taken an aversive technique to such extremes that it became clearly unethical. For example, *timeout* is a commonly used punishment with children, where the child is removed from the opportunity to earn reinforcement (often by being sent to one's room or standing in a corner). However, there have been cases of parents who have locked their children in closets or trunks for extended periods, all in the name of the behavioral technique of timeout.

It is important to recognize that the potential for abuse of behavioral techniques does not, in itself, mean that the techniques are unethical. After all, virtually any treatment technique can be abused. For example, psychoanalytic therapy involves a long-term relationship in which the client develops strong feelings for the therapist. Unfortunately, some therapists abuse their position by engaging in sexual relationships with their clients. Of course, the fact that some therapists abuse the transference, an essential part of psychoanalytic therapy, does not mean that the treatment itself is unethical.

Similarly, it is important to recognize that the use of aversive techniques is not in itself unethical. After all, many medical procedures, including surgeries, laboratory techniques (such as spinal taps), and treatments (such as radiation therapy and chemotherapy for cancer) are aversive. Similarly, traditional psychoanalytic therapy seeks to help clients gain insight into the nature of their unconscious problems; the recognition of such material is often so painful that the client engages in various forms of resistance to avoid it.

In order to evaluate any treatment, it is necessary to weigh the potential benefits against the potential risks. Then, the client must provide informed consent for the treatment. If the client is informed of the potential risks and benefits of the aversive treatment and alternative treatments and the client consents to the aversive treatment, then the use of aversive techniques is not unethical.

In response to the criticism of their use of aversive techniques, behavior therapists also note that they prefer to use reinforcement over punishment, positive techniques over aversive techniques. In a properly designed behavioral intervention (say, behavioral contract or token economy), the client should experience frequent reinforcements and should earn many more reinforcements than punishments. If this does not occur, then the fault is with the behavior therapist who designed the treatment program, rather than with the behavioral technique itself.

Use of Reinforcement as Bribery Critics of behavior therapy have frequently compared the use of reinforcement to simple bribery: "Clients improve their behavior merely to gain rewards; however, they have not truly experienced an improvement in their inner selves." For example, parents often raise this criticism when behavioral techniques are presented to help them manage their child's behavior.

Behaviorists respond to this criticism by referring to the research literature on the development of self-control in children. Luria (1961) and Vygotsky (1934/1987) have suggested that the development of

self-control usually proceeds through a 3-stage process: (1) external control by others, (2) overt self-control, and (3) covert (or internal) self-control. For example, psychologists have examined the development of children's self-control in academic problem solving. Berk (1984; Bivens & Berk, 1990) has shown that, as children age, they engage in increasing amounts of self-talk when solving problems; in addition, self-talk is related to their performance.

Behavior therapists place their use of external reinforcements in this developmental context. The client has not developed self-control; else, there would be no need of therapy. By providing external control, the behavior therapist is merely initiating the normal process through which people in general develop self-control.

Clearly, most clients will return to settings where there is no therapist to administer concrete reinforcement or punishment, and so they need to develop self-control. However, to start this process with external controls does not mean that internal controls will not develop later. Once the desired behavior is established, concrete reinforcers can be faded out and social and self-reinforcers can be faded in.

Punishment and Reinforcement as Manipulation
A third ethical criticism of behavior therapy is that it is manipulative: clients are conditioned to alter their behavior in ways that are determined by the therapist. Instead of changing the client's *underlying personality* so that the client *truly wants to change* his or her behavior, behavior therapy merely forces the client to behave differently in order to earn rewards or to avoid punishment.

Behavior therapists respond to the general criticism that their therapy is manipulative in several ways. As with the criticism that reinforcement is bribery, behavior therapists respond by noting that external control of behavior is simply the first step in the natural process of developing self-control. After the desired behavior is established and maintained by external contingencies, then concrete controls can be faded out and internal controls faded in. Thus, the end goal of therapy is for the client to gain self-control; external "manipulation" is only the first step on the road to self-control.

A second response to this criticism is that behavior therapy, like all psychotherapy, is presented only after a client has provided informed consent for the treatment. Behavior therapists, like other therapists, present clients with the results of their diagnostic assessment and their treatment recommendations. Prior to beginning behavior therapy, the client should understand the goals, methods, approximate length and cost, and risks of therapy. In addition, the client should have an idea of the other available treatments and their likely costs and benefits. If the client has consented to a behavioral treatment over an alternative treatment, such as long-term psychoanalytic therapy, then behavior therapy is not a form of manipulation. The client has consented to the goals and techniques of behavior therapy.

The criticism that behavior therapy is manipulative was directed perhaps most pointedly in the late-1960s and early-1970s when behavioral methods were used in attempts to change the sexual orientation of homosexuals (Begelman, 1975). Although current evaluations of research in this area indicate that there is no effective psychological procedure for changing a homosexual orientation (e.g., Willerman & Cohen, 1990), behavior therapists in the late-1960s were reporting that behavioral methods (e.g., aversive conditioning) were moderately successful. A heated debate arose, examining the definition of *abnormality* and the ethics of attempting to change a behavior defined as abnormal by deviation from social values, rather than by traditional medical or psychological criteria. The result of this debate was that, in 1974, both the American Psychological Association and American Psychiatric Association agreed to remove homosexuality, per se, from their list of mental disorders.

Although behavior therapists have often been criticized for trying to change the sexual orientation of homosexuals, it is important to note two points. First, behavior therapists were among the psychologists who first raised the ethical issues concerning the treatment of homosexuality (e.g., Davison, 1976, 1978). Indeed, a survey of behavior therapists at this time found that, as a group, behavior therapists did not regard homosexuality as abnormal per se, or even as undesirable (Davison & Wilson, 1973). Second, the ethics of changing the sexual orientation of homosexuals had been a moot point prior to the use of behavior therapy; because other psychological treatments were not effective in changing sexual orientation, the ethical problems that arise from changing the sexual orientation of homosexuals were not recognized as significant. They only became an issue when the field had a treatment that was reported to be effective.

Clearly, there are other criticisms of behavior therapy. There is not sufficient room in this text to consider all of the ethical criticisms that have been directed against this form of therapy. Interested readers should consult other works (e.g., Erwin, 1978; Goldfried & Davison, 1976) for more lengthy discussions of the ethics of behavior therapy.

SCIENTIFIC ISSUES

The most important scientific issue concerning behavior therapy is its effectiveness. Remember that Eysenck (1952a) issued a challenge to clinical psychologists to provide scientific evidence to support their claims of the effectiveness of psychotherapy. After reviewing the research to date, Eysenck (1952a) concluded that there was no scientific evidence that adult neurotics, treated with psychoanalysis or other forms of psychotherapy, had a superior outcome to adult neurotics who received no therapy. However, in response both to Eysenck's challenge and to the formal sanction by the American Psychological Association of the scientist–practitioner model of training, clinical psychologists began to conduct scientific studies of the effectiveness of psychotherapy.

Because behaviorism originally developed to emphasize the scientific foundations of psychology, behaviorally oriented clinical psychologists played a major role in conducting research on the effectiveness of therapy. At this date, there is an enormous research literature available to the field concerning the efficacy of behavioral and cognitive therapies. Many of the behavioral and cognitive therapies described in this chapter were presented along with a summary of the research evaluations of their effectiveness.

The rest of this chapter will summarize the results of reviews of research on the effectiveness of cognitive and behavior therapy. Because of the number of studies in this area, this presentation cannot be exhaustive; however, this presentation will illustrate the conclusions drawn by clinical psychologists regarding the effectiveness of cognitive and behavior therapy.

Early Reviews of the Effectiveness of Behavior Therapy

Eysenck (1960, 1965) updated his review of studies on the effectiveness of psychotherapy to include more recent research. Although he did not modify his evaluation of psychoanalytic or eclectic psychotherapies, Eysenck thought that the scientific evidence now supported claims of the efficacy of behavior therapy. For example, Eysenck (1960) concluded that neurotics, "treated by means of psychotherapeutic procedures based on learning theory, improve significantly more quickly than do patients treated by means of psychoanalytic or eclectic psychotherapy, or not treated by psychotherapy at all" (p. 720).

Of course, Eysenck's criticisms of traditional psychotherapy and his endorsement of behavior therapy did not go unchallenged (see Wierzbicki, 1993a for a detailed discussion of the field's criticisms of and responses to Eysenck's reviews). Still, it is significant that Eysenck, such a rigorous advocate of scientific evaluation, judged any form of therapy to be effective.

Other reviews of the psychotherapy outcome literature soon followed (e.g., Bergin, 1971; Luborsky, Singer, & Luborsky, 1975; Meltzoff & Kornreich, 1970). Although these reviews did not judge psychoanalytic and other traditional psychotherapies as harshly as Eysenck, they generally agreed that behavior therapy is effective. For example, Luborsky and colleagues (1975) reported that 19 direct comparisons of the efficacy of behavioral and psychodynamic therapy resulted in 13 "ties" and 6 comparisons that favored behavior therapy. Although Luborsky and colleagues concluded that there is no difference in effectiveness between the two forms of

therapy, they could as easily have concluded that behavior therapy always equals or surpasses psychodynamic therapy.

Meta-Analytic Reviews

More recently, evidence concerning the relative efficacies of behavior, cognitive, and other forms of therapy can be garnered from a series of meta-analyses. As you recall, meta-analysis is a set of statistical methods that permits a reviewer to combine the results of different studies.

In the initial meta-analysis of over 300 therapy outcome studies (Smith & Glass, 1977), cognitive and behavioral therapies were found to have the three largest mean effect sizes: systematic desensitization (0.91), RET (0.77), and behavior modification (0.76). Smith and Glass later extended their meta-analysis, examining 475 studies (Smith, Glass, & Miller, 1980). They found that behavior and cognitive therapy continued to receive substantial support. For example, the greatest mean effect sizes occurred for cognitive (1.31), cognitive-behavioral (1.24), and behavioral (0.91) therapies. Thus, in the initial meta-analytic reviews of research on the effectiveness of psychotherapy, both cognitive and behavior therapy were evaluated as highly effective.

Many subsequent meta-analyses have evaluated the efficacy of behavior therapy. Andrews and Harvey (1981) examined 81 studies of patients (excluding analogue studies) and found that behavioral therapies (0.97) are more effective than verbal (0.74) and developmental therapies (0.35).

Searles (1985) refined the Andrews and Harvey (1981) meta-analysis, excluding studies of conditions that are not typically regarded as "neurotic" (e.g., homosexuality, underachievement) and excluding studies that compared treatments to one another rather than to a control group. In this way, Searles reduced the Andrews and Harvey sample to 16 studies: 8 of behavior therapy and 8 of psychodynamic therapy. After eliminating several studies due to insufficient data, Searles found that the average effect size of psychodynamic therapy (0.32) is substantially less than that of behavior therapy (0.88).

Searles (1985) also refined a meta-analysis of therapy outcome by Landman and Dawes (1982).

Searles omitted studies if they addressed problems unrelated to neurotic disorders (e.g., study habits, occupational planning). Searles examined 19 behavioral studies and 2 psychodynamic studies, and again found that the average effect size of behavior therapy (1.22) is significantly greater than that of psychodynamic therapy (.27).

Shapiro and Shapiro (1982) conducted a meta-analysis that refined the methodology of Smith and colleagues (1980). Shapiro and Shapiro identified 143 published studies that compared two therapies to one another and to a control condition. Mean effect sizes for therapy types were: mixed behavioral (1.42), behavioral (1.06), cognitive (1.00), unclassified behavioral (0.78), minimal (placebo) treatment (0.71), and dynamic/humanistic (0.40).

Dush, Hirt, and Schroeder (1983) evaluated the efficacy of self-statement training in 69 studies. Mean effect size of this cognitive therapy was significant, compared both to no treatment control groups (0.74) and to other forms of therapy (0.49).

Miller and Berman (1983) evaluated the relative efficacy of cognitive, behavior, and other therapy. Although the mean effect size for cognitive therapy was significant when compared to both no treatment (0.83) and other treatment (0.21 over 36 studies), the effect size of cognitive therapy was not significant when compared to desensitization (0.21 over 13 studies). In a follow-up review, Berman, Miller, and Massman (1985) examined studies that compared cognitive and behavior therapy, and again found a nonsignificant advantage (0.06) for cognitive therapy.

Despite criticisms of the methods and interpretations of these meta-analyses (see Wierzbicki, 1993a for a detailed discussion of these meta-analyses), both behavior and cognitive therapy have generally been evaluated by reviewers of psychotherapy research as effective and appropriate treatments for many conditions. These meta-analytic reviews have agreed that cognitive and behavior therapy are effective and are among the more (if not the most) effective forms of therapy. There is somewhat less agreement on the relative efficacy of cognitive and behavioral therapy, although some reviewers today

are giving the nod to cognitive therapy, especially when treating depression (e.g., Sacco & Beck, 1985).

It should be noted, however, that these comparisons of different forms of therapy do not prove that cognitive and behavior therapy are always as or more effective than other therapies. As discussed in Chapter 8, clinical psychologists have long recognized the uniformity myths of early psychotherapy outcome research. Just because cognitive therapy is effective (and perhaps more effective than other therapies) in treating depression, does not mean that it will be effective (or more effective than other therapies) for other disorders. Similarly, the effectiveness of desensitization in treating phobias does not mean that it is an appropriate treatment for other problems. Clinical psychologists must evaluate each form of therapy in a specific context—as it is used to treat certain types of clients with certain disorders. It is only in this way that clinical psychologists can be sure to provide the most effective treatment to each client.

SUMMARY

Soon after its introduction by Watson in 1913, behaviorism became a leading theory among experimental and academic psychologists. However, behavior therapy did not become an influential treatment approach until the 1950s and 1960s.

Behaviorists assume that abnormal behavior, like normal behavior, develops through conditioning. Behavior therapy is a process of reconditioning in which the basic laws of learning are used to replace maladaptive behavior with adaptive behavior.

Therapy techniques based on classical conditioning include desensitization (and the related techniques of implosive therapy and flooding) and aversive conditioning. Desensitization is a treatment for phobias in which the client is gradually exposed to the feared object. Aversive conditioning is used to reduce the frequency of undesirable behaviors that are immediately reinforcing, such as sexual and substance abuse disorders.

Therapy techniques based on instrumental conditioning include stimulus control, shaping, the token economy, contracting, and child management. All of these techniques use punishment to reduce the frequency of undesired behaviors and reinforcement to increase the frequency of desired behaviors.

Social learning is often used to enhance social and cognitive skills. Coping models, who initially have difficulty performing the adaptive behavior but who talk themselves through a troubling situation, tend to be more effective than mastery models, who perform successfully from the outset.

Cognitive therapy assumes that cognitive processes are inaccurate or ineffective, and so lead to ineffective behavior or troubling emotions. Cognitive therapy tries to revise cognitive processes so that they become more accurate and effective.

There are cognitive analogues of behavior therapy based on the principles of classical conditioning, instrumental conditioning, and social learning. Imaginal desensitization is a cognitive (or covert) form of desensitization; covert sensitization is a cognitive form of aversive conditioning. There are cognitive analogues of instrumental techniques, including covert punishment, reinforcement, and rehearsal. In addition, covert modeling is a cognitive analogue of social learning.

Two other approaches to cognitive therapy are important. Cognitive restructuring is a form of cognitive therapy in which irrational or ineffective beliefs are identified and revised. George Kelly's personal construct psychology, Albert Ellis's rational–emotive therapy, and Aaron Beck's cognitive therapy of depression are examples of this approach.

Cognitive skills training is a form of cognitive therapy in which specific cognitive processes are trained to help the client perform more effectively. George Spivack's problem-solving approach to adjustment and Donald Meichenbaum's self-instruction training for coping with stress are examples of this approach.

After its rise in the 1950s and 1960s, several criticisms were directed against behavior therapy. According to psychoanalytic theory, behavior therapy only addresses the external symptom and not the underlying problem; hence, the real problem persists and may be expressed in a new symptom (i.e., symptom substitution). Research and clinical experience since the 1950s, however, has shown that symptom substitution is not a significant problem, occurring in only a small proportion of clients treated with behavior therapy.

A second criticism of behavior therapy concerns relapse. After returning to an environment in which there is no therapist to reinforce adaptive behavior, a client's behavioral gains may be lost. Behavior therapists employ several techniques to reduce the frequency of problem relapse. These include overlearning; booster sessions; fading out external controls while fading in self- and social reinforcers; use of intermittent reinforcement schedules; and use of cognitive self-control techniques.

Another criticism of behavior therapy concerns its use of analogue subjects. Early studies in behavior and cognitive therapy often employed subjects who did not have a clinical disorder, but who were instead clinical analogues. Behavior and cognitive therapists begin with analogue research for ethical and scientific reasons; however, after demonstrating the effectiveness of therapy in analogue research, they then apply therapy to clinical disorders.

Several ethical criticisms have also been directed against behavior therapy. Behavior therapy has been criticized on the grounds that it uses aversive techniques, that it is simple bribery, and that it is manipulative. Behavior therapists respond to these criticisms in several ways: clients give informed consent prior to any intervention, including aversive techniques; behavior therapy begins by using concrete external reinforcements and punishments, but gradually fade these out while fading in internal and social controls.

Many empirical studies have examined the effectiveness of behavior and cognitive therapy. Reviews of this research have agreed that both cognitive and behavior therapy are effective. They have also generally agreed that cognitive and behavior therapy are among the more, if not the most, effective forms of therapy.

STUDY QUESTIONS

1. What is the traditional behavioral view of the cause of abnormality and the goal of therapy?

2. How does this differ from the psychoanalytic theory of the cause and treatment of abnormality?

3. Describe one behavioral therapy technique associated with each of the three basic forms of conditioning.

4. What is the cognitive view of the cause of abnormality and the goal of therapy?

5. Compare and contrast cognitive and traditional behavioral views of the cause and treatment of abnormality.

6. Compare and contrast the cognitive and psychoanalytic views of the cause and treatment of abnormality.

7. Describe one cognitive therapy technique associated with each of the three basic forms of conditioning. Describe one cognitive restructuring approach to therapy.

8. What practical problems arose in the early treatment efforts of behavior therapists? How did behavior therapists modify their treatments to address these problems?

9. Discuss the ethical criticisms that have been directed against behavior therapy. How do behavior therapists respond to such criticisms?

10. Summarize the scientific evidence concerning the efficacy of behavior and cognitive therapy.

12

Biological Treatment

I. Medical Treatments
   A. Psychiatric Medication
   B. Electroconvulsive Therapy
   C. Psychosurgery
II. Physiologically Oriented Treatments
   A. Introduction to Stress-Related Disorders
   B. Treatment of Stress-Related Disorders
III. Behavioral Medicine
   A. Behavioral Medicine Programs

IV. Applied Issues
   A. Psychologists and Prescription
      Privileges
   B. Social Consequences of the Rise of
      Psychiatric Drugs
V. Scientific Issues
VI. Summary

Historically, the mental health profession has had a long and close association with the medical profession. Sigmund Freud, often regarded as the "father" of psychology and psychotherapy, was a physician; psychoanalysts since Freud's time, especially in the United States, have frequently had medical training. Clinical psychologists, without formal medical training themselves, have long worked beside psychiatrists in mental health settings.

However, the rise in psychoanalytic, behavioral, and humanistic psychology in the first half of the twentieth century led clinical psychologists to de-emphasize the role of biological factors. Psychoanalysts explained psychopathology as the result of early family experiences. Behaviorists viewed be-

havior as determined by environmental influences. Humanists viewed behavior as self-determined.

By mid-century, the major theoretical schools in clinical psychology stressed environmental influences on personality and psychopathology more than biological influences. The biological viewpoint was, at that time, only a minority view.

However, advances since the 1950s have led clinical psychologists to become increasingly aware of the role that biological factors play in influencing personality and psychopathology. Behavior genetics has shown that many forms of both normal and abnormal psychological functioning have genetic influences. Pharmacological advances have produced medications that are effective in treating many mental disorders. Biochemical research has begun to show how neurotransmitters are important in the onset and treatment of various mental disorders. Neurological research has begun to demonstrate that neurological structures and processes are associated with mental disorders.

For all of these reasons, clinical psychologists have become increasingly attentive to biological influences on mental disorders. Clinical psychologists are not trained as physicians, and so they cannot prescribe medical treatments. However, clinical psychologists must be aware of these treatments and the theoretical explanations for their effectiveness.

This chapter introduces the reader to medical and physiologically oriented psychological treatments for mental disorders. There will be a lengthy presentation on medical treatments, such as medications and electroconvulsive therapy (ECT). There will also be a discussion of physiologically oriented therapies, such as biofeedback and progressive muscle relaxation, which have physiological effects as their goal. Finally, this chapter will describe the clinical specialty of behavioral medicine, which uses psychological techniques to assist in the treatment of medical conditions.

MEDICAL TREATMENTS

Psychiatric Medication

One of the most significant developments in the mental health field in the last half-century is the discovery of medications that are effective in treating (or at least managing the symptoms of) mental disorders. This section of the chapter introduces the major classes of psychiatric drugs, describes their presumed mechanisms of action, and summarizes research results concerning their effectiveness. Before discussing the physiological mechanisms of psychiatric drugs, however, it is first necessary to review the biochemical actions of drugs.

Recall from Chapter 3 that nerve impulses are transmitted through electrochemical processes. Most of the psychiatric medications to be discussed are thought to affect the transmission of nerve impulses from one cell to the next, and so affect synaptic transmission.

Neurons are separated by a gap called a *synapse*. When a nerve impulse reaches the end of the presynaptic cell, chemical substances called neurotransmitters are released into the synapse. Neurotransmitters diffuse across the synapse and are taken up by specific receptor sites on the postsynaptic cell. Excess neurotransmitters in the synaptic gap, not taken up at receptor sites, are returned to the presynaptic cell through a process called reuptake.

The effect of neurotransmitters on the postsynaptic cell is additive so that, after a sufficient amount has been taken up at receptors, a new nerve impulse is generated (although some neurotransmitters have an inhibitory effect so that, the more that are taken up, the more difficult it will be for other neurotransmitters to initiate a nerve impulse in that cell.)

Although some medications (and the illnesses treated by them) are thought to have their effect by altering the transmission of impulses along an axon within a neuron, most of the medications used to treat psychiatric disorders and discussed below are thought to work by modifying the transmission of nerve impulses across the synapse. If a disorder is associated with a neurotransmitter excess, then medications that lower the amount and activity of the neurotransmitter should be helpful. Decreases in neurotransmitter action can be produced by drugs that (1) block the synthesis or production of the neurotransmitter in the presynaptic cell; (2) prevent the release of the neurotransmitter from the presynaptic cell; (3) decrease the storage of the neurotransmitter in the presynaptic cell (say, by increasing the degree to which the neurotransmitter is metabolized or broken down into other substances); (4) block receptor sites so that the neurotransmitter cannot act on the postsynaptic cell; and (5) increase the activity of inhibitory neurotransmitters, so that the excess neurotransmitter has a lessened effect.

On the other hand, if a disorder is associated with a neurotransmitter deficit, then drugs that increase the neurotransmitter should be helpful. Increased amount or activity of a neurotransmitter is produced by drugs that: (1) increase the supply of the materials used by the presynaptic cell to synthesize the neurotransmitter; (2) decrease the breakdown of the neurotransmitter in the presynaptic cell; (3) increase the release of the neurotransmitter from the presynaptic cell; and (4) decrease neurotransmitter reuptake, so that the neurotransmitter remains longer in the synaptic gap, increasing the likelihood that it will act on the postsynaptic receptors.

Antipsychotics   One of the most important pharmacological advances in the mental health field occurred in the 1950s in the treatment of schizophrenia. Schizophrenia is a severe mental disorder that often leads patients to be psychotic, or out of touch with reality. It is useful to classify the symptoms of schizophrenia as positive and negative. *Negative symptoms* of schizophrenia reflect the absence of normal functioning, such as lack of emotional responsiveness, lack of motivation and initiative, and social withdrawal. *Positive symptoms* of schizophrenia reflect the presence of abnormal functioning. Delusions (irrational beliefs systems), hallucinations, and disorganized speech are positive symptoms of schizophrenia. Because the positive symptoms of schizophrenia indicate that the patient experiences unusual and disconnected thinking, these are also referred to as thought disorder symptoms.

Because schizophrenia is so severe, schizophrenic patients are generally hospitalized. Prior to the 1950s, the mental health field had no effective treatment for this condition, and so schizophrenic patients tended to be hospitalized for extended periods—years if not for the rest of their lives.

The medication *chlorpromazine* was introduced in the United States in 1954. This drug, often sold under the trade name *Thorazine*, was found to be effective in controlling the positive symptoms of schizophrenia. Chlorpromazine is a member of a class of drugs called the *phenothiazines*. Follow-up research on these drugs showed that they also were effective in controlling schizophrenia. For the first time, schizophrenic patients could be successfully treated and released from the hospital.

Following the discovery of the phenothiazines, other medications were soon found to be effective in treating schizophrenia as well. These medications are often called *antipsychotics* or *neuroleptics*. In the

EXHIBIT 12.1   Antipsychotic Medications

Class	Trade Name
Phenothiazine	
Chlorpromazine	Thorazine
Fluphenazine	Prolixin
Thioridazine	Mellaril
Trifluoperazine	Stelazine
Thioxanthene	
Thiothixene	Navane
Butyrophenone	
Haloperidol	Haldol
Diphenylbutylpiperidine	
Pimozide	Orap
Dibenzodiazepine	
Clozapine	Clozaril
Dibenzoxazepine	
Loxapine	Loxitane
Dihydroindolone	
Molindone	Moban

past, they were also termed *major tranquilizers*. This last term, however, has gone out of favor because it may lead to confusion between antipsychotic medications and the *minor tranquilizers* used to treat anxiety disorders.

To date, several major classes of antipsychotic medications have been identified. Exhibit 12.1 lists the major classes of antipsychotic medications, along with representative drugs (and their trade names) from each class.

Although mental health professionals in the 1950s and 1960s expressed some skepticism about the efficacy of antipsychotics, research by the 1970s was very clear that antipsychotic drugs "worked." Antipsychotics did not, as some early critics alleged, simply tranquilize patients so that it became easier for hospital staff to manage them. Rather, research showed that antipsychotic drugs had their greatest impact on precisely the thought disorder or positive symptoms that are regarded as fundamental to schizophrenia (Snyder, 1974).

Since the 1970s, it has been known that antipsychotic medications have the effect of blocking dopamine receptor sites (Bernstein, 1988). By blocking these sites, they lower the degree to which available dopamine can be taken up by and initiate nerve impulses in postsynaptic neurons. In addition, there is a high correlation between a drug's ability to block dopamine receptor sites and its clinical effectiveness in treating the symptoms of schizophrenia (Bernstein, 1988). Thus, antipsychotic drugs are thought to act by decreasing dopaminergic activity.

This dopamine model of schizophrenia is currently one of the most influential theories for explaining the disorder. It is supported by the observation that drugs that increase dopamine activity, such as amphetamines and L-DOPA, can produce states that mimic schizophrenia. In addition, antipsychotic drugs can cause, as a side effect, motor symptoms like those of Parkinson's Disease, which is associated with deficits in dopamine activity, particularly in motor neural pathways (Bernstein, 1988).

Although antipsychotic medications revolutionized the treatment of schizophrenia, they did not provide a cure for it. These drugs control the symptoms of schizophrenia but do not provide a permanent solution to the excess dopamine activity. Schizophrenic patients need to take these medications, not just to alleviate their symptoms when actively psychotic, but also to prevent future episodes. Patients must continue to take antipsychotics to function outside of hospital settings.

A problem here is that a patient may stop taking the medication and become actively psychotic once again. The last several decades has witnessed the rise of the *revolving door syndrome,* wherein patients hospitalized for psychotic conditions are discharged for periods up to several months until their next psychotic episode. The revolving door syndrome is discussed later in the chapter.

Another problem with antipsychotic medications is that they produce some adverse side effects, including cognitive, anticholinergic, and extrapyramidal effects. Cognitive effects include sedation, confusion, and impaired memory. *Anticholinergic*

effects include dry mouth, dry eyes, blurred vision, constipation, and urinary retention. *Extrapyramidal effects* (seen especially with high dosages or with high potency antipsychotics) are motor symptoms, such as *dystonia* (twisting or spasms of muscle groups), *akathesia* (motor restlessness), and *Parkinsonism* (stiffness, tremor, rigidity) (Bezchlibnyk-Butler & Jeffries, 1991). By far, the most serious potential side effect of antipsychotic medications is *tardive dyskinesia.* This is a permanent condition in which the patient experiences the extrapyramidal symptoms above. Tardive dyskinesia occurs occasionally, usually following the long-term use of antipsychotics.

An exciting recent development in the pharmacological treatment of schizophrenia is the discovery of atypical antipsychotics, the most widely used of which is clozapine (Clozaril). Atypical antipsychotics differ from other antipsychotics in that they produce fewer motor side effects, have a lower risk of tardive dyskinesia, and have been reported to be effective in treating both the positive and the negative symptoms of schizophrenia (Breier, Buchanan, Irish, & Carpenter, 1993). The presumed mechanism of action of atypical antipsychotics is unknown. Still, they provide an option for schizophrenic patients who do not respond to or who experience severe motor side effects as a result of other antipsychotics.

Antidepressants Another disorder successfully treated with medication since the 1950s is depression. Depression is a mood disorder characterized by a set of emotional, physiological, cognitive, and behavioral symptoms. For example, depressed individuals experience sadness and decreased enjoyment of their daily activities. They suffer from sleep and appetite disturbances. They experience low self-esteem and frequently entertain thoughts of death and even suicide. Depressives tend to withdraw from others and to engage in few social and recreational activities. When they move and speak, they often do so slowly and effortfully.

In the mid-1950s, the drug iproniazid was used to treat tuberculosis. However, it was found that this drug significantly elevated patients' mood and energy. This energizing effect led investigators to examine iproniazid as a possible treatment for depression (Noll, Davis, & DeLeon-Jones, 1985). By the early 1970s, research had clearly shown that iproniazid and related drugs were effective in treating depression. This included both severe (even psychotic) depressions as well as less severe depressions that could be treated on an outpatient basis.

Iproniazid is in a class of medications called the *MAO-Inhibitors* (or *MAO-Is*). MAO stands for Monoamine oxidase, an enzyme that helps break down the neurotransmitters serotonin and norepinephrine. MAO-Is inhibit the action of MAO, thereby reducing the breakdown and increasing the available supply of norepinephrine and serotonin. With increased supplies of these neurotransmitters, nerve impulses are transmitted more easily from one neuron to the next.

However, MAO-Is have side effects that complicate their use. Patients who take MAO-Is must follow a very strict diet. MAO-Is combined with a diet rich in tyramines (e.g., aged cheese, sausage, dried fish, sauerkraut, etc.) or certain medications (including narcotics, cold remedies, and stimulants) may precipitate a hypertensive crisis, resulting in stroke, liver damage, heart attack, or other severe problems. Thus, patients must be informed of the foods and medications to avoid while taking MAO-Is.

Another class of antidepressants, the tricyclics, was developed in the late 1950s and early 1960s, partly in an attempt to find antidepressants safer than MAO-Is. *Tricyclics* are thought to increase the available supply of serotonin and norepinephrine by decreasing their reuptake. Thus, these neurotransmitters remain in the synapse for longer periods and so have more time to be taken up by the postsynaptic cell.

Research has shown that from 60 to 95 percent of depressed patients respond favorably to tricyclics (Noll et al., 1985). MAO-Is are about as (or perhaps only slightly less) effective than tricyclics (Davis, 1985). Controlled research has shown that both classes of antidepressants are superior to no treatment, placebos, and alternative medications. Both classes are also effective in decreasing the degree to

EXHIBIT 12.2   Antidepressant Medications

Class	Trade Name
MAO-Inhibitor	
Tranylcypromine	Parnate
Phenelzine	Nardil
Tricyclic	
Amitriptyline	Elavil
Clomipramine	Anafranil
Imipramine	Tofranil
Nortriptyline	Pamelor
Bicyclic	
Fluoxetine	Prozac
Monocyclic	
Bupropion	Wellbutrin
Tetracyclic	
Maprotiline	Ludiomil

which patients suffer future episodes of depression (Noll et al., 1985).

Antidepressant medications produce a number of side effects. For example, tricyclics produce anticholinergic effects (e.g., dry mouth). However, these tend to be relatively minor and usually do not interfere with ongoing treatment. MAO-Is may also produce minor side effects such as dry mouth, restlessness, and insomnia.

Recently, several new types of antidepressants have been discovered. These include the bicyclics, monocyclics, and tetracyclics. Exhibit 12.2 lists the classes of antidepressant drugs, along with representative drugs (and their trade names) from each class.

Of the new antidepressants, by far the most commonly used is the monocyclic fluoxetine. *Fluoxetine (Prozac)* has been available in the United States for treating depression since 1988. Although its mechanism of action is as yet unclear, it is currently thought that fluoxetine increases the available supply of serotonin by selectively inhibiting its reuptake (Bernstein, 1988). Fluoxetine has become the most commonly prescribed antidepressant in the United States

(Wilson, O'Leary, & Nathan, 1992), largely because it is about as effective as the tricyclic antidepressants but has fewer aversive side effects (Cooper, 1988).

Following its rapid rise in popularity, a controversy arose concerning the possibility that Prozac might trigger violent or suicidal behavior. Although some lawsuits occurred and although some physicians now prescribe Prozac more cautiously than in the past, current scientific opinion still supports the use of Prozac (Fava, 1991). There is no scientific evidence that shows that Prozac triggers suicidal behavior. Unfortunately, some depressed individuals do attempt suicide or engage in other destructive behavior. That some patients who have been taking Prozac have engaged in such behaviors does not mean that the medication triggered the behaviors.

One other mood disorder should also be addressed here. Bipolar disorder (or manic-depression) is a mood disorder characterized by severe episodes, at different times, of depression and mania. Bipolar disorder is distinct from depression. Even though patients with bipolar disorder in a depressed phase may resemble patients with depression, they are distinguished by the occurrence of previous manic symptoms. Symptoms of mania are virtually the opposite of those of depression. Thus, manic episodes also include emotional (e.g., feeling buoyant, "high"), physiological (e.g., increased energy, decreased need for sleep), cognitive (e.g., unrealistically optimistic thoughts of one's abilities), and behavioral (e.g., rapid speech, excess motor activity) symptoms.

Lithium was first reported to have an antimanic effect by Cade (1949), and was first approved by the Food and Drug Administration (FDA) for use in the United States in 1969 (Bernstein, 1988). Since then, numerous studies have shown that lithium is effective, helping about 75 percent of bipolar patients (Bernstein, 1988). This research shows that lithium is effective in treating both the depressed and the manic phases of bipolar disorder, and that it is also effective in reducing the frequency of future bipolar episodes. Comparative outcome studies have shown that lithium is superior to placebos, no treatment, other antidepressants, and other types of medication for treating and preventing bipolar episodes (Noll et

al., 1985). For these reasons, lithium is generally regarded as the treatment of choice for bipolar disorder.

At this time, the physiological mechanism of lithium is unknown. There is some suggestion that lithium may help regulate the "ion pump" that restores the baseline electrical charge of a neuron following a nerve impulse; it has also been suggested that lithium stabilizes the activity of catecholamine receptors (Bezchlibnyk-Butler & Jeffries, 1991).

Although lithium is very effective for treating bipolar disorder, it also has aversive side effects. The therapeutic dose of lithium is not much lower than the toxic dose. For this reason, patients who receive lithium should be monitored closely, having their blood lithium levels checked frequently, until a dose is established that maintains their blood lithium level within the therapeutic range. Lithium can also have other adverse side effects, usually early in the course of treatment, including gastrointestinal irritation, restlessness, tremor, and blurred vision (Bezchlibnyk-Butler & Jeffries, 1991).

Anti-Anxiety Agents   Perhaps the most common type of mental problem is anxiety. The diagnostic class of anxiety disorders includes phobia (irrational fears), panic disorder (brief periods of intense physical and psychological symptoms of anxiety), and generalized anxiety disorder (chronic anxiety or worry for no apparent reason). One national study found that, in a given year, about 17 percent of adults in the U.S. report experiencing a significant level of an anxiety disorder (Kessler et al., 1994). Anxiety is one of the most frequently treated complaints by clinical psychologists.

In 1960, a class of drugs called the *benzodiazepines* was introduced for the treatment of anxiety disorders (Sarason & Sarason, 1993). From 1960 to 1980, these tranquilizers became the most commonly prescribed medication in the United States (Green, 1991). For example, in 1978 alone, 68 million prescriptions were written in the United States for benzodiazepines, more than half of which were for *diazepam (Valium)* (Green, 1991).

By the early 1980s, however, mental health professionals began to recognize problems with benzodiazepines. There is a risk of physiological dependency (with consequent withdrawal symptoms) and abuse of tranquilizers (Greenblatt, Shader, & Abernethy, 1983). Also, instead of learning psychological techniques for coping with stressors, many patients simply relied on medications to produce relaxation. For these reasons, prescription of tranquilizers in the 1980s decreased somewhat from earlier levels.

Interestingly, recent work has suggested that the risks of benzodiazepines may have been overstated. The American Psychiatric Association Task Force on Benzodiazepines reported that there is only a low tendency for abuse or for adverse physical effects (cited in Salzman, 1990). In addition, since the recognition of the potential for physiological dependency, standard pharmacological advice has been to use tranquilizers sparingly, to withdraw patients from them gradually, and to transfer patients from one benzodiazepine to diazepam (which has a long half-life) prior to discontinuation, in order to reduce the risk of physical withdrawal (Bezchlibnyk-Butler & Jeffries, 1991). Benzodiazepines continue to be widely used, with approximately 55 million prescriptions written annually in the United States (Breier & Paul, 1990).

The physiological mechanism of the benzodiazepines is, at this time, unclear. However, it is believed that it acts on receptors that form a complex with GABA receptors. GABA is a neurotransmitter that has an inhibitory effect; thus, when GABA and benzodiazepine both occupy the receptor complex, they decrease the number of nerve impulses initiated in the cell. Anti-anxiety agents provide materials that occupy benzodiazepine receptors. Thus, to produce the inhibitory effect, only GABA need cross the synaptic gap and be taken up by the postsynaptic cell (Bernstein, 1988).

Benzodiazepines differ in their potency and duration of action. Psychiatrists often select a benzodiazepine depending on the severity and chronicity of the patient's anxiety and situational stressors. Exhibit 12.3 lists several of the more commonly prescribed benzodiazepines, listing them as a function of both their potency and half-life.

Other Medications In addition to the classes of medications described above, several other drugs are routinely prescribed by psychiatrists. This section introduces several additional medications with which students of clinical psychology should become familiar.

Stimulants Stimulants are the most commonly prescribed psychiatric medication for children. Safer

EXHIBIT 12.3 Commonly Prescribed Benzodiazepines, as a Function of Potency and Half-Life

Potency

Half-life		Less Potent	More Potent
	Shorter	Oxazepam (Serax)	Lorazepam (Ativan) Alprazolam (Xanax)
	Longer	Diazepam (Valium)	Clonazepam (Klonopin)

and Krager (1984) estimated that from 2 to 4 percent of American children receive stimulant medication. Stimulants are used to treat Attention Deficit Hyperactivity Disorder (ADHD). The most commonly used stimulant medication for children is *methylphenidate (Ritalin)*. Two other stimulants, *dextroamphetamine (Dexedrine)* and *magnesium pemoline (Cylert)*, are also widely used to treat ADHD.

Bradley (1937) first reported that amphetamines have a therapeutic effect in treating children with behavior disorders. Research since then has shown that over 70 percent of children with ADHD show behavioral improvement when taking Ritalin (DuPaul, Guevremont, & Barkley, 1991).

It seems paradoxical to treat children who are already overactive with a stimulant; common sense suggests that these children should be "calmed down" rather than stimulated. However, by the 1970s, research demonstrated conclusively that the pathology in this condition is not high activity level but rather a deficiency in the ability to sustain attention (DuPaul et al., 1991). Children with this condition have difficulty attending to the task at hand. They are easily distracted and so have difficulty finishing what they start. Also, because of their attention deficit, they respond to distractors that other children ignore, and so they exhibit a high level of activity in situations that require sustained attention. Thus, when DSM-III (American Psychiatric Association, 1980) was published, the condition was relabelled from *hyperactivity* to Attention Deficit Disorder (ADD); DSM-III-R (American Psychiatric Association, 1987) later modified the label to ADHD, restoring the term hyperactivity in the diagnostic label.

Stimulant medication is thought to increase the child's alertness, thereby helping the child focus and sustain attention. In so doing, stimulants also help to lower the child's level of activity. Numerous studies have demonstrated that stimulants are effective in reducing overactivity and in increasing concentration and attention in children with ADHD (DuPaul et al., 1991).

Despite the success of stimulants in treating ADHD, several criticisms have been directed against the practice of medicating so many children.

These criticisms have addressed (1) the possibility of becoming dependent on medication; (2) the possibility of attributing improvements only to the medication, and not to the child's own efforts; and (3) the risk that stimulants may stunt a child's growth.

Parents commonly express fear that their child may become physically dependent on methylphenidate. However, this is not a realistic concern. Methylphenidate has been widely used to treat ADHD children since the 1960s. To date, neither clinical experience nor controlled studies have reported that children become physically dependent on the medication. For example, Weiss and Hechtman (1986) followed a group of children with ADHD into adulthood and did not find that those children treated with stimulants were at greater risk for later substance abuse than other children with ADHD. Methylphenidate is a very mild stimulant that does not have the mood-altering effects of the more powerful amphetamines that are abused.

Another concern, commonly expressed by mental health professionals, is the possibility that children may attribute their improved behavior and concentration to the medication alone, and so have less motivation to exert effort to learn. I have heard parents tell their children that Ritalin is a "smart pill" or a "good pill" that will make them "act better in school." This description of the medication may lead children to exert less than their best effort, relying on the pill to do their schoolwork.

Although this is a legitimate concern, it can be dealt with simply by informing parents and children of the effects of the drug: the medication helps the child pay attention, but it is still up to the child to learn the material. For example, Milich, Licht, Murphy, and Pelham (1989) found that children with ADHD tended to attribute their performance to their own effort or ability more than to their medication. Thus, although this is a commonly heard criticism (and one that clinical psychologists should anticipate and so try to minimize), it does not seem to be a significant problem in clinical practice.

A third criticism of methylphenidate is the claim that it may stunt a child's growth. It was suggested in the early 1970s that children treated with stimulants over a period of years are shorter and weigh less than matched controls (e.g., Safer, Allen, & Barr, 1972). This stimulated a flurry of investigations that ultimately allayed concerns about the drug. Methylphenidate is an amphetamine. As such, one of its effects is appetite suppression. If children take an appetite suppressor for years, it is possible that they may eat less than they otherwise would during that period and so fail to attain their full height and weight. This potential problem can be avoided by having children take the medication after meals and only when in school (and not in the evenings, on weekends, or during school vacations). Used in this way, children who take methylphenidate do not differ in height or weight from control children (Vincent, Varley, & Leger, 1990). In addition, it has been shown that, once stimulant medication is discontinued, children exhibit an accelerated (or rebound) growth rate that compensates for any slowed growth that occurred while taking stimulants (Klein & Mannuzza, 1988).

Imipramine-Treatment of Enuresis   Enuresis is a condition in which an individual (usually a child) experiences repeated involuntary releases of urine; in other words, the person wets himself. Enuresis can be treated effectively with several behavioral techniques (Doleys, 1989), including bell-and-pad conditioning, retention control training, and contingency management. However, enuresis can also be treated with medication.

The medication most commonly used to treat enuresis is *imipramine (Tofranil)*. Imipramine was first shown to be an effective treatment for enuresis by MacLean (1960) and was approved by the FDA for treating enuresis in 1973 (Gadow & Pomeroy, 1991). Imipramine is a tricyclic antidepressant, often used to treat depression in adults. However, it also has the effect of helping an enuretic individual remain dry. Research suggests that somewhat less than 50 percent of enuretic children become completely continent when treated with imipramine; however, many more children experience partial success with the medication (Gadow & Pomeroy, 1991).

The anti-enuretic effect of imipramine is not clearly understood. It is known that the success of imipramine in treating enuresis is not simply due to

its antidepressant effect (Green, 1991); other antidepressants are not as successful as imipramine in treating enuresis. Thus, its effectiveness is not because it alleviates "underlying" depression.

One of the problems with imipramine treatment of enuresis is that there is a high relapse rate once medication is stopped. For this reason, treatment of enuresis often combines imipramine, to produce short-term gains, with behavior therapy (e.g., bell-and-pad retention control training), to produce long-term benefits. In addition, authorities have recommended that behavioral treatments be used first, and only if they fail should medication be used (Gadow & Pomeroy, 1991).

Clomipramine-Treatment of OCD   Since the early 1980s, antidepressant medications have been known to be effective in treating obsessive-compulsive disorder (OCD) (Bernstein, 1988). Recent attention has focused most strongly on *clomipramine (Anafranil)*. Clomipramine is a tricyclic antidepressant. Although it has been used for decades to treat depression, it was approved by the FDA for use with OCD only recently.

As with many other medications, the reason why clomipramine is an effective treatment for OCD is not clear. Interestingly, its effectiveness in treating OCD does not seem to be a function of its antidepressant properties, because other tricyclics are somewhat less effective in treating OCD (Leonard, Swedo, Rapoport, Koby, Lenane, Cheslow, & Hamburger, 1989).

The success of clomipramine has led to increased interest in possible physiological etiologies of OCD. Recent research has shown that OCD runs in families (Swedo, Rapoport, Leonard, Lenane, & Cheslow, 1989) and that monozygotic twins have a higher concordance rate for OCD than dizygotic twins (Turner, Beidel, & Nathan, 1985). Thus, it appears that there is at least a moderate genetic influence on this condition. However, the specific nature of the underlying biological foundation for OCD is unknown.

Others   In addition to the medications introduced above, clinical psychologists should become familiar with several other commonly used psychiatric medications. For example, *phenytoin (Dilantin)* is an anticonvulsant medication that is commonly used to treat seizure disorders. *Haloperidol (Haldol)*, an antipsychotic, is effective in the treatment of Tourette's Syndrome. *Disulfiram (Antabuse)* is often used in the treatment of alcohol dependence disorders.

Clinical psychologists need to remain abreast of advances in psychiatric medication since so many of their clients will take them. Several good handbooks are available that summarize these medications for psychologists (e.g., Bezchlibnyk-Butler & Jeffries, 1991; Grabowski & VandenBos, 1992; Green, 1991).

Electroconvulsive Therapy

Another medical treatment for depression is *electroconvulsive therapy (ECT)*, or *electroshock therapy (EST)*. ECT was introduced to psychiatric practice in 1934 by Laszlo Von Meduna. He observed that schizophrenic patients experience fewer seizures than expected by chance and so he suggested that seizure activity may somehow counteract the symptoms of schizophrenia. Researchers investigated several methods of inducing seizures, including ECT and insulin injection.

This research eventually showed that ECT is not effective for schizophrenia. However, ECT was found to be effective in treating severe depression. Comparative outcome studies have reported that, for severe depression, ECT is about as effective as the major classes of antidepressant medications (Noll et al., 1985).

Historically, many explanations for the effectiveness of ECT have been proposed (Noll et al., 1985). For example, some suggested that ECT satisfies depressed patients' need for punishment so they no longer have to suffer the self-destructive symptoms of depression; because ECT produces memory loss, some suggested that ECT alleviates depression by leading depressives to forget why they are depressed. Of course, such explanations are now considered quaint, given the current understanding of the role of neurotransmitters in depression. Although the exact mechanism of ECT is unclear, it is believed that ECT works through a process similar to that of antidepressant medication; that is, ECT in-

creases the amount or activity of the neurotransmitters norepinephrine and serotonin (Noll et al., 1985).

Despite the fact that ECT is about as effective as antidepressant medication, medication remains the preferred treatment for most depressed patients. ECT has several major side effects: confusion, loss of memory, impairment of fine motor coordination, and so on. Although these side effects are temporary, they are often more serious than the side effects of antidepressant medications. In addition, if the patient receives a large number of sessions of ECT, these side effects may become permanent (Breggin, 1979).

Much of the criticism of ECT stems from its overuse in the 1940s and 1950s. It was not uncommon for patients at that time to receive scores of sessions of shock; in a lifetime, patients may have received hundreds of sessions. When patients receive so many sessions of ECT, the risk of permanent brain damage increases significantly. There were cases in the 1950s of patients who suffered permanent confusion and loss of memory due to excessive ECT. In the 1950s, it was also common for patients to receive shock without first being given muscle relaxants. In this case, the convulsions could be so severe that patients injured themselves (Breggin, 1979).

Current administration of ECT (no pun intended) lowers these risks. Muscle relaxants decrease the intensity of muscular convulsions. Electrical current is passed through only one brain hemisphere to reduce the severity of confusion and loss of memory. The number of sessions of ECT is carefully monitored so that patients receive only a small number of sessions during a single episode of depression, and a limited number of sessions throughout their lifetime. In these ways, the risks of ECT are much lower than they were several decades ago.

Still, despite the lowered risk of adverse side effects, ECT remains more controversial than antidepressant medications. For most depressed patients, antidepressant medications are preferred over ECT. Yet, there is a small group of depressed patients for whom ECT is the treatment of choice. Some severely depressed patients do not respond to antidepressant medications; failure to respond to antidepressants during prior episodes of depression is one indicator

for ECT. Some depressed patients respond in idiosyncratic ways to antidepressant medications. Just as
some people are allergic to penicillin and other antibiotics, some depressed patients exhibit extreme responses to antidepressants; for these patients, ECT is
safer than medication.

Finally, antidepressant medications usually take
some time (from 10 to 14 days) to begin to have a
therapeutic effect; this delay may be dangerous for
suicidal patients. If there is an immediate risk of suicide, some mental health professionals think that it is
more ethical to use ECT (which tends to have almost
immediate effects) than medication. Of course, one
could start the patient on antidepressants and place
the patient on a *suicide watch*, so that special precautions are taken to prevent suicide attempts. However,
such precautions are not foolproof. Every clinical
psychologist knows of cases where patients attempted or committed suicide while on a suicide
watch. For this reason, it may be safer for extremely
suicidal patients to be given ECT than antidepressant
medications.

Psychosurgery

Psychosurgery refers to surgical procedures, usually
involving the nervous system, to treat emotional and
behavioral disorders. Psychosurgery is used relatively rarely today. Because neural tissue does not re-
generate, psychosurgical procedures are irreversible
and so tend to be used as a last resort. However, in the
1930s and 1940s, psychosurgery was used quite frequently. Perhaps the most common (and infamous)
form of psychosurgery used historically was the lobotomy.

Antonio Moniz, a Portuguese psychiatrist, introduced the *prefrontal leucotomy (or lobotomy)* in
1935, thinking that it might be helpful in reducing
the frenetic and uncontrolled behavior of schizophrenic patients. The lobotomy involves the destruc-
tion of neural pathways that connect the frontal lobes
to other parts of the brain. The purpose of this procedure was to calm the patient's violent and uncontrollable behavior, severing the connections between the
brain's intellectual and emotional centers (Valenstein, 1973).

Following its introduction, thousands of mental
patients received lobotomies. For example, Freeman

and Watts (1942) reported that they alone had performed over 3,000 lobotomies. The technique was so
widely used and highly regarded that Moniz received the Nobel Prize for medicine in 1949.

By the 1950s, however, mental health professionals recognized problems with the lobotomy. Lobotomized patients became apathetic and listless;
some lobotomized patients became mute; many exhibited a significant decrease in intellectual and
other cognitive functioning. Also, in the mid-1950s,
antipsychotic medications were introduced that permitted schizophrenic patients to be treated with
drugs (a reversible procedure) rather than psychosurgery. In addition, the ethical principles of psychologists, which were being debated and developed
at that time, increasingly clarified the rights of patients to informed consent, the responsibility of therapists to be accountable for their actions, and the
guideline that therapists work in the best interests of
the patient. Because lobotomies carry so many adverse side effects, do not actually "cure" the patient's
mental disorder, and are irreversible, the field decreased its acceptance and performance of lobotomies. The number of lobotomies was drastically reduced by the late-1950s (Valenstein, 1973).

Today, relatively few psychosurgical procedures are performed in this country. Valenstein
(1973) quoted a President of the International Society of Psychosurgery as indicating that only about
600 psychosurgeries are performed annually. When
psychosurgery is performed today, it tends to be for
severe conditions that are debilitating and have not
responded to other treatments (e.g., chronic pain,
OCD, epilepsy). Of course, contemporary psychosurgery is more selective and accurate than in the
past, leading to less neural tissue damage and fewer
adverse side effects (Wilson et al., 1992).

PHYSIOLOGICALLY ORIENTED TREATMENTS

In addition to the medical treatments prescribed by
psychiatrists, mental health professionals also use a
variety of physiologically oriented forms of psychotherapy. Many of these treatments reduce physiological arousal and so are used to alleviate physical conditions associated with stress. This section of the
chapter presents a brief introduction to the role of

stress in the onset of physiological disorders and de-scribes several treatments designed to lower physio-logical stress.

Introduction to Stress-Related Disorders

Stress has become recognized by both the medical and mental health professions as a major factor in producing, maintaining, and exacerbating physio-logical disorders. Several factors contributed to clin-ical psychologists becoming increasingly involved in the treatment of stress-related disorders. First, the-oretical models, such as Selye's General Adaptation Syndrome, were developed to provide a way for ex-plaining the relation between psychological stress and physiological disorders. Second, research since the 1960s consistently demonstrated an association between stress and both physiological and psycho-logical problems. Third, following the rise of the community mental health movement in the early-1960s, clinical psychologists became increasingly interested in the prevention of disorders; because stress is associated with (and may cause) many health problems, it was natural for clinical psychologists to develop stress-management techniques to limit the development of such conditions.

General Adaptation Syndrome   One reason for the development of psychological treatments to combat physiological stress was the development of theoretical models that explain the relation between stress and illness. Perhaps the most influential of these models is that of Hans Selye.

Selye introduced his concept of the *General Ad-aptation Syndrome (GAS)* in 1936. This syndrome is a physiological reaction to stress, consisting of three stages: (1) alarm and mobilization; (2) resistance; and (3) exhaustion (Selye, 1956).

In the alarm and mobilization stage, an organism responds to a stressor with a generalized increase in arousal and activity. If this is not sufficient to cope (say, if the stressor is especially intense or pro-longed, or if additional stressors are introduced), then the organism enters the second stage.

In the resistance stage, the organism slows down physiological activity, attempting to cope as effi-ciently as possible. In this way, resources are con-served and the organism may be able to withstand the stressor for a longer period of time.

If this is not sufficient, then the organism enters the third stage. In the exhaustion stage, resources be-come depleted, organ systems become overbur-dened, and physical damage occurs. Exhibit 12.4 provides several illustrations of Selye's GAS.

Selye's GAS provides a useful way of conceptu-alizing how both physical and psychological stres-sors may adversely affect physical health. The GAS suggests that some tissue damage will occur after one's physical resources have become overburdened or depleted. The model does not predict what kind of physical problem will result, only that some damage will eventually occur. The specific physical problem that develops depends on the person's physical his-tory (i.e., constitutional vulnerabilities, prior medi-cal history). One person may be most vulnerable, for genetic or other reasons, in the gastrointestinal sys-tem whereas another person may suffer damage to the respiratory or cardiovascular system.

A physical disorder thought to be caused, at least in part, by psychological factors is called *psycho-physiological* or *psychosomatic*. These disorders in-clude migraine and tension headaches, some forms of ulcer and hypertension, colitis, and so on. These are organic disorders that, in some cases, are entirely due to physical factors. In other cases, however, psy-chological factors such as stress play a significant role, either in initiating or exacerbating the disorder. When psychological factors play a significant role, the disorder is considered psychophysiological.

In DSM-IV (American Psychiatric Association, 1994), these disorders are diagnosed in the following way. On Axis I, the client receives the label, *Psycho-logical Factor Affecting a Medical Condition*; the client's physical problem is then identified on Axis III. This label for psychophysiological disorders was introduced by DSM-III (American Psychiatric As-sociation, 1980). It helps avoid the common miscon-ception that psychophysiological (or psychoso-matic) conditions are imaginary.

EXHIBIT 12.4   Illustrations of Selye's General Adaptation Syndrome

1. Consider a person exposed to Arctic cold. Initially, the person experiences increased arousal and activity—flapping arms, stamping feet, shivering. If the intense cold continues, the person experiences a lowered metabolic rate that conserves bodily resources. If the cold continues, the person eventually experiences tissue damage, such as frostbite.

2. Seligman (1968) exposed dogs to inescapable shock. At first, the dogs bit the cage, jumped, and showed other signs of arousal. However, after learning that they were helpless, they gave up trying to escape and simply lay on the floor while being shocked. In this study, Seligman did not continue shocking the dogs to the point that physical damage occurred. However, if he had, the dogs may have developed burns or other tissue damage.

3. Suppose you are given too many jobs at work to complete in a short time. Initially, you experience an increase in arousal; pulse, blood pressure, and respiration increase as you try to get everything done. However, if this is not successful, you are then likely to experience a lowering of arousal. You may rank order the tasks and only work on the most important; you may delegate the assignments to your colleagues; you may calm down by telling yourself that no one could finish all this work. However, if the strain continues for a long time, you may eventually develop a stress-related disorder, such as a headache or upset stomach.

Stress and Illness   Perhaps the most well-known demonstrations of the association between stress and illness are the life stress research of Holmes and Rahe (1967) and the personality type A research of Friedman and Rosenman (1974). Holmes and Rahe determined the severity of a set of life changes (including both positive and negative changes, and both mild and severe events). They then examined the relation between health problems and stress (defined in terms of life change units, which consider both the number and severity of life changes). They observed a modest but significant correlation between stress and illness; subjects with the greatest number of life changes had the most (and most severe) health problems.

Following the initial research by Holmes and Rahe, literally hundreds of studies have examined the relation between stress and illness. This research has generally shown that people who experience more stress in fact experience more health problems.

Life stress research has also been refined in numerous ways since the early work of Holmes and Rahe. For example, researchers have developed measures of life stressors that are commonly experienced in specific populations, such as children and adolescents (Johnson, 1986), and measures of daily hassles rather than major life changes (Kanner, Coyne, Schaefer, & Lazarus, 1981). Researchers have also investigated the variables that moderate the influence of life stress, such as social support (Sarason, Sarason, Potter, & Antoni, 1985), coping skills (Lazarus, & Folkman, 1984), and psychological *hardiness* or *resiliency* (Kobasa, Maddi, & Kahn, 1982).

However, life stress research is correlational and so does not prove that stress causes illness. There are alternative possible explanations of the relationship: perhaps developing health problems lead one to experience more life changes; perhaps those who experience more stress drink more alcohol and smoke more cigarettes, and these factors (rather than stress) cause health problems; perhaps unknown third variables (such as genetic or environmental factors) lead people to experience increases in both stress and health problems. For these reasons, life stress research does not prove that stress causes illness.

Clinical psychologists have also investigated the relation between personality and illness. Hundreds of studies have examined the relation between stress disorders and *personality type A*. Type A individuals are competitive, pursue high goals, become involved in many activities, and set strict schedules; they are popularly referred to as "workaholics." On the other hand, individuals with the *type B personality* are more "laid back;" they are less competitive, achievement-oriented, and "driven" than type A individuals (Friedman & Rosenman, 1974).

Early studies in this area tended to find that type A persons exhibit greater physiological reactivity to stress (e.g., Glass et al., 1980; MacDougall, Dembroski, & Krantz, 1981) and experience more cardiovascular and other stress-related disorders than type B individuals (e.g., Rosenman, Brand, Jenkins, Friedman, Straus, & Wurm, 1975).

However, this research, like the life stress research, is correlational, and so does not prove that personality type A causes health problems. Other factors, such as increased smoking and drinking, poorer diet, and reduced exercise may account for at least some of the increased health risk of type A persons. As was the case with life stress research, many factors, including age, sex, reaction to the diagnosis of a disorder, and social support, may moderate the degree to which type A persons develop stress-related disorders.

In addition, research from the 1980s seriously questioned previous research results. For example, Ragland and Brand (1988) examined the long-term outcome of type A and B men who already had heart attacks and found that type As are actually at lower risk for dying than type Bs. Dimsdale (1988) examined the recent research on the relation between coronary heart disease and type A personality and concluded that the concept of type A is actually quite heterogeneous and that the results are mixed.

Treatment of
Stress-Related Disorders

Because the research on life stress and personality type A suggested that these psychological variables are related to health problems, psychologists became very interested in applying psychological interventions in the treatment of health problems. The rise of the community mental health movement in the 1960s also contributed to clinical psychology's interest in the treatment of stress-related problems. One of the emphases of the community psychology movement is prevention. Because stress was perceived as one of the possible causes of physical and psychological problems, and because psychological techniques could be employed in the control of stress, it was natural for clinical psychologists to become involved in stress management.

Biofeedback, relaxation training, and other stress management techniques became widely used by clinical psychologists in the 1960s and 1970s. These techniques, discussed in more detail below, also influenced the rise of the clinical specialty of behavioral medicine. This specialty will be examined in detail later in the chapter.

Biofeedback   Biofeedback was introduced in the 1960s and became a popular form of treatment for stress-related disorders in the 1970s. *Biofeedback* involves the use of a machine that monitors and provides feedback to the client about a physiological state. The client uses this feedback in efforts to voluntarily produce a desired physiological state.

Prior to the 1960s, it was thought that physiological states controlled by the autonomic nervous system (such as the increases in pulse and blood pressure that accompany stress) could not be controlled voluntarily (Kimble, 1961). Hence, such states could only be conditioned classically and not instrumentally. However, by the mid- to late-1960s, research began to suggest that autonomically controlled responses could be influenced by reinforcement (Reed, Katkin, & Goldband, 1986). Thus, clinical investigators began to examine the possible therapeutic uses of such training in the treatment of stress-related disorders.

Biofeedback is usually used to monitor physical states associated with physiological arousal. For example, it is common for biofeedback devices to monitor muscle tension, respiratory rate, pulse rate, blood pressure, and so on.

Biofeedback is used to treat stress-related disorders in the following way. Suppose a client has a stress-related disorder such as tension headaches.

Tension headaches are thought to result from prolonged states of high muscle tension. Some people, when stressed, frown in concentration or hold their heads at an angle, tensing their neck muscles. This prolonged muscle tension ultimately results in the headache. Biofeedback treatment of tension headaches uses a machine to monitor and provide feedback regarding tension in the muscles across the forehead or in the neck. Feedback can be provided by a digital display or in the form of a tone (higher tension is indicated by a higher pitch) or a light (higher tension is indicated by a red light, lower tension by a blue light). The client practices with the machine, trying to produce and maintain feedback indicating the desired state of relaxation. Initially, the client may use trial-and-error to try to control the feedback. By breathing more slowly, closing one's eyes, or relaxing the arm muscles, the client may lower the muscle tension in the neck and head, perhaps even without being aware of what was successful in lowering tension. Later, by discussing these efforts with the therapist, the client may come to understand the techniques used to produce relaxation. Through biofeedback training, the individual learns to recognize muscle tension and to produce voluntarily a state of relaxation.

Biofeedback can be used to treat a variety of problems. Reed and colleagues (1986) indicated that biofeedback has primarily been used to treat three classes of conditions: anxiety disorders (e.g., generalized anxiety), cardiovascular disorders (e.g., migraine headache, hypertension), and neuromuscular disorders (e.g., tension headache). However, biofeedback has also been used to treat conditions that have clear physical foundations but are exacerbated by psychological stress. For example, biofeedback has been used to treat asthma and epilepsy. Of course, many times these disorders are not related to stress; however, if the condition is exacerbated by stress, then biofeedback may be helpful in lowering the frequency and severity of the episodes.

Reed and colleagues (1986) noted that research prior to 1980 tended to provide only modest scientific support for biofeedback. However, by 1986, Reed and colleagues concluded that the research had

shown biofeedback to be an effective alternative for the treatment of stress-related disorders.

Of course, biofeedback, like other treatments, must be used with a recognition of its limitations. Reed and colleagues (1986) observed that no aspect of biofeedback training is unique to biofeedback—other relaxation procedures provide the same benefits. Because biofeedback requires special equipment, biofeedback training may be more costly than other relaxation training procedures. Because biofeedback training requires this special equipment, gains made during biofeedback training may not generalize to other settings; thus, therapists must include the generalization of therapeutic gains as a goal from the start of therapy. Individual differences (perhaps related to expectations about the efficacy of biofeedback) may also affect treatment success (Reed et al., 1986).

Another potential problem concerns the general skepticism that many individuals—including some health professionals—have about biofeedback. Some skepticism may be due to the exaggerated and sensationalistic claims made about biofeedback in the 1970s. For example, I have seen popular books and local advertisements claim that biofeedback can increase one's creativity, enhance one's ESP, make one a better lover, boost one's spirituality, increase one's confidence, and so on. Alleviating a painful condition through biofeedback training certainly enables one to work more creatively and confidently. However, sensationalistic claims about the efficacy of biofeedback are not based on such prosaic explanations. Consumers should be wary of such exaggerated claims regarding biofeedback, and clinical psychologists should be aware that some clients (and health professionals) will have unrealistic expectations about biofeedback because of such claims.

Progressive Muscle Relaxation Another relaxation technique widely used to treat stress-related disorders is *progressive muscle relaxation*. This was introduced in 1938 by Jacobson, a physiologist, and is sometimes referred to simply as Jacobsonian relaxation. This technique involves training the client to relax the major muscles in the body. As in biofeedback, the client learns both to recognize the physiological sensations of tension and then to produce voluntarily the state of relaxation.

Muscle relaxation training begins by having the client sit or lie in a relaxed position. Anything that may interfere with relaxation (such as heavy jewelry or tight shirt collars) is removed or loosened. The client then lies in a relaxed state, listening to and following the directions of the therapist.

The therapist has the client tense one muscle group (such as the dominant hand and forearm) for about 10 seconds; the muscles in this group are then relaxed for about 30 seconds. The client then repeats this sequence, first tensing the muscles for about 10 seconds and then relaxing them for about 45 seconds. During this period, the therapist instructs the client to focus on and to notice the differences between the sensations of muscle tension and relaxation. The therapist uses a slow monotonic delivery so as not to disrupt the client's relaxation. After completing the tense-relax-tense-relax sequence with the first muscle group, the client proceeds to the next, while maintaining the relaxation in the first group.

At the start of progressive muscle relaxation training, the client's body is divided into 16 major muscle groups. The client systematically tenses and relaxes each muscle group in turn. By the end of the therapy session, the client should be in a state of deep relaxation. The client practices this technique at home, twice a day. After several weeks, the client becomes sufficiently proficient at relaxation that several muscle groups can be combined. Eventually, the client can relax the entire body at will. Exhibit 12.5 illustrates the 16 muscle groups that are tensed and relaxed, first in isolation and then later in combination (Bernstein & Borkovec, 1973).

Progressive muscle relaxation training, like biofeedback, has two major goals. First, it teaches the client to recognize the state of muscle tension. Second, it teaches the client to relax voluntarily. Now, when the client experiences muscle tension, the client not only recognizes it but can take active steps to counteract it. For example, a person who becomes tense at work can recognize the symptoms of muscle tension and take several minutes to relax, thereby lowering the risk of developing a tension headache or another stress-related problem.

Research on progressive muscle relaxation training has consistently shown that it is an effective method of managing stress. For example, in Jacobson's (1938) original description of the technique, he reported that 21 of 23 patients with anxiety disorders improved following progressive relaxation training. Wolpe (1954) incorporated relaxation training in the systematic desensitization of phobias. Recent research has also supported the efficacy of Jacobsonian relaxation. Research reviews have reported that progressive relaxation training is helpful in treating generalized anxiety (Emmelkamp, 1986), pain (Hollon & Beck, 1986), and other stress-related disorders (Pomerlau & Rodin, 1986).

Although muscle relaxation is simple and effective, some clients may have difficulty mastering the procedure. In these cases, the therapist needs to identify the source of the difficulty and then overcome or bypass the problem. For example, some clients have a physical disability that prevents them from tensing a particular muscle group; other clients may experience painful cramping when tensing certain muscles. In such cases, the therapist may skip these muscle groups or modify the procedure so that only partial tension-relaxation is achieved in these groups.

Another potential difficulty is that some clients become uncomfortable if a therapist directs them to lie down and loosen restrictive clothing. A therapist should be sensitive to such discomfort and establish a trusting relationship before beginning training. Client fears can be allayed by information about the method or by providing safeguards for especially reluctant clients (e.g., keeping the office door propped open; leaving lights on).

Some personality type A clients may have trouble relaxing. Because they try to do well at everything, they exert effort to succeed at therapy. This may lead to their becoming caught in a trap of *working* at relaxation—by trying too hard to relax, they cannot relax. Here, the therapist may incorporate cognitive relaxation techniques (e.g., imagery, distraction) to help take the client's mind off the goal of succeeding at relaxation.

Other Relaxation Techniques   Biofeedback and progressive muscle relaxation are perhaps the most thoroughly studied and well-supported relaxation

EXHIBIT 12.5   Progressive Muscle Relaxation Training: Muscle Groups and Training Sequence

Muscles					Session	Focus
1	1	1	Dominant hand, forearm		1–3	16 Groups T/R
		2	Dominant biceps		4–5	7 Groups T/R
	2	3	Nondominant hand, forearm		6–7	4 Groups T/R
		4	Nondominant biceps		8	4 Groups R
2	3	5	Forehead		9	4 Groups R
		6	Upper cheeks, nose		10	Relax via counting
		7	Lower cheeks, jaw			
	4	8	Neck, throat			
3	5	9	Chest, shoulders, upper back			
		10	Abdominal or stomach region			
4	6	11	Dominant thigh			
		12	Dominant calf			
		13	Dominant foot			
	7	14	Nondominant thigh			
		15	Nondominant calf			
		16	Nondominant foot			

Note: T/R = Tense/relax sequence. R = Relax only. Rc = Relax as the therapist counts from 1 to 10.
Source: Adapted from Bernstein & Borkovec (1973).

methods. However, other relaxation methods can be used as well. Cognitive and cognitive–behavioral techniques, such as self-instruction, stress inoculation, imagery, and distraction, described in Chapter 11, are often used to manage stress. Alternatives to biofeedback and muscle relaxation that are primarily directed toward managing the physiological symptoms of stress include breathing exercises and meditation.

Relaxation techniques often incorporate breathing exercises. Breathing exercises are easily added to other relaxation techniques, such as progressive muscle relaxation. However, breathing exercises can also be used independently. Clients are instructed to breathe deeply, hold their breath, and then exhale slowly. As this is repeated, clients gradually hold their breaths for longer periods. Such *deep or slow breathing* produces physiological relaxation, including lowered heart rate, lowered blood pressure, and reduced muscle tension.

One potential problem with breathing exercises is hyperventilation, due to breathing deeply too rapidly. However, this is easily avoided. The therapist should initially monitor the client's rate of breathing and watch for the physical symptoms of hyperventilation (e.g., dizziness, light-headedness, increased heart rate). Before the client is sent home to practice the breathing exercise, the therapist should observe the client practicing the breathing exercise. If the client breathes too rapidly, the therapist should intervene and provide explicit instructions for slowing one's breathing. In addition, the therapist should inform the client about the possibility of hyperventilation and provide the client with the knowledge to both recognize and counter hyperventilation should it occur.

Perhaps the most well-known application of breathing exercises is *Lamaze training*. Often called *natural childbirth classes*, Lamaze training teaches pregnant women to cope with the early symptoms of labor through deep breathing. As labor intensifies, women use rapid shallow breathing to manage the increasing pain and accompanying arousal. Lamaze training employs several psychological techniques in addition to breathing (e.g., distraction, focusing on objects outside oneself, modifying the expectancies that one will experience pain). Still, deep breathing is an important component of Lamaze.

Meditation is another popular relaxation technique. As was noted in Chapter 10, some meditation exercises are based on Eastern philosophical or religious systems (e.g., transcendental meditation or TM). However, meditation can be analyzed in purely physiological and psychological terms.

In meditation, the subject sits in a relaxed position. Lights are lowered and other possible distractions are removed. The subject then closes her eyes, breathes deeply, and concentrates on a repetitive stimulus (the *mantra* in TM) or keeps her mind as "blank" as possible. Such conditions produce physiological relaxation. For example, research has shown that meditators experience about as deep a state of physiological relaxation as do subjects who are resting (Holmes, 1984).

I have worked with clients whose religious beliefs are incompatible with the religious or philosophical underpinnings of TM and other Eastern approaches to meditation. However, in these cases, I have presented the steps of meditation as purely physical exercises that produce physiological relaxation. One does not have to accept the philosophical assumptions of TM to meditate successfully.

Another technique that can be used to produce relaxation is *hypnosis*. Among the several competing psychological theories of hypnosis is the view that it is a method of enhancing both relaxation and suggestibility (Barber, 1969). At the start of the hypnotic induction, clients are instructed to breathe deeply and slowly, to free their minds of distractions, and to concentrate only on the words of the hypnotist. As subjects follow these instructions, they experience physiological relaxation. Such hypnotically induced relaxation may be helpful for clients who are experiencing anxiety or stress-related disorders.

Of course, hypnosis involves more than simple relaxation. Hypnosis uses methods to increase the client's compliance with suggestions. Heightened suggestibility may help clients comply with a treatment regimen for a specific problem (such as a stimulus control program for weight loss). However, the heightened suggestibility of hypnosis is not relevant to the discussion of relaxation exercises and so will not be addressed further here.

BEHAVIORAL MEDICINE

There is a relatively new specialty area within clinical psychology that focuses on patients who have physiological problems: behavioral medicine. *Behavioral medicine* is the application of psychological principles in the treatment of patients with medical conditions.

This specialty arose in the late-1960s and early-1970s. Blanchard (1982) suggested that two trends at this time led to the development of behavioral medicine. First, both medical and mental health professionals recognized that psychological factors, such as stress, contributed significantly to medical health problems. Selye's general adaptation syndrome, the life stress research of Holmes and Rahe, and the personality type A research by Friedman all suggested that stress plays an important role in the development of health problems.

Second, psychologists had developed a variety of treatments, especially behavioral techniques, that were effective in changing behavior. Because many physical health problems were thought to be associated with stress and because psychologists were now able to help clients modify stress-related behaviors, psychologists began to work alongside physicians in treating physical disorders.

Although behavioral medicine appeared only recently, it has grown into a major and significant specialty within clinical psychology. Many clinical psychologists work in medical settings, not simply to treat psychiatric patients, but to assist in the treatment of medical patients. Like other major clinical specialties, professional organizations and journals devoted to behavioral medicine have been founded.

Examples of behavioral medicine interventions will be presented in the following section. Throughout this discussion, it should be stressed that clinical psychologists do *not* provide medical treatment for patients. This would be both unethical and illegal, because psychologists are not trained to practice medicine. In behavioral medicine, clinical psychologists provide psychological interventions to supplement the medical treatment of patients and to address psychological problems that arise during the course of a medical condition. Still, it should be noted that, for some physical conditions, research has shown that psychological interventions may actually be more effective than traditional medical treatments (Blanchard, 1992a).

Behavioral Medicine Programs

Spiegler and Guevremont (1993) suggested that clinical psychologists provide four types of services in behavioral medicine: (1) treatment; (2) increasing adherence to medical treatments; (3) helping patients cope with treatment; and (4) prevention. Examples of each are presented below.

There are many applications of psychological techniques to assist in the treatment of physiological conditions. Relaxation techniques, such as biofeedback, are often used by psychologists to treat physical symptoms related to stress, including hypertension, tachycardia, migraine and tension headache, and Raynaud's syndrome (Reed et al., 1986).

Another interesting and important application of psychological principles in the treatment of medical conditions is pain control. Turk adapted Meichenbaum's stress inoculation model to treat pain (Turk & Genest, 1979; Turk, Meichenbaum, & Genest, 1983). Patients are trained to use self-instruction to anticipate pain, to cope with the physiological and psychological arousal that occurs when in pain, and to monitor their performance and reinforce themselves for successful management of pain. In addition, patients learn other cognitive techniques, such as distraction, fantasy, and relabeling, to help them cope with pain. These cognitive–behavioral techniques have become widely used by psychologists who treat patients experiencing chronic pain (Keefe, Dunsmore, & Burnett, 1992; Phillips, 1988).

A second application of behavioral medicine is to increase patient compliance with a medical regimen. One of the most significant examples of this is the treatment of diabetes. Clinical psychologists have recognized that diabetes has a significant behavioral component (Cox & Gonder-Frederick, 1992). Diabetic patients should closely monitor diet and exercise and must receive daily blood glucose tests and insulin injections. Because of the complexity and demands of treatment, diabetic patients—especially children and adolescents—often have difficulty complying with this regimen.

Clinical psychologists have identified several factors that are related to decreased compliance with the diabetic regimen, including anxiety/depression, deficient coping skills, low self-efficacy, lack of family support, and poor patient–physician relationship (Cox & Gonder-Frederick, 1992). Psychologists have targeted these factors for change, usually with cognitive–behavioral techniques, in order to increase compliance. For example, Lowe and Lutzker (1979) increased a diabetic child's compliance with treatment using the operant conditioning techniques of cueing and reinforcement.

A third application of behavioral medicine is to help clients cope with treatment. This is especially helpful when treatment is painful or frightening. For example, many patients have fears of surgery, hospitalization, dental procedures, chemotherapy, and other medical interventions (Diener & Redd, 1987). Clinical psychologists have treated such patients by lowering the perceived threat of these procedures. Education, modeling of coping skills, relaxation training, pain control, and other cognitive–behavioral techniques are commonly used (Diener & Redd, 1987). For example, Ludwick-Rosenthal and

Neufeld (1993) demonstrated that cardiac-catheterization patients experience less anxiety during this procedure and that this procedure requires less time when they are presented with information that matches their pretreatment desire for information.

The fourth application of behavioral medicine is prevention. Psychologists have become active in training people to engage in healthy behaviors to decrease risk for future health problems. For example, psychologists have provided programs designed to help individuals lose weight (Brownell & Wadden, 1992), stop smoking (Lichtenstein & Glasgow, 1992), and exercise regularly (Dubbert, 1992). In addition, many programs have attempted to educate individuals regarding the risks of drugs and unprotected sexual activity, so as to lower the incidence of substance abuse and AIDS (e.g., Kelly & Murphy, 1992).

Although it is difficult to assess the degree to which such programs in fact prevent the development of future medical problems, evaluations typically find that they are effective in altering the targeted health-related behaviors (Blanchard, 1992b). This application of psychological treatments to improve the physical health of clients is sometimes called *health psychology*.

In addition to these applications of behavioral medicine, clinical psychologists also treat patients who have difficulty coping with their medical condition. For example, patients diagnosed with cancer commonly experience significant emotional, cognitive, and behavioral distress. Although some types of cancer now have extremely high treatment success rates, many cancer patients fear that they have a possibly life-threatening condition; other cancer patients who receive extensive radiation therapy or chemotherapy must cope with aversive side effects of treatment, such as hair loss, nausea, and fatigue.

Andersen (1992) discussed how psychologists can contribute to the treatment of cancer patients. Psychological treatment can help cancer patients reduce their emotional distress, increase their coping skills, and improve their general "adjustment" to their condition, all of which enhance their "quality of life" (Andersen, 1992).

APPLIED ISSUES

Two applied issues regarding physiological treatments will be discussed in this section of the chapter. The first concerns whether psychologists should be permitted to prescribe medications for psychological or behavioral disorders. The second concerns the social consequences of the rise of psychiatric medications, especially with respect to the revolving door syndrome.

Psychologists and Prescription Privileges

Since the mid-1980s, some clinical psychologists have been trying to obtain the privilege to prescribe medications (DeLeon, Fox, & Graham, 1991). Many clinical psychologists have extensive experience with psychiatric medications. They work in treatment teams alongside psychiatrists who prescribe medication. Many psychologists recognize those clients who may benefit from drugs and so direct them to a psychiatrist for a medication referral. In my own experience, I have referred many children with ADHD and adults with depression, bipolar disorder, and schizophrenia to psychiatrists. Quite often, the medication prescribed by the psychiatrist matched my informed but nonmedical opinion as to what type of medication the patient may require.

Health professionals other than physicians currently prescribe drugs in many states. For example, DeLeon and associates (1991) noted that prescription privileges are enjoyed by optometrists in all 50 states and by nurse practitioners in 28 states. For this reason, some clinical psychologists have argued that it is appropriate for states to consider granting prescription privileges to psychologists.

Prescription privileges for psychologists may carry economic and social benefits. It is more cost-effective for patients whose mental disorders require medication to be treated by only a single doctoral-level professional. Because psychologists would not be so dependent on psychiatrists, the two professions could then provide services to a larger segment of the community.

It should quickly be noted that not everyone agrees on this issue. Physicians have strongly resisted efforts by other professions to obtain prescription privileges (DeLeon et al., 1991). Even clinical psychologists have opposed this movement, because prescription privileges might deter them from pursuing theoretical developments and social concerns that have traditionally distinguished psychology from psychiatry (May & Belsky, 1992).

The arguments against psychologists receiving prescription privileges are not limited to economic and social factors. A strong case can be made against psychologists prescribing medication on the basis of their professional training (Kingsbury, 1992a, 1992b). The effects of many psychiatric drugs, including antidepressants, anti-anxiety agents, and antipsychotics, are not limited to a circumscribed part of the body or to a single set of symptoms. These medications influence systems throughout the body; they also affect mood, alertness and other states that, in turn, affect a wide range of behaviors. In these ways, psychiatric medications may differ from the kinds of drugs commonly prescribed by optometrists or nurse practitioners. For this reason, the use of psychiatric medications requires more knowledge of human physiology and more extensive knowledge of possible drug interactions than is the case for medications such as antibiotics or local anasthetics.

Although clinical psychologists may receive some formal training in psychopharmacology and receive extensive experience with psychiatric medications through their clinical practice, they do not attend medical school. Psychologists have not received the formal training in physiology, pharmacology, neuroanatomy, and internal medicine that all medical students receive. Thus, despite their "hands-on" training and best intentions, psychologists may simply not be capable of recognizing the medical conditions that mimic psychological disorders and the physical symptoms that contraindicate the use of medications.

Because of the strength of the medical lobby and because of the lack of consensus on this issue among clinical psychologists, I do not think that it is likely that psychologists will obtain prescription privileges, as independent practitioners who are not directly under the supervision of psychiatrists, in the near future. Still, it will be interesting to see how this debate develops in the next decade.

Social Consequences of the Rise of Psychiatric Drugs

A second issue regarding the practical consequences of physiological treatments of mental disorders concerns the social consequences of the use of psychiatric medications. The introduction of psychiatric medications had a profound impact on the delivery of mental health services. Prior to the 1950s, the mental health profession did not have effective treatments for the most severe mental disorders, such as schizophrenia, bipolar disorder, and psychotic depression. The introduction of antipsychotics, antidepressants, and lithium revolutionized the treatment of patients with these conditions. Whereas they previously had to be hospitalized for extended periods of time, they could now be treated successfully and released from the hospital within a matter of weeks to months.

Perhaps the most profound change resulting from the introduction of medication occurred in the treatment of schizophrenia. In 1955, there were about 560,000 hospitalized mental patients in this country; mental patients occupied about one-half of the hospital beds in the entire country (Rosenhan & Seligman, 1989). Of these mental patients, a large proportion were diagnosed as schizophrenic.

Schizophrenia is so severe that it usually requires hospitalization. Schizophrenia also has a persistent course so that, in the absence of treatment, patients may remain unable to care for themselves for extended periods of time. Because there was no effective treatment for schizophrenia prior to the 1950s, schizophrenic patients at the time often remained hospitalized for lengthy periods—for years if not the rest of their lives.

Following the introduction of chlorpromazine, schizophrenic patients could for the first time be treated successfully and released from inpatient settings. From 1954 to 1971, the number of hospitalized mental patients decreased to about 300,000 (Rosenhan & Seligman, 1989); by 1985, the number of patients in inpatient state hospitals had decreased to fewer than 125,000 (Comer, 1992).

Although the discovery of antipsychotics revolutionized the treatment of schizophrenia, it did not cure schizophrenia. Antipsychotics control the symptoms of schizophrenia but do not provide a permanent solution to the patient's biological disorder. Schizophrenic patients must continue to take these medications, even when not currently psychotic, to prevent future episodes.

A problem here is that a patient may stop taking the medication and become actively psychotic once again. For example, one early study on the long-term outcome of schizophrenic patients who received antipsychotics showed that, over a 2-year period, about 45 percent experienced relapses and had to be rehospitalized (Hogarty, Goldberg, Schooler, Ulrich, & the Collaborative Study Group, 1974). The last several decades have witnessed the rise of the *revolving door syndrome*, wherein patients hospitalized for severe conditions are discharged for periods up to several months until their next psychotic episode. The revolving door of mental disorders continues to be major problem today.

Several factors contributed to the revolving door problem. First, following the introduction of psychiatric medications in the 1950s, the emphasis in mental health service delivery shifted from an inpatient to an outpatient model. Unfortunately, when formerly psychotic patients were released from the hospitals, the mental health field simply did not yet have the facilities or expertise to provide the services essential to the aftercare of these patients.

Second, economic factors have also contributed to the revolving door syndrome. For example, May (1968) conducted an influential study of the relative efficacies of five treatments for schizophrenia: antipsychotic medication, psychodynamic psychotherapy, medication plus psychotherapy, ECT, and milieu therapy (that is, exposure to a therapeutic hospital environment). Outcome was assessed using nursing staff evaluations, therapist evaluations, and cost and length of hospitalization. May found that the best outcome was obtained in the two groups that received antipsychotic medications. In addition, psychotherapy alone (along with milieu therapy) yielded less successful outcome than other treatments. In fact, medication plus psychotherapy was not superior to medication alone. Because the average cost of treatment was far greater for psychotherapy than medication, May concluded that the most cost-effective treatment for schizophrenia was medication alone.

This conclusion was evidently shared by many practitioners, since psychiatric hospitals have frequently treated schizophrenia with medication alone, without emphasizing psychotherapy. This is unfortunate because research and practice have now shown that psychotherapy can be effectively combined with medication in the treatment of schizophrenia. For example, following release from the hospital, a higher probability of relapse has been found to be associated with families that express higher levels of emotion (Vaughn & Leff, 1976). This suggests that family interventions designed to lower familial stress and to alter the family's communication of emotion may be helpful in reducing relapse rates (Falloon et al., 1985). Such family interventions can also include education about the genetics of schizophrenia (to reduce the family's blaming itself) and the importance of taking medication as prescribed (Sarason & Sarason, 1993). Although such forms of psychotherapy are quite different from traditional psychodynamic therapy, they may be exactly what must be combined with antipsychotic medication in order to slow the psychiatric hospital's revolving door.

SCIENTIFIC ISSUES

As with other forms of therapy, the most pressing scientific issue concerning physiological treatment is its effectiveness. Because the success of medications and other physiological treatments was noted as these treatments were introduced, this section will only present a brief overview of the effectiveness of physiological treatments.

Psychiatric medications, like all medications and other medical treatments, must meet Food and Drug Administration (FDA) standards. The FDA was established in 1906 with the enactment of the Pure Food and Drug Act under President Theodore Roosevelt. Although this law initially emphasized consumer-related issues, such as adulteration or misbranding of drugs (Gibson, 1976), the FDA gradually increased its control over the evaluation of medications. In 1938, the Food, Drug, and Cosmetic Act gave the FDA the authority to require proof of the efficacy of marketed drugs (Gibson, 1976). In addition, this law gave the FDA the authority to designate experts to study the safety of experimental drugs (Mintz, 1967).

This means that a new drug must be evaluated in experimental research before it is approved for general use as a medical treatment. Such research usually involves a double-blind design, in which the new medication is compared with a placebo and/or a drug already used to treat the condition. Through repeated experiments, the short- and long-term effectiveness of the experimental drug can be compared with that of no treatment, placebo treatment, and the standard treatments already used. Similarly, experimental studies with animals are conducted to test the safety of the drug, both in isolation and in combination with other commonly used medications. Following such experimental demonstrations that the new medication is both safe and effective, the FDA approves the drug for use by physicians.

The FDA laws ensure that the psychiatric medications in general use have met scientific standards for being both safe and effective. However, it should quickly be noted that the Food and Drug Laws do not guarantee that the medications are completely safe. There are many examples of drugs (e.g., Thalidomide) that received FDA approval but were later found to be harmful. After all, medications may have side effects that are not discovered until they have been used for extended periods. One example of this with psychiatric medications is the problem of tardive dyskinesia resulting from long-term use of antipsychotics.

Also, the FDA laws do not address whether psychiatric medications are more effective than psychological treatments or whether medications can be combined with psychotherapy to enhance their effectiveness. Research by psychologists in collaboration with psychiatrists is necessary to determine the efficacy of psychotherapy and pharmacotherapy, in isolation as well as in combination (e.g., Elkin et al., 1989).

The psychological approaches discussed above do *not* have to meet FDA standards. Instead, psychologists are bound by professional ethical standards to keep current with research on the efficacy of psychological treatments, to conduct evaluations of their services, and to serve the "best interests" of their clients (APA, 1992).

The effectiveness of biofeedback, progressive muscle relaxation, and other stress management techniques have been well documented in controlled studies. The effectiveness of the cognitive–behavioral techniques typically employed in behavioral medicine have also been well documented (see Chapter 11). Thus, the physiological treatments examined in this chapter, including psychiatric medications, psychological treatments with a physiological focus, and behavioral medicine, are generally regarded as meeting empirical standards for being effective.

SUMMARY

Because many clients with psychological disorders receive medication, clinical psychologists should be familiar with psychiatric drugs, their presumed mechanisms of action, and their side effects.

Many drugs are thought to work because they increase or decrease the activity of neurotransmitters. Antipsychotics, such as chlorpromazine, decrease dopamine activity by blocking dopamine receptors, and are effective in controlling the positive symptoms of schizophrenia. The antidepressants—MAO-Is, tricyclics, and fluoxetine—work in different ways to increase the supply of norepinephrine and/or serotonin. The anti-anxiety agents, benzodiazepines, increase the degree to which the neurotransmitter GABA has its inhibitory effect.

Two childhood disorders can be treated with medication. ADHD is due to a deficit in the ability to sustain attention, and is treated with stimulants such as methylphenidate. Enuresis may be treated with imipramine, although there is a high relapse rate when the drug is discontinued.

Other psychiatric conditions can also be treated with medication. OCD has been treated with clomipramine, seizure disorders with phenytoin, Tourette syndrome with haloperidol, and alcohol dependence with disulfiram.

ECT is about as effective as medications in treating depression. However, because its side effects are more severe, ECT is used less commonly than antidepressants. Psychosurgery, once very common, is used only rarely today.

Selye's General Adaptation Syndrome is a useful way to explain the relation between stress and illness. This response to stress occurs in three stages: (1) *alarm*, in which there is an increase in arousal and activity; (2) *resistance*, in which there is a decrease in arousal so as to conserve resources; and (3) *exhaustion*, in which bodily resources are depleted and tissue damage occurs.

Two research programs have been influential in examining the relation between stress and illness. Life stress research has found that when stress, defined in terms of life changes, is high, then level of mental and medical health problems is also high. Personality type A, commonly described as the "workaholic" type, was initially found to be related to increased risk of stress disorders; however, recent research has questioned the relation between personality type A and health problems.

Clinical psychologists have developed several effective methods of managing stress. Biofeedback uses machines that monitor physical states to teach clients to recognize and control physical states associated with stress. Progressive relaxation training consists of having clients systematically tense and relax various muscle groups in the body; like biofeedback, this helps clients learn to recognize and reduce muscle tension.

Other psychological techniques can also be used to cope with stress. Slow breathing, meditation, hypnosis, and cognitive–behavioral techniques have all been used to reduce stress.

Behavioral medicine is a relatively new specialty in clinical psychology. In behavioral medicine, psychological techniques are used to treat clients who have physical disorders. In this way, psychologists (1) treat physical conditions (e.g., use biofeedback to treat tension headaches); (2) increase compliance with a medical treatment program (e.g., the daily blood tests and insulin injections required of diabetic patients); (3) help clients cope with treatment (e.g., reducing clients' fears of dental or surgical procedures); and (4) help prevent the occurrence of disorders (e.g., through weight control or smoking cessation). In addition, psychologists work with clients who have psychological problems related to their medical condition (e.g., depression experienced by cancer patients).

Recently, some clinical psychologists have sought prescription privileges for psychologists. They argue that psychologists are knowledgeable about psychiatric medications and that this would enable psychologists and psychiatrists to increase the number of clients they can treat. In addition, health professionals other than physicians already have limited prescription privileges in many states. Against this position are the arguments that psychologists have not received medical training and that they are not trained to recognize physical disorders that resemble psychiatric conditions or may contraindicate the use of medication. There are also economic stakes that lead many physicians to oppose prescription privileges for psychologists.

The rise of psychiatric medications has had a significant impact on the delivery of mental health services. The greatest impact is perhaps in the treatment of schizophrenia. Before the introduction of antipsychotics, schizophrenic patients occupied many of the hospital beds in the country. Today, schizophrenic patients are treated with medication and shortly released from the hospital. Unfortunately, antipsychotic medications do not cure schizophrenia. These patients would benefit from aftercare services. However, aftercare services have not been adequate to meet the demand. Many schizophrenic patients experience the revolving door syndrome, in which they are released from the hospital for only a brief period before they are readmitted with their next schizophrenic episode.

Psychiatric drugs, like other medications, have met FDA standards for safety and effectiveness. Still, FDA tests do not typically address the relative effectiveness of medication and psychological treatments. In addition, these tests do not guarantee that the drugs are completely safe. Clinical psychologists need to be aware of the side effects of these medications, and should conduct research to examine the relative efficacies of psychiatric drugs and psychological treatments.

STUDY QUESTIONS

1. Summarize the ways in which medications may increase or decrease the supply of neurotransmitters.
2. What are the major classes of medications used to treat schizophrenia, depression, or anxiety disorders? Summarize the presumed physiological action of these medications.
3. Select one of the childhood disorders that is successfully treated with medication. Describe the medication and its effects on this disorder.
4. Discuss how either ECT or psychosurgery has been used historically. What are its risks and benefits?
5. Describe the stages of Selye's General Adaptation Syndrome. How can this be used to explain the development of psychophysiological disorders?
6. Describe the research programs that have examined the relation between stress and illness. What are the limits of the correlational nature of this research? What variables may moderate the relation between stress and illness?
7. Describe the treatment of stress-related disorders with either biofeedback or progressive relaxation training.
8. Describe the clinical specialty of behavioral medicine. What types of psychological treatments are employed in this specialty? What types of disorders are treated?
9. Discuss the arguments for and against psychologists obtaining prescription privileges.
10. Discuss the social consequences of the increased use of psychiatric medications.

13

Child, Family, and Group Therapy

I. Child Therapy
   A. Historical Introduction
   B. Theoretical Approaches
   C. Applied Issues
   D. Scientific Issues
II. Family Therapy
   A. Historical Introduction
   B. Theoretical Approaches

C. Applied Issues
D. Scientific Issues
III. Group Therapy
   A. Historical Introduction
   B. Theoretical Approaches
   C. Applied Issues
   D. Scientific Issues
IV. Summary

Previous chapters have examined the major theoretical schools of psychotherapy. The views of Freud, Rogers, and other influential theorists concerning the goals and techniques of psychotherapy have been presented.

Most of the major approaches to psychotherapy were developed in the context of treating individual adults. However, after these schools of therapy were established, their theoretical concepts and therapeutic techniques could be applied to clients in other contexts. Clinical psychologists today often see clients whose presenting problems require something other than individual adult psychotherapy.

For example, many clinical psychologists treat children and adolescents. In these cases, it is important for treatment to be modified from adult therapy so that it is suited to the age and developmental level of the client. Many clients seek therapy because of a problem in their family or marriage. In these cases, it may be appropriate to treat the entire family or couple as the "client." Finally, many clients seek therapy because of problems in their social interactions. For these clients, a group therapy format may be appropriate, so that they develop more effective ways of interacting with other people.

This chapter will discuss child, family, and group therapy. The chapter will present a brief historical overview, a review of theoretical approaches and treatment techniques, a discussion of the practical issues, and conclude with a summary of the empirical evidence concerning the efficacy of each form of therapy.

CHILD THERAPY

Historical Introduction

According to Achenbach (1982), only a few works during the 1800s addressed childhood psychopathology. Certainly, society had been concerned with the problem of mental retardation in children since Itard's description of the "Wild Boy of Aveyron" in 1799. For example, by the mid-1800s, Edward Seguin had established centers to study and treat the mentally retarded in both France and the United States (Achenbach, 1982). However, the problem of childhood psychopathology received relatively little attention at that time.

As noted in previous chapters, Lightner Witmer founded the first psychological clinic in 1896. Witmer attempted to apply the results of psychological research to the treatment of children. Although Witmer's work was an important step toward understanding and treating childhood problems, it was rather limited in that it primarily addressed educational problems.

In 1909, William Healy established the first *child guidance clinic*—the Juvenile Psychopathic Institute (now called the Institute for Juvenile Research) in Chicago (Morris & Kratochwill, 1991). This clinic adopted an interdisciplinary approach in its work with juvenile offenders. Hence, it addressed, more than Witmer's clinic, the emotional and psychodynamic functioning of its child clients.

Although Freud's psychoanalytic theory was finding a receptive audience in the early 1900s, psychoanalysts had not yet devoted much attention to childhood disorders. Freud published his only case study involving the treatment of a child (Little Hans) in 1909 (Freud, 1909/1963). Interestingly, Freud himself did not treat Hans. Instead, Freud directed the child's father in the psychoanalysis of Hans (Morris & Kratochwill, 1991).

Still, even though there was little theoretical attention to childhood psychopathology at this time, the mental hygiene social movement, stimulated by the book by Clifford Beers (1908), *A Mind that Found Itself: An Autobiography,* became popular in the United States and led to the development of child guidance clinics across the country. This interest in mental health was accompanied by the founding of professional mental health associations devoted to the mental health of children, including the American Orthopsychiatry Association in 1924, the American Association of Psychiatric Clinics for Children in 1945, and the American Academy of Child Psychiatry in 1953 (Freedman, Kaplan, & Sadock, 1976).

Today, child clinical psychology is a major specialty. The American Psychological Association has several groups devoted to the care of children, including the Division of Clinical Psychology Section on Clinical Child Psychology, the Division of Clinical Psychology Section on Pediatric Psychology, and the Division of Child, Youth, and Family Services. According to statistics cited by Weisz, Weiss, and Donenberg (1992), approximately 12 percent of the 63 million children and adolescents in the United States experience significant behavioral or emotional problems, of whom about 2.5 million receive treatment.

Theoretical Approaches

Psychoanalytic   As noted above, Freud restricted his caseload primarily to adults and published only a single case study of the psychoanalytic treatment of a child. It took several decades for the psychoanalytic community to accept the notion that their principles and techniques could be applied to children.

The first major proponent of the psychoanalysis of children was Melanie Klein. (Although Hug-Hellmuth [1921] had previously advocated child psychoanalysis, Klein had a more significant impact on the field than Hug-Hellmuth.) As early as 1932, Klein stated that psychoanalysis can be conducted with children in the form of *play therapy*. Remember that Freud called free association the "fundamental rule" of psychoanalysis. Freud believed that clients could gain insight into the nature of their unconscious troubling material by freely associating, or saying whatever comes to mind without making any deliberate effort to monitor or control their speech. Klein (1932) argued that play is a child's most natural form of expression. During play, children do not consciously control or monitor their statements and actions. Rather, they respond freely, analogously to an adult's verbal free associations. Thus, according to Klein, children's actions and words during play may suggest the nature of their underlying problems.

In psychoanalytic play therapy, a child selects freely from a choice of play materials, including puppets, Bobo dolls, blocks, costumes, and other toys that permit a child to exhibit a range of emotions and to act out scenarios involving family and peer relationships. The therapist monitors the child's statements and actions. Psychoanalysts use children's free play just as they would an adult's free associations—to assess the nature of underlying problems and then to help the client "work through" these issues. See Exhibit 13.1 for an example of how play therapy may lead to insights about a child's underlying problems.

Other psychoanalysts followed Klein in applying Freudian ideas to the treatment of children. For example, Anna Freud (1946) adopted a more classical psychoanalytic approach, emphasizing children's development along traditional developmental stages. Karen Horney (1937, 1939) examined the

psychodynamic relationship between mother and child, stressing the positive and therapeutic aspects of the relationship. Margaret Mahler (1952), an influential object relations theorist known for her views of the development of personality disorders, provided a psychoanalytic model of psychotic childhood disorders. For example, Mahler introduced the term *symbiotic psychosis* to refer to a severe childhood disorder that occurs when the parent-child relationship is overly close and does not permit the child to develop adequate ego boundaries.

Erik Erikson is another important psychoanalytic theorist. Erikson extended Freud's stages of psychological development through adolescence and adulthood. However, whereas Freud developed his ideas primarily from interviews with adults, Erikson actually observed and interviewed children. One of Erikson's contributions, which supports other psychoanalysts' use of play therapy, was his use of play as a projective assessment technique.

Remember that projective personality tests are those in which a subject is presented with a vague or ambiguous stimulus that must be interpreted or orga-

EXHIBIT 13.1   Example of a Psychodynamic Interpretation from Play Therapy

Joey was an 8-year-old boy with severe ADHD and moderate LD. His parents were divorced and his mother had recently remarried. Joey had begun to exhibit oppositional and defiant behavior at home, particularly with his stepfather. Joey had been in a special education classroom for children with LD for two years during which time he had been taking Ritalin. Because his ADHD and LD were being treated appropriately through his special education classroom, the primary focus of the current treatment with Joey was his misconduct.

During an early session, the therapist had Joey play with a set of puppets. Joey selected one which he identified as Superboy. He then spent several minutes in which Superboy performed heroic deeds, saving the other puppets. However, Joey soon began to make believe that Superboy was unhappy. Joey said that the other puppets disliked Superboy because, with his super strength, he

smashed things even though he did not mean to. Joey said that, because Superboy broke so many things, the people were mad at Superboy and so Superboy was lonely.

It did not take much analytic acumen to interpret Joey's play. Joey was severely hyperactive. He had many accidents as he raced around the house. Joey's new stepfather was not used to such behavior and was reacting negatively to Joey. In turn, Joey felt sad and lonely.

The focus of therapy was modified to address Joey's sadness and his stepfather's interactions with him. The stepfather was provided with educational material about ADHD and was trained in child management techniques that are useful with ADHD children. Joey's sadness was addressed by having both the therapist and Joey's mother discuss with Joey her continuing love of him, despite her new marriage.

nized in some way. The way in which one responds to the stimulus can be interpreted as representing one's underlying psychological processes.

Erikson (1963) suggested that children's play can be used as a projective technique. For example, he thought that children's play with blocks reflected their psychological make-up; Erikson (1963) observed that boys tend to build towers (phallic symbols that he thought reflected their striving for achievement) whereas girls tend to make household interiors (vaginal symbols that he thought symbolized their striving for home and family).

Perhaps the therapist who is most well known for the psychoanalytic treatment of children is Bruno Bettelheim. Bettelheim founded the Orthogenic School in Chicago, a setting in which he provided inpatient psychoanalytic treatment for severely disturbed children. Bettelheim (1967) viewed severe childhood disorders, such as autism, as caused by a hostile family environment that leads the child to withdraw from reality. In the Orthogenic School, Bettelheim provided children with a safe environ-

ment and loving "mother-figures" who provided the ego support that the children lacked in their own families. According to Bettelheim, such treatment, over a period of several years, eventually permits the children to navigate successfully the early stages of psychosexual development and to outgrow their disorders. Despite recent criticism (see Exhibit 13.2), Bettelheim remains one of the giants in the psychoanalytic treatment of children.

Humanistic   Just as Melanie Klein viewed play therapy as the childhood analogue of psychoanalytic free association, so did Virginia Axline (1947) view play therapy as the childhood version of Rogerian client-centered therapy. Remember that, according to Rogers, the "active ingredient" in psychotherapy is a client-therapist relationship characterized by unconditional positive regard. By expressing genuineness, warmth, and empathy, the Rogerian therapist establishes the atmosphere in which this therapeutic relationship can develop.

EXHIBIT 13.2   Recent Criticism of Bruno Bettelheim

Bruno Bettelheim died in March 1990. Following his death, an obituary by the *New York Times* hailed his work as "major contributions to therapy for children;" another obituary by the *Washington Post* praised him for "the originality, warmth and wisdom he brought to the study of the minds and emotions of children" (cited in Beck, 1990, p. 15).

However, shortly after Bettelheim's death, Ronald Angres, who had been a patient in Bettelheim's Orthogenic School for 12 years, presented a very different picture of the man. Angres (1990) wrote that Bettelheim slapped children, called them names, and publicly humiliated them. Following this report, other criticisms of Bettelheim appeared. Charles Pekow (1990), another former resident of the school, wrote that, on one occasion, Bettelheim pulled a naked girl out of a shower and beat her in front of a room full of people.

Although such criticisms might be dismissed as inaccurate perceptions of disturbed children, other

reports followed, including those of former staff members. Indeed, I know members of the mental health community in Chicago who referred to Bruno Bettelheim as "Brutal Benoheim."

Of course, it is not fair to condemn a person on the basis of rumor and innuendo. I do not intend to imply that these rumors are true—only that such criticisms have occurred. Even if the rumors are accurate, this would not diminish the impact that Bettelheim has had in terms of his founding of the Orthogenic School and his theoretical writings on the psychoanalytic therapy of children.

Still, it appears that sufficient questions have been raised by both former patients and staff members of the Orthogenic School to recognize that there are significant problems with how Bettelheim interacted with child patients. Although he endorsed a caring and nurturing environment for children, he may not always have succeeded in contributing to such an environment.

Axline (1947) argued that play therapy can be used as the childhood analogue of Rogerian therapy. The therapist provides a set of toys for the child and then uses the Rogerian active listening techniques (open-ended statements, reflection of feeling, paraphrasing, and interpretation) while interacting with the child at play. Axline thought that such Rogerian techniques help to establish an accepting relationship between the child and therapist. In this way, the atmosphere of unconditional positive regard is established and the therapeutic process is activated.

Although other humanistic psychologists have endorsed Axline's model of client-centered play therapy for children (e.g., Dorfman, 1951; Moustakas, 1959), they have not significantly modified this form of therapy.

Cognitive-Behavioral The third major school of therapy is behaviorism, and its contemporary form of cognitive behaviorism. Behavioral and cognitive–behavioral techniques have been used with children from the very beginning of these movements. For example, one of the very first demonstrations of the effectiveness of therapy based on conditioning principles was that of Mary Cover Jones (1924a, 1924b). Following a suggestion of Watson and Rayner (1920), who had used classical conditioning to instill a learned fear in an infant, Jones successfully treated children's fears by pairing the feared object with food when the children were hungry. Jones (1924b) described in detail the case of Peter, a 3-year-old boy who was one of her "most serious" cases. Peter recovered after two months of daily treatment.

Another early classical conditioning therapy for children was the bell-and-pad treatment of bedwetting (Mowrer & Mowrer, 1938). This is an alarm device placed under a child's bedsheets. The alarm, triggered by urine, immediately wakes the child. Through repeated pairing of the alarm and waking with the sensations associated with starting to urinate, the child learns to awaken when feeling a full bladder and the urge to urinate.

Instrumental conditioning techniques (using reinforcement and punishment) have also been used extensively with children. A widely used application of instrumental conditioning is child management. Here, parents are trained in the principles of instrumental conditioning so that they manage their child's behavior more successfully. Much of what is presented in self-help books for parents on how to manage their child's behavior clearly represents an instrumental conditioning orientation. Exhibit 13.3 summarizes some of the instrumental conditioning principles that often appear in child management training.

EXHIBIT 13.3 Instrumental Conditioning Principles Often Used in Parent Training

1. Administer punishments and reinforcements immediately following the behavior to be decreased or increased.
2. Use social reinforcements (smiles, verbal praise) and punishments (frowns, verbal reprimands), since these are readily available and can be administered immediately.
3. Break down large tasks into many small tasks, each of which can receive a small reinforcement.
4. Enforce a rule consistently, reinforcing or punishing every instance of the behavior to be increased or decreased, until it has been learned.
5. Do not establish so many rules that it is difficult for a child to follow them all. This would ensure that the child will fail and should be punished. Instead, start with a small number of rules that the child can readily learn. Then, as the initial simpler rules are mastered, additional and more complex rules can be added.
6. State rules of behavior clearly, so that children know what is expected of them and what the consequences are for following and for not following the rule.
7. When punishing a child, make sure that the child knows what behavior is being punished, and what alternative behavior should have been performed.

One of the most dramatic examples of treatment of children based on instrumental conditioning is Ivar Lovaas's work with children who are autistic. Autism is a disorder that is characterized by severe impairments in social and language development. Autism is considered a pervasive developmental disorder, meaning that it develops early in life and has a profound impact on most areas of functioning. After autism was first identified in the 1940s, research in the 1950s and 1960s showed that communicative language by age five years was one of the best predictors of autistic children's progress (e.g., Rutter, Greenfeld, & Lockyer, 1967).

Lovaas adapted Skinner's (1957) theory of the development of verbal behavior to shape the speech of children with autism. This treatment, described in Chapter 11, uses simple reinforcement and punishment to train children both to pronounce words and to understand their meaning. Lovaas (1966, 1977) showed that behavior therapy is an effective way to teach basic language skills to children with autism. He also used operant techniques to train social skills other than language and to eliminate self-stimulatory behaviors in children who are psychotic and children who are mentally retarded (e.g., Lovaas, Koegel, Simmons, & Long, 1973; Lovaas & Simmons, 1969).

Social learning or modeling techniques are often used with child clients, especially for training social and cognitive coping skills. For example, George Spivack pioneered problem-solving therapy, in which clients are simply taught to improve their problem-solving skills. Spivack and his colleagues (e.g., Spivack, Platt, & Shure, 1976; Spivack & Shure, 1974) demonstrated that children and adolescents who are aggressive, impulsive, and overactive have problem-solving deficits relative to other children. Following therapy that included training in problem-solving skills, Spivack and colleagues found not only that the clients' problem-solving skills improve, but also that their clinical disorders decrease in severity. Modeling of effective problem-solving skills is a significant aspect of this therapy.

Another early cognitive–behavioral therapist was Donald Meichenbaum, who pioneered self-instructional training as a form of therapy. Meichen-baum (1977) showed that childhood behavior problems, such as overactivity and impulsivity, can be reduced through self-instruction training. In such treatment, children are trained to stop and say to themselves statements that instruct them in how to cope more effectively with a troubling situation (e.g., Stop and think. What else can I try? What will happen to me if I hit that child?).

Since the initial work of Spivack and Meichenbaum, many other clinical psychologists have developed cognitive–behavioral treatments for childhood and adolescent problems. In all of these cases, behavioral training techniques are used to train clients to think differently. After their thinking becomes more effective or more accurate, their behavior becomes more effective, and so they are less likely to experience behavioral or emotional problems.

Applied Issues

The practice of child therapy raises two important issues. The first concerns developmental differences between children and adults that make child therapy different from adult therapy. The second concerns ethical issues that occur when treating children.

Differences between Adult and Child Clients   It takes only a moment's reflection to recognize that children differ from adults in many respects—cognitive complexity, emotional control, dependency on others, and so on. These developmental differences lead to important differences between the treatment of children and adults.

For example, children's meta-cognitive abilities are more limited than those of adults; hence, children are less able than adults to monitor and interpret their psychological experiences. Children's vocabulary is less sophisticated than that of adults; for this reason, children are less able than adults to make discriminations among their emotional states and to describe their experiences. The schemata used by children to understand the world are less complex than those of adults; hence, children have a more limited understanding than adults of the world around them and of the effect that their behavior has on others.

Because adults monitor their inner worlds in a more complex way than children, they are more likely than children to recognize that they have a problem and to interpret it as a psychological problem. When adults enter psychotherapy, they generally are self-referred, seeking help because they know they have a problem and are motivated to change it. On the other hand, when children enter therapy, it is usually because an adult—parent, teacher, or court authority—has identified the problem and brings the child for treatment. The child may not recognize that there is a problem; if the problem is one in which the child's behavior causes difficulty for others (e.g., overactivity, aggression), the child may not be suffering and so may not be motivated to change.

Another difference between children and adults is their dependency on the environment. Whereas adults are relatively independent and able to control many aspects of their environments (e.g., sleep schedules, diet, self-reinforcement for progress toward a goal), children are much more dependent on others and have less control over their environments. Thus, if therapy involves changing the child's environment, then the child's parents must play an important role in therapy.

All of these factors lead to significant differences in the conduct of therapy with children and adults. Because of children's limited insight and vocabularies, psychologists must rely on behavioral observations and the report of others more with children than with adults. Because of children's limited motivation and control over their environment, psychologists must work with individuals other than the clients themselves more with child than adult clients. Because of their limited psychological mindedness and control of their environment, psychologists must employ behavioral treatments more with child than adult clients.

Ethical Issues Several ethical issues are of special concern in child psychotherapy: informed consent, confidentiality, and possible conflicts of interests.

The ethical standards of psychologists APA (1992) state that psychologists must obtain a client's informed consent before providing therapy. Obtaining informed consent generally means that the psychologist explains the type of service to be provided, along with its goals, techniques, length, approximate cost, and potential risks and benefits. Of course, when the client is an adult, such explanations are relatively straightforward. Adult clients generally enter therapy voluntarily and so have at least some idea about the services they are about to receive.

The situation is more complex with child clients. Children generally do not seek therapy on their own but instead tend to be referred by others. They may not know they have a problem, they may be unmotivated to change their behavior, and they may have no idea about the nature of psychotherapy. Thus, it is sometimes tricky to obtain informed consent from children prior to therapy.

My practice is to try to obtain consent from all child clients. I first explain to children, in terms that they understand, the purpose and nature of therapy. Even with very young children, it is usually possible to obtain a verbal agreement to begin therapy. With older children, I try to obtain their written permission below their parents' signatures on the treatment contract. My experience is that children feel proud to be treated in such an adult manner.

Another special ethical issue that sometimes occurs in treating children concerns confidentiality. Confidentiality is one of the basic ethical principles of psychotherapy. Again, with adult clients, this principle is clear. The psychologist does not divulge any information revealed in the therapy room except under extreme circumstances (which were listed in Chapter 8: child abuse, imminent danger to self or others, and a legitimate court order).

However, the situation becomes cloudy when working with minors. Because parents typically refer their child for treatment, are significantly affected by their child's problem, and are responsible for paying for their child's therapy, they expect to be kept informed of their child's progress. However, for many parents, this means wanting to know the content of their child's sessions as well as the progress their child is making.

In many cases, children are not sensitive about what they discuss with a therapist. In such cases, the children may describe the therapy sessions to their parents or give permission to the therapist to discuss the material with their parents. However, in other cases, children may not want their parents to know what they have revealed to the therapist. In my experience, this usually arises with preteen and teenage clients who engage in activities that they think violate their parents' sensibilities. When children and adolescents discuss with a therapist their sexual activity, substance use, and illegal activity (such as shoplifting), they frequently do not want their parents to be told of their behavior.

If minors believe that their discussions with the therapist are completely private and the therapist violates this trust by discussing the material with the parents, then they are likely to react negatively—they may no longer trust the therapist and so no longer comply with therapy. On the other hand, if parents expect to be informed about everything their child reveals and are surprised by the therapist's unwillingness to do so, they may discontinue the child's treatment and seek another therapist.

These problems can be minimized by establishing, prior to therapy, ground rules regarding confidentiality. Parents and children should be informed that the content of the child's sessions will be kept confidential, except when the child reveals information that indicates that the child is being abused or is in danger (and so when the therapist must take steps to safeguard the child). Thus, parents will not be informed of the material discussed in most sessions. However, if the child reports being abused or engaging in activities that are life-threatening (e.g., playing Russian roulette, injecting drugs with shared needles, driving while intoxicated), the parent will be informed.

In such cases, the therapist should prepare the child for the breach of confidentiality. A therapy session may be spent with the child to discuss how the parents should be told. In some cases, the child may then decide to tell the parents. If so, perhaps a joint session in which the parents and child meet with the therapist can be arranged. In other cases, the child may give the therapist permission to reveal the information.

(3) A third ethical problem in child psychotherapy is a possible conflict of interest between parent and child. As noted earlier, most child clients are referred by adults, such as their parents. The parents may perceive the child as having a problem, which they expect the therapist to fix. In many cases, this perception is accurate—the child may have a behavioral, emotional, or academic problem that can be addressed directly by the psychologist. However, in some cases, the child's presenting symptom reflects a problem of the parents or the entire family. For example, if parents constantly fight or belittle a child, the child may exhibit depression or decreased academic performance. In such cases, in order for the child to get better, the parents or family must change.

APA ethical standards dictate that psychologists work in the best interests of their clients. However, in such cases, the identity of the client may become clouded. Is the client the child or the parents? The best interests of the child (i.e., change in the parents or family) may not always coincide with the stated interests of the parents.

When such conflicts occur, it is important that the psychologist address explicitly the identity of the client and the goals of therapy. If these issues are not discussed directly, then therapy with the child is likely to be ineffective because the basic problem is not being addressed. Also, if parents expect the therapist to work exclusively with the child's problem and the therapist shifts the focus toward the parents, then parents may think that the therapist is blaming them for the child's problem and resent the therapist.

Of course, if the psychologist perceives the parents as playing a role in the child's problem, this conceptualization must be presented gently. I have seen parents respond extremely defensively to the suggestion that they may have to change their behavior in order to help their child, even to the point that they left the room immediately and terminated the relationship with the therapist. It may be helpful to explain that involving the parents in therapy does not mean that they are to blame for their child's problem—that because the therapist spends only about one hour a week with the child whereas the parents may be with the child the other 167 hours, it is often the most effective form of child therapy to train the parents how to interact with the child in a more effective or therapeutic way. Other suggestions concerning the involvement of the family in therapy will be discussed below in the section on family therapy.

Scientific Issues

The most important scientific issue concerning child psychotherapy is its effectiveness—does it work? As with questions about the efficacy of other forms of psychotherapy, this is a complex issue and is not very easy to answer.

Research on the effectiveness of psychotherapy with children parallels closely the research with adult clients. Following Eysenck's (1952a) initial challenge to the field to provide scientific evidence of the effectiveness of psychotherapy, Levitt (1957) examined the issue of the effectiveness of therapy with children. Levitt reviewed child psychotherapy outcome studies and reported that children who receive psychotherapy have outcomes similar to those of untreated children.

As occurred after Eysenck's (1952a) review, Levitt's analysis was followed by criticisms of its methodology (e.g., Hood-Williams, 1960), subsequent reviews that reached both favorable (e.g., Heinicke & Goldman, 1960; Hood-Williams, 1960) and unfavorable (e.g., Barrett, Hampe, & Miller, 1978; Levitt, 1963, 1971) conclusions concerning the effectiveness of child therapy, and ultimately to more and better designed outcome studies.

Most recently, quantitative reviews using meta-analysis have been conducted (e.g., Casey & Berman, 1985; Durlak, Fuhrman, & Lampman, 1991; Grossman & Hughes, 1992; Kazdin, Bass, Ayers, & Rodgers, 1990; Weiss & Weisz, 1990; Weisz & Weiss, 1989; Weisz, Weiss, Alicke, & Klotz, 1987). As was the case with adult psychotherapy, most of the meta-analytic reviews have concluded that child therapy is effective, although there have been exceptions (e.g., Weisz & Weiss, 1989). However, they have not achieved a consensus on the issue of the relative efficacies of different types of therapy. Meta-analyses of child therapy outcome studies have concluded either that behavioral and nonbehavioral therapies are about equally effective (e.g., Casey & Berman, 1985) or that behavioral therapies are somewhat more effective than nonbehavioral therapies (e.g., Weisz et al., 1987). Meta-analytic reviews of cognitive–behavioral therapies (Durlak et al., 1991) and self-control interventions (which are generally cognitive–behavioral) (Grossman & Hughes, 1992) have found that these approaches are highly effective for treating childhood disorders.

FAMILY THERAPY

Historical Introduction

Family therapy, like child therapy, is another fairly recent development in clinical psychology. Although Olson (cited in Gurman & Kniskern, 1978) reported that couples had been counseled jointly as early as 1932, it was first in the 1950s that systematic approaches to family therapy received wide attention. Gurman and Kniskern (1978) noted that, although family therapy is a rather new development (e.g., most of the professional journals dealing with family therapy were founded in the period from 1963 to 1978), the professional community has accepted family therapy as a legitimate form of treatment.

Several factors influenced the development of family therapy. First, classical psychoanalysis, with its emphasis on long-term treatment and the understanding of the individual's psychodynamics, was being challenged. As discussed in Chapter 9, offshoots of psychoanalysis, such as ego psychology, object relations theory, and psychoanalytically oriented psychotherapy, employed variants of traditional psychoanalytic techniques so as to shorten the length of therapy. As psychoanalysts experimented with techniques other than long-term psychoanalysis, it became natural for them to consider the possibility of treating clients within the family context, especially because they considered the individual's early family experiences to be crucial in the development of psychopathology.

Second, as noted above, child therapy was becoming accepted within the professional community. With this acceptance, clinical psychologists began treating children in the family context. Since children were being treated within a family context, it was natural to extend this to include the treatment of adults within the family context.

Third, the 1950s saw the rise of the school of humanism. As discussed in Chapter 3, humanism focuses on health rather than pathology and stresses a holistic approach to the clinical conceptualization of the individual. These emphases are consistent with family therapy. Rather than view a client's symptoms as indicative of underlying pathology, a humanist may view them as the natural result of being in a disturbed environment—such as the family. Rather than try to treat the individual in isolation from the family, humanists adopt a holistic approach, trying to treat the "whole" person. If they view the client's problems as due to a disturbed family environment, then it is natural for humanists to bring the entire family in for therapy.

By the 1960s, then, many theoretical approaches had been developed as the basis for family psychotherapy. Many of the approaches to family therapy are based on *systems theory*. Systems theory has been attributed to the biologist and philosopher of science, Ludwig von Bertalanffy (Oltmanns & Emery, 1995). It arose in the mid-1900s in conjunction with the rise of cybernetics and ecology. Systems theory is based on the following principles:

1. A system consists of a set of elements.
2. Each element interacts reciprocally with other elements.
3. A system acts to maintain a steady state *(homeostasis)*.
4. A system employs well-defined procedures to maintain its integrity, both in the interactions of the elements within the system and in the interactions of the system with other systems.

It is easy to see how systems theory can be applied to families. Each family member is an element of the family system. Each family member interacts with one another. The family develops patterns of interaction to maintain its integrity. These patterns include how family members interact both with one another and with outside influences.

Family systems theory suggests that an individual's symptom cannot be understood and treated in isolation; instead, the individual must be evaluated within the family system and the symptom must be

understood according to its role in the family interaction.

In this way, family systems theory clearly has both psychoanalytic and humanistic features. It shares with psychoanalysis the notion that an individual's presenting symptom is caused by some underlying problem—in this case, a family pattern of interaction, rather than an unconscious problem resulting from childhood trauma. Family systems theory also shares with humanism an emphasis on holism—the notion that "the whole is greater than the sum of its parts." Whereas humanistic psychologists resist the idea of breaking down the individual client into various components that are understood separately (such as conscious and unconscious, body and mind), the family systems therapist similarly resists evaluating the individual client in isolation from his or her family.

Levant (1984) suggested that the various schools of family therapy can be categorized using three groups: historical, experiential, and structure/process. These clusters correspond roughly (though not exactly) to the major schools of therapy discussed in previous chapters, namely psychoanalytic, humanistic, and cognitive–behavioral. These approaches to family therapy are presented below.

Theoretical Approaches

Psychoanalytic   One major theoretical approach to family systems therapy is psychoanalysis. Interestingly, classical psychoanalysis did not admit the possibility that family problems can be treated effectively within a family format. Rather, classical psychoanalysts interpreted family problems as resulting from the family members' individual problems which must be treated individually. Murray Bowen (1972), an early proponent of psychoanalytically oriented family therapy noted that, when he began to speak out in favor of family therapy, he was told by another analyst that his interest in family therapy was the product of Bowen's own neurosis.

However, by the 1950s, variants of classical psychoanalysis, such as ego psychology, objects relations theory, and psychoanalytically oriented psychotherapy, had been accepted by the psychoanalytic community. In that era of psychoanalytic diversification, two figures developed influential psychoanalytic approaches to family therapy: Murray Bowen and Nathan Ackerman.

Bowen developed his interest in family therapy from a traditional psychoanalytic perspective. He viewed schizophrenia (and other disorders) as resulting from disturbed early family relationships. For example, Bowen (1960) observed that families of schizophrenic patients were typically characterized by the classic "schizophrenogenic" pattern, with overinvolved mothers, detached fathers, and helpless patients. Because disturbed family relationships not only occurred in early childhood but continued into the present, Bowen thought that therapy that addressed current family interactions can be effective in helping the client gain awareness of the origins of his or her condition.

Bowen (1966) assumed that a client's symptoms are due to the individual's enmeshment in disturbed multigenerational family dynamics—what he called an "undifferentiated ego mass." Bowen's goal in therapy is to help individual family members to differentiate from the family. He does this by working most intensely with the client (or the most mature parent) through both individual and family sessions. Bowen attempts to help the targeted individual recognize the futility of trying to change the rest of the family. Once the individual stops trying to change the other family members and starts to change himself or herself, the traditional family patterns are disrupted. This leads to a period of confusion and readjustment as other family members react to the individual who has changed. With the therapist's guidance, the family can establish more healthy patterns of interaction.

Nathan Ackerman is another major psychoanalytic family therapist. Ackerman's approach to family therapy is perhaps most known for his active, interpretative style. Ackerman (1966) assumed that, like individuals, families employ defensive coping mechanisms. As in traditional psychoanalysis, Ackerman thought that these coping mechanisms, if used so extensively that they become automatic, may lead to the symptoms exhibited by individual family members.

Ackerman's therapeutic method is to evoke family conflicts and coping mechanisms (what he called "tickling the defenses" of the family). Ackerman (1966) described this approach as "catching the family members by surprise, by exposing dramatic discrepancies between their self-justifying rationalizations and their subverbal attitudes" (p. 97). For example, if a family has a rule of avoiding discussion of a subject, then Ackerman provokes a discussion of the topic; if a couple avoids talking about sex, Ackerman initiates an intimate interaction (Beels & Ferber, 1972).

In these ways, Ackerman actively confronts families with their defenses. He then uses therapy techniques such as confrontation (to force the family to recognize their coping patterns) and interpretation (to help the family understand the reasons for the ineffective patterns of interaction). Along traditional psychoanalytic lines, Ackerman's interpretations highlight themes of sexuality, aggression, and dependency. Throughout, Ackerman sees the therapist as playing the role of a "parent figure," who is empathetic and caring. It is essential that the therapist establish a sound rapport with the family, since triggering of family conflict will raise strong feelings.

Humanistic   A second approach to family therapy has a humanistic foundation. Remember that humanistic therapy emphasizes health, growth, and openness. All of these features are useful when working with families.

Levant (1984) used the term experiential to refer to the second major cluster of models of family therapy. According to Levant, this type of family therapy emphasizes the following:

1. A here-and-now orientation
2. Intense affective experiences for family members
3. Active-encountering, that is, family members participate actively in genuine activities

Levant (1984) included himself, a Rogerian, in this category, as well as Kempler (1974), who adapted Gestalt therapy to family therapy. Because

Gestalt therapy and Rogerian nondirective therapy have already been discussed in Chapter 10, and because these forms of therapy can be applied without modification to families, they will not be discussed further.

Another experiential family therapist is Virginia Satir. Satir (1967, 1972) is concerned with family communications. She views dysfunctional families as characterized by rigid patterns of communication that lead them to be closed to experience. During her initial evaluation, Satir monitors the family's seating arrangements, nonverbal behavior, and reactions to one another. She then attempts to identify the various roles played by family members in these dysfunctional relationships, including those of "blamer," "placater," and "distracter."

Satir views the therapist as a teacher and communication expert (Beels & Ferber, 1972). Her goal is to train the family to use a new and more effective way of communicating. She accomplishes this by providing straightforward explanations of how poor family interactions can cause symptoms in individual family members, making interpretations of ongoing family interactions, and assigning family exercises that force family members to modify their roles and become aware of their ineffective patterns of interaction. For example, after identifying a family's ineffective pattern of communicating (father as blamer, mother as placater), Satir assigned the family the task of reversing these roles for 15 minutes (Satir, Stachowiak, & Taschman, 1975).

Cognitive-Behavioral   Levant's (1984) third cluster of family therapies are those he termed structure/process. This approach to family therapy emphasizes the ways in which family members interact. This cluster includes cognitive–behavioral family therapies, which employ traditional behavioral approaches to conceptualizing, assessing, and modifying specific types of interactive behavior. However, this cluster also includes several approaches to family therapy that focus expressly on family interactions, though they do not stem from the cognitive–behavioral tradition.

Among the more traditional behavioral family therapists are Neil Jacobson (Jacobson & Margolin, 1979) and James Alexander (Alexander & Parsons, 1973). Since the 1970s, these psychologists have shown that behavioral methods are effective in treating, respectively, marital and family problems. The behavioral approach to family therapy has identified several basic skills (such as communication and problem-solving skills) that, if deficient, are associated with family problems (Gottman, 1979). Behavioral family therapy then uses traditional training methods (including modeling, shaping, graduated homework assignments, and contracting) to help family members enhance these skills.

Levant listed two other influential family therapists in the structure/process category, even though they would not consider themselves to be cognitive behaviorists. Salvador Minuchin (1974) developed a family systems approach to therapy which he called *structural therapy*. In structural therapy, Minuchin attempts to modify the family's patterns of interaction that cause and maintain the members' symptoms. Interestingly, Minuchin maintains that, to change the family structure, the therapist must first join the structure. Hence, Minuchin's approach to family therapy is a highly active one in which the therapist joins the family and assigns tasks that force the family out of their former patterns.

For example, Minuchin (Minuchin, Rosman, & Baker, 1978) used structural therapy to treat adolescents' eating disorders. Minuchin assumes that the eating disorder serves some function within the family. For example, the adolescent may refuse to eat to the point that she is near starvation; as a result, the parents understandably become upset and organize family activities around their child in an effort to help her gain weight. In this way, the adolescent gains a significant measure of control over the family.

Minuchin, like Satir and Ackerman, is highly active in working with families. He tries to modify the existing family structures that maintain an individual's symptom by joining the system himself, and then modifying its rules of interaction. For example, in a family in which the parents fought constantly and united only to blame an adolescent child, Minuchin had the parents attend therapy only with their preschool children; in this way, they were forced to interact in new ways (Minuchin, 1974).

Jay Haley (1963, 1976) is another important family systems therapist who characterized his approach as problem-solving therapy. Haley's goal is to improve the family's understanding of their interactions. Like Minuchin, he assigns tasks to family members that force them to interact in new ways. However, Haley also uses a number of techniques (such as reframing) that make his therapy more closely aligned with cognitive–behavioral than other forms of therapy. Perhaps Haley's most interesting therapy technique is *paradox*. Paradoxical interventions are those in which the therapist encourages clients to engage in or to exaggerate the very symptoms that they have been trying to avoid.

For example, suppose a family seeks help because two brothers constantly fight, disrupting family activities. If Haley's assessment determines that the fighting is not caused by some other treatable problem (such as attention deficit hyperactivity) but instead serves some function within the family (such as distracting the parents from their own marital dissatisfaction), then Haley might employ the paradoxical intervention of having the boys schedule a daily fight. The therapist can provide a plausible-sounding rationale for the prescription, such as gaining a more accurate description of the boys' fighting from the parents who must now merely observe and not intervene. When the boys engage in a planned fight, the traditional family pattern (parents intervening, everyone getting upset) has been disrupted. The fighting no longer serves the function it used to serve in maintaining the family system, and so the family has the opportunity to recognize and modify their ineffective patterns of interaction.

It should be recognized that the descriptions of the family therapists above have been necessarily brief. Readers who are interested in more detailed presentations of the different forms of family therapy should consult the references cited.

Applied Issues

Individual versus Family Therapy   The first practical problem in family therapy is to determine when to treat cases in a family rather than an individual format. Some therapists have adopted extreme positions on both sides of the question. For example, I once knew a psychiatrist who had been trained by Bowen and who attempted to treat every client using family therapy. This was often difficult because the psychiatrist worked at the student health center of a large residential university at which very few students' families lived locally and could attend family therapy sessions. The psychiatrist involved families using letters, long-distance phone conversations, homework to be done when students were on vacation, and occasional family sessions when families visited the campus. Although the psychiatrist's commitment to the Bowenian position is admirable, the approach was not well suited to the population.

I have also known psychotherapists trained as classical psychoanalysts who held that clients cannot benefit from family therapy unless they have first resolved their individual issues. Thus, even when couples and families approached these therapists with the express purpose of receiving family or marital therapy, the therapists recommended that every family member receive individual psychoanalytic therapy before addressing family issues.

Of course, these positions are both so extreme that they cause unnecessary problems. I use a more reasonable approach for recommending individual versus family therapy. I consider first the presenting problem. Often, clients seek help expressly for a family problem; if the initial assessment suggests that the presenting problem and expressed goal are accurate, then family therapy should be recommended. If a client reports an individual problem, but the clinical conceptualization of the case suggests that the pathology and/or etiology involve family interactions, then family therapy should again be considered. However, if the pathology and etiology do not have a clear family basis, then I recommend individual therapy.

For example, suppose a couple seeks marital therapy and it becomes apparent that the wife is experiencing dysthymia (chronic mild depression). It is important to identify the cause of both the depression and the marital dissatisfaction. In some cases, the depression may be the result of the marital problems, and so marital therapy is appropriate. However, in other cases, the woman's depression may be one of the reasons for the marital problems; here, individual therapy is appropriate (perhaps in conjunction with or as a prelude to later marital therapy).

Of course, the initial conceptualization of the case may not be so clear. An individual problem and a family problem may co-exist and exacerbate one another. In addition, one of the problems may be secondary to the other (say, depression occurring as a consequence of a family problem). In some cases, a problem may be secondary to another condition, but it may now be so severe (say, suicidal depression) that it demands immediate attention.

In addition to deciding between individual and family therapy, the clinical psychologist must also recognize that some families should not enter family therapy. Ackerman (1966) listed several contraindications for family therapy:

1. A family so close to breakup that it is too late to reverse the process
2. The presence of one or more family members who have a strong destructive motivation, so that they would sabotage family therapy
3. A parent who is paranoid, psychopathic, criminal, or sexually deviant
4. One or more parents who are dishonest and deceitful
5. The existence of a valid family secret
6. A strong cultural, religious, or other prejudice against family therapy
7. The presence of such an extremely rigid defense that, if broken, the person may develop a psychosis or become assaultive
8. The presence of an organic condition that would preclude participation by a family member

The Goal of Family Therapy   One of the most significant issues in family therapy is selection of a common goal. This is important so that the entire family is motivated to work on their problem.

Unfortunately, when a family seeks treatment, members may not agree on the need for or goals of therapy. For example, it is common for some family member (e.g., an adolescent, a spouse) to be a reluctant participant, attending sessions only at the insistence of another family member. In such cases, simply proceeding without addressing the member's lack of motivation is unlikely to be helpful. The unwilling participant may exhibit resistance, disrupting therapy sessions, interfering with homework assignments between sessions, belittling the process, and lowering other family members' motivation to participate in therapy.

It is also common for two family members to have mutually exclusive expectations about and goals of therapy. For example, parents who are having conflicts with their adolescent children may enter family therapy; however, parents and adolescents may each have as their initial goal of treatment a change in the other. Similarly, couples may enter treatment with very different goals. For example, I have seen couples in which one member seeks a reconciliation but the other hopes to prepare for separation.

For these reasons, it is important that, prior to starting therapy, the psychologist clarify the goals. It is important to stress that the therapist will not take sides in family disputes or try to change one family member at the request of another. The goal of treatment will be to improve the family interactions, which should lead to increased individual satisfaction. In cases where a family member remains reluctant to participate, the psychologist can act as a mediator, identifying the goals of this member and then negotiating compromises with other family members.

If the family still cannot agree on a goal, the therapist can spend several sessions with the family in an attempt to have the family negotiate a common goal. This may be helpful in teaching the family both communication and problem-solving skills.

Of course, even this may not work, in which case family therapy should be discontinued. It is possible to continue working with an individual member of the family (say, a wife who is upset with her husband who is not willing to try therapy). However, the goal of individual therapy in such cases is not to try to change the resistant family member. Rather, the goal should be to try to help the individual client how to better cope with his or her situation.

Scientific Issues

Methodological Difficulties   To date, there is relatively less empirical evidence concerning the efficacy of family therapy than for individual adult and child psychotherapy. Gurman and Kniskern (1978) noted three historical reasons for the limited amount of family therapy outcome studies. First, family therapists stem from multiple disciplines, including social work, psychiatry, psychology, and sociology; because of the autonomy of these disciplines, many family therapists developed systems that parallelled but were unrelated to those of others. Hence, there was less systematic critical self-examination in this field as might have occurred if family therapists represented a single discipline.

Second, many family therapists represent disciplines, such as social work and psychiatry, which place less emphasis than clinical psychology on the scientific evaluation of treatment. Similarly, many family therapists work in agencies, such as child guidance clinics and family service agencies, which are primarily service- rather than research-oriented. Hence, family therapy arose in settings and was practiced by professionals that placed less emphasis on outcome research than clinical psychologists.

Third, family therapy initially was influenced by psychoanalytic and humanistic theories, which have traditionally placed little emphasis on scientific evaluations of treatments.

In addition to these historical reasons, there are many methodological factors that make it difficult to conduct adequate family therapy outcome studies. These include the heterogeneity of subjects and the operationalization of family therapy techniques. It is easy to see how each of these factors makes it difficult to conduct adequate outcome studies on family therapy.

Remember that, in order to conduct experimental research that can show causal effects, it is necessary to start with equivalent comparison groups. It often is difficult to conduct experimental outcome studies in clinical populations because many uncontrolled factors (e.g., age, socioeconomic status (SES), physical health, marital status, etc.) are related to clients' functioning. When working with families, there are even more variables to consider (e.g., the number of children, the gender and age of children, age differences between children, etc.). In order to obtain comparable groups, one must either select families very carefully, to ensure their comparability, or use extremely large samples. Both options are difficult to carry out in practice.

The second major methodological problem with family therapy outcome studies is the operationalization of treatment. In order to evaluate some form of therapy, it is necessary to describe the treatment in operational terms so that other researchers and therapists can duplicate the treatment. Such operationalization is straightforward when using a relatively simple procedure with an individual client, such as biofeedback or muscle relaxation. However, it is much more difficult to operationalize a treatment when it is directed at a group of family members. There are multiple ways in which the family may respond to the therapist, misinterpret an assignment, interact with one another, and so on.

Empirical Evaluations   Still, despite the difficulty, several researchers have conducted family therapy outcome studies. This section of the chapter will summarize the conclusions of several of the major reviews of this research.

Before 1970, research on family therapy was sparse and poorly designed. Early reviewers (Massie & Beels, 1972; Olson, 1970; Wells, Dilkes, & Trivelli, 1972; Winter, 1971) did not reach very positive conclusions about the scientific evidence for the efficacy of family therapy.

However, more and better designed studies were conducted in the 1970s. DeWitt (1978) examined 31 studies of nonbehavioral family therapy. Of 23 uncontrolled studies, 72 percent reported that family therapy is successful; of 8 studies with control groups, 5 found that family therapy is superior to no treatment. Thus, DeWitt (1978) concluded that, although controlled research was still sparse, nonbehavioral family therapy is likely to be effective.

Gurman and Kniskern (1978) conducted a review of over 200 family therapy studies, critically evaluating their methodologies. They found that, for nonbehavioral treatments, marital therapy was superior to control conditions in 10 of 15 comparisons (with communication training showing the most consistently positive results) and family therapy was superior to no treatment in 8 of 16 comparisons. Behavioral marital therapy (BMT) was superior to control conditions in 7 of 11 studies and to alternative treatments in 8 of 16 comparisons, while behavioral family therapy was superior to no treatment in 5 of 5 studies and superior to alternative treatments in 5 of 6 comparisons. Although this type of box score evaluation is questionable, Gurman and Kniskern generally concluded that family therapy is effective and a sound alternative to individual therapy.

Gurman, Kniskern, and Pinsof (1986) updated their review a few years later. They now considered behavioral therapy to have been sufficiently demonstrated by controlled outcome studies, both for treating marital problems as well as a variety of child behavior problems. In general, Gurman and colleagues (1986) considered the efficacy of behavioral approaches to have been more well demonstrated than that of any other approach to family therapy.

Of all the various approaches to family therapy, perhaps the most thoroughly investigated has been BMT. Baucom and Hoffman (1986) and Hahlweg and Markman (1988) reviewed the research on BMT, concluding that it is significantly more effective than wait-list control groups. Perhaps of most interest is the meta-analysis by Hahlweg and Markman (1988), which found that, relative to control or placebo control groups, the average effect size of BMT is 0.95. That is, "the average person who had received BMT was better off at the end of treatment than 83% of the people who had received either no treatment or a placebo treatment" (p. 443).

Recent reviews have also examined nonbehavioral family therapy. For example, Hazelrigg, Cooper, and Borduin (1987), Markus, Lange, and Pettigrew (1990), and Shadish, Montgomery, Wilson, Wilson, Bright, and Okwumabua (1993) published meta-analytic reviews of family therapy outcome studies. Hazelrigg and colleagues identified 20 controlled studies of family therapy and found that family therapy is superior to no treatment and to alternative treatments. Markus and colleagues (1990)

examined 19 studies of family therapy and found that family therapy is superior to control conditions at post-treatment and at follow-up. Markus and colleagues observed that "the average patient who received family therapy is better off than 76% of the patients in the various control groups" (p. 209). Shadish and colleagues (1993) examined 163 studies of marital and family therapy, addressing possible differences across theoretical schools. They found, first, that family and marital therapy are effective (the average treated patient was better off than 70 percent of untreated controls). In addition, they found that, although many types of family and marital therapy are effective, "behavior therapies do better than other therapies" (p. 998). For example, Shadish and colleagues reported that behavioral treatments are at or near the top of the list of treatment effect sizes when considering treatment of children's conduct problems, measuring global satisfaction with therapy, and assessing specific therapy techniques.

Today, most clinical psychologists who have reviewed the research on family and marital therapy recognize that these therapies work. Research has gone beyond merely asking whether family and marital therapy are effective, to examining more specific issues such as the process of family therapy and the assignment of patients with different characteristics to different forms of therapy. In addition, research has also examined the effectiveness of family and marital therapy for specific populations and purposes, such as families with adolescents as patients (Breunlin, Breunlin, Kearns, & Russell, 1988), couples that are seeking divorce (Sprenkle & Storm, 1983), and families that are seeking enrichment rather than treatment (Giblin, 1986; Giblin, Sprenkle, & Sheehan, 1985).

GROUP THERAPY

Historical Introduction

As the field of psychotherapy was developing in the early 1900s, it is unclear who first introduced group therapy. Actually, group therapy refers to a very broad range of treatments. For example, Yalom (1975) noted that group therapy includes groups of well-functioning outpatients in a therapist's private office, groups designed to help pregnant women at a prenatal clinic, groups of schizophrenic patients on an inpatient ward, and groups of parolees at a probation officer's office.

Rosenbaum (1978) referred to group psychotherapy as a uniquely American phenomenon, attributing the origins of group therapy to a Boston physician named Joseph Pratt. Pratt was treating tuberculosis patients, attempting to address both its medical and psychological aspects. In 1905, Pratt started a tuberculosis class, in which groups of 25 patients met to discuss their condition. According to Rosenbaum (1978), Pratt observed that patients rarely discuss their symptoms, developing a strong social bond and a camaraderie that lifts their spirits. Although Pratt saw himself as a physician rather than a psychotherapist, Pratt's later writings recognized that psychological influences play an important role in patients' recovery (Rosenbaum, 1978).

Rosenbaum (1978) also identified several physicians who experimented with group therapy in the early 1900s. For example, Lazell presented lectures to groups of schizophrenic patients. Marsh, drawing on his experiences as a revivalist minister, presented inspirational lectures to groups of psychiatric patients. Dreikurs (cited in Rosenbaum, 1978) noted that European psychotherapists were providing group therapy by 1930.

Perhaps the most well-known psychotherapist who used group therapy at this time was Alfred Adler. Adler was a psychiatrist who often treated low-income patients. He employed group techniques to make therapy more readily available to working-class patients. As was presented in Chapter 9, Adler defined neurosis in terms of a life style that interferes with the expression of one's social interest. Thus, it was natural for Adler to treat clients in groups so as to be better able to help them to interact effectively with other people.

Another well-known psychotherapist who used group techniques during this period was Jacob Moreno. According to Rosenbaum (1978), Moreno claimed to have used group therapy as early as 1910 and to have introduced the term *group therapy* in 1932. Moreno pioneered *psychodrama,* a therapy in which clients role-play or act out troubling scenes from their lives. Psychodrama stems from the psychoanalytic tradition, substituting acting for free association. When clients act out a role or enact a troublesome episode from their lives, they have the opportunity to gain insight into underlying problems and to express pent-up emotions.

By the 1930s to 1940s, psychotherapists from all major schools of therapy were regularly using group therapy. As variants to traditional individual adult psychotherapy, including child and family therapy, had gained acceptance, so had group psychotherapy. By the 1940s, leading psychotherapists such as Carl Rogers and Fritz Perls had established followings of therapists who used group therapy. New models of psychotherapy, such as Eric Berne's transactional analysis, were developed that were commonly delivered to clients in groups.

With the rise of humanism in the 1950s and 1960s, there was an increased emphasis on the healthy rather than the sick. Hence, this period also saw the rise of encounter groups, designed to provide growth or enrichment experiences to people who were not expressly seeking treatment for a disorder.

The 1960s saw the rise of the community mental health movement. This movement attempted, among other things, to make psychological services more readily available to people, including those in lower income groups. Because group therapy is less expensive than individual therapy, it is more affordable to low-income clients.

By the 1970s, group therapy had been widely accepted among psychologists as a legitimate and cost-effective treatment mode. Yalom (1975) identified over 18 different forms of group therapy and noted that there were at least 75 centers around the country that provided encounter groups or group therapy. By the 1990s, Scheidlinger (1994) reported that more than half of all inpatient psychiatric facilities in the United States provide group therapy.

Theoretical Approaches

Yalom (1975) identified eleven "curative" influences in group psychotherapy: (1) instillation of hope; (2) universality; (3) imparting of information; (4) altruism; (5) corrective recapitulation of the primary family group; (6) development of socializing techniques; (7) imitative behavior; (8) interpersonal learning; (9) group cohesiveness; (10) catharsis; and (11) existential factors.

Many of these are familiar from the presentations in previous chapters on nonspecific factors in and the techniques of specific theoretical approaches to therapy. Imparting information, training in social skills, and social learning are important aspects of cognitive–behavioral therapy. Examination of one's family relations and catharsis are essential features of psychoanalysis. Existential factors (i.e., learning in the here and now) is an important element of humanistic therapy.

However, some of Yalom's curative factors of group therapy are not necessarily found in individual therapy. For example, groups instill hope and provide clients with the sense that they are not alone—that others have experienced comparable problems and recovered. Groups provide clients with a sense of camaraderie and fellowship and the opportunity to focus on something other than one's own problems by helping others. Regardless of whether one has a psychoanalytic, behavioral, or humanistic approach to psychotherapy, it is clear that such general factors can only benefit treatment.

Just as was the case with family and child therapy, so can group therapy be provided along psychoanalytic, humanistic, or cognitive–behavioral lines. The following section of the chapter introduces several significant approaches to group therapy that represent the three major schools of therapy.

Psychoanalytic   Ernest Jones (cited in Wolf & Kutash, 1990) suggested that psychoanalytic group therapy may have begun when Freud, Jung, and Ferenczi analyzed one another's dreams on their ocean voyage to the United States in 1909. Although classical psychoanalysts treat clients using individual long-term analysis, variants of classical psychoanalysis became widespread within the psychoanalytic community by the 1950s. Psychoanalytically oriented psychotherapy modified traditional psychoanalysis by making the therapist more active so that therapy can be completed more quickly; object rela-

tions therapists emphasized the client's social relationships. Such modifications of traditional psychoanalysis opened the door for group and other variants from traditional individual psychoanalysis.

Alexander Wolf is perhaps the foremost proponent of group psychoanalysis. Following his participation in a psychodrama group led by Moreno, Wolf instituted a series of psychoanalytic groups in 1938 (Wolf & Kutash, 1990).

According to Wolf and Kutash (1990), psychoanalytic group therapy uses many of the techniques of traditional individual psychoanalysis. Dream interpretation, free association, and working through transference and resistance all can occur within the group context.

The major difference between individual and group psychanalysis, according to Wolf and Kutash (1990), is the activity level of both therapist and client. In group psychoanalysis, the therapist must respond to and interpret the expressions of an entire group of clients; hence, the therapist is more active in group than individual analysis. In addition, in group psychoanalysis, clients have the opportunity to observe the therapist's relationship to several clients, not just to themselves; hence, clients have more opportunity to "reality test" the transference fantasies they develop regarding the therapist. The client also must attend to the emotions and dynamics of others. Hence, the client is less passive and introspective in group than individual analysis.

Wolf's goal in group psychoanalysis is the same as in individual psychoanalysis: insight into the unconscious determinants of one's problems. He uses traditional analytic techniques, but in an active group setting.

Object relations theory is an offshoot of psychoanalysis that stresses relationships to others. According to object relations theory, social relations, rather than the expression of the instincts of sex and aggression, determine psychological health. Since this variant of psychoanalysis places so much emphasis on healthy social ties, it is understandable that object relations therapists have employed group therapy (Kutash & Wolf, 1990). Through analysis and working through of group relationships, object relations therapists hope to help their clients achieve healthier functioning.

Humanistic Humanistic therapy, more than psychoanalysis and cognitive–behavior therapy, has traditionally been closely associated with group therapy. From its very introduction, humanistic psychotherapy was widely delivered in a group format. Remember that humanism tends to focus on the here and now. For this reason, humanistic therapies, including Rogerian, Gestalt, and existential, have all won large followings among group therapists.

Carl Rogers held that the active ingredient in psychotherapy is unconditional positive regard—a client–therapist relationship in which the therapist expresses genuineness, warmth, and empathy. In his major book on client-centered therapy, Rogers (1951) acknowledged that client-centered therapy is effective in a group format.

Hobbs (1951) discussed at length the similarities and dissimilarities between individual and group client-centered therapy. Similarities include the therapist's acceptance of clients and the therapeutic techniques (reflection of feeling, clarification, etc.) used to demonstrate this acceptance. Differences between individual and group client-centered therapy include the facts that individual therapy has more direction and singleness of purpose (since the therapist is working with only a single client) than group therapy; that group therapy brings into focus the adequacy of the clients' interpersonal relationships; that group therapy provides the opportunity for more satisfying ways of relating to others; and that group therapy provides the opportunity for clients to give help as well as receive it.

Two variants of humanistic therapy discussed in Chapter 10 are Gestalt and existential therapy, both of which have been widely offered in groups. For example, Yontef (1990) noted that Gestalt therapists were in the forefront of the movement in the 1960s to popularize group therapy. Frew (cited in Yontef, 1990) surveyed Gestalt therapists and found that 98 percent of Gestalt therapists received some training in Gestalt group therapy and 85 percent had more than half of their training in groups.

Remember that Gestalt therapy emphasizes awareness—of one's current emotions, behavior, and interactions with others. Gestalt therapists use a variety of directive exercises to enhance awareness. These techniques are readily used in groups. Clients learn to be aware of their feelings and behaviors, through their interactions with the therapist and other clients.

For example, one commonly used Gestalt technique is confrontation. Because one of the problems of substance abusers is denial, group therapists in drug treatment programs commonly use confrontation to help clients recognize their problem.

Existential psychology, like Gestalt therapy, emphasizes the here and now—the individual's current existence. According to Holt (1990), the traditional emphases and techniques of individual existential therapy readily apply to group existential therapy. For example, existential psychology identifies three modes of existence: Umwelt (the physical world), Mitwelt (the social world), and Eigenwelt (the inner, psychological world). Existential group therapy examines clients' manners of relating in these three modes, through their group interactions. Yalom (1980) is an influential existential therapist who also is well known for his works on the theory and outcome of group therapy.

A major type of group therapy, also stemming from humanistic psychology, is the encounter group. According to Yalom (1975), Carl Rogers coined the term *encounter group* in the 1960s. Previously, the term *T-group* (*T* for training in human relations) was used. The first T-group was held in 1946, when Kurt Lewin established a series of small group discussions of members' everyday problems, so that he and other social psychologists could observe the process and outcome of group interactions (Yalom, 1975). Lewin is perhaps best known for his *field theory of personality,* an ecological approach that emphasizes the individual's relationships to the environment. According to Yalom (1975), observers described the group interactions as "electric." Participants not only became actively involved in group discussions, they also participated enthusiastically in later discussions of the group interactions. Subjects benefited from the opportunity to be confronted with observations of their behavior and its effects on others. As Yalom (1975) noted, the researchers serendipitously discovered "a powerful technique of human relations education—experiential learning" (p. 460).

Several participants in this initial study went on to promote the use of experiential learning groups. By 1950, the National Training Laboratory was established by the National Education Association to support and promote experiential learning (Yalom, 1975). By the late-1950s, T-groups had become popular forums for the enhancement of communication skills.

By the 1960s, such groups were promoted, not simply as ways of improving relationship skills, but as "therapy for normals." This shift in emphasis from training to therapy for normals was associated with the rise of humanistic psychology. Humanism focuses on psychological health rather than pathology. Rogerian mechanisms for promoting growth were assumed to work in any helping relationship—a clinical psychologist working with a patient or a nonprofessional supporting a friend. Offshoots of humanism, such as Gestalt and existential therapy, also focused on the normal rather than the pathological. For example, Polster and Polster (1973) wrote that one of the basic tenets of Gestalt therapy is that "therapy is too good to be limited to the sick" (p. 7). For these reasons, the encounter group movement arose, until it reached, by the late-1960s, "near epidemic proportions" (Lieberman, Yalom, & Miles, 1973, p. 6).

Cognitive–Behavioral   The third major theoretical approach to psychotherapy, cognitive behaviorism, also has been implemented widely in group format. Cognitive–behavioral therapy uses basic conditioning techniques to train clients to think and behave more successfully. Such training techniques are readily adapted to group formats. Hence, much cognitive–behavioral therapy has been done in groups. For example, training parents in child management skills, children in problem-solving skills, and inpatients in basic social skills have all been done successfully in groups.

Perhaps most notable among cognitive–behavioral group therapies has been the treatment of depression. As discussed in Chapter 11, Beck's cognitive model of depression assumes that depression results from negativistic and ineffective thinking and so can be treated by training to think in more accurate and effective ways. Beck's therapy of depression has repeatedly been shown to be effective, not only in individual but also in group formats (e.g., Vandervoort & Fuhriman, 1991; Wierzbicki & Bartlett, 1987). Similarly, Lewinsohn's behavioral therapy assumes that depression results from low reinforcement and so can be treated by increasing reinforcement through both social skills training and activity scheduling. Lewinsohn has developed a set of materials to be used in a course format to help depressed individuals cope with their problems (Lewinsohn, Antonuccio, Steinmetz, & Teri, 1984). Lewinsohn has shown, in several controlled studies, that this course—which is a form of psychoeducational group therapy—is effective in alleviating outpatient depressions (Hoberman & Lewinsohn, 1985).

Self-Help Groups   An important approach to group therapy that does not fit neatly into the three theoretical schools above is the self-help group. The most well-known self-help group is Alcoholics Anonymous (AA), founded in 1935 as a group to be run by and for alcoholics. AA is based on an inspirational—even a religious model. AA outlines twelve steps that alcoholics must take in order to attain and maintain their sobriety. These steps include admitting that one is powerless over alcohol; believing that a power greater than oneself is necessary to recovery; making amends to people whom one has wronged; and taking a personal inventory, admitting when one is wrong.

AA meetings generally begin with a brief discussion of one of the twelve steps and then have a series of participants testify, describing themselves, their problems, and how they have tried to cope with alcoholism. Groups members share their experiences, give advice and encouragement, and remind newcomers that the only way to improve their lives is to take the twelve steps and remain sober. Since its inception, AA has grown tremendously. It has over 30,000 chapters and more than one million participants (Davison & Neale, 1994). Exhibit 13.4 presents a brief evaluation of the effectiveness of AA.

Following the model of AA, many other self-help or *twelve-step programs* have appeared. Lieberman (1990) noted that one directory lists over 400 types of self-help groups. Self-help groups have been developed for problems ranging from narcotics abuse to gambling to child abuse to epilepsy to mental illness to divorce and unemployment. Based on two large national surveys and a study of the use of self-help groups in California, Lieberman and Snowden (1993) estimated that 7.5 million adults in the United States participated in a self-help group in 1992.

Although it is clear that not all of these groups are effective or necessary, and in some cases may even foster dependency on a group (see Kaminer, 1992 for an incisive and entertaining criticism of the risk of becoming overreliant on twelve-step groups), self-help groups are an important resource for many people. They are less expensive than professional care, are more readily available than a private therapist (e.g., some self-help groups provide participants with sponsors who can be called any time—day or night—if one needs help), and provide elements of group therapy (camaraderie, shared experiences,

---

EXHIBIT 13.4   Effectiveness of Alcoholics Anonymous (AA)

AA is by far the most well-known and widespread self-help group. It is an important resource for clinical psychologists who work with clients who abuse or are dependent on alcohol. Although AA is considered by many lay people to be the most effective treatment for alcoholics, the empirical research on the efficacy of AA is less clear.

For example, the "big book" of AA (AA, 1955) suggests that AA yields about a 75 percent recovery rate, with additional participants improving without attaining sobriety. However, it has been difficult to verify this claim. Surveys of individuals who attend AA meetings may indeed find that they have a relatively high rate of sobriety; however, such surveys do not include individuals who have stopped attending AA, perhaps because they have relapsed, and so they are not included in the reported data.

Most of the controlled research on the treatment of alcoholism has examined AA as only one aspect of an entire inpatient or outpatient alcohol treatment program; although such research reports a 40 to 50 percent improvement rate (Miller & Hester, 1980), such research says little about the effectiveness of AA in isolation.

Other studies have reported that participation in AA is associated with more successful outcome. However, a problem with such studies is that they are correlational and so do not permit causal conclusions. It is possible that alcoholics who are motivated to attain sobriety, who receive more social support to get help, or who are less severely impaired and so are more capable of seeking help, are the very ones who attend AA. These factors are likely to be related to more successful outcome regardless of whether clients attend AA or some other form of treatment.

Only a handful of controlled studies have examined the effectiveness of AA. Miller and Hester (1980) summarized several of these studies and observed that AA tends to have a high dropout rate and to be associated with a more moderate outcome than is reported in the AA literature.

It is important to remember that such studies do not represent a refutation of the possible effectiveness of AA. My opinion is that, even if AA is not as effective as is popularly believed, it still represents an extremely important resource for patients who have problems with alcohol. In most major cities, alcoholics can find AA meetings throughout the day, every day of the week. If alcoholics are tempted to drink, they can call their sponsor (or, in a strange city, an AA hotline) to find someone who will encourage them to abstain. No matter how much social standing or income alcoholics have lost, AA meetings are in their price range. For these reasons, AA is a useful supplement to other forms of treatment for alcoholism.

etc.) that may not be available from individual therapy.

Applied Issues

Suitability of Clients for Group Therapy   The first practical decision for clinical psychologists who provide group therapy is to decide which clients are suitable candidates for groups. According to Yalom (1975), there is "considerable clinical consensus" that poor candidates for intensive outpatient group therapy include brain-damaged, paranoid, extremely narcissistic, hypochondriacal, suicidal, acutely psychotic, psychopathic, and substance-addicted individuals. It is clear why such patients are poor candidates for intensive group therapy. They are unlikely to be able to participate in the basic activities of the group: to attend to the group discussion, take turns speaking, and interact with others in therapeutic ways (i.e., offering advice, support, interpretations).

Of course, depending on the nature of the group, such individuals may be treatable in a group format. For example, in inpatient psychiatric settings, groups may be designed for suicidal or formerly psychotic patients. In these cases, the group is likely to be more structured and directive than outpatient intensive group therapy. Similarly, both inpatient and outpatient drug treatment programs commonly use group therapy as one part of treatment. However, such groups, designed to treat a single type of problem, are easier to structure so that low-functioning patients can benefit more from group discussions than in intensive outpatient group therapy.

Yalom (1975) also identified several inclusion criteria when selecting clients for group therapy. Of these, the most important is client motivation for group therapy. It is clear that if a client is not motivated to change in therapy, no treatment—group or individual—is likely to be very helpful. In addition, if a client is motivated to enter therapy but is unwilling to participate in a group (say, due to shame or embarrassment), than it will not be helpful to induce the client to join a group against his or her wishes.

Yalom (1975) also noted that other factors, such as the client's ability to participate in group activities and comply with group rules and the therapist's

judgment as to whether the client will "fit in" with other group members, are important. In one study, Yalom, Houts, Zimerberg, and Rand (1967) attempted to identify client factors that predict outcome of group therapy. They found that psychological sophistication and demographic variables are unrelated to outcome, whereas the client's attraction to the group (an index of the client's motivation to participate) and popularity in the group are positively related to outcome. Although the results of this study are limited by the homogeneity of the clients (adult, middle-class, well-educated, only mildly disturbed), the results are still quite intriguing.

Homogeneity of Group Composition   A second practical consideration when conducting group therapy is to decide on the mix of clients within the group. According to Yalom (1975), heterogeneous groups are superior to homogeneous groups when conducting intensive interactional group therapy. The reasoning here is that a mixture of clients (by age, gender, diagnosis, severity) is more likely to provide an atmosphere in which a variety of social conflicts can emerge. By becoming aware of and working through social interactions within the group, clients learn how to deal with their problems affecting social relationships in their daily functioning.

Of course, other types of groups may benefit from a more homogeneous composition. For example, psychoeducational groups are likely to have a homogeneous composition; because such groups train clients to cope with a specific problem, they require that clients share a common problem. Similarly, self-help groups, which provide a sense of camaraderie and the opportunity to learn how others have resolved similar problems, also tend to have homogeneous group memberships.

Open versus Closed Membership   A third practical consideration when forming groups is to decide whether group membership will be open or closed. That is, once the group starts, will new group members be added as old members leave or will all group members start and stop treatment at the same time?

This decision again rests largely on the purpose of the group. If the group is psychodynamically oriented, it is likely to require more time for clients to reach the goal of insight and personality restructuring than other forms of therapy. In such cases, a client may be in the group for a year or more. Because clients achieve their goals at different rates, it makes sense for this type of group to add new members as members leave. Groups in inpatient settings also tend to have open memberships, in that new group members are added as old members are discharged from the hospital. For example, I once worked on an alcohol treatment unit in an inpatient hospital, where patients stayed for at most 30 days. One part of treatment was daily group therapy. The group composition was constantly changing, with newly admitted patients participating minimally and patients about to be discharged spending the most time addressing the problems they were about to face when they left the hospital.

Of course, when groups have open memberships, the therapist must take steps to ensure that new members are accepted. The therapist should ensure that new members know the guidelines of the group and that the old group members are willing to admit new members. Such acceptance is easier if group rules have clearly indicated that new members will join and if there is a history of periodic new memberships, so that group members are at different stages of therapy.

Other groups are closed to new members. Briefer and more structured forms of group therapy, such as cognitive-behavioral and psychoeducational approaches, may meet a relatively small number of times, say from 6 to 20 sessions. In such instances, it makes sense for all group members to start and end therapy at the same time, so that new members are not permitted to enter in the middle of the program.

Number of Group Members   Yalom (1975) wrote that the "ideal size of an interactional therapy group is approximately seven, with an acceptable range of five to ten members" (p. 284). When groups become too small (say, three or four members), the type and complexity of group interactions are lim-

ited, and so intensive and experiential groups lose effectiveness. Conversely, if the group size becomes too large (more than twelve), then it becomes difficult for the therapist to monitor all of the members' reactions and for each group member to participate actively.

Of course, different types of groups permit varying sizes. Psychoeducational groups may be able to succeed with larger group sizes than insight-oriented psychodynamic groups. For example, Lewinsohn has shown that his Coping With Depression program is effective as a treatment for depression when delivered in a course format; hence, the group leader may be able to train 20 or more clients with the assistance of several co-therapists. Similarly, self-help groups, such as Alcoholics Anonymous, often meet with 50 or more members in attendance. In self-help groups, a leader starts the meeting with announcements, delivers a brief presentation concerning one of the twelve steps, and then introduces a series of group members who speak about their own experiences. Many group members may not actively participate, but they still may benefit from the fellowship and the presentations.

My experience has been that groups (both nondirective experiential groups and directive cognitive–behavioral or psychoeducational groups) are most effective with from seven to twelve members. I have found that I can work with groups (or families) with six or fewer members on my own; however, when groups reach seven or more members, I prefer to work with a co-therapist. One of the basic aspects of applied clinical training is how to work with a co-therapist. Exhibit 13.5 presents a brief set of tips for working with a co-therapist with either group or family therapy.

Scientific Issues

Methodological Difficulties   As was the case with family therapy, group therapy presents more methodological obstacles than individual therapy to the conduct of sound experimental research. Because group therapy, by definition, involves multiple clients, the issues of group heterogeneity, comparabil-

---

EXHIBIT 13.5   How to Work with a Co-Therapist

Part of one's basic training in becoming a psychotherapist is to learn how to work with a co-therapist. Co-therapy usually is conducted within the context of family or group therapy, when there is a sizable number of clients that may be too difficult for a single therapist to handle. Co-therapy also is commonly used in the training of psychotherapists. The following are several tips to keep in mind when working with a co-therapist.

1. Discuss the functions each co-therapist will serve prior to the session. It may be helpful to assign some preliminary functions (e.g., introductions, statement of ground rules) so that they are about equally active at the beginning of the session.

2. Complement your co-therapist. If your co-therapist is serving one function (e.g., emotional stimulation), then you should address another, complementary function, such as providing caring or meaning attribution. If one co-therapist is providing an interpretation or is explaining some complex material, the co-therapist should attend to the clients' nonverbal reactions to gauge their acceptance and understanding of the material.

3. Always remain active. Even if a co-therapist is silent, he or she should remain alert, monitoring the group interaction.

4. Model social skills along with your co-therapist. Since one of the curative factors in group is social learning, it is important that co-therapists model appropriate social skills. For example, if the co-therapists disagree about which direction to move in, they should demonstrate how to express disagreements politely but assertively, examine possible solutions, and reach a compromise.

5. Avoid becoming an advocate for one member of the group. If this happens, then the co-therapists may be drawn into taking sides in group or family disputes.

6. Conduct post-mortems of sessions with your co-therapist. It is important to discuss therapy sessions with your co-therapist as soon after the session as possible. Differences in the co-therapists' interpretations of the session and plans for the next session should be addressed. Also, significant concerns about how the co-therapists work together can be resolved.

---

ity of control groups, and subject attrition are more telling obstacles than in studies of individual therapy. Because group therapy involves interactions among many individuals, the issues of the operationalization of treatment methods, homogeneity of treatment techniques across groups, and the measurement of group process become important.

Finally, because many approaches to group therapy stem from psychoanalysis and humanism, two schools that traditionally have devoted less effort to research and to the operationalization of theoretical constructs than other schools, many of the commonly used forms and concepts in group therapy are not readily assessed. For example, Bednar and Lawlis (1971) reviewed the empirical evaluations of group therapy to date and reported that theoretical differences between types of group therapy were "largely unstudied" (p. 814). In addition, Bednar and Lawlis noted that biased sampling, rater contamination, and spontaneous remissions make it difficult to evaluate many studies, and that few of the well-designed studies of group therapy have been replicated. For all of these reasons, research on group therapy has tended to lag behind that on individual psychotherapy.

Empirical Evaluations   Although adequate scientific evaluations of group therapy are difficult to conduct, a significant amount of research on the effectiveness of group therapy has appeared.

One of the most ambitious (and well-designed) studies of the process and outcome of group therapy was conducted by Lieberman and colleagues (1973).

They assigned 69 students to a control condition and another 210 students to 18 encounter groups, representing 10 theoretical approaches (e.g., Gestalt, transactional analysis, psychodrama, psychoanalytically oriented, etc.). Subjects were evaluated before, after, and six months following the group experience. Subject functioning was assessed on several indices, including self-report questionnaires and reports by significant others. Lieberman and colleagues also evaluated the characteristics of the group leaders.

Lieberman and colleagues (1973) found that about two-thirds of the participants reported that the group experience was beneficial; however, on more objective measures, only about one-third of participants experienced positive change. In addition, about eight percent of subjects actually experienced such considerable negative change over the course of their participation that they could be considered "casualties."

Another interesting and important finding was that the theoretical perspective of the group leader is unrelated to outcome. However, when Lieberman and colleagues examined the specific functions served by group leaders, they found that meaning attribution and caring are positively associated with outcome, and that emotional stimulation and executive function (i.e., setting limits, pacing, managing time) are curvilinearly related to outcome. That is, both too little and too much of both emotional stimulation and executive functioning were associated with poorer outcome. These results are very important, given the theoretical bases of the major schools of psychotherapy, which stress some of these functions at the expense of others.

Although the Lieberman and colleagues (1973) study is a classic, it by no means represents all of the research conducted on group therapy. What follows is a summary of several major reviews of the research on group therapy.

Perhaps the most noted figure in the area of reviewing the research on group therapy is Richard Bednar. Bednar, along with several colleagues, has published a series of critical reviews of the research on the process and outcome of experiential group therapy.

Bednar and Lawlis (1971) noted a relative lack of studies and methodological problems with existing studies. Still, they thought that the evidence suggests that group therapy can have both positive and negative effects on people, with the most successful results occurring for individuals with mild or "neurotic" disorders. Bednar and Kaul (1978) updated the previous review, noting an increasing number of empirical studies. Bednar and Kaul (1978) concluded that group therapy has been shown to be more effective than no treatment, placebo treatments, and nonspecific treatment; however, they were cautious about the "curative factors" involved in group therapy. "Causal statements about the curative forces operating in the group context, the circumstances under which they may be brought to bear, or the form in which they may be expressed cannot be supported on the basis of the available literature" (Bednar & Kaul, 1978, p. 793).

Kaul and Bednar (1986) updated the review once again. However, their conclusions at this time were quite cautious. They noted a dramatic decrease in the number of controlled outcome studies and repeatedly expressed frustration with the field's lack of clarity in defining important concepts, such as cohesion. With some chagrin, Kaul and Bednar (1986) suggested that psychologists address such basic questions as "What is a group?" and "What constitutes group treatment?" They thought that psychologists have not sufficiently operationalized these basic constructs and so it is difficult for researchers to investigate them scientifically.

Bednar and Kaul (1994) recently updated their review. They remained cautious about the results of the research. For example, they reiterated that few group therapy constructs have been defined clearly enough to permit adequate scientific measurement. "Generally speaking, it seems that group research has not yet achieved a level of semantic and measurement precision sufficient to allow for the clear specification of the primary treatment variables it is investigating" (p. 658).

Although Bednar's conclusions may seem harsh, students should be aware that he is a group therapist who has repeatedly challenged the field to conduct better designed studies. His purpose is to improve the quality of studies so that clinical psychologists can base group therapy on firm scientific foundations, rather than on theoretical speculation and clinical lore.

It should also be noted that Bednar's reviews only examined experiential group therapy. Other forms of group therapy have been examined empirically, with more optimistic results. For example, Vandervoort and Fuhriman (1991) reviewed studies of group therapy of depression and found that this treatment (largely cognitive and behavioral) is effective. Similarly, group presentations of cognitive or behavioral therapy have been successful for many other problems, including social anxiety, snake phobias, weight loss, and smoking (Davison & Neale, 1994). Because cognitive and behavior therapists have traditionally had a stronger commitment to research than experiential therapists, because cognitive and behavioral concepts are more readily measured than other theoretical constructs, and because cognitive and behavioral treatments are more readily operationalized than other treatments, cognitive and behavioral group therapists have been able to conduct more and better designed studies than other group therapists. Of course, this does not prove that cognitive–behavioral group therapy is more effective than other forms of group therapy, only that these treatments have more empirical support to date than other forms of group therapy.

SUMMARY

In addition to individual adult psychotherapy, many clinical psychologists provide treatment to children, families, or groups. These approaches to therapy developed several decades after the rise of individual adult psychotherapy; however, they are all widely practiced by contemporary clinical psychologists.

Child therapy can be provided according to psychoanalytic, humanistic, or cognitive–behavioral lines. Melanie Klein popularized the use of play therapy as the childhood analogue to the psychoanalytic technique of free association. Other influential psychoanalysts who worked with children include Anna Freud, Erik Erikson, Karen Horney, Margaret Mahler, and Bruno Bettelheim. Bettelheim founded

the Orthogenic School in Chicago, a setting in which he provided long-term psychoanalytic treatment for seriously disturbed children.

Virginia Axline suggested that play therapy can be used as the childhood analogue to Rogerian therapy. Through nondirective play, Axline thought that the therapist can express unconditional positive regard, the curative factor in Rogerian therapy.

Behavior therapy with children has been conducted following each of the different types of conditioning. Mary Cover Jones and Mowrer used classical conditioning techniques to treat, respectively, phobic and enuretic children. Ivar Lovaas used instrumental conditioning to shape language and self-care skills in autistic children. Social learning is often used to train social and coping skills in children. Cognitive–behavioral therapies commonly used with children include George Spivack's problem-solving training and Donald Meichenbaum's self-instruction training.

Clinical psychologists who work with children must recognize that children differ from adults in many ways—self-monitoring, vocabulary, insight, dependency, and so on. These factors sometimes make it difficult to treat children, who may have less motivation to change and less awareness of what occurs in therapy than adults. Therapists also must be aware of special ethical issues that arise in treating children, including informed consent, confidentiality, and possible conflicts of interests.

The effectiveness of child therapy has been investigated. Early reviews of the research by Levitt (1957, 1963) found little scientific evidence that children who receive treatment are better off than untreated children. However, later and better designed studies support a more favorable conclusion. Recent meta-analyses of child psychotherapy have generally concluded that child therapy is effective; however, there is little consensus about the relative efficacies of different forms of child therapy.

Family therapy often is based on systems theory, which adopts the holistic assumption that the whole is greater than the sum of its parts and so holds that the family must be treated as a unit in order to help a single family member. Family therapy can be presented along psychoanalytic, humanistic, and cognitive–behavioral lines.

Murray Bowen and Nathan Ackerman developed psychoanalytic approaches to family therapy. Bowen interprets the multigenerational family relationships along traditional psychoanalytic lines; Ackerman evokes family conflicts in order to challenge the family's defenses and force them to become aware of their ineffective patterns of interaction.

Humanistic approaches to family therapy also are popular. Rogerian and Gestalt therapy have been widely used to treat families. Virginia Satir is a humanistic family therapist who stresses the family's communication patterns; Satir tries to improve the family patterns of communication to make it more open to experience.

Neil Jacobson uses traditional behavioral techniques, such as communication and problem-solving training, to treat couples. James Alexander uses similar behavioral methods to treat families.

Salvador Minuchin developed an approach called structural therapy, in which the therapist joins the structural patterns of the family in order to change them. Jay Haley uses an approach he calls problem solving, to enhance the family's interactions; one technique frequently used by Haley is paradox.

Clinical psychologists must evaluate clients to determine whether individual or family treatment should be provided. The agreement of the family on the need for and goals of treatment, the ability of family members to participate actively, and the severity of individual members' symptoms must be considered.

Research on family therapy has lagged behind that on individual adult therapy. Family therapy is more difficult to study than individual therapy because the greater number of clients makes it more difficult to obtain homogeneous treatment groups and equivalent comparison groups. Also, family therapy has traditionally been more closely associated with mental health professionals who do not have as strong a research orientation as scientist–practitioner clinical psychologists (e.g., social work-

ers, humanistic psychologists, etc.); hence, many constructs in theories of family therapy have not been sufficiently operationalized so that they can be studied empirically.

Reviews in the 1970s of the research on the effectiveness of family therapy reached negative conclusions, due to inconsistent results and a limited number of well-controlled studies. In the 1970s and 1980s, more and better designed studies were conducted so that recent reviews have generally concluded that family therapy is superior to no therapy and, in some cases, to alternative treatments such as individual therapy. Although there is no clear consensus on the relative efficacies of family therapy stemming from different theoretical perspectives, behavioral approaches to family and to marital therapy have been supported by more studies than other theoretical approaches.

Group therapy also has become a popular mode of treatment. Group therapy provides several therapeutic factors not present in individual therapy (e.g., learning from other patients who have similar problems, a sense of group cohesion or camaraderie, benefiting from helping others); however, group therapy also enables therapists to employ the curative factors present within the various forms of individual therapy. Hence, group therapy can be provided within the three major schools of therapy.

Alfred Adler is a psychoanalyst who treated patients in groups. Jacob Moreno introduced psychodrama, a group psychoanalytic treatment in which role playing and acting take the place of free association.

Alexander Wolf may be the foremost proponent of group psychoanalysis, using traditional psychoanalytic methods (e.g., dream analysis, free association, interpretation of resistance and transference) in a group format.

Humanistic therapists use an existential approach, stressing the here and now. Such an emphasis fits well with group therapy, where much of the therapy occurs as a result of becoming aware of one's interactions with others. Rogers provided client-centered therapy in groups. Gestalt therapy, using confrontation and exercises to enhance client awareness, often is provided in groups. Existential therapists, such as Irwin Yalom, also frequently employ groups.

Another emphasis of humanists is health. Humanists have led T-groups or encounter groups, which are designed to enhance human relations skills (such as communication). After the introduction of T-groups, some humanistic therapists came to regard them as a type of group therapy for healthy people.

Behavior therapy has also been provided in groups. For example, behavioral groups have been used to train people to cope with specific problem behaviors, such as smoking and overeating. Cognitive–behavioral groups also have been successful in training clients to change specific problems, such as depression.

Another kind of group is the self-help group. AA was the initial self-help group, founded by alcoholics for alcoholics. AA members adopt a twelve-step approach in which they admit their inability to control alcohol and make amends to those they have wronged. Because of the popularity and success of AA, many other twelve-step self-help groups have now been established.

Clinical psychologists who provide group therapy must evaluate clients for their suitability for groups. Clients who are so severely impaired that they will not be able to participate actively in group activities (say, because of psychosis or brain damage) should be excluded from groups. Therapists must also decide on the basic structure of the group, addressing such issues as the size and homogeneity of the group and whether group membership will be open or closed. Larger groups should be treated by co-therapists.

Research on group therapy is difficult to conduct. The greater number of clients in group therapy makes the issues of group homogeneity, comparability of groups, and attrition more troublesome than in studies of individual therapy. Also, many of the theoretical constructs concerning group process have not been sufficiently operationalized to permit their measurement in research.

In a classic study of encounter groups, Lieberman and colleagues (1973) found that, although two-thirds of participants reported that they had benefited, more objective measures showed that only about one-third had actually improved. In addition, Lieberman and colleagues found that the leadership functions of caring and meaning attribution are positively related to outcome, whereas the leadership functions of emotional stimulation and executive function are curvilinearly related to outcome.

Richard Bednar has published several critical reviews of the research on experiential group therapy. Bednar has repeatedly expressed frustration over the lack of well designed studies in this area, largely because the theoretical constructs, even such fundamental concepts as "group" and "group cohesion," have not been well operationalized. However, research on other forms of group therapy, such as cognitive–behavioral therapy for depression and behavior therapy for weight loss, smoking, phobias, and child management, has shown that these treatments are effective.

STUDY QUESTIONS

1. Discuss the historical factors that led to the rise of alternatives to individual adult psychotherapy, including child, family, and group therapy.
2. Select one of the major theoretical schools of psychotherapy (psychoanalysis, humanism, behaviorism). Discuss how this form of therapy can be provided to children.
3. Discuss the differences between child and adult clients that affect how a therapist treats them.
4. Discuss three ethical issues that may pose more of a problem when working with child than adult clients.
5. Is psychotherapy effective with children? Support your answer, noting the difficulties faced when attempting to answer this question.
6. Summarize systems theory and apply it to families.

7. Select one of the major theoretical schools of psychotherapy (psychoanalysis, humanism, behaviorism). Discuss how this form of therapy can be provided to families.

8. What methodological problems make it more difficult for psychologists to conduct research on family therapy (or group therapy) than on individual therapy?

9. Select one of the major theoretical schools of psychotherapy (psychoanalysis, humanism, behaviorism). Discuss how this form of therapy can be provided in groups.

10. What practical decisions must a clinical psychologist make when considering whether a client is suitable for group therapy and deciding on the composition of a group?

14

Training and Professional Roles of Clinical Psychologists

I. *Graduate School Training*
   A. *History*
   B. *Current Programs*
II. *Professional Roles*
   A. *History*
   B. *Work Settings and Activities*
   C. *Recent Trends*
III. *Applied Issues*
   A. *Selecting Clinical Psychology versus Other Mental Health Fields*

B. *Applying to Graduate School in Clinical Psychology*
IV. *Scientific Issues*
   A. *Evaluation of Graduate Training and Career Choice*
   B. *Evaluation of the Boulder and Vail Models of Training*
V. *Summary*

Previous chapters discussed the history of clinical psychology—from the founding of the first psychological clinic by Witmer in 1896 to the increase in the number of clinical psychologists from World War II to the present. As clinical psychology grew as a profession, it formalized its standards and practices, as illustrated by the development of ethical principles. This growth as a profession also led to the development of formal standards for training clinical psychologists and for regulating the practice of clinical psychology.

This chapter discusses the training and professional roles of clinical psychologists, including both their historical development and current status. Following these presentations, this chapter will address both applied and scientific issues concerning the choice and evaluation of training programs in clinical psychology.

GRADUATE SCHOOL TRAINING

History

Witmer established the first psychological clinic and introduced the term *clinical psychologist* in 1896. Witmer's clinic was affiliated with the University of Pennsylvania and staffed primarily by faculty and students at the school. According to Edelstein and Brasted (1991), four of five psychological clinics established in the next 15 years were similarly affiliated with academic departments of psychology. Training for students to work in these clinics varied, with most of the departments requiring that students complete a clinical internship after receiving training in general psychology (Edelstein & Brasted, 1991).

Shakow (1976, 1978) referred to clinical training at that time as following a "do-it-yourself" model, in which students received traditional scientific training in experimental psychology followed by one or more experiences in applied clinical work. For example, following Shakow's own graduate training in which he conducted research in a traditional area of experimental psychology, he accepted a position as a schizophrenia researcher in a state hospital. He then went on to become a leading figure both in the cognitive functioning of people diagnosed as schizophrenic and in the training of clinical psychologists.

Edelstein and Brasted (1991) noted several other significant steps in the evolution of the training of clinical psychologists. For example, a clinical section was established in the APA in 1919. Five years later, this clinical group recommended to the APA that clinical psychologists should have a Ph.D. (rather than a master's degree); four years of clinical experience, at least one of which is supervised; and a balance of scientific and applied training.

In 1931, the APA established a Committee on Standards of Training for Clinical Psychologists. This committee made its initial report to the APA in 1935. However, although its recommendations echoed earlier calls for a doctorate and a combination of scientific and professional training, this report had little impact at the time (Edelstein & Brasted, 1991).

Shakow (1938) recommended that clinical psychologists receive a one-year internship as part of their training. He suggested that the internship should take place in a psychiatric hospital or other clinical setting and serve four major training functions: (1) to further develop clinical techniques that students have already learned; (2) to provide students with experience in the practical aspects of psychopathology; (3) to further develop an experimental-scientific attitude toward applied psychology; and (4) to expose students to the methods and attitudes of other mental health professionals. Most subsequent accounts of the nature and purposes of the clinical internship have echoed Shakow's (1938) recommendations.

It remained for external incentives to motivate psychologists to formalize their training requirements. During World War II, many psychologists provided clinical services to soldiers and, as a result, decided to work in applied rather than research settings. In addition, following World War II, many distressed soldiers sought clinical services through the Veterans Administration system. Darley and Wolfle (1946) estimated that the VA system needed an additional 4,700 clinical psychologists to provide the assessment and intervention services that the influx of World War II veterans demanded. For these reasons, the VA and the U.S. Public Health Service requested that the APA specify the nature of adequate clinical training and identify the programs that met these criteria (Edelstein & Brasted, 1991; Shakow, 1978).

In response to this external incentive, the APA established the Committee on Training in Clinical Psychology, chaired by David Shakow. This committee made its recommendations to the APA in 1947 (Shakow, Hilgard, Kelly, Luckey, Sanford, & Shaffer, 1947). This report stressed several general principles, including the following: (1) a clinical psychologist is first and foremost a psychologist; (2) training in clinical psychology should be as rigorous as for a traditional doctorate, combining both academic and clinical training in at least a four-year program; (3) training should be broad and directed toward research and professional goals, rather than technical goals; (4) and training should include contact with clinical material through all four years of graduate training. The committee report identified six major areas of study to be included in clinical training: (1) general psychology, (2) psychodynamics of behavior; (3) diagnostic methods; (4) research methods; (5) related disciplines, and (6) therapy. Finally, the report required that clinical psychology students complete a one-year internship (usually in the third year of training), to gain practical experience with diagnostic and treatment issues with a variety of clients.

Two later reports from the Committee on Training in Clinical Psychology followed (1948, 1949), in which issues surrounding the evaluation of programs were discussed in detail. At the time of these reports, 22 universities in the United States had doctoral programs in clinical psychology (Reisman, 1981). Representatives from those schools, the APA Committee on Training in Clinical Psychology, and other interested parties attended a two-week conference on training in clinical psychology in 1949 in Boulder, Colorado. The result of this conference was the unanimous endorsement of the scientist–practitioner model of clinical training, which has come to be known as the Boulder Model. This model is based on the 1947 recommendations of the Committee on Training in Clinical Psychology. That is, clinical psychologists were to be trained as psychologists first and foremost, with training, not only in clinical techniques, but also in general psychology and the research methods used to acquire basic psychological knowledge. In addition, clinical techniques were presumed to be based on psychological facts and principles, as derived from scientific psychological research.

According to the report of this conference (Raimy, 1950), the Boulder Model was supported because of the fundamental lack of scientific knowledge concerning clinical practice and the need for researchers to have a clinical background so that researchers have a better understanding of and increased interest in clinical research issues.

Since 1949, there have been several other major conferences on graduate training in clinical psychology. These include meetings at Stanford University in 1955 (Strother, 1957), in Miami in 1958 (Roe, Gustad, Moore, Ross, & Skodak, 1959), Chicago in 1965 (Clark, 1965), Vail, Colorado in 1973 (Korman, 1974), and Salt Lake City in 1987 (Bickman,

1987). Each of these conferences continued to recognize scientific principles and findings as the basis for clinical practice.

However, the Vail and Salt Lake City conferences also endorsed a professional training model as an alternative to the scientist–practitioner model. There are several reasons for the acceptance of a second model of training. First, from the 1940s to the 1980s, there was a dramatic increase in the demand for applied clinical services (Pryzwansky & Wendt, 1987), with a corresponding increase in the number of clinical psychologists employed in practice settings rather than research or university settings. The shift in the work settings and professional roles of clinical psychologists will be documented later in the chapter.

Second, some clinical psychologists expressed dissatisfaction with the scientific components of their graduate training (Garfield & Kurtz, 1976), noting that the time spent on research detracted from their applied clinical training. Several surveys addressing the satisfaction of psychologists with their graduate training will also be examined later in the chapter.

Third, Frank (1984) argued that, prior to 1947, APA committees on graduate training in clinical psychology had recommended that "clinical training should be grounded *in* and *on* research in psychology," but that Shakow's 1947 committee report changed this emphasis by recommending that clinical psychologists "should be trained to *do* research" (Frank, 1984, p. 425).

For these reasons, the Vail and Salt Lake City conferences endorsed a professional model as an alternative to the scientist–practitioner model. Still, it should be noted that these conferences recognized that clinical practices must be founded on scientifically demonstrated principles and techniques. Even though a psychologist may not be conducting research in his or her own clinical practice, it is assumed that the clinical techniques used have a grounding in empirical science. For this reason, the Vail model could be regarded as a practitioner–scientist model.

The practitioner–scientist model is the basis for Psy.D. training programs. The Psy.D. degree as an applied degree distinct from the Ph.D. was suggested by Poffenberger as early as 1938, and was first attempted unsuccessfully at the University of Montreal in the late-1940s (Holt, 1971). The first Psy.D. program in the United States was established in 1968 at the University of Illinois (Peterson, 1968). Shortly thereafter, Psy.D. programs were introduced at Baylor University and the University of Denver (Lutzker, Olmedo, & Persico, 1987). Even though the original Psy.D. program at the University of Illinois has been discontinued, the Psy.D. has become well established as an alternative form of clinical training. By 1987, 45 professional schools of psychology had been established, with 22 of them having APA accreditation (Strickland, 1988).

The philosophies underlying the Boulder Model and Vail Model of training will be discussed later in the chapter, in the section on scientific issues concerning the training of clinical psychologists. The next section of the chapter addresses current training programs in clinical psychology.

Current Programs

As of 1995, there were 185 APA-accredited doctoral programs in clinical psychology (APA, 1995a). About 80 percent of these were Ph.D. programs, with the remaining 20 percent being Psy.D. programs (APA, 1995a). There is a small number of additional Ph.D. and Psy.D. programs that are not APA accredited—some because they are relatively new and have not yet received accreditation, others because they have not met the standards required for APA accreditation. For example, in a survey of doctoral clinical psychology programs in 1992–1993, Norcross, Hanych, and Terranova (1996) reported that there were 26 nonaccredited Ph.D. programs and 28 nonaccredited Psy.D. programs.

The current standards for APA accreditation of doctoral programs (APA, 1995b) resemble those first proposed by Shakow's committee (Shakow et al., 1947). For example, current APA standards, like Shakow's 1947 recommendations, include the general principles that doctoral training be "broad and professional" rather than "narrow and technical," and that training programs must include both science

and practice elements (APA, 1995b). However, current standards are somewhat more general than the initial standards in that they recognize that degree-granting institutions have different missions and that doctoral clinical programs may be based on different training models; hence, current accrediting standards require that a program should be evaluated according to the mission of the institution and that training model of the program. For example, a large, state-supported, research-oriented university (such as the University of Wisconsin) may have different training goals from a private, urban university (such as Marquette University) or a free-standing professional school (such as the Illinois Institute of Technology); the APA evaluates each doctoral program according to the extent to which the program meets the unique goals of its institution and training program.

Current accreditation standards also specify that a coherent curriculum be presented that includes the following:

1. "The breadth of scientific psychology, its history and development, its research methods, and its applications. To achieve this end, the students shall be exposed to the current body of knowledge in at least the following areas: biological aspects of behavior; cognitive and affective aspects of behavior; social aspects of behavior; history and systems of psychology; psychological measurement; research methodology; and techniques of data analysis" (APA, 1995b, p. 6). In practice, this criterion generally translates into a sequence of courses in research design and statistics, a series of research requirements (such as first- and second-year research projects and a dissertation), and courses in core areas such as cognitive, biological, and social psychology.

2. "The scientific, methodological, and theoretical foundations of practice in [clinical psychology]. To achieve this end the students shall be exposed to the current body of knowledge in at least the following areas: individual differences in behavior; human development; dysfunctional behavior or psychopathology; and professional standards and ethics" (APA, 1995b, p. 6). In practice, this criterion is generally met by courses in developmental psychology, theories of personality, and abnormal psychology. In addition, courses, training workshops, or significant sections of courses may address professional and ethical issues.

3. "Diagnosing or defining problems through psychological assessment and measurement and formulating and implementing intervention strategies (including training in empirically supported procedures). To achieve this end, the students shall be exposed to the current body of knowledge in at least the following areas: theories and methods of assessment and diagnosis; effective intervention; consultation and supervision; and evaluating the efficacy of interventions" (APA, 1995b, p. 6). In practice, this criterion is generally met by a sequence of courses in assessment and another series of courses in intervention.

4. "Issues of cultural and individual diversity that are relevant to all of the above" (APA, 1995b, p. 6). This criterion is often met by discussions of cultural diversity in appropriate classes or training workshops. For example, racial differences in intelligence can be discussed in classes on the assessment of psychological abilities, sex differences in the manifestation of psychopathology can be addressed in abnormal psychology classes, and socioeconomic aspects of psychotherapy (such as differential dropout rates across income groups) can be addressed in courses and practica on psychological intervention.

5. "Attitudes essential for life-long learning, scholarly inquiry, and professional problem-solving as psychologists in the context of an evolving body of scientific and professional knowledge" (APA, 1995b, p. 6). Although no single course sequence can ensure such a life-long attitude in students, this criterion can be evaluated by the degree to which a training program consistently adheres to a scientist–practitioner or practitioner–scientist philosophy, both of which endorse the founding of clinical practice on empirical findings that constantly evolve.

Another criterion for APA accreditation is that programs provide "adequate and appropriate practicum experiences" (APA, 1995b, p. 6). To this end, practicum placements should be made in settings that are committed to training, provide adequate supervision, and provide a wide range of experiences. In addition, applied practicum training should be integrated with the didactic portion of the curriculum.

In 1986, the APA required that doctoral students receive at least 400 hours of practicum experience, including at least 150 hours of direct service to clients and at least 75 hours in formal supervision (APA, 1986). There have been subsequent discussions of the practicum requirement, including attempts to clarify the meaning of practicum training and to expand the number of practicum hours (Belar, Bielauskas, Larsen, Mensh, Poey, & Roelke, 1989). In addition, a survey of Directors of APA-accredited Ph.D. programs and internships found that the APA requirement of 400 hours is below what many programs require of their students (Hecker, Fink, Levasseur, & Parker, 1995). For example, Hecker and colleagues reported that 56 APA-accredited Ph.D. programs required, on average, 900 practicum hours (median = 840 hours); in addition, Hecker and colleagues found that 150 APA-accredited internships required, on average, over 700 hours (median = 675 hours) of practicum experience. Thus, many clinical training programs provide much more than the minimum 400 hours of practicum training.

A final requirement for a doctorate in clinical psychology is the completion of an internship. This usually takes the form of a full-time placement over an entire year (2,000 hours) in a clinical setting. Like practicum experiences, the internship must be completed in a setting that provides a variety of training experiences (assessment, intervention, consultation), adequate supervision, and the opportunity to integrate didactic information with applied experience. As of 1995, there were 439 agencies that provided APA-approved internships in clinical psychology (APA, 1995c). In addition, there are many additional agencies that provide doctoral internships that are not APA-accredited.

Different clinical training programs have different missions and are based on different training models. In addition, they may choose to meet a criterion in different ways (e.g., a course on ethics versus sections on ethics across several courses). For these rea-

EXHIBIT 14.1   Curricula of Selected APA-accredited Ph.D. and Psy.D. Programs

Indiana University (Ph.D.)	Illinois School of Professional Psychology (Psy.D.)
1. 90 Semester hours	108 Quarter hours
2. Qualifying exam	Comprehensive exam
3. Two-course statistics sequence Research seminar 1st-year research project 2nd-year research project	Two-course statistics/design sequence
4. Four courses in core areas (e.g., Social, Cognitive, Developmental, Learning)	Three-course developmental sequence Social bases of behavior Biological bases of behavior
5. Assessment sequence Psychotherapy sequence Psychopathology	Assessment sequence Psychotherapy sequence Psychopathology sequence
6. Four credits (semesters) of clinical practicum	Six quarters of clinical practicum
7. 9–12 hours in a minor in another department or area of psychology	13 quarter hours of electives
8. Dissertation	Clinical research project
9. 12-month internship	12-month internship

Note: Program summaries are based on recent program descriptions
from Indiana University and the Illinois School of Professional Psychology.

sons, no single set of courses can be presented as a template against which to judge whether a program meets APA accreditation standards. Still, it may be helpful for students to see the curricula of two APA-accredited training programs. Exhibit 14.1 summarizes the curricula of one APA-accredited Ph.D. program and one APA-accredited Psy.D. program.

PROFESSIONAL ROLES

History

Witmer and Binet were among the first psychologists who attempted to apply psychological principles to solving practical problems. They were experimental psychologists who were asked by others

whether psychology could be useful in assessing and helping children (Frank, 1987). Early clinical psychologists, like other psychologists, tended to work in academic settings. For example, in 1947, the APA had about 4,600 members, of whom about 85 percent were academics (Young, 1992). Clinical practice primarily consisted of psychological assessment and was largely confined to hospitals, schools, and prisons (Abt, 1992).

World War I led to an increase in the roles psychologists played and the settings in which they worked (Frank, 1987). For example, psychologists were asked by the military to assist in the screening of recruits for possible psychopathology and in the assessment of soldiers who were discharged due to emotional problems. As a result, clinical psychologists worked in more hospital settings and in the military more in the 1910s and 1920s than they had previously (Frank, 1987).

World War II led to a further increase in the roles of clinical psychologists. The military again asked that psychologists assist in the assessment of psychological disorders in recruits and veterans (Frank, 1987). However, following the war, it also requested assistance in the treatment of distressed soldiers (Hawley, 1946). Although Abt (1992) recalled that clinical psychologists performed little psychotherapy except under medical supervision during the war, it is clear that, following World War II, psychotherapy became recognized as one of the major roles of clinical psychologists.

With clinical psychologists providing treatment as well as assessment services, the number of agencies in which they could be employed increased. With increased marketability went increased numbers of psychologists. Woodworth (1937) evaluated the need for applied clinical services and estimated that the future would see an increase in the number of clinical psychologists from the hundreds to the thousands. However, he greatly underestimated the increase. According to Sechrest (1992), whereas the population of the United States doubled from 1937 to 1992, the number of psychologists increased twenty-fold. By 1985, the number of licensed psychologists was about 46,000 (Sechrest, 1992).

Work Settings and Activities

Garfield and Kurtz (1976) published a well-known study of the activities and work settings of clinical psychologists. They surveyed 855 members of the APA Division of Clinical Psychology and presented an interesting picture of the clinical psychologist of the 1970s. According to Garfield and Kurtz, the mean age of clinical psychologists was 46.8 years; 84 percent of clinical psychologists were male. The primary work settings of clinical psychologists were as follows: private practice (23.27 percent), university psychology department (21.99 percent), university, mental hospital (8.42 percent), medical school

(7.95 percent), community mental health center (7.48 percent), university, other (7.02 percent), general hospital (5.97 percent), outpatient clinic (5.15 percent), none (1.17 percent), and other (11.58 percent).

Garfield and Kurtz found that the activities of clinical psychologists broke down as follows: individual psychotherapy (25.07 percent), teaching (13.82 percent), administration (13.21 percent), diagnosis/assessment (9.79 percent), clinical supervision (7.78 percent), research (7.04 percent), community consultation (5.23 percent), group psychotherapy (4.35 percent), scholarly writing (3.77 percent), research supervision (2.71 percent), behavior modification (2.00 percent), sensitivity group (0.40 percent), and other (4.82 percent).

So, by the 1970s, the modal clinical psychologist had moved from academia and the psychiatric hospital to private practice; the modal clinical activity had changed from research, teaching, and assessment to psychotherapy.

Many subsequent surveys of clinical psychologists have been conducted, often addressing some subset of clinical psychologists such as academicians (e.g., Shemberg & Leventhal, 1978), part-time practitioners (e.g., Norcross, Nash, & Prochaska, 1985), and Psy.D.s (e.g., Peterson, Eaton, Levine, & Snepp, 1982). These surveys have generally confirmed the increasing number of clinical psychologists who are in private practice and who provide psychotherapy as their primary activity. For example, in a survey of 479 members of the APA Division of Clinical Psychology, Norcross and Prochaska (1982) found that 62.8 percent view themselves as clinical practitioners, 31.1 percent are in private practice, and only 16.9 percent are affiliated with a department of psychology in a university. In a later survey of members of this division, Norcross, Prochaska, and Gallagher (1989) found that 35 percent of clinical psychologists are primarily involved in private practice while about 17 percent work in a university department of psychology. In a smaller survey of 87 recent clinical graduates, Walfish, Moritz, and Stenmark (1991) found that clinical psychologists spend 71 percent of their time in clinical practice (with only 15 percent in academic research) and that private practice is the most common work setting (45 percent), followed respectively by hospitals (19 percent) and universities (15 percent).

Students should be aware that even clinical practitioners do not spend all of their time providing psychotherapy. For example, suppose a clinical psychologist provides outpatient psychotherapy and assessment services in a community mental health center. It is likely that this psychologist will spend up to several hours daily in activities other than direct provision of services. For example, for every several hours of individual, group, or family/marital therapy provided, there will be at least an hour of report writing and administrative work. For every several hours of psychological testing, there will be an hour or two of test scoring, interpretation, and report writing. It is also likely that some time every week will be spent in case staffings, supervision, and consultation with other agencies. Thus, even though a psychologist's primary activity may be psychotherapy, up to 25 percent of the work week will likely be taken up with other activities.

Employment in other work settings similarly carries other nontherapy responsibilities. For example, psychologists who work in medical centers not only provide clinical services, they also conduct research and are involved in training; for example, they may lecture to trainees, conduct training sessions observed by students, and supervise the work of psychology interns. Psychologists who work in state mental hospitals are likely to be involved in planning and evaluating treatment programs as well as in providing therapy and assessment services.

Recent Trends

The surveys of clinical psychologists cited in the previous section document several trends in the practice of clinical psychologists over the last several decades:

1. There has been an increase in the number and percentage of clinical psychologists who work in private practice.
2. There has been an increase in the degree to which clinical psychologists provide treatment services rather than other services, such as diagnosis and assessment.
3. There has been a shift away from clinical psychologists being affiliated with research settings (universities, medical schools) to applied clinical settings.
4. There has been an increase in the number of women who are receiving doctorates in clinical psychology.

In addition, there have been several other changes in the types of services provided by clinical psychologists in recent decades. For example, when Garfield and Kurtz (1976) surveyed clinical psychologists in the 1970s, they found that only about 12 percent described their theoretical orientation as cognitive (RET) or behavioral; however, by the late 1980s, Zook and Walton (1989) found that a full 34.5 percent of clinical psychologists endorsed a behavioral or cognitive–behavioral orientation. Interestingly, Zook and Walton further considered the variable of age as a correlate of theoretical orientation. They found that younger clinical psychologists (40 years and younger) were more likely to have a behavioral (or cognitive–behavioral) orientation and less likely to have either a psychodynamic or humanistic orientation than older clinical psychologists. This suggests a fifth trend in clinical psychology over the last several decades:

5. There has been a substantial increase in the cognitive–behavioral theory of explaining and treating psychopathology.

Another change in the thinking of clinical psychologists in recent decades is the increased attention to biological models of explaining and treating disorders. Edelstein and Brasted (1991) noted this increased attention to biological factors as one of the most significant recent trends in the training of clinical psychologists. That is, many clinical programs have developed specializations in behavioral medicine, neuropsychology, pediatric psychology, and clinical gerontology, all of which can be considered as representing the increased awareness of the role of biological influences on psychological problems. Thus, a sixth recent trend in the roles of clinical psychologists is:

6. There has been an increased attention to biological factors and their role in the cause and treatment of psychological problems.

APPLIED ISSUES

Selecting Clinical Psychology versus Other Mental Health Fields

I have often found that undergraduate students are not aware of the differences among the major mental health professions, as well as those among the various applied professional areas within psychology. Perhaps the most frequently asked question I hear from students (as well as nonstudents I see in social settings) concerns the difference between psychology and psychiatry. As an academic advisor, I have encountered many students who say that they intend to pursue a doctoral degree in clinical psychology; yet, when we discuss their career interests, it often turns out that they wish to work as a counseling psychologist or as a social worker—they simply did not understand the differences among the professions.

A psychiatrist is a medical doctor and so has earned an M.D., followed by postgraduate training (a residency) in the diagnosis and treatment of mental disorders. As a physician, a psychiatrist can prescribe medications and other medical interventions. The ability to prescribe medications makes psychiatrists unique among mental health professionals (although some clinical psychologists have been lobbying to gain prescription privileges. See Chapter 12 for a discussion of this movement.)

Psychiatrists do receive training in psychotherapy and so may provide any of a number of types of verbal therapy. I have known psychiatrists, for example, with behavioral, humanistic, family systems, and psychodynamic orientations to explaining and treating psychopathology. However, a common perception among psychologists is that many psychiatrists limit their treatment of patients to medical interventions, providing only minimal psychotherapy as they manage their patients' medication. Another common perception is that psychiatrists retain a stronger tie than clinical psychologists to traditional Freudian models of conceptualizing psychopathology.

Kingsbury (1987) (who received training in both clinical psychology and psychiatry) identified several cognitive differences between psychiatrists and clinical psychologists that result from their different courses of training:

1. *The nature of science.* Whereas psychologists are trained in the methods of science, and so are trained to think theoretically and probabilistically, psychiatrists are trained to view science as a collection of facts and documented procedures.

2. *Clinical conceptualizations.* Whereas clinical psychologists view the disease model of psychopathology as only one of many competing models, psychiatrists accept the medical model as the most appropriate way of interpreting data.

3. *Training experience.* Psychiatrists' training after their second year of medical school is primarily experiential, whereas clinical psychologists' practicum training is usually graduated over four years of academic training, followed by a one-year internship.

For these reasons, students who hold a strong biological perspective to explaining and treating mental disorders and who seek a more practice-oriented approach to learning how to work with clients may prefer psychiatry over clinical psychology.

Another important distinction is that between clinical and counseling psychology. Watkins (1983) discussed several differences between the two areas, perhaps the most important of which concerns their origins. According to Watkins, clinical psychology's beginnings were tied to the mental health movement and the treatment of patients in psychiatric settings; hence, early clinical psychologists were significantly influenced by Freudian theory. On the other hand, Watkins noted that counseling psychology is rooted in attempts to provide vocational guidance to nonpatients and that counseling psychology grew as a specialty at the time that Rogers's model of psychotherapy was becoming influential. For these reasons, clinical psychology has traditionally stressed psychopathology (e.g., differential diagnosis, etiological theories, and treatment), whereas counseling psychology has traditionally emphasized the counseling of normal individuals who are experiencing problems in living.

Watkins (1990) argued that clinical and counseling psychology have converged so that both can be trained in an integrated curriculum. There is some evidence to support this. For example, Stapp and Fulcher (1982) and Stedman, Neff, and Morrow (1995) reported that clinical and counseling psychologists follow similar career paths, in terms of employment setting.

However, such comparisons are simplistic, overlooking possible differences in theoretical orientation and type of work performed. Johnson and Brems (1991) surveyed clinical and counseling psychologists and found that the groups differ in their theoretical approaches. Compared to clinical psychologists, counseling psychologists place significantly less emphasis on biological factors, environmental determinants, and endogenous factors; in addition, counseling psychologists endorse more holistic approaches to conceptualizing cases than clinical psychologists (Johnson & Brems, 1991). Thus, as a group clinical psychologists stress psychopathology and adopt a more scientific orientation to explaining and treating psychopathology than counseling psychologists. In this way, clinical psychologists should be expected to have more psychodynamic, behavioral, and biopsychological orientations whereas counseling psychologists are more likely to have humanistic orientations. This was partly confirmed by Zook and Walton (1989), who found that clinical psychologists prefer behavioral and psychodynamic approaches about equally, whereas counseling psychologists prefer behavioral and humanistic approaches about equally.

A common perception among psychologists is that clinical psychology training programs stress scientific training and the scientific foundations of clinical practice more than do counseling psychology programs.

Thus, students who wish to "counsel" individuals for common problems of living (e.g., educational, vocational, marital counseling), who view abnormality in terms of normal reactions to stress, and who have limited interest in a scientist–practitioner model of clinical work would likely prefer counseling over clinical psychology programs. Conversely, students who have an interest in the scientific foundation of clinical practice, who view psychopathology as being more than a normal reaction to stress, and who are interested in adopting a variety of theoretical models to explaining and treating psychopathology would do well to choose clinical over counseling psychology.

Social work is another mental health profession. Social workers usually have an M.S.W., which is typically a two-year degree following college. Social workers are trained to perform psychotherapy, and in this way resemble psychologists and psychiatrists. However, social workers differ from other mental health professionals in they are also trained to work with social support agencies to enlist the help that a client may require, such as financial assistance or shelter. Social workers tend to view psychological problems in terms of their impact on social functioning; hence, social workers often adopt a systems approach (which views a problem in the family context) to explain disorders.

The training of clinical psychologists and social workers differs in two important respects. Clinical psychologists learn to conduct and interpret research and to apply research results in clinical practice; however, social workers receive little training in science and its application to clinical work. A second difference is in the breadth of training. Clinical psychologists receive training across the breadth of psychology—cognition, learning, social processes, physiological influences, and other areas. Social work is an applied field rather than a science. As such, social work training is much more focused on applied techniques than the training of clinical psychologists.

For these reasons, students who have a limited interest in a theoretical approach to conceptualizing psychopathology, little interest in a scientific foundation for applied practice, and who wish to receive practice-oriented training might prefer training in social work to clinical psychology.

Applying to Graduate School in Clinical Psychology

Psychology is one of the more popular undergraduate majors. For example, in the mid-1980s, there were approximately 40,000 undergraduate psychology majors in the United States (Hogan & Sexton, 1991). About 8,000 students in the United States receive master's degrees in psychology annually (Hogan & Sexton, 1991), while another 2,500 to 3,000 receive doctorates in psychology (Norcross et al., 1996; Rosenzweig, 1991). Of the doctorates, by far the largest specialty area is clinical psychology, accounting for from 37 to 45 percent of psychology doctoral students (Norcross et al., 1996; Rosenzweig, 1991).

However, although there are about 200 doctoral programs in clinical psychology, which grant doctorates to well over a thousand students annually, it is important for students to know that admission to doctoral clinical programs is highly competitive. This section of the chapter summarizes some of the facts about admissions rates and requirements for doctoral programs in clinical psychology.

The APA publishes an annual guide to graduate study in psychology (APA, 1996). This book lists all of the programs in North America that offer graduate programs in psychology and categorizes them according to type of degree offered and area of specialization. For each program, statistics from recent years are provided concerning the number of students who applied and were admitted to the program; in addition, information concerning the admitted students' qualifications (e.g., mean grade point average, GRE scores, etc.) are provided. Information is provided concerning the number of openings for the coming year and the amount and type of financial support available to incoming students. This enables potential applicants to judge the competitiveness of the program (e.g., ratio of applicants to admissions; mean test scores), to compare their own qualifications to those of previously accepted students, and to make initial judgments about the likelihood that they may be admitted to a program.

Norcross and colleagues (1996) summarized the information on doctoral clinical psychology programs listed in the APA 1992–1993 guide to graduate school. This information is very useful for students who are contemplating applying to graduate school. On average, APA-accredited Ph.D. programs received 232.7 applications for 11.1 openings, whereas APA-accredited Psy.D. programs received 241.2 applications for 22.8 openings (nonaccredited Ph.D. and Psy.D. programs received, respectively, 40.0 applications for 6.7 openings and 57.3 applications for 17.8 openings) (Norcross et al., 1996). These results show that APA-accredited programs receive more applications than nonaccredited programs and that Psy.D. programs have larger class sizes than Ph.D. programs. They are also consistent with earlier reports (e.g., Stoup & Benjamin, 1982) that the acceptance rate is about from 3 to 5 percent for APA-accredited programs and from 8 to 14 percent for nonaccredited programs.

Norcross and colleagues (1996) also summarized the admission requirements for doctoral clinical programs. They found that most (93 percent) require the GRE General Test, about half (49 percent) require the GRE Advanced Psychology Test, and most require a specified set of undergraduate psychology courses, including, in the order most frequently cited as a requirement: Statistics/Research Design, Abnormal, Personality, Developmental, Testing, Learning, Laboratory, Physiological, and History/Systems. For doctoral programs that require the GRE General Test, the mean minimum score on the Verbal and Quantitative Tests combined was 1,090, although the mean score of admitted students was 1,206. Similarly, the mean minimum undergraduate GPA was 3.09, whereas the mean GPA of admitted students was 3.50.

Mayne, Norcross, and Sayette (1994) surveyed directors of APA-accredited doctoral programs in clinical psychology, asking about the acceptance rates and admissions requirements of programs. However, Mayne and colleagues also presented this information as a function of whether the program offers the Psy.D or Ph.D. and whether a Ph.D. program is described by its director as research- or practice-oriented. Across 129 programs, the mean preferred GRE Verbal, Quantitative, Analytical, and Psychology scores were, respectively, 581, 580, 579, and 587. The mean preferred undergraduate GPA was

3.3. Interestingly, Mayne and colleagues found slight differences across types of programs in the preferred qualifications of students. Research-oriented Ph.D. programs tend to have higher preferred scores, whereas Psy.D. programs tend to have lower preferred scores. In addition, Psy.D. programs have substantially larger class sizes and acceptance-to-application ratios than Ph.D. programs.

This suggests that scores on the GRE General and Advanced Psychology Tests of 600-plus and an undergraduate GPA of about 3.5 make one a likely candidate for acceptance into a doctoral clinical program. Clearly, admission to more prestigious and competitive programs requires stronger qualifications. Still, the common rumor among undergraduates that, to be admitted to a doctoral clinical program, one must have GRE Verbal and Quantitative scores of 1,400 and a GPA of 4.0 is false and should be dispelled by faculty advisors.

Graduate programs do not simply consider objective criteria such as test scores and undergraduate grades. Norcross and colleagues (1996) reported that the following nonobjective criteria, listed in order of importance, are also considered: personal statement, letters of recommendation, research experience, interview, work experience, public service, and extracurriculars. Of these, the first four were weighed substantially higher than the others.

So, when considering applying to graduate clinical programs, students should try to match their own academic qualifications with the average qualifications of students who have been admitted previously into a program. Several sources are available for undergraduates to help them evaluate their credentials and select an appropriate graduate program. These include the *Insider's Guide to Graduate Programs in Clinical Psychology* (Sayette, Mayne, & Norcross, 1992), *The Complete Guide to Graduate School Admission: Psychology and Related Fields* (Keith-Spiegel, 1991), and *Getting In: A Step-by-Step Plan for Gaining Admission to Graduate School in Psychology* (APA, 1993).

However, students also should try to select a program that matches their personal interests and professional goals. Several sources provide information about the emphases and unique training opportunities of individual programs. First, program descriptions can be obtained from the addresses listed in the APA guide to graduate study. The faculty, their research and professional interests, the emphases of the program, and the clinical training opportunities available should be summarized in program descriptions.

Second, the *Insider's Guide to Graduate Programs in Clinical Psychology* (Sayette et al., 1992) summarizes information on doctoral clinical programs in the APA guide to graduate study, along with information obtained from the programs themselves on the theoretical orientations and research interests of the faculty, clinical training opportunities, and self-rating of the program along a practice-research continuum.

Finally, surveys have been conducted of clinical doctoral programs that enable one to draw some generalizations concerning the nature of various training programs. For example, Wisocki, Grebstein, and Hunt (1994) surveyed directors of clinical doctoral programs and found that their primary theoretical orientation is cognitive–behavioral (55 percent), followed by psychodynamic (23 percent), applied behavioral (11 percent), humanistic–existential (10 percent), systems (8 percent), and other (18 percent).

In their survey of directors of doctoral clinical training programs, Mayne and colleagues (1994) found significant differences in the theoretical orientations of faculty across various types of training programs. For example, practice-oriented Ph.D. programs have a higher percentage of faculty with a psychodynamic orientation (55.4 percent) than Psy.D. programs (32.6 percent), equal-emphasis Ph.D. programs (27.9 percent), and research-oriented Ph.D. programs (17.6 percent). On the other hand, research-oriented Ph.D. programs have a significantly higher percentage of faculty with a cognitive–behavioral orientation (62.7 percent), than the other types of programs (ranging from 31.4 to 46.5 percent).

Sayette and Mayne (1990) surveyed APA-accredited clinical doctoral programs and found that Ph.D. programs are more research oriented than Psy.D. programs, and that Ph.D. programs have more faculty with cognitive–behavioral orientations than Psy.D. programs. In addition, they reported that the most frequently reported areas of faculty research interest are, in order, behavioral medicine, family research, depression, substance abuse, childhood psychopathology, therapy process, and neuropsychology. The researchers also noted that the most commonly reported areas of clinical training opportunities are, in order, family therapy, behavioral medicine, neuropsychology, marital/couples therapy, community psychology, eating disorders, and anxiety disorders.

These surveys show that Ph.D. programs are more research oriented than Psy.D. programs. This certainly is no surprise, since Psy.D. programs were introduced expressly to reduce the emphasis on scientific training in clinical programs. However, these surveys also reveal several trends that are not so obvious but may be helpful when students must decide to which programs to apply: (1) Ph.D. programs fall along a continuum, from strongly research oriented through placing equal emphases on research and practice, to being practice oriented; (2) practice-oriented programs tend to have more faculty with a psychodynamic orientation whereas research-oriented programs tend to have more faculty with a cognitive–behavioral orientation; (3) specific clinical training opportunities (e.g., domestic abuse, AIDS, gerontology) are available across the spectrum of programs, and are more a function of the interests of the faculty than the research–practice orientation of the program.

SCIENTIFIC ISSUES

Evaluation of Graduate Training and Career Choice

It is difficult to measure the quality or effectiveness of graduate training. As observed above, students differ in their career goals and psychologists differ in their views of the most appropriate model of clinical training and practice. For these reasons, it is not possible to judge a graduate program against a template to determine its quality. As incorporated into current APA accreditation guidelines, programs must be judged individually, according to their own stated goals and philosophy of training.

Many researchers have surveyed clinical psychologists to determine their satisfaction with their own training and career. Such "consumer satisfaction" surveys may not be the most scientifically valid measure of the quality of training. Still, they provide a useful perspective of opinions within the field.

In an early study on this topic, Kelly and Goldberg (1959) followed up a sample of psychologists who trained within the VA system and found a very interesting result. A full 40 percent of clinical psychologists expressed some dissatisfaction with their career choice and almost 50 percent indicated that, if given the chance to live their life over again, they would choose a career other than clinical psychology.

The apparent dissatisfaction of clinical psychologists with their careers was both surprising and disappointing. However, students should take heart. Kelly and Goldberg (1959) assessed career satisfaction by asking subjects whether, if they had their lives to live over again, they would select a career as a clinical psychologist or another profession, including high status professions such as law, medicine, and business. This wording likely led more subjects to select a career other than psychology than if a more straightforward question had been asked in which subjects simply rated career satisfaction.

Subsequent surveys have found that clinical psychologists are quite satisfied with their careers. For example, Garfield and Kurtz (1976) observed that only about 10 percent of their sample of clinical psychologists express dissatisfaction with their career and that about 70 percent of clinical psychologists would repeat their career choice. (As an interesting aside, Garfield and Kurtz observed that academic clinical psychologists express significantly more satisfaction with their career choice than clinical practitioners, and that Rogerian-oriented clinical psychologists are less satisfied with their career choice than clinical psychologists of other theoretical persuasions.)

Subsequent surveys of clinical psychologists have consistently shown that most are satisfied with their career choice. For example, from 76 percent (Norcross et al., 1989) to 90 percent (Norcross & Prochaska, 1982b; Walfish et al., 1991) of clinical psychologists are satisfied with their career choice, even though as many as 40 percent might choose another career (Norcross & Prochaska, 1982b; Norcross et al., 1989). This holds for those who have received the Psy.D. degree as well as the Ph.D. (Hershey, Kopplin, & Cornell, 1991; Peterson et al., 1982).

Another set of studies has reported the satisfaction of clinical psychologists with their graduate training. Many of these studies have been used in discussions of the appropriateness of the scientist–practitioner model of training and the suitability of alternative models of training.

Garfield and Kurtz (1976), in their classic survey of clinical psychologists in the 1970s, reported that about 77 percent of clinical psychologists express satisfaction with their graduate training and only about 11 percent express significant dissatisfaction. The mean rating of satisfaction was 4.46 on a 6-point scale, corresponding to a point about midway between "satisfied" and "quite satisfied." Interestingly, academic clinical psychologists expressed significantly more satisfaction with their graduate training than did clinical practitioners, which may reflect practitioners' dissatisfaction with the scientific components of training. When Garfield and Kurtz asked subjects to suggest areas of improvement in graduate training, the greatest number of suggestions spoke to increased clinical training and a decreased scientific component. These results are frequently cited in discussions of the need for a practitioner model of clinical training as an alternative to the scientist–practitioner model.

Comparable results have been reported by Norcross and Prochaska (1982a) and Norcross and colleagues (1989). In general, most clinical psychologists are satisfied with their graduate training, with only a minority expressing any dissatisfaction. When asked how to change graduate training, the most frequently made suggestions concern an increase in applied clinical experiences. Interestingly, clinical psychologists who receive the Psy.D. degree

are as about as satisfied with their graduate training as those who receive a Ph.D. (Hershey et al., 1991; Peterson et al., 1982); however, these surveys of psychologists who receive the Psy.D. did not report their suggestions for improving graduate training.

Norcross, Prochaska, and Gallagher (1989) reported an important result. They surveyed clinical psychologists about their views of graduate training, as a function of the psychologists' own training. About 50 percent preferred the Boulder Model, about 14 percent preferred the Vail Model, and the remaining 36 percent approved about equally of the two models. They found that the preferred training model is significantly related to one's own training. Of those trained in a strong Boulder Model, only 7 percent preferred the Vail Model; of those trained in a strong Vail Model, only 10 percent preferred the Boulder Model. Students who prefer one model of training over the other select programs based on their preferred model; in addition, exposure to a model may increase one's preference for it. Hence, this result, though unsurprising, is important in that it shows that both training models have broad support among clinical psychologists.

Evaluation of the Boulder and Vail Models of Training

The Boulder or scientist–practitioner model has historically been the one in which most clinical psychologists have been trained. As described by Shakow's 1947 committee report, and as elaborated by Thorne (1947), the scientist–practitioner adopts a scientific approach to working with clients. Individual cases are regarded as N-of-one studies in which a scientific (i.e., critical, objective, empirical) approach is taken with regard to assessment, differential diagnosis, theoretical conceptualization, treatment selection, and follow-up evaluation. Each case is viewed as part of a larger sample of cases, so that data collected from individual clients can be aggregated to perform statistical analyses on groups of cases. In this way, clinical psychologists operate as scientists even when working as practitioners.

Working as a scientist–practitioner has several advantages. First, the psychologist can use treatments that have been shown in controlled research to be effective. By relying on research evidence rather than "intuition" or "clinical experience" to select treatments, one has more assurance that the treatment used will be effective. The APA has recognized about two dozen psychotherapies as having been empirically validated (Task Force on Promotion and Dissemination of Psychological Procedures, 1995). APA accreditation standards recommend that training include exposure to empirically validated procedures (APA, 1995b). Although practitioner-oriented training programs can and should include exposure to such empirically validated treatments, it seems likely that training programs that stress research more strongly will also stress research-based treatments. (Crits-Christoph, Frank, Chambless, Brody, & Karp [1995] surveyed Directors of Clinical Training at 135 APA-accredited doctoral programs concerning the degree to which students receive training in empirically validated treatments. Unfortunately, they did not report results separately for Psy.D. and Ph.D. programs. However, they concluded that, in general, training programs do a good job of exposing students to these treatments.)

A second advantage of adopting a scientific approach to clinical practice is the effectiveness of its problem-solving method. By adopting a scientific approach to solving clinical questions, one should be able to develop more accurate clinical conceptualizations (diagnosis, theoretical explanation, treatment selection) and do so more efficiently than using other approaches.

The scientific method involves forming alternative hypotheses and then considering the evidence that supports or disconfirms each; it does *not* mean that the clinician should form a hypothesis and then simply look for evidence to confirm it alone. Such a confirmatory bias has been demonstrated to occur in the thinking of people in general (e.g., Wason, 1960) as well as in the thinking of people who are asked to make clinical-like judgments about others (Snyder & Swann, 1978), and may occur in the way that professional clinicians assign diagnoses (Elstein, Shulman, & Sprafka, 1978; Sandifer, Hordern, & Green, 1970).

Another advantage of the scientific approach to clinical practice is its empirical emphasis. The scientist–practitioner establishes treatment goals that are measurable. Hence, both the therapist and the client can monitor progress toward the goal. The therapist does not rely solely on subjective outcome measures (such as client's self-report or therapist's judgment) that are more likely than objective measures to be biased by influences such as demand characteristics or self-fulfilling prophecies. Because both client and therapist can monitor progress, both parties are in a position, if they do not see clear improvements, to request that the treatment plan be reviewed and renegotiated. By using objective outcome measures, scientist–practitioners become more accountable for the treatment they provide.

However, these advantages of a scientific foundation for clinical practice do not preclude alternative models of clinical training. The Vail Model of training, with its emphasis on clinical practice, continues to stress the scientific foundations of clinical practice, even though its students are not trained to perform research to the extent that occurs in the Boulder Model.

Frank (1984, 1986a, 1986b, 1987) has written extensively about the limits of the Boulder Model. Although Frank agrees that clinical practice should be grounded in and on research, he does not think that it is necessary for clinical psychologists to be trained to do research (Frank, 1984).

Meltzoff (1984) discussed nine major criticisms of the Boulder model. These criticisms are summarized below.

1. *Research training dilutes clinical training.* This argument states that, because so much has been discovered in recent years about the causes and effective treatments of psychopathology, any time spent on research training will necessarily detract from the time spent on and the quality of the clinical training.

The response to this criticism is straightforward. The purpose of graduate training in clinical psychology has never been to produce master clinicians. Rather, the purpose of graduate training is to provide a foundation for continued professional development throughout one's career. Specialized training (say, in neuropsychology) can well be obtained in one's internship or postdoctoral training.

2. *Including research training adds to the expense of training.* Meltzoff (1984) acknowledged that research training costs more than no training. However, he did not think that it costs more than clinical training. If research training were replaced by additional clinical training, then there would be no savings.

3. *Research training is not relevant to clinical practice.* Unfortunately, there is some truth to this point. Frank (1984), for example, argued that there is no evidence that scientific training improves one's clinical efficacy.

However, the reply to this argument is that there is also little evidence that clinical training improves one's effectiveness (Dawes, 1994). Studies have consistently shown that clinical practitioners make little use of research findings in their practice (Morrow-Bradley & Elliott, 1986). Barlow (1986) summarized this literature with an oft-quoted conclusion: "At present, clinical research has little or no influence on clinical practice" (p. 147).

However, simply because practitioners do not employ results from clinical research does not mean that the problem lies in the research—perhaps the problem lies with the practitioners. There has been an increase among clinical psychologists to identify empirically validated treatments and to ensure that students are exposed to such treatments in their training. This effort may help to improve clinical practice by increasing practitioners' use of research-supported treatments.

4. *Research training is unnecessary for the jobs that clinical psychologists will be hired to perform.* Even though the job descriptions of most clinical psychologists in applied settings do not include the conduct of research, this does not mean that research training is unnecessary. APA ethical standards state that psychologists "rely on scientifically and professionally derived knowledge when making scientific or professional judgments or when engaging in scholarly or professional endeavors" (APA, 1992, p. 1600). For practitioners to be able to select effective treatments from among the many "pop psychology

fads" that are marketed requires training in how to evaluate evidence.

5. *There is a conflict between the research and clinical modes of thought.* Frank (1984) stressed this point and summarized the research evidence that suggests that there are cognitive and personality differences between clinicians and scientists. Some differences have been documented. For example, Conway (1988) surveyed clinical psychologists who presented themselves as either practitioners or scientists and found that practitioners more frequently describe themselves as warm and agreeable, whereas scientists present themselves more as conscientious.

One response to this criticism is that people shift between roles all the time (Meltzoff, 1984). During the course of a day, a clinical practitioner may serve as psychotherapist, supervisor, administrator, and consultant. Each role requires its own skills, which can be trained or acquired independently. The skills necessary to succeed in the role of researcher can also be acquired.

6. *The research requirement is exclusionary.* Some fear that students who have the potential to become good clinicians may not have the skills needed to conduct research and so may fail to complete a dissertation and receive the doctorate.

Meltzoff (1984) responded to this criticism by noting that any student bright enough to get into graduate school can learn how to conduct research. Completing a dissertation requires that one defines a problem, attacks it critically, and is motivated to carry the project through its completion. These skills are important in any graduate student, even those who do not intend to become researchers. Interestingly, in a survey of directors of training at Psy.D. programs, Sanchez-Hucles and Cash (1992) found no relationship between a program's having a dissertation requirement and its rate of students who fail to complete the degree.

7. *Students do not want research training.* Meltzoff's (1984) response here is apt. What students want is not necessarily what is good for them nor what they need. Psychologists who have worked as trainers of clinical psychologists are in a much better position than students to recognize what is important in a training program.

8. *Other mental health practitioner fields do not require research training.* For example, medicine does not require that medical students receive research training, even though medical practice should be based on scientifically validated techniques. Why should psychology be different?

Meltzoff (1984) pointed out the different evolutionary paths of medicine and clinical psychology. Medicine developed first as an applied field; its scientific foundation was added later, as the related fields of chemistry, physiology, and pharmacology developed into distinct sciences. Psychology, however, began as a science and then only later developed clinical applications. To separate clinical psychology from its scientific psychological roots would violate the basic premise on which it was founded.

9. *The definition of research is too restricted.* Some have argued that requiring research to be experimental or quasi-experimental "drains the richness and meaning out of personality and clinical research" (Meltzoff, 1984, p. 207). If research is defined narrowly, then clinical research may be trivial and unrelated to actual clinical problems.

Meltzoff's (1984) reply to this criticism is again apt. It is the research question and not the scientific method that is narrow or broad. The scientific method is a method of answering questions. If one applies the scientific method to narrow questions, then the fault is in the researcher and not in the research.

Meltzoff's responses to the criticisms of the Boulder model are well taken. Despite Frank's (1984) argument that scientific and clinical skills are distinct, many clinicians today recognize that the two approaches go hand-in-hand. For example, the APA conferences on clinical training that endorsed the practitioner model as an alternative to the Boulder Model stated that clinical practice should be founded on scientifically documented psychological principles.

Beutler, Williams, Wakefield, and Entwistle (1995) published a recent study that speaks against Frank's (1984) separation of clinical and scientific training. Beutler and colleagues surveyed 325 clinical psychologists, dividing them into academics and practitioners. They found, as expected, that academic clinicians read and value research articles more than do practitioners. However, they also found that clinical practitioners value scientific research and consider their clinical practice to be augmented by scientific findings. This result has been reported in other research (e.g., Beutler, Williams, & Wakefield, 1993; Dent & Ormiston, 1979; Kazdin, Siegel, & Bass, 1990), and suggests that clinicians are not as unreceptive to research results as was formerly believed.

SUMMARY

The first psychological clinic in the United States was established by Witmer in 1896. This and other early clinics were associated with academic psychology departments and staffed primarily by faculty and students. Early clinical psychologists were typically trained in existing doctoral programs in psychology. However, there was some debate over the amount of applied training that clinical psychology students should receive and whether they should receive a master's rather than a doctoral degree. In 1919, 1931, and 1947, committees recommended that clinical psychologists should receive doctorates and receive a combination of both scientific and applied training. In 1949, an APA conference in Boulder, Colorado endorsed the scientist–practitioner model of clinical training, which holds that clinical psychologists are, first and foremost, psychologists, and so should be trained in scientific methods as well as the breadth of psychology.

Since 1949, the APA has also accepted the practitioner–scientist (or Vail) training model as an alternative to the Boulder Model. This training model holds that clinical practice is based on scientific foundations, but does not require that clinical psychologists be trained to conduct scientific research. The Vail Model is the basis of training in Psy.D. programs.

Currently, there are about 200 APA-accredited doctoral programs in clinical psychology, about 80 percent of which are Ph.D. programs and the remaining 20 percent being Psy.D. programs. APA accreditation standards resemble those adopted at the 1949

Boulder conference, requiring that training be broad and professional, rather than narrow and technical, and that training include both science and practice elements. In addition, APA standards require that students receive training in the breadth of psychology, scientific and methodological foundations of psychology, methods of diagnosing and treating problems, and applied practicum experiences. Another requirement is the completion of a one-year internship, during which students work full-time in a clinical setting that provides a variety of training experiences in assessment and treatment. However, APA standards also recognize that training institutions have different missions, and so flexibility is allowed in terms of how different training programs meet these requirements.

Witmer and other early clinical psychologists tended to work primarily in academic and medical settings. The primary activity of early clinical psychologists was assessment. However, World Wars I and II led to recognition of the need for additional providers of clinical services and to clinical psychologists becoming more involved in treating clients. Throughout the twentieth century, clinical psychologists gradually moved away from research settings to private practice and other clinical settings. In addition, there has been an increase in cognitive (and cognitive–behavioral) and biological models of explaining and treating disorders.

Clinical psychology is one of several mental health professions. Clinical psychology differs from psychiatry in several respects. Clinical psychologists are not trained as physicians and so cannot prescribe medications. Psychiatrists are not trained in experimental methods and the breadth of psychology. Training in psychiatry tends to be more practice oriented than in clinical psychology.

Clinical psychology differs from counseling psychology in several ways. Clinical psychology places more emphasis on the scientific study of psychopathology whereas counseling psychology places more emphasis on understanding psychological difficulties as the result of problems in living. As a result, clinical psychologists emphasize scientific training, diagnosis of psychopathology, and behav-

ioral, biopsychological, and psychodynamic theories, whereas counseling psychologists place less emphasis on scientific training and diagnosis and more emphasis on Rogerian theory.

Social workers typically have a two-year master's degree. Social workers are trained to provide psychotherapy and to help clients within a social context, often enlisting assistance from social agencies. Social work is an applied rather than a scientific field. For this reason, social workers receive less training than clinical psychologists in research methods, theoretical models of psychopathology, and the importance of a scientific foundation for clinical practice.

Graduate programs in clinical psychology are highly competitive. Programs typically require minimum GRE Verbal and Performance scores of about 550 and undergraduate GPAs of about 3.1. However, admitted students are more likely to have GRE Verbal and Performance Test scores of about 600 and a GPA of about 3.5. Programs also typically consider several nonobjective admission criteria, such as a personal statement, letters of recommendation, research experience, and an interview.

Students should attempt to match their qualifications to those of applicants previously admitted to a program. The APA publishes an annual guide to graduate programs that lists statistics from recent years concerning each program's number of applicants, number of openings, and admitted students' mean GRE scores and GPAs. Other sources, such as Sayette and colleagues (1992) and individual program descriptions, provide additional information about the theoretical orientation, research emphasis, and unique training opportunities at each training program.

Typically, Ph.D. programs have smaller class sizes, larger application-to-admission ratios, a greater research emphasis, and a larger proportion of faculty with cognitive–behavioral orientations than Psy.D. programs. In addition, research-oriented Ph.D. programs tend to require higher GRE scores and to have more faculty with cognitive–behavioral orientations than practice-oriented Ph.D. and Psy.D. programs.

Clinical psychologists are generally happy with their career choice. Although one survey in the 1950s found significant dissatisfaction, later surveys typically reported that from 76 to 90 percent of clinical psychologists are satisfied with and would repeat their career choice. This holds for psychologists with both Ph.D. and Psy.D. degrees.

Surveys have similarly found that clinical psychologists are satisfied with their graduate training. Dissatisfaction with graduate training typically is expressed in terms of a desire for additional applied clinical experiences. This desire for increased applied clinical training, usually at the expense of scientific training, is one of the reasons for the development of the Vail Model as an alternative to the scientist–practitioner training model.

A scientific approach to clinical practice has several benefits. It ensures that clinical assessment and intervention procedures have been shown empirically to be effective. It provides a systematic method for solving clinical questions. It uses empirical measures to assess treatment progress and outcome.

However, some psychologists criticized the scientist–practitioner model, arguing that psychologists can base clinical practice on scientific principles without having to be trained to conduct research themselves. Others argued that scientific training detracts from clinical training and that the skills necessary to become an effective researcher are inconsistent with those essential in a good clinician.

Despite these criticisms, the Boulder Model remains popular among clinical training programs. Recent research has suggested that clinical practitioners value research and consider their practice to be based on scientific findings more than was suggested in the past.

STUDY QUESTIONS

1. Summarize the general principles and areas of study that were recommended by Shakow and colleagues' (1947) committee on training in clinical psychology.
2. Discuss the influences that led the APA to formalize the standards of training of clinical psychologists.
3. What criteria must be met for a doctoral clinical psychology training program to receive current APA accreditation.
4. Select a mental health profession other than clinical psychology. Compare and contrast clinical psychology to this other profession in terms of training, clinical services provided, and general principles underlying clinical practice.
5. Discuss the criteria used by graduate training programs to evaluate and admit applicants. How do Ph.D. and Psy.D. programs differ in their admissions policies?
6. Summarize the research on clinical psychologists' satisfaction with their training and career choice.
7. How do the Vail and Boulder Models of clinical training differ?
8. Summarize the criticisms of the Boulder Model of training that led to the development of the Vail model.
9. How can a scientist–practitioner respond to these criticisms of the Boulder Model?
10. Discuss the benefits of having a scientific foundation for clinical practice.

Glossary

ABAB reversal design   A single-subject study design in which a researcher observes a client's improvement across four periods: baseline (A), treatment (B), removal of treatment and return to baseline (A), and re-implementation of the treatment (B).

absolutistic thinking   Thinking in "all-or-none" terms; according to Beck, a depressogenic thinking error.

achievement test   A test that measures the extent to which one has mastered the information concerning a particular subject.

acquiescence   A response set in which individuals tend to agree more than disagree with selfstatements, regardless of the item content; also called yea-saying.

activity   One's motor level; a basic dimension of temperament, according to Buss and Plomin.

adoption study   A study in which the similarity of adoptees to their adoptive and biological families is compared; used to estimate the heritability of traits.

akathesia   Motor restlessness; an extrapyramidal side effect of antipsychotic medication.

alternate form reliability   The degree to which two versions of a test agree with one another.

anal character   A cluster of traits, including excessive neatness and orderliness, which Freud considered to be associated with problems the anal stage of development.

analogue study   A study whose subjects only resemble in some way the population to which the investigator wishes to generalize the results.

anal stage   In psychoanalytic theory, the second or toddlerhood stage of psychosexual development, in which one gratifies instincts by anal means; the stage in which the ego develops.

analytical psychology   The psychoanalytic school founded by Carl Gustav Jung.

anticholinergic effects   A set of side effects of medications that lower catecholamine activity, including dry mouth, dry eyes and blurred vision, constipation, and urinary retention.

antipsychotic   A medication used to treat schizophrenia, thought to work by blocking dopamine receptor sites.

aphasia   Inability to name objects.

aptitude test   A test of a general ability that is used to predict future learning or performance.

arbitrary inference   Drawing a conclusion without sufficient evidence to support it; according to Beck, a depressogenic thinking error.

archetypes   Universal symbols, according to Jungian theory.

asthenic body type   The thin, frail physique, considered by Kretschmer as one of the three basic body types.

athletic body type   The hard, muscular physique, considered by Kretschmer as one of the three basic body types.

autonomic system   The division of the peripheral nervous system that connects the central nervous system to the glands and organs of the body; its functions are largely involuntary.

aversive conditioning   A treatment in which an aversive response is classically conditioned to occur in response to a stimulus that formerly triggered an undesirable behavior.

Barnum effect   The tendency for people to accept barnum statements as true about themselves.

Barnum statement   A vague or ambiguous statement that can be interpreted as true of almost everyone.

baseline   A stage of behavioral assessment in which the target behavior is recorded prior to an intervention.

base rate   The percentage of individuals in a group who exhibit the trait of interest.

base rate (BR) score   A score, used on the MCMI, which reflects the prevalence of a symptom in a population and so is interpreted in terms of the likelihood that a symptom is a problem or the major problem for a subject.

basic needs   According to Maslow, a set of needs that must be met in order, or else the person experiences distress and is unable to become self-actualized.

becoming   Allport's term to describe experience as a process of constant growth and development.

behavioral deficit   An adaptive behavior that does not occur frequently or strongly enough, so that a person experiences problems as a result.

behavioral excess   A maladaptive behavior that occurs more frequently or more strongly than is typical, and that causes problems for a person.

behavioral medicine   The application of psychological principles in the treatment of patients with medical conditions.

behavior checklist   A list of behavioral symptoms that are rated for occurrence and/or severity; sometimes called a behavior rating scale.

behavior genetics   A field that studies genetic influences on both normal and abnormal behavior.

behavior rating scale   A list of target behaviors that are rated for severity or frequency.

behavior repertoire   The set of behaviors that an individual is capable of exhibiting.

behavior therapy   The application of conditioning principles in efforts to modify problem behaviors; the attempt to alter human behavior and emotion in a beneficial manner according to the laws of learning theory.

bell-and-pad   An alarm device, triggered by urine, used to treat enuresis; thought to work through classical conditioning.

benzodiazepine   A class of anti-anxiety drugs, thought to work by increasing the degree to which GABA has its inhibitory effect on the postsynaptic cell.

biofeedback   A treatment in which a machine monitors and provides feedback about a physiological state, enabling the client to learn how to voluntarily produce a desired physiological state, usually relaxation.

birth order   Adler's notion that early family experiences, associated with one's order of birth in the family, have a significant influence on the development of personality.

black box   A complex mechanism whose inner workings are unknown so that observers can see only the input entering the mechanism and the output exiting the mechanism.

blocking   Being unable to complete a sentence; an indicator of a client's underlying troubling material.

booster session   Additional training session scheduled after the end of regular treatment.

Boulder Model   A model of training clinical psychologists, which holds that clinical psychologists are psychologists first and clinicians second. As psychologists, clinical psychologists should be trained in scientific methods, general psychological principles, and then in applied clinical techniques. Also called the scientist–practitioner model.

case study   An intensive investigation of an individual subject.

castration anxiety   In psychoanalytic theory, a boy's fear, during the Oedipal Conflict, of being castrated by father.

catharsis   The release of pent-up psychic energy; one of the goals of psychoanalysis.

central nervous system   The brain and spinal cord; the major communication system of the body.

cerebral cortex   The highly wrinkled part of the forebrain that ties just beneath the surface of the skull and that regulates higher mental processes, such as memory and perception.

cerebrotonia   The temperament type identified by Sheldon that is characterized by inhibition and restraint.

chaining   The training of separate behaviors that are then combined to form a complex behavior.

child management   A behavior therapy technique in which parents are trained to use principles of instrumental conditioning to manage their children's behavior more effectively.

chlorpromazine (thorazine)   An antipsychotic medication, in the class of phenothiazines, that is used to treat schizophrenia.

classical conditioning   A form of conditioning in which a previously neutral stimulus comes to elicit a response that had automatically been elicited by another stimulus; also called respondent conditioning.

client-centered therapy   A term for Rogerian therapy that reflects his emphasis on the therapeutic client–therapist relationship.

clinical prediction   A judgment about a person based on a clinician's subjective evaluation.

clinical psychology   The branch of psychology that is concerned with the scientific study of abnormal behavior and mental processes; a term introduced by Witmer.

clomipramine (Anafranil)   A tricyclic antidepressant that is also effective in treating obsessive-compulsive disorder.

cognitive dissonance   An aversive state that occurs when important cognitions (beliefs, perceptions) are in conflict.

cognitive dissonance theory   A theory, developed by Festinger, that holds that people act to reduce cognitive dissonance.

cognitive restructuring   A cognitive therapy that is designed to correct a set of faulty or maladaptive beliefs.

cognitive skills training   A cognitive therapy that is designed to train clients to think in more effective ways, so that they experience fewer behavioral and emotional problems.

comparison   An Adlerian therapy technique in which the therapist compares himself to the client and asks what goals he would be seeking if he behaved like the client.

comprehensiveness   The range of observations that a theory can explain; a criterion used to evaluate scientific theories.

concurrent validity   The extent to which a test agrees with measures of the construct or related construct that are assessed concurrently.

conditional positive regard   An environment in which a person is accepted only when meeting the conditions of others; according to Rogers, fosters unhealthy psychological development.

conditioned reflex therapy   Salter's term for the use of classical conditioning to treat clinical disorders.

conditioned response (CR)   In classical conditioning, a response that is trained to occur to a conditioned stimulus.

conditioned stimulus (CS)   In classical conditioning, the neutral stimulus that, through repeated pairing with the unconditioned stimulus, is conditioned to elicit a response similar to the original unconditioned response.

condition of worth   A belief that one must meet some standard, adopted from others, in order to be a worthy person.

confabulation   A response on the Rorschach test in which the examinee identifies two distinct percepts and then combines them inappropriately; traditionally interpreted as an indicator of psychosis.

confidence interval   A range of scores within which one can state with a certain degree of probability that a true score lies.

confound   An uncontrolled factor that co-varies with a variable in a study and so limits the internal validity of the study.

confrontation   A therapeutic technique in which the therapist brings to the client's attention some aspect of functioning that the client is unaware of or has been denying.

conscience   The part of the superego that, following the violation of a moral value, makes one feel guilty.

consensual drift   A form of observer drift in which a set of observers no longer use the original scoring criteria but continue to show good inter-rater reliability with one another.

construct   Kelly's term for a cognitive dimension along which people interpret, classify, and evaluate experience.

construct validity   The extent to which theoretical relationships between a construct, as measured by the assessment instrument and other constructs are supported.

contact   A person's relatedness to the world; in Gestalt therapy, awareness of one's contact is an index of psychological health.

content validity   The extent to which an assessment instrument has sampled from the entire domain of interest.

continuous reinforcement   A schedule of reinforcement in which every instance of the target behavior is reinforced or punished.

contracting   A therapy technique in which the client and therapist form a contract, so that the client earns reinforcement for making progress toward a behavioral goal.

control   The fourth stage of science in which empirically supported principles are applied in specific circumstances to obtain desired results.

control group   In an experiment, a group of subjects that is not exposed to the experimental manipulation.

conversion   A defense mechanism, through which painful psychic material is exhibited symbolically in physiological symptoms.

conversion disorder   A disorder characterized by physical symptoms, with no physical basis, that are caused by psychological factors; originally called hysterical conversion disorder.

coping model   A model who initially experiences the same problem as the client but who gradually performs successfully, demonstrating methods of coping with fear, doubt, and other obstacles to successful performance.

correlational study   A study in which the investigator measures the relationship between naturally occurring variables.

correlation coefficient   A measure of the strength of the relation between two variables.

counterconditioning   A term for systematic desensitization.

countertransference   The emotional reactions of a therapist toward a client; interpreted by Freud as representing feelings the therapist had for significant others earlier in life.

coverant   A covert operant; Lloyd Homme's term for a cognitive process that he thought is a form of behavior and so follows the principles of behaviorism.

covert modeling   A cognitive therapy technique in which a client imagines someone engaging in an adaptive behavior.

covert punishment   A cognitive therapy technique in which a client imagines himself engaging in a maladaptive behavior that is followed by punishment.

covert rehearsal   A cognitive therapy technique in which a client imagines himself performing an adaptive behavior.

covert reinforcement   A cognitive therapy technique in which a client imagines himself engaging in an adaptive behavior that is followed by reinforcement.

covert sensitization   A cognitive version of aversive conditioning, in which the imaginal occurrence of an undesired behavior is paired with imagined aversive consequences; introduced by Cautela.

craniology   The view that cranial capacity is related to brain size and so can be used as a sign of intelligence.

craniometry   Measuring cranial capacity (brain size) as an index of intelligence.

criterion-related validity   The extent to which a test agrees with other measures of the construct, or with other measures of constructs that are theoretically related to the construct.

cross-lag correlational study   A correlational research design that examines the association between two variables at two (or more) points in time and compares the correlations between variables assessed and subsequently.

cross-validation   A procedure in which statistical results in one sample are tested in an independent sample before applying the results to the general population; this procedure reduces the likelihood that results due to random variation in the initial sample will be included in the final results.

crystallized intelligence   Specific abilities one has already learned, which enable one to solve familiar problems.

deep (slow) breathing   A relaxation technique in which one breathes deeply, holds one's breath, and exhales slowly, gradually slowing one's respiration rate.

defense mechanism   An unconscious ego process that serves to protect the individual from threatening material.

deficiency (d-) needs   Another term for Maslow's basic needs.

delayed treatment group   A control group in psychotherapy outcome studies in which subjects are placed on a waiting list so that they are assured of receiving treatment in the future.

demoralization   According to Frank, the experience common to all therapy clients subsequent to becoming aware that they have failed to cope with their life problems and no longer having the expectancy that they will be able to cope on their own.

denial   A defense mechanism, through which threatening material is prevented from entering awareness.

dependent variable (DV) The variable that is measured and compared across groups at the end of an experiment to determine whether the independent variable has a causal effect.

dereflection A therapy technique, introduced by Frankl, in which the therapist helps the client focus attention outside of the self, so that excessive self-observation no longer interferes with functioning.

describe The first stage of science in which initial observations are made.

determinism The philosophical assumption that all events have causes.

deviation IQ A measure of intelligence determined by one's performance on an intelligence test relative to age-peers; generally has a mean of 100 and a standard deviation of 15.

diagnostic efficiency The percentage of individuals who are correctly classified by a test.

diazepam (Valium) A commonly prescribed benzodiazepine.

difficult temperament A cluster of behavioral and emotional tendencies in infants that makes it difficult for parents to care for them; identified by Chess and Thomas.

discriminant analysis A complex statistical technique that identifies variables that discriminate between groups.

discrimination A phenomenon of learning in which a behavior is conditioned to occur in response to specific stimulus and not in response to other similar stimuli.

displacement A defense mechanism, through which unacceptable impulses are directed toward more acceptable targets.

dissociation A form of psychological disorder in which troubling ideas are split from the rest of consciousness; studied by Janet.

disulfiram (antabuse) A medication used in the treatment of alcohol abusers, which, when combined with alcohol, causes severe nausea and vomiting.

dizygotic (DZ) twins Fraternal twins, who share, on average, about 50 percent of their genes.

double-blind study A design, used in placebo studies, in which neither the subject nor the person administering the treatment knows whether the subject is receiving a placebo or an experimental treatment; controls for expectation and suggestion effects.

dystonia Twisting and spasmodic movements of muscle groups; an extrapyramidal side effect of antipsychotic medication.

easy temperament A cluster of behavioral and emotional tendencies in infants that makes it easy for parents to care for them; identified by Chess and Thomas.

eclecticism The view that different theoretical approaches may be most appropriate for different cases.

ectomorphy The thin, frail body type, considered by Sheldon to be associated with cerebrotonia.

effect size A measure of the strength of the observed results of a study; used in meta-analytic reviews as a measure common to all studies.

ego In psychoanalytic theory, the realistic component of personality.

ego ideal The values and ideals to which one aspires.

ego psychology A Neo-Freudian movement, which places a greater emphasis on ego than id functioning, leading to a greater focus than classical psychoanalysis on conscious motivations, healthy functioning, and the integrity of personality.

electroconvulsive therapy (ECT) A treatment for severe depression, in which seizures are induced by passing a mild electrical current through the brain.

emotionality The degree to which one responds physiologically to emotion; a basic dimension of temperament, according to Buss and Plomin.

empathy An element of unconditional positive regard in Rogerian therapy, in which the therapist understands what the client is experiencing and communicates this understanding to the client.

empiricism The assumption that science restricts its attention to observables or measurables.

endomorphy The round, soft body type, considered by Sheldon to be associated with viscerotonia.

epistemology The philosophy of knowledge, which addresses issues concerning the acquisition, nature, and certainty of knowledge.

etiology The initial cause of a disorder.

existentialism A school of philosophy that focuses on the problems of human existence, such as pain, loneliness, death, and responsibility.

experiment   A study in which the investigator randomly assigns subjects to groups and then manipulates one or more variables, while controlling other variables; enables the investigator to draw causal conclusions.

explain   The second stage of science in which possible explanations are proposed for the initial observations.

external validity   The degree to which the results of a study can be generalized to other subjects and situations; a function of the degree to which the subjects and situations in a study are representative of the subjects and situations to which the investigator wishes to generalize the results.

extrapyramidal effects   A set of motor side effects of antipsychotic medication, including dystonia, akathesia, and Parkinsonism.

factor analysis   A multivariate technique that examines the interrelationships among a set of variables to identify the basic dimensions that contribute to scores on the variables.

fading   The gradual removal of concrete or salient cues that are used during behavior therapy.

false negative   A test result that indicates that a person does not have a trait when in fact he has it.

false positive   A test result that incorrectly indicates that a person has a trait when in fact he does not have it.

falsifiability   Ability of a theory to generate testable predictions; the defining feature of scientific theories, according to Karl Popper.

family study   A research method used to determine whether a trait runs in families.

field theory of personality   An ecological theory of personality, developed by Lewin, which emphasizes the person's relationships to his or her environment.

fixation   The cessation of psychosexual development in an early stage.

fixed-role therapy   A therapy technique in which the client plays the role of a fictional character, whose cognitive construct system was scripted by the client and therapist, between therapy sessions; introduced by George Kelly.

flooding   A treatment for phobias, based on extinction, in which the client experiences prolonged exposure to the feared object.

fluid intelligence   The general capacity to learn, which enables one to adapt to new situations.

fluoxetine (Prozac)   A monocyclic antidepressant, thought to work through selectively inhibiting the re-uptake of serotonin.

forebrain   The most recently evolved part of the human brain that controls higher mental functions, such as memory and perception.

free association   A psychoanalytic therapy technique in which the client says whatever comes to mind, making no conscious effort to inhibit or censor the speech; the "fundamental rule" of psychoanalysis.

functional analysis   Skinner's term for behavioral assessment, in which behavior is explained as a function of the antecedent stimuli that cue it and the consequent stimuli that punish or reinforce it.

general (g) factor   According to Spearman, a general factor of intelligence which contributes to level of performance across a variety of tests.

general adaptation syndrome   A physiological response to stress, described by Selye, consisting of three stages: alarm and mobilization, resistance, and exhaustion.

generalization   A phenomenon of learning in which a response, originally learned in one situation, is trained to occur in other similar situations.

generalization gradient   The tendency for generalized responses to be greater in the presence of stimuli that more strongly resemble the stimulus in the presence of which the response was originally learned.

general paresis   A physical disorder characterized by progressive loss of motor and psychological functions; caused by deterioration of the central nervous system due to action of spirochetes, the infectious agent in syphilis.

genital stage   In psychoanalytic theory, the fifth, adult stage of psychosexual development.

genuineness   An element of unconditional positive regard in Rogerian therapy, in which the therapist is honest and open in expressing his or her own thoughts and feelings.

gestalt   The German word for "pattern" or "whole."

Gestalt therapy   A form of therapy, developed by Fritz Perls, which stresses the individual's awareness of one's current experience and relatedness to the external world.

goodness-of-fit   A developmental model that states that a child's development is optimal when there is a match between the child's temperament and environment.

graphology   Interpreting personality from handwriting.

haloperidol (Haldol)   An antipsychotic medication that is also effective in the treatment of Tourette's Syndrome.

health psychology   The use of psychological interventions to improve physical health, such as weight loss.

heritability coefficient   An estimate of the degree to which genes influence a trait and which can be estimated from adoption and twin studies; ranges from zero to one, with a coefficient of zero meaning no genetic influence and a coefficient of one meaning no environmental influence.

heuristic value   The ability of a scientific theory to be applied to multiple problem areas or contexts.

hindbrain   The part of the brain that lies above and is connected to the spinal cord; controls the most basic bodily functions, such as breathing and swallowing.

homeostasis   The tendency for a system to act to maintain its steady state.

hypnosis   A psychological treatment that enhances both relaxation and suggestibility.

hypothalamus   A brain structure important in regulating drive-related behavior, such as hunger and sexual activity.

hypothesis   A statement of a potential empirical relationship between variables.

hypothetical construct   A nonobservable construct that is presumed to exist and that is theoretically related to constructs that can be observed.

hysterical conversion disorder   Physical symptoms for which there is no physical cause but which instead are produced by psychological factors.

id   In psychoanalytic theory, the animalistic side of personality driven by the biological instincts of sex and aggression.

illusory correlation   A mistakenly perceived association between events that in fact have no statistical association.

imipramine (Tofranil)   A tricyclic antidepressant that is also used to treat enuresis.

implosive therapy   A treatment for phobias in which the client experiences prolonged exposure to the feared object, along with visual imagery of and psychodynamic images related to the object; introduced by Stampfl.

independent variable (IV)   In an experiment, the variable manipulated by the investigator so that different groups are exposed to different levels of the IV.

individual psychology   The psychoanalytic school founded by Alfred Adler.

inferiority complex   According to Adler, a real or perceived inferiority that leads to efforts to compensate for the deficiency.

inhibited temperament   A temperament type, identified by Kagan, characterized by high distress in response to novel stimuli.

insight   Bringing unconscious troubling material to consciousness; the primary goal of psychoanalysis.

instrumental conditioning   The conditioning of voluntary responses through their positive or negative consequences; also called operant conditioning.

intellectualization   A defense mechanism, through which an individual acknowledges an unacceptable impulse or action, without recognizing its emotional content.

intelligence   The capacity to learn from experience and adapt to the environment.

intelligence quotient (IQ)   A measure of intelligence, introduced in the Stanford-Binet (1916), and calculated by the formula: IQ = 100 ×[(Mental Age)/(Chronological Age)].

intermittent reinforcement   A schedule of reinforcement in which not every instance of the target behavior is followed by a consequence; also called partial reinforcement.

internal consistency   A characteristic of a theory to generate predictions that are not contradictory; a theory that is internally inconsistent is not falsifiable; the degree to which subsections of a test agree with one another.

internal validity   The extent to which the observed results of a study were caused by the experimental treatment; a function of the degree to which the investigator has controlled for and so ruled out alternative possible explanations for the results.

interpretation   The therapist's referring to something the client has said or done in such a way as to identify features of the behavior of which the client had not been fully aware.

inter-rater reliability The degree to which two judges produce consistent evaluations of a subject.

interval schedule An intermittent schedule of reinforcement in which a certain amount of time must elapse following a reinforcement before the next instance of the target behavior will be reinforced.

intervening variable A construct that is used simply to summarize a set of empirical observations or principles; does not convey any meaning other than what can be directly observed.

introversion/extraversion The degree to which one enjoys quiet and introspective versus active and stimulating activities; according to Eysenck, a basic dimension of personality that is related to cortical arousal.

item analysis Statistical techniques used to evaluate and select items for a test.

item-total correlation A measure of the association between the score on a single item and the score on the sum of the remaining items of a test; measures the degree to which each item is related to the entire test.

kappa coefficient A measure of agreement, independent of chance, on assignment to categories.

Lamaze training Natural childbirth training, in which pregnant women learn to manage the pain and arousal of labor through breathing exercises and psychological methods such as distraction.

latency stage In psychoanalytic theory, the fourth or school-age stage of psychosexual development.

law of parsimony The principle that, all else being equal, scientists prefer the simplest theory.

libido Sexual energy in psychoanalytic theory.

life lie Adler's term for neurosis, referring to a style of life that reflected a poorly developed social interest.

limbic system A part of the midbrain that is important in the regulation of emotion.

lithium A medication used to treat bipolar disorder.

lobotomy A surgical procedure, introduced by Moniz, in which neural pathways that connect the frontal lobes to other parts of the brain are severed.

logotherapy A form of existential therapy, developed by Viktor Frankl, which is designed to help clients find meaning in their lives.

mainstream The educational practice of using the least restrictive intervention possible when providing special educational services, so that the child is placed as much as possible with nondisabled children.

Malleus Malleficarum (The Witches' Hammer) A book written In 1486 to guide the clergy in identifying individuals who consorted with witches; initiated the Spanish Inquisition.

MAO-Inhibitor (MAO-I) A class of antidepressant medications that inhibit an enzyme used to break down serotonin and norepinephrine, thereby increasing the supply of these neurotransmitters.

mastery model A model who performs a target behavior successfully from the outset, without exhibiting the problems experienced by the client.

maximization/minimization Overemphasizing the negative aspects of experience while overlooking the positive; according to Beck, a depressogenic thinking error.

medical model An approach to pathology that assumes that patients with common symptoms have a common disorder, including their pathology, etiology, and prognosis.

meditation A transpersonal therapy in which physical and psychological exercises are used in order to heighten attention and enhance mental functioning.

mental age (mental level) The age at which normal children are expected to pass specified items of the Binet-Simon (1908) test.

mental status examination An interview in which the client's current psychological functioning is assessed, including appearance, behavior, affect, and cognitive processes.

mesmerism The original form of hypnotism, believed by Mesmer to be based on "animal magnetism."

mesomorphy The hard, muscular body type, considered by Sheldon to be associated with somatotonia.

meta-analysis A set of statistical procedures designed to enable reviewers to combine data across studies.

metaphorical medical model Freud's generalization of the medical model, in which he limited his attention to underlying psychological, rather than physiological, pathology.

method of contrasted groups An empirical method of test development in which many items are administered to groups and those items are selected to which members of different groups respond differentially.

methylphenidate (Ritalin) A mild amphetamine that is widely used to treat children with attention deficit hyperactivity disorder.

midbrain The part of the brain that lies above the hindbrain and is involved with the control of drive-related behavior and the regulation of emotions.

milieu therapy A treatment used in inpatient settings in which every aspect of the environment is designed to be therapeutic.

minimal treatment group A control group in psychotherapy outcome studies in which subjects receive a minimal intervention (e.g., support, information); they may receive the experimental treatment at a later time.

monozygotic (MZ) twins Identical twins, who share 100 percent of their genes.

moral treatment A treatment, introduced by Pinel, in which mental patients were released from chains and treated humanely.

Morgan's Canon A statement of the law of parsimony by Lloyd Morgan.

mortido Aggressive energy, in psychoanalytic theory.

multiple baseline design A single-subject design in which different symptoms are treated sequentially; differential improvement of targeted and nontargeted symptoms is taken as evidence of the effectiveness of treatment.

multiple correlation A correlational research design in which the association between a criterion and a set of predictor variables is measured.

mutual analysis Term used to describe Jungian analysis, stressing the fact that the Jungian analyst may suggest interpretations based on a symbol's meaning for the therapist.

naturalistic observation Monitoring behavior in its natural setting.

nay-saying Another term for the response set of nonacquiescence.

negative symptoms of schizophrenia Symptoms of schizophrenia that reflect the absence of normal functioning, such as lack of emotional responsiveness, lack of motivation and initiative, and social withdrawal.

neologism Words that a person makes up or uses idiosyncratically; often associated with severe psychological disorders such as schizophrenia.

neuro-hypnotism A term used by Braid to suggest that mesmerism is a neurological state akin to sleep; later shortened to "hypnotism."

neuroleptic A term for antipsychotic medication.

neurology The medical specialty that studies and treats disorders of the nervous system.

neuroticism According to Eysenck, a basic dimension of personality, associated with physical emotional reactivity.

neurotransmitter A chemical that crosses a synapse and activates nerve impulses in the postsynaptic cell.

nominalism A logical fallacy in which the naming of a phenomenon is thought to explain it.

nonacquiescence A response set in which individuals tend to disagree more than agree with self-statements, regardless of the item content; also called nay-saying.

nondirective therapy Rogerian therapy in which the therapist does not dictate the course or methods of therapy.

nonparticipant observer A person, such as the psychologist or a clinic assistant, who is not generally in the client's natural environment and who records the client's problem behavior.

nonspecific elements of therapy Common factors, such as client, therapist, and relationship variables, that may contribute to the effectiveness of all forms of psychotherapy.

normal science According to Kuhn, a process of "puzzle-solving" wherein scientists pursue mundane questions within a paradigm rather than attempt to refute the paradigm.

noumena Kant's terms for objective reality.

object relations theory A Neo-Freudian movement, which emphasizes social and other object-related motivations that do not simply serve to gratify sexual and aggressive instincts.

observer drift A threat to the accuracy of behavioral observations that occurs when observers, following training, introduce idiosyncratic modifications of the recording system.

Occam's razor A statement of the law of parsimony by William of Occam.

Oedipal conflict (neurosis, complex) In psychoanalytic theory, the process during the phallic stage when the child experiences incestuous wishes for the opposite-sex parent, ultimately resolved by identifying with the same-sex parent.

open-ended statement   A therapy technique in which the therapist indicates the topic of conversation but does not set limits on how the client may respond, leaving the development of the topic to the client.

operant   A voluntary behavior that can be conditioned to increase or decrease in frequency by its consequences.

operant conditioning   See instrumental conditioning.

operational definition   A specification of a concept in terms of the operations or procedures used to measure the concept.

oral character   A cluster of traits, including selfishness and love of oral gratification, which Freud considered to be associated with problems during the oral stage of development.

oral stage   In psychoanalytic theory, the first or infancy stage of psychosexual development, in which one gratifies instincts by oral means.

order   The philosophical assumption that the universe is lawful—that nature is orderly.

overconditioning   The process of developing abnormal behavior by being conditioned to exhibit problem behaviors not found in others.

overgeneralization   Drawing a general conclusion on the basis of a single incident; according to Beck, a depressogenic thinking error.

overlearning   A conditioning technique in which training continues long after initial criteria for success are attained.

paradigm   The prevailing theory within a science.

paradox   A treatment intervention in which the therapist encourages clients to engage in or to exaggerate the very symptoms they have been trying to avoid.

paradoxical intention   A treatment technique, introduced by Frankl, in which the therapist encourages the client to exhibit a problem behavior or symptom that he fears and has been trying to avoid.

parallel forms   Alternative versions of a test that have the same psychometric characteristics, including mean score, reliability, and validity.

paraphrasing   A therapy technique in which the therapist summarizes the content of what the client has said.

parapraxis   A "Freudian slip;" interpreted by Freud as caused by unconscious influences.

paraprofessional   An individual who does not have formal training in a profession, but who receives specialized training and then works alongside professionals.

Parkinsonism   Stiffness, tremor, and rigidity, caused as a side effect of antipsychotic medication.

parsimony   Simplicity; a criterion used to evaluate scientific theories.

partial reinforcement   See intermittent reinforcement.

participant observer   A person, such as a spouse, parent, or teacher, who already is in the client's natural environment and who records the target behavior.

pathognomonic symptom   A symptom that is both a necessary and sufficient criterion for a disorder; the presence of such a symptom therefore determines the client's diagnosis.

pathology   The immediate cause of the patient's symptoms; the problems in the patient's psychodynamics, physiology, or environment that leads to the patient's symptoms.

penis envy   In psychoanalytic theory, a girl's sense of inferiority because she lacks a penis, experienced at the start of the Phallic stage.

peripheral nervous system   The section of the nervous system that connects the brain and spinal cord to the organs, muscles, and senses of the rest of the body.

perseveration   Nonpurposive repetition of words, phrases, or behaviors.

personality disorder   A personality trait that is inflexible, maladaptive, and causes significant distress or impaired functioning.

personality trait   A tendency to behave in functionally equivalent ways across situations.

personality type A   A set of behavioral traits, including competitiveness, setting strict schedules, and becoming involved in many activities, which may lead a person to be at increased risk for stress-related disorders.

personality type B   A set of behavioral traits, including low competitiveness and low achievement-orientation, which may lead a person to be at decreased risk for stress-related disorders.

personalization   Interpreting events as personal affronts or obstacles; according to Beck, a depressogenic thinking error.

phallic stage   In psychoanalytic theory, the third stage of psychosexual development, around ages 5 to 6 years, in which one gratifies instincts by phallic means; the stage in which the superego develops through resolution of the Oedipal conflict.

phenomena   Kant's term for an individual's subjective experience of the external world.

phenomenology   The philosophical approach, introduced by Husserl, which states that the only way to understand a person is through the person's subjective experience.

phenothiazines   A class of antipsychotic medications.

phenytoin (Dilantin)   An anticonvulsant medication commonly used to treat seizure disorders.

philosophy of science   A branch of epistemology concerned with the philosophical foundations of science; addresses the assumptions, methods, and logic of science.

phrenology   The practice of judging one's personality and faculties through reading the bumps on their head; introduced by Franz Joseph Gall.

physiognomy   The practice of determining character from a person's physical appearance; the study of the relationship between physical appearance and psychological characteristics.

placebo   An inert or inactive treatment.

play therapy   A form of psychotherapy with children in which the primary form of client–therapist interaction is play; used both by psychoanalytic and humanistic therapists.

pleasure principle   In psychoanalytic theory, the principle underlying the functioning of the id— namely, that the id seeks to maximize immediate gratification.

polarity   An artificial distinction drawn by a person between different aspects of self; considered by Gestalt therapists as an indication of neurosis.

positive symptoms of schizophrenia   Symptoms of schizophrenia that reflect the presence of abnormal functioning, including delusions, hallucinations, and loose associations.

practitioner–scientist model   A model of training clinical psychologists, which holds that clinical psychologists should be trained primarily in applied techniques. Rather than conduct research themselves, practitioner–scientists should provide services that have a scientific foundation. Also called the Vail Model.

predictive validity   The degree to which a test provides measures of a construct that are related to future measures of the trait or related constructs.

prefrontal leucotomy   Another term for lobotomy.

primary mental abilities   According to L. L. Thurstone, the seven basic dimensions of intelligence.

prognosis   The future course of the condition.

progressive muscle relaxation   A treatment, introduced by Jacobson, in which the client systematically tenses and relaxes muscle groups, thereby learning to distinguish between muscle tension and relaxation and to relax voluntarily.

projection   A Freudian defense mechanism in which one attributes one's own threatening thoughts or impulses to others.

projective personality test   A test, based on Freudian principles, that is designed to understand a person's personality from that person's unique responses to ambiguous test items.

projective test   A personality test consisting of vague or unstructured stimuli to be interpreted or organized by the examinee; the examinee's underlying personality is interpreted from the person's unique responses to test stimuli.

proprium   The developing self; a term used by Allport to emphasize the dynamic nature of experience.

psychic determinism   Freud's assumption that all actions are caused, often by unconscious influences from early childhood.

psychoanalysis   Freudian insight-oriented psychotherapy, designed to bring the client's unconscious problems to consciousness.

psychoanalytically oriented psychotherapy   A variation of Freudian therapy, introduced by Alexander, which is briefer and more flexible than classical psychoanalysis.

psychodrama   A form of psychotherapy, introduced by Moreno, in which clients role-play or act out troubling scenes from their lives; an early form of group therapy.

psychology   The scientific study of behavior and mental processes.

psychometrics   The statistical theory of psychological assessment.

psychophysiological disorder   A physical disorder that is caused, at least in part, by psychological factors.

psychosomatic disorder   Another term for psychophysiological disorder.

psychosurgery   A surgical procedure, usually involving the nervous system, to treat emotional and behavioral disorders.

psychoticism   According to Eysenck, a basic dimension of personality, associated with eccentricity of thinking.

punishment   An undesirable consequence that, following a behavior, decreases the frequency of the behavior.

pyknic body type   The round soft physique, considered by Kretschmier as one of the three basic body types.

Q-sort   A research technique in which subjects sort self-statements, printed on cards, into piles, according to the degree to which they accurately describe the self or self-ideal.

rapid smoking   A treatment in which a client inhales cigarette smoke every six to eight seconds until becoming ill; after several sessions, a classically conditioned aversive response to cigarettes is established.

rapport   The quality of an interpersonal relationship, considered to be an important factor in psychotherapy outcome.

ratio schedule   An intermittent schedule of reinforcement in which a target behavior must occur a certain number of times before the next instance of the behavior is reinforced.

rational-emotive therapy (RET)   A cognitive therapy based on the assumption that emotional disorders result from irrational cognitions; treats emotional problems by helping clients revise or replace irrational cognitions; introduced by Albert Ellis.

rationalization   A defense mechanism, through which unacceptable impulses or actions are justified through implausible excuses.

reaction formation   A defense mechanism, through which an unacceptable impulse is expressed as its direct opposite.

reactivity   The tendency for people to respond differently when observed than at other times; a potential problem of behavioral assessment.

reality principle   In psychoanalytic theory, the principle underlying the functioning of the ego, namely that the ego seeks to maximize gratification given the constraints of reality.

receptor site   A structure on the postsynaptic cell that takes up specific neurotransmitters.

reciprocal inhibition   Wolpe's term for the treatment of phobias in which the feared object is paired with muscle relaxation, which is incompatible with the physiological arousal that accompanies fear.

reflection   A therapy technique in which the therapist recognizes in some way the feeling or attitude expressed by the client.

regression   A return to the psychosexual functioning associated with a previously completed stage of development.

reinforcement   A desirable consequence that, following a behavior, increases the frequency of the behavior.

reliability   The extent to which assessment instruments provide stable or consistent results.

repression   A defense mechanism, through which threatening material is simply blocked out of awareness.

resistance   Anything the client does to interfere with therapeutic progress; according to Freud, a common occurrence in therapy when the client begins to approach recognition of the unconscious troubling material.

respondent   A response that is elicited reflexively by a stimulus.

respondent conditioning   Another term for classical conditioning.

response set   A pattern of responding to structured test items, not because of item content, but because of a general response style; a commonly raised criticism of structured personality inventories.

reticular activating system   A formation in the midbrain and part of the hindbrain that regulates state of alertness.

reuptake   A process through which excess neurotransmitters in the synapse are taken up by and returned to the presynaptic cell.

revolving door syndrome   The problem where patients hospitalized for psychotic disorders are treated with medication and released but become psychotic and must be hospitalized once again when they discontinue the medication.

sample approach The model of psychological assessment that assumes that test responses are samples of one's general behavior and in which no inferences are drawn about underlying characteristics.

schema A set of cognitive statements that an individual uses to help organize and interpret experience.

scientist–practitioner model See Boulder Model.

selective abstraction Focusing on a detail taken out of context; according to Beck, a depressogenic thinking error.

self According to Rogers, a person's subjective view of self, or one's self-image.

self-actualization According to humanists, a basic human motivation to develop all of one's potentialities.

self-efficacy One's perception of his or her ability to perform effectively in a given situation; the expectation that one can perform successfully in a given situation; increased self-efficacy was considered by Bandura to be the basis for all forms of psychotherapy.

self-ideal The self (or self-image) one would most like to have.

self-monitoring A form of assessment in which clients attend to and record their problem cognitions or behaviors.

sensitivity The ability of a test to correctly identify people who have the trait of interest.

shaping The systematic reinforcement of successive approximations to a desired behavior.

sibling rivalry Adler's notion that early conflicts with siblings have an important influence on the development of personality.

sign approach The model of psychological assessment that assumes that test responses are outward manifestations of underlying characteristics.

slow-to-warm-up temperament The temperament type characterized by a tendency for infants to withdraw from and show distress in response to a new stimulus; identified by Chess and Thomas.

sociability The degree to which one approaches or withdraws from others; a basic dimension of temperament, according to Buss and Plomin.

social desirability A response set in which the individual tends to respond to test items by selecting the most socially desirable option.

social learning Learning through the observation of other people's behavior; also called modeling, imitative learning, vicarious learning, and observational learning.

social reinforcement Reinforcement provided naturally in social interactions, such as smiles and verbal praise.

somatic system The division of the peripheral nervous system that connects the central nervous system to the muscles and senses of the body; largely controls voluntary functions.

somatization disorder A condition characterized by multiple conversion-like symptoms; that is, the client reports one physical symptom after another, each without a physical basis.

somatotonia The temperament type identified by Sheldon that is characterized by love of vigorous activity and risk-taking.

specific (s) factors According to Spearman, specific dimensions of intelligence that each contribute to performance in a specific area.

specificity The ability of a test to correctly identify individuals who do not have the trait of interest.

spontaneous remission rate The percent of untreated patients who improve without receiving formal treatment.

standard error of measurement (SEM) The standard deviation of a set of observed scores for an individual; a useful statistic in judging the accuracy of the estimate of a true score.

standardized behavioral assessment An approach to evaluating behavior in which client behavior is observed in a standardized setting, rather than its natural setting.

statistical prediction A judgment about a person based on quantitative information, using formulas derived from empirical research with other subjects.

stimulus control Behavior therapy technique in which the antecedent and consequent stimuli that control a problem behavior are modified.

stress inoculation A cognitive therapy in which clients learn to instruct themselves to prepare to confront and then cope more effectively with a stressor; introduced by Meichenbaum.

structural therapy Minuchin's family systems therapy, in which the therapist joins the family structure in order to change it.

structuralism   A school of psychology, introduced by Wundt, which attempted to understand mental processes in terms of their most basic elements.

structured interview   An interview in which the interviewer follows a script that determines the wording of questions and the sequence of questions, depending on the client's responses.

sublimation   A defense mechanism, through which an unacceptable impulse is expressed symbolically; a healthy defense that permits people to express instinctive urges in prosocial ways.

superego   In psychoanalytic theory, the part of personality that operates using abstract morals and values.

symbiotic psychosis   A psychoanalytic concept; introduced by Mahler, referring to a severe childhood disorder caused by an overly close maternal relationship that does not permit the child to develop adequate ego boundaries.

symptom substitution   A criticism of behavior therapy raised by psychoanalysts, that by treating only symptomatic behavior, behavior therapy ignores the underlying problem that persists and may begin to manifest itself in another symptom.

symptomatology   The presenting symptoms of a patient.

synapse   The gap between nerve cells across which nerve impulses are transmitted by neurotransmitters.

systematic desensitization   A treatment for phobias, based on classical conditioning, in which the phobic object is gradually presented to the client, while the client remains relaxed.

systems theory   A theoretical view that holds that elements must be understood in the context of the systems in which they operate; a basis for many approaches to family therapy.

talking cure   An early form of psychotherapy, introduced by Josef Breuer, in which he engaged patients in discussions about their conversion symptoms.

tardive dyskinesia   A permanent condition, caused occasionally by antipsychotic medication, in which the patient experiences extrapyramidal symptoms such as akathesia, dystonia, and Parkinsonism.

teleology   The notion that events are influenced by future states, such as goals.

temperament   The physiological aspects of behavioral and emotional responding.

termination   The final stage of psychotherapy, in which the course of therapy is reviewed and the client is prepared to cope with future problems independently.

test–retest reliability   The consistency of test results across time.

thought sampling   A cognitive assessment technique in which the client is cued, at random intervals, to record the thoughts he or she is experiencing at the moment.

timeout   A punishment, where the individual is removed from the environment where he has the opportunity to earn reinforcement; for example, being sent to one's room or standing in a corner.

token economy   A treatment technique used to modify the behavior of groups of people in institutional settings, in which behavior is reinforced with tokens, which can he saved and exchanged for later reinforcements.

transactional analysis   A contemporary variant of Freudian therapy, introduced by Eric Berne; describes personality in terms of child, parent, and adult and considers neuroses as maladaptive games.

transference   The feelings that a client develops for a therapist; interpreted by psychoanalysts as an index of the client's feelings toward significant others earlier in life.

transpersonal therapy   A form of psychotherapy that is based on Asian philosophies or religions and that emphasize the here and now, self-determinism, and consciousness.

trephining   An ancient surgical process that removed portions of the skull; thought to permit the release of "evil spirits" that inhabited the individual.

tricyclics   A class of antidepressant medication that is thought to increase the available supply of serotonin and norepinephrine by decreasing their reuptake.

true negative   A test result that accurately indicates that a person does not have a trait.

true positive   A test result that accurately indicates that a person does have a trait.

true score   The actual value of a trait for an individual, which is presumed to exist and which a test attempts to measure.

T- (training) group   A group experience for nonpatients, designed to enhance one's interpersonal skills and self-awareness; also called encounter, growth, or sensitivity groups; later developed into a form of group therapy for patients.

twelve-step program A self-help group, modeled after the twelve steps of Alcoholics Anonymous, in which participants acknowledge that they are powerless over their problem.

unconditional positive regard An environment in which a person is accepted, without having to meet the conditions of others; according to Rogers, fosters healthy psychological development; the experience of caring for and accepting a person regardless of what the person says or does; the "active ingredient" in Rogerian psychotherapy.

unconditioned response (UCR) In classical conditioning, a response that is automatically elicited by an unconditioned stimulus.

unconditioned stimulus (UCS) In classical conditioning, a stimulus that automatically elicits a response and is paired with a neutral stimulus.

unconscious Psychological processes that are outside the awareness of the individual.

underconditioning Failing to be conditioned to exhibit normal behaviors.

undoing A defense mechanism, through which an individual engages in behaviors that symbolically atone for an unacceptable impulse or action.

uninhibited temperament A temperament type, identified by Kagan, characterized by low distress in response to novel stimuli.

Vail Model See practitioner–scientist model.

validity The accuracy of an assessment instrument; the degree to which a test actually measures what it purports to measure.

validity scale A scale on a structured test that helps determine whether an examinee's responses are accurate.

viscerotonia The temperament type identified by Sheldon that is characterized by love of comfort and sociability.

wait-list treatment group A control group in psychotherapy outcome studies in which subjects are placed on a waiting list so that they are assured of receiving treatment in the future.

warmth An element of unconditional positive regard in Rogerian therapy, in which the therapist expresses unconditional caring for the client.

willful concentration A technique in which a therapist exerts mild pressure on the client's head and suggests that troubling psychological material will be released when the physical pressure is released.

YAVIS client The ideal client in insight-oriented therapy; stands for young, attractive, verbal, intelligent, and successful.

yea-saying Another term for the response set of acquiescence.

yoga A transpersonal therapy in which one combines meditation with study, ethical training, and changes in life style in order to increase one's mental discipline and consciousness.

References

Abell, S. C., Heiberger, A. M., & Johnson, J. E. (1994). Cognitive evaluations of young adults by means of human figure drawings: An empirical investigation of two methods. *Journal of Clinical Psychology, 50,* 900–905.

Abikoff, H., Gittelman-Klein, R., & Klein, D. (1977). Validation of a classroom observation code for hyperactive children. *Journal of Consulting and Clinical Psychology, 45,* 772–783.

Abt, L. E. (1992). Clinical psychology and the emergence of psychotherapy. *Professional Psychology: Research and Practice, 23,* 176–178.

Achenbach, T. M. (1978). The child behavior profile: I. Boys aged 6–11. *Journal of Consulting and Clinical Psychology, 46,* 478–488.

Achenbach, T. M. (1982). *Developmental psychopathology* (2nd ed.). New York: Wiley.

Achenbach, T. M., & Edelbrock, C. S. (1979). The child behavior profile: II. Boys aged 12–16 and girls aged 6–11 and 12–16. *Journal of Consulting and Clinical Psychology, 47,* 223–233.

Ackerman, N. (1966). *Treating the troubled family.* New York: Basic Books.

Adler, A. (1979). The differences between individual psychology and psychoanalysis. In H. L. Ansbacher & R. R. Ansbacher (Eds. and Trans.), *Superiority and social interest: A collection of later writings* (3rd rev. ed., pp. 205–218). New York: Viking. (Original work published in 1931).

Agnew, N. M., & Pyke, S. W. (1969). *The science game: An introduction to research in the behavioral sciences.* Englewood Cliffs, NJ: Prentice-Hall.

Aiken, L. R. (1985). Review of ACT Assessment Program. *Ninth mental measurements yearbook* (Vol. 1), 29–31.

Aiken, L. R. (1996). *Rating scales and checklists: Evaluating behavior, personality, and attitude.* New York: Wiley.

Alcoholics Anonymous. (1955). *Alcoholics Anonymous: The story of how many thousands of men and women have recovered from alcoholism.* New York: AA World Services.

Alden, L., & Safran, J. (1978). Irrational beliefs and nonassertive behavior. *Cognitive Therapy and Research, 2,* 357–364.

Alden, L., Safran, J., & Weideman, R. (1978). A comparison of cognitive and skills training strategies in the treatment of unassertive clients. *Behavior Therapy, 9,* 843–846.

Alexander, F., & French, T. M. (1946). *Psychoanalytic therapy.* New York: Ronald Press.

Alexander, J. F., & Parsons, B. (1973). Short-term behavioral intervention with delinquent families: Impact on family process and recidivism. *Journal of Abnormal Psychology, 81,* 219–225.

Allport, G. W. (1937). *Personality: A psychological interpretation.* New York: Holt.

Allport, G. W. (1953). The trend in motivational theory. *American Journal of Orthopsychiatry, 25,* 107–119.

Allport, G. W. (1955). *Becoming.* New Haven, CT: Yale University Press.

Allport, G. W. (1961). *Pattern and growth in personality.* New York: Holt, Rinehart and Winston.

Allport, G. W., & Odbert, H. S. (1936). Trait-names: A psycho-lexical study. *Psychological Monographs, 47* (No. 211), 1–171.

American Psychiatric Association. (1980). *Diagnostic and statistical manual of mental disorders* (3rd ed.). Washington, DC: American Psychiatric Association.

American Psychiatric Association. (1987). *Diagnostic and statistical manual of mental disorders* (3rd rev. ed.). Washington, DC: American Psychiatric Association.

American Psychiatric Association. (1994). *Diagnostic and statistical manual of mental disorders* (4th ed.). Washington, DC: American Psychiatric Association.

American Psychological Association. (1954). Technical recommendations for psychological tests and diagnostic techniques [Supplement]. *Psychological Bulletin, 51* (2, Pt. 2).

American Psychological Association. (1966). *Standards for educational and psychological tests and manuals.* Washington, DC: American Psychological Association.

American Psychological Association. (1974). *Standards for educational and psychological tests.* Washington, DC: American Psychological Association.

American Psychological Association. (1977). *Standards for providers of psychological services.* Washington, DC: American Psychological Association.

American Psychological Association. (1981). Specialty guidelines for the delivery of services by industrial/organizational psychologists. *American Psychologist, 36,* 664–669.

American Psychological Association. (1982). *Report of the task force on the evaluation of education, training, and service in psychology.* Washington, DC: American Psychological Association.

American Psychological Association. (1985). *Standards for educational and psychological tests.* Washington, DC: American Psychological Association.

American Psychological Association. (1986). *Careers in psychology* (4th rev. ed.). Washington, DC: American Psychological Association.

American Psychological Association. (1987). *General guidelines for providers of psychological services.* Washington, DC: American Psychological Association.

American Psychological Association. (1992). Ethical principles of psychologists and code of conduct. *American Psychologist, 47,* 1612–1628.

American Psychological Association. (1993). *Getting in: A step-by-step plan for gaining admission to graduate school in psychology.* Washington, DC: American Psychological Association.

American Psychological Association. (1995a). APA-accredited doctoral programs in professional psychology: 1995. *American Psychologist, 50,* 1069–1080.

American Psychological Association. (1995b). *Guidelines and principles for accreditation of programs in professional psychology.* Washington, DC: American Psychological Association.

American Psychological Association. (1995c). APA-accredited predoctoral internships for doctoral training in psychology: 1995. *American Psychologist, 50,* 1050–1068.

American Psychological Association. (1996). *Graduate study in psychology.* Washington, DC: American Psychological Association.

Ames, L. B. (1970). Projecting the future of a projective technique. *Journal of Projective Techniques and Personality Assessment, 34,* 359–365.

Anastasi, A. (1988). *Psychological testing* (6th ed.). New York: Macmillan.

Anastopoulos, A. D., & Barkley, R. A. (1988). Biological factors in attention deficit-hyperactivity disorder. *Behavior Therapist, 11,* 47–53.

Andersen, B. L. (1992). Psychological interventions for cancer patients to enhance the quality of life. *Journal of Consulting and Clinical Psychology, 61,* 552–568.

Anderson, H. H. (1951). Human behavior and personality growth. In H. H. Anderson & G. L. Anderson (Eds.), *An introduction to projective techniques* (pp. 3–25). New York: Prentice-Hall.

Andrews, G., & Harvey, R. (1981). Does psychotherapy benefit neurotic patients? A reanalysis of the Smith, Glass, and Miller data. *Archives of General Psychiatry, 38,* 1203–1208.

Angres, R. (1990, October). Who, really, was Bruno Bettelheim? *Commentary, 90,* 26–30.

Archer, R. P. (1992). *MMPI-A: Assessing adolescent psychopathology.* Hillsdale, NJ: Erlbaum.

Archer, R. P., Griffin, R., & Aiduk, R. (1995). MMPI-2 clinical correlates for ten common codes. *Journal of Personality Assessment, 65,* 391–407.

Aronow, E., & Reznikoff, M. (1973). Attitudes toward the Rorschach test expressed in book reviews: A historical perspective. *Journal of Personality Assessment, 37,* 309–315.

Astin, A. W., Green, K. C., & Korn, W. S. (1987). *The American freshman: Twenty year trends 1966–1985.* University of California: Cooperative Institutional Research Program, American Council on Education.

Axline, V. M. (1947). *Play therapy.* Boston: Houghton Mifflin.

Ayllon, T., & Azrin, N. H. (1968). *The token economy: A motivational system for therapy and rehabilitation.* New York: Appleton-Century-Crofts.

Azrin, N. H., Naster, B. J., & Jones, R. (1973). Reciprocity counseling: A rapid learning-based procedure for marital counseling. *Behavioral Research and Therapy, 11,* 365–382.

Baars, B. J. (1986). *The cognitive revolution in psychology.* New York: Guilford.

Bandura, A. (1969). *Principles of behavior modification.* New York: Holt, Rinehart and Winston.

Bandura, A. (1973). *Aggression: A social learning analysis.* Englewood Cliffs, NJ: Prentice-Hall.

Bandura, A. (1977). Self-efficacy: Toward a unifying theory of behavioral change. *Psychological Review, 84,* 191–215.

Bandura, A. (1986). *Social foundations of thought and action: A social cognitive theory.* Englewood Cliffs, NJ: Prentice-Hall.

Barber, T. X. (1969). *Hypnosis: A scientific approach.* New York: Van Nostrand Reinhold.

Barber, T. X. (1976). *Pitfalls in human research: Ten pivotal points.* New York: Pergamon.

Barber, T. X., & Silver, M. J. (1968). Fact, fiction, and the experimenter bias effect. *Psychological Bulletin* (Monograph Supplement), *33* (No. 6, Pt. 2), 1–29.

Barlow, D. H. (1986). On the relation of clinical results to clinical practice: Current issues, new directions. *Journal of Clinical and Consulting Psychology, 49,* 147–155.

Barlow, D. H., Hayes, S. C., & Nelson, R. O. (1984). *The scientist practitioner: Research and accountability in clinical and educational settings.* New York: Pergamon.

Barrett, B. H., Johnston, J. M., & Pennypacker, H. S. (1986). Behavior: Its units, dimensions, and measurement. In R. O. Nelson & S. C. Hayes (Eds.), *Conceptual foundations of behavioral assessment* (pp. 156–200). New York: Guilford Press.

Barrett, C. L., Hampe, I. E., & Miller, L. C. (1978). Research on child psychotherapy. In S. L. Garfield & A. E. Bergin (Eds.), *Handbook of psychotherapy and behavior change: An empirical analysis* (2nd ed., pp. 411–435). New York: Wiley.

Baucom, D. H., & Hoffman, J. A. (1986). The effectiveness of marital therapy: Current status and application to the clinical setting. In N. S. Jacobson & A. Gurman (Eds.), *Clinical handbook of marital therapy* (pp. 597–620). New York: Guilford.

Beck, A. T. (1967). *Depression: Clinical, experimental, and theoretical aspects.* New York: Hoeber.

Beck, A. T. (1976). *Cognitive therapy and the emotional disorders.* New York: International Universities Press.

Beck, A. T., & Emery, G. (1985). *Anxiety disorders and phobias: A cognitive perspective.* New York: Basic Books.

Beck, A. T., Rush, A. J., Shaw, B. F., & Emery, G. (1979). *Cognitive therapy of depression.* New York: Guilford.

Beck, A. T., Steer, R. A., & Garbin, M. G. (1988). Psychometric properties of the Beck Depression Inventory: Twenty-five years of evaluation. *Clinical Psychology Review, 8,* 77–100.

Beck, A. T., Ward, C. H., Mendelson, M., Mock, J., & Erbaugh, J. (1961). An inventory for measuring depression. *Archives of General Psychiatry, 4,* 561–571.

Beck, J. (1990, October 1). Bettelheim led us cruelly down wrong road for children. *Chicago Tribune,* p. 15.

Bednar, R. L., & Kaul, T. J. (1978). Experiential group research: Current perspectives. In S. L. Garfield & A. E. Bergin (Eds.), *Handbook of psychotherapy and behavior change: An empirical analysis* (2nd ed., pp. 769–815). New York: Wiley.

Bednar, R. L., & Kaul, T. J. (1994). Experiential group research: Can the canon fire? In A. E. Bergin & S. L. Garfield (Eds.), *Handbook of psychotherapy and behavior change* (4th ed., pp. 631–663). New York: Wiley.

Bednar, R. L., & Lawlis, G. F. (1971). Empirical research in group psychotherapy. In A. E. Bergin & S. L. Garfield (Eds.), *Handbook of psychotherapy and behavior change: An empirical analysis* (pp. 812–838). New York: Wiley.

Beecher, H. K. (1955). The powerful placebo. *Journal of the American Medical Association, 159,* 1602–1606.

Beels, C., & Ferber, A. (1972). What family therapists do. In A. Ferber, M. Mendelsohn, & A. Napier (Eds.), *The book of family therapy* (pp. 168–232). Boston: Houghton Mifflin.

Beers, C. W. (1908). *A mind that found itself: An autobiography.* New York: Doubleday and Company.

Begelman, D. A. (1975). Ethical and legal issues of behavior modification. In R. M. Eisler & P. M. Miller (Eds.), *Progress in behavior modification* (Vol. 1, pp. 159–190). New York: Appleton-Century-Crofts.

Belar, C. D., Bielauskas, L. A., Larsen, K. G., Mensh, I. N., Poey, K., & Roelke, H. K. J. (1989). The national conference on internship training in psychology. *American Psychologist, 44,* 60–65.

Bell, G. O. (1981). Astrology. In G. O. Bell & B. Singer (Eds.), *Science and the paranormal: Probing the existence of the supernatural* (pp. 70–94). New York: Scribners.

Bell, J. E. (1948). *Projective techniques: A dynamic approach to the study of the personality.* New York: Longmans, Green.

Bellack, A. S., & Hersen, M. (1985). General considerations. In M. Hersen & A. S. Bellack (Eds.), *Hand-*

book of clinical behavior therapy with adults (pp. 1–19). New York: Plenum.

Bellak, L. (1950). On the problems of the concept of projection. In L. E. Abt & L. Bellak (Eds.), *Projective psychology: Clinical approaches to the total personality* (pp. 7–32). New York: Knopf.

Bellak, L. (1986). *The Thematic Apperception Test, the Children's Apperception Test, and the Senior Apperception Technique in clinical use* (4th ed.). Orlando, FL: Academic.

Bem, S. L. (1984). Androgyny and gender schema theory: A conceptual and empirical integration. In R. A. Dienstbier & T. B. Sonderegger (Eds.), *Nebraska Symposium on Motivation* (Vol. 34, pp. 179–226). Lincoln, NE: University of Nebraska Press.

Bender, L. (1938). A visual motor Gestalt test and its clinical use. *American Orthopsychiatric Association Research Monographs,* No. 3.

Ben-Porath, Y. S., & Butcher, J. N. (1989). Psychometric stability of rewritten MMPI items. *Journal of Personality Assessment, 53,* 645–653.

Ben-Porath, Y. S., & Butcher, J. N. (1991). The historical development of personality assessment. In C. E. Walker (Ed.), *Clinical psychology: Historical and research foundations* (pp. 121–156). New York: Plenum.

Bentler, P. M. (1968a). Heterosexual behavior—I. Males. *Behavior Research and Therapy, 6,* 21–25.

Bentler, P. M. (1968b). Heterosexual behavior assessment—II. Females. *Behavior Research and Therapy, 6,* 27–30.

Berg, E. A. (1948). A simple objective test for measuring flexibility in thinking. *Journal of General Psychology, 39,* 15–22.

Bergin, A. E. (1971). The evaluation of therapeutic outcomes. In A. E. Bergin & S. L. Garfield (Eds.), *Handbook of psychotherapy and behavior change: An empirical analysis* (pp. 217–270). New York: Wiley.

Bergin, A. E., & Garfield, S. L. (Eds.). (1971). *Handbook of psychotherapy and behavior change: An empirical analysis.* New York: Wiley.

Bergin, A. E., & Garfield, S. L. (Eds.). (1994). *Handbook of psychotherapy and behavior change* (4th ed.). New York: Wiley.

Berk, L. E. (1984). Relationship of elementary school children's private speech to behavioral accompaniment to task, attention, and task performance. *Developmental Psychology, 22,* 671–680.

Berk, L. E. (1994). *Child development* (4th ed.). Boston: Allyn and Bacon.

Berman, J. S., Miller, R. C., & Massman, P. J. (1985). Cognitive therapy versus systematic desensitization: Is one treatment superior? *Psychological Bulletin, 97,* 451–461.

Berne, E. (1958). Transactional analysis: A new and effective method of psychotherapy. *American Journal of Psychotherapy, 12,* 735–743.

Berne, E. (1964). *Games people play.* New York: Grove Press.

Berne, E. (1976). *Beyond games and scripts.* New York: Ballantine.

Bernstein, D. A., & Borkovec, T. D. (1973). *Progressive relaxation training: A manual for the helping professions.* Champaign, IL: Research.

Bernstein, J. G. (1988). *Handbook of drug therapy in psychiatry* (2nd ed.). Littleton, MA: PSG.

Bettelheim, B. (1967). *The empty fortress.* New York: Free Press.

Bettelheim, B. (1982). *Freud and man's soul.* New York: Knopf.

Beutler, L. E., Crago, M., & Arizmendi, T. G. (1986). Research on therapist variables in psychotherapy. In S. L. Garfield & A. E. Bergin (Eds.), *Handbook of psychotherapy and behavior change* (3rd ed., pp. 257–310). New York: Wiley.

Beutler, L. E., Williams, R. E., & Wakefield, P. J. (1993). Obstacles to disseminating applied psychological science. *Journal of Applied and Preventive Psychology, 2,* 53–58.

Beutler, L. E., Williams, R. E., Wakefield, P. J., & Entwistle, S. R. (1995). Bridging scientist and practitioner perspectives in clinical psychology. *American Psychologist, 50,* 984–994.

Bezchlibnyk-Butler, K. Z., & Jeffries, J. J. (Eds.). (1991). *Clinical handbook of psychotropic drugs* (3rd rev. ed.). Toronto: Hogrefe & Huber.

Bickman, L. (1987). Proceedings of the National Conference on Graduate Education in Psychology, University of Utah, Salt Lake City, June 13–19, 1987 [Special issue]. *American Psychologist, 42*(12).

Bivens, J. A., & Berk, L. E. (1990). A longitudinal study of the development of elementary school children's private speech. *Merrill-Palmer Quarterly, 36,* 443–463.

Blanchard, E. B. (1982). The role of biofeedback in behavioral medicine. *American Journal of Clinical Biofeedback, 5,* 126–130.

Blanchard, E. B. (1992a). Introduction to the special issue on behavioral medicine: An update for the 1990s. *Journal of Consulting and Clinical Psychology, 60,* 491–492.

Blanchard, E. B. (Ed.). (1992b). Behavioral medicine: An update for the 1990s [special issue]. *Journal of Consulting and Clinical Psychology, 61,* 491–643.

Blum, G. (1950). *The Blacky Pictures.* New York: Psychological Corporation.

Bolton, B. (1992). Review of the California Psychological Inventory, Revised Edition. In J. Kramer & J. C. Conoley (Eds.), *Eleventh mental measurements yearbook* (pp. 138–141). Lincoln, NE: University of Nebraska Press.

Bonato, D., Cyr, J., Kalpin, R., Prendergast, P., & Sanhueza, P. (1988). The utility of the MCMI as a DSM-3 Axis I diagnostic tool. *Journal of Clinical Psychology, 44,* 867–875.

Bookbinder, L. J. (1962). Simple conditioning vs. the dynamic approach to symptoms and symptom substitution: A reply to Yates. *Psychological Reports, 10,* 71–77.

Boring, E. G. (1923, June). Intelligence as the tests test it. *New Republic, 35,* 35–37.

Boring, E. G. (1929). *A history of experimental psychology.* New York: Appleton-Century-Crofts.

Boring, E. G. (1940). Was this analysis a success? *Journal of Abnormal and Social Psychology, 35,* 4–10.

Boring, E. G. (1950). *A history of experimental psychology* (2nd ed.). New York: Appleton-Century-Crofts.

Bornstein, M. R., Bellack, A. S., & Hersen, M. (1977). Social skills training for unassertive children: A multiple baseline analysis. *Journal of Applied Behavior Analysis, 10,* 183–195.

Botwin, M. D. (1995). Review of the Revised NEO Personality Inventory. In J. C. Conoley & J. C. Impara (Eds.), *Twelfth mental measurements yearbook* (pp. 862–863). Lincoln, NE: University of Nebraska Press.

Bouchard, T. J., Jr., & McGue, M. (1981). Familial studies of intelligence: A review. *Science, 250,* 223–228.

Bowen, M. (1960). A family concept of schizophrenia. In D. D. Jackson (Ed.), *The etiology of schizophrenia* (pp. 346–388). New York: Basic Books.

Bowen, M. (1966). The use of family therapy in clinical practice. *Comprehensive Psychiatry, 7,* 345–374.

Bowen, M. (1972). Panel discussion on being and becoming a family therapist. In A. Ferber, M. Mendelsohn, & A. Napier (Eds.), *The book of family therapy* (pp. 135–154). Boston: Houghton Mifflin.

Bowers, T. G., & Clum, G. A. (1988). Relative contribution of specific and nonspecific treatment effects: Meta-analysis of placebo-controlled behavior therapy research. *Psychological Bulletin, 103,* 315–323.

Bradley, C. (1937). The behavior of children receiving Benzedrine. *American Journal of Psychiatry, 94,* 577–585.

Breggin, P. R. (1979). *Electroshock: Its disabling effects.* New York: Springer-Verlag.

Brehm, S. S., & Kassin, S. M. (1993). *Social psychology* (2nd ed.). Boston: Houghton Mifflin.

Breier, A., Buchanan, R. W., Irish, D., & Carpenter, W. T. (1993). Clozapine treatment of outpatients with schizophrenia: Outcome and long-term response patterns. *Hospital and Community Psychiatry, 44,* 1145–1149.

Breier, A., & Paul, S. M. (1990). The GABA/benzodiazepine receptor: Implications for the molecular basis of anxiety. *Journal of Psychiatric Research, 24,* 91–104.

Brems, C., Thevenin, D. M., & Routh, D. K. (1991). The history of clinical psychology. In C. E. Walker (Ed.), *Clinical psychology: Historical and research foundations* (pp. 3–35). New York: Plenum.

Breuer, J., & Freud, S. (1955). Studies on hysteria. In J. Strachey (Ed. and Trans.), *The standard edition of the complete psychological works of Sigmund Freud* (Vol. 2, pp. 1–251). London: Hogarth. (Original work published in 1893–1895).

Breunlin, D. C., Breunlin, C., Kearns, D. L., & Russell, W. P. (1988). A review of the literature on family therapy with adolescents 1979–1987. *Journal of Adolescence, 11,* 309–334.

Brody, N. (1992). *Intelligence* (2nd ed.). San Diego: Academic.

Bromberg, W. (1975). *From shaman to psychotherapist: A history of the treatment of mental illness.* Chicago: Henry Regnery Company.

Brown, D. T. (1989). Review of the Jackson Vocational Interest Survey. In J. C. Conoley & J. J. Kramer (Eds.), *The tenth mental measurements yearbook* (pp. 401–403). Lincoln, NE: University of Nebraska Press.

Brownell, K. D., & Wadden, T. A. (1992). Etiology and treatment of obesity: Understanding a serious, prevalent, and refractory disorder. *Journal of Consulting and Clinical Psychology, 61,* 505–517.

Buck, J. (1948). The H-T-P test. *Journal of Clinical Psychology, 4,* 151–159.

Buck, J. (1981). *The House-Tree-Person technique: A revised manual.* Los Angeles: Western Psychological Services.

Burns, R. C., & Kaufman, S. H. (1970). *Kinetic family drawings (K-F-D): An introduction to understanding children through kinetic drawings.* New York: Brunner/Mazel.

Buros, O. K. (1951). *Fourth mental measurements yearbook.* Highland Park, NJ: Gryphon Press.

Buros, O. K. (Ed.). (1959). *Fifth mental measurements yearbook.* Highland Park, NJ: Gryphon Press.

Buros, O. K. (1985). *Ninth mental measurements yearbook.* Highland Park, NJ: Gryphon Press.

Buss, A. H., & Plomin, R. (1975). *A temperament theory of personality development.* New York: Wiley.

Buss, A. H., & Plomin, R. (1984). *Temperament: Early developing personality traits.* Hillsdale, NJ: Erlbaum.

Butcher, J. N. (Ed.). (1972). *Objective personality assessment: Changing perspectives.* New York: Academic.

Butcher, J. N. (1994). Psychological assessment by computer: Potential gains and problems to avoid. *Psychiatric Annals, 24,* 20–24.

Butcher, J. N., Dahlstrom, W. G., Graham, J. R., Tellegen, A., & Kaemmer, B. (1989). *Manual for the restandardized Minnesota Multiphasic Personality Inventory: MMPI–2. An administrative and interpretive guide.* Minneapolis, MN: University of Minnesota Press.

Butcher, J. N., Williams, C. L., Graham, J. R., Archer, R. P., Tellegen, A., Ben-Porath, Y. S., & Kaemmer, B. (1992). *MMPI–A (Minnesota Multiphasic Personality Inventory–Adolescent): Manual for administration, scoring, and interpretation.* Minneapolis, MN: University of Minnesota Press.

Butler, J. M., & Haigh, G. V. (1954). Changes in the relation between self-concepts and ideal concepts consequent upon client-centered counseling. In C. R. Rogers & R. F. Dymond (Eds.), *Psychotherapy and behavior change: Coordinated studies in the client-centered approach* (pp. 55–76). Chicago: University of Chicago Press.

Cade, J. F. J. (1949). Lithium salts in the treatment of psychotic excitement. *Medical Journal of Australia, 2,* 349–352.

California School of Professional Psychology. (1991–1992). *System clinical Psy.D. and Ph.D. programs.* San Francisco: California School of Professional Psychology.

Campbell, D., Sanderson, R. E., & Laverty, S. G. (1964). Characteristics of a conditioned response in human subjects during extinction trials following a single traumatic conditioning trial. *Journal of Abnormal and Social Psychology, 68,* 627–639.

Campbell, D. E., & Beets, J. L. (1978). Lunacy and the moon. *Psychological Bulletin, 85,* 1123–1129.

Campbell, D. P. (1971). *Handbook for the SVIB.* Stanford, CA: Stanford University Press.

Campbell, D. T., & Stanley, J. C. (1966). *Experimental and quasi-experimental designs for research.* Chicago: Rand McNally.

Canter, S., & Canter, D. (1982). Professional psychology. In S. Canter & D. Canter (Eds.), *Psychology in practice: Perspectives on professional psychology* (pp. 1–22). New York: Wiley.

Carey, G., & Gottesman, I. I. (1978). Reliability and validity in binary ratings: Areas of common misunderstanding in diagnosis and symptom ratings. *Archives of General Psychiatry, 35,* 1454–1459.

Carlson, C. G., Hersen, M., & Eisler, R. M. (1972). Token economy programs in the treatment of hospitalized adult psychiatric patients: Current status and recent trends. *Journal of Nervous and Mental Disease, 155,* 192–204.

Casey, R. J., & Berman, J. S. (1985). The outcome of psychotherapy with children. *Psychological Bulletin, 98,* 388–400.

Cattell, R. B. (1951). Principles of design in "projective" or misperception tests of personality. In H. H. Anderson & G. L. Anderson (Eds.), *An introduction to projective techniques* (pp. 55–98). New York: Prentice-Hall.

Cautela, J. R. (1966). Treatment of compulsive behavior by covert sensitization. *Psychological Record, 16,* 33–41.

Cautela, J. R. (1967). Covert sensitization. *Psychological Reports, 20,* 459–468.

Chambers, W. J., Puig-Antich, J., Hirsch, M., Paez, P., Ambrosini, P. J., Tabrizi, M. A., & Davies, M. (1985). The assessment of affective disorders in children and adolescents by semistructured interview: Test-retest reliability of the Schedule for Affective Disorders and Schizophrenia for School-Age Children, Present Episode version. *Archives of General Psychiatry, 42,* 696–702.

Chambless, R. D., Caputo, G. C., Bright, P., & Gallagher, R. (1984). Assessment of fear in agoraphobics: The Body Sensations Questionnaire and the Agoraphobic Cognitions Questionnaire. *Journal of Consulting and Clinical Psychology, 52,* 1090–1097.

Chambless, D. L. (1985). Agoraphobia. In M. Hersen & A. S. Bellack (Eds.), *Handbook of clinical behavior therapy with adults* (pp. 49–87). New York: Plenum.

Chapman, L. J. (1967). Illusory correlation in observational report. *Journal of Verbal Learning and Verbal Behavior, 6,* 151–155.

Chapman, L. J., & Chapman, J. P. (1967). Genesis of popular but erroneous psychodiagnostic observations. *Journal of Abnormal Psychology, 72,* 193–204.

Chapman, L. J., & Chapman, J. P. (1969). Illusory correlation as an obstacle to the use of valid psychodiagnostic signs. *Journal of Abnormal Psychology, 74,* 271–280.

Clark, D. M. (1983). On the induction of depressed mood in the laboratory: Evaluation and comparison of the Velten and musical procedures. *Advances in Behavior Research and Therapy, 5,* 27–49.

Clark, K. E. (1965). Committee on the scientific and professional aims of psychology: Preliminary report. *American Psychologist, 20,* 95–100.

Coe, W. C. (1980). Expectations, hypnosis and suggestion in change. In F. H. Kanfer & A. P. Goldstein (Eds.), *Helping people change: A textbook of methods* (2nd ed., pp. 423–469). New York: Pergamon.

College Entrance Examination Board. (1987). *ATP guide for high schools and colleges.* Princeton, NJ: Educational Testing Service.

Comer, R. J. (1992). *Abnormal psychology.* New York: Freeman.

Committee on Training in Clinical Psychology. (1948). Clinical training facilities: 1948. *American Psychologist, 3,* 317–318.

Committee on Training in Clinical Psychology. (1949). Doctoral training programs in clinical psychology: 1949. *American Psychologist, 4,* 331–341.

Conners, C. K. (1969). A teacher rating scale for use in drug studies with children. *American Journal of Psychiatry, 126,* 884–888.

Conners, C. K. (1970). Symptom patterns in hyperactive, neurotic and normal children. *Child Development, 41,* 667–682.

Conners, C. K. (1973). Rating scales for use in drug studies with children. *Psychopharmacology Bulletin, 9,* 24–84.

Conway, J. B. (1988). Differences among clinical psychologists: Scientists, practitioners, and scientist-practitioners. *Professional Psychology: Research and Practice, 19,* 642–655.

Cooper, A. M., Kernberg, O. F., & Person, E. S. (Eds.). (1989). *Psychoanalysis: Toward the second century.* New Haven, CT: Yale University Press.

Cooper, G. L. (1988). The safety of fluoxetine—An update. *British Journal of Psychiatry* (Suppl. 3), *153,* 77–86.

Cook, T. D., & Leviton, L. C. (1980). Reviewing the literature: A comparison of traditional methods with meta-analysis. *Journal of Personality, 48,* 449–472.

Connolly, A. J., Nachtman, W., & Pritchett, E. M. (1976). *KeyMath Diagnostic Arithmetic Test.* Circle Pines, MN: American Guidance Service.

Cordasco, F. (1976). *A brief history of education* (2nd rev. ed.). Towata, NJ: Littlefield, Adams, and Co.

Corsini, R. J. (Ed.). (1981). *Handbook of innovative psychotherapies.* New York: Wiley.

Corulla, W. J. (1987). A psychometric investigation of the Eysenck Personality Questionnaire (Revised) and its relationship to the I.7 Impulsiveness Questionnaire. *Personality and Individual Differences, 8,* 651–658.

Costa, P. T., Jr., & McCrae, R. (1992). *NEO-PI-R test manual.* Port Huron, MI: Sigma Assessment Systems.

Costello, E. J., Edelbrock, C. S., Dulcan, M. K., & Kalas, R. (1984). *Testing of the NIMH Diagnostic Interview for Children (DISC) in a clinical population. Final report to the Center for Epidemiological Studies, National Institute for Mental Health.* Pittsburgh: University of Pittsburgh.

Cox, D. J., & Gonder-Frederick, L. (1992). Major developments in behavioral diabetes research. *Journal of Consulting and Clinical Psychology, 60,* 628–638.

Craig, P. L. (1979). Neuropsychological assessment in public psychiatric hospitals: The current state of the practice. *Clinical Neuropsychology, 1,* 1–7.

Crits-Christoph, P. (1992). The efficacy of brief dynamic psychotherapy: A meta-analysis. *American Journal of Psychiatry, 149,* 151–158.

Crits-Christoph, P., Frank, E., Chambless, D., Brody, C., & Karp, J. F. (1995). Training in empirically validated treatments: What are clinical psychology students learning? *Professional Psychology: Research and Practice, 26,* 514–522.

Cronbach, L. J., Rajaratnam, N., & Gleser, G. C. (1963). Theory of generalizability: A liberalization of reliability theory. *British Journal of Statistical Psychology, 16,* 137–163.

Crowne, D. P., & Marlowe, D. (1960). A new scale of social desirability independent of psychopathology. *Journal of Consulting Psychology, 24,* 349–354.

Culver, R. B., & Ianna, P. A. (1979). *The Gemini syndrome: Star wars of the oldest kind.* Tucson, AZ: Pachart.

Dahlstrom, W. G., Welsh, G. S., & Dahlstrom, L. E. (1972). *An MMPI handbook: Volume 1: Clinical interpretation.* Minneapolis, MN: University of Minnesota Press.

Dana, R. H. (1993). *Multicultural assessment perspectives for professional psychology.* Boston: Allyn and Bacon.

Danaher, B. G. (1977). Research on rapid smoking: Interim summary and recommendations. *Addictive Behaviors, 2,* 151–166.

Darley, J. G., & Wolfle, D. (1946). Can we meet the formidable demand for psychological services? *American Psychologist, 1,* 179–180.

Davis, J. M. (1985). Antidepressant drugs. In H. I. Kaplan & B. J. Sadock (Eds.), *Comprehensive textbook of psychiatry* (Vol. 1), (4th ed., pp. 1513–1547). Baltimore, MD: Williams & Wilkins.

Davison, G. C. (1976). Homosexuality: The ethical challenge. *Journal of Consulting and Clinical Psychology, 44,* 157–162.

Davison, G. C. (1978). Not can but ought: The treatment of homosexuality. *Journal of Consulting and Clinical Psychology, 46,* 170–172.

Davison, G. C., & Neale, J. M. (1990). *Abnormal psychology* (5th ed.). New York: Wiley.

Davison, G. C., & Neale, J. M. (1994). *Abnormal psychology* (6th ed.). New York: Wiley.

Davison, G. C., & Wilson, G. T. (1973). Attitudes of behavior therapists toward homosexuality. *Behavior Therapy, 4,* 686–696.

Dawes, R. M. (1994). *House of cards: Psychology and psychotherapy built on myth.* New York: Free Press.

Dean, G. A. (1992). The bottom line: Effect size. In B. L. Beyerstein & D. F. Beyerstein (Eds.), *The write stuff* (pp. 269–341). Buffalo, NY: Prometheus Press.

Deblinger, E., McLeer, S. V., & Henry, D. (1990). Cognitive behavioral treatment for sexually abused children suffering from post-traumatic stress: Preliminary findings. *Journal of the American Academy of Child and Adolescent Psychiatry, 29,* 747–752.

de Groot, A. D. (1965). *Thought and choice in chess.* The Hague: Mouton.

DeLeon, P. H., Fox, R. E., & Graham, S. R. (1991). Prescription privileges: Psychology's next frontier? *American Psychologist, 46,* 384–393.

DeMaster, B., Reid, J., & Twentyman, C. (1977). The effects of different amounts of feedback on observer's reliability. *Behavior Therapy, 8,* 317–329.

Dent, O. B., & Ormiston, D. W. (1979). Training, role models, and research activity among clinical psychologists. *Journal of Clinical Psychology, 35,* 226–240.

Derogatis, L. R. (1977). *SCL-90 administration, scoring and procedures manual-I.* Baltimore, MD: Johns Hopkins University Press.

DeWitt, K. N. (1978). The effectiveness of family therapy: A review of outcome research. *Archives of General Psychiatry, 35,* 549–561.

Diener, C., & Redd, W. H. (1987). Anxiety associated with chemotherapy and other noxious medical procedures. In L. Michelson & L. M. Ascher (Eds.), *Anxiety and stress disorders: Cognitive-behavioral assessment and treatment* (pp. 502–519). New York: Guilford.

Dimsdale, J. E. (1988). A perspective on Type A behavior and coronary disease. *New England Journal of Medicine, 318,* 110–112.

Doleys, D. M. (1989). Enuresis and encopresis. In T. H. Ollendick & M. Hersen (Eds.), Handbook of child psychopathology (2nd ed., pp. 291–314). New York: Plenum.

Donlon, T. F. (Ed.). (1984). *The College Board technical handbook for the Scholastic Aptitude Test and achievement tests.* New York: College Entrance Examination Board.

Dorfman, E. (1951). Play therapy. In C. R. Rogers, *Client-centered therapy: Its current practice, implications, and theory* (pp. 235–277). Boston: Houghton Mifflin.

Doyle, K. O., Jr. (1974). Theory and practice of ability testing in ancient Greece. *Journal of the History of the Behavioral Sciences, 10,* 202–212.

Dubbert, P. M. (1992). Exercise in behavioral medicine. *Journal of Consulting and Clinical Psychology, 61,* 613–618.

DuBois, P. H. (1970). *A history of psychological testing.* Boston: Allyn and Bacon.

Dunn, L. M., & Dunn, L. M. (1981). *Peabody Picture Vocabulary Test—Revised: Manual for forms L and M.* Circle Pines, MN: American Guidance Service.

Dunn, L. M., & Markwardt, F. C., Jr. (1970). *Peabody Individual Achievement Test.* Circle Pines, MN: American Guidance Service.

DuPaul, G. J., Guevremont, D. C., & Barkley, R. A. (1991). Attention-deficit hyperactivity disorder. In T. R. Kratochwill & R. J. Morris (Eds.), *The practice of child therapy* (2nd ed., pp. 115–144). New York: Pergamon.

Durlak, J. A. (1979). Comparative effectiveness of paraprofessional and professional helpers. *Psychological Bulletin, 86,* 80–92.

Durlak, J. A., Fuhrman, T., & Lampman, C. (1991). Effectiveness of cognitive-behavior therapy for maladapting children: A meta-analysis. *Psychological Bulletin, 110,* 204–214.

Dusay, J. M., & Dusay, K. M. (1989). Transactional analysis. In R. J. Corsini & D. Wedding (Eds.), *Current psychotherapies* (4th ed., pp. 405–453). Itasca, IL: Peacock.

Dush, D. M., Hirt, M. L., & Schroeder, H. (1983). Self-statement modification with adults: A meta-analysis. *Psychological Bulletin, 94,* 408–422.

Dyer, C. O. (1985). Jackson Personality Inventory. In D. J. Keyser & R. C. Sweetland (Eds.), *Test critiques* (Vol. II), (pp. 369–375). Kansas City, MO: Test Corporation of America.

D'Zurilla, T. J., & Goldfried, M. R. (1971). Problem solving and behavior modification. *Journal of Abnormal Psychology, 78,* 107–126.

D'Zurilla, T. J., & Nezu, A. M. (1990). Development and preliminary evaluation of the Social Problem-Solving Inventory. *Psychological Assessment, 2,* 156–163.

Edelstein, B. A., & Brasted, W. S. (1991). Clinical training. In M. Hersen, A. E. Kazdin, & A. S. Bellack (Eds.), *The clinical psychology handbook* (2nd ed., pp. 45–65). New York: Pergamon.

Educational Testing Service. (1994). *GRE 1994–1995 guide to the use of the Graduate Record Examinations Program.* Princeton, NJ: Educational Testing Service.

Edwards, A. L. (1959). *Edwards Personal Preference Schedule.* New York: Psychological Corporation.

Eisler, R. M. (1988). Behavioral Assertiveness Test—Revised. In M. Hersen & A. S. Bellack (Eds.), *Dictionary of behavioral assessment techniques* (pp. 48–50). New York: Pergamon.

Eisler, R. M., Hersen, M., Miller, P. M., & Blanchard, E. B. (1975). Situational determinants of assertive behaviors. *Journal of Consulting and Clinical Psychology, 43,* 330–340.

Elkin, I., Shea, M. T., Watkins, J. T., Imber, S. D., Sotsky, S. M., Collins, J. F., Glass, D. R., Pilkonis, P. A., Leber, W. R., Docherty, J. P., Fiester, S. J., & Parloff, M. B. (1989). National Institute of Mental Health treatment of depression collaborative research program: General effectiveness of treatments. *Archives of General Psychiatry, 46,* 971–982.

Ellenberger, H. (1970). *The discovery of the unconscious.* New York: Basic Books.

Ellenberger, H. (1972). The story of Anna O.: A critical review with new data. *Journal of the History of the Behavioral Sciences, 8,* 267–279.

Ellis, A. (1962). *Reason and emotion in psychotherapy.* Secaucus, NJ: Lyle Stuart.

Ellis, A., & Yeager, R. J. (1989). *Why some therapies don't work.* Buffalo, NY: Prometheus Books.

Elstein, A. S., Shulman, L. S., & Sprafka, S. A. (1978). *Medical problem solving: An analysis of clinical reasoning.* Cambridge, MA: Harvard University Press.

Emmelkamp, P. M. G. (1986). Behavior therapy with adults. In S. L. Garfield & A. E. Bergin (Eds.), *Handbook of psychotherapy and behavior change* (3rd ed., pp. 385–442). New York: Wiley.

Endicott, J., & Spitzer, R. L. (1978). A diagnostic interview: The Schedule for Affective Disorders and Schizophrenia. *Archives of General Psychiatry, 35,* 837–844.

Erikson, E. (1951). Sex differences in play configurations of preadolescents. *American Journal of Orthopsychiatry, 21,* 667–692.

Erikson, E. H. (1963). *Childhood and society* (2nd ed.). New York: Norton.

Erwin, E. (1978). *Behavior therapy: Scientific, philosophical, and moral foundations.* Cambridge: Cambridge University Press.

Esveldt-Dawson, K., Wisner, K. L., Unis, A. S., Matson, J. L., & Kazdin, A. E. (1982). Treatment of phobias in a hospitalized child. *Journal of Behavior Therapy and Experimental Psychiatry, 11,* 77–83.

Evans, R. G. (1982). Clinical relevance of the Marlowe-Crowne Scale: A review and recommendations. *Journal of Personality Assessment, 46,* 415–425.

Exner, J. E. (1993). *The Rorschach: A comprehensive system* (3rd ed.). New York: Wiley.

Exner, J. E. (Ed.). (1995). *Issues and methods in Rorschach research.* Hillsdale, NJ: Erlbaum.

Eyberg, S. M. (1980). Eyberg Child Behavior Inventory. *Journal of Clinical Child Psychology, 9,* 29.

Eysenck, H. J. (1947). *Dimensions of personality.* London: Routledge and Kegan Paul.

Eysenck, H. J. (1952a). The effects of psychotherapy: An evaluation. *Journal of Consulting Psychology, 16,* 319–324.

Eysenck, H. J. (1952b). *The scientific study of personality.* London: Routledge and Kegan Paul.

Eysenck, H. J. (1960). The effects of psychotherapy. In H. J. Eysenck (Ed.), *Handbook of abnormal psychology: An experimental approach* (pp. 697–725). New York: Basic.

Eysenck, H. J. (1964). The nature of behaviour therapy. In H. J. Eysenck (Ed.), *Experiments in behaviour therapy: Readings in modern methods of treatment of mental disorders* (pp. 1–15). New York: Pergamon.

Eysenck, H. J. (1965). The effects of psychotherapy. *International Journal of Psychiatry, 1,* 99–142.

Eysenck, H. J. (1967). *The biological basis of personality.* Springfield, IL: Charles C. Thomas.

Eysenck, H. J. (1983). Special review: M. L. Smith, G. V. Glass, and T. I. Miller: The benefits of psychotherapy. *Behaviour Research and Therapy, 21,* 315–320.

Eysenck, H. J., & Kamin, L. (1981). *The intelligence controversy.* New York: Wiley.

Eysenck, S. B., Eysenck, H. J., & Barrett, P. (1985). A revised version of the Psychoticism scale. *Personality and Individual Differences, 6,* 21–29.

Falloon, I. R. H., Boyd, J. L., McGill, C. W., Williamson, M., Razani, J., Moss, H. B., Gilderman, A. M., & Simpson, G. M. (1985). Family management in the prevention of morbidity of schizophrenia. *Archives of General Psychiatry, 42,* 887–896.

Fava, M. (1991). Does fluoxetine increase the risk of suicide? *Harvard Mental Health Letter, 7*(7), 8.

Feigl, H., & Brodbeck, M. (Eds.). (1953). *Readings in the philosophy of science.* New York: Appleton-Century-Crofts.

Feldt, L. S., Forsyth, R. A., Ansler, T. N., & Alnot, S. D. (1994). *ITED interpretive guide for teachers and counselors.* Chicago: Riverside.

Festinger, L. (1958). *A theory of cognitive dissonance.* Stanford, CA: Stanford University Press.

Fiedler, F. E. (1950). The concept of an ideal therapeutic relationship. *Journal of Consulting Psychology, 14,* 239–245.

Fisher, S., & Greenberg, R. (1977). *The scientific credibility of Freud's theories and therapy.* New York: Basic Books.

Ford, D. H., & Urban, H. B. (1963). *Systems of psychotherapy: A comparative study.* New York: Wiley.

Forer, B. R. (1949). The fallacy of personal validation: A classroom demonstration of gullibility. *Journal of Abnormal and Social Psychology, 44,* 118–123.

Foster, S. L., Bell-Dolan, D. J., & Burge, D. A. (1988). Behavioral observation. In A. S. Bellack & M. Hersen (Eds.), *Behavioral assessment: A practical handbook* (3rd ed., pp. 119–160). New York: Pergamon.

Frank, G. (1984). The Boulder Model: History, rationale, and critique. *Professional Psychology: Research and Practice, 15,* 417–435.

Frank, G. (1986a). The Boulder Model revisited: The training of the clinical psychologist for research. *Psychological Reports, 58,* 579–585.

Frank, G. (1986b). The Boulder Model revisited. *Psychological Reports, 59,* 407–413.

Frank, G. (1987). Clinical psychology in a new context. *Psychological Reports, 60,* 3–8.

Frank, J. D. (1961). *Persuasion and healing.* Baltimore: Johns Hopkins University Press.

Frank, L. K. (1939). Projective methods for the study of personality. *Journal of Psychology, 8,* 389–409.

Frank, L. K. (1948). *Projective methods.* Springfield, IL: Charles C. Thomas.

Frankl, V. (1963). *Man's search for meaning: An introduction to logotherapy.* New York: Pocket Books.

Frankl, V. (1965). *The doctor and the soul: From psychotherapy to logotherapy.* New York: Vintage Books.

Frankl, V. (1969). *The will to meaning.* New York: World Publishing.

Franzen, M. D. (1989). *Reliability and validity in neuropsychological assessment.* New York: Plenum Press.

Franzen, M. D., & Robbins, D. E. (1989). The Halstead-Reitan neuropsychological battery. In M. D. Franzen, *Reliability and validity in neuropsychological assessment* (pp. 91–107). New York: Plenum.

Freedman, A. M., Kaplan, H. I., & Sadock, B. J. (Eds.). (1976). *Modern synopsis of comprehensive textbook of psychiatry* (2nd ed.). Baltimore: Williams and Wilkins.

Freeman, W., & Watts, J. W. (1942). *Psychosurgery: Intelligence, emotional and social behavior following prefrontal lobotomy for mental disorder.* Springfield, IL: Charles C. Thomas.

Freud, A. (1946). *The psycho-analytical treatment of children.* London: Imago.

Freud, S. (1950). Project for a scientific psychology. In J. Strachey (Ed. and Trans.), *The standard edition of the complete psychological works of Sigmund Freud* (Vol. 1, pp. 295–397). London: Hogarth (Original work written in 1895).

Freud, S. (1953). The interpretation of dreams. In J. Strachey (Ed. and Trans.), *The standard edition of the complete psychological works of Sigmund Freud* (Vol. 5, pp. 339–627). London: Hogarth. (Original work published in 1900).

Freud, S. (1959). The question of lay analysis. In J. Strachey (Ed. and Trans.), *The standard edition of the complete psychological works of Sigmund Freud* (Vol. 20, pp. 183–250). London: Hogarth. (Original work published in 1926).

Freud, S. (1960). The psychopathology of everyday life. In J. Strachey (Ed. and Trans.), *The standard edition of the complete psychological works of Sigmund Freud* (Vol. 6, pp. 1–279). London: Hogarth. (Original work published in 1901).

Freud, S. (1960). Jokes and their relation to the unconscious. In J. Strachey (Ed. and Trans.), *The standard* edition of the complete psychological works of Sigmund Freud (Vol. 8, pp. 9–236). London: Hogarth. (Original work published in 1905).

Freud, S. (1961). Civilization and its discontents. In J. Strachey (Ed. and Trans.), *The standard edition of the complete psychological works of Sigmund Freud* (Vol. 21, pp. 64–145). London: Hogarth. (Original work published in 1930).

Freud, S. (1962). On the grounds for detaching a particular syndrome from neurasthenia under the description "anxiety neurosis." In J. Strachey (Ed. and Trans.), *The standard edition of the complete psychological works of Sigmund Freud* (Vol. 3, pp. 90–115). London: Hogarth. (Original work published 1895).

Freud, S. (1962). Further remarks on the neuro-psychoses of defense. In J. Strachey (Ed. and Trans.), *The standard edition of the complete psychological works of Sigmund Freud* (Vol. 3, pp. 162–185). London: Hogarth. (Original work published 1896).

Freud, S. (1963). Analysis of a phobia in a five-year-old boy. In J. Strachey (Ed. and Trans.), *The standard edition of the complete psychological works of Sigmund Freud* (Vol. 10, pp. 3–149). London: Hogarth. (Original work published in 1909).

Freud, S. (1963). Introductory lectures in psychoanalysis. In J. Strachey (Ed. and Trans.), *The standard edition of the complete psychological works of Sigmund Freud* (Vol. 16, pp. 241–489). London: Hogarth. (Original work published in 1917).

Freud, S. (1964). New introductory lectures on psychoanalysis. In J. Strachey (Ed. and Trans.), *The standard edition of the complete psychological works of Sigmund Freud* (Vol. 22, pp. 7–182). London: Hogarth. (Original work published in 1933).

Freud, S. (1964). An outline of psycho-analysis. In J. Strachey (Ed. and Trans.), *The standard edition of the complete psychological works of Sigmund Freud* (Vol. 23, pp. 144–207). London: Hogarth. (Original work published in 1940).

Freud, S. (1964). Constructions in analysis. In J. Strachey (Ed. and Trans.), *The standard edition of the complete psychological works of Sigmund Freud* (Vol. 23, pp. 255–269). London: Hogarth. (Original work published 1937).

Fried, M. N., & Fried, M. H. (1980). *Transitions: Four rituals in eight cultures.* New York: Norton.

Friedman, A. F. (1984). Eysenck Personality Questionnaire. In D. J. Keyser & R. C. Sweetland (Eds.), *Test critiques* (Vol. I, pp. 279–283). Kansas City, MO: Test Corporation of America.

Friedman, M., & Rosenman, R. H. (1974). *Type A behavior and your heart.* New York: Knopf.

Gadow, K. D., & Pomeroy, J. C. (1991). An overview of psychopharmacotherapy for children and adolescents. In T. R. Kratochwill & R. J. Morris (Eds.), *The practice of child therapy* (2nd ed., pp. 367–409). New York: Pergamon.

Gandour, M. J. (1989). Activity level as a dimension of temperament in toddlers: Its relevance for the organismic specificity hypothesis. *Child Development, 60,* 1092–1098.

Garfield, S. L. (1986). Research on client variables in psychotherapy. In S. L. Garfield & A. E. Bergin (Eds.), *Handbook of psychotherapy and behavior change* (3rd ed., pp. 213–256). New York: Wiley.

Garfield, S. L., & Bergin, A. E. (Eds.). (1978). *Handbook of psychotherapy and behavior change: An empirical analysis* (2nd ed.). New York: Wiley.

Garfield, S. L., & Bergin, A. E. (Eds.). (1986). *Handbook of psychotherapy and behavior change* (3rd ed.). New York: Wiley.

Garfield, S. L., & Kurtz, R. M. (1976). Clinical psychologists in the 1970s. *American Psychologist, 31,* 1–9.

Garner, D. M., & Garfinkel, P. E. (1979). Eating Attitudes Test: An index of the symptoms of anorexia nervosa. *Psychological Medicine, 9,* 273–279.

Gay, P. (1988). *Freud: A life for our time.* New York: Norton.

Geer, J. H. (1965). The development of a scale to measure fear. *Behavioral Research and Therapy, 3,* 45–53.

Genest, M., & Turk, D. C. (1981). Think-aloud approaches to cognitive assessment. In T. V. Merluzzi, C. R. Glass, & M. Genest (Eds.), *Cognitive assessment* (pp. 233–269). New York: New York University Press.

Giblin, P. (1986). Research and assessment in marriage and family enrichment: A meta-analysis study. *Journal of Psychotherapy and the Family, 2,* 79–96.

Giblin, P., Sprenkle, D. H., & Sheehan, R. (1985). Enrichment outcome research: A meta-analysis of premarital, marital, and family interventions. *Journal of Marital and Family Therapy, 11,* 257–271.

Gibson, J. T. (1976). *Medication law and behavior.* New York: Wiley.

Gilberstadt, H., & Duker, J. (1965). *A handbook for clinical and actuarial MMPI interpretation.* Philadelphia: W. B. Saunders.

Glass, C. R., Merluzzi, T. V., Biever, J. O., & Larsen, K. H. (1982). Cognitive assessment of social anxiety: Development and validation of a self-statement questionnaire. *Cognitive Therapy and Research, 6,* 37–55.

Glass, D., Krakoff, L. R., Contrada, R., Hilton, W. F., Kehoe, K., Manucci, E. G., Collins, C., Snow, B., & Elfing, E. (1980). Effect of harassment and competition upon cardiovascular and catecholamine responses in Type A and Type B individuals. *Psychophysiology, 17,* 453–463.

Goldberg, E. E., & Alliger, G. M. (1992). Assessing the validity of the GRE for students in psychology: A validity generalization approach. *Educational and Psychological Measurement, 52,* 1019–1027.

Goldberg, L. R. (1978). Review of Jackson Personality Inventory. In O. K. Buros (Ed.), *Eighth mental measurements yearbook* (Vol. 1, pp. 867–871). Highland Park, NJ: Gryphon.

Goldberg, P. A. (1965). A review of sentence completion methods in personality assessment. *Journal of Projective Techniques and Personality Assessment, 29,* 12–45.

Goldfried, M. R., & Davison, G. C. (1976). *Clinical behavior therapy.* New York: Holt, Rinehart and Winston.

Goldfried, M. R., & Kent, R. N. (1972). Traditional versus behavioral assessment: A comparison of methodological and theoretical assumptions. *Psychological Bulletin, 77,* 409–420.

Goldfried, M. R., & Sprafkin, J. N. (1976). Behavioral personality assessment. In J. T. Spence, R. C. Carson, & J. W. Thibaut (Eds.), *Behavioral approaches to therapy* (pp. 295–321). Morristown, NJ: General Learning.

Golden, C. J., Purisch, A. D., & Hammeke, T. A. (1985). *Luria-Nebraska Neuropsychological Battery: Forms I and II (Manual).* Los Angeles: Western Psychological Services.

Goldstein, G. (1992). Historical perspectives. In A. E. Puente & R. J. McCaffrey (Eds.), *Handbook of neuropsychological assessment: A biopsychosocial perspective* (pp. 1–10). New York: Plenum.

Goodenough, F. L. (1926). *Measurement of intelligence by drawings.* New York: Harcourt, Brace, and World.

Goodenough, F. L. (1949). *Mental testing: Its history, principles, and applications.* New York: Rinehart.

Gottman, J. M. (1979). *Marital interaction: Experimental investigations.* New York: Academic.

Gough, H. G. (1957). *California Psychological Inventory manual.* Palo Alto, CA: Consulting Psychologists Press.

Gough, H. G. (1975). *California Psychological Inventory (revised manual).* Palo Alto, CA: Consulting Psychologists Press.

Gough, H. G. (1987). *California Psychological Inventory manual.* Palo Alto, CA: Consulting Psychologists Press.

Gould, S. J. (1981). *The mismeasure of man.* New York: W. W. Norton.

Goy, R. W., & Goldfoot, D. A. (1974). Experiential and hormonal factors influencing development of sexual behavior in the male rhesus monkey. In R. O. Schmidt & F. G. Worden (Eds.), *The Neurosciences* (pp. 571–581). Cambridge, MA: MIT Press.

Goyette, C. H., Conners, C. K., & Ulrich, R. F. (1978). Normative data on revised Conners Parent and Teacher Ratings Scales. *Journal of Abnormal Child Psychology, 6,* 221–236.

Grabowski, J., & VandenBos, G. R. (Eds.). (1992). *Psychopharmacology: Basic mechanisms and applied interventions.* Washington, DC: American Psychological Association.

Graham, J. R. (1990). *MMPI-2: Assessing personality and psychopathology.* New York: Oxford University Press.

Green, W. H. (1991). *Child and adolescent clinical psychopharmacology.* Baltimore, MD: Williams & Wilkins.

Greenblatt, D. J., Shader, R. I., & Abernethy, D. R. (1983). Current status of benzodiazepines. *New England Journal of Medicine, 309,* 354–358.

Gregory, R. J. (1992). *Psychological testing: History, principles, and applications.* Boston: Allyn and Bacon.

Gregory, R. J. (1996). *Psychological testing: History, principles, and applications* (2nd ed.). Boston: Allyn and Bacon.

Gross, M. L. (1978). *The psychological society: A critical analysis of psychiatry, psychotherapy, psychoanalysis and the psychological revolution.* New York: Simon and Schuster.

Grossman, P. B., & Hughes, J. N. (1992). Self-control interventions with internalizing disorders: A review and analysis. *School Psychology Review, 21,* 229–245.

Grotevant, H. D., & Cooper, C. (1988). The role of family experience in career exploration during adolescence. In P. Baltes, D. Featherman, & R. Lerner (Eds.), *Lifespan development and behavior* (Vol. 8, pp. 231–258). Hillsdale, NJ: Erlbaum.

Grunbaum, A. (1984). *The foundations of psychoanalysis: A philosophical critique.* Berkeley, CA: University of California Press.

Grusec, J. E., & Skubiski, S. L. (1970). Model nurturance, demand characteristics of the modeling experiment, and altruism. *Journal of Personality and Social Psychology, 14,* 352–359.

Gurman, A. S., & Kniskern, D. P. (1978). Research on marital and family therapy: Progress, perspective, and prospect. In S. L. Garfield & A. E. Bergin (Eds.), *Handbook of psychotherapy and behavior change: An empirical analysis* (2nd ed., pp. 817–901). New York: Wiley.

Gurman, A. S., Kniskern, D. P., & Pinsof, W. M. (1986). Research on the process and outcome of marital and family therapy. In S. L. Garfield & A. E. Bergin (Eds.), *Handbook of psychotherapy and behavior change* (3rd ed., pp. 565–624). New York: Wiley.

Guy, J. D., Stark, M. J., & Poelstra, P. L. (1988). Personal therapy for psychologists before and after entering professional practice. *Professional Psychology, 19,* 474–476.

Hahlweg, K., & Markman, H. J. (1988). Effectiveness of behavioral marital therapy: Empirical status of behavioral techniques in preventing and alleviating marital distress. *Journal of Consulting and Clinical Psychology, 56,* 440–447.

Haley, J. (1963). *Strategies of psychotherapy.* New York: Grune & Stratton.

Haley, J. (1976). *Problem-solving therapy.* New York: Harper & Row.

Hall, C. S., & Lindzey, G. (1978). *Theories of personality* (3rd ed.). New York: Wiley.

Hall, M. H. (1967). An interview with "Mr. Psychology" Edwin G. Boring. *Psychology Today, 1*(5), 16–19, 65–67.

Halstead, W. C. (1947). *Brain and intelligence.* Chicago: University of Chicago Press.

Hansen, J. C., & Campbell, D. P. (1985). *Manual for the Strong Interest Inventory Form T235 of the Strong Vocational Interest Blank* (4th ed.). Stanford, CA: Stanford University Press.

Hare, R. D. (1970). *Psychopathy: Theory and research.* New York: Wiley.

Harlow, H. F., & Zimmerman, R. (1959). Affectional responses in the infant monkey. *Science, 130,* 421–432.

Harris, D. B. (1963). *Children's drawings as measures of intellectual maturity: A revision and extension of the Goodenough Draw-a-Man-Test.* New York: Harcourt, Brace, and World.

Harris, D. B. (1972). Review of the DAP. In O. K. Buros (Ed.), *The seventh mental measurements yearbook* (pp. 401–405). Highland Park, NJ: Gryphon.

Harris, T. (1969). *I'm OK, you're OK.* New York: Harper and Row.

Harrower, M. (1976). Rorschach records of the Nazi war criminals: An experimental study after thirty years. *Journal of Personality Assessment, 40,* 341–351.

Hartlage, L. C., & Telzrow, C. F. (1980). The practice of clinical neuropsychology in the U.S. *Clinical Neuropsychology, 2,* 200–202.

Hartman, L. M. (1984). Cognitive components of anxiety. *Journal of Clinical Psychology, 40,* 137–139.

Hartmann, H. (1958). *Ego psychology and the problem of adaptation.* New York: International Universities Press.

Hathaway, S. R., & McKinley, J. C. (1940). A multiphasic personality schedule (Minnesota): I. Construction of the schedule. *Journal of Psychology, 10,* 249–254.

Hathaway, S. R., & McKinley, J. C. (1943). *The Minnesota Multiphasic Personality Inventory.* Minneapolis, MN: University of Minnesota Press.

Hawley, P. R. (1946). The importance of clinical psychology in a complete medical program. *Journal of Consulting Psychology, 10,* 292–300.

Haworth, M. R. (1970). House-Tree-Person projective technique. In O. K. Buros (Ed.), *Personality tests and reviews* (pp. 1240–1241). Highland Park, NJ: Gryphon.

Hayes, S. C., Nelson, R. O., & Jarrett, R. B. (1986). Evaluating the quality of behavioral assessment. In R. O. Nelson & S. C. Hayes (Eds.), *Conceptual foundations of behavioral assessment* (pp. 463–503). New York: Guilford.

Haynes, S. N., & Horn, W. F. (1982). Reactivity in behavioral observation: A review. *Behavioral Assessment, 4,* 369–386.

Hazelrigg, M. D., Cooper, H. M., & Borduin, C. M. (1987). Evaluating the effectiveness of family therapies: An integrative review and analysis. *Psychological Bulletin, 101,* 428–442.

Heaton, R. K. (1981). *Wisconsin Card Sorting Test manual.* Odessa, FL: Psychological Assessment Resources.

Heaton, R. K., Baade, L. E., & Johnson, K. L. (1978). Neuropsychological test results associated with psychiatric disorder in adults. *Psychological Bulletin, 85,* 141–162.

Hecker, J. E., Fink, C. M., Levasseur, J. B., & Parker, J. D. (1995). Perspectives on practicum: A survey of directors of accredited Ph.D. programs in internships (or, what is a practicum hour, and how many do I need?).

Professional Psychology: Research and Practice, 26, 205–210.

Hedberg, A. G. (1981). Professional and ethical issues in providing clinical services. In C. E. Walker (Ed.), *Clinical practice of psychology: A guide for mental health professionals* (pp. 367–396). New York: Pergamon.

Heinicke, C. M., & Goldman, A. (1960). Research on psychotherapy with children: A review and suggestions for further study. *American Journal of Orthopsychiatry, 30,* 483–494.

Hempel, C. G. (1965). *Aspects of scientific explanation and other essays in the philosophy of science.* New York: Free Press.

Hendrick, I. (1967). *Facts and theories of psychoanalysis* (3rd ed.). New York: Knopf.

Henry, W. P., Strupp, H. H., Schacht, T. E., & Gaston, L. (1994). Psychodynamic approaches. In A. E. Bergin & S. L. Garfield (Eds.), *Handbook of psychotherapy and behavior change* (4th ed., pp. 467–508). New York: Wiley.

Heppner, P. P., & Peterson, C. H. (1982). The development and implications of a personal problem solving inventory. *Journal of Counseling Psychology, 29,* 66–75.

Herrnstein, R. J., & Boring, E. G. (Eds.). (1966). *A sourcebook in the history of psychology.* Cambridge, MA: Harvard University Press.

Hersen, M., & Bellack, A. S. (Eds.). (1988). *Dictionary of behavioral assessment techniques.* New York: Pergamon.

Hersen, M., Bellack, A. S., Himmelhoch, J. M., & Thase, M. E. (1984). Effects of social skills training, amitryptaline, and psychotherapy in unipolar depressed women. *Behavior Therapy, 15,* 21–40.

Hershey, J. M., Kopplin, D. A., & Cornell, J. E. (1991). Doctors of Psychology: Their career experiences and attitudes toward degree and training. *Professional Psychology: Research and Practice, 22,* 351–356.

Hetherington, E. M., Stouwie, R. J., & Ridberg, E. H. (1971). Patterns of family interaction and child-rearing attitudes related to three dimensions of juvenile delinquency. *Journal of Abnormal Psychology, 78,* 160–176.

Hill, W. F. (1971). *Learning: A survey of psychological interpretations* (rev. ed.). Scranton, OH: Chandler.

Hobbs, N. (1951). Group-centered psychotherapy. In C. R. Rogers, *Client-centered therapy: Its current practice, implications, and theory* (pp. 278–319). Boston: Houghton Mifflin.

Hoberman, H. M., & Lewinsohn, P. M. (1985). The behavioral treatment of depression. In E. E. Beckham & W. R. Leber (Eds.), *Handbook of depression: Treatment, assessment, and research* (pp. 39–81). Homewood, IL: Dorsey.

Hogan, J. D., & Sexton, V. S. (1991). Some additional comments on training. *Psychological Science, 2,* 21–22.

Hogarty, G. E., Goldberg, S. C., Schooler, N. R., Ulrich, R. F., & the Collaborative Study Group. (1974). Drug and sociotherapy in the aftercare of schizophrenic patients: II. Two-year relapse rates. *Archives of General Psychiatry, 31,* 603–608.

Hollandsworth, J. G., Jr., Glazeski, R. C., Kirkland, K., Jones, G. E., & Van Norman, L. R. (1979). An analysis of the nature and effects of test anxiety: Cognitive, behavioral, and physiological components. *Cognitive Therapy and Research, 3,* 165–180.

Holliman, B. B., & Guthrie, P. C. (1989). A comparison of the Millon Clinical Multiaxial Inventory and the California Psychological Inventory in assessment of a nonclinical population. *Journal of Clinical Psychology, 45,* 373–382.

Hollon, S. D., & Beck, A. T. (1986). Cognitive and cognitive-behavioral therapies. In A. E. Bergin & S. L. Garfield (Eds.), *Handbook of psychotherapy and behavior change* (3rd ed., pp. 443–482). New York: Wiley.

Hollon, S. D., & Kendall, P. C. (1980). Cognitive self-statements in depression: Development of an Automatic Thoughts Questionnaire. *Cognitive Therapy and Research, 4,* 383–395.

Holmes, D. S. (1984). Meditation and somatic arousal reduction: A review of the experimental evidence. *American Psychologist, 39,* 1–10.

Holmes, T. H., & Rahe, R. H. (1967). The social readjustment rating scale. *Journal of Psychosomatic Research, 2,* 213–218.

Holt, H. (1990). Existential group analysis. In I. L. Kutash & A. Wolf (Eds.), *The group psychotherapist's handbook: Contemporary theory and technique* (pp. 175–190). New York: Columbia University Press.

Holt, R. R. (Ed.). (1971). *New horizons for psychotherapy.* New York: International Universities Press.

Holt, R. R., & Luborsky, L. (1958). *Personality patterns of psychiatrists.* New York: Basic Books.

Holtzman, W. H. (1961). *Guide to administration and scoring: Holtzman Inkblot Technique.* New York: Psychological Corporation.

Honigfeld, G., Gillis, R. O., & Klett, C. J. (1966). NOSIE-30: A treatment-sensitive ward behavior scale. *Psychological Reports, 19,* 180–182.

Hood-Williams, J. (1960). The results of psychotherapy with children: A revaluation. *Journal of Consulting Psychology, 24,* 84–88.

Homme, L. E. (1965). Perspectives in psychology: XXIV. Control of coverants, the operants of the mind. *Psychological Record, 15,* 501–511.

Honaker, L. M., & Fowler, R. D. (1990). Computer-assisted psychological assessment. In G. Goldstein & M. Hersen (Eds.), *Handbook of psychological assessment* (2nd ed., pp. 521–546). New York: Pergamon.

Hook, S. (Ed.). (1958). *Determinism and freedom in the age of modern science.* New York: New York University Press.

Hook, S. (1959). Science and mythology in psychoanalysis. In S. Hook (Ed.), *Psychoanalysis, scientific method, and philosophy* (pp. 212–224). Washington Square, NY: New York University Press.

Hooper, S. R., & Layne, C. C. (1983). The Common Belief Inventory for Students: A measure of rationality in children. *Journal of Personality Assessment, 47,* 85–90.

Horkheimer, R., Abell, S. C., & Nguyen, S. (1995, May). *Intellectual evaluations of adolescents using human figure drawings: An empirical investigation of two methods.* Paper presented at the meeting of the Midwestern Psychological Association, Chicago, IL.

Horney, K. (1937). *The neurotic personality of our time.* New York: Norton.

Horney, K. (1939). *New ways in psychoanalysis.* New York: Norton.

Hug-Hellmuth, H. V. (1921). On the technique of child analysis. *International Journal of Psychoanalysis, 2,* 287–305.

Huitema, B. E., & Stein, C. R. (1993). Validity of the GRE without restriction of range. *Psychological Reports, 72,* 123–127.

Hulse, W. C. (1951). The emotionally disturbed child draws his family. *Quarterly Journal of Child Behavior, 3,* 152–174.

Hurlburt, R. T. (1979). Random sampling of cognitions and behavior. *Journal of Research in Personality, 13,* 103–111.

Ishiyama, F. (1986). Positive reinterpretation of fear of death: A Japanese (Morita) psychotherapy approach to anxiety treatment. *Psychotherapy, 23,* 556–562.

Jackson, D. N. (1976). *Jackson Personality Inventory manual.* Port Huron, MI: Research Psychologists Press.

Jackson, D. N. (1977). *Jackson Vocational Interest Survey manual.* Ontario: Research Psychologists Press.

Jackson, D. N. (1991). *Jackson Vocational Interest Survey manual* (3rd ed.). Port Huron, MI: Research Psychologists Press.

Jacobson, E. (1938). *Progressive relaxation.* Chicago: University of Chicago Press.

Jacobson, N. S., & Margolin, G. (1979). *Marital therapy: Strategies based on social learning and behavior exchange principles.* New York: Brunner/Mazel.

Jastak, S., & Wilkinson, G. (1984). *The Wide Range Achievement Test—Revised: Administration manual.* Wilmington, DE: Jastak Associates.

Jensen, A. R. (1959). The reliability of projective techniques: Review of the literature. *Acta Psychologica, 16,* 108–136.

Jensen, A. R. (1969). How much can we boost IQ and scholastic achievement? *Harvard Educational Review, 39,* 1–123.

Jensen, A. R. (1980). *Bias in mental testing.* New York: Free Press.

Jensen, A. R. (1981). *Bias in mental testing.* New York: Free Press.

Jerome, L. E. (1977). *Astrology disproved.* Buffalo, NY: Prometheus.

Johnson, J. H. (1986). *Life events as stressors in childhood and adolescence.* Beverly Hills, CA: Sage.

Johnson, M. E., & Brems, C. (1991). Comparing theoretical orientations of counseling and clinical psychologists: An objective approach. *Professional Psychology: Research and Practice, 22,* 133–137.

Jones, E. (1953). *The life and work of Sigmund Freud: The formative years and the great discoveries* (Vol. 1). New York: Basic Books.

Jones, M. C. (1924a). The elimination of children's fears. *Journal of Experimental Psychology, 7,* 383–390.

Jones, M. C. (1924b). A laboratory study of fear: The case of Peter. *Journal of Genetic Psychology, 31,* 308–315.

Jones, R. R., Reid, J. B., & Patterson, G. R. (1975). Naturalistic observation in clinical assessment. In P. McReynolds (Ed.), *Advances in psychological assessment* (Vol. 3, pp. 42–95). San Francisco: Jossey-Bass.

Jung, C. G. (1910). The association method. *American Journal of Psychology, 21,* 219–235.

Jung, C. G. (1974). *The psychology of dementia praecox.* (R. F. C. Hull, Trans.). Princeton, NJ: Princeton University Press. (Original work published 1907).

Juni, S. (1995). Review of the Revised NEO Personality Inventory. In J. C. Conoley & J. C. Impara (Eds.), *Twelfth mental measurements yearbook* (pp. 863–868). Lincoln, NE: University of Nebraska Press.

Kagan, J. (1992). Behavior, biology, and the meanings of temperamental constructs. *Pediatrics, 90,* 510–513.

Kagan, J., & Snidman, N. (1991). Temperamental factors in human development. *American Psychologist, 46,* 856–862.

Kaminer, W. (1992). *I'm dysfunctional, you're dysfunctional: The recovery movement and other self-help fashions.* Reading, MA: Addison-Wesley.

Kanner, A. D., Coyne, J. C., Schaefer, C., & Lazarus, R. S. (1981). Comparison of two modes of stress measurement: Daily hassles and uplifts versus major life events. *Journal of Behavioral Medicine, 4,* 1–39.

Kaplan, E. F., Goodglass, H., & Weintraub, S. (1983). *The Boston Naming Test* (2nd ed.). Philadelphia: Lea and Febiger.

Kaufman, A. S., & Kaufman, N. L. (1977). *Clinical evaluation of young children with the McCarthy Scales.* New York: Grune and Stratton.

Kaufman, A. S., & Kaufman, N. L. (1983a). *Kaufman Assessment Battery for Children: Administration and scoring manual.* Circle Pines, MN: American Guidance Service.

Kaufman, A. S., & Kaufman, N. L. (1983b). *Kaufman Assessment Battery for Children: Interpretive manual.* Circle Pines, MN: American Guidance Service.

Kaufman, A. S., & Kaufman, N. L. (1985). *Kaufman Test of Educational Achievement.* Circle Pines, MN: American Guidance Service.

Kaul, T. J., & Bednar, R. L. (1986). Experiential group research: Results, questions, and suggestions. In S. L. Garfield & A. E. Bergin (Eds.), *Handbook of psychotherapy and behavior change* (3rd ed., pp. 671–714). New York: Wiley.

Kazdin, A. E. (1986). The evaluation of psychotherapy: Research design and methodology. In S. L. Garfield & A. E. Bergin (Eds.), *Handbook of psychotherapy and behavior change* (3rd ed., pp. 23–60). New York: Wiley.

Kazdin, A. E., Bass, D., Ayers, W. A., & Rodgers, A. (1990). Empirical and clinical focus of child and adolescent psychotherapy research. *Journal of Consulting and Clinical Psychology, 58,* 729–740.

Kazdin, A. E., & Bootzin, R. R. (1972). The token economy: An evaluative review. *Journal of Applied Behavior Analysis, 5,* 343–372.

Kazdin, A., Siegel, T. C., & Bass, D. (1990). Drawing on clinical practice to inform research on child and adolescent psychotherapy: Survey of practitioners. *Professional Psychology: Research and Practice, 21,* 189–198.

Keefe, F. J., Dunsmore, J., & Burnett, R. (1992). Behavioral and cognitive-behavioral approaches to chronic pain: Recent advances and future directions. *Journal of Consulting and Clinical Psychology, 60,* 528–536.

Keith-Spiegel, P. (1991). *The complete guide to graduate school admission: Psychology and related fields.* Hillsdale, NJ: Erlbaum.

Kelly, G. A. (1955). *The psychology of personal constructs* (Vols. 1, 2). New York: Norton.

Kelly, J. A., & Murphy, D. A. (1992). Psychological interventions with AIDS and HIV: Prevention and treatment. *Journal of Consulting and Clinical Psychology, 61,* 576–585.

Kelly, L., & Goldberg, L. R. (1959). Correlates of later performance and specialization in psychology. *Psychological Monographs, 73* (Whole No. 482).

Kempler, W. (1974). *Principles of Gestalt family therapy.* Salt Lake City, UT: Desert.

Kendall, P. C. (1987). Cognitive processes and procedures in behavior therapy. In G. T. Wilson, C. M. Franks, P. C. Kendall, & J. P. Foreyt (Eds.), *Review of behavior therapy: Theory and practice* (Vol. 11, pp. 114–153). New York: Guilford.

Kendall, P. C., & Norton-Ford, J. D. (1982). *Clinical psychology: Scientific and professional dimensions.* New York: Wiley.

Kendall, R. E., Cooper, J. E., Gourlay, A. J., & Copeland, J. R. M. (1971). Diagnostic criteria of American and British psychiatrists. *Archives of General Psychiatry, 25,* 123–130.

Kent, R. N., & Foster, S. L. (1977). Direct observation procedures: Methodological issues in applied settings. In A. Ciminero, K. S. Calhoun, & H. E. Adams (Eds.), *Handbook of behavioral assessment* (pp. 279–328). New York: Wiley.

Kernberg, O., Burstein, E., Coyne, L., Appelbaum, A., Horwitz, L., & Voth, H. (1972). Psychotherapy and psychoanalysis: Final report of the Menninger Foundation's Psychotherapy Research Project. *Bulletin of the Menninger Clinic, 36,* 1–275.

Kessler, R. C., McGonagle, K. A., Zhao, S., Nelson, C. B., Hughes, M., Eshleman, S., Wittchen, H., & Kendler, K. S. (1994). Lifetime and 12-month prevalence of DSM-III-R psychiatric disorders in the United States: Results from the National Comorbidity Survey. *Archives of General Psychiatry, 51,* 8–19.

Kiernan, V. (1995, January 21). "Cheats" outwit computerized exam. *New Scientist, 145* (No. 1961), 11.

Kifer, E. (1985). Review of ACT Assessment Program. *Ninth mental measurements yearbook* (Vol. 1), 31–46.

Killian, G. A. (1984). House-Tree-Person Technique. In D. J. Keyser & R. C. Sweetland (Eds.), *Test critiques* (Vol. 1, pp. 338–353). Kansas City, MO: Test Corporation of America.

Kimble, G. A. (1961). *Hilgard and Marquis' conditioning and learning* (2nd ed.). New York: Appleton-Century.

Kingsbury, S. J. (1987). Cognitive differences between clinical psychologists and psychiatrists. *American Psychologist, 42,* 152–156.

Kingsbury, S. J. (1992a). Some effects of prescribing privileges. *Professional Psychology: Research and Practice, 23,* 3–5.

Kingsbury, S. J. (1992b). Some effects of prescribing privileges. *American Psychologist, 47,* 426–427.

Kirk, S. A., McCarthy, J. J., & Kirk, W. D. (1968). *The Illinois Test of Psycholinguistic Abilities.* Urbana: University of Illinois Press.

Klein, M. (1932). *The psycho-analysis of children.* London: Hogarth.

Klein, R. G., & Mannuzza, S. (1988). Hyperactive boys almost grown up: III. Methylphenidate effects on ultimate height. *Archives of General Psychiatry, 45,* 1131–1134.

Kline, P. (1972). *Fact and fantasy in Freudian theory.* London: Methuen.

Klopfer, W. G., & Taulbee, E. S. (1976). Projective tests. *Annual Review of Psychology, 27,* 543–567.

Kluger, R. (1975). *Simple justice: The history of Brown v. Board of Education and Black America's struggle for equality.* New York: Knopf.

Knoff, H. M. (1989). Review of the Personality Inventory for Children, Revised Format. In J. C. Conoley & J. Kramer (Eds.), *Tenth mental measurements yearbook* (pp. 625–630). Lincoln, NE: University of Nebraska Press.

Kobasa, S. C., Maddi, S. R., & Kahn, S. (1982). Hardiness and health: A prospective study. *Journal of Personality and Social Psychology, 42,* 168–177.

Koppitz, E. M. (1963). *The Bender Gestalt test for young children.* New York: Grune and Stratton.

Korman, M. (1974). National conference on levels and patterns of professional training in psychology. *American Psychologist, 29,* 441–449.

Kraepelin, E. (1962). *One hundred years of psychiatry* (W. Baskin, Trans.). New York: Citadel. (Original work published in 1917).

Kris, E. (1947). Round table discussion: Problems in clinical research. *American Journal of Orthopsychiatry, 17,* 196–230.

Kuder, G. F. (1939). *Kuder Preference Record.* Chicago: Science Research Associates.

Kuder, G. F. (1975). *General Interest Survey (Form E)—Manual.* Chicago: Science Research Associates.

Kuder, G. F., & Diamond, E. E. (1979). *Kuder Occupational Interest Survey: General manual.* Chicago: Science Research Associates.

Kuder, G. F., & Richardson, M. W. (1937). The theory of estimation of test reliability. *Psychometrika, 2,* 151–160.

Kuhn, T. S. (1962). *The structure of scientific revolutions.* Chicago: University of Chicago Press.

Kutash, I. L., & Wolf, A. (1990). Object relational groups. In I. L. Kutash & A. Wolf (Eds.), *The group psychotherapist's handbook: Contemporary theory and technique* (pp. 99–115). New York: Columbia University Press.

Lachar, D. (1974). *The MMPI: Clinical assessment and automated interpretation.* Los Angeles: Western Psychological Services.

Lahey, B. B., & Piacentini, J. C. (1985). An evaluation of the Quay-Peterson Revised Behavior Problem Checklist. *Journal of School Psychology, 23,* 285–289.

Lakin, M. (1988). *Ethical issues in the psychotherapies.* New York: Oxford University Press.

Lambert, M. J., & Bergin, A. E. (1992). Achievements and limitations of psychotherapy research. In D. K. Freedheim, H. J. Freudenberger, J. W. Kessler, S. B. Messer, D. R. Peterson, H. H. Strupp, & P. L. Wachtel (Eds.), *History of psychotherapy: A century of change* (pp. 360–390). Washington, DC: American Psychological Association.

Lambert, M. J., Shapiro, D. A., & Bergin, A. E. (1986). The effectiveness of psychotherapy. In S. L. Garfield & A. E. Bergin (Eds.), *Handbook of psychotherapy and behavior change* (3rd ed., pp. 157–211). New York: Wiley.

Landman, J. T., & Dawes, R. M. (1982). Psychotherapy outcome: Smith and Glass' conclusions stand up under scrutiny. *American Psychologist, 37,* 504–516.

Lazarus, A. A. (1971). *Behavior therapy and beyond.* New York: McGraw-Hill.

Lazarus, A. A. (1973). Multimodal behavior therapy: Treating the BASIC I.D. *Journal of Nervous and Mental Disease, 156,* 404–411.

Lazarus, R. S., & Folkman, S. (1984). *Stress, appraisal, and coping.* New York: Springer-Verlag.

LeCroy, C. W. (Ed.). (1994). *Handbook of child and adolescent treatment manuals.* New York: Lexington.

Leonard, H. L., Swedo, S. E., Rapoport, J. L., Koby, E. V., Lenane, M. C., Cheslow, D. L., & Hamburger, S. D. (1989). Treatment of obsessive-compulsive disorder with clomipramine and desipramine in children and adolescents: A double-blind crossover comparison. *Archives of General Psychiatry, 46,* 1088–1092.

Levant, R. F. (1984). *Family therapy: A comprehensive overview.* Englewood Cliffs, NJ: Prentice-Hall.

Levitt, E. E. (1957). The results of psychotherapy with children: An evaluation. *Journal of Consulting Psychology, 21,* 189–196.

Levitt, E. E. (1963). Psychotherapy with children: A further evaluation. *Behaviour Research and Therapy, 1,* 45–51.

Levitt, E. E. (1971). Research on psychotherapy with children. In A. E. Bergin & S. L. Garfield (Eds.), *Handbook of psychotherapy and behavior change: An empirical analysis* (pp. 474–494). New York: Wiley.

Levitzky, A., & Perls, F. (1970). The rules and games of Gestalt therapy. In J. Fagan & I. Shepherd (Eds.), *Gestalt therapy now.* Palo Alto, CA: Science and Behavior Books.

Levy, L. (1962). The skew in clinical psychology. *American Psychologist, 17,* 244–249.

Lewinsohn, P. (1974). A behavioral approach to depression. In R. J. Friedman & M. M. Katz (Eds.), *The psychology of depression: Contemporary theory and research* (pp. 157–178). Washington, DC: Winston-Wiley.

Lewinsohn, P. M., & Amenson, C. S. (1978). Some relations between pleasant and unpleasant mood-related events and depression. *Journal of Abnormal Psychology, 87,* 644–654.

Lewinsohn, P. M., Antonuccio, D. O., Steinmetz, J. L., & Teri, L. (1984). *The Coping with Depression course: A psychoeducational intervention for unipolar depression.* Eugene, OR: Castalia.

Lewinsohn, P. M., Biglan, A., & Zeiss, A. M. (1976). Behavioral treatment of depression. In P. O. Davidson (Ed.), *Behavioral management of anxiety, depression, and pain* (pp. 91–146). New York: Brunner/Mazel.

Lezak, M. D. (1976). *Neuropsychological assessment.* New York: Oxford University Press.

Lichtenstein, E., & Brown, R. A. (1980). Smoking cessation methods: Review and recommendations. In W. R. Miller (Ed.), *The addictive behaviors: Treatment of alcoholism, drug abuse, smoking, and obesity* (pp. 169–206). New York: Pergamon.

Lichtenstein, E., & Glasgow, R. E. (1992). Smoking cessation: What have we learned over the past decade? *Journal of Consulting and Clinical Psychology, 61,* 518–536.

Lick, J., & Bootzin, R. (1975). Expectancy factors in the treatment of fear: Methodological and theoretical issues. *Psychological Bulletin, 82,* 917–931.

Lieberman, M. A. (1990). A group therapist perspective on self-help groups. *International Journal of Group Psychotherapy, 40,* 251–278.

Lieberman, M. A., & Snowden, L. R. (1993). Problems in assessing prevalence and membership characteristics of self-help group participants. *Journal of Applied Behavioral Science, 29,* 166–180.

Lieberman, M. A., Yalom, I. D., & Miles, M. B. (1973). *Encounter groups: First facts.* New York: Basic Books.

Lindzey, G. (1952). Thematic Apperception Test: Interpretive assumptions and related empirical evidence. *Psychological Bulletin, 49,* 1–25.

Lindzey, G. (1961). *Projective techniques and cross-cultural research.* New York: Appleton-Century-Crofts.

Lipinski, D. P., & Nelson, R. O. (1974). The reactivity and unreliability of self-recording. *Journal of Consulting and Clinical Psychology, 42,* 118–123.

Lombroso, C. (1910). *The man of genius.* New York: Scribner.

Lord, F. M., & Novick, M. R. (1968). *Statistical theories of mental test scores.* Reading, MA: Addison-Wesley.

Louttit, C. M., & Browne, C. G. (1947). The use of psychometric instruments in psychological clinics. *Journal of Consulting Psychology, 11,* 49–54.

Lovaas, O. I. (1966). A program for the establishment of speech in psychotic children. In J. K. Wing (Ed.), *Early childhood autism* (pp. 115–144). London: Pergamon.

Lovaas, O. I. (1977). *The autistic child.* New York: Irvington.

Lovaas, O. I. (1987). Behavioral treatment and normal educational and intellectual functioning in young autistic children. *Journal of Consulting and Clinical Psychology, 55,* 3–9.

Lovaas, O. I., Koegel, R., Simmons, J. Q., & Long, J. S. (1973). Some generalizations and follow-up measures on autistic children in behavior therapy. *Journal of Applied Behavior Analysis, 6,* 131–166.

Lovaas, O. I., & Simmons, J. Q. (1969). Manipulation of self-destruction in three retarded children. *Journal of Applied Behavior Analysis, 2,* 143–157.

Lovaas, O. I., Smith, T., & McEachin, J. J. (1989). Clarifying comments on the Young Autism Study: Reply to Schopler, Short, and Mesibov. *Journal of Consulting and Clinical Psychology, 57,* 165–167.

Lowe, K., & Lutzker, J. (1979). Increasing compliance to a medical regimen with a juvenile diabetic. *Behavior Therapy, 10,* 57–67.

Lubin, B., Larsen, R. D., & Matarazzo, J. D. (1984). Patterns of psychological test usage in the United States: 1935–1982. *American Psychologist, 39,* 451–454.

Lubin, B., Wallis, R. R., & Paine, C. (1971). Patterns of psychological test usage in the United States: 1935–1969. *Professional Psychology, 2,* 70–74.

Luborsky, L. (1954). A note on Eysenck's article "The effects of psychotherapy: An evaluation." *British Journal of Psychology, 45,* 129–131.

Luborsky, L., Singer, B., & Luborsky, L. (1975). Comparative studies of psychotherapies: Is it true that "everyone has won and all must have prizes"? *Archives of General Psychiatry, 32,* 995–1008.

Luborsky, L., & Spence, D. P. (1971). Quantitative research on psychoanalytic therapy. In A. E. Bergin & S. L. Garfield (Eds.), *Handbook of psychotherapy and behavior change: An empirical analysis* (pp. 408–438). New York: Wiley.

Luborsky, L., & Spence, D. P. (1978). Quantitative research on psychoanalytic therapy. In S. L. Garfield & A. E. Bergin (Eds.), *Handbook of psychotherapy and behavior change: An empirical analysis* (2nd ed., pp. 331–368). New York: Wiley.

Ludwick-Rosenthal, R., & Neufeld, R. W. J. (1993). Preparation for undergoing an invasive medical procedure: Interacting effects of information and coping style. *Journal of Consulting and Clinical Psychology, 61,* 156–164.

Luria, A. R. (1961). *The role of speech in the regulation of normal and abnormal behavior.* New York: Pergamon.

Lutzker, J. R., Olmedo, E. L., & Persico, C. F. (1987). The professional schools: Problems or panaceas? *The Behavior Therapist, 10,* 11–13.

MacCuorquodale, K., & Meehl, P. E. (1948). On a distinction between hypothetical constructs and intervening variables. *Psychological Review, 55,* 95–107.

MacDougall, J., Dembroski, T., & Krantz, D. (1981). Effects of types of challenge on pressor and heart rate responses in Type A and B women. *Psychophysiology, 18,* 1–9.

Macfarlane, J. W., & Tuddenham, R. D. (1951). Problems in the validation of projective techniques. In H. H. Anderson & G. L. Anderson (Eds.), *An introduction to projective techniques* (pp. 26–54). New York: Prentice-Hall.

Machover, K. (1949). *Personality projection in the drawing of a human figure.* Springfield, IL: Charles C. Thomas.

MacLean, R. E. G. (1960). Imipramine hydrochloride and enuresis. *American Journal of Psychiatry, 117,* 551.

Maddi, S. R. (1996). Personality theories: A comparative analysis (6th ed.). Pacific Grove, CA: Brooks/Cole.

Mahler, M. S. (1952). On child psychosis and schizophrenia. *Psychoanalytic Study of the Child, 7,* 286–305.

Mahoney, M. J. (1974). *Cognition and behavior modification.* Cambridge, MA: Ballinger.

Mahoney, M. J. (1976). *Scientist as subject: The psychological imperative.* Cambridge, MA: Ballinger.

Mahoney, M. J., & Arnkoff, D. B. (1978). Cognitive and self-control therapies. In S. L. Garfield & A. E. Bergin (Eds.), *Handbook of psychotherapy and behavior change: An empirical analysis* (2nd ed., pp. 689–722). New York: Wiley.

Marks, I. M. (1975). Behavioral treatment of phobic and obsessive-compulsive disorders: A critical appraisal. In M. Hersen, R. M. Eisler, & P. M. Miller (Eds.), *Progress in behavior modification* (Vol. 1, pp. 65–158). New York: Appleton-Century- Crofts.

Marks, I. (1978). Behavioral psychotherapy of adult neurosis. In S. L. Garfield & A. E. Bergin (Eds.), *Handbook of psychotherapy and behavior change: An empirical analysis* (2nd ed., pp. 493–547). New York: Wiley.

Marks, P. A., Seaman, W., & Haller, D. L. (1974). *The actuarial use of the MMPI with adolescents and adults.* New York: Oxford University Press.

Markus, E., Lange, A., & Pettigrew, T. F. (1990). Effectiveness of family therapy: A meta-analysis. *Journal of Family Therapy, 12,* 205–221.

Markwardt, F. C. (1989). *Peabody Individual Achievement Test—Revised.* Circle Pines, MN: American Guidance Service.

Mash, E. J., & Hunsley, J. (1990). Behavioral assessment: A contemporary approach. In A. S. Bellack, M. Hersen, & A. E. Kazdin (Eds.), *International handbook of behavior modification and therapy* (2nd ed., pp. 87–106). New York: Plenum.

Maslow, A. H. (1962). *Toward a psychology of being.* New York: Van Nostrand.

Massie, H. N., & Beels, C. C. (1972). The outcome of the family treatment of schizophrenia. *Schizophrenia Bulletin, 6,* 24–36.

Masson, J. M. (1990). *Final analysis: The making and unmaking of a psychoanalyst.* New York: Addison-Wesley.

Matarazzo, R. G. (1971). Research on the teaching and learning of therapeutic skills. In A. E. Bergin & S. L. Garfield (Eds.), *Handbook of psychotherapy and behavior change: An empirical analysis* (pp. 895–924). New York: Wiley.

Matarazzo, R. G. (1978). Research on the teaching and learning of therapeutic skills. In S. L. Garfield & A. E. Bergin (Eds.), *Handbook of psychotherapy and behavior change: An empirical analysis* (pp. 941–966). New York: Wiley.

Matarazzo, R. G., & Patterson, D. (1986). Methods of teaching therapeutic skill. In S. L. Garfield & A. E. Bergin (Eds.), *Handbook of psychotherapy and behavior change* (3rd ed., pp. 821–843). New York: Wiley.

May, P. R. A. (1968). *Treatment of schizophrenia: A comparative study of five treatment methods.* New York: Science House.

May, W. T., & Belsky, J. (1992). Response to "Prescription privileges: Psychology's next frontier?" or the siren call: Should psychologists medicate? *American Psychologist, 47,* 427.

Mayne, T. J., Norcross, J. C., & Sayette, M. A. (1994). Admission requirements, acceptance rates, and financial assistance in clinical psychology programs: Diversity across the practice-research continuum. *American Psychologist, 49,* 806–811.

McCall, R. B. (1977). Childhood IQs as predictors of adult educational and occupational status. *Science, 197,* 482–483.

McCarthy, D. A. (1972). *Manual for the McCarthy Scales of Children's Abilities.* San Antonio, TX: The Psychological Corporation.

McGrew, M. W., & Teglasi, H. (1990). Formal characteristics of Thematic Apperception Test stories as indices of emotional disturbance in children. *Journal of Personality Assessment, 54,* 639–655.

McGuire, W. (Ed.). (1974). *The Freud/Jung letters: The correspondence between Sigmund Freud and C. J. Jung.* Princeton, NJ: Princeton University Press.

McMahon, R. J., & Forehand, R. (1988). Conduct disorders. In E. J. Mash & L. G. Terdal (Eds.), *Behavioral assessment of childhood disorders: Selected core problems* (2nd ed., pp. 105–153). New York: Guilford.

McNamara, J. R., & Barlow, A. G. (Eds.). (1982). *Critical issues, developments, and trends in professional psychology.* New York: Praeger.

McNamara, J. R., Jones, N. F., & Barclay, A. G. (1982). Contemporary professional psychology. In J. R. McNamara & A. G. Barclay (Eds.), *Critical issues, developments, and trends in professional psychology* (pp. 1–28). New York: Praeger.

McReynolds, P. (1975). Historical antecedents of personality assessment. In P. McReynolds (Ed.), *Advances in psychological assessment* (Vol. 3, pp. 477–532). San Francisco: Jossey-Bass.

Meehl, P. E. (1954). *Clinical versus statistical prediction.* Minneapolis, MN: University of Minnesota Press.

Meehl, P. E. (1957). When shall we use our heads instead of the formula? *Journal of Counseling Psychology, 4,* 268–273.

Meehl, P. E., & Hathaway, S. R. (1946). The K factor as a suppressor variable in the MMPI. *Journal of Applied Psychology, 30,* 525–564.

Meichenbaum, D. (1971). Examination of model characteristics in reducing avoidance behavior. *Journal of Personality and Social Psychology, 17,* 198–307.

Meichenbaum, D. (1977). *Cognitive-behavior modification: An integrative approach.* New York: Plenum.

Meichenbaum, D. (1985). *Stress inoculation training.* New York: Pergamon.

Meichenbaum, D., & Turk, D. (1976). The cognitive-behavioral management of anxiety, anger, and pain. In P. O. Davidson (Ed.), *The behavioral management of anxiety, depression and pain* (pp. 1–34). New York: Brunner/Mazel.

Meltzoff, J. (1984). Research training for clinical psychologists: Point-counterpoint. *Professional Psychology: Research and Practice, 15,* 203–209.

Meltzoff, J., & Kornreich, M. (1970). *Research in psychotherapy.* New York: Atherton.

Miale, F. R., & Selzer, M. (1975). *The Nuremberg mind: The psychology of the Nazi leaders.* New York: Quadrangle.

Miele, F. (1979). Culture bias in the WISC. *Intelligence, 3,* 149–164.

Milich, R., Licht, B. G., Murphy, D. A., & Pelham, W. E. (1989). Attention-deficit hyperactivity disordered boys' evaluations of and attributions for task performance on medication versus placebo. *Journal of Abnormal Psychology, 98,* 280–284.

Miller, R. C., & Berman, J. S. (1983). The efficacy of cognitive behavior therapies: A quantitative review of the research evidence. *Psychological Bulletin, 94,* 39–53.

Miller, W. R., & Hester, R. K. (1980). Treating the problem drinker: Modern approaches. In W. R. Miller (Ed.), *The addictive behaviors: Treatment of alcoholism, drug abuse, smoking, and obesity* (pp. 11–141). New York: Pergamon.

Millon, T. (1977). *Manual for the Millon Clinical Multiaxial Inventory (MCMI).* Minneapolis, MN: National Computer Systems.

Millon, T. (1981). *Disorders of personality: DSM-III, Axis II.* New York: Wiley.

Millon, T. (1984). On the renaissance of personality assessment and personality theory. *Journal of Personality Assessment, 48,* 450–466.

Millon, T. (1987). *Manual for the Millon Clinical Multiaxial Inventory-II (MCMI-II).* Minneapolis, MN: National Computer Systems.

Millon, T. (1990). *Toward a new personology.* New York: Wiley.

Millon, T. (1994). *Manual for the Millon Clinical Multiaxial Inventory-III (MCMI-III).* Minneapolis, MN: National Computer Systems.

Mills, D. H. (1982). Ethical standards in professional psychology. In J. R. McNamara & A. G. Barlow (Eds.), *Critical issues, developments, and trends in professional psychology* (pp. 270–294). New York: Praeger.

Mintz, M. (1967). *By prescription only.* Boston: Beacon.

Minuchin, S. (1974). *Families and family therapy.* Cambridge, MA: Harvard University Press.

Minuchin, S., Rosman, B., & Baker, L. (1978). *Psychosomatic families.* Cambridge, MA: Harvard University Press.

Mischel, W. (1968). *Personality and assessment.* New York: Wiley.

Mischel, W. (1973). Toward a cognitive social learning reconceptualization of personality. *Psychological Review, 80,* 252–283.

Monte, C. F. (1987). *Beneath the mask: An introduction to theories of personality* (3rd ed.). New York: Holt, Rinehart and Winston.

Moore, D. R. (1988). Family Interaction Coding System. In M. Hersen & A. S. Bellack (Eds.), *Dictionary of behavioral assessment techniques* (pp. 210–212). New York: Pergamon.

Morgan, C. D., & Murray, H. A. (1935). A method for investigating fantasies: The thematic apperception test. *Archives of Neurology and Psychiatry, 34,* 289–306.

Morris, R. J., & Kratochwill, T. R. (1991). Introductory comments. In T. R. Kratochwill & R. J. Morris (Eds.), *The practice of child therapy* (2nd ed., pp. 3–5). New York: Pergamon.

Morrison, R. L. (1988). Structured interviews and rating scales. In A. S. Bellack & M. Hersen (Eds.), *Behavioral assessment: A practical handbook* (3rd ed., pp. 252–277). New York: Pergamon.

Morrow-Bradley, C., & Elliott, R. (1986). Utilization of psychotherapy research by practicing psychotherapists. *American Psychologist, 41,* 188–197.

Moustakas, C. E. (1959). *Psychotherapy with children: The living relationship.* New York: Harper and Row.

Mowrer, O. H., & Mowrer, W. M. (1938). Enuresis: A method for its study and treatment. *American Journal of Orthopsychiatry, 8,* 436–459.

Mulhern, J. (1959). *A history of education: A social interpretation.* New York: Ronald.

Murray, H. A. (1938). *Explorations in personality.* New York: Oxford University Press.

Murray, H. A. (1943). *Thematic Apperception Test—Manual.* Cambridge: Harvard University Press.

Myers, D. G. (1989). *Psychology* (2nd ed.). New York: Worth.

Myerson, A. (1939). The attitude of neurologists, psychiatrists and psychologists toward psychoanalysis. *American Journal of Psychiatry, 96,* 623–641.

Nagel, E. (1961). *The structure of science: Problems in the logic of scientific explanation.* New York: Harcourt, Brace, and World.

New York Times. (1994, February 28). The SAT. *New York Times, 143,* A12.

Nezu, A. M., Nezu, C. M., & Perri, M. G. (1989). *Problem-solving therapy for depression: Theory, research, and clinical guidelines.* New York: Wiley.

Nickell, J. (1992). A brief history of graphology. In B. L. Beyerstein & D. F. Beyerstein (Eds.), *The write stuff* (pp. 23–29). Buffalo, NY: Prometheus.

Noll, K. M., Davis, J. M., & DeLeon-Jones, F. (1985). Medication and somatic therapies in the treatment of depression. In E. E. Beckham & W. R. Leber (Eds.), *Handbook of depression: Treatment, assessment, and research* (pp. 220–315). Homewood, IL: Dorsey.

Norcross, J. C. (1987). A rational and empirical analysis of existential psychotherapy. *Journal of Humanistic Psychology, 27,* 41–68.

Norcross, J. C., Hanych, J. M., & Terranova, R. D. (1996). Graduate study in psychology: 1992–1993. *American Psychologist, 51,* 631–643.

Norcross, J. C., Nash, J. M., & Prochaska, J. O. (1985). Psychologists in part-time independent practice: Description and comparison. *Professional Psychology: Research and Practice, 16,* 565–575.

Norcross, J. C., & Prochaska, J. O. (1982a). A national survey of clinical psychologists: Affiliations and orientations. *The Clinical Psychologist, 35*(3), 1, 4–5.

Norcross, J. C., & Prochaska, J. O. (1982b). A national survey of clinical psychologists: Characteristics and activities. *The Clinical Psychologist, 35*(3), 5–8.

Norcross, J. C., & Prochaska, J. O. (1984). Where do behavior (and other) therapists take their troubles?: II. *The Behavior Therapist, 7,* 26–27.

Norcross, J. C., Prochaska, J. O., & Gallagher, K. M. (1989). Clinical psychologists in the 1980s: I. Demographics, affiliations, and satisfactions. *The Clinical Psychologist, 42,* 29–39.

Novaco, R. W. (1978). Anger and coping with stress: Cognitive behavioral interventions. In J. P. Foreyt & D. P. Rathjen (Eds.), *Cognitive behavior therapy: Research and applications* (pp. 135–173). New York: Plenum.

Nurius, P. S., & Yeaton, W. H. (1987). Research synthesis reviews: An illustrated critique of "hidden" judgments, choices, and compromises. *Clinical Psychology Review, 7,* 695–714.

O'Donnell, W. E., & Reynolds, D. McQ. (1983). *Neuropsychological Impairment Scale manual.* Annapolis, MD: Annapolis Neuropsychological Services.

O'Donnell, W. E., Reynolds, D. McQ., & DeSoto, C. B. (1983). Neuropsychological Impairment Scale (NIS): Initial validation study using Trailmaking Test (A&B) and WAIS Digit Symbol (Scaled score) in a mixed grouping of psychiatric, neuropsychological, and normal patients. *Journal of Clinical Psychology, 39,* 746–748.

Ollendick, T. H. (1986). Child and adolescent behavior therapy. In A. E. Bergin & S. L. Garfield (Eds.), *Handbook of psychotherapy and behavior change* (3rd ed., pp. 525–564). New York: Wiley.

Olson, D. H. (1970). Marital and family therapy: Integrative review and critique. *Journal of Marriage and the Family, 32,* 501–530.

Oltmanns, T. F., & Emery, R. E. (1995). *Abnormal psychology.* Englewood Cliffs, NJ: Prentice-Hall.

Orlinsky, D. E., & Howard, K. I. (1986). Process and outcome in psychotherapy. In S. L. Garfield & A. E. Bergin (Eds.), *Handbook of psychotherapy and behavior change* (3rd ed., pp. 311–381).

Parloff, M. B., Waskow, I. E., & Wolfe, B. E. (1978). Research on therapist variables in relation to process and outcome. In S. L. Garfield & A. E. Bergin (Eds.), *Handbook of psychotherapy and behavior change: An empirical analysis* (2nd ed., pp. 233–282). New York: Wiley.

Pascal, G. R., & Suttell, B. J. (1951). *The Bender-Gestalt Test: Quantification and validity for adults.* New York: Grune and Stratton.

Patterson, G. R., Ray, R. S., Shaw, D. A., & Cobb, J. A. (1969). *Manual of Coding of Family Interactions.* New York: Microfiche.

Paul, G. (1966). *Effects of insight, desensitization, and attention placebo treatments of anxiety.* Stanford, CA: Stanford University Press.

Pavlov, I. P. (1934). An attempt at a physiological interpretation of obsessive neurosis and paranoia. *Journal of Mental Science, 80,* 187–197.

Pavlov, I. P. (1941). *Conditioned reflexes and psychiatry* (W. H. Gantt, Trans.). New York: International Universities Press.

Pekarik, G., & Wierzbicki, M. (1986). The relationship between clients' expected and actual treatment duration. *Psychotherapy, 23,* 532–534.

Pekow, C. (1990, August 26). The other Dr. Bettelheim. *Washington Post,* p. C1.

Perls, F. (1969a). *Gestalt therapy verbatim.* Lafayette, CA: Real People.

Perls, F. (1969b). *In and out of the garbage pail.* Lafayette, CA: Real People.

Perry, N. W. (1979). Why clinical psychology does not need alternative training models. *American Psychologist, 34,* 602–611.

Peterson, D. R. (1968). The doctor of psychology program at the University of Illinois. *American Psychologist, 23,* 511–516.

Peterson, D. R. (1985). Twenty years of practitioner training in psychology. *American Psychologist, 40,* 441–451.

Peterson, D. R., Eaton, M. M., Levine, A. R., & Snepp, F. P. (1982). Career experiences of Doctors of Psychology. *Professional Psychology, 13,* 268–277.

Peterson, R. A. (1978). Review of the Rorschach. In O. K. Buros (Ed.), *The eighth mental measurements yearbook* (pp. 1042–1045). Highland Park, NJ: Gryphon.

Phillips, H. C. (1988). *The psychological management of chronic pain: A treatment manual.* New York: Springer.

Piaget, J. (1952). *The origins of intelligence in children.* New York: International Universities Press.

Piotrowski, C., & Keller, J. W. (1989). Psychological testing in outpatient mental health facilities: A national study. *Professional Psychology: Research and Practice, 20,* 423–425.

Piotrowski, Z. (1937). The reliability of Rorschach's Erlebnistypus. *Journal of Abnormal and Social Psychology, 32,* 439–445.

Piotrowski, Z. A. (1964). A digital computer administration of inkblot data. *Psychiatric Quarterly, 38,* 1–26.

Piotrowski, Z. A. (1965). The Rorschach inkblot test. In B. B. Wolman (Ed.), *Handbook of clinical psychology* (pp. 522–561). New York: McGraw-Hill.

Planck, M. (1949). *Scientific autobiography and other papers* (F. Gaynor, Trans.). New York: Philosophical Library.

Platt, J. J., & Spivack, G. (1972). Problem-solving thinking of psychiatric patients. *Journal of Consulting and Clinical Psychology, 39,* 148–151.

Platt, J. J., & Spivack, G. (1974). Means of solving real-life problems: I. Psychiatric patients versus controls, and cross-cultural comparisons of normal females. *Journal of Community Psychology, 2,* 45–48.

Platt, J. J., & Spivack, G. (1975). *Manual for the Means-Ends Problem-Solving Procedure (MEPS): A measure of interpersonal cognitive problem-solving skills.* Philadelphia: Hahnemann Medical College and Hospital.

Platt, J. J., & Spivack, G. (1985). *Manual for the Means-Ends Problem-Solving Procedure (MEPS): A measure of interpersonal cognitive problem-solving skills.* Philadelphia: Hahnemann Community Mental Health/Mental Retardation Center.

Polster, E., & Polster, M. (1973). *Gestalt therapy integrated.* New York: Random House.

Pomerlau, O. F., & Rodin, J. (1986). Behavioral medicine and health psychology. In S. L. Garfield & A. E. Bergin (Eds.), *Handbook of psychotherapy and behavior change* (3rd ed., pp. 483–522). New York: Wiley.

Popper, K. R. (1959). *The logic of scientific discovery.* London: Hutchinson.

Popper, K. R. (1963). *Conjectures and refutations: The growth of scientific knowledge.* New York: Harper and Row.

Prioleau, L., Murdock, M., & Brody, N. (1983). An analysis of psychotherapy versus placebo studies. *Behavioral and Brain Sciences, 6,* 275–310.

Prior, M., & Werry, J. S. (1986). Autism, schizophrenia, and allied disorders. In H. C. Quay & J. S. Werry (Eds.), *Psychopathological disorders of childhood* (3rd ed., pp. 156–210). New York: Wiley.

Prochaska, J. O. (1984). *Systems of psychotherapy: A transtheoretical analysis.* Homewood, IL: Dorsey.

Pryzwansky, W. B., & Wendt, R. N. (1987). *Psychology as a profession: Foundations of practice.* New York: Pergamon.

Psychological Corporation. (1992). *Wechsler Individual Achievement Test manual.* San Antonio, TX: Psychological Corporation.

Quay, H. C. (1965). Psychopathic personality as pathological stimulus seeking. *American Journal of Psychiatry, 122,* 180–183.

Quay, H. C., & Peterson, D. R. (1987). *Manual for the Revised Behavior Problem Checklist.* Miami: Authors.

Quay, L. C. (1974). Language dialect, age, and intelligence—test performance in disadvantaged black children. *Child Development, 45,* 463–468.

Rabin, A. J. (1968). Projective methods: An historical introduction. In A. I. Rabin (Ed.), *Projective techniques in personality assessment: A modern introduction* (pp. 3–17). New York: Springer.

Rachman, S. (1971). *The effects of psychotherapy.* New York: Pergamon.

Rachman, S. J., & Wilson, G. T. (1980). *The effects of psychological therapy* (2nd ed.). New York: Pergamon.

Ragland, D. R., & Brand, R. J. (1988). Type A behavior and mortality from coronary heart disease. *New England Journal of Medicine, 318,* 65–69.

Raimy, V. C. (1950). *Training in clinical psychology (Boulder Conference).* New York: Prentice-Hall.

Rajaratnam, N. (1960). Reliability formulas for independent decision data when reliability data are matched. *Psychometrika, 25,* 261–271.

Rangell, L. (1954). Similarities and differences between psychoanalysis and dynamic psychotherapy. *Journal of the American Psychoanalytic Association, 2,* 734–744.

Raskin, N. J., & Rogers, C. R. (1989). Person-centered therapy. In R. J. Corsini & D. Wedding (Eds.), *Cur-

rent psychotherapies (4th ed., pp. 155–194). Itasca, IL: Peacock.

Reed, S. D., Katkin, E. S., & Goldband, S. (1986). Biofeedback and behavioral medicine. In F. H. Kanfer & A. P. Goldstein (Eds.), *Helping people change* (3rd ed., pp. 381–436). New York: Pergamon.

Rehm, L. P., Kornblith, S. J., O'Hara, M. W., Lamparski, D. M., Romano, J. M., & Volkin, J. (1981). An evaluation of major components in a self-control behavior therapy program for depression. *Behavior Modification, 5,* 459–489.

Rehm, L. P., & Marston, A. R. (1968). Reduction of social anxiety through modification of self-reinforcement: An instigation therapy technique. *Journal of Consulting and Clinical Psychology, 32,* 565–574.

Reisman, J. M. (1981). History and current trends in clinical psychology. In C. E. Walker (Ed.), *Clinical practice of psychology: A guide for mental health professionals* (pp. 1–32). New York: Pergamon.

Reitan, R. M., & Davison, L. A. (1974). *Clinical neuropsychology: Current status and applications.* Washington, DC: Winston.

Rexford, L., & Wierzbicki, M. (1989). An attempt to predict change in mood in response to Velten-like mood induction procedures. *Journal of Psychology, 123,* 285–294.

Reynolds, D., & Kiefer, C. (1977). Cultural adaptability as an attribute of therapies: The case of Morita therapy. *Culture, Medicine, and Psychiatry, 1,* 395–412.

Rhoads, J. M., & Feather, B. (1974). Application of psychodynamics to behavior therapy. *American Journal of Psychiatry, 131,* 17–20.

Richards, M. S. (1986). *Behavioral therapy research and the treatment of autistic children.* Unpublished manuscript, Washburn University.

Rimm, D. C., & Masters, J. C. (1974). *Behavior therapy: Techniques and empirical findings.* New York: Academic.

Ritzler, B. A. (1978). The Nuremberg mind revisited: A quantitative approach to Nazi Rorschachs. *Journal of Personality Assessment, 42,* 344–353.

Roback, H. B. (1968). Human figure drawings: Their utility in the clinical psychologist's armamentarium for personality assessment. *Psychological Bulletin, 70,* 1–19.

Robins, L. N., Helzer, J. E., Croughan, J., & Ratcliff, K. S. (1981). National Institute of Mental Health Diagnostic Interview Schedule: Its history, characteristics, and validity. *Archives of General Psychiatry, 38,* 381–389.

Roe, A., Gustad, J. W., Moore, B. V., Ross, S., & Skodak, M. (1959). Graduate education in psychology. *Report of the Conference on Graduate Education in Psychology.* Washington, DC: American Psychological Association.

Rogers, C. R. (1942). *Counseling and psychotherapy: Newer concepts in practice.* Boston: Houghton Mifflin.

Rogers, C. R. (1951). *Client-centered therapy: Its current practice, implications, and theory.* Boston: Houghton Mifflin.

Rogers, C. R. (1957). The necessary and sufficient conditions of therapeutic personality change. *Journal of Consulting Psychology, 21,* 95–103.

Rogers, C. R. (1959). A theory of therapy, personality, and interpersonal relationships as developed in the client-centered framework. In S. Koch (Ed.), *Psychology: A study of a science* (Vol. 3, pp. 184–256). New York: McGraw-Hill.

Rogers, C. R. (1961). *On becoming a person.* Boston: Houghton Mifflin.

Rogers, C. R., & Dymond, R. F. (Eds.). (1954). *Psychotherapy and behavior change: Coordinated studies in the client-centered approach.* Chicago: University of Chicago Press.

Rogers, T. R. (1995). *The psychological testing enterprise: An introduction.* Pacific Grove, CA: Brooks/Cole.

Rorschach, H. (1942). *Psychodiagnostics: A diagnostic test based on perception* (P. Lemkau & B. Kronenburg, Trans.). New York: Grune and Stratton. (Original work published 1921).

Rosen, A. J. (1988). Observational Record of Inpatient Behavior. In M. Hersen & A. S. Bellack (Eds.), *Dictionary of behavioral assessment techniques* (pp. 320–322). New York: Pergamon.

Rosen, A. J., Tureff, S. E., Daruna, J. H., Johnson, P. B., Lyons, J. S., & Davis, J. M. (1980). Pharmacotherapy of schizophrenia and affective disorders: Behavioral correlates of diagnostic and demographic variables. *Journal of Abnormal Psychology, 89,* 378–389.

Rosen, R. D. (1975). *Psychobabble.* New York: Avon Books.

Rosenbaum, M. (1978). Group psychotherapy: Heritage, history, and the current scene. In H. Mullan & M. Rosenbaum (Eds.), *Group psychotherapy: Theory and practice* (2nd ed., pp. 3–30). New York: Free.

Rosenberg, L. A. (1962). Idealization of self and social adjustment. *Journal of Counseling Psychology, 26,* 487.

Rosenhan, D. L., & Seligman, M. E. P. (1989). *Abnormal psychology* (2nd ed.). New York: Norton.

Rosenman, R. H., Brand, R. J., Jenkins, C. D., Friedman, M., Straus, R., & Wurm, M. (1975). Coronary heart disease in the Western Collaborative Group Study: Final follow-up experience of 8½ years. *Journal of the American Medical Association, 233,* 872–877.

Rosenthal, R. (1966). *Experimenter effects in behavioral research.* New York: Appleton-Century-Crofts.

Rosenthal, R., & Jacobson, L. (1968). *Pygmalion in the classroom: Teacher expectation and pupils' intellectual development.* New York: Holt, Rinehart and Winston.

Rosenzweig, M. R. (1991). Training in psychology in the United States. *Psychological Science, 2,* 16–18.

Rothermel, R. D., & Lovell, M. R. (1985). Personality Inventory for Children. In D. J. Keyser & R. C. Sweetland (Eds.), *Test critiques* (Vol. 2), (pp. 570–578). Kansas City, MO: Test Corporation of America.

Rotter, J. B. (1954). *Social learning and clinical psychology.* Englewood Cliffs, NJ: Prentice-Hall.

Rotter, J. B., & Rafferty, J. E. (1950). *Manual: The Rotter incomplete sentences blank.* New York: Psychological Corporation.

Rozeboom, W. W. (1966). *Foundations of the theory of prediction.* Homewood, IL: Dorsey.

Russell, B. (1945). *A history of Western philosophy.* New York: Simon and Schuster.

Rutter, M., Greenfeld, D., & Lockyer, L. (1967). A five-to-fifteen-year follow-up study of infantile psychosis: II. Social and behavioral outcome. *British Journal of Psychiatry, 113,* 1183–1199.

Rychlak, J. F. (1981). *Introduction to personality and psychotherapy: A theory-construction approach* (2nd ed.). Boston: Houghton Mifflin.

Sacco, W. P., & Beck, A. T. (1985). Cognitive therapy of depression. In E. E. Beckham & W. R. Leber (Eds.), *Handbook of depression: Treatment, assessment, and research* (pp. 3–38). Homewood, IL: Dorsey.

Safer, D., Allen, R. P., & Barr, E. (1972). Depression of growth in hyperactive children on stimulant drugs. *New England Journal of Medicine, 287,* 217–220.

Safer, D. J., & Krager, J. M. (1984). Trends in medication treatment of hyperactive school children: Results of six biannual surveys. *Clinical Pediatrics, 22,* 500–504.

Salter, A. (1949). *Conditioned reflex therapy: The direct approach to the reconstruction of personality.* New York: Farrar, Straus, and Giroux.

Salter, A. (1963). *The case against psychoanalysis.* New York: Harper and Row.

Salzman, C. (1990). Benzodiazepine dependency: Summary of the APA task force on benzodiazepines. *Psychopharmacology Bulletin, 26,* 61–62.

Sanchez-Hucles, J., & Cash, T. F. (1992). The dissertation in professional programs: 1. A survey of clinical directors on requirements and practices. *Professional Psychology: Research and Practice, 23,* 59–62.

Sanderson, R. E., Campbell, D., & Laverty, S. G. (1963). An investigation of a new aversive conditioning treatment for alcoholism. *Quarterly Journal of Studies on Alcohol, 24,* 261–275.

Sandifer, M. G., Hordern, A., & Green, L. M. (1970). The psychiatric interview: The impact of the first three minutes. *American Journal of Psychiatry, 126,* 968–973.

Sandifer, M. G., Hordern, A., Timbury, G. C., & Green, L. M. (1968). Psychiatric diagnosis: A comparative study in North Carolina, London and Glasgow. *British Journal of Psychiatry, 114,* 1–9.

Sarason, I. G., & Sarason, B. R. (1993). *Abnormal Psychology: The problem of maladaptive behavior* (7th ed.). Englewood Cliffs, NJ: Prentice-Hall.

Sarason, I. G., Sarason, B. R., Potter, E. H., III, & Antoni, M. H. (1985). Life events, social support, and illness. *Psychosomatic Medicine, 47,* 156–163.

Satir, V. (1967). *Conjoint family therapy: A guide to theory and technique.* Palo Alto, CA: Science and Behavior Books.

Satir, V. (1972). *Peoplemaking.* Palo Alto, CA: Science and Behavior Books.

Satir, V., Stachowiak, J., & Taschman, H. A. (1975). *Helping families to change.* New York: Jason Aronson.

Sattler, J. M. (1982). *Assessment of children's intelligence and special abilities* (2nd ed.). Boston: Allyn and Bacon.

Sattler, J. M. (1992). *Assessment of children* (3rd rev. ed.). San Diego: Jerome M. Sattler.

Sattler, J. M., & Covin, T. M. (1986). Comparison of the Slosson Intelligence Test, Revised Norms, and WISC-R for children with learning problems and for gifted children. *Psychology in the Schools, 23,* 259–264.

Sattler, J. M., & Gwynne, J. (1982). White examiners generally do not impede the intelligence test performance of black children: To debunk a myth. *Journal of Consulting and Clinical Psychology, 50,* 196–208.

Sayette, M. A., & Mayne, T. J. (1990). Survey of current clinical and research trends in clinical psychology. *American Psychologist, 45,* 1263–1266.

Sayette, M. A., Mayne, T. J., & Norcross, J. C. (1992). *Insider's guide to graduate programs in clinical psychology* (1992/1993 ed.). New York: Guilford.

Scarr, S., & Kidd, K. K. (1983). Developmental behavior genetics. In M. M. Haith & J. J. Campos (Eds.), *Handbook of child psychology: Vol. 2. Infancy and developmental psychopathology* (pp. 345–433). New York: Wiley.

Scheidlinger, S. (1994). An overview of nine decades of group psychotherapy. *Hospital and Community Psychiatry, 45,* 217–225.

Schofield, W. (1950). Research trends in clinical psychology. *Journal of Clinical Psychology, 6,* 148–152.

Schofield, W. (1952). Research in clinical psychology: 1951. *Journal of Clinical Psychology, 8,* 255–261.

Schofield, W. (1964). *Psychotherapy: The purchase of friendship.* Englewood Cliffs, NJ: Prentice-Hall.

Schopler, E., Reichler, R. J., DeVellis, R. F., & Daly, K. (1980). Toward objective classification of childhood autism: Childhood Autism Rating Scale (CARS). *Journal of Autism and Developmental Disorders, 10,* 91–103.

Schopler, E., Short, A., & Mesibov, G. (1989). Relation of behavioral treatment to "normal functioning": Comment on Lovaas. *Journal of Consulting and Clinical Psychology, 57,* 162–164.

Schretlen, D. (1990). A limitation of using the Wiener and Harmon obvious and subtle subscales to detect faking on the MMPI. *Journal of Clinical Psychology, 46,* 782–786.

Schroeder, H. E., & Black, M. J. (1985). Unassertiveness. In M. Hersen & A. S. Bellack (Eds.), *Handbook of clinical behavior therapy with adults* (pp. 509–530). New York: Plenum.

Schroeder, S. R., Rojahn, J., & Mulick, J. A. (1978). Ecobehavioral organization of developmental day care for the chronically self-injurious. *Journal of Pediatric Psychology, 3,* 81–88.

Schwartz, G. E., Davidson, R. J., & Goleman, D. J. (1978). Patterning of cognitive and somatic processes in the self-regulation of anxiety: Effects of meditation versus exercise. *Psychosomatic Medicine, 40,* 321–328.

Schwartz, R. M., & Gottman, J. M. (1976). Toward a task analysis of assertive behavior. *Journal of Consulting and Clinical Psychology, 44,* 910–920.

Searles, J. S. (1985). A methodological and empirical critique of psychotherapy outcome meta-analysis. *Behaviour Research and Therapy, 23,* 453–463.

Sears, R. R. (1943). *Survey of objective studies of psychoanalytic concepts.* New York: Social Science Research Council.

Sechrest, L. (1992). The past future of clinical psychology: A reflection on Woodworth (1937). *Journal of Consulting and Clinical Psychology, 60,* 18–23.

Seligman, M. E. P. (1968). Chronic fear produced by unpredictable shock. *Journal of Comparative and Physiological Psychology, 66,* 402–411.

Seligman, M. E. P., Abramson, L. Y., Semmel, A., & von Baeyer, C. (1979). Depressive attribution style. *Journal of Abnormal Psychology, 88,* 242–247.

Seligman, M. E. P., Peterson, C., Kaslow, N. J., Alloy, L. B., & Abramson, L. Y. (1984). Explanatory style and depressive symptoms among school children. *Journal of Abnormal Psychology, 93,* 235–238.

Selye, H. (1936). A syndrome produced by diverse nocuous agents. *Nature, 138,* 32.

Selye, H. (1956). *The stress of life.* New York: McGraw-Hill.

Selzer, M. L. (1971). The Michigan Alcoholism Screening Test: The quest for a new diagnostic instrument. *American Journal of Psychiatry, 127,* 89–94.

Shadish, W. R., Montgomery, L. M., Wilson, P., Wilson, M. R., Bright, I., & Okwumabua, T. (1993). Effects of family and marital psychotherapies: A meta-analysis. *Journal of Consulting and Clinical Psychology, 61,* 992–1002.

Shakow, D. (1938). An internship year for psychologists (with special reference to psychiatric hospitals). *Journal of Consulting Psychology, 2,* 73–76.

Shakow, D. (1968). The development of orthopsychiatry: The contributions of Levy, Menninger, and Stevenson. *American Journal of Orthopsychiatry, 38,* 804–809.

Shakow, D. (1976). Reflections on a do-it-yourself program in clinical psychology. *Journal of the History of the Behavioral Sciences, 12,* 14–30.

Shakow, D. (1978). Clinical psychology seen some 50 years later. *American Psychologist, 33,* 148–157.

Shakow, D., Hilgard, E. R., Kelly, E. L., Luckey, B., Sanford, R. N., & Shaffer, L. F. (1947). Recommended graduate training program in clinical psychology. *American Psychologist, 2,* 539–558.

Shapiro, A. K., & Morris, L. A. (1978). The placebo effect in medical and psychological therapies. In S. L. Garfield & A. E. Bergin (Eds.), *Handbook of psycho-*

therapy and behavior change: An empirical analysis (2nd ed., pp. 369–410). New York: Wiley.

Shapiro, D. A., & Shapiro, D. (1982). Meta-analysis of comparative therapy outcome studies: A replication and refinement. *Psychological Bulletin, 92,* 581–604.

Shea, S. C. (1988). *Psychiatric interviewing: The art of understanding.* Philadelphia: W. B. Saunders.

Sheldon, W. H., & Stevens, S. S. (1942). *The varieties of temperament: A psychology of constitutional differences.* New York: Harper.

Sheldon, W. H., Stevens, S. S., & Tucker, W. B. (1940). *The varieties of human physique: An introduction to constitutional psychology.* New York: Harper.

Shemberg, K. M., & Leventhal, D. B. (1978). A survey of activities of academic clinicians. *Professional Psychology, 9,* 580–586.

Shepard, J. W. (1989). Review of the Jackson Vocational Interest Survey. In J. C. Conoley & J. J. Kramer (Eds.), *The tenth mental measurements yearbook* (pp. 403–404). Lincoln, NE: University of Nebraska Press.

Shorkey, C. T., & Whiteman, V. L. (1977). Development of the Rational Behavior Inventory: Initial validity and reliability. *Educational and Psychological Measurement, 37,* 527–534.

Shostrom, E. L. (1963). *Personality Orientation Inventory.* San Diego, CA: Educational and Industrial Testing Service.

Siegel, L. J., & Smith, K. E. (1991). Somatic disorders. In T. R. Kratochwill & R. J. Morris (Eds.), *The practice of child therapy* (2nd ed., pp. 222–256). New York: Pergamon.

Sifneos, P. (1972). *Short-term psychotherapy and emotional crisis.* Cambridge, MA: Harvard University Press.

Sifneos, P. (1979). *Short-term dynamic psychology therapy: Evaluation and technique.* New York: Plenum.

Skinner, B. F. (1953). *Science and human behavior.* New York: Macmillan.

Skinner, B. F. (1957). *Verbal behavior.* New York: Appleton-Century-Crofts.

Slosson, R. L. (1961). *Slosson Intelligence Test for children and adults.* East Aurora, NY: Slosson Educational.

Slosson, R. L. (1983). *Slosson Intelligence Test (SIT) and Oral Reading Test (SORT) for children and adults.* East Aurora, NY: Slosson Educational.

Smith, M. C., & Thelen, M. H. (1984). Development and validation of a test for bulimia. *Journal of Consulting and Clinical Psychology, 52,* 863–872.

Smith, M. L. (1980). Meta-analysis of research on teacher expectations. *Evaluation in Education, 4,* 53–55.

Smith, M. L., & Glass, G. V. (1977). Meta-analysis of psychotherapy outcome studies. *American Psychologist, 32,* 752–760.

Smith, M. L., Glass, G. V., & Miller, T. I. (1980). *The benefits of psychotherapy.* Baltimore, MD: Johns Hopkins University Press.

Smye, M. D., & Wine, J. D. (1980). A comparison of male and female adolescents' social behavior and cognitions. *Sex Roles, 6,* 213–230.

Snyder, C. R., Shenkel, R. J., & Lowery, C. R. (1977). Acceptance of personality interpretations: The "Barnum effect" and beyond. *Journal of Consulting and Clinical Psychology, 45,* 104–114.

Snyder, M., & Swann, W. B. (1978). Hypothesis-testing processes in social interaction. *Journal of Personality and Social Psychology, 36,* 1202–1212.

Snyder, S. H. (1974). Catecholamines as mediators of drug effects in schizophrenia. In F. O. Schmitt & F. Worden (Eds.), *Neurosciences: Third study program* (pp. 721–732). Cambridge, MA: MIT Press.

Sobell, M. B., Schaefer, H. H., & Mills, K. C. (1972). Differences in baseline drinking behavior between alcoholics and normal drinkers. *Behaviour Research and Therapy, 10,* 257–267.

Spanos, N. P., & Gottlieb, J. (1976). Ergotism and the Salem village witch trials. *Science, 194,* 1390–1394.

Spence, D. P. (1982). *Narrative truth and historical truth: Meaning and interpretation in psychoanalysis.* New York: Norton.

Spiegler, M. D., & Guevremont, D. C. (1993). *Contemporary behavior therapy* (2nd ed.). Pacific Grove, CA: Brooks/Cole.

Spielberger, C. D., Gorsuch, R. C., & Lushene, R. E. (1970). *Manual for the State-Trait Anxiety Inventory.* Palo Alto, CA: Consulting Psychologists Press.

Spielberger, C. D., Jacobs, G., Russel, S., & Crane, R. S. (1983). Assessment of anger: The State-Trait Anger Scale. In J. N. Butcher & C. D. Spielberger (Eds.), *Advances in Personality Assessment* (Vol. 2, pp. 159–187). Hillsdale, NJ: Erlbaum.

Spitzer, R. L., Endicott, J., & Robins, E. (1978). Research diagnostic criteria: Rationale and reliability. *Archives of General Psychiatry, 35,* 773–782.

Spitzer, R. L., Williams, J. B. W., Gibbon, M., & First, M. B. (1990). *Structured Clinical Interview for DSM-III-R (SCID).* Washington, DC: American Psychiatric Association.

Spivack, G., Platt, J. J., & Shure, M. B. (1976). *The problem-solving approach to adjustment.* San Francisco: Jossey-Bass.

Spivack, G., & Shure, M. B. (1974). *Social adjustment of young children.* San Francisco: Jossey-Bass.

Spivack, G., & Spotts, J. (1965). The Devereux Child Behavior Rating Scale: Symptom behaviors in latency age children. *American Journal of Mental Deficiency, 69,* 839–853.

Spreen, O., & Strauss, E. (1991). *A compendium of neuropsychological tests: Administration, norms, and commentary.* New York: Oxford University Press.

Sprenkle, D. H., & Storm, C. L. (1983). Divorce therapy outcome research: A substantive and methodological review. *Journal of Marital and Family Therapy, 9,* 239–258.

Stampfl, T. G., & Levis, D. J. (1967). Essentials of implosive therapy: A learning-theory-based psychodynamic behavior therapy. *Journal of Abnormal Psychology, 72,* 496–503.

Stapp, J., & Fulcher, R. (1982). The employment of 1979 and 1980 doctorate recipients in psychology. *American Psychologist, 39,* 1408–1423.

Stedman, J. M., Neff, J. A., & Morrow, D. (1995). Career pathways and current practice patterns of clinical and counseling psychologists: A follow-up study of former interns. *Journal of Clinical Psychology, 51,* 441–448.

Stern, W. L. (1914). The psychological methods of testing intelligence (G. M. Whipple, Trans.). *Educational Psychology Monographs* (No. 13). Baltimore: Warwick and York. (Original work published in 1912).

Stoup, C. M., & Benjamin, L. T., Jr. (1982). Graduate study in psychology. *American Psychologist, 37,* 1186–1202.

Strickland, B. R. (1977). Approval motivation. In T. Blass (Ed.), *Personality variables in social behavior* (pp. 315–356). Hillsdale, NJ: Erlbaum.

Strickland, B. R. (1987). On the threshold of the second century of psychology. *American Psychologist, 42,* 1055–1056.

Strickland, B. R. (1988). Clinical psychology comes of age. *American Psychologist, 43,* 104–107.

Strong, E. K. (1927). *Vocational Interest Blank.* Stanford, CA: Stanford University Press.

Strong, E. K. (1955). *Vocational interests 18 years after college.* Minneapolis, MN: University of Minnesota Press.

Strother, C. R. (Ed.). (1957). *Psychology and mental health: A report of the Institute on Education and Training for Psychological Contributions to Mental Health, Held at Stanford University in August 1955.* Washington, DC: American Psychological Association.

Strube, M. J., & Hartmann, D. P. (1983). Meta-analysis: Techniques, applications, and functions. *Journal of Consulting and Clinical Psychology, 51,* 14–27.

Stuart, R. B. (1971). A three-dimensional program for the treatment of obesity. *Behavior Research and Therapy, 9,* 177–186.

Stuart, R. B., & Davis, B. (1973). *Slim chance in a fat world.* Champaign, IL: Research Press.

Suinn, R. M. (1988). *Fundamentals of abnormal psychology: Updated.* Chicago: Nelson-Hall.

Sundberg, N. D. (1954). A note concerning the history of testing. *American Psychologist, 9,* 150–151.

Suzuki, T. (1989). The concept of neurasthenia and its treatment in Japan. *Culture, Medicine, and Psychiatry, 13,* 187–202.

Svartberg, M., & Stiles, T. C. (1991). Comparative effects of short-term psychodynamic psychotherapy: A meta-analysis. *Journal of Consulting and Clinical Psychology, 59,* 704–714.

Swartz, J. D. (1978). Review of the TAT. In O. K. Buros (Ed.), *Eighth mental measurements yearbook* (pp. 1127–1130). Highland Park: NJ: Gryphon.

Swedo, W. E., Rapoport, J. L., Leonard, H. L., Lenane, M., & Cheslow, D. (1989). Obsessive-compulsive disorder in children and adolescents: Clinical phenomenology of 70 consecutive cases. *Archives of General Psychiatry, 46,* 335–341.

Swensen, C. H. (1957). Empirical evaluations of human figure drawings. *Psychological Bulletin, 54,* 431–466.

Swensen, C. H. (1968). Empirical evaluations of human figure drawings: 1957–1966. *Psychological Bulletin, 70,* 20–44.

Task Force on Promotion and Dissemination of Psychological Procedures. (1995). Training in and dissemination of empirically validated psychological treatments: Report and recommendations. *The Clinical Psychologist, 48*(1), 3–23.

Teasdale, J. D., & Bancroft, J. (1977). Manipulation of thought content as a determinant of mood and corrugator electromyographic activity in depressed patients. *Journal of Abnormal Psychology, 86,* 235–241.

Tennenbaum, D. L. (1988). Marital Interaction Coding System. In M. Hersen & A. S. Bellack (Eds.), *Dictio-*

nary of behavioral assessment techniques (pp. 291–293). New York: Pergamon.

Terman, L., & Oden, M. H. (1959). *Genetic studies of genius: Vol. 4. The gifted group at midlife.* Stanford, CA: Stanford University Press.

Thomas, A., & Chess, S. (1977). *Temperament and development.* New York: Brunner/Mazel.

Thomas, A., & Chess, S. (1984). Genesis and evolution of behavioral disorders: From infancy to early adult life. *American Journal of Psychiatry, 141,* 1–9.

Thompson, L. L., & Heaton, R. K. (1989). Comparison of different versions of the Boston Naming Test. *Clinical Neuropsychologist, 3,* 184–192.

Thorndike, R. L., Hagen, E. P., & Sattler, J. M. (1986). *The Stanford-Binet Intelligence Scale: Fourth Edition: Guide for administering and scoring.* Chicago: Riverside.

Thorndike, A. M., & Lohman, D. F. (1990). *A century of ability testing.* Chicago: Riverside.

Thorne, F. C. (1947). The clinical method in science. *American Psychologist, 2,* 161–166.

Thornton, E. M. (1983). *The Freudian fallacy: An alternative view of Freudian theory.* Garden City, NY: Dial.

Tomkins, S. S. (1947). *The Thematic Apperception Test.* New York: Grune and Stratton.

Torrey, E. F. (1992). *Freudian fraud: The malignant effect of Freud's theory on American thought and culture.* New York: HarperCollins.

Truax, C. B., & Carkhuff, R. R. (1967). *Toward effective counseling and psychotherapy: Training and practice.* Chicago: Aldine.

Truax, C. B., & Mitchell, K. M. (1971). Research on certain therapist interpersonal skills in relation to process and outcome. In A. E. Bergin & S. L. Garfield (Eds.), *Handbook of psychotherapy and behavior change: An empirical analysis* (2nd ed., pp. 299–344). New York: Wiley.

Tryon, W. W. (1984). Principles and methods of mechanically assessing motor activity. *Behavioral Assessment, 6,* 129–140.

Turk, D. C. (1978). Cognitive behavioral techniques in the management of pain. In J. P. Foreyt & D. P. Rathjen (Eds.), *Cognitive behavior therapy: Research and applications* (pp. 199–232). New York: Plenum.

Turk, D. C., & Genest, M. (1979). Regulation of pain: The application of cognitive and behavioral techniques for prevention and remediation. In P. Kendall & S. Hollon (Eds.), *Cognitive behavioral interventions: Theory, research and procedures* (pp. 287–318). New York: Academic.

Turk, D. C., Meichenbaum, D., & Genest, M. (1983). *Pain and behavioral medicine: A cognitive behavioral perspective.* New York: Guilford.

Turkat, I. D., & Maisto, S. A. (1985). Personality disorders: Application of the experimental method to the formulation and modification of personality disorders. In D. H. Barlow (Ed.), *Clinical handbook of psychological disorders: A step-by-step treatment manual* (pp. 502–570). New York: Guilford.

Turner, R. H., & Vanderlippe, R. H. (1958). Self-ideal congruence as an index of adjustment. *Journal of Abnormal and Social Psychology, 40,* 1126–1136.

Turner, S. M., Beidel, D. C., & Nathan, R. S. (1985). Biological factors in obsessive-compulsive disorders. *Psychological Bulletin, 97,* 430–450.

Twentyman, C. T., & McFall, R. M. (1975). Behavioral training of social skills in shy males. *Journal of Consulting and Clinical Psychology, 43,* 384–395.

Valenstein, E. S. (1973). *Brain control.* New York: Wiley.

VandenBos, G. R., Cummings, N. A., & DeLeon, P. H. (1992). A century of psychotherapy: Economic and environmental influences. In D. K. Freedheim, H. J. Freudenberger, J. W. Kessler, S. B. Messer, D. R. Peterson, H. H. Strupp, & P. L. Wachtel (Eds.), *History of psychotherapy: A century of change* (pp. 65–102). Washington, DC: American Psychological Association.

Vandervoort, D. J., & Fuhriman, A. (1991). The efficacy of group therapy for depression: A review of the literature. *Small Group Research, 22,* 320–338.

van Hutton, V. (1990). Test review: The California Psychological Inventory. *Journal of Counseling and Development, 69,* 75–77.

Vaughn, C. C., & Leff, J. P. (1976). The influence of family and social factors on the course of psychiatric illness: A comparison of schizophrenic and depressed neurotic patients. *British Journal of Psychiatry, 129,* 125–137.

Velten, E. (1968). A laboratory task for induction of mood states. *Behaviour Research and Therapy, 6,* 473–482.

Vincent, J., Varley, C. K., & Leger, P. (1990). Effects of methylphenidate on early adolescent growth. *American Journal of Psychiatry, 147,* 501–502.

Voegtlin, W. L. (1940). The treatment of alcoholism by establishing a conditioned reflex. *American Journal of the Medical Sciences, 199,* 802–810.

Vogler, R. E., Lunde, S. E., Johnson, G. R., & Martin, P. L. (1970). Electrical aversion conditioning with chronic alcoholics. *Journal of Consulting and Clinical Psychology, 34,* 302–307.

Vygotsky, L. S. (1987). Thinking and speech. In R. W. Rieber, A. S. Carton (Eds.), & N. Minick (Trans.), *The collected works of L. S. Vygotsky: Vol. 1. Problems of general psychology* (pp. 37–285). New York: Plenum. (Original work published 1934).

Wade, T. C., & Baker, T. B. (1977). Opinions and use of psychological tests: A survey of clinical psychologists. *American Psychologist, 32,* 874–882.

Walfish, S., Moritz, J. L., & Stenmark, D. E. (1991). A longitudinal study of the career satisfaction of clinical psychologists. *Professional Psychology: Research and Practice, 22,* 253–255.

Wallace, R. K., & Benson, H. (1972). The physiology of meditation. *Scientific American, 226*(2), 84–90.

Walsh, R. (1989). Asian psychotherapies. In R. J. Corsini & D. Wedding (Eds.), *Current psychotherapies* (4th ed., pp. 547–559). Itasca, IL: Peacock.

Wampler, L. D., & Strupp, H. H. (1976). Personal therapy for students in clinical psychology: A matter of faith? *Professional Psychology, 7,* 195–201.

Wason, P. C. (1960). On the failure to discriminate hypotheses in a conceptual task. *Quarterly Journal of Experimental Psychology, 12,* 129–140.

Wason, P. C., & Johnson-Laird, P. N. (1972). *The psychology of reasoning.* Cambridge, MA: Harvard University Press.

Watkins, C. E. (1983). Counseling psychology versus clinical psychology: Further explorations on a theme, or once around the identity "Maypole" with gusto. *The Counseling Psychologist, 11,* 76–92.

Watkins, C. E. (1990). Reflections on uncomplemented philosophies, integrated curriculums, and words that bind and separate in counseling and clinical psycholgy. *Counseling Psychology Quarterly, 3,* 101–108.

Watkins, C. E., Jr., Campbell, V. L., Nieberding, R., & Hallmark, R. (1995). Contemporary practice of psychological assessment by clinical psychologists. *Professional Psychology: Research and Practice, 26,* 54–60.

Watson, J. B. (1913). Psychology as a behaviorist views it. *Psychological Review, 20,* 158–177.

Watson, J. B. (1924). *Behaviorism.* Chicago: University of Chicago Press.

Watson, J. B., & Rayner, R. (1920). Conditioned emotional reactions. *Journal of Experimental Psychology, 3,* 1–14.

Wechsler, D. (1981). *Wechsler Adult Intelligence Scale—Revised: Manual.* New York: Psychological Corporation.

Wechsler, D. (1987). *Wechsler Memory Scale—Revised: Manual.* San Antonio, TX: Psychological Corporation.

Wechsler, D. (1989). *Wechsler Preschool and Primary Scale of Intelligence—Revised: Manual.* New York: Psychological Corporation.

Wechsler, D. (1991). *Wechsler Intelligence Scale for Children—Third edition: Manual.* New York: Psychological Corporation.

Wechsler, D., & Stone, C. P. (1973). *Wechsler Memory Scale Manual.* New York: Psychological Corporation.

Wegner, K. W. (1992). California Psychological Inventory, 1987 Revised Edition. In D. J. Keyser & R. C. Sweetland (Eds.), *Test critiques* (Vol. 7), (pp. 66–75). Kansas City, MO: Test Corporation of America.

Weiner, I. B. (1975). *Principles of psychotherapy.* New York: Wiley.

Weiss, B., & Weisz, J. R. (1990). The impact of methodological factors on child psychotherapy outcome research: A meta-analysis for researchers. *Journal of Abnormal Child Psychology, 18,* 639–670.

Weiss, G., & Hechtman, L. T. (1986). *Hyperactive children grown up: Empirical findings and theoretical considerations.* New York: Guilford.

Weiss, R. L., & Summers, K. J. (1983). Marital Interaction Coding System-III. In E. E. Filsinger (Ed.), *Marriage and family assessment* (pp. 85–116). Beverly Hills, CA: Sage.

Weissman, A., & Beck, A. T. (1978, November). *Development and validation of the Dysfunctional Attitude Scale (DAS).* Paper presented at the 12th annual meeting of the Association for the Advancement of Behavior Therapy, Chicago, IL.

Weissman, A. N. (1979) *The Dysfunctional Attitude Scale: A validation study.* Unpublished doctoral dissertation, University of Pennsylvania, Philadelphia.

Weisz, J. R., & Weiss, B. (1989). Assessing the effects of clinic-based psychotherapy with children and adolescents. *Journal of Consulting and Clinical Psychology, 57,* 741–746.

Weisz, J. R., Weiss, B., Alicke, M. D., & Klotz, M. L. (1987). Effectiveness of psychotherapy with children and adolescents: A meta-analysis for clinicians. *Journal of Consulting and Clinical Psychology, 55,* 542–549.

Weisz, J. R., Weiss, B., & Donenberg, G. R. (1992). The lab versus the clinic: Effects of child and adolescent psychotherapy. *American Psychologist, 47,* 1578–1585.

Wells, R. A., Dilkes, T. C., & Trivelli, N. (1972). The results of family therapy: A critical review of the literature. *Family Process, 11,* 189–207.

Wertheimer, M. (1978). Humanistic psychology and the humane but tough-minded psychologist. *American Psychologist, 33,* 739–745.

Wetzler, S. (1990). The Millon Clinical Multiaxial Inventory (MCMI): A review. *Journal of Personality Assessment, 55,* 445–464.

Wheelis, A. (1973). *How people change.* New York: Harper and Row.

Whipple, G. M. (1910). *Manual of mental and physical tests.* Baltimore: Warwick and York.

White, R. W. (1963). Ego and reality in psychoanalytic theory: A proposal regarding independent ego energies. *Psychological Issues* (Monograph No. 11). New York: International Universities Press.

Widiger, T. A. (1985). Review of Millon Clinical Multiaxial Inventory. In J. V. Mitchell (Ed.), *Ninth mental measurements yearbook* (pp. 986–988). Lincoln, NE: University of Nebraska Press.

Wiener, D. (1948). Subtle and obvious keys for the Minnesota Multiphasic Personality Inventory. *Journal of Consulting Psychology, 12,* 164–170.

Wierzbicki, M. (1993a). *Issues in clinical psychology: Subjective versus objective approaches.* Boston: Allyn and Bacon.

Wierzbicki, M. (1993b, April). *The psychological adjustment of adoptees: A meta-analysis.* Paper presented at the meeting of the Midwestern Psychological Association, Chicago, IL.

Wierzbicki, M. (1993c). The relationship between MCMI subtlety and severity. *Journal of Personality Assessment, 61,* 259–263.

Wierzbicki, M. (1993d). Use of MCMI subtle and obvious subscales to detect faking. *Journal of Clinical Psychology, 49,* 809–814.

Wierzbicki, M. (1995a). Use of subtle and obvious scales to detect faking on the MCMI-II. *Journal of Clinical Psychology,* in press.

Wierzbicki, M. (1995b, May). *A comparison of random and selective assignment to cognitive or behavioral therapy of depression.* Paper presented at the meeting of the Midwestern Psychological Association, Chicago, IL.

Wierzbicki, M., & Bartlett, T. S. (1987). The efficacy of group and individual cognitive therapy for mild depression. *Cognitive Therapy and Research, 11,* 337–342.

Wierzbicki, M., & Gorman, J. L. (1995). Correspondence between students' scores on the Millon Clinical Multiaxial Inventory—II and Personality Diagnostic Questionnaire—Revised. *Psychological Reports, 77,* 1079–1082.

Wierzbicki, M., & Howard, B. J. (1992). The differential responding of male prisoners to subtle and obvious MCMI scales. *Journal of Personality Assessment, 58,* 115–126.

Wierzbicki, M., Westerholm, P., & McHugh, K. (1994). A comparison of cognitive and behavioral inductions of negative mood. *Journal of Psychology, 128,* 651–657.

Willerman, L., & Cohen, D. B. (1990). *Psychopathology.* New York: McGraw-Hill.

Williams, B. W., Mack, W., & Henderson, V. W. (1989). Boston Naming Test in Alzheimer's disease. *Neuropsychologia, 27,* 1073–1079.

Williams, J. A., & Williams, J. D. (1985). Kuder General Interest Survey, Form E. In D. J. Keyser & R. C. Sweetland (Eds.), *Test critiques* (Vol. II), (pp. 395–401). Kansas City, MO: Test Corporation of America.

Williams, S. L. (1985). On the nature and measurement of agoraphobia. *Progress in Behavior Modification, 19,* 109–144.

Williams, S. L., & Watson, N. (1985). Perceived danger and perceived self-efficacy as cognitive determinants of acrophobic behavior. *Behavior Therapy, 16,* 136–146.

Williamson, D. A., Moody, S. C., Granberry, S. W., Letherman, V. R., & Blouin, D. C. (1983). Criterion-related validity of a role-play social skills test for children. *Behavior Therapy, 14,* 466–481.

Wilson, G. T., O'Leary, K. D., & Nathan, P. (1992). *Abnormal psychology.* Englewood Cliffs, NJ: Prentice-Hall.

Winter, W. D. (1971). Family therapy: Research and theory. In C. D. Spielberger (Ed.), *Current topics in clinical and community psychology* (Vol. 3, pp. 95–121). New York: Academic.

Wirt, R. D., Lachar, D., Klinedinst, J. K., & Seat, P. D. (1984). *Multidimensional description of child personality: A manual for the Personality Inventory for Children.* Los Angeles: Western Psychological Services.

Wisocki, P. A., Grebstein, L. C., & Hunt, J. B. (1994). Directors of clinical training: An insider's perspective. *Professional Psychology: Research and Practice, 25,* 482–488.

Withers, E., & Hinton, J. (1971). Three forms of the Clinical Tests of the Sensorium and their reliability. *British Journal of Psychiatry, 119,* 1–8.

Wolf, A., & Kutash, I. L. (1990). Psychoanalysis in groups. In I. L. Kutash & A. Wolf (Eds.), *The group psychotherapist's handbook: Contemporary theory and technique* (pp. 11–45). New York: Columbia University Press.

Wolpe, J. (1954). Reciprocal inhibition as the main basis of psychotherapeutic effects. *Archives of Neurology and Psychiatry, 72,* 205–266.

Wolpe, J. (1958). *Psychotherapy by reciprocal inhibition.* Stanford, CA: Stanford University Press.

Wolpe, J. (1982). *The practice of behavior therapy* (3rd ed.). New York: Pergamon.

Wood, J. M., Nezworski, M. T., & Stejskal, W. J. (1996). The comprehensive system for the Rorschach: A critical examination. *Psychological Science, 7,* 3–10.

Woodcock, R. W. (1977). *Woodcock-Johnson Psycho-Educational Battery: Technical report.* Boston: Teaching Resources.

Woodcock, R. W., & Mather, N. (1989). *Woodcock-Johnson Tests of Achievement.* Allen, TX: DLM Teaching Resources.

Woodworth, R. S. (1920). *Personal data sheet.* Chicago, IL: Stoeling.

Woodworth, R. S. (1937). The future of clinical psychology. *Journal of Consulting Psychology, 1,* 4–5.

Worthen, B. R., & Sailor, P. (1995). Review of the Strong Interest Inventory. In J. C. Conoley & J. C. Impara (Eds.), *The twelfth mental measurements yearbook* (pp. 999–1003). Lincoln, NE: University of Nebraska Press.

Wortman, C. B., & Loftus, E. F. (1992). *Psychology* (4th ed.). New York: McGraw-Hill.

Wyss, D. (1973). *Psychoanalytic schools from the beginning to the present.* New York: J. Aronson.

Yalom, I. D. (1975). *The theory and practice of group psychotherapy* (2nd ed.). New York: Basic Books.

Yalom, I. D. (1980). *Existential psychotherapy.* New York: Basic Books.

Yalom, I. D., Houts, P. S., Zimerberg, S. M., & Rand, K. H. (1967). Prediction of improvement in group therapy. *Archives of General Psychiatry, 17,* 159–168.

Yates, A. J. (1958). Symptoms and symptom substitution. *Psychological Review, 65,* 371–374.

Yates, A. J. (1970). *Behavior therapy.* New York: Wiley.

Yates, A. J. (1975). *Theory and practice in behavior therapy.* New York: Wiley.

Yontef, G. (1990). Gestalt therapy in groups. In I. L. Kutash & A. Wolf (Eds.), *The group psychotherapist's handbook: Contemporary theory and technique* (pp. 191–210). New York: Columbia University Press.

Yontef, G. M., & Simkin, J. S. (1989). Gestalt therapy. In R. J. Corsini & D. Wedding (Eds.), *Current psychotherapies* (4th ed., pp. 323–361). Itasca, IL: Peacock.

Young, F. A. (1992). APA and AP. *Professional Psychology: Research and Practice, 23,* 436–438.

Youngstrom, N. (1990, December). Settlement compliance is lagging, plaintiffs say. *APA Monitor, 21*(12), 17.

Zigler, E. F., & Seitz, V. (1982). Social policy and intelligence. In R. J. Sternberg (Ed.), *Handbook of human intelligence* (pp. 586–641). Cambridge: Cambridge University Press.

Zillmer, E. A., Harrower, M., Ritzler, B. A., & Archer, R. A. (1995). *The quest for the Nazi personality: A psychological investigation of Nazi war criminals.* Hillsdale, NJ: Erlbaum.

Zook, A., II, & Walton, J. M. (1989). Theoretical orientations and work meetings of clinical and counseling psychologists: A current perspective. *Professional Psychology: Research and Practice, 20,* 303–315.

Zubin, J. (1954). Failures of the Rorschach technique. *Journal of Projective Techniques, 18,* 303–315.

Zubin, J., Eron, L. D., & Schumer, F. (1965). *An experimental approach to projective techniques.* New York: Wiley.

Zuckerman, M. (1989). Personality in the third dimension: A psychobiological approach. *Personality and Individual Differences, 10,* 391–418.

Name Index

Abell, S. C., 107
Abernethy, D. R., 291
Abikoff, H., 143
Abramson, C., 68, 153
Abt, L. E., 346, 347
Achenbach, T. M., 3, 145, 312
Ackerman, N., 226, 321, 322, 324, 337
Adler, A., 221, 222, 223, 228, 233, 337
Agassiz, L., 99
Agnew, N. M., 16
Aiduk, R., 177
Aiken, L. R., 112, 145, 146
Alden, L., 150
Alexander, F., 224, 225
Alexander, J. F., 322, 337
Alicke, M. D., 319
Allen, R. P., 293
Alliger, G. M., 112
Alloy, L., 68
Allport, G. W., 44, 61, 62, 65, 161, 167
Alnot, S. D., 109
Amenson, C. S., 28
Ames, 179
Anastasi, A., 105, 110, 116, 179
Anastopoulos, A. D., 73
Andersen, B. L., 304
Andrews, G., 281
Angres, R., 314
Ansler, T. N., 109
Antoni, M. H., 297
Antonuccio, D. O., 330
Appelbaum, A., 228
Archer, R. A., 168, 169

Archer, R. P., 177
Arizmendi, T. G., 196
Arnkoff, D. B., 269
Aronow, E., 166, 168, 178
Axline, V. M., 314, 315, 336
Ayers, W. A., 319
Ayllon, T., 258, 262, 263
Azrin, N. H., 258, 262, 263

Baade, L. E., 117
Baars, B. J., 66
Back, A. T., 273
Baker, L., 322
Baker, T. B., 117
Bancroft, J., 67
Bandura, A., 58, 66, 68, 266, 267, 276
Barber, T. X., 122, 302
Barclay, A. G., 3
Barkley, R. A., 73, 292
Barlow, A. G., 3
Barlow, D. H., 11, 39, 356
Barr, E., 293
Barrett, B. H., 156
Barrett, C. L., 319
Barrett, P., 174
Bartlett, T. S., 330
Bass, D., 38, 319, 357
Baucom, D. H., 326
Beck, A. T., 28, 67, 146, 148, 153, 265, 267, 271, 272, 273, 282, 283, 300
Beck, G. A., 67
Beck, J., 314
Bednar, R. L., 334, 335, 336, 338
Beecher, H. K., 32

Beels, C. C., 321, 325
Beers, C., 312
Beets, J. L., 164
Begelman, D. A., 280
Beidel, D. C., 293
Belar, C. D., 345
Bell, J. E., 165, 179
Bellack, A. S., 133, 144, 157, 265
Bellak, A. L., 166, 170, 171
Bell-Dolan, D. J., 141
Belsky, J., 305
Bem, S. L., 67
Bender, L., 11, 116, 117
Benjamin, L. T., 351
Ben-Porath, Y. S., 165, 167, 172, 173, 175, 176
Benson, H., 247, 248
Bergin, A. E., 198, 201, 203, 231, 232, 244, 251, 281
Berk, L. E., 224, 279
Berman, J. S., 282, 319
Berne, E., 225, 327
Bernheim, H., 217
Bernstein, D. A., 288, 300, 301
Bernstein, J. G., 289, 290, 291, 293
Bettelheim, B., 230, 314, 336
Beutler, L. E., 38, 196, 357
Bezchlibnyk-Butler, K. Z., 288, 290, 291, 294
Bickman, L., 11, 343
Bielauskas, L. A., 345
Biever, J. O., 153
Biglan, A., 146
Binet, A., 82, 101, 102, 103, 126
Binswanger, L., 242
Bivens, J. A., 279

Black, M. J., 265
Blanchard, E. B., 144, 302, 304
Blouin, D. C., 144
Blum, G., 170
Bolton, B., 174
Bonato, D., 178
Bookbinder, L. J., 274
Bootzin, R. R., 196, 276
Borduin, C. M., 326
Boring, E. G., 2, 20, 81, 119, 231
Borkovec, T. D., 300, 301
Bornstein, M. R., 144
Boss, M., 242
Botwin, M. D., 174
Bouchard, T. J., 101
Bowen, M., 226, 320, 321, 323, 337
Bowers, T. G., 32
Bradley, C., 292
Brand, R. J., 298
Brasted, W. S., 342, 348
Breggin, P. R., 294
Brehm, S. S., 196, 197
Breier, A., 288, 291
Brems, C., 8, 193, 350
Breuer, J., 217
Breunlin, 326
Bright, I., 326
Bright, P., 153
Broca, P., 99, 110
Brodbeck, M., 16
Brody, C., 355
Brody, N., 32, 119
Bromberg, W., 3, 4, 5, 7
Brown, D. T., 113
Brown, R. A., 261
Browne, C. G., 166, 170, 173, 178
Brownell, K. D., 304
Buchanan, R. W., 288
Buck, J., 171
Burge, D. A., 141
Burnett, R., 303
Burns, R. C., 171
Buros, O. K., 166, 179
Burstein, E., 228
Buss, A. H., 74
Butcher, J. N., 165, 167, 172, 173,
    175, 176, 177, 189, 190
Butler, J. M., 65, 252, 288

Cade, J. F. J., 290
Campbell, D., 261
Campbell, D. E., 164
Campbell, D. P., 113
Campbell, D. T., 30
Campbell, V. L., 170
Canter, D., 11
Canter, S., 11
Caputo, G. C., 153
Carey, G., 87
Carkhuff, R. R., 64, 65, 248, 253,
    255
Carlson, C. G., 276
Carnap, R., 15
Carpenter, W. T., 288
Casey, R. J., 319
Cash, T. F., 40, 356
Cattell, J. M., 81, 82, 99, 101
Cattell, R. B., 166
Cautela, J. R., 269
Chambers, W. B., 141
Chambless, D., 278, 355
Chambless, R. D., 153
Chapman, J. P., 182
Chapman, L. J., 182
Cheslow, D., 293
Chess, S., 73, 74, 75
Clark, K. E., 343
Clum, G. A., 32
Cobb, J. A., 143
Coe, W. C., 196
Cohen, D. B., 75, 76, 83, 280
Comer, R. J., 306
Conners, C. K., 145
Connolly, A. J., 109
Conway, J. B., 39, 356
Cook, T. D., 201, 202
Cooper, A. M., 225
Cooper, C., 119
Cooper, G. L., 290
Cooper, H. M., 326
Cooper, J. E., 154
Copeland, J. R. M., 154
Cordasco, F., 106
Cornell, J. E., 354
Corsini, R. J., 194
Corulla, W. J., 174
Costa, P. T., 174

Costello, E. J., 141
Covin, T. M., 107
Cox, D. J., 303
Coyne, J. C., 297
Coyne, L., 228
Crago, M., 196
Craig, P. L., 117
Crits-Christoph, P., 233, 355
Cronbach, L. J., 88, 89
Croughan, J., 141
Crowne, 188
Culver, R. B., 164
Cummings, N. A., 194
Cyr, J., 178

Dahlstrom, W. G., 176
Daly, K., 146
Dana, R. H., 125
Danaher, B. G., 261
Darley, J. G., 342
Daruna, J. H., 143
Darwin, C., 20
Davidson, R. J., 153
Davies, R., 220
Davis, B., 146
Davis, J. M., 143, 289
Davison, G. C., 3, 75, 141, 156, 240,
    280, 331, 336
Davison, L. A., 114
Dawes, R. M., 232, 281, 356
Dean, G. A., 165
Deblinger, E., 278
de Groot, A. D., 149
DeLeon, P. H., 194, 304, 305
DeLeon-Jones, F., 289
DeMaster, B., 155
Dembroski, T., 298
Dent, O. B., 38, 357
Derogatis, L. R., 148
DeSoto, C. B., 118
DeVellis, R. F., 146
DeWitt, K. N., 325
Diamond, E. E., 113
Diener, C., 303, 304
Dilkes, D. C., 325
Dimsdale, J. E., 298
Doleys, D. M., 262, 276, 293
Donenberg, G. R., 312

Donlon, T. F., 111
Donnell, W. E., 118
Dorfman, E., 315
Doyle, K. O., 98
Dreikurs, 327
Dubbert, P. M., 304
DuBois, P. H., 98, 106, 165, 166, 167, 172, 173, 189
Duker, J., 175
Dulcan, M. K., 141
Dunn, L. M., 107, 108
Dunsmore, J., 303
DuPaul, G. J., 292
Durlak, J. A., 250, 319
Dusay, J. M., 225
Dusay, K. M., 225
Dush, D. M., 282
Dyer, C. O., 174
Dymond, R. F., 252
D'Zurilla, T. J., 150, 273

Eaton, M. M., 347
Ebbinghaus, H., 172
Edelbrock, C. S., 141, 145
Edelstein, B. A., 342, 348
Edwards, A. L., 186, 188
Eisler, R. M., 144, 276
Elkin, I., 273, 307
Ellenberger, H., 51, 194
Elliott, R., 39, 356
Ellis, A., 66, 67, 150, 248, 251, 267, 271, 272, 283
Elstein, A. S., 355
Emery, G., 146, 271, 272
Emery, R. E., 320
Emmelkamp, P. M. G., 260, 300
Endicott, J., 139
Entwistle, S. R., 38, 357
Erbaugh, J., 28, 148
Erikson, E., 167, 313, 314, 336
Eron, L. D., 166
Erwin, E., 276, 280
Esveldt-Dawson, K., 144
Evans, R. G., 188
Exner, J. E., 167, 168
Eyberg, S. M., 145
Eysenck, H. J., 38, 72, 73, 75, 99, 117, 174, 198, 200, 201, 203, 204, 212, 213, 231, 258, 280, 281, 319
Eysenck, S. B., 174

Fairbairn, R., 224
Falloon, I. R. H., 306
Fava, M., 290
Feather, B., 276
Fechner, G., 81
Feigl, H., 15, 16
Feldt, L. S., 109
Ferber, A., 321
Ferenczi, 328
Festinger, L., 68
Fiedler, F. E., 253
Fink, C. M., 345
Fisher, S., 54, 232
Folkman, S., 297
Ford, D. H., 37, 156, 215
Forer, B. R., 181
Forsyth, R. A., 109
Foster, S. L., 141, 152, 153, 154, 155
Fowler, R. D., 189, 190
Fox, R. E., 304
Frank, E., 355
Frank, G., 38, 39, 178
Frank, J. D., 195, 196
Frank, L. K., 166, 167, 343, 346, 347, 355, 356, 357
Frankl, V., 243, 244
Franzen, M. D., 110, 114, 115, 116, 117
Freedman, A. M., 133, 228, 312
Freeman, W., 295
French, T. M., 225
Freud, A., 228, 313, 336
Freud, S., 6, 12, 19, 25, 26, 45, 49, 50, 52, 53, 55, 58, 61, 66, 83, 166, 167, 197, 215, 216, 217, 218, 219, 220, 221, 222, 223, 224, 225, 228, 230, 231, 233, 234, 248, 285, 311, 312, 328
Frew, 329
Fried, M. H., 98, 131
Fried, M. N., 98, 131
Friedman, A. F., 174
Friedman, M., 297, 298, 302

Fromm, E., 228
Fuhriman, A., 330, 336
Fuhrman, T., 319
Fulcher, R., 350

Gadow, K. D., 293
Gall, F. J., 164
Gallagher, K. M., 347, 354
Gallagher, R., 153
Galton, F., 81, 82, 99, 165, 172
Gandour, M. J., 75
Gannon, 246
Garbin, M. G., 148
Garfield, S. L., 196, 201, 211, 232, 343, 347, 348, 353, 354
Garfinkel, P. E., 153
Garner, D. M., 153
Gaston, L., 230
Gay, P., 53, 226, 229
Genest, G. E., 149
Genest, M., 303
Giblin, 326
Gibson, J. T., 307
Gilberstadt, H., 175
Gillis, R. O., 146
Gittelman-Klein, R., 143
Glasgow, R. E., 304
Glass, C. R., 153, 298
Glass, G. V., 200, 201, 203, 213, 232, 251, 252, 260, 271, 277, 281
Glazeski, R. C., 149
Gleser, G. C., 88
Goldband, S., 298
Goldberg, E. E., 112
Goldberg, L. R., 172, 174, 249, 353
Goldberg, S. C., 306
Golden, C. J., 114
Goldfoot, D. A., 224
Goldfried, M. R., 132, 141, 150, 155, 156, 240, 273, 280
Goldman, A., 319
Goldstein, K., 110, 244
Goleman, D. J., 153
Gonder-Frederick, L., 303
Goodenough, F. L., 102, 107, 171
Goodglass, H., 115
Gorman, J. L., 178

Gottesman, I. I., 87
Gottlieb, J., 4
Gottman, J. M., 149, 153, 322
Gough, H. C., 174
Gould, S. J., 99
Gourlay, A. J., 154
Goyette, C. H., 145
Grabowski, J., 294
Graham, J. R., 176, 185, 186
Graham, S. R., 304
Granberry, S. W., 144
Grebstein, L. C., 352
Green, L. M., 154, 355
Green, W. H., 290, 293, 294
Greenberg, R., 54, 232
Greenblatt, D. J., 291
Greenfeld, D., 316
Gregory, R. J., 82, 99, 102, 168, 190
Griffin, R., 177
Gross, M. L., 251
Grossman, P. B., 319
Grotevant, H. D., 119
Grunbaum, A., 53
Grusec, J. E., 197
Guest, J., 216
Guevremont, D. C., 258, 292, 303
Gurman, A. S., 319, 325, 326
Gustad, J. W., 343
Guthrie, P. C., 178
Guy, J. D., 229
Gwynne, J., 125

Hagen, E. P., 103
Hahlweg, K., 326
Haigh, G. V., 65, 252
Haley, J., 323, 337
Hall, C. S., 163, 164, 194
Haller, D. L., 177
Hallmark, R., 170
Halstead, W., 114
Hamburger, S. D., 293
Hammeke, T. A., 114
Hampe, I. E., 319
Hansen, J. C., 113
Hanych, J. M., 11, 344
Hare, R. D., 73
Harlow, H. F., 224
Harris, T., 107, 171

Harrower, M., 168, 169
Hartlage, L. C., 117
Hartman, L. M., 153
Hartmann, D. P., 202
Hartmann, H., 223
Harvey, R., 281
Harvey, S., 232
Hathaway, S. R., 173, 185
Hawley, P. R., 347
Haworth, M. R., 172
Hayes, S. C., 11, 156
Haynes, S. N., 152
Hazelrigg, M. D., 326
Healy, W., 312
Heaton, R. K., 115, 117
Hechtman, L. T., 292
Hecker, J. E., 345
Hedberg, A. G., 210
Heiberger, A. M., 107
Heidegger, M., 242
Heinicke, C. M., 319
Helzer, J. E., 141
Hempel, C. G., 15, 16
Henderson, V. W., 115
Hendrick, I., 225
Henry, D., 278
Henry, W. P., 230
Heppner, P. P., 149
Herrnstein, R. J., 20
Hersen, M., 133, 144, 157, 265, 276
Hershey, J. M., 354
Hester, R. K., 261, 269, 331
Hetherington, E. M., 144
Hilgard, E. R., 11, 36, 342
Hill, W. F., 66
Himmelhoch, J. M., 265
Hinton, J., 118
Hirt, M. L., 282
Hobbs, N., 329
Hoberman, H. M., 330
Hoffman, J. A., 326
Hogan, J. D., 351
Hogarty, G. E., 306
Hollandsworth, J. G., 149
Holliman, B. B., 178
Hollon, S. D., 153, 265, 300
Holmes, D. S., 247, 248, 302
Holmes, T. H., 297

Holt, H., 329, 344
Holt, R. R., 249
Holtzman, W. H., 167
Homme, L. E., 66, 267
Honaker, L. M., 189, 190
Honigfeld, G., 146
Hood-Williams, J., 319
Hook, S., 16, 53
Hooper, S. R., 150
Hordern, A., 154, 355
Horkheimer, R., 107
Horn, W. F., 152
Horney, K., 313, 336
Horwitz, L., 228
Houts, P. S., 332
Howard, B. J., 186
Howard, K. I., 253
Hug-Hellmuth, H. V., 312
Hughes, J. N., 319
Huitema, B. E., 112
Hulse, W. S., 171
Hunsley, J., 156
Hunt, J. B., 352
Hurlburt, R. T., 150
Husserl, E., 61

Ianna, P. A., 164
Irish, D., 288
Ishiyama, F., 247, 248
Itard, 12

Jackson, D. N., 113, 174
Jacobson, E., 299, 300
Jacobson, L., 122
Jacobson, N. S., 322, 337
James, W., 66
Jarrett, R. B., 156
Jastak, S., 108
Jeffries, J. J., 288, 290, 291, 294
Jenkins, C. D., 298
Jensen, A. R., 101, 117, 124, 171
Jerome, L. E., 164
Johnson, G. R., 276
Johnson, J. E., 107, 297
Johnson, K. L., 117
Johnson, M. E., 350
Johnson, P. B., 143
Johnson-Laird, P. N., 24

Johnston, J. M., 156
Jones, E., 328
Jones, G. E., 149
Jones, M. C., 258, 315, 336
Jones, N. F., 3
Jones, R. R., 143
Jung, C. G., 165, 167, 220, 221, 223, 228, 233
Juni, S., 174

Kaemmer, B., 176
Kagan, J., 74
Kahn, S., 297
Kalas, R., 141
Kalpin, R., 178
Kamin, L., 99, 117
Kaminer, W., 331
Kanner, A. D., 297
Kant, I., 61
Kaplan, E. F., 115
Kaplan, H. I., 133, 228, 312
Karp, J. F., 355
Kaslow, N. J., 68
Kassin, S. M., 196, 197
Katkin, E. S., 298
Kaufman, A. S., 105, 106, 109
Kaufman, N. L., 105, 106, 109
Kaufman, S. H., 171
Kaul, T. J., 335
Kazdin, A. E., 38, 144, 196, 276, 319, 357
Kearns, D. L., 326
Keefe, F. J., 303
Keller, J. W., 170, 171, 172, 178, 179, 182
Kelly, E. L., 11, 36, 342
Kelly, G., 66, 67, 267, 270, 271, 283
Kelly, J. A., 304
Kelly, L., 249, 353
Kempler, W., 322
Kendall, P. C., 38, 153, 267
Kendall, R. E., 154
Kent, R. N., 155
Kernberg, O. F., 224, 225, 228
Kessler, R. C., 290
Kidd, K. K., 101
Kiefer, C., 247
Kiernan, V., 112

Kifer, F., 112
Killian, G. A., 172
Kimble, G. A., 298
Kingsbury, S. J., 305, 349
Kirk, S. A., 109
Kirk, W. D., 109
Kirkland, K., 149
Klein, D., 143
Klein, M., 224, 228, 312, 313, 336
Klein, R. G., 293
Klett, C. J., 146
Kline, P., 54, 231, 232
Klinedinst, J. K., 174
Klopfer, B., 167
Klopfer, W. G., 171
Klotz, M. L., 319
Kluger, R., 125
Kniskern, D. P., 319, 325, 326
Knoff, H. M., 174
Kobasa, S. C., 297
Koby, E. V., 293
Koegel, R., 263, 316
Kohut, H., 224
Koppitz, E. M., 116
Kopplin, D. A., 354
Korman, M., 11, 343
Kornblith, S. J., 153
Kornreich, M., 281
Kraepelin, E., 3, 6
Krager, J. M., 292
Krantz, D., 298
Kratochwill, T. R., 312
Kretschmer, E., 163, 164
Kris, E., 230
Kuder, G. F., 85, 113
Kuhn, T., 23, 24, 25, 41
Kurtz, R. M., 343, 347, 348, 353, 354
Kutash, I. L., 328

Lachar, D., 174, 175
Lahey, B. B., 145
Lakin, M., 208
Lambert, M. J., 203, 251
Lamparski, D. M., 153
Lampman, C., 319
Landman, J. T., 232, 281
Lange, A., 326

Larsen, K. G., 345
Larsen, K. H., 153
Larsen, R. D., 175
Laverty, S. G., 261
Lawlis, G. F., 334, 335
Layne, C. C., 150
Lazarus, A. A., 133
Lazarus, R. S., 276, 297
Lazell, 327
LeCroy, C. W., 204
Leff, J. P., 306
Leger, P., 293
Lenane, M. C., 293
Leonard, H. L., 293
Letherman, V. R., 144
Levant, R. F., 320, 321, 322
Levasseur, J. B., 345
Leventhal, D. B., 347
Levine, A. R., 347
Levis, D. J., 260
Leviton, L. C., 201, 202
Levitsky, A., 245
Levitt, E. E., 319, 336
Levy, L., 39, 271
Lewin, K., 329
Lewinsohn, P. M., 28, 146, 272, 330, 333
Lezak, M. D., 114
Licht, B. G., 292
Lichtenstein, E., 261, 304
Lick, J., 196
Lieberman, M. A., 250, 330, 331, 334, 335, 338
Lindsley, O., 258
Lindzey, G., 163, 164, 171
Lipinski, D. O., 154
Lockyer, L., 316
Loftus, E. F., 2
Lohman, D. F., 101, 102, 103
Lombroso, C., 164
Long, J. S., 263, 316
Lord, F. M., 88, 89
Louttit, C. M., 166, 170, 173, 178
Lovaas, O. I., 263, 264, 276, 278, 316, 336
Lovell, M. R., 174
Lowe, K., 303
Lowery, C. R., 182

Lubin, B., 117, 171, 172, 175, 176, 182
Luborsky, L., 198, 201, 230, 231, 232, 249, 281
Luckey, B., 11, 36, 342
Ludwick-Rosenthal, R., 304
Lunde, S. E., 276
Luria, A. R., 279
Lutzker, J. R., 303, 344
Lyons, J. S., 143

MacCorquodale, K., 17, 56, 155
MacDougall, J., 298
Macfarlane, J. W., 179
Machover, K., 166, 171, 172, 178
Mack, W., 115
MacLean, R. E. G., 293
Maddi, S. R., 68, 297
Mahler, M., 224, 313, 336
Mahoney, M. J., 24, 268, 269, 274
Maisto, S. A., 278
Mannuzza, S., 293
Margolin, G., 322
Markman, H. J., 326
Marks, I., 260, 268
Marks, P. A., 177
Markus, E., 326
Markwardt, F. C., 108
Marlowe, D., 188
Marston, A. R., 144
Martin, P. R., 276
Mash, E. J., 156
Maslow, A. H., 61, 62, 63, 65
Massie, H. N., 325
Massman, P. J., 282
Masson, J. M., 229
Masters, J. C., 141, 258, 260, 265
Matarazzo, J. D., 175
Matarazzo, R. G., 249, 250, 252
Mather, N., 108
Matson, J. L., 144
Maudsley, H., 6
May, R., 242
May, W. T., 305, 306
Mayne, T. J., 351, 352
McCall, P. B., 119
McCarthy, D. A., 105, 106
McCarthy, J. J., 109
McCrae, R., 174

McEachin, J. J., 264
McFall, R. M., 144
McGrew, M. W., 171
McGue, M., 101
McGuire, W., 220
McHugh, K., 33
McKinley, J. C., 173
McLeer, S. V., 278
McNamara, J. R., 3, 10
McReynolds, P., 163, 164
Meehl, P. E., 17, 56, 155, 185, 176, 190, 191
Meichenbaum, D., 265, 266, 274, 283, 303, 316, 336
Meltzoff, J., 39, 40, 281, 355, 356, 357
Mendelson, M., 28, 148
Mensh, I. N., 345
Merluzzi, T. V., 153
Mesibov, G., 264
Miale, F. R., 168
Miele, F., 124
Miles, M. B., 250, 330
Milich, R., 292
Miller, L. C., 319
Miller, P. M., 144
Miller, R. C., 282
Miller, T. I., 200, 251, 281
Miller, W. R., 261, 269, 331
Millon, T., 177, 178, 185
Mills, D. H., 210
Mills, K. C., 144
Mintz, M., 307
Minuchin, S., 322, 323, 337
Mischel, W., 66, 267
Mitchell, K. M., 253
Mock, J., 28, 148
Moniz, A., 295
Monte, C. F., 217
Montgomery, L. M., 326
Moody, S. C., 144
Moore, B. V., 343
Moore, D. R., 143
Moreno, J., 327, 328, 337
Morgan, C. D., 170
Morgan, C. L., 20
Morganthaler, W., 167
Morita, S., 247, 248
Moritz, J. L., 347

Morris, L. A., 32, 196
Morris, R. J., 312
Morrison, R. L., 141
Morrow, D., 350
Morrow-Bradley, C., 39, 356
Moustakas, C. E., 315
Mowrer, 336
Mowrer, O. H., 262, 315
Mowrer, W. M., 262, 315
Mulhern, J., 106
Mulick, J. A., 143
Murdock, M., 32
Murphy, D. A., 292, 304
Murray, H. A., 11, 166, 170, 171, 186
Myerson, A., 231

Nachtman, W., 109
Nagel, E., 15, 16
Nash, J. M., 347
Nathan, P., 290
Nathan, R. S., 293
Neale, J. M., 3, 75, 331, 336
Neff, J. A., 350
Nelson, R. O., 11, 154, 156
Neufeld, R. W. J., 304
Nezu, A. M., 150, 274
Nezu, C. M., 150, 274
Nezworski, M. T., 168
Nguyen, S., 107
Nickell, J., 164
Nieberding, R., 170
Noll, K. M., 289, 290, 294
Norcross, J. C., 11, 82, 229, 242, 243, 344, 347, 351, 352, 354
Norton-Ford, J. D., 38
Novaco, R. W., 274
Novick, M. R., 88, 89
Nurius, P. S., 202

O'Hara, M. W., 153
O'Leary, K. D., 290
Odbert, H. S., 161
Oden, M. H., 119
Okwumabua, T., 326
Ollendick, T. H., 260
Olmedo, E. L., 344
Olson, D. H., 319, 325

Oltmanns, T. F., 320
Orlinsky, D. E., 253
Ormiston, D. W., 38, 357

Paine, C., 117, 171
Parker, J. D., 345
Parloff, M. B., 65, 253
Parsons, B., 322
Pascal, G. R., 116
Patterson, D., 249, 250
Patterson, G. R., 143
Paul, G., 31, 32
Paul, S. M., 291
Pavlov, I. P., 258
Pekarik, G., 196
Pekow, C., 314
Pelham, W. E., 292
Pennypacker, H. S., 156
Perls, F., 244, 245, 246, 254, 327
Perri, M. G., 150, 274
Persico, C. F., 344
Person, E. S., 225
Peterson, C. H., 68, 149
Peterson, D. R., 145, 168, 344, 347, 354
Peterson, R. A., 11
Pettigrew, T. F., 326
Phillips, H. C., 303
Piacentini, J. C., 145
Piaget, J., 68
Pinel, P., 5, 12
Pinsof, W. M., 326
Piotrowski, C., 170, 171, 172, 178, 179, 182, 183
Piotrowski, Z. A., 94, 167, 190
Planck, M., 24
Platt, J. J., 149, 267, 316
Plomin, R., 74
Poelstra, P. L., 229
Poey, K., 345
Polster, E., 245, 250, 330
Polster, M., 245, 250, 330
Pomerlau, D. F., 300
Pomeroy, J. C., 293
Popper, K. R., 15, 21, 22, 23, 24, 25, 41, 53, 230
Potter, E. H., 297
Pratt, J., 327
Prendergast, P., 178

Prioleau, L., 32
Prior, M., 263
Pritchett, E. M., 109
Prochaska, J. O., 82, 224, 229, 244, 246, 347, 354
Pryzwansky, W. B., 11, 205, 210, 343
Purisch, A. D., 114
Pyke, S. W., 16

Quay, H. C., 73, 125, 145

Rabin, A. J., 82, 165, 170
Rachman, S. J., 203, 278
Rafferty, J. E., 166, 172
Ragland, D. R., 298
Rahe, R. H., 297, 302
Raimy, V. C., 343
Rajaratnam, N., 88, 89
Rand, K. H., 332
Rangell, L., 230
Rank, O., 228
Rapaport, D., 167
Rapoport, J. L., 293
Raskin, N. J., 235
Ratcliff, K. S., 141
Ray, R. S., 143
Rayner, R., 59, 258, 315
Redd, W. H., 303, 304
Reed, S. D., 298, 299, 303
Rehm, L. P., 144, 153
Reich, W., 244
Reichler, R. J., 146
Reid, J. B., 143, 155
Reisman, J. M., 11, 36, 194, 343
Reitan, R. M., 114
Rexford, L., 33
Reynolds, D., 118, 247
Reznikoff, M., 166, 168, 178
Rhoads, J. M., 276
Richards, M. S., 264
Richardson, M. W., 85
Ridberg, E. H., 144
Rieff, P., 215
Rimm, D. C., 141, 258, 260, 265
Ritzler, B. A., 168, 169
Roback, H. B., 171
Robbins, D. E., 114
Robins, E., 139

Robins, L. N., 141
Rodgers, A., 319
Rodin, J., 300
Roe, A., 343
Roelke, H. K. J., 345
Rogers, C. R., 61, 62, 63, 64, 65, 82, 235, 236, 237, 238, 240, 241, 245, 248, 249, 250, 251, 252, 254, 311, 327, 329, 337
Rogow, 227
Rojahn, J., 143
Romano, J. M., 153
Rorschach, H., 166, 167
Rosen, A. J., 143, 251
Rosenbaum, M., 327
Rosenberg, L. A., 65
Rosenhan, D. L., 305
Rosenman, R. H., 297, 298
Rosenthal, R., 122
Rosenzweig, M. R., 2, 351
Rosman, B., 322
Ross, S., 343
Rothermel, R. D., 174
Rotter, J. B., 66, 166, 172, 271
Routh, D. K., 8, 193
Rozeboom, W. W., 88
Rush, A. J., 146, 271
Russell, B., 16, 20, 326
Rutter, M., 316

Sacco, W. P., 273, 282
Sadock, B. J., 133, 228, 312
Safer, D. J., 291, 293
Safran, J., 150
Salter, A., 231, 258
Salzman, C., 291
Sanchez-Hucles, J., 40, 356
Sandifer, M. G., 154, 355
Sanford, R. N., 11, 36, 342
Sanhueza, P., 178
Sarason, B. R., 297, 306
Sarason, I. G., 290, 297, 306
Sarason, R. R., 290
Sartre, J. P., 242
Satir, V., 322, 337
Sattler, J. M., 103, 106, 107, 108, 117, 119, 123, 124, 125
Sayette, M. A., 351, 352, 358

Scarr, S., 101
Schacht, T. E., 230
Schaefer, C., 297
Schaefer, H. H., 144
Scheidlinger, S., 327
Schofield, W., 179, 204, 228
Schooler, N. R., 306
Schopler, E., 146, 264
Schretlen, D., 186
Schroeder, H. E., 265, 282
Schroeder, S. R., 143
Schumer, F., 166
Schwartz, G. E., 153
Schwartz, R. M., 149, 153
Seaman, W., 177
Searles, J. S., 203, 232, 281, 282
Sears, R. R., 53
Seat, P. D., 174
Sechrest, L., 347
Seguin, E., 312
Seitz, V., 119
Seligman, M. E. P., 68, 153, 297, 305, 306
Selye, H., 296, 297, 308
Selzer, M., 168
Semmel, N. J., 153
Sexton, V. S., 351
Shader, R. I., 291
Shadish, W. R., 326
Shaffer, L. F., 11, 36, 342
Shakow, D., 7, 11, 36, 342, 344, 354
Shapiro, A. K., 32, 196
Shapiro, D. A., 203, 232, 251, 282
Shaw, B. F., 146, 271
Shaw, D. A., 143
Shea, S. C., 133, 134
Sheehan, R., 326
Sheldon, W. H., 163, 164
Shemberg, K. M., 347
Shenkel, R. J., 182
Shepard, J. W., 113
Shorkey, C. T., 150
Short, A., 264
Shostrom, E. L., 65
Shulman, L. S., 355
Shure, M. B., 266, 267, 273, 316
Siegel, L. J., 276
Siegel, T. C., 38, 357

Sifneos, P., 225
Silver, M. J., 122
Simkin, J. S., 244
Simmons, J. Q., 263, 316
Simon, 101, 102
Singer, B., 201, 281
Skinner, B. F., 25, 56, 132, 258, 263, 316
Skodak, M., 343
Skubiski, S. L., 197
Slosson, R. L., 107
Smith, K. E., 276
Smith, M. L., 122, 200, 201, 203, 213, 232, 251, 252, 260, 271, 277, 281, 282
Smith, T., 264
Smye, M. D., 149
Snepp, F., 347
Snidman, N., 74
Snowden, L. R., 331
Snyder, C. R., 182
Snyder, M., 355
Snyder, S. H., 288
Sobell, M. B., 144
Spanos, N. P., 4
Spearman, C., 99
Spence, D. P., 230, 231, 232
Spiegler, M. D., 258, 303
Spitzer, R. L., 139, 140
Spivack, G., 145, 149, 266, 267, 273, 274, 283, 316, 336
Spock, B., 215
Spotts, C., 145
Sprafka, S. A., 355
Sprafkin, J. N., 132
Spreen, O., 108, 115, 116
Sprenkle, D. H., 326
Stachowiak, J., 322
Stampfl, T., 260
Stanley, J. C., 30
Stapp, J., 350
Stark, M. J., 229
Stedman, J. M., 350
Steer, R. A., 148
Stein, C. R., 112
Steinmetz, J. L., 330
Stejskal, W. J., 168
Stenmark, D. E., 347

Stern, W. L., 103
Stevens, S. S., 163
Stone, C. P., 115
Storm, C. L., 326
Stoup, C. M., 351
Stouwie, R. J., 144
Straus, R., 298
Strauss, E., 108, 115, 116
Strickland, B. R., 2, 3, 10, 11, 188, 344
Strother, C. R., 343
Strube, M. J., 202
Strupp, H. H., 229, 230
Stuart, R. B., 146
Suinn, R. M., 3
Summers, K. J., 144
Sundberg, N. D., 166, 178, 182
Suttell, B. J., 116
Suzuki, T., 247, 248
Svartberg, M., 232
Swann, W. B., 355
Swartz, J. D., 171
Swedo, S. E., 293
Swensen, C. H., 171, 172

Taschman, H. A., 322
Taulbee, E. S., 171
Teasdale, J. D., 67
Teglasi, H., 171
Tellegen, A., 176
Telzrow, C. F., 117
Tennenbaum, D. L., 144
Teri, P. M., 330
Terman, L., 119, 126
Terranova, R. D., 11, 344
Thase, M. E., 265
Thevenin, D. M., 8, 193
Thomas, A., 73, 74, 75
Thompson, L. L., 115
Thorndike, A. M., 101, 102, 103, 117
Thorndike, R. L., 103, 118
Thorne, F. C., 36, 354
Thornton, E. M., 51
Thurstone, L. L., 99
Tillich, P., 242
Timbury, G. C., 154
Tomkins, S. S., 179

Torrey, E. F., 215, 226, 227, 228
Trivelli, N., 325
Truax, C. B., 64, 65, 248, 253, 255
Tryon, W. W., 142
Tucker, W. B., 163
Tuddenham, R. D., 179
Tureff, S. E., 143
Turk, D. C., 274, 303
Turk, L. R., 149
Turkat, I. D., 278
Turner, R. H., 65
Turner, S. M., 293
Twentyman, C. T., 144, 155

Ulrich, R. F., 145, 306
Unis, A. S., 144
Urban, H. B., 37, 156, 215

Valenstein, E. S., 295
van Hutton, V., 174
Van Norman, L. R., 149
VandenBos, G. R., 194, 294
Vanderlippe, R. H., 65
Vandervoort, D. J., 330, 336
Varley, C. K., 293
Vaughn, C. C., 306
Velten, E., 33
Vincent, J., 293
Voegtlin, W. L., 261
Vogler, R. E., 276
Volkin, J., 153
von Baeyer, C., 153
von Helmholtz, H., 6
Von Meduna, L., 294
Voth, H., 228
Vygotsky, L. S., 279

Wadden, D. A., 304
Wade, T. C., 117
Wakefield, P. J., 38, 357
Walfish, S., 347, 354
Wallace, R. K., 247, 248
Wallis, R. R., 117, 171
Walsh, R., 247
Walton, J. M., 348, 350
Wampler, L. D., 229

Ward, C. H., 28, 148
Waskow, I. E., 65, 253
Wason, P. C., 24, 355
Watkins, 171, 182
Watkins, C. E., 170, 178, 179, 349
Watkins, J. B., 172
Watson, J. B., 54, 58, 59, 60, 132, 257, 258, 282, 315
Watson, N., 143
Watts, J. W., 295
Weber, E., 81
Wechsler, D., 103, 115, 117, 118, 126
Wegner, K. W., 174
Weideman, R., 150
Weiner, D., 219
Weinstock, 231
Weintraub, S., 115
Weiss, B., 312, 319
Weiss, G., 292
Weiss, R. L., 144
Weissman, A. N., 153, 272
Weisz, J. R., 312, 319
Wells, R. A., 325
Wendt, R. N., 11, 205, 210, 343
Wernicke, K., 110
Werry, J. S., 263
Wertheimer, M., 252
Westerholm, P., 33
Wetzler, S., 178
Weyer, J., 194
Wheelis, A., 278
Whipple, G. M., 165
White, R., 223
Whiteman, V. L., 150
Widiger, T. A., 178
Wiener, I. B., 186
Wierzbicki, M., 11, 28, 33, 35, 37, 38, 60, 61, 133, 141, 156, 157, 168, 173, 176, 178, 179, 186, 191, 196, 198, 203, 204, 281, 282, 330
Wilkinson, G., 108
Willerman, L., 75, 76, 83, 280
Williams, B. W., 115
Williams, J. A., 113

Williams, J. D., 113
Williams, R. E., 38, 357
Williams, S. L., 143
Williamson, D. A., 144
Wilson, G. T., 203, 290, 295
Wilson, M. R., 326
Wine, J. D., 149
Winter, W. D., 325
Wirt, R. D., 174
Wisner, K. L., 144
Wisocki, P. A., 352
Withers, E., 118
Witmer, L., 12, 82, 312, 341, 342, 357
Wolf, A., 328
Wolfe, B. E., 253
Wolfle, D., 342
Wolpe, J., 258, 259, 260
Wood, J. M., 168
Woodcock, R. W., 108
Woodworth, R. S., 347
Woodworth, S., 173
Wortman, C. B., 2
Wundt, W., 12, 66, 81, 82, 99
Wurm, M., 298
Wyss, D., 225

Yalom, I. D., 242, 250, 326, 327, 328, 329, 330, 332, 333, 338
Yates, A. J., 59, 141, 146, 257, 274
Yeager, R. J., 248, 251
Yeaton, W. H., 202
Yontef, G. M., 244, 329
Young, F. A., 346
Youngstrom, N., 229

Zeiss, A. M., 146
Zigler, E. F., 119
Zilboorg, G., 226
Zillmer, E. A., 168, 169
Zimerberg, S. M., 332
Zimmerman, R., 224
Zook, A., 348, 350
Zubin, J., 166
Zuckerman, M., 73

Subject Index

ABAB reversal design, 26, 27, 199
Ability testing (*see* Psychological ability, assessment of)
Abnormal behavior:
    ancient views of, 3–12
    modern views, 4
    physiological model, 4, 5–6
    psychological model, 6–7
    and reinforcement, 59
    religious model, 3
    social model, 4
Abstract conceptualization, 19
Academic assessment, 106–110
    achievement tests, 107, 108–109
    aptitude tests, 110
Acetylcholine, 71
Achievement tests, 107, 108–109, 127
Acquiescence, 187
Active-encountering, 321
Active listening skills, 240
Adler, Alfred, 221
Adoption study, 34, 72
Aggressive personality, 155
Akathesia, 288
Alcoholics Anonymous (AA), 330, 333
Allport's Ascendance-Submission Test, 173
Allport-Vernon Study of Values, 173
Alternate form reliability, 85
Alternative hypothesis, 22
American Association for Applied Psychology (AAAP),
    formation of, 8
American Association of Clinical Psychology (AACP),
    formation of, 8
American College Testing Program (ACT), 111
American Educational Research Association, 93
American Psychological Association, formation of, 8

American Psychological Society, formation of, 8
Amphetamines, 288
Anafranil, 293
Anal character, 50
Anal stage of development, 46, 50
Analogue study, 32–34
Analogue subjects, 283
    in behavioral therapy, 277
Analytical psychology, 220, 233
Anna O., case of, 51
Antabuse, 294
Antecedent stimuli, 132
Anti-anxiety agents, 290
Anticholinergic effects, 288
Antidepressants, 288–290
Anti-diagnosis movement, 156
Antipsychotics, 287–288
Antisocial personality disorder, 162
Anxiety disorders, 71, 247
Aphasia, 114, 139
Applied value, 20
    of behaviorism, 60
    of biological theory, 77
    of cognitive theory of personality, 70
    of humanism, 64
    of psychoanalysis, 52
Aptitude tests, 108, 110, 111, 127
Arbitrary inference, 272
Archetypes, 220
Army Alpha and Beta Tests, 9
Assertiveness training, 149, 265
Assessment (*see* Clinical assessment; Psychological ability, assessment of)
Attention deficit hyperactivity disorder (ADHD), 73, 292
Autism, 316

Autonomic system, 71
Aversive conditioning, 261, 278, 282
    ethical concerns, 262
Aversive stimulus, 56
Avoidant personality disorder, 162
Axon, 286

Barnum effect, 181, 182
Base rate, defined, 86
Baseline period, 132
Basic needs, in humanistic view, 63
Beck Depression Inventory (BDI), 148
Beck's cognitive therapy of depression, 271–272
Bedside manner, 197
Behavior checklist, 144, 157
Behavior genetics, 72
Behavior rating scales, 145
Behavior repertoire, 55
Behavior therapy, Eysenck definition, 258
Behavioral Assertiveness Test–Revised (BAT–R), 144
Behavioral assessment, 12, 84, 131–158
    assumptions of, 155
    cognitive assessment, 149–152
    interview, 133–141
    observation, 141–148
    reactivity to measurement, 152
    reliability of, 155–157, 158
    selection of observers, 153
    self-assessment, 146
    self-monitoring, 146
    Skinner, B. F., 132
    standardized, 143
    training of observers, 153
    validity of, 155–157, 158
Behavioral deficit, 259
Behavioral excess, 258
Behavioral marital therapy (BMT), 326
Behavioral medicine, 302–304
Behavioral observation, 141–148, 157
    naturalistic observation, 143
Behavioral symptoms, 59
Behavioral therapy, 257–266
    effectiveness of, 280–282
    ethical problems, 278–280
    goals of, 259
    instrumental conditioning, 262–265
    meta-analysis, 281–282

relapse, 276
    social learning, 265–266
    techniques, 259–266
    theory of pathology, 258–259
Behaviorism, 54–61, 78
    and abnormal behavior, 59
    applied value, 60
    and clinical psychology, 61
    comprehensiveness of, 60
    determinism, 54
    empiricism, 54
    evaluation of, 60
    falsifiability of, 61
    heuristic value of, 60
    hypothetical constructs, 54
    internal consistency of, 60
    intervening variable, 55
    and nocturnal enuresis, 59
    and order, 54
    parsimony of, 60
    personality development, 56
    personality dynamics, 58
    personality structure, 55
    and psychopathology, 58
    and punishment, 60
    and reinforcement, 60
    Skinner, B. F., 57
    treatment, 60
    Watson, John, 54
Bell-and-pad treatment, 262
Bender-Gestalt Test, 9, 116, 117, 127
Benzodiazepines, 290, 291
Bernreuter's Personality Inventory, 173
Binet, Alfred, 10, 101, 126
Binet-Simon Intelligence Test, 102
Biofeedback, 76, 237, 298
Biological theory of personality, 70–78
    applied value of, 77
    attention deficit hyperactivity disorder (ADHD), 73
    comprehensiveness of, 76
    Eysenck's physiological theory, 72
    falsifiability of, 77
    heuristic value of, 77
    internal consistency of, 77
    parsimony of, 77
    personality development, 74
    personality dynamics, 75

personality structure, 72
and psychopathology, 75
and schizophrenia, 76
and temperament, 73
and treatment, 76
Biological treatment, 285–309
anti-anxiety agents, 290–291
antidepressants, 288–290
antipsychotics, 287–288
behavioral medicine, 302–304
clomipramine-treatment of OCD, 293
effectiveness of, 306
electroconvulsive therapy, 294–295
imipramine-treatment of enuresis, 293
medical treatment, 286–295
psychosurgery, 295
of schizophrenia, 287
stimulants, 291–293
stress-related disorders, 296–302
Bipolar disorder, 290
Birth order, 221
Black box, 132
Blocking, 217
Booster sessions, 276
Borderline personality disorder, 162, 163
Boston Naming Test (BNT), 115
Boulder Model, 11, 38, 39 (*see also* Scientist–practitioner
    model)
    training, 354
Brain, structure of, 71

California Psychological Inventory (CPI), 174
Capacity for future learning, 99
Case study, defined, 41
Castration anxiety, 47
CAT scan, 72
Catastrophizing, 271
Catecholamine receptors, 290
Categorical trait, 34
Category test, 114
Catharsis, 194, 216
Cattell, James McKean, 81
Central nervous system, 71
Cerebral cortex, 71
Cerebrotonia, 164
Chaining, 57
Child abuse and confidentiality, 206
Child Behavior Checklist (CBCL), 84, 145

Child management, 283
Child therapy, 311–319
    cognitive-behavioral theory, 315–316
    comparison of adult and child clients, 316–317
    effectiveness, 319
    ethical issues, 317–319
    history, 312
    humanistic theory, 314–315
    psychoanalytic theory, 312–314
Childhood Autism Rating Scale (CARS), 145
Chlorpromazine, 287
Classical conditioning, 56, 258, 259, 282
    and child therapy, 315
    defined, 56
    Eysenck's theory, 72
Classical test theory, 88
Client-centered therapy, 64, 78
    example of, 241
    training in, 248
Client–therapist relationship, 197, 217, 219, 253
Clinical analogues, 277, 283
Clinical assessment, 81–96
    advances in, 9
    base rate problem, 87
    behavioral, 84
    Binet, Alfred, 82
    Cattell, James McKean, 81
    classical test theory, 88
    clinical interview, 84
    criteria for evaluating tests, 84
    direct observation, 84
    ethical issues, 93
    Galton, Francis, 81
    generalizability theory, 89
    history of, 3, 81–82
    intellectual, 83
    internal consistency, 85
    inter-rater reliability, 85
    personality testing, 84
    standardized tests, 84, 89–91
    test reliability, 85
    test theory, 88
    test validity, 86, 87
    types of, 82–84
Clinical interview, 84, 131–141
    client appearance, 137
    client attitude, 137
    client cognitive functioning, 138

client history, 135
client perception, 135
client/psychologist relationship, 135
client verbal behavior, 138
example of, 136
outline, 134
structured interview, 139–141
Clinical prediction, 190
Clinical psychology:
defined, 2
development of, 8
graduate school training, 342–346
graduate training, evaluation of, 353
history of, 2–7
introduction of, 194
modern developments, 7–12
professional roles 346–349
psychiatry vs. psychology, 349
research methods, 25–36
scientist–practitioner model, 36–40
theoretical advances in, 9
work settings, 347
Clinical psychology, scientific foundations of, 15–42
assumptions, 16–17
philosophy of science, 15–25
progress, 21–25
research methods, 25–36
scientist–practitioner model, 36–40
stages, 17–19
theories, 20–21
Clinical Tests of the Sensorium (CTS), 118
Clomipramine (Anafranil), 293
Clozapine (Clozaril), 288
Cognitive assessment, 12, 157, 149–152
Cognitive–behavioral therapy, 197
Cognitive behaviorism, defined, 66
Cognitive consonance, 68
Cognitive development, 68
Cognitive dissonance theory, 68
Cognitive models in clinical psychology, 66
Cognitive restructuring, 270, 283
Cognitive self-assessment, 150
Cognitive skills:
assessment, 149
training, 273, 283
Cognitive theory of personality, 65–70, 78
applied value of, 70
comprehensiveness, 69

evaluation, 69
falsifiability of, 70
heuristic value of, 70
internal consistency of, 70
parsimony of, 70
personality development, 68
personality dynamics, 68
personality structure, 67
psychopathology, 69
treatment, 69
Cognitive therapy, 69, 266–283
cognitive analogues of behavior therapy, 268–270
covert techniques, 268
meta-analysis, 281–282
techniques, 268–274
theory of psychopathology, 267–268
College Entrance Examination Board (CEEB), 106
Community Mental Health Centers Act, 8
Community mental health movement, 327
Complex, 47
Comprehensiveness:
of behaviorism, 60
of cognitive theory of personality, 69
of humanism, 64
of psychoanalysis, 52
Concurrent validity, 86
Conditional positive regard, 62, 78, 236
Conditioned reflex therapy, 258
Conditioned response (CR), 56, 262
Conditioned stimulus (CS), 56, 262
Conditioning, 56, 78
and child therapy, 315
Confabulation, 180
Confession, and Jungian therapy, 221
Confidence interval, defined, 88
Confidentiality, and psychotherapy, 206
Confrontation, in Gestalt therapy, 245
Conjectures, 22
Conscience, 46
Consensual drift, 154
Consequent stimuli, 132
Construct validity, 86
Constructs, defined, 67, 270
Contact, in Gestalt therapy, 245
Content validity, 86
Continuous reinforcement schedules, 277
Continuous schedule, 57
Continuous trait, 34

Contracting, 283
    and instrumental conditioning, 264
Control group, 25, 199
Conversion, 49, 51
Conversion disorder, 45, 83 (*see also* Hysterical
    conversion disorder)
Coping model, 266, 283
Correlation coefficient, 27
Correlational study, 27, 41
Cortical arousal, 73
Co-therapist, working with, 334
Counterconditioning, 259
Countertransference, 218
Covert modeling, 270
Covert punishment, 269
Covert rehearsal, 269
Covert reinforcement, 269
Covert sensitization, 269
Craniology, 98
Craniometry, 98
Criterion-related validity, 86
Critical flicker fusion test, 114
Cross-lag correlational studies, defined, 29
Cross-validation, 92
Crystallized intelligence, 99
Cylert, 292

Daydreams, and Freudian psychoanalysis, 217
Deduction, 19
Defense mechanism, 48, 49, 50, 166, 216
Delayed (or wait-list) treatment group, 199
Delusion, defined, 75
Demoralization, 195
Denial, 48, 49
Dependent personality disorder, 162, 163
Dependent variable (DV), 30
Depression, 176, 288
    and cognitive therapy, 272
    and personality disorder, 163
Depression Scale, 93
Depressogenic thinking errors, 272
Dereflection, 243, 244
Desensitization, 259, 268, 282
Determinism, 16, 54
Developmental psychologist, defined, 2
Devereux Child Behavior Rating Scale (DCBRS), 145
Deviant conditioning process, 59
Deviation IQ, 103

Dextroamphetamine (Dexedrine), 292
Diagnostic Interview Schedule (DIS), 141
Diagnostic Interview Schedule for Children (DISC), 141
*Diagnostic and Statistical Manual of Mental Disorders
    (DSM)*, publication of, 8
Diazepam (Valium), 290
Dilantin, 294
Discriminant analysis, 92
Discrimination, 57
Displacement, 48, 49
Dissociation, 7
Disulfiram (Antabuse), 294
Dizygotic (DZ) twins, 35
D-needs, 63
Dopamine, 71, 288
Dopamine receptor sites, 288
Double-blind study, 31
Draw-a-Family Test, 171
Draw-a-Person Test (DAP), 9, 94, 166, 171
Dream analysis, 51
    and Freud, 217
Dysfunctional Attitude Scale, 272
Dysthymia, 323
Dystonia, 288

Eclecticism, 44
Ectomorphy, 164
Education, and Jungian therapy, 221
Educational Testing Service (ETS), 107
Effect size, 202
Ego, 46, 77, 216, 222
Ego ideal, 46
Ego psychology, 223
Ego strength, 228
Egocentricity, 68
Eigenwelt, 329
Electroconvulsive therapy (ECT), 76, 294
Electroshock therapy (EST), 294
Elucidation, and Jungian therapy, 221
Emotional stimulation, 335
Encounter groups, 250, 329
Endomorphy, 163
Enrichment, 63
Enuresis, 293
Error variance, 88
Executive function, 335
Existential therapy, 242–244, 254
Exner Scoring System, 91

Exorcism, 3, 4
Experiment, and research methods of clinical
        psychology, 30
Experimental manipulation, 30, 31
External reinforcements, 279
External validity:
        and analogue studies, 33
        and case study, 26
        defined, 25
Externalizing, 145
Extrapyramidal effects, 288
Extreme determinism, 220
Eyberg Child Behavior Inventory (ECBI), 145
Eysenck, Hans, 198
        physiological theory, 72
Eysenck Personality Questionnaire–Revised (EPQ–R),
        174

Face validity, 200
Factor analysis, defined, 30
Fading, 276
False negatives, 87
False sciences, 21
Falsifiability, 20, 22, 41
        of behaviorism, 61
        of biological theory, 77
        of cognitive theory of personality, 70
        defined, 21
        of humanism, 64
        of psychoanalysis, 53
Family Conflict and Dominance Code (FCDC), 144
Family Interaction Coding System (FICS), 143
Family study, 34, 72
Family systems therapy, 226, 233
Family therapy, 319–326
        cognitive-behavioral, 322–323
        comparison of individual and family, 323–324
        contraindications, 324
        eating disorders, 322
        empirical evaluations, 325–326
        goal of, 324
        history of, 319–320
        humanistic theory, 321–322
        methodological difficulties, 325
        psychoanalytic theory, 320–321
Fantasies, and Freudian psychoanalysis, 217
Field theory of personality, 329
Finger oscillation test, 114

Fixation, 50
Fixed-role therapy, 270
Flooding, 260
Fluid intelligence, 99
Fluoxetine (Prozac), 289
Forebrain, 71
Fragmentation of personality, 222
Fraternal twins, 35
Free association, 51, 167, 217
Freud, Sigmund (*see also* Psychoanalysis):
        defense mechanisms, 49
        developmental stages, 50
Freudian drive theory, 224
Freudian slip, 217
Freudian theory, internal inconsistency in, 53
Frontal lobe, 72
Functional analysis, 132, 157
Functional equivalence, 162

GABA receptors, 291
Galen, and personality assessment, 163
Galton, Francis, 81
Galvanic skin response (GSR), 73
Gamma-aminobutyric acid (GABA), 71
General adaptation syndrome (GAS), 296, 297
General Cognitive Index (GCI), 106
General factor, of intelligence, 99
General paresis, 5, 6
Generalizability theory, 95
Generalization, 56
Generalization gradient, 57
Genetic research, 34–36
Genital stage, 48, 50
Gestalt therapy, 244–247, 254
        in family therapy, 322
        techniques, 245–246
Goodness-of-fit, 75
Graduate Record Examination (GRE), 110, 112, 351
Graduate school training of clinical psychologists,
        342–346
        accreditation standards, 344–345
        history, 342–344
        programs, 344–346
Graphology, 164
Group psychoanalysis, 328
Group therapy, 326–336
        Alcoholics Anonymous (AA), 331
        cognitive-behavioral theory, 330

empirical evaluations, 334–336
existential psychology, 329
Gestalt therapy, 329
history, 326–327
humanistic theory, 329–330
psychoanalytic theory, 328
self-help groups, 330
suitability of client, 332

Hallucination, defined, 75
Haloperidol (Haldol), 294
Halstead Battery, 114
Halstead-Reitan, 114
Handwriting analysis, 167
Hartford Retreat, 5
Health psychology, 304
Heritability coefficient, 34, 36
Heuristic value, 21
    of behaviorism, 60
    of biological theory, 77
    cognitive theory of personality, 70
    of humanism, 64
    of psychoanalysis, 52
Hindbrain, 71
Hippocrates, 4
    and personality assessment, 163
Histrionic personality disorder, 162
Homeostasis, 320
House-Tree-Person Technique (HTP), 171
Human figure drawing tests, 107, 171
Human nature, Freudian vs. Adlerian views, 222
Humanism, 61–65
    Allport, Gordon, 61
    applied value of, 64
    comprehensiveness of, 64
    evaluation of, 64
    falsifiability of, 64
    heuristic value of, 64
    internal consistency of, 64
    parsimony of, 64
    personality development, 62
    personality dynamics, 62
    personality structure, 62
    phenomenology, 61
    philosophical roots, 61
    psychopathology, 63
    Rogers, Carl, 61
    treatment, 63

Humanistic psychology, 78, 236
Humanistic therapy, 235–255 (*see also* Rogerian
        therapy)
    effectiveness of, 252
    existential therapy, 242–244
    Gestalt therapy, 244–247
    goal of, 236–237
    and the healthy, 250–251
    influence of Rogerian qualities, 252–254
    psychopathology, 236
    techniques, 237–240
    training of psychotherapists, 248–250
    transpersonal therapy, 247–248
Huntington's chorea, 1
Hyper-reflection, 244
Hypnosis, 7, 194, 217, 222, 302
Hypochondriasis, 175
Hypomania, 175
Hypothalamus, 71
Hypothetical constructs, 17, 54, 55, 67
Hysteria, 175
Hysterical conversion disorder, 7, 45 (*see also*
        Conversion disorder)

Id, 45, 77, 216
Identical twins, 35
Illinois Test of Psycholinguistic Abilities (ITPA), 109
Illusory correlation, 182
Imaginal desensitization, 268
Imipramine (Tofranil), 293
Imitative learning, 265
Implosive therapy, 260
In vivo desensitization, 268, 277
Incomplete Sentences Blank (ISB), 166, 172
Independent variable (IV), 30
Individual psychology, 221, 233
Induction, 19
Inferiority complex, 221
Informed consent, 209
Inkblots, 82
Inoculation training, self-statements used in, 275
Insight-oriented therapy, 233
Insomnia, 71
Instinctual gratification, 224
Instrumental conditioning, 56, 59, 258, 262, 282 (*see also*
        Operant conditioning)
    and child therapy, 315
Intellectual assessment, 11, 90, 99–106

Intellectualization, 49
Intelligence, 99
  defined, 126
  environmental relationship, 101
  genetic studies, 101
  measurement of, 83
  psychological models, 100
Intelligence quotient (IQ), defined, 102
Intelligence tests, 82, 101–106
  Binet, 101
  Kaufman Assessment Battery for Children, 105
  McCarthy Scales of Children's Abilities, 105
  reliability of, 117
  test bias, 122–126
  validity of, 118
  Wechsler, 103
Intermittent schedule, 57, 277
Internal arousal, 73
Internal consistency, 20, 21
  of behaviorism, 60
  of biological theory, 77
  of cognitive theory of personality, 70
  defined, 85
  in Freudian theory, 53
  of humanism, 64
  of psychoanalysis, 52
Internal validity:
  and case study, 26
  defined, 25
Internalizing, 145
Interpretation:
  and Freudian psychoanalysis, 219
  in Rogerian therapy, 239
Inter-rater reliability, 85
Interval schedule, 57
Intervening variable, 55
Interview, 131
  clinical, 134
  goals of, 133
Introversion–extraversion, 72
Iowa Tests of Basic Skills (ITBS), 109
Iowa Tests of Educational Development (ITED), 109
Iproniazid, 288, 289
Irrational Beliefs Inventory (IBI), 150
Item analysis, 92
Item-total correlation, 92

Jackson Personality Inventory (JPI), 174

Jackson Vocational Interest Survey (JVIS), 113
Jung, Carl Gustav, 220
Jungian therapy, 220–221
Juvenile Psychopathic Institute, 312

K scale, 185
Kappa coefficients, 140
Kaufman Assessment Battery for Children (K-ABC), 105
KeyMath Diagnostic Arithmetic Test (KMDAT), 109
Kiddie-SADS (K-SADS), 140
Kinetic Family Drawing, 171
Kuder General Interest Survey (KGIS), 113
Kuhn, Thomas, 21, 23

La Bicetre lunatic asylum, 5
Lamaze training, 302
Latency stage of development, 48, 50
Law of parsimony, 20
L-DOPA, 288
Learning, 56
Learning disability, 83, 120
Learning disorder, diagnostic criteria for, 121
Legal competency, 120
Libido, 48
Life lie, 221, 222
Limbic system, 71
Lithium, 290
Little Hans, 312
Lobotomy, 295
Logotherapy, 243
Luria Nebraska Neuropsychological Battery (LNNB), 114

Magnesium pemoline (Cylert), 292
Magnetic Resonance Imaging (MRI), 72
Major tranquilizers, 287
Malleus Malleficarum (The Witches' Hammer), 3
Manic depression, 290
Manticore, The, 220
MAO-Inhibitors (MAO-Is), 289
Marital Interaction Coding System (MICS), 144
Marital therapy, 326
Mastery model, 266
Maximization/minimization, 272
McCarthy Scales of Children's Abilities (MSCA), 105
Means-Ends Problem Solving Procedure (MEPS), 149, 273
Meditation, 247, 302

Melancholia, 163
Mental age, 102
Mental chemistry, 7
Mental level, 102
Mental Measurements Yearbook, 178
Mental retardation, diagnostic criteria for, 121
Mental status examination, 137
Mental test, 82
Mesmer, Franz Anton, 7
Mesomorphy, 163
Meta-analysis, 201, 202, 213, 232
    of cognitive and behavioral therapies, 281–282
Metaneeds, 63
Method of contrasted groups, 91
Methylphenidate (Ritalin), 292
Metropolitan Achievement Tests (MAT), 109
Midbrain, 71
Milieu therapy, 5
Millon Clinical Multiaxial Inventory (MCMI-III), 177,
    185
Minimal treatment group, 199
Ministry for Public Education, 101
Minnesota Multiphasic Personality Inventory (MMPI), 9,
    176, 183, 184, 185
    clinical scales of, 175
    MMPI-2, 89, 173, 177
    MMPI-A, 177
Minor tranquilizers, 287
Mitwelt, 329
Modeling, 69, 265
Monoamine oxidase, 289
Monozygotic (MZ) twins, 35
Moral treatment, 5
Morita therapy, 247
Mortido, 48
Multiple baseline design, 27, 199
Multiple correlation, defined, 29
Muscle relaxation, 76
Mutual analysis, 220

Narcissism, 222
Narcissistic neuroses, 228
Narcissistic personality disorder, 162
National Council on Measurements Used in Education,
    94
Naturalistic observation, 143
Naturalistic treatments, 4
Nay-saying, 187

Negative cognitive schema, 68
Negative correlation:
    defined, 27
    examples of, 28
Negative punishment, 56
Negative reinforcement, 56
Negative symptoms of schizophrenia, 287
Negative transference, 218
Neo-Freudian schools, 233
Neo-Freudian therapies, 223
Nerve impulses, 6, 286, 288
Nervous system, 71
Neuro-hypnotism, 7
Neuroleptics, 287
Neurology, 6
    defined, 45
Neurons, 70, 286
Neuropsychological assessment, 12, 110–117
    neuropsychological tests, 114
    screening instruments, 118
    specific cognitive abilities, 115
Neuropsychological Impairment Scale (NIS), 118, 128
Neurosis, 47, 225
Neuroticism, 72
Neurotransmitters, 71, 286
Neutral stimulus, 56
Nocturnal enuresis, 52, 59, 262
Nominalism, 54
Nonacquiescence, 187
Nondirective counselor, 240
Nondirective therapy, 64
Nonobservables, 17
Nonparticipant observer, 153, 154
Nonspecific elements of therapy, 196
Norepinephrine, 71, 289
Normal science, 23
Noumena, and humanism, 61
Null hypothesis, 22
Nurse's Observational Scale for Inpatient Evaluation
    (NOSIE), 146

Obesity, 146
Object relations theory, 223, 224, 233, 328
Observational learning, 265
Observational Record of Inpatient Behavior (ORIB), 143
Observer drift, 154, 155
Obsessive-compulsive disorder (OCD), 162, 243, 293
    Freudian explanation, 52

Occam's Razor, 20
Occipital lobe, 72
Oedipal conflict, 47, 218, 222
Open-ended statement, 238
Operant conditioning (*see* Instrumental conditioning)
Operational definition, 17, 18
Operationalization of treatment, 325
Oral character, 50
Oral stage of development, 46, 50
Order, as an assumption of science, 17
Orthogenic School, 314
Overconditioning, 59
Overgeneralization, 272
Overlearning, 276

Paradigm, defined, 23, 41
Paradoxical intention, 243
Paradoxical intervention, 323
Parallel forms, defined, 85
Paranoid delusions, Freudian explanation, 52
Paranoid personality disorder, 162
Paraphrasing, in Rogerian therapy, 239
Parapraxis, 217
Paraprofessional, 250
Parapsychology, 21
Parental psychopathology, 27
Parietal lobe, 72
Parkinsonism, 288
Parsimony:
    biological theories, 77
    of behaviorism, 60
    of cognitive theory of personality, 70
    defined, 20
    of humanism, 64
    of psychoanalysis, 52
Partial reinforcement schedule, 277
Partial schedule, 57
Participant observer, 153, 154
Pathognomonic symptom, 91
Pathology, defined, 44
Pavlov, Ivan, 56, 258
Pavlovian conditioning, 56 (*see also* Classical
        conditioning)
Peabody Individual Achievement Test (PIAT), 108
Peabody Picture Vocabulary Test, 107
Penis envy, 47
Peripheral nervous system, 71
Perseveration, 139

Personal analysis, 219
Personal construct psychology, 270
Personality, Allport definition, 44
Personality, meaning of, 161–162
Personality assessment, 161–192
    history, 163–165
    personality testing, 162–163
    projective tests, 166–172
    structured, 172–184
Personality development:
    behaviorist view, 56
    biological theory, 74
    cognitive theory, 68
    humanistic view, 62
    psychoanalytic view 46–48
Personality disorders, 162, 177
Personality dynamics:
    behaviorist view, 58
    biological theory, 75
    cognitive theory, 68
    humanistic view, 62
    psychoanalytic view, 48–50
Personality inventories, structured, 173
Personality Inventory for Children (PIC), 174
Personality structure:
    behaviorist view, 55
    biological theory, 72
    cognitive theory, 67
    humanistic view, 62
    psychoanalytic view, 45–46
Personality testing, 84, 162–163
Personality theories, 43–79
    behaviorism, 54–61
    biological, 70–77
    cognitive, 65–70
    Freud, Sigmund, 45–54
    humanism, 61–65
    psychoanalysis, 45–54
Personality trait, defined, 161
Personalization, 272
Ph.D. programs, APA accredited, 346
Phallic stage of development, 47, 50
Phenomena, and humanism, 61
Phenomenology, 236
Phenothiazines, 287
Phenytoin (Dilantin), 294
Philosophy of science, 15–25
Phobia, 73, 243

and classical conditioning, 259
Freudian explanation, 52
Phobic avoidance behaviors, 73
Phrenology, 164
Physiognomy, 164
Physiological reductionism, 6
Piaget, Jean, 68
Placebo, 31–32, 41, 200
    defined, 31
    effectiveness of, 32
    treatment group, 200
Play therapy, 312
    psychodynamic interpretation, 313
Pleasure principle, 45
Polarity, 244
Popper, Karl, 21, 22, 41
Positive correlation:
    defined, 27
    examples of, 28
Positive punishment, 56
Positive reinforcement, 56
Positive symptoms of schizophrenia, 287
Positive transference, 218
Postsynaptic cell, 286
Postsynaptic neurons, 288
Post-traumatic stress syndrome, 173
Practitioner model, 38
Practitioner–scientist model, 11, 354
Predictive validity, 86
Prefrontal leucotomy (lobotomy), 295
Presynaptic cell, 71, 286
Primitive medications, 4
Problem-focused assessment techniques, 69
Problem relapse, 283
Problem-solving ability, 149
Problem Solving Inventory (PSI), 150
Problem-solving therapy, 273
Progressive muscle relaxation, 299
Projection, 48, 49, 166
Projective human figure drawing, 171
Projective personality assessment, 165
Projective personality tests, 9, 11, 37, 82, 165, 166–172, 191
    computerized interpretations of, 188
    evaluation of, 178
    faking, 184
    and Freudian theory, 218
    reliability of, 179

validity of, 179
validity scales, 184
Projective play, 167
Proprium, 62
Prozac, 289, 290
Pseudosciences, 21
Psi-missing, 21
Psy.D. programs, APA accredited, 346
Psychasthenia, 175, 176
Psychiatric drugs, social consequences, 305
Psychiatric medication, 286–294
Psychic determinism, 50, 165, 166, 218
Psychic energy, 216
Psychoanalysis, 45–54, 77, 215–234
    applied value of, 52
    benefits of, 227
    comprehensiveness of, 52
    cost of, 226
    developmental stages, 77
    dream analysis, 51
    empirical evaluation, 231
    evaluating treatment, 229
    evaluation of, 52
    falsifiability of, 53
    free association, 51
    Freudian, 216–220
    goals of, 216
    heuristic value of, 52
    internal consistency of, 52
    length of, 226
    parsimony of, 52
    personality development, 46–48
    personality dynamics, 48–50
    personality structure, 45–46
    provider and training requirements, 228
    psychopathology, 50
    techniques, 216–220
    treatment, 51
Psychoanalytically oriented psychotherapy, 224, 225, 233
Psychodiagnostic assessment, 11
Psychodynamic therapy, 225
Psychoeducational groups, 333
Psychological ability, assessment of, 97–128
    academic, 106–110
    diagnosis planning, 120
    history, 98–99
    intelligence tests, 101–106

labeling, 122
neurological disorders, 121
neuropsychological, 110–117
test bias, 122
treatment planning, 120
Psychological disorders, 193
Psychological game, 225
Psychological health, 254
Psychological incongruence, 236, 254
Psychological tests:
    development of norms, 92
    ethical issues, 93
    guidelines, 94–95
    test construction, 91
Psychological treatment, 193–213
    accountability, 210
    case management, 210–211
    confidentiality, 206–209
    effectiveness, 199
    ethical issues, 204–206
    history, 193–195
    informed consent, 209–210
    initial contact, 211
    major achievements, 203
    monitoring client progress, 211
    nonspecific factors, 196–197
    outcome studies 200–204
    provider guidelines, 207–208
    relative efficacies, 201
    termination, 211–212
Psychology, defined, 2
Psychometrics, 95
Psychopathic deviate, 175
Psychopathology:
    behaviorist view, 54–61
    biological theory, 70–77
    causal models, 32
    cognitive theory, 65–70
    defined, 36
    demographic correlates of, 5
    Freudian explanations of, 52
    humanistic view, 61–65
    psychoanalytic theory, 45–54, 216
    and stress, 29
Psychophysiological disorders, 296
Psychosexual development, 216
Psychosomatic disorders, 296
Psychosurgery, 295

Psychotherapy (*see also* Psychological treatment):
    Freudian approaches, 216–226
    humanistic approaches, 236
    psychoanalytically oriented, 224
Psychoticism, 73
Punishment, 60
    and instrumental conditioning, 56, 262
Pygmalion in the Classroom effect, 122
Pyknic, 163

Q-sort methodology, 65
Quasi-experiment, 30
Quasi-random sampling, 93

Random sampling, 92
Ratio schedule, 57
Rational-emotive therapy (RET), 271
Rationalization, 49
Reaction formation, 48, 49, 53
Reactivity to measurement, 152
Reality principle, 46
Receptor sites, 71, 286
Reciprocal inhibition, 258
Reconditioning, 78
Reflection, in Rogerian therapy, 238
Regression, 50
Rehearsal, 69
Reinforcement, 56, 60
    and abnormal behavior, 59
    and ethics, in behavioral therapy, 279
    and instrumental conditioning, 262
Relapse, and behavioral therapy, 276
Reliability, defined, 37, 41
Repression, 48, 49
Research Diagnostic Criteria (RDC), 139
Research methods, in clinical psychology, 25–36,
    adoption study, 34
    analogue study, 32–34
    case study, 26
    control group, 25
    correlational study, 27–31
    cross-lag correlational studies, 29
    double-blind study, 31
    experimental research, 27–31
    factor analysis, 30
    family study, 34
    genetic research, 34–36
    multiple correlation, 29

placebo study, 31
single-subject designs, 26
twin study, 35
Resistance, 219
Respondents, defined, 56
Response sets, 184, 186
Reticular activating system, 71
Reuptake, 71, 286
Revised NEO Personality Inventory (NEO-PI-R), 174
Revolving door syndrome, 288
Rhythm test, 114
Rogerian therapy, 197, 235 (*see also* Humanistic
        therapy)
Role-play, 69, 144, 270
Rorschach Inkblot Test, 9, 89, 94, 166, 178

Sample approach of assessment, 155, 158
Schedule for Affective Disorders and Schizophrenia
        (SADS), 139
Schema, defined, 67
Schizoid personality disorder, 162
Schizophrenia, 75, 175
    biological theory of, 76
    and biological treatment, 287
Schizotypal personality disorder, 162
Scholastic Aptitude Test (SAT), 110, 111
Scientific model, and study of psychopathology, 36
Scientist-practitioner model, 11, 41, 211, 36–40 (*see also*
        Boulder Model)
    training, 36
Secondary drive, 224
Seizure disorders, 1
Selective abstraction, 272
Self, and humanism, 62
Self-actualization, 62, 78, 236, 254
Self-efficacy, 68
Self-fulfilling prophecies, 252
Self-help groups, 330
Self-ideal, and humanism, 62
Self-instruction training, 274
Self-monitoring, 69, 150, 157, 264
Self-observation, 154
Self-realization, and Jungian therapy, 221
Self-report, 69
Self/self-ideal congruence, 65
Self-statements, 177
Self-talk, 265
Senior Apperception Technique, 171

Sensation seeking, 73
Sentence completion tests, 172
Serotonin, 71, 289
Sexual dysfunction, 141
Sexual orientation, and behavior therapy, 280
Shamanism, 195
Shaping, 57, 263, 282
Shell shock, 173
Short-term gratification, 224
Short-term psychodynamic psychotherapy (STPP), 232
Sibling rivalry, 221
Sign approach of assessment, 155, 158
Simon, Theodore, 101
Simulated environment, 144
Single-subject design, 26, 41
Slosson Intelligence Test, 107
Smoking, rapid, 261
Social desirability, 188
Social introversion, 175
Social learning, 56, 58, 265, 266
Social Problem-Solving Inventory (SPSI), 150
Social psychologist, defined, 2
Social reinforcement, 277
Social work, 350
Somatic system, 71
Somatization disorder, 83
Somatotonia, 164
SORC (Situational influences, Organismic variables, Re-
        sponse characteristics, and Consequences), 132
Speech sounds perception test, 114
Spirochetes, 6
Spontaneous remission rate, 198
Standard error of measurement (SEM), 88
Standardized behavioral assessment, 143
Standardized tests, 84–91 (*see also* Psychological tests)
Stanford-Binet, 9, 83, 102
Statistical hypothesis testing, 22, 23
Statistical norms, 92
Statistical prediction, 190
Statistical tests, 22
Stimulants, 291
Stimulus control, 282
Story-telling tests, 170
Stratified random sampling, 93
Stress:
    and illness, 297
    and psychopathology, 29
    reduction of, 4

Stress inoculation, 274
Stress-related disorders, 296, 298
Strong Interest Inventory (SII), 113
Structural therapy, 322
Structuralism, 7
Structured Clinical Interview for *DSM-III-R* (SCID), 141
Structured interview, 139
Structured personality inventories, 12, 172–184, 191, 192
    evaluation of, 182–184
Subclinical populations, 32
Sublimation, 48, 49
Sugar pill, 31 (*see also* Placebo)
Suggestibility, 217
Suicide watch, 295
Superego, 46, 77
Surgery, 76
Symbiotic psychosis, 313
Symbolism, in dreams, 217, 218
Symptom Checklist (SCL), 148
Symptom substitution, 274
Symptomatology, defined, 44
Synapse, 71, 286
Syphilis, 6
Systematic desensitization, 237, 259, 300
Systems theory, 320

Tactual performance test, 114
Talking cure, 45
Tardive dyskinesia, 288
Target behavior, in behavioral observation, 141
Teleological alternative, 220
Temperament, 73
    and environment, 75
    in infants, 74
    types, 74
Temporal lobe, 72
Tension headaches, and biofeedback, 299
Terman, Lewis, 10
Test interpretation, computerized, 190
Test reliability, 95
Test validity, 95
Testability, 21
Testing hypotheses, efficiency of disconfirmation in, 24
Test–retest reliability, 85
T-group, 250, 329
Thematic Apperception Test (TAT), 9, 170–171, 178
    examples of responses, 170
Therapeutic relationships, 195

Thorazine, 287
Thought sampling, 150
Thurstone's Personality Schedule, 173
Time sense test, 114
Tofranil, 293
Token economy, 262, 282
Trail Making Test, 114
Transactional analysis, 225, 233
Transference, 218
Transformation, and Jungian therapy, 221
Transpersonal therapy, 247–248, 254
Treatment (*see also* Psychological treatment):
    behaviorism, 60
    biological theory, 76
    cognitive theory, 69
    history of, 3, 10
    humanism, 63
    psychoanalysis, 51–52
Trephining, 3
Tricyclics, 289
TRIN scale, 188
True negatives, 87
True positives, 87
True Response Inconsistency (TRIN), 186
T-score, defined, 175
Twelve-step programs, 331
Twin study, 35, 36, 72
Type A personality, 298
Type B personality, 298

Umwelt, 329
Unconditional positive regard, 62, 237, 254
Unconditioned response (UCR), 56, 262
Unconditioned stimulus (UCS), 56, 262
Unconscious defensive functioning, 216
Unconscious, defined, 45, 218
Unconscious material, 217
Underconditioning, 59
Undoing, 49

V profile, 175
Vail Model (*see* practitioner–scientist model)
Validity, 41
    defined, 37
Validity scales, 184, 192
Valium, 290
Variable Response Inconsistency (VRIN), 185
Velten mood induction procedure, 33

Vicarious conditioning, 265
Viscerotonia, 163
Visual imagery, 260

Wait-list treatment group, 199
War neurosis, 173
Watson, John, 54
Wechsler, David, 126
Wechsler Adult Intelligence Scale (WAIS), 9, 104
Wechsler Adult Intelligence Scale–Revised (WAIS–R), 83, 182
Wechsler-Bellevue Test, 9, 103, 126
Wechsler Individual Achievement Test (WIAT), 108
Wechsler Intelligence Scale for Children (WISC), 104
Wechsler Memory Scale (WMS), 115

Wechsler Primary and Preschool Scale of Intelligence (WPPSI), 9
Weyer, Johann, 194
Wide Range Achievement Test (WRAT), 108
"Wild Boy of Aveyron," 5, 312
Willful concentration, 217
Wisconsin Card Sorting Test (WCST), 115
Woodcock-Johnson Psycho-Educational Battery, 108
Woodworth Personal Data Sheet, 173
Word association test, 165, 167
Word pairs, and personality tests, 182

YAVIS client, 227, 228, 233
Yea-saying, 187
York Retreat, 5